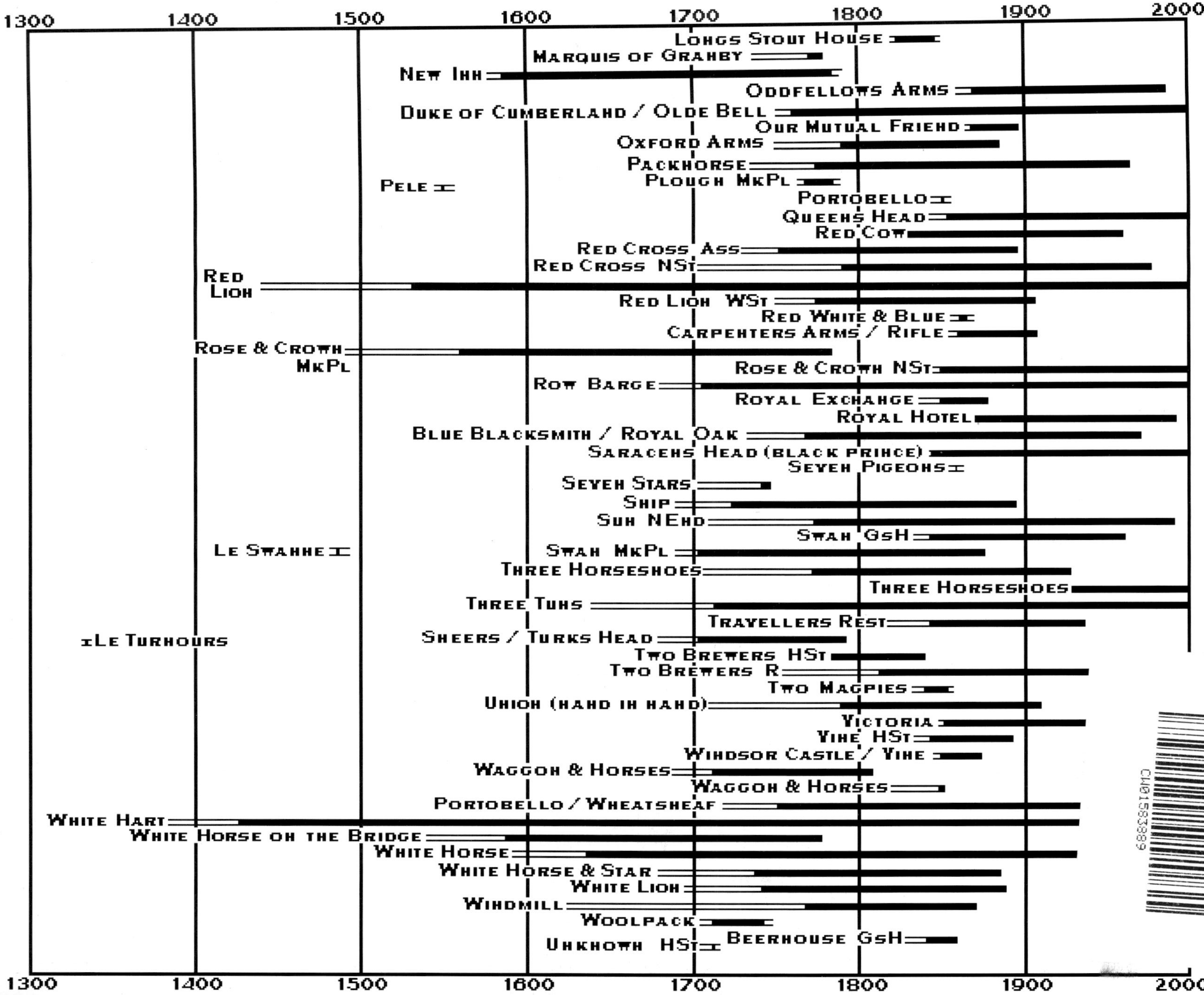
1300
1400
1500
1600
1700
1800
1900
2000
Longs Stout House
Marquis of Granby
New Inn
Oddfellows Arms
Duke of Cumberland / Olde Bell
Our Mutual Friend
Oxford Arms
Packhorse
Plough MkPl
Pele
Portobello
Queens Head
Red Cow
Red Cross Ass
Red Cross NSt
Red Lion
Red Lion WSt
Red White & Blue
Carpenters Arms / Rifle
Rose & Crown MkPl
Rose & Crown NSt
Row Barge
Royal Exchange
Royal Hotel
Blue Blacksmith / Royal Oak
Saracens Head (black prince)
Seven Pigeons
Seven Stars
Ship
Sun NEnd
Swan GsH
Le Swanne
Swan MkPl
Three Horseshoes
Three Horseshoes
Three Tuns
Travellers Rest
Le Turnours
Sheers / Turks Head
Two Brewers HSt
Two Brewers R
Two Magpies
Union (hand in hand)
Victoria
Vine HSt
Windsor Castle / Vine
Waggon & Horses
Waggon & Horses
Portobello / Wheatsheaf
White Hart
White Horse on the Bridge
White Horse
White Horse & Star
White Lion
Windmill
Woolpack
Unknown HSt
Beerhouse GsH

Frontispiece Henley on Thames O.S.Map of 1884

THE HOSTELRIES OF HENLEY

or
an account of the
Alehouses, Beerhouses, Breweries, Hostelries,
Hotels, Inns, Malthouses, Public houses,
Taverns and Typpling houses
in the Town of
Henley on Thames

ANN H G COTTINGHAM

2000 A.D.

First published in 2000
by
Ann H G Cottingham
Heathfield, ReadingRd,
Shiplake,Oxon RG9 3JN

ISBN No. 0-9538376-0-2

Printed in Great Britain
by
Parchment Oxford
Printworks
Crescent Road
Cowley
Oxford OX4 2PB

This book is dedicated to the memory of my father, G L Graham Rodger, who had fond memories of the pubs of Henley, which he sampled in the early 1920s when he coxed for London Rowing Club.

I wish to thank most particularly my husband **Kenneth Cottingham** for his patience and encouragement throughout the years that this book has been in preparation.

I also wish to thank the many people of Henley and members of the Henley Archaeological & Historical Group who have assisted me with information. Most especially I wish to thank the following (placed in alphabetical order) :-

Mr Peter Anderson for the use of his photographs.

Mr M Chalcraft late of Brakspear's Brewery for supplying information on the *A E Hobbs,* and the names of licensees of their current pubs.

Mr John Crocker for allowing me the use of his transcripts of Henley Rentals and other works, and also for supplying many snippets of information from his recollections from his long life in the town.

Miss Joan Dils and her evening class of 1984-5 for the use of their transcripts of 17th century Wills and Inventories.

Mrs Hilary Fisher for much information from her own researches and also for the use of her valuable Post Card collection.

Mr Alun Jones for allowing me to see round his house which was once part of the *Bell Inn.*

Mrs Ruth Gibson for allowing me to use her researches on buildings.

Ms Christine Price, Clerk to the Magistrates Court, and her assistants for allowing me access to the Registers of Licenses held at the Court, and to the Magistrates Special Sessions Minute Book beginning in 1870.

Miss Ivy Reeves for information on 17th century families in the town.

The late **Miss Sybil Reeves** for photos taken by her father and her father's list of by-gone pubs.

Mrs Annette Rosen for allowing me to see round her house which was once part of the *Bell Inn.*

The Hon Georgina Stonor for supplying me with information on the priests at the *Bull.*

Mrs Elizabeth Young for her assistance with the medieval Latin of the Borough Records, and for information from her researches into Apprentice Records.

The late **Mr Brian Young** for very kindly allowing me to publish the letter of John Strange to be found on pages 14-15.

Ownership of Illustrations

Unless listed below the illustrations are either drawings, tracings, or photographs of mine.

Photos loaned to me by **Mrs Hilary Fisher**
Fig. Nos. 1, 2, 3, 5, 9, 10, 14, 15, 19, 20, 25, 26, 28, 35, 43, 49, 51, 55, 57, 58

Photos by **Mr Peter Anderson**
Fig. Nos. 16, 45

Plan of **Simmons & Sons**
Fig. No. 39

Photo by the late **Mr W G Reeves** given to me by the late **Miss Sybil Reeves**
Fig. No. 48

Contents

Page 1 Introduction

Page27 Pubs open in 2000 in Bold

86	The Portobello	Reading Road
87	The Portobello	Reading Road
	The Queen's Arms	Market Place
88	**The Queen's Head**	Duke Street
89	The Red Cow	West Street
90	The Red Cross	Assendon
91	The Red Cross	New Street
92	**The Red Lion**	Hart Street/Riverside
93	The Red Lion	West Street
94	The Red White and Blue	Reading Road
95	The Rifle	Greys Road
96	The Rose and Crown	Market Place
97	**The Rose and Crown**	New Street
98	**The Row Barge**	West Street
99	The Royal Exchange	New Street
100	The Royal Hotel	Station Road
101	The Royal Oak	Greys Road
102	**The Saracen's Head**	Greys Road
103	The Seven Pigeons	Station Road
104	The Seven Stars	Market Place
105	The Sheers	Market Place
106	The Ship	Riverside/Wharf Lane
107	The Sun	Market Place/West Street
108	The Sun	Northfield End
109	The Swan	Greys Hill
110	The Swan	Market Place
111	The Three Horseshoes	Reading Road
112	**The Three Horseshoes**	Reading Road
113	**The Three Tuns**	Market Place
114	The Travellers Rest	Fairmile
115	The Turk's Head	Market Place
116	Le Turnours	Market Pl /Middle Row?
117	The Two Brewers	Hart Street
118	**The Two Brewers**	Remenham
119	The Two Magpies	Northfield End
120	The Union	Hart Street
121	**The Victoria**	Market Pl /Middle Row
122	The Vine	Hart Street
123	The Vine	Northfield End
124 & 125	The Waggon and Horses	Market Place/Middle Row
126	The Waggon and Horses	Market Place
	(The Welcome Tavern	West Street)
127	**The Wheatsheaf**	Reading Road
128	The White Hart	Hart Street
129	The White Horse	Bridge
130	**The White Horse**	Northfield End
131	The White Horse and Star	Northfield End
132	The White Lion	Friday Street
133	The Windmill	Badgemore
134	The Windsor Castle	Northfield End
135	The Woolpack	Market Place
136	Beerhouse (no name)	Greys Hill
137	Unknown (Longlands)	Hart Street

Page 271 Breweries & Malthouses

M1	27 Bell Street now W H Smith
M2	43 Bell Street
M3	63 & 63a Bell Street
B1	67-9 Bell Street, Brewhouse
M4	77-9 Bell Street , the Bear
M5	85 Bell Street
M6	91 Bell Street
M7	Somewhere at Northfield End
M8	18-20 Bell Street
M9	36,38,40 Bell Street
M10	42 Bell Street
M11	62 Bell Street
M12	74,76,78 Bell Street
B2	2,4,6 Duke Street & 1,3 Market Pl
B3	The Union Brewery, Duke Street
M13	Somewhere in Duke St/Reading Rd
M14	31,33 Friday Street
B4	45 Friday Street
M15	67,69,71 Friday Street
M16	12 Friday Street once Ye Lion
M17	Malthouse on site of Queen Street
M18	14 Friday Street
M19	South side of Friday Street
B5 & M20	Greys Brewery & Malthouse
M21	Malthouse at Dirty Bottom
M22	27 Hart Street
M23	31,33 Hart Street
B6 & M24	Adjoining the Church yard
M25	6,8 Hart St, Malt Mill & Malthouse
?	10.12 Hart Street ?
M26	14,16 Hart Street
M27	18 Hart Street
(B3) & M28	20 Hart Street
M29	40 Hart Street
M30	9 Market Place
B7	Cannon Brewery, 15 Market Pl
M31	21, 23 Market Place
M32	29, 31 Market Place

List of Illustrations

Breweries & Malthouses

INTRODUCTION

Lines written on a pane of window glass at the *Red Lion*,
by William Shenstone (b.1714, d 11 Feb 1763)

'To thee, fair Freedom, I retire,
From flattery, cards, and dice, and din;
Nor art thou found in mansions higher
Than the low cot, or humble Inn.'

'Tis here with boundless power I reign,
And every health which I begin,
Converts dull Port to bright Champagne
Such freedom crowns it at an Inn.'

'I fly from pomp; I fly from state;
I fly from falsehood's special grin;
Freedom I love and form I hate,
And choose my lodgings at an Inn.'

'Here, Waiter ! take my sordid ore,
Which lackeys else might hope to win:
It buys what Courts have not in store;
It buys me freedom at an Inn.'

'Whoe'er has travelled life's dull round;
Where'er his stages may have been;
May sigh to think he still has found
His warmest welcome at an Inn.'

Dr Samuel Johnson in 1776
according to Boswell stayed at the
'Inn at Henley where Shenstone wrote these lines'

Earlier in February 1775 in a letter to James Macpherson,
Dr Johnson declared :-

'There is nothing which has yet been contrived by man, by which so much happiness is produced as by a good tavern or Inn.'

THE HOSTELRIES OF HENLEY

or an account of the Alehouses, Beerhouses, Breweries, Hostelries, Hotels, Inns, Malthouses, Public houses, Taverns and Typpling houses in the Town of Henley on Thames.

The variation of name as shown in the secondary title is often a matter of period. Since Registers of Licenses have been kept from 1870, there has been a very clear distinction between houses with Alehouse and Victuallers Licenses and those known as beerhouses, which hold licenses to sell beer only. Those with full Alehouse and Victuallers Licenses are sometimes referred to as inns or hotels and sometimes as public houses. The tendency since the end of the 19th century is for a closure of some beerhouses by their owners in exchange for the grant of full licenses to their remaining beerhouses. The result today is that there are no beerhouses left in Henley, but only hotels or public houses, most often called pubs.

Earlier the definitions between the various types of houses are not as clear, whether a particular tavern or hostelry was an alehouse or beerhouse is often uncertain. It would seem that hostelries, hotels and inns supplied beds, food and drink, and often stabling as well. Beerhouses supplied only beer to drink, though many of them were also lodging houses. Some of the present day pubs without yards or extensive back quarters started their existence as beerhouses, later being promoted to full Alehouse and Victuallers status. Since the definition is so indistinct in early records, for the purposes of this book I have generally used the modern term of 'pubs' for all types of houses.

The pubs named in this book are those in the Town centre, in the eastern end of what used to be Rotherfield Greys going west as far as Elizabeth Road, in Northfield End and the Fairmile, and over the bridge three pubs in Remenham.

The further end of the Fairmile coincides with the Parish boundary as shown in the 1843 Tithe Map, this means that although the *Travellers Rest* and the *Assendon Cross* or *Red Cross* are included as being in the Parish of Henley, neither the *Golden Ball* nor the *Rainbow* on the western side of the Assendon Road are mentioned, they were in the Parish of Bix. Unfortunately one has to stop somewhere. The pubs in Remenham are the *Angel,* the *Two Brewers* and the late *Carpenters Arms*, all three of which though in Remenham and Berkshire are so close to Henley as to have been always within the social orbit of the town.

Brewers, Breweries and Malthouses Breweries and malthouses are interwoven with the history of pubs, and in Henley on Thames have always in the past formed an important part of the town's activities. In fact brewing and malting might have been termed the main industry of Henley, it rivalled and was also part of Henley's other industry, that of river transport. Part of the barge trade of Henley was concerned with carrying not only grain and timber down river, but also malted barley [1]

1 Dils, Joan 'Henley & the River Trade in the Pre-Industrial Period' Journal of the Henley Archaeological & Historical Group No 5 1987

Dr Plot in the 17th century[2] said 'the malt kilns of Henley are so thriftily contrived that the kiln holes are placed in the backs of their kitchen chimnies, so that, drying their malt with wood the same fire serves for that, and all other uses of their kitchen besides.'

In the P.O. Street Directory of 1854 it says 'considerable trade carried in corn, flour, malt and beechwood. Upwards of 30,000 quarters of malt are annually made here. There is a large silk mill and five breweries.'

Apart from the trade in malt to other towns, there was also a large amount used by the local breweries, of which there have been many. In recent years there has been only one brewery, that of Brakspear, situated in New Street on the south side of the street near the river. The company was founded in 1779, when Robert Brakspear came to Henley, and entered into a partnership with his uncle by marriage, Richard Hayward[3]. At that time their brewery was in Bell Street, the premises now known as Brakspears were in 1715 occupied by the brewer Benjamin Sarney, who built the Old Brewery House now 86 New Street. In 1739 the premises became the property of Daniel Sarney, brewer, who dying in 1747, left the property to his brother Peter, who bought the house and malt kiln adjoining on the west, now Brakspear's offices. In 1775 the brewery was leased to Robert Appleton and John Shaw, brewers. Peter Sarney died in 1783, and left the brewery to his nephew Joseph Benwell, who in 1812 entered a partnership with William Brakspear, son of Robert. They then took over the brewery in New Street, employing Appleton and Shaw as brewers. The property was later leased by Benwell to Brakspear, and it was finally bought by W H Brakspear and Sons in 1856[4].

In 1961 Whitbreads bought up 15% of Brakspears company, but Brakspears remained in control and continued to brew its own beer and run its pubs. Brakspears has, in its two hundred years in Henley, taken over several of the other Henley breweries. Richard Hayward as early as 1772 had taken over Brooks Brewery and several of its pubs.

The owning or sponsoring of pubs or tied houses seems to have been a practice that began a long time ago. Early records of pubs show that owners, leaseholders or occupants were often brewers and maltsters, often with interests in more than one pub. In some records the description brewers and maltsters seems to be interchangeable. Strictly speaking a brewer is one who is in charge of a brewery and the whole brewing process, while a maltster is concerned with the production of malt from grain. The two activities were often combined, or partnerships were made between brewers and maltsters to form a company. In property records it is not always clear on what terms the brewers or maltsters owned or leased the property, whether as in the case of pubs they sub-let to a landlord, or whether the property was part of a brewery, or if the property was where the brewer or maltster actually lived. All one can be sure of is that their properties were connected primarily with the making or consumption of beer, ale and probably other drinks and victuals.

The father of James Brooks who sold out in 1772 to Richard Hayward, was a William Brooks who began as a brewer in Henley in 1720. He had a family connection with Richard Fisher who was a brewer in the early 1700s [5], Richard Hayward apart from his partnership with Robert Brakspear, was also in partnership in 1776[6] with William Newell, and in 1791[7] with Benjamin Moorhouse, who in 1796 was referred to as a wine merchant, while Hayward and Brakspear were

---

2 Burn, John S 'History of Henley on Thames' 1861, p81

3 Sheppard, Francis 'Brakspear's Brewery. 1779-1979.'

4 & 5 as note 3

6 Hughes, M W 'List of the Archives of Henley on Thames' compiled 1928-30 (not in chronological order but later given Ancient Document numbers (AD) by the Bodlieian in correct order) now in O.R.O. MS DD Henley Nos 181 AD657 & 91 AD661

7 Hughes, M W 'List of Archives' (see note 6) No 110 AD692

called brewers. Other names, which come from Hughes List of Archives, were in 1808 John Berris maltster, in 1784 Anne Geere widow brewer, in 1756 John Brigstock brewer, in 1750 John Blackman brewer, in 1741 Robert Cluett and in 1738 and 1727 Charles Brigstock.

In Pigot & Co's Street Directory of 1823 there were twelve maltsters listed. Hugh Barford, Hart Street; William Cooper, Market Place; George Day, Bell Street; William Dobson, High Street; John Paulin, Northfield End; Richard Pickman New Street; Riggs & Son, New Street; James Roomes, West Street; James Sharp senior, New Street; James Sharp junior, Market Place; Widow Smith, New Street; and John Waite, Bell Street. By 1830 a similar directory shows that the number of maltsters had dwindled to nine. Hugh Barford, Hart Street; Joseph Benwell & Co, New Street; William Cooper, Market Place; William Dobson, High Street; Richard Pickman, New Street; Thomas Riggs, New Street; James Roomes, Greys Lane; John Sharp, New Street; and Hugh Waite, Bell Street.

Some of the brewers and maltsters already mentioned can be connected to specific properties, many of them are to be found in the later part of this book which describes individual malthouses. Some however it has not been possible to place exactly. Others such as John Berris may be placed at a location, but one with no apparent associations with pubs or malthouses. John Berris, maltster, is recorded in 1808[8] as having taken the lease of what is now 19 Gravel Hill, known as Button Jugs or Juggs, at that time two cottages. Despite the name being suggestive of a pub, there is no proof that either of the cottages were a pub, although it is possible that a malthouse did exist behind the cottages. It may be that John Berris was living in one or both of the cottages, the present single house was probably built soon after 1825 (Fig 66). In September of that year the two cottages 'called Button Jugs' were advertised[9] as 'To be let on a building lease'. Both cottages were given to the town as part of the Barnaby Bridge Book Charity of 1582, and were always linked together. The name if not that of a pub may derive from the various meanings of the words 'button' and 'jug' as defined in the greater Oxford Dictionary. 'Button' may describe something of small value, while the word 'jug' or 'jugg' may lead to 'double jug' or things yoked together. Thus 'Button Jugs' may simply mean two cottages of small value linked together.

Concerning the brewers, Charles Brigstock leased the *Rose and Crown* Market Place in 1727 and 1738, and in 1756 John Brigstock leased the same pub. John Blackman had connections in 1726 and 1748 with the *Blue Bell* and also a brewhouse. In 1764 the *Crown and Thistle* was left to Blackman's daughter Sarah Painter by her aunt Susanna Cluett, the widow of Robert Cluett, who had owned the *Crown and Thistle* or the *Black Horse and Farrier* as it was previously known, till his death in 1743[10].

Of the maltsters, Hugh Barford was connected to malthouses at 18 and 27 Hart Street and to others in the town. William Cooper was at 29 Market Place, a property now demolished for the entrance to Greys Road Car Park. The Market Place was often in the past referred to as the High Street, though since the High Street also sometimes included Hart Street and Gravel Hill, the name can be confusing. There are also occasions when property at the upper end of the Market is termed Gravel Hill. William Dobson had malthouses at 21 and 55/57 Market Place. Riggs & Son, the son of whom may be the later Thomas Riggs, seem to have had their main malthouse at 44 New Street, as well as being concerned with other houses in the town. James Roomes lived and also had a malthouse at the site of what was later to be Albion Place in West Hill or Street, another in New Street, and another in Dirty Bottom, or the lower end of Greys Road. The name Dirty Bottom was

8 Hughes, M W 'List ofArchives' (see note 6) 149 AD725

9 Reading Mercury & Oxford Gazette 26 Sep 1825

10 See entries for the *Black Horse and Farrier,* the *Blues Bell,* the *Crown and Thistle* and the *Rose & Crown*

probably because the Town Ditch crossed the roadway at the junction of Greys Road with Duke or Duck Street. The malthouse at 33 New Street was later to be that of John and/or James Sharp, later still like many of the malthouses it became the property of Brakspear.

Malthouses in the 17th century as implied by the earlier quotation from Dr Plot, were at that time small domestic concerns, but by the 18th century, purpose built malthouses were of larger dimensions, and obviously more commercial. Some of the 18th and 19th century houses lasted till the end of the century, and feature on the large scale O.S. map of 1879. Some however by then had already vanished, as can be found by comparing the number on the map with the number that are recorded in various documents and other sources. So far in researches of Henley properties forty two malthouses have been located for certain, with a further two probable, and there are possibly more to be found. There were eleven in Bell Street, one in Northfield End, eight or maybe nine in Hart Street, six or seven in the Market Place, two on Gravel Hill, seven in Friday Street, four in New Street, one at the bottom of Greys Road, one in Duke Street or possibly Reading Road, and one in West Hill.

At the end of the 19th century when Brakspears had become the largest brewery in the town, having taken over and closed its only serious rival, Greys Brewery in 1896, they seem to have decided to rationalise the malting process. In 1900 Brakspears built the very large malthouse on the north side of New Street opposite the brewery. This large malthouse (Fig 67) was big enough for all their requirements, and Brakspears then sold off or leased out various properties and malthouses around the town. Malting ceased in 1972, and the malthouse has now become offices, while the stables, built at the same time, have been converted into living accommodation. Although malting no longer takes place in Henley, malt being brought in from elsewhere, Brakspears continue to brew, using their own supply of water from an artesian well deep beneath the brewery.

In the 19th century as stated in the P.O. Directory of 1854 there were five breweries. Brakspears has already been described, Greys Brewery, bought and closed in 1896 by Brakspears, was situated in Friday Street on the south side (Figs 64 & 65) behind the houses on the west side of the *Anchor,* a pub which was known as Greys Brewery Tap (Fig 1). A tap was the name often given to a pub near to a brewery, which served that brewery's beer, and which by its position was never short of supplies. Greys Brewery can be traced back to the early 19th century. The name is derived from its location, being on the south side of Friday Street it was until 1892 in Rotherfield Greys and not in Henley.

Greys Brewery was at one time almost as large as Brakspears, indeed it had pubs distributed over a wide area, including several in Wokingham and Reading. It however had a weakness in that the majority of its pubs were leasehold and not freehold, as were many of Brakspears[11]. James Brooks had had long leaseholds and freeholds which were bought by Hayward, who left them to Robert Brakspear, who then left them to W H Brakspear. Other pubs had been owned by the Sarneys and then Benwell, who in 1812 amalgamated his brewery with that of Brakspear, eventually selling his share to Brakspear, and also selling off his pubs, some of which were bought by Brakspear, while others were bought by Brakspear in later years. Henry Nathaniel Byles who started Greys Brewery, left it to his son, but later it was being run by managers, which may have left it vulnerable to a take over by Brakspear.

Other breweries in the 19th century were the Cannon Brewery behind the *Cannon Inn*, now the *Argyll* (Figs 6,23 & 26), the Crown Brewery in the Market Place; the Union Brewery which may have started behind the *Union* public house and then moved behind the *Queen's Head*;

11 'Greys Brewery Rent Ledger. 1885-96' O.R.O. Brakspear IV/ii/1 & ' Inventory & Valuation of the Brewery, New Street, the property of Joseph Benwell & W H Brakspear. 1826' O.R.O. Brakspear VI/1

and the Ives Brewery later at 39 Market Place. This last named continued till about 1920. There were also breweries in nearby towns who owned or leased pubs in Henley, firms such as Simonds Brewery of Reading, Hewett & Son of Reading, Fuller & Co of Maidenhead, Leadbetter & Bird of High Wycombe, the Watlington Brewery, the Wallingford Brewery, and the Goring Brewery, which became the property of Mrs Ann Gundry. After Mrs Gundry's death, her pubs and the Goring Brewery were bought by Brakspears in November 1940[12].

The Early Pubs of Henley The earliest mention of what may well have been a pub is 21 October 1337, when Thom Schireburne and Elizabeth his wife paid a rent of 13s 4d to the Warden of the Town for a tenement called *Le Turnours* in the High Street[13]. Unfortunately its location is unknown, and at that date the High Street may have included both Hart Street and the Market Place, and even perhaps Gravel Hill.

In 1359 Thom Huberd left property in the town, among which was a tavern with solar and shop in the middle of the High Street[14]. The middle of the High Street refers to houses which were later called Middle Row, and were down the centre of the Market Place and across into Hart Street to about opposite where the *Catharine Wheel* now stands. Middle Row was finally demolished at the end of the 18th century (Fig 23). From later references one gathers that the early Guildhalls, one was newly created in 1486, were situated at or just above the main cross roads. It also appears that a pub, known as the *Feathers* or the *Plume of Feathers* was alongside the Guildhall, in one reference being on the line of and seeming to be a continuation of Duke Street[15]. This pub was demolished when the old Guildhall (possibly the one of 1486) was taken down and a new Town Hall of 1796 was erected on the site now occupied by its successor, the present Town Hall of 1899/1901.

The position of the 18th century *Feathers* makes it possible that it could have been the same tavern left to the town by Thom Huberd in 1359. The name of the pub is of interest. Feathers or a plume of feathers are by tradition the emblem of the Princes of Wales, two Princes of Wales have been connected with Henley, oddly neither of them became king. The second Prince of Wales, Frederick, son of George II, lived at Park Place from about 1738 to his death in 1752. It is true that the name of the *Feathers* is only mentioned in about 1750, but the pub is known to have existed before that, and it is not uncommon in the records for the name of a pub not to be recorded. The other Prince of Wales was the son of Edward III, Edward the Black Prince, who in 1356 had a resounding victory at Poitiers. In 1337 his father had conferred the Duchy of Cornwall on Edward, and this duchy included the Manors of Wallingford and Bensington (Benson), which he held till his death in 1376. The town of Henley was at the extreme south east corner of the land of the Manor of Bensington[16]. Northfield End was still in the Manor of Bensington in the early 19th century, but in 1337 Henley itself no longer seems to have been part of Bensington. However the connection of the Black Prince with Henley is a strong one, since the Manor of Henley was held by the Duchy of Cornwall. Add this connection to his popular image as a successful soldier, it is not unlikely that the tavern of Thom Huberd might have been called the *Plume of Feathers.*

---

12 Henley Standard 22 Nov 1940

13 Hughes, M W 'List of Archives'(see note 6, P2) 624 AD40 The Warden was the equivalent of the Mayor

14 Hughes, M W 635 AD89

15 Henley Rentals 1745 & Journal of the Henley Archaeological & Historical Group No 12 Spring 1997, see also plan of Middle Row Fig 23, original plan in Town Hall

16 Pearman, Rev M T 'History of the Manor of Bensington' 1896

Names of Pubs. Sometimes it seems that pub names were changed by the whim of the landlord or owner. On the north side of the Market Place there was the *Sheers* or *Shears* which changed to the *Turk's Head*, on the south side there was the *Black Horse and Farrier* which became the *Crown and Thistle.* Near to it there was the *North Star,* which became the *Cannon Inn,* then the *Hop Leaf* and then the *Argyll,* still trading under that name. In Greys Road there was the *Blue Blacksmith* which became the *Royal Oak* (Fig 45). In Reading Road the *Portobello* is now the *Wheatsheaf,* and in Bell Street the *Duke of Cumberland* is now *Ye Olde Bell* (Fig 32).

Other name changes such as the *Plough* becoming the *Black Horse*, the *Waggon and Horses* becoming briefly the *Six Bells* and then the *Eight Bells*, and the *Saracen's Head* being for a short time the *Black Prince,* may have been caused by local interpretations of the inn signs. A plough may have been shown pulled by a black horse, a waggon and team may have been shown with eight horses and a bell on each harness hame. A picture of a saracen might easily be called a black prince, though this was a name which did not stick, the pub remains the *Saracen's Head* to this day. The other two remained the *Black Horse* and the *Eight Bells* till they closed 90-100 years after the change of name.

There were often two pubs of the same name operating in and around Henley at the same time; while other names have been transferred from one location to another, like the *Rose and Crown* and the *Bell.* Even today there are two *Angels*, one on the bridge and the other across the bridge in Remenham. There were also till quite recently two *White Harts*, one being referred to as the *Little White Hart* while the other was often called the *Old White Hart*. During the 1850s there were three *Cannons*, two in the Market Place and one in Northfield End.

Tracing the names of the smaller pubs in the 19th century is difficult, as they were sometimes described simply as beerhouses with no name attached. The street directories tend to give the names of beerhouse keepers as 'beer retailers' with no pubs named. If a publican was long lived or his widow took over the premises, it has sometimes been possible to place some of the beerhouse keepers at a definite pub from later editions of the directories. The Census Returns have also been useful in placing beerhouse keepers. The street directories after about 1883 begin to put street numbering in the addresses, but the early numbering does not always agree with that after about 1900. For instance what is now the *Olde Bell* and was then the *Duke of Cumberland,* has at various times been listed as 16,18,20 & 22 Bell Street. The south side of New Street was even more drastically changed, number 32 became 48, and 40 became 56. This was due to the later numbering including the houses in the back alleys. Before street numbering the method used to describe property was to state what street it was in, and then say who owned the properties to the east and west, or north and south. Sometimes the description goes further and says in what direction the property lay to the street, or as at *Ye Cocke* what lay behind it. This at least places the property on one side of the street for certain.

Laws and Licenses. Pubs both large and small have always been the subject of laws and regulations. In recent times there have been various licensing acts and laws regulating not only the behaviour of landlords and customers, but also times of opening and services supplied. These laws are by no means a modern invention.

In 1438 on Wednesday 14 May a notice was published and recorded in the Henley Borough Records[17]. 'Notice for bakers and for hostelers (pistoribus et hostilariis)' this was a declaration by the bakers before the Warden and Burgesses as to the price they would sell 'Horse bread XV loaves for 2 pence and no more (pro duodena et non ultra)' and all the hostelers promised that they would

17 Briers, P M 'The Henley Borough Records. Assembly Books, 1395-1543' pub by Oxfordshire Record Society 1960

not bake horse bread in their hostelries (hospitiis). Horse bread and the sale of it is mentioned in edicts of 1474, 1494 and 1513.

Horse bread is a bread made of beans, bran etc. for horses, still made in some parts of Europe. In 1753 horse bread was given to horses to strengthen them. The edicts against inn keepers making horse bread seem to have been general. In 1467 'that non baker that shalle bake eny horsebrede, kepe eny hostre' and again in 1540 'No hosteler or Innholder should make any horse breadde.' In Webb's Travels of 1590 it says 'the food which I and others did eat was very blacke, far worse than horse breade.' Ben Jonson has the last word in 'Every Man out of Humour' in 1599, when as a term of abuse a character says 'You thread-bare horse-bread eating rascals' [18].

It seems likely from these comments that the poorest people probably ate horse bread, but that it was generally unsavoury and possibly downright dangerous. It probably included a lot of impurities and being of a dark colour, perhaps disguising inclusions such as ergot, might if baked in the same oven as ordinary bread have contaminated it. One is left wondering though why the bakers were allowed to bake horse bread in their ovens, perhaps the law was only to prevent innkeepers from serving it to their customers.

In 1532 or 1533 in the Henley Borough Records the following notice is to be found:-

> 'Be it known that it is ordenyd and made by the Warden and his brethren that all these persons ffolleing are admitted to be typplers within the towne and to sell ale and lodge according to the statute, and for the same they have putt in suretes whose namys ffolleith with the typpler:-
>
> Primus (in margin) Rob. Strong, plegges Tho. Lewes and John Fowle; Hen. Pyrry, plegges Joh. Fowle and Olyver Lylly; Ric. Lyde plegges — — (page torn) — — — Hen. Luen and Matilda Saunder; John West, plegges Jamys Cramford and John Chastelene; Matilda Coke, plegges Thomas Lewes and Hen. Luen; Wil. Atkyn, John Fowle and Thomas Stone; John Gregory, Hen. Luen and Tho. Lewes; Rob. Nichollas, plegges Hen. Luen and Tho. Ro; Joh. Peynter, John Chastelen and Olyver Lylly; Tho. Chesildene, Mr Aysheby and Tho. Lewes; Annes Revers, plegges John Ansty and W. Abery; Bonour (?), Wil. Assinden and Tho. Lewes; Wil. Browne, plegges Hen. Luen and W.Woderoff; John Foster, plegges John Chastelen and Hen. Luen; Rob. Eton, John Chastelen and Wil. Lowthman; Annes Rutter, plegges Tho. Ro and J Chastelen; John Chattall, plegges John Chastelen and Ric. Smyth; Hen. Losewell, plegges W. Schomaker and John Chastelen; all these suretes are bound to the Kyng in £X and every of them and allso John Olyver's wyff, plegges Rob Rawlynsum and Wil. Abery ' [19]

It is interesting to note that the word 'typplers' is here used to denote the seller of ales, the innkeeper or landlord, and not its modern meaning of one who drinks to excess. Also the custom of innkeepers needing two persons to stand surety for them for the sum of £10 each, a considerable sum in 1532/3. The system of landlords being vouched for is still present in the 18th and early 19th centuries. In the Victuallers Recognizances 1753-1822 every landlord is vouched for by two persons, the amount being still £10 each. In neither case is it clear whether the money had to be paid over immediately, or whether it was only a surety for good behaviour.

The names of innkeepers in the 1532/3 list cannot be connected to specific pubs, except

18 The Greater Oxford Dictionary

19 Briers, P M 'The Henley Borough Records- Assembly Books 1395-1543' Ox. Record Soc. 1960

for possibly Ric Lyde who may have been at the *Catharine Wheel* (Fig 20), grandson of John Lyde who left his tenement the *'Katheryne Whyll'* in his will of 1499 [20]. Another is Matilda Coke, was she a widow or daughter of Tho Coke carpenter and victualler in New Street in 1494 ? (see *Ye Cocke*). It is a great misfortune that the Parish Registers only start in 1558. Another recognised name is Thomas Lewes one of those standing surety, who was probably a brewer living at what is now Longlands (see unknown pub No 137, B6 & M24).

Among the names of those standing surety John Chastelen (Chastelene) appears eight times, Hen (Henry) Luen six times, Tho (Thomas) Lewes five times, John Fowle three, Thomas Ro (Rowe ?) three, Olyver Lylly twice, and W Abery twice. There are eighteen publicans named, none of them more than once, and none of them standing surety. This may mean that in 1532/3 there were eighteen public houses in central Henley, which might have included Northfield End. It may also mean that those standing surety were men of greater means, who either owned the houses, or were brewers or maltsters; certainly several of the names appear in the Borough Records of the same date listed as burgesses of the town. Those standing surety in the 18th century were often brewers or maltsters, though by then publicans sometimes vouched for each other.

Licensing in the 17th century In 1605 and 1608 the Privy Council issued orders to 'every Quarter Sessions in England' and therefore, according to Mrs Mary Sturge Gretton in her book on 'Justices of the Peace in the 17th Century', the orders must have been sent to Oxfordshire Quarter Sessions, although no copy has come to light in Oxfordshire. In June 1605 instructions were sent to the Justices of the Peace, these particular ones were taken from a document in Exeter [21]. The justices had to see that various statutes were observed, these included :-

> 'The Statutes concerning Alehouses & Typlers the statutes of the assize of bread and drink...... But especially such as keepe Ale houses without Lycense may there be examined & presently punished according to the lause. And that such as having Lycense doe abuse the same or not observe these Articles to bee put doune and proceeded with upon their recognisance & such like.'
>
> '........the Constable of the Hundred.......and the pettie Constables & other inferiour officers......to deliver their knowledges touching the premisses......and to bring...... such as offend in remissness or otherwise, touching roages & idlers, or in keeping of typling houses without lawfull license, or wch doe not observe the Articles & orders prescribed unto them.......Item that at these Assemblies they punish......such as be comon drunkerdes, and all comon haunters of Alehouses......'

Three years later in June 1608 apparently conditions in alehouses were still not as they should be. The Privy Council issued further licensing directions, the following is from a Devon manuscript. It was said that 'the directions of 1605 have failed to suppress lewdness and disorder in Alehouses.' So specific rules were laid down :-

> '1 Licenses to be annual only. To be renewed at every Easter Sessions.
>
> 2 Where a licence has been granted by two Justices it must be brought to the next Quarter Sessions to be sealed by the Clerk of the Peace.

---

20 Weaver, J R H & Beardwood, A 'Some Oxfordshire Wills' Ox. Record Soc. 1958

21 Gretton, Mrs Mary Sturge 'Oxfordshire Justices of the Peace in the 17th Century' Ox. Record Soc. 1934 ppxxv-xxvii

3 The Clerk of the Peace is to keep a register, to be signed by four Justices, two of whom must be of the Quorum, of all licences granted.
4 The Articles of Good Order, to be observed by their Alehouse keepers must be drawn up by the Justices and forwarded to the Privy Council that the Council may add to or amend them if necessary.
5 A list of all licensed houses is to be kept, and the number of them is to be diminished rather than increased.'

The Articles of Good Order as instructed in Clause 4, were duly drawn up by the Devon Justices and were as follows :-

'That such as shalbe lycensed to keepe typling houses to be bound in X£ themselves with two sureties V£ apiece to observe these Articles following viz :-
1 That they suffer no nyhbors Children or tenantes nor any dwelling in the same toune to tipple in their houses.
2 That none be suffered to tipple in their houses in any one day above one hour.
3 That none be suffered to tipple in their houses on the Sabboth & festivall daies at the time of Sermons or Service, nor at any time after nyne of the Clock at nyht.
4 That if any Vagabondes or suspitious persons com to their houses they shall acquaint the officers with yt, and so if any goodes be offered in their houses to be sold by any.
5 That they suffer no Carding dicing or other play in their houses.
6 That they suffer no drunkenness or dissolute order to be in their houses & if any happen to be, to acquainte the Constable of the toune wth it that the offenders may be punished.
7 That they shall not Brew in their houses but shall take their drinke from the Brewer when it may be had & the best to be but at 6s the Barrell and the small at 4s the Barrell.
8 That they drawe out their drinke by the Ale quart & not by Jugges or Cuppes and sell the best after the rate of 3d the gallon and the worst at the rate of 2d the gallon. And such as must needbe Brewe themselves to make it so they may sell at the price aforesaid.
9 That no Alehouse be erected in anie Limit but by the Justices is assigned to that lymit that thereupon they may be charged wth what falleth out amiss therein.
10 That if any of them offend in any of the articles they be forthwth putt downe & no more suffered to keep anie more typpling house & their bondes certified to be put in suit and themselves bound to the good beghaviour.
11 That none be admitted to keep Alehouse or tiplinge but such as have bin knowne of good behaviour & conversacon and such as are not retainers to anye.
12 That none be suffered but in the bodies of good Tounes & through faires & the number still to be as few as may be.
13 The Justice of the Assize to be certified at everye Assizes what number of Typling houses bee licenced within anie division & in what tounes and places.
14 That no brewer be suffered to be retayner to any Justices of the Cuntrye & that all Brewers have a rate or size set doune to them by the Magistrates of Citties and Tounes corporate and by the Justices of the Cuntrie according to the statute for selling their Beers & Ale.'

Mrs Gretton continues in her book by quoting from a paper which was found among papers on Eynsham, Oxfordshire[22] which contains similar directions to the Devon examples. It is entitled 'License to keepe a Tipling House 1617'. The License is a clerk's copy, but nevertheless it appears to be a valid statement about laws pertaining to Oxfordshire. Following the license, which is one issued to 'Egerly of Brittington husbandman to sell ale & beere..... for the space of one whole year next ensusing', directions are given as to behaviour.

> '1 Imprimis that he shall suffer no Neighbours children or servants or any other dwelling in the same parish to tipple in his house.
> 2 Item that none be suffered to tipple in his said house on the Sabboth or Festivall dayes, at the sermon or service tyme, nor in any other day above one hower, nor at any tyme after 9 of the clocke at night.
> 3 That he suffer no diceing, carding, playing at Tables, or any other unlawfull game to be used in his house.
> 4 That he suffer no drunkerds, drunkenness, or any other evill rule to be in his house, if any happen to be, he shall presently accquaint the constable, or other officer with it, that such offenders may be punished, and such abuses reformed.
> 5 That if any vagabonds or any other suspitious persons come to his house and doe there offer any goods to be sold, he shall presently acquaint the constable, or other officer therewithall, that such persons may be apprehended and brought before some Justice of the peace to be examined if there be cause.
> 6 That he brue his drinke, that he may sell the best at 6s the barrell and the small at 3s.
> 7 That he draw out his drinke and sell it by the Alequart and Alepinte, and not by cupps and Juggs, and sell the best for 3d the aleggallon, and the small at 2d the Alegallon.'

It can easily be seen how similar the directions are in both the Devon and the Eynsham lists, and there is no reason to suppose that Henley publicans did not have the same instructions. The first clause in both lists is hard to understand, unless one was supposed to be a traveller before being allowed to 'tipple'. If so it had a modern equivalent in the only recently abolished Sunday laws in Scotland. One wonders how the various houses maintained their business with such a prevention on local custom. In other respects the directions seem very much to be the basis of modern licensing laws, many of the points made are virtually unaltered today. One thing is made very clear that it has always been the landlord's responsibility to maintain order, and that he may refuse to serve customers if he regards them as being 'drunkerds' or otherwise of 'evill rule.'

Later in the 17th century, in 1682, a book was published for Henry Twyford of Vine Court, Middle Temple, called 'List of Proceedings for J.P.s.' It is a set of instructions to magistrates categorising various offences and giving the penalties to be imposed for the offences. Mrs Gretton has again quoted the text in full, and certain aspects of it are recorded here. The offences were divided into three sections.

Firstly there were offences against God and his Church. This included invoking spirits, witch craft and sorcery whereby any person is 'killed, destryed or lamed' (Penalty: Death without benefit of clergy). Attempting by witchcraft etc to find treasure, unlawful love or hurting a man's goods (Penalty: for first offence imprisonment for a year with once a quarter six hours in the pillory and there confessing. Second offence Death without clergy). Then there was perjury, and Drawing

22 'Papers concerning Eynsham' O.R.O. MSS Top Oxon c118, quoted in 'Oxfordshire Justices....' see note 21

a weapon in church or churchyard (Penalty: Forfeit an ear or, if ears are lacking, brand right cheek with letter F for fray-maker). Absenting from church for a month (Penalty: £20 or two parts of offender's whole estate when it has been divided into three parts). There then follow various other transgressions against God and his Church.

Secondly the category of offences against the King and his government, which included treason, murder, manslaughter, house burning, robbery with violence etc. The penalty for these crimes was generally Death, with or without clergy depending on degree of the offence, such as the difference between murder and manslaughter. This section oddly included neglecting to bury in a wool shroud and to line the coffin with wool (Penalty: £5), scandalising magistrates and selling corrupt meat, these last two had penalties of fines and imprisonment.

Finally in the third category there are offences against the Country, and amidst poaching offences, breaking down of pond heads, and common scolds, one comes to 'Disordered Victallers..... those who have agreed to sell their victuals at certain prices' (Penalty : '£10 or if that sum not paid within six days twenty days imprisonment with only bread and water; second offence pay £20 with pillory; third offence pay £40 or if not paid within six days loose one of his ears in pillory and be infamous'). Then there were also 'Disorderly Ale-house-keepers.' Those suffering 'Common bawdery, common gaming, common drunkards' within their houses (Penalty: 'Fine and imprisonment and to be bound to the Good Behaviour').

Licensing in the 18th & 19th Centuries At the beginning of the 18th century according to the Corporation Records[23] newcomers to the town had to pay a fine to the Corporation to be free to exercise their trade in the town. There were various trades mentioned such as a bobbin maker, a cutler, a baker and a couple of goldsmiths, who paid 40s, as did Mr Rames on 28 August 1713 when he was granted the liberty to exercise his trade as a distiller, though it is not clear whether he was distilling liquors or perhaps scents from the lavender fields then around the town. On 12 January 1721 Edward Bolton on payment of three guineas was allowed to follow the distillers and strong water trade. It is possible that he was the same man who appears in a Victuallers Recognizance List as a Henley publican in 1753 though he is then named Edward Bolter, unfortunately neither in 1721 or 1753 is a pub mentioned. Neither Rames nor Bolton can be placed at a locality.

During the 18th century some records of licensees were made, the first remaining records for Henley and district are of 1753 when following an act in the 26th year of George II, the licensing of ale houses and the conviction of persons selling ale and other liquors without a license became law. The returns made to the Clerk of the Peace were termed Registers of Recognizance and it is by the name Victuallers Recognizances that the eighteenth century records are known.

In Henley the lists of 1753 and 1754 are only of use if a publican's name is already known, since both these lists contain merely the names of the licensees and no pubs are mentioned. It is not till 1774 that another list survives for Henley, a mere two names, identifiable as the publicans of the *Bell* and the *Windmill*, by this time two guarantors are named each standing for the sum of 10s. In 1775 while listing again the same two landlords and mentioning the pubs by name a note was made

> 'Be it remembered that at the Bell Inn in Henley on Thames in the County of Oxford on Thursday the 7th day of September 1775. The several alehouse keepers within the said hundred did appear before this two of his Majesty's Justices of the Peace.'

The lists presumably made of these alehouse keepers and their pubs in that year and following years do not survive except for two lists of 1815[24] and another of 1817. That of 1815

23 Holton, S J 'Ledger containing Transcription of the Corporation Records 1687-c.1858' Town Hall 4/11/12

24 O.R.O. F114 & F115 AXVI 30/1

gives the landlords with their guarantors each for 10s, while that of 1817 gives the names of the landlords and their pubs.

Victuallers Recognizances do however exist for parishes and areas outside Henley, for example Northfield End, Assendon, Bix, Rotherfield Greys and Shiplake. Most of these start in 1753 and then continue with a few years missing, through to 1822 when all the Recognizances seem to cease. The Recognizances for the places outside Henley except for Northfield End start to mention pubs by name in 1775, Northfield End only mentions the pubs by name in the last entry of 1822.

Acts to regulate licensing were made in the 9th Year of George IV (1829), the 1st, 4th and 5th year of William IV (1830-36), these were summarised in the Reading Mercury & Oxford Gazette of 22 June 1839, when much discussion was still going on about the acts and what they meant, and who benefited and who did not.

The Licensed Victuallers were considered first, the holders of full food and drink licenses, the regulations for them were explained as follows:-

1. **Obtaining the License**. Applicant is required to give notice of his intention to the Overseer and Constable and exhibit a copy on the church door and another on his own door. No certificate of any kind is demanded by law, and even character forms no essential part for a new license.
2. **Security for good behaviour.** The licensed victualler is not required to give a bond for good behaviour nor find security for payment of penalties incurred by transgressions.
3. **Price of a victuallers license.** A return of 22 February 1839 shows that out of 55,750, 39,926 paid one guineau per annum, and of the remainder none paid more than one guineau.
4. **Hours for business.** With the exception of the hours of Divine Service licensed victuallers may be open unlimited time and even at night. Sundays except as above they may open all the time.
5. **Fines etc..** Imposed by the Magistrates, usually for a few shillings.
6. **Transfer of licenses.** Licenses may be transferred to members of the family, if need be several times in a year.
7. **Forfeiture of license.** The licensee may transgress with impunity, the license cannot be forfeited.
8. **Measures.** Licensed victuallers cannot be compelled to use standard measures unless demanded by the customers.

The regulations as laid down for Licensed Beersellers were far more stringent as will be seen in the following list :-

1 **Obtaining the license.** Applicant has to produce a certificate of character signed by six inhabitants of the same parish. A fresh certificate each year. (The necessity of getting six persons to sign is sometimes a great difficulty in a small parish.)

2 **Bond and security.** Beerseller has to give personal bond as well as additional security for good behaviour and for payment of any penalties.

3 **Price of a license.** Beersellers license charged at £3 5s 0d p.a., those only selling beer and not licensed for beer to be drunk on the premises pay £1 1s 0d p.a.

4 **Hours of business** limited by local magistrates, in some places only up to 8.0 in the evening. Power to extend the hours to 11.0 allowed by law.
5 **Sunday opening.** Beerhouses not to open on Sundays and Fast days till 1.0.p.m., nor between 3.0.p.m. and 5.0.p.m., must close by 10.0.p.m. or earlier if directed locally.
6 **Penalties.** The penalty for the most trivial offence fixed at 40s with costs, sometimes as much as £5. So serving a neighbour a few minutes after time may cost 40s and £5. No appeal allowed.
7 **Transfer of licenses.** The license not transferable not even to a widow or family.
8 **Forfeiture.** The license forfeited for any conviction.
9 **Measures.** Beersellers compelled to use standard measures.
10 **Billetting soldiers.** Both licensed victuallers and beersellers are obliged to conform unless the local laws prohibit.

Comparing the two sets of regulations it is easy to see why the beersellers felt that they were hard done by and clamoured for greater equality. However in spite of their reservations about the laws it was in the 1830s, 1840s and 1850s that beerhouses increased in number. Before this time houses selling beer only, were practically unknown, and would be beersellers had to obtain a victuallers license, which was not easy to do for someone who had limited resources and did not want to sell either food, wine or spirits. So these acts of the 1830s while allowing more people to become purveyors of beer, at the same time made sure that a tight control was maintained over them, and that it was possible and indeed easy to remove any beer license if the beerseller proved unworthy.

It is surprising that it was only the beersellers who had to use standard measures, since before this time measures had been under the control of the Court Leets of the various manors, and in Henley the Court Leet's officers made regular checks on measures used by both innkeepers and shop keepers. During the period from 1800 to about 1830 most of the licensed victuallers of the town were fined at some time or other for inadequate measures.

The confusion about measures seems to have continued, in June 1855[25] it was reported that fourteen publicans were charged with having incorrect measures for the sale of beer. Many of them had common straight pint cups which they had assumed to be correct measures, all were fined 5s with 10s costs. In the County Bench there were a further similar twenty one cases, and their fines ranged from 20s to £5. One was fined 30s plus £5 costs for putting the cups back on his shelf after they were tested.

The regulations were again altered in an act of 1870, and all licensees had to serve standard measures, which again resulted in a spate of convictions of publicans whose measures were incorrect. It is also from 1870 that licenses began to be recorded by the Licensing Magistrates, at first in Henley in a book named the Magistrates Special Sessions Minute Book, which also contained other matters dealt with by the magistrates. Later books were provided where a continuing record was kept of all licensed victuallers, a separate record of beerhouse keepers and another list of shop keepers with licensed premises. Licenses for the town of Henley were termed the Henley Borough records and licenses for the surrounding district were called the Rural records, a system which continues to the present day.

---

25 Reading Mercury & Oxford Gazette 23 Jun 1855

Problems with the Military In the Appendix to Mrs Gretton's book among miscellaneous petitions of 1689 is the following:-

> 'Petition of John Lane, James Harrison, Frances Worley widow, Richard Johnson and William Usher, innholders and victuallers of Henley, signed also by Richard Frost, Warden of Henley, for an order to the constables of Henley to make a rate to reimburse them for moneys spent on firing and candles for 'Gaurds of horse and dragoones' quartered in the town by order of the Earl of Dumbarton 3rd December 1688. Lieftinant Generall of the forces of the late King James the second. Noted - Referred to the Warden & Sir Ed Warcupp & Mr Stone or any two of them to examine and allow what they find cause.'

Attached to the petition was the Warrant signed 'Dumbarton' from 'Redding 3rd December 1688.' Which addressed to the Warden, Constable or Chief Magistrate of Henley, required him to furnish the firing and candles.

Unfortunately it does not say whether the innholders were reimbursed before the town of Henley was welcoming William and Mary in 1689. Frances Worley widow was at the *Red Lion,* William Usher was at the *White Horse* on the bridge, and it is possible that James Harrison was at the *Catharine Wheel.*

Just over a hundred years later there were still difficulties between innkeepers and soldiers, as shown by the following letter [26] which was addressed to :-

> 'Major Lee, commanding the 16th or Queen's Light Dragoon Guards, Beaconsfield, Bucks.'
>
> 'Honored Sir,'
>
> 'I consider myself under many obligations by your trouble in writing to me and beg you will have the goodness to excuse me taking the liberty to answer your letter.'
>
> 'I have been for many years keeper of the House I now live in and so far has been my conduct from keeping a disorderly House that it has been my study continually to avoid it and the Gents of this Corporation, Parish Officers and most of the principal inhabaitants of this town emply me in my business of a Bricklayer and I never yet had a soldier drunk in my House so as to be incapable of Duty or that was ever confined for such a fault for I never suffered a Man to drink to excess.'
>
> 'The Store being kept at my House of course the greater part of the Troops quartered in this town frequented my House more than any other and the men being no in my Debt there is no doubt but they will make use of any unfair advantage to avoid paying their just demands and I flatter myself that no soldier can (to my Face) say I have used any Allurement whatever to tempt him to drink and on that Account will myself waint' (sic) 'on your Honour on Monday next for the very purpose of vindicating my character from the very unjust Reports that has been made reflecting me.'
>
> 'Corporal Smith when on a Pass in this Town having no Money I advanced him seven shillings to follow the Troop and I have not since heard of

26 Letter in private hands - the property of the late Brian Young of Shiplake

him and Duffin always informed me he had Money in your Hands considerably more than was sufficient to satisfy my Demands on him.'

'I hope your Honour will consider the peculiar Hardships of Publicans in general and the burthen they have been to me and that I have a very large family and that such a sum that is justly due to me will be a very considerable Object.'

'I am Hon^{d} Sir

Your very obed ((covered by seal))

Jno Strange

Henley 25 May 1797.'

John Strange was at the *King's Arms* in 1791 (Fig 30), and possibly a few years before that. The Street Directory of about 1793 just says John Strange victualler and bricklayer, but an entry in the Reading Mercury & Oxford Gazette for 17 June 1793 advertised 'An Annual Subscription Pink Meeting of 5s each which will be held at Mr Strange's the *King's Arms* on Friday 28 June instant, where the attendance of Florists and others will be esteemed a favour. To show 7 blooms of 7 different sorts and the subscription money will be divided into 6 handsome pieces of plate......' It was evidently a club meeting of flower enthusiasts and their annual show.

John Strange was buried on the 28 November 1809 aged 62, and it was his son John Strange who in 1814 was at the house later to be known as the *Rose and Crown* New Street (Fig 7). In 1823 the son was listed in a street directory as a bricklayer and plasterer, and there is no evidence that the *Rose and Crown* existed while he was there, or that he was a publican or beer seller.

A later occasion in Henley concerned with the army was less a problem and more of an entertainment. In the Reading Mercury & Oxford Gazette of 10 September 1859 it was said that there had been a visit to Henley of detachments of the 11th Hussars, whose late Colonel had been the Earl of Cardigan, and who had been engaged in that 'memorable cavalry charge at Balaklava'. Their headquarters had been set up for the few days at the *Red Lion* (Cover photo), then newly re-opened by Mrs Williams (see the *Red Lion*). On the Tuesday that they were there, the Hussar's band played lively and popular music outside the *Red Lion* in the moonlight. A concert much enjoyed by a large crowd who had gathered around the bridge.

Gaming in the pubs of Henley Although some games have always been, and still are allowable in pubs such as darts, billiards, shove halfpenny, dominoes, skittles and bowling as at the *White Horse* in the Fairmile, and at the *Broad Gates* in the 18th century - as long as no bets were taken. Games of chance played for money using dice or cards have always been frowned upon, as can be seen by the licensing laws of 1608 and 1617. The account of 1800 which follows, records a 'Meeting of the Magistrates of the town for the purpose of an inquiry into the conduct of publicans of the said town and to arrange such plan as may be requisite to enforce orderly conduct'[27].

'7th January 1800'

'John Arundell the Watchman was examined who deposed that he particularly recollect about a month or six weeks ago about two or three o'clock on a Sunday morning, as he was going his round when he came to Mr Burrett he heard a loud conversation which induced him to stop and' (listen ?) - 'that a party appeared playing at cards and that he does not know what was won or lost but that

27 O.R.O. MS DD Hen J29 1800

he heard the money often sound on the table - that one person was Mr Tho Piercey but he was not certain as to any other person.'

'That he has frequently heard the same at very late hours - that as he has gone his round he has frequently heard at Mr Marclues persons playing at cards at very late hours - that he recollects hearing a person as he came out of the house say he had won a guineau and a half.'

'Corporal Crabtree says that on Friday morning last after one o'clock he was at the *White Hart* that Thos Piercey, Mr Henry Allnutt, Mr Appleton, and Mr Burrett were playing at cards in the Bars and this deposee was in the kitchen. Mr Piercey and Mr Burrett came into the kitchen and Mr Piercey bragged that he had some money and as this deposee understood about £8. Mr Allnutt came into the kitchen and asked them to come in again and Mr Piercey told Mr Allnutt that he owed him one guineau and a half and as this deposee understood the words that he had won it and he said I do win or lose - that this deposee offered to take a hand with Mr Piercey for a crown, that he apprehends Mr Piercey did not hear him, but that Mr Burrett did who answered - "Man - we do not play for crowns here, but for guineaus or a Bullseye which I ' (Burrett) 'call a hundred pound note." '

'William Tonnjon corroborates the above being present.'

'James Rogers, Private in the 3rd Dragoons says that on Friday morning about one o'clock he was at the *White Hart* that as he passed by the Bar he saw a party playing at cards that they were Mr Thos Piercey, Mr Appleton, Mr Burrett and a fourth person, but whom the fourth person was he was not certain - but he heard it was Mr Allnutt in the morning - that Mr Burrett and Mr Piercey came into the kitchen where this deponent was and Mr Piercey said he was about seven guineaus in pocket - that Mr Appleton came and desired them to play again - which they refused to do - Mr Burrett saying that he would not unless Mr Burrett' (Piercey ?) 'went with them - that Mr Appleton repeated his request more than once but was still refused - this deponent then went to bed.'

'Richd Taylor /the watchman /was with Arnold' (Arundell ?) 'on this Sunday morning - when he heard the card playing at Mr Burrett and deposes the same effect and he particularly recollects hearing persons say - you owe some money - as at different times - and in as large sums as ten pounds and the least he recollects is two guineaus - that he recollects Mr Piercey's name being mentioned as one of the party.'

'That he has often heard and been convinced that cards were playing at Mr Burretts of very large sums.'

'That he has repeatedly heard at Mr Marklew's at the *Wheel* persons playing at cards - at very late hours that he has heard persons as they came out of the house mention that they had won or lost such as a guineau or two.'

'Examinations taken today - Mr Bradshaw assisted me to write to Sir C Willoughby again - but I apprehend it is useless - as he has I suppose determined either to come or not and my writing will have no effect.'

On this rather defeated note the article ends, obviously whoever was taking the depositions despaired of any notice being taken. Mr Marclue, Mr Piercey, Mr Allnutt, Mr Appleton and Mr Burrett were all well off and well connected gentlemen and most likely well known and friendly with the Magistrates, so that the whole business was probably a bit of an embarrassment. Mr Marclue (Marklow/Marklew) was in 1800 landlord of the *Catharine Wheel*, while Mr Burrett was landlord of the *White Hart.* Mr Appleton was the brewer in partnership with Mr Shaw, Mr Allnutt was an attorney and an auctioneer, and Mr Piercey was a gentleman.

In an Inventory of Brakspear's Brewery taken in 1826[28] when Joseph Benwell and William Henry Brakspear were in partnership, the various inns and beerhouses were listed noting which the company held freehold or leasehold, which were held by Joseph Benwell and which by Brakspear alone. To arrive at a valuation of the houses concerned, mention was made of the facilities of each pub. Note was taken of the amount of stabling, storage sheds, piggeries, yards etc. In three houses, the *Crown and Thistle,* the *Union,* and the *Windmill* there were skittle grounds. The first two were in the Market Place and Hart Street, and presumably catered to customers who had time on their hands during market activities. Neither of the pubs were of the status of the larger coaching inns, and perhaps they catered to the working men or servants of the wealthier farmers, who may have had to wait around while their masters transacted business elsewhere. The *Windmill* was out of town up Gravel Hill and probably catered to those with business at the mill, who perhaps also had to wait about.

In 1870 the game of skittles was being played in several pubs, in 1860 when the *Basketmakers Arms* was offered for sale a skittle alley was included. Another pub for sale in 1863 was the *Broad Gates*, where a 'covered skittle alley' was advertised. At the Annual General Licensing meeting in August 1870 'a general caution' was issued to alehouse and beerhouse keepers in the town against the practice of 'gambling which is now carried on by persons playing skittles and other games at these houses'[29]. Today there is a skittle alley at the *Bull*, whether there was one there in 1870 is not known, there are no references to it before the last few years.

Betting of all kinds was and is illegal in pubs, in 1921 three publicans were cautioned and their licenses suspended for a month, for allowing bookmakers to do business in their pubs. They were Joseph Massie Furnival of the *Anchor*, Elizabeth Ann Hewlett of the *King's Arms*, and Brigid Ayres of the *Three Horseshoes.* All three took notice and their licenses were continued on the understanding that they would lose the licenses if the bookmakers returned.

Although betting and bookmakers are illegal in pubs, one form of gambling has been allowed in recent years, and that is with the introduction of licenses for Gaming machines or Fruit machines as they are sometimes called. Most of the pubs in Henley and district applied for permission to have one or more machines on their premises in 1970, either in April or in June of that year [30].

The only hint of theatrical performances in the pubs of Henley, is at the *Broad Gates*. It is said that performances took place there, before the building of the theatre in New Street. The theatre was built in 1805 by Sampson Penley and John Jonas on the site where the old workhouse had been. Penley and Jonas may previously have performed at the *Broad Gates* [31].

Other activities often associated with pub yards were cock fighting, bear and bull baiting. Bull baiting was still practised at the end of the 18th century, for instance in 1786 it occurred in the Market Place at Wokingham, and at Thatcham, when the owner of the dog that ran the longest received one guineau[32]. This event was at the *Plough* at Thatcham, but so far no advertisement for a similar event in Henley has been found.

Cock fighting also seems to have been held at pubs, though again there is no mention of

28 Inventory of the Brewery 1826 see note 11
29 Henley Advertiser 20 Aug 1870
30 Henley Magistrates Court, 'Henley Borough & Rural Registers of Licenses 1962-1973'
31 Burn, John S 'History of Henley on Thames' 1861 p21
32 Reading Mercury & Oxford Gazette Nov-Dec 1786

Henley as a venue. In August of 1787 'a Great Main of Cocks' was advertised to be held at the *Cross Keys* in Reading, on each morning of the races[33]. It was to be between the Gentlemen of Oxfordshire and Berkshire and the Gentlemen of Middlesex and Hampshire, for ten guineas a battle and one guinea the odd battle. The only indication that there may have been cock fighting nearer to Henley, is in the Inventory of Thomas Leay/ Lea in 1664 (see the *White Horse,* Fairmile) when in the 'Chamber over the Kitchin & Garrett' there was a 'sett of cock pens, one tub and some small olde lumber.'

Accommodation at Inns and Pubs A study of available 17th century inventories of innkeepers in Henley[34], show that there was not a great deal of room in the inns nor very many beds. Though here it must be said that there were no inventories included for the larger inns such as the *Red Lion,* the *Bell* or the *White Hart.*

The other source of information on accommodation in the 17th century is the Hearth Tax list of 1665. At the *Red Lion* Nathaniel Worley is listed as having thirteen hearths, this means that he had more than thirteen rooms, as attics and small or unimportant rooms would not have had hearths. To put the thirteen hearths in context, the average number of hearths for houses in the town was three. Only two people are listed as having more than Nathaniel Worley, Henry Boler gent had seventeen hearths and Richard Ellian eighteen. Where these two lived is unknown, could either of them have been at the *Bell* or the *White Hart ?*

The *Bell* in the 17th and 18th centuries must have had a large number of rooms, including as it did the whole block of buildings on the north west corner of Bell Lane, it could easily have had eighteen hearths. Similarly the *White Hart* had extensive accommodation, part of the old pub shows the remains of an open gallery which had doors opening into individual rooms. The *White Hart* now closed, is smaller than it once was, and it is probable that the gallery extended round the courtyard on the west side, and had more rooms opening from it (see the *White Hart*).

The Hearth Tax list is only of use if the landlord of the pub is already known. In 1665 Henry Godfrey was at the *Bear* which then had five hearths. In 1683 John Dolton also of the *Bear* left a will and inventory. He had six chambers with ten 'bedsteds' plus one trundle bed. Presumably the innkeeper his wife and family used one if not two beds, so the number left for guests was not large. However it is probable that the servants never had proper beds, but scrounged straw and old rags and slept where they could. In the inventory two of the chambers had 'an irons' or andirons, one of the two had also 'fire shouffels and tongues', while another room had a 'paire of iron doggs'. So three of the five hearths were in bedchambers, but the hall had 'one paire of an irons', and the kitchen also had a 'paire of grates fire shoffel and tongues'. Which looks as though by 1683 there were six hearths.

Robert Shard in 1665 at the *White Horse* on the bridge, had three hearths. The will and inventory of Roger Sharde of 1628, proved in 1631, shows that it then had five rooms used as bedchambers, in which there were four 'joyned bedsteds' three trundle beds and two 'boorded bedsteds'. The hall had 'two payre of bellowes' and two of the bedchambers had fire irons. A kitchen is not listed, but under the heading 'Iron', which included a 'dryppinge pann', 'spittes' etc, there were 'two paire of Iron dogges, one paire of racke Andirons, two fyer shovells, two pair of tonges.' The hall probably served as a communal room and kitchen.

The will and inventory of Thomas Gorroway of 1668 cannot be linked to any specific pub, though there is the possibility that his inn was on the south side of the Market Place, somewhere

33 Reading Mercury & Oxford Gazette Aug 1787
34 Wills & Inventories transcribed by the evening class taken by Miss Joan Dils

between the *Broad Gates* at what is now 45-7 and the *Chequers* at 61-3 Market Place, now Waldens. Henley Rentals for the south side of the Market in 1713/4 has the entry 'Thomas Garroway for his house and more for an encroachment 10d, and more for a tenement in occupation Rob Cooper 8d'. The rentals in that year seem to have been made starting at the west end of the market, and this entry follows that for Mr Sayer's house, which appears to have been where the Baptist Chapel now stands, and behind which there was a malthouse (see Malthouses M34). This places Gorroway's inn at either 51 or 53 Market Place. If at 51 it would have been in the building or on the site of what later became the *Cannon* beerhouse. There is known to have been at least one cottage in the yard behind, which could possibly account for the mention of the tenement held by Rob Cooper. However it is unlikely that the beerhouse was a continuation of Gorroway's inn, since it would then have been listed in the 19th century as an inn rather than a beerhouse.

According to the rentals a Thomas Garroway was in the same place in 1721/2, his widow in 1733/4, and by 1737 a William Garroway was there. The differences in spelling at that date is usual, the name was spelt variously Gorroway, Goroway, Goraway, Garroway and Garawaye.

The Thomas who died in 1668 was termed in the Burial Register Thomas 'the elder'. This pre-supposes that he was survived by a son of the same name, possibly the Thomas who became the father of a Thomas baptised in 1674. This grandson of the Thomas of 1668 may well have been the Thomas of the rentals of 1713/4, and who died in 1724.

In the inventory accompanying the will of Thomas Gorroway in 1668, there is mention of four bedchambers, of which two were called 'men's chambers' and one of which contained 'fyre shovell tongs and irons'. Another chamber had '1 paire of iron dogges' but there is no other mention of hearth equipment. The kitchen however did have 'other Ironworks' which may have included fire shovells etc. Three years before in 1665 in the Hearth Tax, Thomas Gorroway was listed as having eight hearths. The inventory does seem rather sparse, either the writer of it could not be bothered with details, in two rooms 'etc' was added, or the beneficiary of the will had already claimed some of the possessions.

It may be that the inn of Thomas Gorroway in the 1660s occupied the site of what are now 51 and 53 Market Place, and might well have had four bedchambers and eight hearths. It may have ceased being an inn even before the last of the Gorroways were in the vicinity in the 18th century. In the 19th century the *Cannon* beerhouse at 51 was both a beerhouse and a lodging house.

These inventories are the only ones which at the moment it has been possible to link with both the Hearth Tax and an actual pub or building. Other inventories of innkeepers show much the same pattern, bedchambers usually seem to have had one large bedstead and sometimes a trundle bed as well. In a few cases there seem to have been two bedsteads to a room, but when the number of rooms are counted, and allowance made for the landlord and his family, there was not much room for guests. Sharing of both rooms and beds must have been usual, a room or a bed to oneself must have been the height of luxury, and probably regarded as quite unnecessary. Certainly the sharing of a double bed between those of the same sex was regarded as normal till well into the 20th century. The use of the term 'men's chamber' seems to suggest it was common for men to share a room if not a bed.

The sharing of rooms between couples seems also to have been a practice[35] at the *Red Lion* beerhouse, which was also a lodging house. In 1863 it led to an unfortunate incident. One of the men concerned was found almost dead from loss of blood from an injury sustained in a quarrel. The injured man was an itinerant china and glass mender named James Walker, who with his wife

35 Reading Mercury & Oxford Gazette 12 Sep 1863

had gone to the room where they were to sleep. Another couple were already there, and the women started an argument. The second man named William Hayward alias Barnay Jennings, attacked Walker, threw him on the bed, and tried to garrotte him. This caused a rupture in his throat and extensive bleeding. The following week it was said that Walker was still very ill, and that Hayward had been sent to trial at the Quarter Sessions in Oxford. It is not mentioned in the account as to whether the couples were merely sharing a room, or were to share a bed.

Although most of the inventories list such items as feather-beds, blankets, pillows and in some cases linen sheets, one wonders what state they may have been in when in use. Very probably some of the items would have been washed once or twice a year if then. Probably they waited for fine weather and then washed what they could.

By the beginning of the 19th century Mrs Dixon at the *Red Lion* Waterside, was celebrated for her 'lavender scented sheets'[36]. The fact that they were worthy of note, rather implies that they were unusual at that time.

Even later, in the 20th century there is an interesting inference in an article written in December 1922[37]. It is a piece eulogising the management and the facilities of the *Spread Eagle* in Thame. It had recently been taken over by John Fothergill, who was as the article says keeping all the best traditions and spirit of the past alive. There was old fashioned furniture, traditional meals with 'no modern nonsense', and pictures in the house were by Augustus John. The article then continues 'At night a hot water bottle is put in every bed as a matter of course. Sheets are not merely turned and ironed. Clean ones are given to every visitor.' Evidently an unusual state of affairs !

So far accommodation has been considered in the light of a passing guest or chance visitor, but many pubs provided lodgings for long term residents. The earliest evidence for this is at the *Clubhouse*, Rotherfield Greys. Entries of Baptisms and Burials in the Parish Registers from 1818 to the mid century show that several families were living at the pub, the fathers listed in the Baptism entries were all agricultural labourers.

The Census Returns of the 19th century also indicate that whole families were living at pubs. In 1871 the *Horse and Groom*, New Street had four lodgers, one of whom had a wife and son. In the same year just down the road at the *Rose and Crown* there were five lodgers, one of whom had a wife two sons and a daughter, while another lodger also had a wife.

The *Red Lion* West Street in the 1871 Census was termed a lodging house - at that time there were twelve lodgers, while in 1881 the number had risen to nineteen. It was not a large house, which perhaps explains the room sharing already mentioned earlier.

In 1892[38] it was stated that there were four licensed lodging houses in the Borough, the *Red Lion* and the *Jolly Farmer* in West Street, the *Cannon* in the Market Place, and the *Duke's Head* in Duke Street. The necessity of being licensed as a lodging house was made clear in 1878[39] when William McDermott was charged with keeping an unlicensed lodging house in West Hill (Street). A Charles Thornett, hawker of oranges, said he stayed there ten days paying 4d a night. He said there were about a dozen tramps in the kitchen and in the house every night, and also there were German musicians in the house. The report went on that the house had been regarded as a refuge for thieves, tramps and suspicious characters for a long time. A license had been refused as the rooms were too small. McDermott was fined £5 and 19s 6d costs, or a term of two months imprisonment, the highest penalty allowed. In which house did McDermott live ? Was it a lot

36 Climenson, Mrs Emily J 'Guide to Henley on Thames' 1896 p25 quoted from Jesse's 'Angler's Rambles'

37 Henley Standard 8 Dec 1922

38 Henley Standard 14 May 1892

39 Henley Standard 2 Mar 1878

smaller than the *Red Lion* with its nineteen lodgers and only five bedrooms, one of which must surely have been occupied by the landlord ?

Priests and Packhorses. During the 16th and 17th centuries and for many years before that, packhorses were in general use by many people for transporting both their own belongings and their trade goods. Coaches up to the end of the 17th century were lumbering affairs with no springs, and little better than covered carts. Most travellers unless aged or infirm would have preferred riding, taking their luggage on packhorses. That is if they had to go by road, and were not able to go by water.

Pubs and inns would have provided stopping places for the packhorses, one pub in Henley was called the *Packhorse*. Two others which are known to have catered to packhorse travellers were the *Bear* and the *Bull* in Bell Street. Both were owned by the Stonor family[40] and both catered to a special kind of packhorse traveller.

During the 16th and 17th centuries the Roman Catholic religion was outlawed, and Catholic priests were forbidden entry to the country. The headquarters of the Jesuit order in England was secretly established at Mapledurham, and priests arriving from abroad congregated there, and were sent out from there on packhorses to travel the country ministering to Catholics.

According to the Hon. Georgina Stonor the priests regularly used both the *Bear*(Fig 9) and the *Bull* (Fig 16), often holding services at the pubs for local Catholics. Since many of the priests were strangers to the country, they tended to meet one another for companionship, which in some cases proved their downfall, as it became known which pubs they frequented.

Coaches and Waggons. The main coaching period was a brief fifty or sixty years from about 1785 to the coming of the railways. Coaches were in use during the 17th century, but most at that time would have been privately owned. Henley would have known them being on the route from London to Oxford and places further west. Trade tokens in use in Henley in the 17th century include one of John Hathaway in 1668, which shows on it a man driving a carriage and pair. It has been said that he was landlord of the *White Hart*, however no John Hathaway appears in the Hearth Tax list of 1665, which he would have done had he been an innkeeper. A John Hathaway buried in 1700[41] was listed as a coachman, and not an innkeeper. He may have run a coach service from the *White Hart*.

The *White Hart* (Figs 54, 55 & 56) apart from being the oldest pub on record in Henley until recently still trading, was also the main public coaching inn. The *Bell* and the *Red Lion* were the inns frequented by the gentry in the 17th and 18th centuries, and they would have been busy with private coaches. Indeed the *Red Lion* at the end of the 18th century considerably enlarged its stables.

In 1717 an advertisement (Fig 56) announced the commencement of a coaching service by John Alleway, of coaches from the *White Hart* to London every Monday and Friday, returning every Wednesday and Saturday [42].

In November 1785 the Reading Mercury & Oxford Gazette advertised 'The Henley Machine'. 'Richard Taylor most respectfully informs his friends and the public in general that his coaches will set out from the *White Hart* Inn, Hart Street, Henley, on Monday, Tuesday, Wednesday,

40 Papers belonging to the Stonor family are not available

41 Henley Parish Burial Register 1653-1703

42 Henley Standard 13 Jan 1961

Thursday and Friday mornings at eight o'clock and Sunday mornings at ten o'clock to the *Angel* Inn behind St Clements Church in the Strand, London, and will return from thence every morning (Sunday excepted) at ten o'clock.' A street directory of about 1793 advertised that coaches go daily from the *White Hart.*

The traffic in Henley was obviously increasing as the 18th century ended. In September 1787 the Henley Corporation found it necessary to insert the following notice in the Reading Mercury & Oxford Gazette :-

> 'Whereas Coachmen, Drivers of Post Chaises and persons riding upon horseback do frequently in passing through the said Town, go at a very furious rate, thereby creating great danger, both to themselves, the passengers in such carriages, and to the foot passengers along the streets of the said Town. Notice is therefore hereby given, that all, and every person and persons who shall henceforth be guilty of such offence will be proceeded against and punished for the same as the law directs. And Drivers of Post Chaises are particularly hereby cautioned against permitting their horses, when returning without carriages to go loose through the said Town, as they will be severely punished for so doing.'

This last directive suggests that horses were not always kept at the stables of various pubs, but were taken through the town to graze in nearby fields.

By 1830[43] in the heyday of coaching, about fifteen public coaches arrived and departed day and night at the *White Hart.* Four went to the *Catharine Wheel*, three to the *Red Lion*, two to the *Bull* and two to the *Bell* Northfield End. Also in 1830 carriers called at the *Three Tuns* on two days a week, while the *Bear* was busier with eight carriers a week. The *White Horse and Star*, long known as a Waggon Inn, had a twice daily waggon service from London going on to Sodbury. The *Swan* also had a service to London on Fridays.

By 1850 the Great Western Railway was at Twyford and Reading, the branch line to Henley opened in 1856, and in Henley there was a dramatic drop in the number of public coaches, and probably also in the number of private coaches passing through the town. At the *White Hart* there were only coaches to Marlow and High Wycombe on Tuesdays and Fridays, to Reading on Mondays, Wednesdays, Thursdays and Saturdays, and also now carriers to London on Mondays and Thursdays. The *Catharine Wheel* had neither coaches nor carriers: The *Red Lion* had three coaches a day, two of which were Train Coaches to Twyford, all three having started out from the *Bell Tap* calling at the *Red Lion* 'en route'. The *Three Tuns* had a coach every afternoon (Sundays excepted) to Reading[44].

Although there seems to have been a distinct lessening of the numbers of coaches by 1850, the carriers remained busy. At the *Three Tuns* there was a daily van for passengers and goods to Reading, the *Bull* had six carriers a week to Bensington (Benson), Oxford, Wallingford, and Watlington. The *Bear* had daily carriers to Reading and Twyford, Thursdays and Saturdays excepted. The *Packhorse* six a week to High Wycombe, Reading and Twyford, and the *Broad Gates* a carrier to Wargrave on Thursdays and Saturdays.

By 1883[45] there were no public coaches, the *White Hart* had carriers to London Mondays and Thursdays. The *Bull* had five a week to Binges (misprint for Fingest ?), Lane End, Hambleden, Nettlebed and Watlington. The *Three Tuns* had carriers to Hambleden on Thursdays, and the *Broad Gates* to Hare Hatch also on Thursdays. (For more details of the various services see entries for

43 Pigot & Co's Directory 1830

44 Slater's Directory 1850

45 Kelly's Directory 1883

individual pubs.)

The destinations of the coaches from the *White Hart* in 1830 were as far flung as Holyhead, Birmingham and Shrewsbury, by 1850 they had dwindled to local journeys. The change from cross country coaches to local and railway connected traffic was an immediate result of the coming of the railways. The ensuing change to the town's importance and prosperity must have been appalling, apart from what must have been a drop in sales of goods and provision of accommodation, there must also have been an immediate and devastating drop in employment.

Indeed as reported in the Reading Mercury & Oxford Gazette of the 1 July 1848, a petition was sent to the House of Commons by the inhabitants of Henley on Thames.

This stated —

> 'that in consequence of the diversion of road traffic which once passed through the town, but is now conveyed by the Great Western Railway, the trade of the town has very materially decreased, that the burthen of the poor has at the same time very much increased. That your petitioners have felt the Income Tax to press heavily upon them, and while they would express their loyalty to the illustrious house seated on the throne of Great Britain, they pray that your honourable house would take into its consideration the whole question of taxation, with a view to every practical reduction......'

What result this petition had is not recorded.

Beer Houses in the 19th century. The recession in the fortunes of Henley caused by the end of the coaching era in the 1840s and 50s, though it obviously affected trade in the larger inns, does not seem to have lowered the consumption of beer in the town. Indeed it is during the same period that the beerhouses proliferated, aided by a change in license regulations as described earlier in the section on 'Licensing in the 18th & 19th Centuries'. For the first time beer was allowed to be sold on its own without a full victuallers license. There was also a lowering of taxation on beer. The keeping of a beerhouse seems to have been very much a secondary occupation, very often run by wife and daughters, the man is nearly always listed in Census Returns and street directories as having another trade or occupation. The keeping of a beerhouse was a home based industry which supplemented the income of the main wage earner, and gave the women of the family a chance to earn while staying in their own home, though probably the amount earned was very small.

At the *Cannon* beerhouse in the Market Place in 1906 it was said that they 'did four barrels a week,' but by 1931, when closure was being considered, the amount was down to one and a half barrels a week, except in the Summer and Regatta time, when there was an increase[46]. The *Cannon* was by no means one of the smallest beerhouses, and its position in the market would ensure plenty of custom on market days. Again there is the account of the publican of the *Oxford Arms* who in 1871 was summoned for selling beer after hours. His defence was that he had fallen asleep, the pub being empty, and had not noticed the time when a customer came in and asked for beer. In neither case did the pubs appear to be having a lucrative trade.

In 1885 there was a proposal at the Annual Brewster Sessions to withold licenses from the *Cannon* and the *Victoria*, as apparently they had little trade, however the licenses were renewed a month later. Again the following year there was another proposal to close the *Victoria* as it was claimed that no beer had been sold there for years. The following month the license was renewed.

---

46 Henley Standard 2 Mar 1906 & 13 Mar 1931

Many beerhouses started trading in about 1840 or just before, while records of others only go back to the 1850s or 1860s. Many of them continued into this century, and a few like the *Queen's Head*, the *Victoria,* the *Horse and Groom* and the *Rose and Crown* are still trading. Others like the *Half Way House* only survived for about thirty years, the small beerhouses were a prime target for the activities of the various temperance societies.

The Temperance Movement The temperance movement started in America in 1808, by 1829 societies had sprung up in England, Scotland and Ireland[47]. The drunkeness of Noah was often quoted as being the first illustration of the evils of alcohol. The first World's Temperance Convention was held in 1846.

One of the leading temperance societies locally was the Henley Total Abstinence Society, who very actively campaigned for a reduction in the number of beerhouses. In 1884 when the subject of license transfers were brought before the Magistrates, and the license of the *Red Lion* West Hill was being transferred from Mrs Emma Rawlings to William Poffley, Mr Knight suggested that the *Red Lion* was not needed. He went on to say that with 'so many public houses in the town and that so much misery and crime were caused by them, he thought the Bench should adopt some plan which would reduce the number by half.....' There followed a lengthy discussion both for and against the motion. It was terminated by the Clerk pointing out that legally a beerhouse could not be closed on the grounds that there was no need for it, especially if an old beerhouse was concerned. The only way it could be closed was if the holder of the license conducted the house improperly[48].

Charles Clements a builder of the town, who was Mayor three times, was a leading member of the temperance lobby, and he appears to have had several clashes with William Henry Brakspear. In the Henley Advertiser of 28 April 1888 he is found refuting remarks about 'a well known brewer in the town' which the paper alleged he had made. Clements claimed that he was supposed to have said that the 'well known brewer in the town who had no less than 40 public houses' would be 'pleased to see this number reduced by half as he should do quite as much business by the result, simply because of the taxes, as he would then only have to pay half the number as he does now.' Clements continued that the report was incorrect, that the brewer had not expressed such views, but had said 'many men frequent public houses for the company to be found in them and would be tempted to drink more in a house where company was found ...... the result would be that the brewer would do as much business ...... for this advantage we the rate payers would be burdened with taxes to pay compensation.'

This shows that even for those in the temperance ranks there would be problems in the wholesale closure of pubs. Other problems seem to have arisen for Mr Clements. On one of his trips to London to lobby Parliament on a bill to limit the hours of drinking, during his absence his building sheds and materials caught fire. There was a rumour in the town that the fire was not entirely accidental !

Pub Closures By the end of the 1890s several pubs had closed, quite a few closing in 1897. After that the closures came more slowly but still steadily. By 1918 there were said to be 29 fully licensed houses and 8 beerhouses in the Borough[49]. While in 1885[50] there had been 36 fully licensed houses and 19 beerhouses in the town and Northfield End, which did not include any premises south of the middle of Friday Street, along the Reading Road or up Greys Road. Now in

47 'The Illustrated Encyclopaedia of Universal Knowledge' 1879

48 Henley Advertiser 27 Sep 1884

49 Henley Standard 8 Feb 1918 50 Henley Advertiser 29 Aug 1885

1999 in the whole Henley district covered by this book, a larger area than the Borough, there are only 21 public houses and 2 over the bridge in Remenham.

The pubs open in the 1920s gave rise to an entertaining article listing the pubs then open, which was quoted in the Henley Standard of 12 January 1990. The list was supplied by Mr Hammant, by whose kind permission it is quoted here. It came to Mr Hammant from his uncle Henry Goddard of the *Argyll*, and was written by E J Darby.

> 'Whilst standing by the river bank I saw the *Two Brewers* loading up *Three Tuns* from a *Row Barge* called the *Saracen's Head,* while the *Jolly Waterman* whose name was *Argyll*, was getting up the *Anchor* with the aid of the *Basket Maker's Arms*. So I left those *Oddfellows* with the *Swan* to keep them company and leaving the *Bird in Hand* I made for the Fair ground on which was a menagerie which contained the *Red Lion*, the *Bull,* the *Bear*, the *Fox,* the *White Hart* with a *Little White Hart,* the *Red Cow* and *Ye Lion* which looked the fiercest of the lot.'
>
> 'Further along by the *Wheatsheaf* I saw a *White Horse* known as a *Packhorse*, so I went up to the *Horse and Groom* and asked him the name of the horse and he said the *Angel* because she had got *Three Horse Shoes* and the *Red Cross.* I said she ought to have *Five Horse Shoes* to make one for luck.'
>
> 'Soon after that the *Sun* came out, so I stood beneath the *Royal Oak* where the *Travellers Rest* and watched a man at a waxworks show bang at *Ye Olde Bell* on which was painted the *Rose and Crown.*'
>
> 'So I went inside but all I saw was the *Royal - Imperial - Crown* that *Victoria* wore on the *Duke's Head* and the *Queen's Head* laying in the *King's Arms.*'
>
> 'Just then the *Cannon* went off and I turned a *Catherine Wheel* and woke up to find myself in the *Carpenter's Arms.*'

This list includes the *Fox* at Bix and the late *Five Horseshoes* on Remenham Hill, neither of which are included in this book. The date of the composition must have been between 1920 and 1930. *Ye Olde Bell* was only known as that from 1920, and the *Cannon* was closed in May 1931, but had been shut since January 1931.

Since 1889, forty three pubs have closed, including the *Carpenter's Arms* across the bridge, while in the same period only two new ones have opened. The *A E Hobbs* opened in 1968 and the *Imperial* in 1903. When the *Imperial* opened it was as a hotel and the license was for residents at the hotel and their guests only. A full license and permission for a bar open to the public was obtained only 1931. Another pub built in 1899, the *Three Horseshoes*, was refused a license until 1930, when the license of the old *Three Horseshoes* was transferred, together with the name and the licensee.

If this trend continues, pubs will become things of the past, and beer, wines and spirits will only be obtainable from super-markets and off-licenses.

PUBS

Abbreviations after Landlord's Names after each pub entry

They show the various sources from which names have been found

AKL	Alehouse Keepers List 1817 (O.R.O. A XVI 30 F115)
AucC	Auction Catalogue
BaReg	Henley Parish Baptism Registers
BR	Borough Records (Briers P M 1960)
BRB	Bridge Rent Book 1886
BReg	Henley Parish Burial Registers
BRO	Berkshire Record Office
C	Census Returns
CB	Court Baron Book 1785
CL	Book of the Court Leet of the Manor of Henley 1787-c.1868
GB/R	Greys Brewery Rent Ledger
HA	Henley Advertiser
HL	Hughes Lists
HS	Henley Standard
HT	Hearth Tax 1665
HTom	H Tomalin
JSB	J S Burn 'History of Henley' 1861
MReg	Henley Parish Marriage Registers
OJ	Jackson's Oxford Journal
ORO	Oxfordshire Record Office
PF	Pew Faculties 1820, 1834-5
PI	Private information from, friends or relatives
R	Henley Rentals
RE	Royal Exchange Insurance Register O.R.O.
RL	Registers of Licenses
RM	Reading Mercury & Oxford Gazette
SD	Street Directories
SL	Stonor Letters
SSM	Magistrates Special Sessions Minute Book
THD	Documents belonging to Town Council kept in Town Hall
TM	Tithe Maps & Tithe Returns
USC	Documents of United Schools Charities
VR	Victuallers Recognizances
WHB/C	Information from W H Brakspear & Sons Plc supplied by Mr Chalcraft
WHB/I	Inventory & Valuation of the Brewery 1826
WHB/R	Brakspear's Rent Ledgers O.R.O.

Dates in the Lists of Landlords/Tenants marked by a * mean that it is possible that the Landlord or Tenant was there before a known date or there afterwards, that the known date is of occupation and not arrival or departure.

1

The A E Hobbs

Valley Road

This is the newest of all the Henley pubs, it opened on Friday 22 November 1968, the first licensee being William Christopher Cattell.

Throughout the 1960s there were discussions about the need for a new pub to cater for the growing population in the housing estates behind Henley. Places that were suggested were at Ridgeway or Wootton Manor. In February 1962 a provisional license was granted to H R Emmett a tenant of Messrs Brakspear, for a pub to be built in Greys Road. In 1964 application was made for a pub in Valley Road, which was refused. In 1966 at the Licensing Session it was pointed out that though a provisional license was issued in 1962, no pub had yet been built. Finally a provisional license was granted for April 1967-April 1968 to Alan Thomas Farmer for the present pub, which was then being built.

The name of A E Hobbs is to commemorate a man who was a notable figure in Henley. He was an architect, who while working for Brakspears, was responsible for either altering or entirely rebuilding the following pubs and houses :-

Everley House in Hart Street (until recently Brakspear's Off License premises), the *Old White Horse,* the *Golden Key* at Caversham, the *Fox* at Bix, the *Land's End* at Woodley, the *Wendover Arms* High Wycombe, the *Travellers Rest* Caversham, and the *Butcher's Arms* Widmore Pond.

A E Hobbs other claim to fame was as a trout fisherman, he was credited with having caught over 800 large Thames trout in his day. It was said that he had an arrangement with various lock keepers, who informed him if they spotted any large trout passing through their locks. The other part of the legend was that if a large trout was seen and reported to him, he would drop everything and rush to a suitable location, returning to work after making his catch.

When the *A E Hobbs* was opened, a statue was placed in the entrance, which showed Hobbs in his fishing gear, with his characteristic button hole which he always wore, and holding not only a rod but also a large trout. The statue was created from a photograph taken soon after the last war, and when it was put in place there was much speculation about the size of the fish, and what its weight might have been. The general consensus was that he held a trout weighing about 14lbs. Sadly the statue has been vandalised and the trout removed from his grasp, and it no longer presides over the entrance.

It seems that the A E stood for Albert Edward, but there is some confusion as to where he was born. Enquiries at Brakspears received the answer that he was born across the road from the brewery at Bishop's House or 55 New Street in 1871. However the Census of 1871 reveals that the house at that time was occupied by the Misses Latter and one servant, who were there both before and after the date of the Census according to other references. In 1871 Henry Edward Hobbs was at the *Ship*, Wharf Lane, but his sons were Henry Edward, Frank, Ernest James, Frederic and lastly in 1880 Albert Edwin. He was an A E Hobbs, but was not the special A E.

The Census of 1881 reveals that a Benjamin Hobbs, master carpenter employing three men and one boy, was living at the house now 30 Hart Street. He had two sons and one daughter, the eldest son being Benjamin Henry aged 17, and the younger son Albert Edward aged 10. Both boys are listed as being born in Henley, but the actual place is not mentioned.

Street directories list Benjamin Hobbs builder at 30 Hart Street until 1924, and Albert Edward Hobbs architect and surveyor as at 28 Hart Street from 1895-1928 and in 1935 at 30a Hart Street. In 1907 he is listed also as a private resident at 17 New Street. This would seem to confirm that this was the A E Hobbs of Brakspears. Born in 1871 he would have already been 24 in 1895, and may well have started his career as a general builder and architect in premises next door to his father. Architects at that period often had no formal training and became architects by trial and error, and actual practice.

Landlords/ Tenants of the *A E Hobbs*

Nov 1968-74	William Christopher Cattell
Jan 1974-85	Bessie Gwendolen Barefield & John Barefield (RL)
Dec 1985-9	Peter David John Weston (RL)
Nov 1989-91	Ian Barry Jones (RL)
Mar 1991-95	Barry Armstrong (RL)
Feb 1995-99-	William David Thurston (RL) & Mrs Julie Hawkins (HS)

2

The Anchor

58 Friday Street

The Rotherfield Greys Tithe Map of 1844 (Fig 64) includes the south side of Friday Street, as up to 1892 the boundary between Henley and Rotherfield Greys, which then stretched down to the river, ran down the roadway of Friday Street. A portion of this map defines the houses along Friday Street, and shows the house, yard and brewery of Greys Brewery (see also Fig 65), owned by Thomas Soundy and let to H N Byles, who in the 1841 Census was living at the house adjoining the brewery. On the river side of the brewery in 1844 there is shown another yard entrance and then two cottages owned by the Rev Deacon Morrell and let to William Woodley and others. In the Census of 1841 William Woodley aged 60 fisherman was in one cottage, with his wife and five children ages 15-3. The second cottage was occupied by Charles Trotman aged 65 agricultural labourer, his wife and two lodgers. Adjoining the cottages on the tithe map were two houses, one with its length to the street, and the other end on to the street. These two houses are now 60 Friday Street and Baltic Cottage. The building now known as the *Anchor* was in 1844 two cottages, although when it was bought by Deacon Morrell in the same sale as he bought the Old Rectory in 1813, it was described as a cottage and farm buildings in Friday Street[51]. So part of the present building may have originated as a shed or barn.

Whether in the early 1840s one or other of the cottages was already in use as a beerhouse is not known. Since the *Anchor* was in Rotherfield Greys, if it had been trading before 1823, there would have been mention of it in the Victuallers Recognizances for Rotherfield Greys which go up to 1822, and by that date, and for some time before that mention all the pubs by name. H N Byles was at Greys Brewery in 1821, although he and Thomas Soundy may have started the brewery in about 1803, so possibly a nearby cottage began selling their beers. A street directory of 1844 gives the name Henry Gillett as a beer retailer in Friday Street, and he cannot be placed at the other pubs in the street. Maybe by then he had moved into the second cottage, and was one of the 'others'

51 Sheppard, Francis 'The History of the Old Rectory' H.A.&H.G. Journal, Summer 1986, No4

mentioned in the Tithe Returns. Another directory of 1847 gives Mrs Elizabeth Martin as at the *Anchor* in Friday Street. This is the earliest positive reference to there being a pub of that name in Friday Street.

By the time of the 1851 Census the Byles family were still occupying the house belonging to the brewery, while the two cottages had become one household again, occupied by James Wilder aged 38 bricklayer, his wife and two lodgers. Street directories show that Wilder was landlord of the *Anchor* from 1850-68.

Although the *Anchor* is no great age as a public house, the building is much older. The cottages may have been built in the early 18th century, the 17th century or just possibly even earlier. The dating of timber framed houses is always difficult, especially as it was common practice to use beams from previous buildings, which in spite of popular belief were hardly ever ship's timbers.

Fig 1 The Anchor, Friday Street in about 1890, the words 'Greys Brewery Tap' are painted on the side (see also Figs 64 & 65)

There are photographs, one probably taken in the 1880s, and another in about 1890, which show that by that time the *Anchor* was known as the Brewery Tap (Fig 1). This meant a pub next to, or on the premises of a brewery, which sold the products of that brewery, and which by its position never ran out of beer.

Miss Lucy Cooper, whose paintings are in the Mayor's Parlour in the Town Hall, made two paintings of the end of Friday Street, which show part of the frontage of the *Anchor*. The first is dated 1894, and the second undated was probably between 1900 and 1915. The part of the building which can be seen is the projecting bay, in the first painting the windows are small paned, the wall between the upper and lower windows is the same as the rest of the house, and the roof over the bay runs parallel to the street. In the second painting the windows are larger, with a large lower panel, and a slightly smaller pane at the top. The wall between the top and bottom windows is tile hung, the roof above the bay has a gable facing the street, and the lower part of the bay at pavement level seems to project a little more.

Fig 2 The front of the Anchor after alterations done in about 1900. It is probably Mrs Furnival standing outside

The alterations were possibly made during the tenure of Joseph Massie Furnival, landlord for 29 years (Fig 2). He took over from Reginald G H Ward in 1900, after Mrs Ward had explained to the Magistrates that her husband would be no longer able to run the pub, as he had gone to South Africa with the Oxfordshire Yeomanry[52].

In 1921 Mr Furnival was one of three landlords in the town reprimanded for allowing bookmakers to do business at their pubs. His license was suspended for a month, but was renewed on the understanding that the license would be removed if the bookmakers returned[5.3].

The *Anchor* was probably purchased by Greys Brewery in the mid 19th century, it was part of the Greys Brewery property when Greys Brewery and all its pubs were bought by Brakspear & Sons Ltd in 1896.

Landlords/ Tenants of the *Anchor*

?1841-4?	WilliamWoodley (C, TM)fisherman
? 1844	Henry Gillett (SD)
1847	Mrs Elizabeth Martin (SD)
1850-68	James Wilder (C,SD) bricklayer
1869-77	William Spicer (HA,SD)
*1882-3	Alfred Parrott (RL,SD)
Nov 1883-7	James Carpenter (RL)
Apr 1887- 8	Henry Large (RL,SD)
Nov 1888-92	Henry Bates (RL,SD)
Dec 1892-3	Frederick William Norman Clarke (RL)
Aug 1893-4	James Frederick Cox (R
Sep 1894-9	Friedich August Hugo Keil (RL)
Mar 1899-1900	Reginald George Harvey Ward (RL,HS)
May 1900-29	Joseph Massie Furnival (RL,HS,WHB/C)
Jul 1929-31	Albert Edward Arlett (RL,HS,WHB/C)
Apr 1931-2	George Francis Heath (RL,HS,WHB/C)
Feb 1932-5	Edwin Thomas Arthur Mills (RL,HS,WHB/C)
Jan 1935-6	Ernest Thomas Thornton Adams (RL,HS,WHB/C)

53 & 54 Henley Standard 20 Apr 1900, 11 Feb 1921

Sep 1936-40	Henry Foreman Steer (RL,SD,HS,WHB/C)
Sep 1940-5	Cresswell Clarence Ward (RL,WHB/C)
Apr 1945-52	Henry Foreman Steer (RL,WHB/C)
Feb 1952-62	George Henry Mowbray (RL,WHB/C)
Jan 1962-70	John Frederick Carpenter (RL,WHB/C)
Sep 1970-3	Clive Sarsfield Martin (RL,WHB/C)
Mar 1973-4	George Anthony John Hutton (RL,WHB/C)
Jul 1974-8	David Edward Chacksfield (RL,WHB/C)
Apr 1978-90	Mrs Jill Angela Chacksfield (RL,WHB/C)
Apr 1990-99-	Gary Arthur Ion-Savage (RL,WHB/C)

3

The Anchor

Waterside - S E corner of New Street

Fig 3 The Anchor, Riverside north, from an engraving by Hay from a drawing by J P Neale for the 'Beauties of England and Wales' c.1813

This pub was on the corner of New Street and Waterside, Thameside or Riverside as it is variously known. There is a print of about 1813-20 showing the pub, with a man sitting on a bench outside (Fig 3). The shape of the building is similar to the cottages still there, numbers 27 & 28 Riverside North, only those cottages have had their lower floors built out in line with the jetty.

Appleton and Shaw brewers at the brewery now Brakspears, are said to have purchased the property consisting then of four cottages fronting the river, one of which was known as the *Anchor*, some time between 1765 and 1812[54]. Most probably after 1793 as at that date a plan[55] was drawn up of the riverside properties, when the river embankment wall was being constructed, and the property at the corner of New Street was labelled as owned by Mr Clements (Fig 31).

In 1826 the cottages were included amongst the property listed in the Inventory of the Brewery as being held freehold by Joseph Benwell and W H Brakspear. The end cottage which had been the *Anchor* was described as 'A cottage near the Waterside at extremity of New Street brick and timber built but in bad repair and at present untenanted - 3 rooms.' 'Cottage of the same size adjoining occupied by Mrs Ivermee, cottage of same size adjoining occupied by Edwd Pearce, and cottage of the same size occupied by J Buckett.'

From this one may assume that the end cottage had ceased being a pub by 1826, and it is likely that it was soon after that that the end cottage was replaced by the red brick building with the curved corner which is there today.

In the Bridge Rent Book of 1886 the entry says 'Messrs Brakspear & Sons formerly Flight for the tenements at the south east corner of New Street.' Going back in the Henley Rentals from 1842 to 1779, the names of past owners and landlords are stated, as shown in the list of landlords below.

Landlords/ Tenants of the *Anchor*

1779	Mr Davis occ by Widow Banks (R)
1785-90	Sam Clements in occ of his father (R)
1793	Bealey late Clements (R)
1795	Bealey late Davis (R)
1800	Bealey late Davis late Clements (R)
1807	Mr Bealey in occ Flight (R)
1828-42	Benwell (R)

— Closed —

4

The Angel on the Bridge

S W end of the bridge

The building of the *Angel* probably dates from the beginning of the 18th century, though it may not have been a pub till later in the century. In the paintings of Henley by Jan Siberechts of about 1690[56] there is no sign of any building on the south west side of the bridge. The painting shows the old bridge, wooden in its centre spans, but with two stone arches at the east end and a single arch at the west end.

54 Sheppard, Francis 'Brakspear's Brewery 1779-1979' 1979

55 Plan among documents in Town Hall, also H.A.&H.G. Journal No 12 Spring 1997

56 Painting by Jan Siberechts of Henley from south east, copy in the Mayor's Parlour, Town Hall

When the *Carpenter's Arms* at the south east end of the bridge was demolished in 1984 a flint and stone arch was revealed which is thought to date from about 1170. It was part of the old bridge, against which the *Carpenter's Arms* had been built, and was almost certainly one of the two arches depicted by Siberecht. The *Angel* was also built against the old bridge (Fig 4) and the arch at the west end forms part of the cellarage of the *Angel.* On examination it has been shown to be similar to the arch at the east end of the bridge, therefore the *Angel* can claim an ancient cellar. The cellar lies under the pavement on the north side of the pub, between the line of the present bridge and the pub.

The north side of the *Angel* facing the main road has had changes in its appearance, a photograph of about 1912 shows a plain wall without the later mock timbering, and the portico with its two pillars was an addition made between 1836 and 1868. The Court Leet of 1868 charged the Trustees a Quit Rent of 6d p.a. owed to the Lord of the Manor for projecting a portico with two pillars in front of the house at the Bridgefoot known as the *Angel.* At the previous meeting of the Court in 1836 there was no mention of it.

Fig 4 Line of the face of the old bridge arch found 1984, showing how the Angel on the Bridge was built right up against the side of the old bridge

Another change in the building seems to have been made when the present bridge was being built. On 25 March 1786[57] it was agreed in a meeting of the council that since damages had occurred to the house under lease to Mr Hayward and occupied by Mrs Toomer, by the building of a wall to the south west corner of the new bridge, that the house should be restored by either building two rooms at the top of the 'new part of the house' or that four rooms should be added over the whole of the house. If one looks at the present building it would seem that the option of building the two rooms was the one chosen, as the north part nearest to the bridge is of three storeys, while the other end, with its roof ridge running from south to north, is of two storeys with only an attic room. It would also seem that perhaps the north part of the house may have been re-built at about that time, as it is described as the 'new part of the house', so the large bay windows facing the river may date from about 1786 or just before that (See back cover photo).

The *Angel* belongs to Henley Corporation as part of their Charity Trusts, being on land given to the town as part of Longland's Charity in 1547. In 1887 the Henley Advertiser of August 6 announced 'It will be seen by an advertisement that this well known and favourite hotel

57 Holton, S J Ledger containing transcription of Corporation Records 1687-c.1858. Town Hall 4/11/12

will be let at the next meeting of the Trustees of Henley Charities. The form of letting has always been by open bidding in the room, and presumably this will be the 'modus operandi' on the present occasion. A three minute 'sandglass' represents the auctioneer, and is started afresh after each bidding, and of course if the sand all runs through without a fresh bidding, the sale or rather the letting is concluded in favour of the last bidder.'

On August 27 1887 the same paper reported that 'Bids were invited for 21 years lease of the *Angel* (option of terminating in 7 years). Bidding started slowly, began at £50 p.a. Lease signed by Mr Blackall as agent for Messrs Holmes & Harper & Co' (Greys Brewery) 'at £210 p.a. Surprise was expressed at such high bidding.'

Though Greys Brewery gained the lease in 1887, the lease has often been held by others, like Brakspears who hold it today.

On 8 August 1728 the Mayor, Corporation etc leased to Mary Simmons for 11 years a messuage on the south part of the bridge[58] . Mary Simmons elsewhere is described as a maltster, so it is possible that it could have been a pub at that date, and this may have been soon after the pub was built.

On 13 January 1742 the Mayor etc leased to Henry Chipp of Henley grocer for 11 years a messuage on the south part of the foot of the bridge[59].

On 6 March 1780 the Mayor etc leased to Rich Hayward of Henley brewer for 11 years a messuage or public house known as the *Angel* at the foot of the bridge on the south side thereof [60]. This is the first definite mention of a pub called the *Angel* on this site.

Henley Rentals in 1745 and 1749 give rentals for two houses at the bridge, Rob Usher in his own occupation and Widow Simmons at Bridgefoot now Chip. Rob Usher was a hosteler, but he is known to have been at the *White Horse* on the bridge, which was situated on the north side of the west end of the bridge (see entry for the *White Horse on the Bridge*). It may well be that Henry Chipp/Chip was a victualler or hosteler as well as being a grocer.

Rentals of 1775 give Mr David Toomer in one tenement John Allen for a tenement late in his own occupation now Toomer. In 1770 and 1771 the name David Toomer appears in a list of Henley victuallers, unfortunately the pubs are not named in the list, but it seems probable that Toomer was at the *Angel.*

On 25 October 1787 the Mayor Aldermen Bridgemen and Burgesses of Henley were insuring the premises with the Royal Exchange Insurance Co for the sum of £150[61]. 'A tenement situate near the bridge, tenant Hanah Toomer victualler and known by the sign of the *Angel.*' In the year before, in 1786, the wall and embankment were built from the bridge through the garden in the occupation of Mrs Hannah Toomer to the watering place at Friday Street[62].

In 1788 according to the Brakspear Rent Ledgers[63], Hayward & Co who then held the lease gave Mrs Toomer £10 to quit and give possession to John Halley, a condition of which was that Halley gained the right of a premium from the tenant to succeed him.

Henley Rentals of 1790 say Hayward in occupation Halley late Toomer, in 1795 they say Hayward for a house called the *Angel,* formerly two houses occupied by Toomer and Pratt . In 1800 and 1807 the entry says Brakspear for a house called the *Angel* in occupation John Halley, formerly two houses in occupation D Toomer and T Pratt.

The Rentals from 1745 seem to indicate that the building now known as the *Angel* was

---

58, 59 & 60 Hughes List 119 AD570, 101 AD592, 182 AD663

61 Royal Exchange Insurance Register O.R.O. Brakspear X/1

62 Holton, S J Ledger containing transcription of Corporation Records 1687-c.1858. Town Hall 4/11/12

63 O.R.O. Brakspear IV/1/1-2

divided into two houses, although Rob Usher is known to have been at the *White Horse* he may have also rented one of them either privately or as an extension of his pub. Or it may be that the division was only from about 1775 up to the arrival of John Halley and the entries of 1745 and 1749 refer to the *Angel* as one house and Usher as being at a separate house.

In the Court Leet book[64] of 10 October 1801 John Halley was reprimanded for not paying his acknowledgement to the Lord of the Manor of 1s, that being due for the permission given to erect 'posts and rails at the Bridge foot upon the embankment of the Thames near his garden for fastening the Barge horses.' Evidently the pub at that time was much in use by bargemen travelling up and down the river.

In the Alehouse Keeper's list of 1817[65] John Halley is named as at the *Angel*, and in a Pew Faculty list for Henley Church in 1820 as John Halley of the *Angel* at the foot of the bridge. In the Inventory of the Brewery in 1826, under leaseholds held by Joseph Benwell and W H Brakspear it says 'Public house in occupation of John Halley with stabling, garden etc , held at will. Rent £35 p.a. Quit Rent 2s.'

After John Halley a street directory of 1830 places Thomas Page at the *Angel*, but some time in the 1830s John Hobbs took over, he was there in 1838 when the crews of two boats dined there after a race. His son managed the boat hiring trade which for a long time was a side line to the pub. The son in March 1840 had a tragic accident while sailing near Fawley Court, and was drowned. Soon after, in May 1840 the *Angel* was advertised to let, since the present occupier, Mr Hobbs, was wishing to leave due to the loss of his son, upon whom the management of the boat business entirely depended.

Apart from the hiring out of fishing boats, the Regatta having started as an annual event in 1839, the *Angel* was well placed to hire boats to spectators. In the words of May 1840 'The recent established and great success of the Annual Regatta , on the beautiful reach of water, the abundance of Fish (the result of the efforts of the Henley Fishing Society established for the preservation of the fish) have already brought Henley into good notoriety.' It appears that in spite of wanting to leave, John Hobbs was still at the *Angel* in 1842 and 1844, according to street directories.

In 1844 when Henry Rogerson had become the new landlord, the Regatta took place on the 25 and 26 June. In the Reading Mercury & Oxford Gazette of 22 June Henry Rogerson advertised that he wished to inform 'Visitors to the Regatta that he intended making ample provision for the accommodation of those who may please to favour him with their patronage.' He went on that 'A cold collation consisting of poultry, hams, tongues, boiled and roast joints etc will be provided in a spacious room, commanding extensive views of the River Thames and its beautiful scenery both above and below the Bridge and from which the whole of the interesting contests may be witnessed. Refreshment Tickets 3s 6d.'

By the following April in the same paper, his widow Mary Rogerson, was thanking their friends for their patronage and support of her late husband during the short time he carried on the business, and was assuring them that she intended to carry on. She had also added to her stock 'several safe and commodious Pleasure Boats; also a variety of smaller ones;' and had availed herself of 'a very respectable person' who will attend to the comfort etc of ladies and gentlemen wishing to engage 'Pleasure Boats or Fishing Punts.'

In 1854 an Indenture[66] recites how in 1844 William Brakspear and Peter S Benwell (since deceased) had taken an 11 year lease on the condition that they would lay out a large sum on improvements, and so they had spent £100 on repairs to 'all that messuage called by the name of

---

64 'The Court Leet of the Manor of Henley' book in Town Hall recording transactions of the Manor Court

65 O.R.O. AX VI 30 F115

66 O.R.O. Cooper & Caldecott C18 (20)

the *Angel* occupied by Henry Rogerson afterwards by Mary Rogerson, and now by Edward Johnson.'

In 1865 the *Angel* was leased for 11 years to Edward Johnson innkeeper[67] at a rent of £50 p.a. now in the occupation of Edward Johnson. This lease had a clause allowing access by the stone steps on the north east corner for viewing and repairing the bridge. (The present bridge was completed in 1786.)

It has often been said that during the 1914-18 war feelings ran high against those whose names were of German origin, it is seldom that one finds proof of this. In 1915 when the licenses were renewed a note was made signed by J D Cooper, Clerk of the Licensing Justices that 'a Deed Poll produced to me this day duly executed by the within named Frederick Herman Richard Scheibner and dated 9 July 1915 he assumed the name of Frederick Herman Richard Brice by which name he is to be hereafter called and known.'

Frederick Herman Richard Scheibner had already held the license for the *Angel* in 1913 and 1914. In spite of this and the Deed Poll and the fact that he had taken out British citizenship in 1912, when it came to renewing the license in 1917, there were objections made because he was German. Mrs Brice then asked for the license to be granted to her. There followed a barrage of questions including whether she was pro-German. She pointed out that she was British born and bred, had married here and lived in this country all her life. Finally she was granted the license[68] . Sadly the Brice's ten year old son was buried in June 1918[69] , and the following month the Brices left the *Angel.*

After the Brices there were three licensees in quick succession, and Mr Fryer who held a sub-lease from Brakspears had difficulty finding a tenant. After holding the license for a few months himself, he persuaded Miss Woodbridge who had been Manageress of the *White Hart* to take the license. In January 1923 Brakspears whose lease was to end in March 1924, started negotiating for a continuance of the lease. They suggested that in return for extensive renovations they should receive a lease at a lower rent, they were then paying £65 p.a. The Trustees declined the offer as they wished to oversee renovations themselves, so that the character of the building was preserved. By January 1924 several applicants had applied for the new lease, and as was customary it was put to auction. Brakspears offer went up to £145 p.a., but they were beaten by a Mr Tilbury of London who offered £150 p.a.[70]

By the time of the Licensing or Brewster Sessions of February 1925 Mr Tilbury had brought a court action to evict Miss Woodbridge from the *Angel.* However the Court left the matter undecided, as the claims of Mr Tilbury and Miss Woodbridge that it was their livelihood, appeared to balance. So the Bench renewed the license to Miss Woodbridge in March, but in May judgement was made against Miss Woodbridge, who yet retained the license till after an appeal. Perhaps the fact that she married on 19 October 1925, led to her appeal being dismissed. At any rate by March 1926 Herbert Johnson held the license.

Landlords/ Tenants of the *Angel on the Bridge*

1728	Mary Simmons (HL)
1742-9	Henry Chipp (HL,R) grocer
1770-5	David Toomer (R,VR)
*1786- 8	Hanah/Hannah Toomer (RE,WHB/R)

67 O.R.O. Cooper & Caldecott C18 (21)

68 Henley Standard 9 Mar 1917

69 Henley Parish Registers. Burials 1884-1944

70 Henley Standard 22 Sep 1922, 27 Oct 1922, 3 Nov 1922, 5 Jan 1923, 4 Jan 1924, 6 Feb 1925, 1 May 1925, 3 Dec 1926, 7 Jan 1927

1788-1826*	John Halley (R,WHB/R,AKL,CL,PF,WHB/I)
1830	Thomas Page (SD
*1838-44	John Hobbs (RM,SD)
1844-5	Henry Rogerson (ORO,RM)
1845-52*	Mary Rogerson (ORO,RM,SD)
*1854-74	Edward Johnson (ORO,SSM,SD,BReg)
1874-87	Mary Elizabeth Johnson (RL,SD)
Nov 1887-8	George Peacey (RL,HA)
1888-90	Mary Peacey (RL,HA)
Oct 1890-3	Mary McVicker (RL)
Dec 1893-4	Arthur Benjamin Smith (RL)
1894-8	James Whitson Webster (RL)
1898-1901	Richard Clement Court (RL)
Aug 1901-5	Ernest John Clegg (RL)
1905-6	Alfred Wendover Hunt (RL)
1906-Sep	Ernest Barton (RL)
Sep 1906-10	Robert Tenneson Duke (RL)
Jul 1910- Sep	Ernest Barton (RL)
Sep 1910-3	William Finch (RL)
Jul 1913-5	Frederick Herman Richard Scheibner (RL,HS)
Jul 1915-17	Frederick Herman Richard Brice (RL,HS)
Mar 1917-8	Emmie Elizabeth Brice (RL,HS)
Jul 1918-9	Albert Halliday (RL)
Dec 1919-20	Richard Henry Richards (RL,HS,SD)
Oct 1920-1	Arthur Ward Ellis (RL,HS)
Dec 1921-2	William Leslie Mathews (RL,HS)
Sep 1922-Nov	Edward James Fryer (RL,HS)
Nov 1922-6	Winifred Lilian Woodbridge (RL,HS)
	(married 19 Oct 1925 - Winifred Lilian Browne)
Mar 1926-7	Herbert Johnson (RL,HS)
Feb 1927-30	Ralph Bloomfield Cross (RL,HS,SD)
May 1930-Oct	Thomas Thorne (RL,HS)
Oct 1930-2	Frank Adams (RL,HS)
May 1932-7	Capt Philip Horsley Flood Page (RL,HS,SD)
May 1937-Jul	Sydney Harry Herbert (RL)
Jul 1937-8	Bernard Norris (RL)
Sep 1938-9	Leonard Frederick Spray (RL,HS)
Feb 1939-May	Bernard Norris (RL)
May 1939-48	Vera Conti (RL,SD) (married - Vera Ada Warren (RL))
Oct 1948-50	Leslie James Warren (RL,WHB/C)
Jan 1950-6	Herbert George Yarrow (RL,WHB/C)
Sep 1956-7	Harry Findlow (RL,WHB/C)
Mar 1957-72	James Martin Gordon Lamb (RL,WHB/C)
Oct 1972-9	James Graham Talfourd Jones (RL)
Sep 1979-82	Robert John Worsdell (RL,WHB/C)
Sep 1982-91	John Lee Noble (RL,WHB/C)
Jan 1991-99-	Jeremy Drew Buckler (RL,WHB/C)

5

The Angel or the Little Angel

Remenham

This pub is outside of Henley Town and has always been so, the east side of the bridge is in the Parish of Remenham, Berkshire. The county and town boundaries run down the centre of the river, except at the bridge, where the boundary crosses to the Berkshire side, so that the entire bridge and also that part of the land to the south of the present bridge, where the old bridge once stood belongs to Henley and Oxfordshire. However for the purposes of this book the *Angel* or *Little Angel* falls into the social ambience of Henley, as do the *Two Brewers* at the beginning of the Wargrave Road, and the late *Carpenter's Arms* which was at the south east end of the bridge.

The situation of the *Angel* (Fig 50) close to the river and on the flood plain, below the level of the embanked road up White Hill, means that it is susceptible to flooding. In the extensive floods of 1894 it was flooded and a photo of the time shows it surrounded by water (Fig 5).

The *Angel* Remenham was part of the Fawley Court estate up to 1853, and it is shown on two estate maps , one of about 1782 and the other drawn in about 1821, when Admiral Freeman inherited the estate[71]. The Tithe Award for Remenham of 1841 shows it as belonging to William

Fig 5 The Angel or the Little Angel, Remenham, in the floods of 1894 (see also Fig 50)

71 Map c.1782 in River & Rowing Museum, map of c.1821 in private hands

Peer Williams Freeman[72], the then owner of Fawley Court, and the tenant as being James Tallent. In 1853 the whole of the Fawley Court estate was put up for auction, a sales map attached to the catalogue shows the *Angel* as Lot 18. Unfortunately the pages describing Lot 18 in the catalogue are missing, however in a book found among the Town Hall documents belonging to a William Willis, a wheelwright who used the book to jot down what was of interest to him, he included a full list of the 'Important Sale of Estates', which is a list of the Lots sold on 29 June 1853, when the Fawley Court sale took place. Lot 18 as he recorded it was for 'The *Angel* beershop near Henley Bridge let at £1 5s. Sold for £300.'

In 1751 Mary Blandy fled across the bridge to the *Angel* while the inquest and autopsy on her father were being performed. Mary Blandy and her father lived at a house which preceded the one now known as Blandy House or 29 Hart Street. Mary Blandy had poisoned her father Francis Blandy with arsenic supplied by her lover Capt Cranstoun, who had assured Mary that it was a kind of love philtre which would make Francis Blandy look kindly on their marriage. Mary Blandy was held in house arrest until the findings of the inquest were known. In a panic she ran from the house, with apparently a howling mob from the town pursuing her, when she reached the *Angel* the landlady, a Mrs Davis took pity on her and sheltered her in the pub. While there she encountered a couple who happened to be in the pub, a Robert Lane and his wife. The Henley Town Serjeant escorted Mary Blandy from the *Angel* in a chaise, she was later taken to the gaol in Oxford, where she was tried and hanged in April 1752. Cranstoun escaped abroad where he subsequently died[73].

In 1774 the *Angel* was said to be part of the stock in trade when the partnership between James Brooks and Richard Hayward was dissolved[74]. It was possibly held leasehold rather than freehold. Richard Hayward's property was mostly conveyed to his nephew Robert Brakspear, and in about 1790 the *Angel* appears in Brakspear's Rent Ledgers.

There do not seem to be any Victuallers Recognizances for Berkshire before 1815, when William Thackery of Remenham was licensed at the *Angel* with himself and John Cox of Henley cooper both standing surety for £10 each[75]. After this there seem to be no license records for Berkshire until the Register of Licenses in 1887, except for the single year of 1873.

The Inventory of the Brewery in 1826 shows that the property was then held leasehold by Joseph Benwell and W H Brakspear. 'Public house in occupation of James Gibbs with stabling for four horses and small garden. Lease expires 29 September 1837. Rent £15 p.a. Land Tax 18s.'

Whoever bought the *Angel* in the sale of 1853, by 1873 it had become the property of J Pitman of Pitman's Brewery, Goring, and by 1887 was owned by Anne Pitman of Goring[76]. In December 1887 the whole of Pitman's Brewery and thirty seven licensed houses were for sale, three of them in Henley and Remenham. 'Lot 35. The *Angel* Inn, valuable freehold, fully licensed facing the London Road at its junction with Remenham Road, Berks. The house contains - Entrance lobby, small bar, tap room, parlour, private ditto, cellar and kitchen, three bedrooms and two attics. Capital garden, timber built stable for three horses, carthouse, workshop, woodhouse and privy. Let to Mr Charles Butler (held it for 23 years) at nominal rent of £13 p.a. The beer stands, sign etc are the property of the vendor'[77].

72 William Peere Williams Freeman inherited in 1831, grandson of the Admiral of the same names, who inherited in 1821, see also the *Bell*

73 Morgan, Joan 'The Hanging Wood' 1950 pp232-3 (a biographical account in novel form of Mary Blandy)

74 Sheppard, Francis 'Brakspear's Brewery. 1779-1979' 1979

75 B.R.O. Q/MF 16RLv4

76 B.R.O. Registers of Licenses

77 Sales Catalogue Pitman's Brewery 1887 O.R.O. Misc Lee III/ i/ 1

It appears from the license records that the *Angel* was bought by Thomas Gundry brewer of Goring, by 1903 it was the property of Ann Gundry of Goring. In November 1940[78] after the decease of Ann Gundry, her properties were put up for auction, nine fully licensed houses, sixteen beerhouses, four off-license premises, and the Goring Brewery. Twenty five of the houses and the Goring Brewery were purchased by W H Brakspear & Sons Ltd, which included the *Angel.*

Landlords/Tenants of the *Angel* or the *Little Angel*

1751	Mrs Davies
*1791	William Gibbs (WHB/R)
1791-7	Thomas Glover (WHB/R)
1798	John Allen (WHB/R)
Jul 1798-1811*	Richard Talbott (WHB/R)
1815	William Thackery (VR)
1823	John Farley (SD)
1826	James Gibbs (WHB/I)
1830-54	James Tallent (TM,SD)
*1863	Thomas Wise (RM,SD)
1864-96	Charles Butler (RL,AucC)
Dec 1896- 1913	Edgar Butler (RL)
May 1913-39	Martha Butler (RL)
May 1939-50	Edmund Frank Butler (RL)
1950	Ann Martha Griffin (RL)
1951-73	Rupert Vallings Bucknall (RL,WHB/C)
Oct 1973-91	P A Southwood (WHB/C)
1991-	Ashley Bundock (HS)

6

The Argyll

15 Market Place

In 1885 this pub was called the *Hop Leaf* but by 1887 had become the *Argyll.* In the Henley Advertiser of January 1885 it was said that a change of name of the *Hop Leaf* was contemplated, and it was suggested that it should be called the *Bodega*. In the same report which was of the transfer of license, the landlord was given as Thomas Cleaver, however a street directory of 1887 gives his name as William Cleaver, which is the name stated in the Register of Licenses in 1887. When the pub was the *Hop Leaf* it was owned by H & G Simonds of Reading, whose Trade Mark was a hop leaf. Between 1885 and 1887 the pub changed ownership, and in 1887 was the property of Ive Brothers. Unfortunately the Register of Licenses for the Borough from 1882-6 is missing, so the exact date of the transfer is not known definitely, but it may be that it was at the same time as Cleaver became the tenant. At any rate the suggested name of the *Bodega* was not used, though why it was named the *Argyll* is not known.

The building as it is today (Fig 6), with its mock Tudor front, was probably rebuilt in about 1919. Plans for alterations were submitted in 1918, by the then owners Dymore Brown & Sons Ltd, of the Royal Albert Brewery, Queen's Road, Reading[79]. They had owned it since 1913

78 & 79 Henley Standard 22 Nov 1940, 13 Dec 1918

Fig 6 The Argyll, before that the Hop Leaf, the Cannon & the North Star. Four Houses away is the gable of Machins, once the Crown & Thistle, together with the third house which was later the Crown (see also Figs 23 & 26) Photo 1998

when they bought it from Ive Brothers, it is now owned by Morland's Brewery of Abingdon.

The rebuilding radically altered the ground floor of the pub, though it retains vestiges of its carriage entry on the east side, the building was increased in height and the entire front fascia was altered.

There are not many early photos of the south side of the Market Place, probably because it would have meant photographing into the light. The ones that do exist which show 15 Market Place, are firstly one of about 1880, when it was the *Hop Leaf*, and when Simonds' sign can be seen (Fig 26). Secondly there is a photo of about 1910, which shows the same building as in about 1880. It is also the same building as rebuilt by Richard Cox in 1845-6, when it became the *North Star*, a three storied flat fronted brick house with carriage entrance on the east, and the two upper floors having a pair of windows each.

Before becoming the *Argyll* it had been the *Hop Leaf*, before that the *Cannon Inn,* and originally in 1851 or perhaps 1846 it was the *North Star.* Further information is supplied in the accounts of each of these three pubs.

One question still remains, why was it called the *Argyll ?*

Landlords/ Tenants of the *Argyll*

1885-88	William/ Thomas Cleaver (RL,HA,SD)
Mar 1888-9	James William Brasher (RL)
Oct 1889-Oct	Edward Cooper (RL,HA)
Oct 1889-99	William Bridgman (RL,HA,SD)
1899-1905	Henry Foley Norman (RL,SD)
1905-10	Robert Randerson Owen (RL)

1910-14	William Henry Hubbard (RL,SD)
1914-38	Henry Goddard (RL,SD,BReg)
Sep 1938-9	Royle Henry Charles Goddard (RL,SD,PI)
1940-46	Isabel Goddard
1946-74	Royle Henry Charles Goddard (RL,SD,PI)
Sep 1974-91	Ray Kier Boswell (RL) & Veronica Boswell (HS)
Apr 1991-92	Adrian Neil Staley, John Alfred Topping (RL) & AngelaTopping (HS)
Jan 1992-93	Adrian Neil Staley(?Stanley) & S P Lothian (RL)
Mar 1995-Aug	Adrian Neil Staley & Francis Alfred Cobb (RL)
Aug 1995-96	Francis Alfred Cobb & David John Shenton (RL,HS)
Apr 1996-98	David John Shenton & Richard James Turner (RL)
Apr 1998-99-	Richard James Turner & Brian Alfred Birks (RL)

The Armistice Hotel

31-3 Hart Street

This hotel was not a pub, since it was a Temperance Hotel, started in 1918 and continuing till about 1939 under the direction of Mrs M Batty who had previously run other temperance hotels in the town. The Armistice is not included in the numbering.

7

The Barge Pole

Tudor Cottage/ Anne Boleyn Cottage, New Street

This pub is mentioned in the 18th century in Henley Rentals and is not found later. By taking the Rentals in conjunction with the Bridge Rent Book of 1886 and viewing the other entries in the Rentals and Bridge Rent Book, it is possible to narrow down the possibilities of its position. It is almost certain that the Bridge Rent Book entry is for Tudor Cottage, Anne Boleyn Cottage (Fig 7), and the row of cottages behind them, reached by a passage between the two front cottages (Fig 68 O.S.map 1879 the two cottages and the buildings behind may be seen on the left of the house marked 4).

The entry in the Bridge Rent Book, No 111, 1886 is as follows 'Thos A Champion late James Champion formerly Warner for cottages and premises 5s.' (a later pencilled entry says 'Stanley Barrett now D Graham.')

Going back to 1842 and to 1836 the Rentals are 'J Warner own occupation and others 5s. In 1828-23-14 & 07 'Sam Hucks and others 5s.' In 1800-1795-93-90 & 85 'Sam Hucks occupied Bell breeches maker and others.' In 1785 in addition to the Rentals there was also the Court Baron Book, this was a list of rentals in the town composed specially for the use of the Lord of the Manor. It contains some of the same information as the Rentals but sometimes with interesting additions. In this case it says 'Sam Hucks occupied Widow Bell called the *Barge Pole* 5s.'

The Rentals continue back in 1779 and again in 1775 'late Mr Hucks now Sam Hucks occupied Downing and Wells now Bell breeches maker 5s.' In 1769 'Mr Hucks late Downing the *Barge Pole* now Phillips 4½d.' (the cash mentioned for all rents between 1769 & 1758 is much lower throughout, whether they really were or the calculation was different it is hard to say.) In 1765-58 'Mr Hucks late Downing the *Barge Pole* 4½d.' In 1749-5 'Hucks occupied Downing 5s.' In 1737 'Tenement in possession of Downing and for 7 trees.' Finally in 1733/4 'for the tenements in tenure of Downing and others.'

From these entries it seems that the *Barge Pole* was definitely in existence from 1758-85, and most likely for the whole time that Downing was in occupation, if not for many years before that. It is also likely that it continued as a pub until at least 1800 which was the last entry for the Bell who was a breeches maker.

Landlords/ Tenants of the *Barge Pole*

1733-49	Downing (R)
1758-65	Hucks (R)
1769	Phillips(R)
1775-1800	Bell (1785 Widow Bell) (R,CB)

— Closed —

Fig 7 Cottages once the Barge Pole, with beyond them the present day Rose & Crown (see also Fig 68) Photo 1989

8

The Barley Mow

North side of the Market Place

See the entry for the *Sun* on the north side of the Market Place.

— Closed —

9

The Basketmakers Arms

43 Gravel Hill

The *Basketmakers Arms* was a beerhouse and lodging house, records of it go back to 1841, but it may have been a beerhouse slightly before that. In 1960 it gained a full license but it closed on 1 February 1972.

It was situated up Gravel Hill on the south side of the medieval market place, at the west end of the town. Gravel Hill was not originally within the town, it was in medieval times in the parish of Badgemore. Even though in the 19th century the parish of Henley included Badgemore, this did not alter the municipal boundary, which on the O.S. map of 1884 still excluded Gravel Hill. The boundary ran across the fields to where the Market Place becomes Gravel Hill, across the road and then westward up behind the houses on the north side of Gravel Hill to the top of West Hill or Street, along what is now the Hop Gardens, round the then Workhouse now the hospital and down to Bell Lane.

Fig 8 The Basketmakers Arms after closure (see also Fig 66)
Photo 1989

The building which was the *Basketmakers Arms* is in a prominent position, projecting beyond the main building line of the other houses on that side of the hill, its gable end looking down Gravel Hill (Figs 8 & 66). When Ruth Gibson of the Vernacular Buildings Research section of the Henley Archaeological & Historical Group investigated the house, it was found that the oldest part of the building was in fact the part projecting, which consisted of two bays divided by a massive chimney block. This chimney section, virtually a narrow bay, may have been used as a smoke bay, a feature not often found in this district, but common in parts of Surrey. There were also slight signs of smoke blackening in the roof above the more eastern bay, that is the gable end looking down the hill. This may indicate that originally this part could have been an open hall, with an open fire, the chimney being a later addition. The present bedroom floor above this area is supported by beams which are narrower, and appear more recent than those over the other end of the building. There are also fine curved wind braces supporting the roof at the east end, often a feature of an open hall, designed to be seen from below.

Ruth Gibson feels that although the house is listed as 18th century, the front part is actually much older and could be 16th century or even earlier.

How far back it was in use as a beerhouse and lodging house it is impossible to say, though it is unlikely that it was open before the 1820s. Most pubs if they were trading earlier than that were classified as inns and not beerhouses, it also is not listed under the entries in the Victuallers Recognizances which go up to 1822 for the area outside Henley town. That it was a lodging house in the 19th century is clear from the Census Returns, and it is probable that Annie Pigden aged 64 in 1905, and Sarah Clarey aged 86 in 1911, who are recorded in the Burial Register of 1844-1944, with the *Basketmakers Arms* given as their residence, were lodgers. C W Maidment aged 58, buried in 1921 was landlord of the pub.

In 1882 when the *Basketmakers Arms* first appears in the Register of Licenses, it was owned by Brakspears, it is not known when they acquired it, though it may have been in 1860 when the property was offered for sale[80]. At that time Brakspears were leasing the premises and the under tenant was Thomas Usher. It was described as having a parlour, tap room, kitchen, six bedrooms and a cellar, with sheds and a skittle alley at the rear, and side entrance.

One feature shown on the O.S.Map of 1879 (Fig 66) is what appear to be entrance steps in the centre of the east facing gable end. This presumes a door at that point, which indicates that there have been quite major changes to the building in the last hundred years.

Landlords/ Tenants of the *Basketmakers Arms*

1841- 69	Thomas Usher (C,RM,SD)
*1871-Sep 78	Benjamin May (C,SD,BReg)
Sep 1878-85	Jane May (RL,C) widow
Apr 1885-99	John Lewis Coates (RL,HA,SD)
Aug 1899-1903	Emily Coates (RL)
May 1903-21	Charles Walter Maidment (RL,HS,BReg)
May 1921-7	Kate Maidment (RL,HS,SD) widow
Feb 1927-8	Samuel Hunter (RL,HS,SD)
Dec 1928-31	George Francis Heath (RL,HS)
May 1931-8	Sydney Charles Butler (RL,HS,SD)
Jul 1938-40	John Harry Roberts (RL,BaReg,SD)
Feb 1940-1	Harry Facey(Lacey?) Kench (RL)
Feb 1941-2	Elizabeth Caroline Kench (RL)
Dec 1942-6	Eric John Bowery (RL,BaReg)
Feb 1946-53	Hubert Walker/Walters (RL)
Feb 1953-7	Thomas Mann (RL)
Feb 1957-72	Edward John Manley (RL)

— Closed —

80 Reading Mercury & Oxford Gazette 12 May 1860

10

The Bear

77-9 Bell Street

The name of the *Bear* is said by the Hon Georgina Stonor to derive from the badge of the Earls of Oxford, the De Veres, which was a bear with a staff. Before its closure in February 1986 it had for some time incorrectly displayed a polar bear on its sign. In 1900 however it did not appear to have had any pictorial sign (Fig 9).

Fig 9 The Bear in the early 1900s, the entrance to the yard under the central gable

The earliest available record of the *Bear* is a deed of 1666, which concerns not the *Bear* but the property to the south. This says 'to the north Henry Godfrey at the *Bear*.' Henry Godfrey in the Hearth Tax of 1665 had five hearths. A further deed for the same property in 1682 says 'John Dolton on the north at the *Bear*'[81].

In 1683 the Will and Inventory of John Dolton was proved (see p18). From the Inventory[82] the number of rooms can be ascertained, there was a hall, parlour, kitchen, brewhouse, wash house and cellar. There were six chambers - a new chamber, little chamber, chamber over the gatehouse, middle chamber, chamber called 'Ye Captains Chamber,' and 'ye little chamber below.' All the chambers had beds in them, a total of eleven beds, and as previously mentioned three of the hearths seem to have been in the chambers, and three hearths seem to have been in the hall, the parlour and the kitchen, that is going by such items as fire irons etc. So either Henry Godfrey misrepresented

81 Deed between Thomas Shefford bargemaster & Jeffrey Brocke baker & deed of sale by Thomas Shefford the elder to Thomas Shefford the younger. O.R.O. Cooper & Caldecott

82 Will & Inventory transcribed by the evening class of Miss Joan Dils

the number of hearths, or another hearth was added between 1665 and 1683.

In 1683 some of the contents of the rooms are of interest, '3 Hogsheads of beer, 8 emty hogsheads, 3 dozen glass bottles, plates, flagons etc., 18 pairs of sheets, 6 dozen napkins, 8 tablecloths, 6 towels. 2 base viols, 1 harp, 1 sittern and 1 violin.' The musical instruments suggest that the *Bear* might have been the meeting place of a musical group. One can only speculate as to the reason for the name of 'Ye Captains Chamber', perhaps the 'Captain' was a veteran of the Civil War, though if he were, it would be hard to know which side he might have supported given the divided nature of Henley in those times, though with the Stonor connection he might well have been a royalist. Maybe the Captain was a retired army man who had permanent lodgings at the *Bear.*

In the 17th century the *Bear* belonged to the Stonor family, and although it is probable that the *Bear* existed long before 1666 it is not possible to research the details as the Stonor papers are not available to the public. However as previously stated (see p21) in the 17th century the *Bear* like the *Bull* was used by travelling priests, who may have held services at the *Bear.*

In 1686 there is a deed in the Oxford Record Office which says 'John Stonor son and heir of the late Thomas Stonor' granted to William Hyne yeoman of Pishill a messuage called the *Beare* in Henley in Bell Street, together with barns, stables, malting houses etc. In 1714 James Phelps or Philps of Reading labourer leased to John Havergill of Henley innholder a messuage stables and malthouse on the west side of Bell Street known as the *Beare Inne*[83], which was already occupied by Havergill.

Havergill variously spelt as Havergail, Abigail, or Abbegail appears in the Parish Registers. In 1701 John Abigail innholder was the father of a child baptised at that date and of another in 1705/6. John Havergill also had other properties in Henley, two houses which were probably 82 and 84 Bell Street, and the *Butchers* Arms[84].

When the Stonors sold the *Bear* is not known, possibly between 1686 and 1714, by 1732 it was owned by William Brooks brewer, an abstract of title at that time mentions Mrs Anne Brooks, T Fowler and Eliz Havergill as being the parties concerned. Henley Rentals show that either James Brooks or Mrs Brooks paid for the *Bear* from 1745-1800. The Bridge Rent for the *Bear* was one of the more expensive in the town it was set at £1 3s 4d and was finally commuted by Brakspears on 31 March 1967. Brakspears had probably become the owners between 1800 and 1807 when they started paying the Rentals.

The Royal Exchange Insurance Register shows that on the 14 March 1785 Mr Stephen Pauling/Paulin innholder took out a policy on 'His household furniture in his dwelling house lath and plaister built and tiled situate in Bell Street in Henley and known as the *Bear Inn.* £60. Wearing apparel £15. Utensils and stock in trade £40. Utensils and stock in trade in granaries and hay lofts adjoining lath and plaister built and tiled near. £135.' Paulin's insurance continued till July 1806, and there is a pencilled note saying 'now John Heath.'[85]. John Heath's name is not mentioned in other sources so it is probable that he was at the *Bear* from 1806 to before 1812 when George Chalmers according to the Court Leet Book was there, listed as having deficient measures. Stephen Paulin/Pauling was listed in the Henley licenses of 1771 but not those of 1770, so it is likely that he took over the *Bear* in 1771. In the street directory of about 1793 Mary Paulin is listed as at the *Bear.*

The Inventory of Brakspear's brewery in 1826, shows that the freehold of the *Bear* was held by Joseph Benwell and W H Brakspear. 'The *Bear Inn* in occupation of William Wilstead,

---

83 O.R.O. Brooks C3 (1-14)

84 O.R.O. Cooper & Caldecott C57 (1)

85 Royal Exchange Insurance Register O.R.O. Brakspear X/I

numerous rooms, chamber over gateway, good cellars. Open and enclosed stabling for 78 horses. Lofts, cartsheds, poultry house, piggeries, granaries, wash coal and wood houses, yard etc. Also a house adjoining occupied by Goodwyn with a front shop, parlour, chambers and a wash house. Land Tax £1 13s 6d. Bridge Rent £1 3s 4d.'

The house adjoining was possibly the house under the gable to the right of the gateway, (Fig 9) on the north side of the *Bear*, and was earlier mentioned in the Henley Rentals as also being paid for by Mr Brooks in 1745.

The number of horses which could be stabled at the *Bear* indicates something of the trade done at the pub. In the 19th century it was essentially a 'carter's pub', but it is possible that earlier it had catered to the private traveller, it is not mentioned as a stopping place for public coaches. By 1830[86] John Kent was running a carrier service to London on Wednesdays, Fridays and Saturdays, and also a service in the other direction to Abingdon on Tuesdays, Fridays and Saturdays. At the same time Aaron Cooke ran a service to Dorchester on Wednesdays, and Thomas Wilkins to Hendred on Wednesdays. Depending on their loads, waggons may have been pulled by anything from two to eight horses, which would quickly have used up the stabling.

In 1850[87] James Wicks ran a carrier service from the *Bear* to Reading and Twyford daily, Thursdays and Saturdays excepted. By 1850 the railway was impinging on both the coaching and carrier services in the town. The Great Western Railway line from London to the west ran through both Twyford and Reading, the link to Henley from Twyford did not come till 1856.

Although the carrier services dwindled during the 19th century, the *Bear* was probably much used by local farmers and tradesmen from the surrounding countryside, in Henley for business purposes either for the market or for general provisioning. Besides having a large amount of stabling, it is also probable that the field behind, now part of Adam Court, was used as grazing land by the *Bear* and its clients. In 1978 when the Henley Archaeological & Historical Group excavated portions of the field, before Adam Court was built, traces of a wide farm type gateway were found immediately behind the back wall of the *Bear*.

All the activity in the yard did not stop the landlord, James Wigmore, from keeping rabbits[88]. In August of 1883 John Hughes was charged with stealing a tame rabbit from the *Bear*. Alice Wigmore, daughter of James, said she fed the rabbits, and there were four in the hutch, one being black. Later she noticed before going in to dinner that the black one was missing, the hutch door closed but a spar broken. Hughes was seen near the hutch, and later tried to sell a black rabbit to Gabriel Machin junior, who offered 1s for it, which Hughes at first refused but then came back and accepted the shilling. A constable apprehended Hughes, fetched back the rabbit from Machin, and it was returned to the *Bear*. Hughes was sentenced to 21 days hard labour.

A few years before the affair of the rabbit, there was the case of the stolen trousers or trowsers as they were spelt[89]. In 1879 Harriet Adams the housekeeper said that between 8 and 9 o'clock Saturday last, John Robinson came in and called for a pint of mild beer. He sat for a few minutes, then crossed the bar where there was a table with a bundle on it, a mackintosh, a pair of trowsers and a wrapper. Robinson finished his beer, went back and picked up the trowsers which he placed under his jacket and left. The owner of the bundle, James Bartlett of Adwell Square, was in the yard, called in by Mrs Adams he checked the bundle then pursued Robinson, and found the trowsers with him. Robinson was sentenced to two months hard labour.

It is interesting to compare the two sentences, 21days for a rabbit and 2 months for a pair of trousers. (NB. the spelling in the newspaper account was trowsers) It is probable that at that time for a man not very well off, a pair of trousers was a major expense, hence the longer sentence.

86 Pigot & Co Street Directory 1830

87 Slater's Street Directory 1850

88 & 89 Henley Advertiser 18 Aug 1883, 3 Jul 1879

The Census Returns show that John Banbury was landlord in both 1861 and 1871. In 1861 with two sons and two daughters, the sons by 1871 were both whitesmiths, and a lodger with family was also an engineer and whitesmith. They may have carried on their business at the *Bear*, using one of the outhouses or sheds. Whitesmithing is the working of pewter or Britannia metal, as opposed to blacksmithing with iron. Another lodger, a gardener named James Shaw with wife and children, was lodging there in both 1861 and 1871. Proof of the long term residence of some lodgers at pubs.

By the end of the 19th century when Henley was reviving as a holiday and leisure centre, in the 1896 'Guide to Henley' by Emily Climenson, it says 'Mr William Keene who rents the yard, has always horses and carriages of all descriptions to let out, and gives riding and driving lessons as well. Good Hacks and Hunters to be hired. Horses broken to ride.' Mr Keene had moved there from the *Rose and Crown* in New Street in May 1890, when he advertised his move in the Henley Advertiser on the 19th May.

The malthouse (M4) mentioned in the deeds of 1686 and 1714, was probably used as part of Brooks' brewery, but may have fallen into disuse when Brakspears acquired the property soon after 1800. Brakspears had several malthouses scattered round the town in the early 1800s, their chief one being at 74-8 Bell Street, another being at 44 Bell Street, and yet another in Bell Street together with a brewhouse at 67, which also had been Brooks. The malthouse at the *Bear* may not have been needed.

In 1924 at the Henley Brewster Sessions[90] many licensed houses were said to be badly in need of cleaning and decorating. The *Bear* was one of three singled out for having unsatisfactory sanitary accommodation, the others were the *Bull* and the *Red Cow*. The following year in February 1925 it was said that the sanitary accommodation was now satisfactory.

Landlords/ Tenants of the *Bear*

1666	Henry Godfrey (ORO)	
*1682-3	John Dolton (ORO)	
1686*	William Hyne (ORO)	
*1701-22	John Havergill (ORO)	
1722-25*	Thomas Havergill (ORO)	
*1732	Eliz Havergill (ORO)	
1732 ?	T Fowler ? (ORO)	
1771-1806	Stephen & Mary/Ann Paulin/Pauling (VR,SD,RE)	
1806-12*	John Heath (RE,CL))	
1812-17	George Chalmers (AKL,CL) }	This may be the same person
1823	Richard Chalmers (SD) }	an error of christian names
1826-30	William Wilstead/Walstead (WHB/I,SD)	
*1841-7	Joseph Bisley/Biesley/Beisley etc (C,SD,RM) tailor	
*1850	Stephen Boyes (SD)	
1851	John Cole (C)	
1852-4*	Joseph Dance (SD) watchmaker	
*1861-72	John Banbury (C,SD,HA)	
1872-3	Elizabeth Banbury (HA)	
1873-87	John Mosdell Wigmore (RL,C,SD,HA) builder	
1887-97	Mrs Harriet Wigmore (RL)	
Oct 1897-1901	Frederick Drewett (RL)	
Apr 1901-2	George Street (RL)	

90 Henley Standard 8 Feb 1924

Dec 1902-13	Alfred Robert Norcott (RL)
Nov 1913-4	Charles Alfred Young (RL)
Feb 1914-Sep	Mrs Annie Edith Young (RL)
Sep 1914-5	William John Crawford (RL)
Jan 1915-7	Frederick Edward Townsend (RL)
Dec 1917-9	Arthur Lockyer (RL)
Mar 1919-35	Richard Henry Cain (RL,SD) 1920-32 Mrs Alice Cain (SD)
Sep 1935-7	Henry James Keeling (RL)
Oct 1937-48	Leonard George Rumbold (RL)
Sep 1948-50	Arthur Fayze (RL)
Jul 1950-4	Thomas Henry Hayward (RL)
Dec 1954-6	Michael Sporway Holman (RL)
Oct 1956-7	Peter Edward Gates (RL)
Dec 1957-64	Robert Francis Simon (RL)
Feb 1964-6	Walter Frank Barker (RL)
Dec 1966-8	John Graham Carter (RL)
Apr1968-Feb1986	Eduard Rudolph Pfyl (RL)

— Closed —

11

The Bell Inn later the Bell Tap

Northfield End

The *Bell* was one of the most prestigious inns of Henley in the 17th and 18th centuries. It was on the east side of Northfield End on the north west corner of Bell Lane, due to this it was outside Henley town. The town boundary until 1892 crossed Bell Street diagonally from the point still to be seen today on the west side, where Bell Street becomes Northfield End, and then went down Bell Lane to the river.

The *Bell* included the whole of what now appears to be a row of terraced houses with a pediment over the centre, and also the house at the corner of Bell Lane now known as Denmark House (Figs 10 & 11).

The *Bell* was part of the estate of Phyllis/Filletts Court bought in 1632 by James Whitelocke of Fawley Court[91]. The earliest mention of the *Bell* is an entry in the Burial Register in May 1629 'a stranger buried from the *Bell*'. In February 1638 another entry reads 'Richard Foord a stranger dead at the *Bell*'. This stranger was presumably staying at the inn since his name was known, while the earlier one may have just wandered in and been found on the premises, perhaps in an outhouse.

It is said[92] that in 1633 Archbishop Laud and his train stayed at the *Bell*, although Bulstrode Whitelocke tried to persuade him to stay at Fawley Court. Bulstrode's father James had been a student at Oxford with William Laud, a clothier's son from Reading[93].

During the Civil War in 1642 the *Bell* was used for a time as a headquarters by Prince Rupert, who is said to have had a Parliamentary spy hanged on the elm in front of the inn. The remains of the elm tree could still be seen in the garden outside the front of the inn until 1995, when

91 & 93 Spalding, Ruth 'The Improbable Puritan' 1975 p30 & p26
92 Climenson, Mrs Emily J 'Guide to Henley on Thames' 1896

Fig 10 The Bell Inn in c.1900 when it was the Grammar School. On the left is the 19th century schoolroom, and on the right Denmark House. The top of the 18th century wing may be seen over the central pediment. The obelisk in front was removed from the central cross roads in 1885

it was removed. It was known as Rupert's Elm and a portion of it may be seen in the River & Rowing Museum.

In her book 'The Improbable Puritan', a biography of Bulstrode Whitelocke, Ruth Spalding quotes a letter from William Cooke, a tenant farmer probably of Fawley Court Farm, and acting bailiff for Whitelocke. It is dated in early March, so although we now would regard that as being 1644, strictly speaking it was still 1643, until 1753 the new year began on March 25. The letter is as follows:-

> 'Master and Mistress ..... Upon Wenday nite there hapined a nill mischance at the Bell at Henley about to of the cloke in the morning by fire ..... It began at the Yalhouse as we go to Filles Court ..... there is not much of the timber distroyed but the tilles be distroid, the selling bet down, the walls bet down, the woman's household stuff torn and lost to peces of hir great lose but she doth umbelie desier you that you would be pleased to set your helping hand to mend it ..... I ham very willing to have it mended again, and had thought to set upon it without trobilling of you, I have take a nottis of it, about 2 thousens of tilles will heale it again, so that I thinge that the charge will amount to fiftie pounds to mend it if it be suddenlie dun fiftie pounds will do more now than a hundrid will do twelve months hence, and therfore if I do not hear from you to the contrary I will set upon it, to mend it, that I will have it dun with in this month if God will give me leafe .....
>
> I rest your loving servant
>
> William Cooke to command in anything that God shall give me leave .'

The damage had been done by Parliamentary soldiers of whom Whitelocke bitterly complained, saying that he was 'a parliament man' but adding 'common soldiers know no distinction between friends and others'.

From the letter it is clear that the Yalhouse or Alehouse of the inn was on Bell Lane, behind where Denmark House is today, perhaps an extension running down the lane from the corner of the *Bell.* The whole block of property was still being auctioned as one group as late as 1853, at a sale of the Fawley Court estate. A study of the Ordnance Survey map of 1879, a reduced portion of which is illustrated here (Fig 11), suggests that Bell Lane may once have been wider at the west end or lower end on the map. If one imagines the lane without Denmark House it would then have a consistent width throughout. Denmark House is said by J S Burn to have been so named because George of Denmark, husband of Queen Anne, stayed there when it was part of the *Bell.* If it was then the most modern part of the inn, it may well have been built in about 1700, an addition which encroached on the roadway, and which possibly removed the Yalhouse. Since the

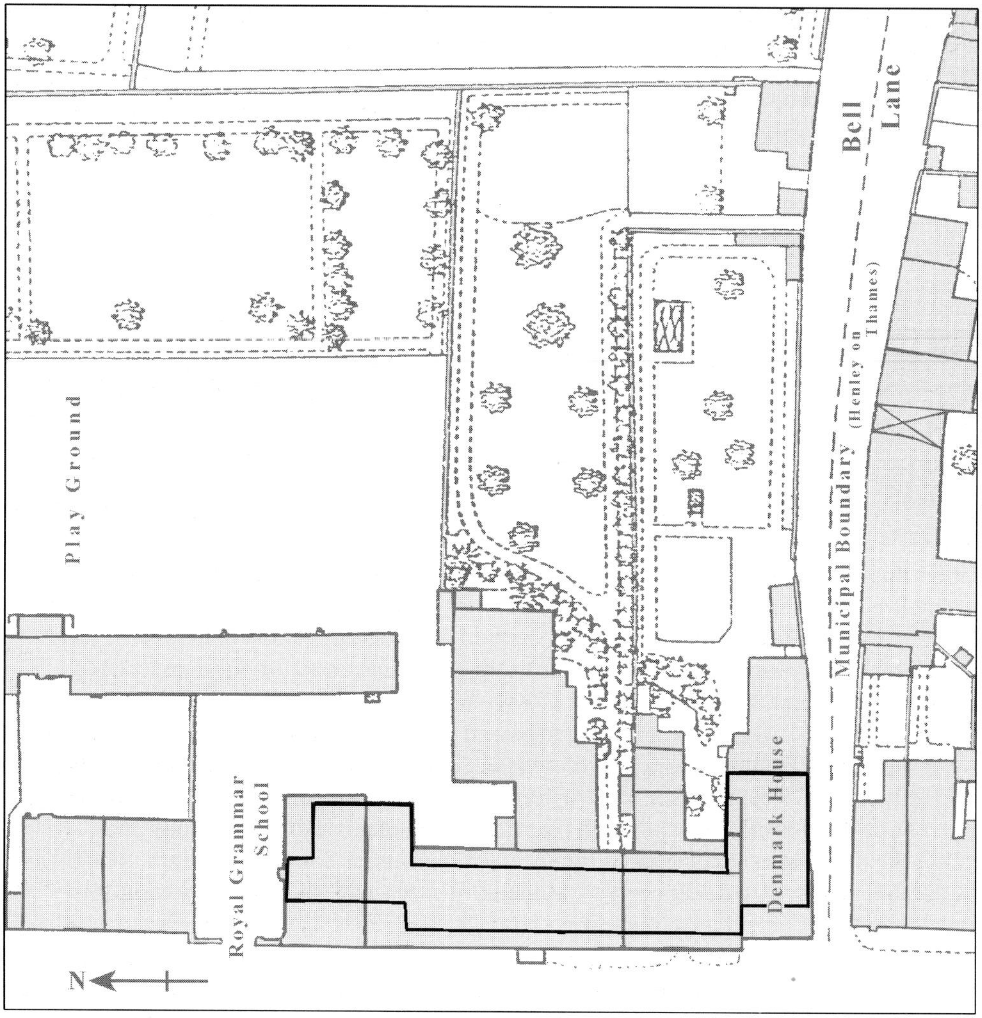

Fig 11 The Bell Inn, O.S. map 1879 much reduced in grey. Possible extent of original inn as indicated on a Fawley Court Estate map c.1782 and as suggested by timbers in 'Rupert's Bell' in black

Lord of the Manor owned the *Bell* at that time he was probably able to build on the lane without any hindrance. If such an encroachment was made by anyone else it would have incurred not only his wrath but also a heavy fine, an encroachment of ten inches for a step incurred an annual fine of 6d.

At the end of the 17th century the Stevens family were innholders at the *Bell*. The Parish Burial Registers in April 1699 have the burial of Elizabeth Stevens daughter of Richard Stevens innholder, in January 1700 Margaret Stevens daughter of Richard Stevens innholder, in February 1701 the burial of 'Richard Stevens innholder of the *Bell*'. This was followed in January 1703 by 'Abraham Stevens son of ye widow at ye *Bell*'. A Mary Stevens widow was buried in 1708.

In 1724 the Fawley Court estate and the Manor of Henley was sold to Gislingham Cooper, and the *Bell Inn* was in the occupation of John Nicoll. In 1751 Jackson's Oxford Journal says that the *Bell Inn* is to let and that the owner (or leaseholder) Wright Burdett is retiring. The Victuallers Recognizances of 1753, 56 and 57 have the name Wright Burdett as an innholder. So maybe he was unable to let and had to postpone his retirement. Unfortunately these early licensing lists do not name the pubs. The lists of 1770 and 1771 both name Thomas Hally as an innholder and from later references he is known to have been at the *Bell*.

In 1775 there is a note in the Victuallers Recognizances book as follows :-

> 'Be it remembered that at the *Bell* in Henley on Thames in the County of Oxford on Thursday 7th day of September 1775 the several alehouse keepers within the said hundred did appear before this two of his Majesty's J.P.s.'

This sounds as though the alehouse keepers of Henley went to the *Bell* and were seen by the magistrates, and that became the custom for some years. Unfortunately no records seem to have been kept or perhaps they have just not survived. The only lists in the 18th century are those already mentioned in 1753, 54, 56, 1770 and 71. The exception to this from the 1770s are the landlords of the *Bell* and the *Windmill*, both pubs were situated outside the town boundary but included in Henley Parish.

In 1768 Fawley Court and the entire estate including the *Bell* was inherited by the Rev. Edward Cooper son of Gislingham Cooper, who immediately sold the property to Sambrook Freeman, who left it to his nephew Strickland Freeman in 1782. Strickland Freeman having no descendants, the property went on his death in 1821 to a cousin, the eldest son of Mrs Mary Williams, who was the daughter of an aunt of Sambrook Freeman. The son, Admiral Williams, took the name Freeman, and became William Peere Williams Freeman. He died in 1831, when his grandson, also a William Peere Williams Freeman, inherited[94].

In 1774 Thomas Hadley was at the *Bell*. The variations of the spelling of the name are many, even in the Victuallers Recognizances in following years there are Hadley, Hallay, Halley and Hally. So it is safe to assume that the Hally of 1770-1 is the same as Hadly in 1774. From 1778-81 Christopher Widmore/Widmer was at the *Bell*, followed in 1782 and 83 by Samuel Bealey, and after him Thomas Tripp 1787 and 89.

Thomas Tripp of Henley innholder took out an insurance policy on 25 July 1787[95], on 'household furniture in his dwelling house brick built and tiled in Henley known as the *Bell Inn* £650, on wearing apparel £20, on plate £30, on utensils and stock in trade £150, and on utensils and stock in trade in the stables, hay lofts, granaries adjoining brick built and weather boarded and tiled situate in the yard near £150.' The insurance seems to have terminated after 1792, and in December of 1793[96] Thomas Tripp was selling his household effects at the *Bell*, so it is probable

94 Burn, John S 'History of Henley on Thames' 1861

95 Royal Exchange Insurance Register No 102820 O.R.O. Brakspear X/1

96 Reading Mercury & Oxford Gazette 16 Dec 1793

that he left the *Bell* at the end of 1793 or the beginning of 1794.

An estate map of about 1782 shows the outline of the *Bell* and Denmark House as being considerably smaller than they appear in the O.S.map of 1879, and Fig 11 demonstrates this.

The Victuallers Recognizances have a gap between 1789 and 1794 when Elizabeth Messenger was at the *Bell*. In the Reading Mercury & Oxford Gazette of 2 June 1794 the leasehold of the *Bell* was offered for sale. The description says 'which is so altered as to make it far more eligible to the coming tenant. It now consists of a spacious ballroom, comfortable sleeping rooms, four parlours, bar, larders, good kitchen, large garden and stabling for forty horses, with every convenience that can recommend it .....' In the same paper on 15 October 1794 William Baylis 'respectfully informs the nobility, the gentry, his friends and the public in general that he has opened the *Bell Inn*. The Assembly Room will be fit for their reception in the first week of November.' (Fig 12). Soon after there was an announcement that the Henley Town Assembly would be held at the *Bell*.

William Baylis was at the *Bell* in 1795-6 according to the Victuallers Recognizances, he was buried on 22 December 1796 aged 39. His widow Ann Baylis took over and appeared in the Recognizances 1797-1808, she almost certainly remained there until her death at the end of 1811 or beginning of 1812. When Joseph Sawer/Sawyer took the *Bell* his announcement in the Reading Mercury & Oxford Gazette of 20 April 1812 said that he would commence on 1 May, and that the *Bell Inn* at present was in the occupation of the daughters of Mrs Ann Baylis deceased.

In March and April of 1814 Mr Sawyer advertised in the same paper, that the *Bell* was again to let, since he had taken up another business. Later in the same year he advertised again, this time adding that the *Bell* was to let with or without a small farm. It seems that there were no takers. Finally on 8 January 1816 Mr Sawyer advertised once more, and it is the first mention of the *Bell Tap*. The *Bell* was to let and to be entered upon immediately. It was in excellent repair, to have a good posting trade, to have an excellent tap, a large garden and about 4 acres of meadow. The rent to be £100 p.a.

In the paper of 19 February 1816 Arthur Venables announced that he had taken the *Bell Inn*. That it had 'recently been fitted up in a style of superior neatness', and that there were 'Neat Post chaises and good horses' and that the 'Holmes Defiance coach' went from the *Bell* 'to London and Oxford every day at one o'clock.'

It was during the 18th century and the very early part of the 19th century that the *Bell* was at its most prosperous, its elegant exterior dates from that time, perhaps it was part of the refurbishing done before the lease was offered for sale in 1794. Mrs Lybbe Powys an indefatigable diarist, who was writing between 1756 and 1808, speaks of balls and suppers at the *Bell*, and especially of a particular one given by Lord Villiers. It was one of the inns frequented by the gentry, and a major stopping place on the road to Oxford and beyond.

Emily Climenson in 1896[97] mentions that the house was panelled throughout, that there was accommodation for 100 horses, and that a great number of coaches stopped there. However a slightly more modest number of horses is suggested by the Brakspear Inventory of 1826. Benwell and Brakspear then held the *Bell* leasehold — 'The *Bell Inn* in occupation of Mrs Dixon with stabling for 54 horses, standing for 8 carriages, double lock-up coach house, large paved yard and garden. Lease expires 29 September 1833. Rent £70 p.a.' The double lock-up coach house supports the idea that it was primarily a stopping place for the travelling gentry, with their own carriages with expensive contents.

The first mention of a public coach stopping at the *Bell* was in 1816 when the Holmes Defiance coach went to London and Oxford daily. In 1830, a coach went to London from the *Bell*

97 Climenson, Mrs Emily J 'Guide to Henley on Thames' 1896

and the *Red Lion* every morning (Sundays excepted) at seven, every Monday morning at five and every Saturday morning at nine (all go through Maidenhead etc)[98]. By 1850[99] the number of coaches had declined and the status of the *Bell* had changed, it was no longer termed the *Bell Inn* but was the *Bell Tap*. The coach service to London, known as Dixon's coach, went from the *Bell* calling at the *Red Lion* every morning at nine. A coach also now went to Twyford called the Train coach, also calling at the *Red Lion* at eight and a quarter before one noon.

By 1853 the Henley Grammar School had taken over the larger part of the buildings and the *Bell Tap* was relegated to the northern side. This is shown on the map accompanying a sales catalogue of 1853, when the Fawley Court estate was for sale by William Peere Williams Freeman[100]. In that sale Lot 7 included the whole block of buildings on the north west of Bell Lane. The *Bell Tap* to the north side had the yard and some of the stables—'5 bedrooms and cellar, wash house, stabling for 20 horses and loft over, coach house and granary over, 12 stall stable, harness room coach house and large yard. Let to Mr Dixon whose tenancy will expire at Christmas next at £40 p.a.' Also part of Lot 7 was 'The Royal Grammar School - 9 bedrooms and 2 small rooms adjoining. Entrance hall, 2 sitting rooms, dining room, kitchen, back ditto, 2 dressing rooms, schoolroom and butler's pantry. Closet, housekeeper's room, knife house, cellar and playground, and ornamental ground in front. Let to the Trustees of the School till 1891.' Also in Lot 7 there was 'A stuccoed Residence known as Denmark House', an adjoining brick built and stuccoed residence and cottage in Bell Lane, two other cottages, and two walled gardens. The whole of these properties were at one time part of the *Bell.*

Mr Dixon whose tenancy expired at 'Christmas next', seems to have been the last landlord of the *Bell*. After 1854 there are no further landlords mentioned, nor does the *Bell* or the *Bell Tap* appear in later street directories. It was probably closed after the sale of 1853 and the expiry of Dixon's lease, and then probably leased by the Grammar School. The *Bell* was almost certainly a victim of the opening of the railways, and the consequent loss to the town of well to do travellers.

The Grammar School moved from the premises in the early 1930s, Simmons & Sons drew up in 1934 a detailed plan of the buildings vacated by the school[101] In this plan (Fig 12) if a comparison is made between the two floors, it is clear that the large room at the north end on the ground floor is an addition to the main building, and when the plans are also considered in relation to the photograph of about 1900 (Fig 10), this room is shown to be the building alongside the main building, which has the appearance of a non-conformist chapel or late 19th century school. This building, which was probably a schoolroom, no longer exists.

The 1934 plan is of the northern part of the *Bell*, the entrance porch to the right on the plan, is at the centre of the building directly under the central pediment. The room to the left of the entrance has a large chimney block and was possibly the main hall of the original building. A large wing projects almost centrally behind the main entrance, and the plan shows that it was in this wing on the upper floor that there was a large room (35ftx20ft), which may most likely be the ball room or Assembly room mentioned in 1794. From the outside it can still be seen that the wing is of a greater height than the front buildings, probably due to higher ceilings inside. Significantly the room is shown on the plan to have at the front what may well have been arches leading to the landing or foyer, which in turn leads to the main stairs reached from the front hallway. Alternatively there was a back entrance from a lobby and a double flight of stairs leading up from a lobby below, with an entrance from the yard where coaches might have arrived. There is also a sizeable room off the same upper lobby which might have been used for either refreshments or card playing .

---

98 Pigot & Co Street Directory 1830

99 Slater's Street Directory 1850

100 W P W Freeman inherited the estate in 1831 from his grandfather Admiral Freeman

101 Simmons & Sons' plan of old Grammar School Buildings 1934. O.R.O. Hen RDC XVII/ ix/ 17

It seems that when the school was in occupation the part of the old building on the south or right hand side was separated off as the house of the headmaster, now known as Ruperts Bell, while Denmark House was occupied for many years by the various estate managers of Edward Mackenzie of Fawley Court, which he purchased in 1853. Neither of these buildings therefore appear on the plan of 1934, nor does the room at the rear or east side as shown on the O.S. map of 1879 (Fig 11).

Two features of the *Bell* are described by Emily Climenson in 1896. 'A very curious sort of crypt or cellar supported by columns, and in the roof is a recess long enough for a man to lie in'[102]. Of the chamber in the roof, Mr John Crocker, a local historian, now in his nineties, says that his uncle Henry Crocker, a builder of Northfield End, showed him the room in the roof, which could only be entered from an attic window. No entry from the house being possible.

Mr Alun Jones who now (1999) owns the whole front part of the building as shown on the plan of 1934 (Fig 12), very kindly took me on a tour of his house, whose rooms still conform to the plan of 1934.

The rooms and their fireplaces would seem to be as they were 'so altered' in 1794, the fireplaces are noteworthy in having matching flat carved stone plinths, while the interiors, or hearth spaces are built of bricks laid so as to form a curved wall enclosing the hearths. There is no longer any trace of any earlier wide or open fireplaces, such as might have been there before the 1790s. There is also no sign of any panelling as mentioned by Emily Climenson, apart from the shutters with their original fastenings on all the front windows, probably installed when the Georgian front was built in the 1790s.

The cellar, now divided in two, has no pillars or vaulting which could suggest it being crypt like, although it does have a curious arched passage under what was once the entrance hall, leading to stairs no longer in use which would have led to the room to the right of the main door as in Fig 12. In 1934 the entrance to the cellar is shown as a curved stair from the yard, and is now altered and replaced by a straight stair from the yard under the lobby, shown as a door entrance next to the curved stair. The cellar is under the back stairs and passageway, and under the large front room and would once have joined what is now a second cellar under the next room with the large fireplace. This part of the cellar is now reached by a trap door set in the floor of the passage alongside the main stairs.

The main staircase although appearing to be a fine example of plain late 17th century or early 18th century pine woodwork, well proportioned and sturdily built, may have been a later insertion possibly of the 1790s. The back wall of the building as shown in the plan of about 1782 (Fig 11) may not have coincided with the back wall in the O.S. map of 1879, which is the same as the wall today.

The roof is constructed with two parallel ridges running along the length of the building, with short ridges across both ends, leaving an enclosed gully within. This gully is drained by a wooden channel lined with lead running across the rear attic, under the back roof ridge, which is lower than the front roof ridge. This pattern of roofing would seem to be typical of the late 17th or 18th centuries, so is of little help in deciding whether the *Bell* was an ancient building.

Little of the original building remains visible, even the roof chamber has lost its mystery, since it can now be reached from a collapsible roof ladder leading to the main attic, from where it is now open to view. The room contains interesting graffitti, mostly from visitors near the end of the 19th century, an exception is an inscription saying 'William Higgins imprisoned here 1701'. If genuine one wonders why the imprisonment, since at that time the house was a normal working inn, and did not have Catholic connections which might have necessitated 'priest holes', or prisons.

102 Climenson, Mrs Emily J 'Guide to Henley on Thames' 1896

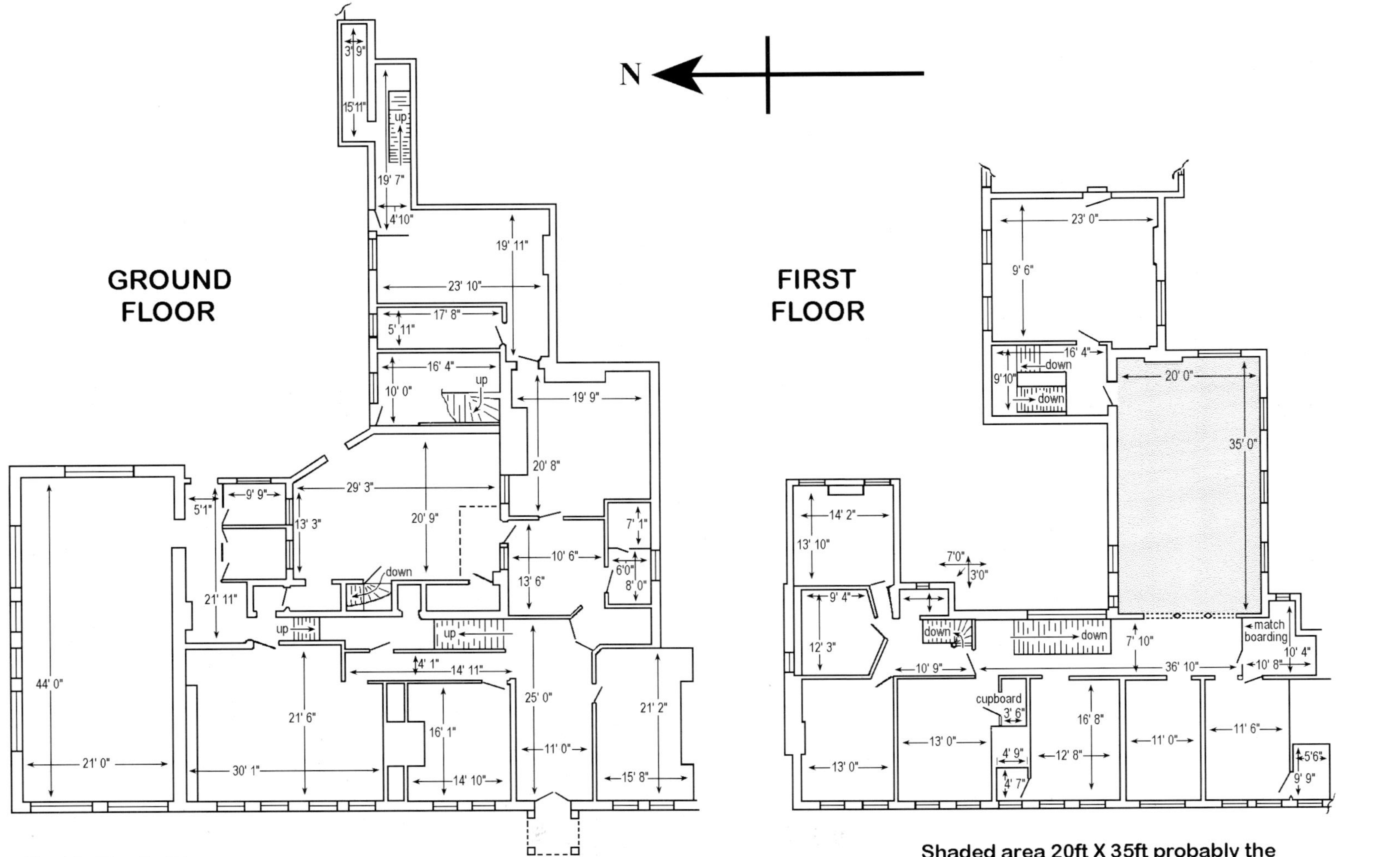

Fig 12 The Bell Inn
Plan of the old Grammar School much reduced
drawn in 1934 by EJH for Simmons & Sons
Document in O.R.O. (XVII/ IX/ 17)

Shaded area 20ft X 35ft probably the ballroom added in c.1794
Large room 21ft X 44ft on ground floor a 19th century addition most likely for a schoolroom

Although in that part of the Bell used by the school there is no sign of a more ancient building; upstairs in the house used by the headmaster, at the south end next to Denmark House, there is old timber work and the remains of panelling. This house now called Rupert Bell is owned by a family named Rosen. Mrs Annette Rosen very kindly allowed me to see round her house, the interior of the roof space and the cellar. The cellar probably once led into the other cellars, the other side of the entrance hall, and also has a blocked passage once leading to a cellar under Denmark House.

In an upstairs front room whose windows are similar to the Georgian windows in the other end of the building, an extremely large upright post is situated about six foot back from the present front wall, with a tie beam running back from it, and above it a principal rafter and collar beam, forming a box frame. On the opposite wall the pattern is repeated so that the size of the present room is still of one bay wide, while its length is extended by six foot towards the front. Continuing the line of this opposite wall into what is now a bathroom, one can see the principal rafter at the other end sloping down to another upright post, with the back of the building beyond it. The width of the box frame suggests that the whole building was narrower than today, and that the shape as suggested by the map of about 1782 (Fig 11) is correct. Which also suggests that the present back wall and the main staircase are part of the rebuilding of the 1790s. The apex of the principal rafters is about level with the ceiling, the present upstairs rooms are the height of what was once the apex of the roof.

In the attic space above these two frames, there is a beam on the floor of the attic which may have been the apex of the original roof, which has been used to support the larger 18th century roof. This roof is a continuation of that already seen at the north end of the building, two roof lines with a gully between.

Judging by the positioning of the box frames it would seem as though the original building was a single frame deep, possibly about 16 to 18 feet wide, with a single pitched roof. If this is an indication of what was once the shape of the *Bell* it may be that the mysterious roof chamber situated as it is within the late 18th century roof is merely an attic bedroom, and the date 1701 claiming it as a prison is a later embellishment.

Landlords/ Tenants of the *Bell*

*1699-1701	Richard Stevens (BaReg,BReg)
1701-1708	Widow Stevens (BReg)
1724	John Nicoll (ORO)
1751-57	Wright Burdett (OJ,VR)
1770-74	Thomas Hadley/Hallay/Halley/Hally (VR)
*1778-81	Christopher Widmore/Widmer (VR)
1782- 3*	Samuel Bealey (VR)
*1787-93	Thomas Tripp (VR,RE,RM)
1794	Elizabeth Messenger (VR)
1795-96	William Baylis/Bayliss (VR,RM)
1796-1811	Ann Baylis/Bayliss (VR,RM)
May 1812-16	Joseph Sawer/Sawyer (RM)
Feb 1816-21*	Arthur Venables (VR,RM)
1823-47	James Dixon (SD) - 1826 Mrs Dixon (WHB/I)
*1850-54	Robert Dixon (SD)

— Closed —

12

The Bird in Hand

55 Greys Road / Lane

The earliest definite mention of this pub is in the Census of 1861, when the *Bird in Hand* was occupied by Valentine Fletcher publican and carrier. Later in the Census of 1871 it was occupied by Joseph Simmons blacksmith. The Post Office street directory of 1869 has Joseph Simmons in Greys Lane but an earlier directory of 1867 places him in the Reading Road. He had therefore probably taken over the *Bird in Hand* in about 1868-9. He may previously, in 1867, have been at the *Red White and Blue.*

In the Henley Advertiser of 2 January 1875 a holdover of the license was reported as being to Henry Everett, but when the report of the confirmation of the license was made in the issue of 30 January it was said to be to Henry Emmett. The Post Office directory of 1877 gives a Henry Everett as a beer retailer in Greys Lane.

William Webb licensee in 1888 was charged with selling beer to William Cordery, who was said to be already under the influence of alcohol[103]. Webb claimed that Cordery came in every evening for his pint, and that on the occasion under discussion he was as usual. Webb was fined £1 and costs, and the license was transferred a couple of months later to William Jarvis .

Ownership of the *Bird in Hand* in the 1880s seems to have been by Richard Lucas of High Wycombe, but by 1892 was by Leadbetter & Bird also of High Wycombe, who held it till 1928. In 1929 Wheeler of Wycombe Breweries held it, and then in 1934 H & G Simonds of Reading. H & G Simonds became Courage, Barclay & Simonds between 1948 and 62, which changed to Courage Brewery in 1973. After this the *Bird in Hand* became the property of Morland's Brewery of Abingdon, who in June 1992 declared that they were selling the *Bird in Hand*, which was to become a Free House with Dave Holland as landlord. However the sale did not go through, and by the Autumn of 1992[104] the premises were closed and boarded up.

A report in the Henley Standard of 15 January 1993 suggested that Morland's Brewery was still hoping to sell the *Bird in Hand* as a Free House. Manager Peter Capon of Morlands was granted a protection order to hold the license till a new owner could be found.

The Henley Standard of 26 November 1993 announced that the *Bird in Hand* had re-opened about three weeks ago. The new landlord Graham Steward and his wife Celia had opened the pub as a Free House, and were still selling Morland's beer as well as other beers, they also were now serving meals as well as drinks.

The *Bird in Hand* remained a beerhouse until 1957, when it was granted a full license[105].

Landlords/Tenants of the *Bird in Hand*

1860-1	Valentine Fletcher (C,RM) carrier
1869-71	Joseph Simmons (C,SD) blacksmith
1875-7*	Henry Everett/Emmett (SD,HA)
*1881-2	John William Cox (RL,C,SD)
Nov 1882-7	Mary Cox (RL)
Apr 1887-8	William Webb (RL,HA)
Sep 1888-93	William Jarvis (RL,HA,SD)
Dec 1893-5	Robert Chapman (RL)

102 Henley Advertiser 30 Jun 1888

103 & 104 Henley Standard 19 Jan 1992, 8 Feb 1957

Dec 1895-1901	Robert Daunsey/Dauncey (RL,SD)
Dec 1901-2	Thomas Hazell (RL)
1904-28	Henry Neate (RL,HS,SD)
Feb 1928-31	William Benjamin Hawkins (RL,SD)
May 1931-51	Arthur Caddy (RL,HS)
Feb 1951-3	William Hack (RL)
Sep 1953-5	Robert William Marsh (RL)
Jul 1955- 65	Alfred George Gibbs (RL)
Apr 1965-92	Mrs Lilian Florence Gibbs (RL,HS)

Nov 1993-99-	David Graham Steward & Celia Beatrice Steward (RL,HS)

13

The Bird In the Bush

West side of Bell Street

This pub is rather elusive, it has only two mentions, one in 1660 in a Henley Rental, and the other in a description of the Town Wards in the Henley Borough Association Minutes of 1677[106]. The entry is as follows:-

1/ From Mr Gledworth's house to the *Bell* on the east side of Bell Street.

2/ From Mr John Freeman's house to the *Bird in the Bush* on the north (sic) side of Bell Street.

The Burgesses for the wards were Mr Ambrose Freeman and William Atkins.

It would help if one could place either Mr Gledworth's house or Mr John Freeman's, the only place of which we can be certain is the *Bell* at Northfield End .

The modern wards cut across Bell Street just south of where the entrance used to be to Waitrose. Perhaps the two wards are the northern half of Bell Street. This would place the *Bird in the Bush* either near the entrance to what is now Boroma Way or where Bell Street becomes Northfield End, and definitely on the west side of the street.

— Closed —

14

The Black Horse

16 Friday Street

This pub on the south side of Friday Street and therefore in Rotherfield Greys until 1892, was before 1804 known as the *Plough* (Figs 13 & 64). It may have changed its name gradually through the pictorial image of its sign, which may have shown a black horse pulling a plough, and which may have been spoken of casually as the black horse.

In the Victuallers Recognizances for Rotherfield Greys Edward Deane was at the *Plough* from 1795 and at the *Black Horse* from 1804-11. In Henley Rentals the change of name seems to

106 O.R.O. Research by Mr Peter Elliman

Fig 13 The Black Horse once the Plough, on far right on the corner of Queen Street the gable end of Ye Lion (see also Fig 64) Photo 1989

have been later, as in 1800-14 Brakspear paid for the *Plough* occupied by Deane.

The freehold of the *Black Horse* in the Inventory of 1826 was held by Henry William Brakspear , not in conjunction with Joseph Benwell, which means that it was most likely one of the pubs inherited from Robert Brakspear, and inherited by him from his uncle Richard Hayward. 'The *Black Horse* at Henley' (sic) 'in occupation of William Browne with wood house, piggery and neat garden. Bridge Rent 1s 8d.'

The 1844 Tithe Returns for Rotherfield Greys say owned by Brakspear occupied by William Brown. The Census of 1851 shows that by then Ann Brown widow aged 60, her grand daughter and a lodger lived there.

The Henley Advertiser of 8 May 1886 contains an account of a disturbance caused by Mrs Sarah Munro of the *Black Horse*. She was said to have been standing in her doorway when she observed Annie Wise and Sarah Hill passing down the street. She called out derogatory remarks to Annie Wise about her 'bastard children'. This caused an uproar and a fight ensued, all three women taking part. All were taken to court and all the participants were fined 5s and the costs were divided. Mrs Munro's husband Donald Munro held the license of the *Black Horse* from March 1883 to April 1887.

The license of the *Black Horse* was discontinued in 1897.

Landlords/ Tenants of the *Black Horse*

1804-14*	Edward Deane (VR,R)
1818-9	Elizabeth Talbot (VR)
1821-44	William Browne/Brown (VR,TM,SD,WHB/I)
1847-54	Ann Brown (C,SD) widow
1863-71	James/John Ashfield (C,SD)
1877	Henry Worskett (SD)
1881	James Meads (C)
1882-3	William Lloyd (RL)
Mar 1883-7	Donald Munro (RL)
Apr 1887-9	John Hayes (RL,HA,SD)

Nov 1889-93	Ralph Harper (RL,HA,SD)
Jul 1893-4	George Chandler (RL)
Nov 1894-5	Edwin Jarrett (RL)
Dec 1895-7	Alfred Joseph Meyer (RL)

— Closed —

15
The Black Horse and Farrier or the Black Horse
7 Market Place

This pub was later to become the *Crown and Thistle,* documents in the Oxford Record Office show that the property now 7 Market Place known as Gabriel Machin's butchers shop (Fig 6), and the neighbouring property, now number 9, were jointly held throughout the 18th and most of the 19th century.

Robert Cluett maltster in a will of 1743 proved in 1744[107] left the properties to his wife Susanna Cluett. Her will proved in 1764[108] left to her niece Sarah Blackman 'the house where I dwell' (No9) and the adjoining house called the *Black Horse* (No 7). Sarah Blackman was the daughter of John Blackman of Henley brewer.

An abstract of title drawn up in about 1833[109] shows that the properties were sold in 1772 by Herald Painter and his wife Sarah (nee Blackman) to Josiah Sarney. The properties were described in 1772 as the messuage next to William Rackstraw hatter on the west (No 11) the messuage late in tenure of Susanna Cluett afterwards Eliz Prince widow and then or late Thomas Gregge <u>and also</u> malthouse granaries storehouses behind and adjoining late in tenure of Susanna Cluett then John Blackman then Josiah Sarney and their undertenants <u>and also</u> on the east side of the aforementioned the messuage called by the name or sign of the *Black Horse and Farrier* and then or late of the *Crown and Thistle* with the yard and garden thereto heretofore in the occupation of Thomas Davis afterwards James Robinson and then or late Lessiter Nichols <u>and also</u> a messuage lying behind the last mentioned in the yard or garden in the tenure of Mary Weller widow her undertenants etc formerly in the tenure of Thomas Messenger and then or late of Richard Geere <u>and also</u> two tenements in Brooke Street (Duke Street) <u>and also</u> all that barn and stable behind the messuage called the *Crown and Thistle* heretofore in the occupation of John Hare afterwards John Blackman and then Josiah Sarney and Richard Geere <u>and also</u> garden and waste ground on the south.

From these documents it can be seen that the building on the east side of the pair (No 7) was the *Black Horse and Farrier* or perhaps less formerly the *Black Horse*. When the change to the *Crown and Thistle* was made is not clear it may not have been till about 1770, or it may have been slightly earlier if the change was in any way a statement of approbation that the Hanoverians had maintained their hold on Scotland.

Reading through the list of properties it is also obvious that it was a large block of buildings in use by maltsters and brewers, John Blackman, Richard Geere and Josiah Sarney were all either brewers or maltsters. Although a malthouse is mentioned as being behind what is now no 9 there is no mention of a brewhouse, so it was not a brewery. However a brewhouse was rented nearby by

---

107 & 108, Wills of Robert 1744 & Susanna Cluett 1764 O.R.O. Cooper & Caldecott C9 (7 &1)

109 Abstract of Title O.R.O. Cooper & Caldecott

John Blackman on the corner of Duke Street with the Market Place (see B2 Breweries & Malthouses).

A Thomas Davis is listed in the Victuallers Recognizances of 1753 and 1754, and in the lists of 1770 and 1771there is a Leicester Nicholls.

Later details of the property can be found under the *Crown and Thistle* and also details of 9 Market Place under the *Crown.*

Landlords/ Tenants of the *Black Horse and Farrier*

1753-4	Thomas Davis (ORO,VR)
- -	James Robinson (ORO)
1770-1	Lessiter/Leicester Nichols/Nicholls (ORO,VR)

— Continued as the *Crown and Thistle* —

The Black Prince

121 Greys Road

In Billing's street directory of 1854 in the Rotherfield Greys section Edmund Butler was given as the landlord of the *Black Prince*. This may have been a colloquial name for the *Saracen's Head*. Edmund Butler is listed as a beer retailer in Greys Lane in 1847, 50, 54 and 69, while in 1863, 67 and 68 he is listed at the *Saracen's Head*, a pub which was not built till after 1844, the Tithe Map of 1844 for Rotherfield Greys shows an empty plot of land (Fig 60).

There is no other reference to the *Black Prince* so it is likely that the name was an error on the part of the compiler of Billing's directory. It is easy to understand how the name might have developed from a pictorial sign, but in this case it did not remain, so the *Black Prince* was never one of Henley's pubs.

16
The Blue Bell, the Bell, the One Bell, the Little Bells or the Little Blue Bell

corner of Hart Street and Duke Street

The property on the corner of Hart Street with Duke Street, which until recently was Foster Bros, and before that for many years was W H Smiths, was built in 1892. It replaced what had been the corner site of the *Blue Bell* and the neighbouring property once 2 Hart Street. A picture of 1888 (Fig 14) shows the two buildings, with the white stuccoed building beyond (4 Hart Street) now Frost Borneo & Gegg opticians. Not only did the rebuilding of 1892 incorporate the two houses fronting Hart Street, but also two cottages in Duke Street adjoining the corner property.

The *Blue Bell* on the corner site as shown in the picture of about 1888 was a rebuilding of 1808[110], as that was when both the Hart Street-Duke Street and the Hart Street-Bell Street corners were altered for street improvements. The Hart Street-Bell Street corner building remains much as it was built in 1808, that is if you look above the modern shop windows and view the exterior of the

110 Tyack, Geoffrey 'The Rebuilding of Henley on Thames 1780-1914' Oxfordshire Local History Assoc. Vol 3 No2

Fig 14 The Blue Bell before the closure in 1890

upper floorand the roof, and it can be seen how similar it is to the photo of the *Blue Bell*. Before the change of 1808 both corners and their opposite corners extended further into the streets (Fig 23), probably in the case of the *Blue Bell* extending into both Hart Street and Duke Street.

The *Blue Bell* seems to have always been at the corner, but at one time seems to have occupied the neighbouring house later 2 Hart Street. The *Blue Bell* site belongs to the Charity of Humphry Newbury set up by his will of 1664, while 2 Hart Street has belonged to the Charity of Thomas Cobb Binfield since the end of the 18th century. Because both properties belonged to Town Charities, the Trustees of the United Charities were enabled to rebuild both sites in 1892 as one property.

The first reference to the corner house[111] is the sale of it to Humphrey Newberry dated 9 October 1633. William Woolley of London haberdasher and Anne his wife to Humfrye Newberrye of Henley on Thames maultster and Jane his wife grant of a corner house in Brooke Street (Duke Street).

The will of Humphrey Newberry dated 16 March 1664[112] left property mainly to enable his charity to set up and maintain almshouses. There are still Humphrey Newberry almshouses on the east side of the churchyard. Among the property was the *Blue Bell* at the corner of Duke Street, with two tenements and a cottage adjoining in Duke Street. It is not quite clear whether at that time the two tenements were also in Duke Street or whether they were on the site of 2 Hart Street, and may have been then in use by the *Blue Bell*. However in later years there were two properties adjoining the *Blue Bell* in Duke Street, which were included with the *Blue Bell* deeds.

A lease of the *Blue Bell* was granted to John Blackman brewer by the Mayor and Corporation on 10 January 1748. It was a lease for eleven years of a messuage called the *Bell* at the corner of Duck Street (Duke Street)[113].

On 13 September 1773[114] the Mayor etc granted to Josiah Sarney of Great Wild Street, Lincoln's Inn Fields, Middx., coach painter a lease for eleven years of a messuage called the *Blue Bell* at the corner of Duck Street.

111, 113 & 114 Hughes List 4 AD476, 141 AD566, 175 AD602

112 Cooper, John 'An Account of the Charities under the Management of the Corporation of Henley on Thames' 1858

On 7 May 1784[115] the Mayor etc granted to Ann Geere of Henley brewer a lease for eleven years of a messuage known as the *Blue Bell* at the corner of Duck Street.

On 11 March 1791[116] the Mayor etc granted to Rich Hayward, Rob Brakspear and Benjamin Moorhouse of Henley brewers a lease for eleven years of a messuage known as the *Blue Bell* at the corner of Duke Street.

Brakspear's Rent Ledgers which start in about 1790, say that the *Blue Bell* was on a lease to be renewed in 1801. The tenants listed are - Lady Day 1791-1801 William Williams, Lady Day 1801-6 George Gregge, Lady Day 1806-10 Wiggins and Hayward and in 1811 John Major. The Alehouse Keepers List of 1817 also has John Major at the *Little Blue Bell.*

A counterpart of a lease of the *Blue Bell* dated 5 October 1804[117] says that the lease for eight years from Michaelmas 1804 granted to Robert Brakspear, as the sole executor and devisee of Richard Hayward, the residue of a second eleven year lease. Also that going back to the covenant of 1791 between Richard Hayward, Robert Brakspear and Benjamin Moorhouse, the last named had assigned his share to Robert Brakspear, who was now the sole leaseholder. The lease of 1804 was for the *Blue Bell* on the corner of Duke Street late in the occupation of Charles Stokes, since of William Williams, and now of George Gregge.

On 25 October 1787[118] The Mayor Aldermen Bridgemen and Burgesses of Henley took out insurance with the Royal Exchange Insurance Co on, among other properties, a 'house situate on the corner of Duke Street and Hart Street, tenant Charles Stokes victualler and known as the *Blue Bell* £80. A tenement adjoining and situate in Duke Street, tenant — £10. A tenement adjoining, tenant Thomas Halley £30.'

By 1826 Joseph Benwell and W H Brakspear were holding the 'public house known as the *Blue Bell* leasehold, in occupation of William Roomes with cottage adjoining of two rooms. Held at will. Rent £25 p.a.'

A lease of 29 August 1845[119] was granted to Benwell and Brakspear of the *Blue Bell* at the corner of Duke Street and Hart Street, and all that cottage or tenement adjoining on the south side late in the occupation of Mark Woodbridge and now partly in occupation of Samuel Lofting and partly untenanted .

The next eleven year lease dated 29 July 1856[120] was granted to W H Brakspear of the *Blue Bell* together with cottage adjoining late in the occupation of Samuel Lofting and partly untenanted, now in the occupation of Samuel Cole and Leaver.

In 1867[121] the eleven year lease was granted to Edmund Tanner brewer (see the *Cannon Inn*), in exchange for covenants and agreements, mostly for repairs. The list of dilapidations was extensive and covered both the *Blue Bell* and the two cottages adjoining. It was also Edmund Tanner who in 1868 was charged by the Court Leet a Quit Rent of 6d p.a. for an encroachment in front of the Blue Bell by opening a cellar flap in Duke Street. This cellar opening may have been part of his improvements.

The *Blue Bell* was another pub which was in use as a lodging house. The Census of 1861 shows that not only did the publican Thomas Waldron live there with his wife, son, daughter, step son and step daughter but also there were eleven lodgers. The lodgers were all men, their ages were 60, 46, 45, 41, 40, 36, 30, 23, 22, 20 and 18. Their occupations were as varied as their ages. There were 2 coal porters, 1 boat builder, 1 shepherd's labourer, 2 bricklayer's labourers, 1 wharf labourer, 1 hay cutter, 1 labourer, 1 engine driver, and 1 machine labourer .

Thomas Waldron was twice brought before the Magistrates for allowing disorderly conduct and drunkenness. In August 1861 it was said by the Magistrate that the house was notoriously

---

115 & 116 Hughes List 114 AD644 / 41 AD645, & 161 AD678

117, 119, 120 &121 O.R.O. Cooper & Caldecott C18 (1), (2), (3), & (4)

noisy. Two years later in August 1863 he was charged with allowing notoriously bad characters to assemble at his house. He was fined £3 and costs[122].

By the 1880s the *Blue Bell* was leased to Simonds Brewery of Reading, as can be seen in the photo of about 1888. In 1880 a complaint was raised at the Licensing Session of the Town Bench[123] that the landlord had allowed card playing in the house. However the landlord was able to prove that it was persons lodging in the house who were playing, and so his license was renewed.

The Bridge Rent Book of 1886 has two entries which mention the *Blue Bell.* No32 says 'The Trustees of Humphrey Newberry's Charity for a house etc adjoining No 31 and now known as the *Blue Bell* public house, it is the corner house on the east side of Duke Street late in the occupation of John Major, since of James Richardson, afterwards of James Brasher and now of — as undertenants of Messrs Simonds & Co.'

Entry No 31 says 'The Trustees of Thomas Cobb Binfield late Mrs Stokes for a house etc formerly the old *Blue Bell* afterwards the *Two Brewers* since a private house, and now a shop formerly in the occupation of Mrs Hiatt since of Josh Jeffreys afterwards A W Awberry then of Miss Peacock and now of Miss Gear.'

This last entry concerns 2 Hart Street. Miss Gear in 1887 was selling ladies' underclothing, as was Miss Peacock in 1883, A W Awberry was a chemist and stationers in 1876, and Josh Jeffreys a grocer in 1863. Mrs Hiatt was a stationer, bookseller, glass and china dealer from 1842-54. So the period in which the house was the *Two Brewers* must have been at the beginning of the 19th century and the end of the 18th century, and it must have been before that , that it was the old *Blue Bell* .

Henley Rentals for the two properties going back from 1842 are as follows, firstly the rentals for the corner house:- 1842 Dixon Treasurer for Humphrey Newberry the *Blue Bell* 5s, plus cottage occupied by Stubbs 2d. 1836 was the same except it was the *Blue Bell* occupied by Woodbridge. 1828, 23, & 14 Trustees of Humphrey Newberry the *Blue Bell* 5s, and cottage occupied by Cox. 1807 *Blue Bell* occupied by Mrs Gregge 5s, and cottage Mrs Cox. 1800, 1795, & 93 Trustees for the *Blue Bell* occupied by Williams and Jos Cox. 1790 Trustees for the *Blue Bell* occupied by Williams 5s, and cottage late London now Cox. 1785 Trustees for *Blue Bell* occupied Charles Stokes 5s, and cottage occupied by London 2d. 1779 Trustees late in occupation Stokes now C Stokes called the *Blue Bell.*

These last entries may have been when the *Blue Bell* was situated in both the corner house and 2 Hart Street. The Rentals for 2 Hart Street are as follows:- 1842-36 Binfield former old *Blue Bell* since *Two Brewers* 10s. 1828 the same but adding now occupied Shepherd 10s. The phrase 'formerly old *Blue Bell* since *Two Brewers*' goes back to 1795. It is therefore probable that the property became the *Two Brewers* in about 1785-90, and before that was part of the *Blue Bell.*

The Binfield Charity dates from 1724, but the property it then owned was in the middle row of the market, in a row of buildings which were situated in the upper part of Hart Street, similar to those shown in the plan of Middle Row (Fig 23), and which were demolished in about 1785-90. It was then that the Binfield Charity bought the property later 2 Hart Street. Rentals earlier than 1779 are confusing, the only clear ones are in 1749 Widow Barrett for the *Blue Bell*, and in 1745 Mr Barrett for the *Blue Bell.*

The closure of the *Blue Bell* was in August 1890. As early as 1871 there were discussions about alterations and the need for massive repairs. The question was whether to close or do the repairs.

In September 1889[124] the problem of the *Blue Bell* was again being considered. By January

---

122 Reading Mercury & Oxford Gazette 31 Aug 1861, 29 Aug 1863

123 & 124 Henley Advertiser 4 Sep 1880 & 21 Sep 1889, 25 Jan 1890, 9 Aug 1890, 13 Jun 1891, 10 Oct 1891, 16 Jan 1892, 26 Mar 1892, final comment 9 Apr 1892

1890 the architect Mr Stallwood of Reading was asked to draw up plans, and in August 1890 it was recommended that the *Blue Bell* should be converted into two business houses, the corner house having a frontage of 16ft to Hart Street and 50ft to Duke Street, while the second house should have a frontage to Duke Street of 20ft and a depth of 35ft. By June 1891 the site was offered for sale on a building lease of 99 years. The tenant to build either one or two houses, to use existing plans or his own, as long as they were approved by the Trustees. There were no takers for this offer as reported on 4 July, and by October complaints were being made about the disgraceful state of the buildings, which were not only dilapidated but covered by fly posters. Finally in January 1892 new plans were proposed, the Trustees decided to rebuild, to include the premises at 2 Hart Street, and then to let the new buildings on lease. In March 1892 an agreement was reached with Mr T Webb for a lease of the new premises - when built. The lease was to be for 21 Years at a rent of £110 p.a. The agreement had a clause that no license should be applied for without the consent of the Trustees.

Rather sadly there is an exultant note in the report in the Henley Advertiser of April 1892. 'It is quite delightful to see the old *Blue Bell* being demolished.'

Landlords/ Tenants of the *Blue Bell*

1745 '	Thomas Barrett (R)
1749	Widow Barrett (R)
pre 1779	Stokes (R)
1779-87	Charles Stokes (R)
*1790-1801	William Williams (R,WHB/R)
1801-9*	George Gregge & Mrs Gregge (R,WHB/R,CL)
1806-10	Wiggins & Hayward (WHB/R)
1811-23	John Major (WHB/R,AKL,CL,RM)
1823-6*	William Roomes (WHB/I,SD)
*1830-45	Mark Woodbridge (ORO,SD,RM)
1845-7*	Samuel Lofting (ORO,SD)
1850-2	William Paul (C,SD)
1854	Mrs Fanny Paul (SD)
1856	Samuel Cole (ORO)
1861-3	Thomas Waldron (C,SD) greengrocer
1868	Moses Butler (SD)
*1869-71	James Richardson (SSM,SD)
1872-9	James William Brasher (RL,SD)
1879	Richard Wood (RL)
1879-82	Joseph Barfoot/Barefoot (RL,SD,HA)
-Oct 1884	Samuel Hunt (HA)
Oct 1884-5	Joseph Foster (HA)
Apr 1885-Sep	George Mattingly Osmond (HA)
Sep 1885-	William Stevens (HA)
Sep 1886-7	Robert Dove Stoke (SSM)
Sep 1887-Nov	James Birt (SSM,RL)
Nov 1887-Dec	Thomas Ryan (RL)
Dec 1887-9	William Bridgman (RL)
Apr 1889-Aug 1890	James William Brasher (RL)

— Closed —

17

The Blue Blacksmith

6 Greys Road

The Victuallers Recognizances of 1769-1811 for Rotherfield Greys list this pub. Having eliminated the other names mentioned, it is very likely that the *Blue Blacksmith* was an early name for the *Royal Oak* at 6 Greys Road (Fig 45). The *Royal Oak* was in Rotherfield Greys prior to 1892, the Henley boundary having come up the centre of Friday Street and across the crossroads as far as Tuns Lane, then went behind the houses on the north side of Greys Road, across the fields along what is now the south edge of Greys Road car park (Fig 64).

The Recognizances having listed the *Blue Blacksmith* up to 1811, this name suddenly disappears and in 1818-21 in its place in the list the *Royal Oak* appears with Joel Perrin as landlord. The names of all the other pubs in Rotherfield Greys remain the same in 1818-21 as they had done previously.

Landlords/ Tenants of the *Blue Blacksmith*

1769-87	John Lewington (VR)
*1789-97	William Leaver (VR)
1798*	Jos Anderson (VR)
1801-04	Thomas Egelton (VR)
1806-11	John Fisher (VR)

— Continued as the *Royal Oak* —

18

The Blue House

Bell Pits, Northfield End

Northfield End in 1815 was part of the Manor of Bensington, which had an outlet to the river down the centre of Bell Lane. In the Manorial Records for 1815 there is an entry for the 'rent of two messuages in Bell Pits once called the *Fox* and the *Blue House*, now the *Sun* and the *Blue House*. W Towsey and the Rev J Joyce.' The Rev J Joyce probably became part owner since he was married to the daughter of Robert Brakspear, and it may have been part of her dowry.

Bell Pits as far as can be ascertained was in the triangular area created by the line of Northfield End and the Marlow Road. It is possible that the *Sun* mentioned was the same pub known as the *Sun* which closed recently. The *Blue House* was probably nearby.

— Closed —

The Boar

Bell Street

This may have been the original name of the *Bear* or it could possibly be a misreading of the *Bear.* The *Boar* was the property of the Stonors and a deed of 1686 describes it as 'the land between Thos Shefford and Webb on the north side house, malting houses, rooms, barns, stables, yards, water pits and lead cistern etc.' It was also said to be opposite the glasshouse. The glasshouse was the workshop of Ravenscroft when he lived in Henley, and made experiments with glass manufacture. There has been much speculation in Henley about the whereabouts of Ravenscroft's glasshouse, it is now thought to have been in Bell Lane.

The deeds already mentioned in the account of the *Bear* of 1666 and 1682 are concerned with the property south of the *Bear*, that of 1666 being the property of Thos Shefford bargemaster, with Henry Godfrey on the north at the *Bear.* The deed of 1682 is a transference of the property from Thos Shefford the elder to Thos Shefford the younger and again has the *Bear* on the north side.

So it would seem that in the second half of the 17th century it was the *Bear* rather than the *Boar*, unless of course Thos Shefford in 1686 had another property in Bell Street perhaps nearer to a position opposite Bell Lane, and the Boar was there. It would help if it was possible to ascertain which house was occupied by Webb.

19

The Boar

Friday Street

There are two mentions of a pub named the *Boar* in Friday Street in the Henley rentals. In 1733/4 the Rentals say 'The *Boar* for sign' and in 1737 'Quit Rent for sign'.

There are no other mentions of this pub, which was perhaps on the north side of the street, as otherwise it would not have been in Henley.

— Closed —

20

The Brewers Arms

Thameside

This is probably an early name for the *Little White Hart*, by its position in the Henley Rental lists it would seem to be on the same site. In the painting of 'Henley with a Rainbow' by Jan Siberechts in the Tate Gallery of about 1699, a beerhouse is shown on Riverside north with barrels outside it, this may have been the *Brewers Arms*.

Henley Rentals of 1713/4 say Rick Fisher for the *Brewers Arms* 3d. In 1721/2 Mr Fisher for the *Brewers Arms* 3d and more for the slipway. In 1727/8 this had become Mr Fisher for the *Brewers Arms* 3d and more for the standing of a chimney 2d; and in 1733/4 it was the same. In 1737 Mr Fisher for his house in occupation of Charles Stock 3d and for chimney 2d. By 1758 the entry is for Rich Hayward for late Facers 3d and for standing of a chimney 2d. In 1765 the rentals says Charles Fracer for Ushers (Fishers?) now Rick Hayward 3d and more for standing of a chimney 2d. By 1769 this had become late Chas Facer for Fishers now Rich Hayward 3d and more for standing of a chimney 2d.

The Court Baron Book of 1785 under the heading of Thameside, has the entry Hayward & Co encroachment of a bow window at the *White Hart Inn* 1s. This entry is not being confused with the *White Hart* in Hart Street, as the entry for that pub is given in the same book under entries for 'Hart Street starting at the church'.

When the change of name occurred is not known but obviously some time between 1733/4 and 1785.

Landlords/ Tenants of the *Brewers Arms*

1737 Charles Stock

— Continued as the *Little White Hart* —

21

The British Workman

44 Bell Street

This beerhouse appears unknown except for some references to the landlord William Bull. It would seem to have been a beerhouse as William Bull was referred to as a landlord, which he would not have been had it been a cafe or temperance restaurant. In the Henley Advertiser of 30 April 1881, William Bull of the *British Workman* Bell Street was charged with stealing a quantity of coal from the premises of Mrs Susanna Terry, value 6d, during the night of the 27th instant. He was remanded till May. The Advertiser of 7 May duly reported that William Bull was also charged with stealing tools from the garden of Mr C Simmons.

Mrs Terry on account of age and precarious health did not wish to press charges, her medical adviser strongly recommended her not to proceed. Mr Simmons also declined, so the case was dismissed, but the magistrate then lectured Mr Bull on his ingratitude and bad behaviour. It was said that Mrs Terry had befriended him, and even subscribed to assisting him with his rent.

It was later in the year in the Advertiser of 8 October that William Bull 'late landlord of the *British Workman*' was charged with non-payment of the Poor Rate. He paid the next week.

The Bridge Rent Book of 1886 for the premises now 44 Bell Street says 'Mr J L Pither late the Reading Building Society late Mr Daniel Burgis late Mr Turrell formerly Robins for a house late in the occupation of Kerrod hatter, since of Mrs Thomas fishmonger, afterwards of William Bull and now of J F Burton.' Frederick James Burton had coffee rooms at 44 Bell Street.

If the *British Workman* was a beerhouse it was of very short duration, perhaps not long enough to gain a license. It does not appear in the License Register of 1877-81.

Landlords/ Tenants of the *British Workman*

1878-81 William Bull

— Closed —

22

The Broad Gates

43-45 Market Place

The building which was once the *Broad Gates* is now used by Stuart Turner, manufacturer and suppliers of pumps of all kinds, as offices. In 1908 as shown in a photo of that time, they were situated next door at 41 Market Place, and were then known as Shiplake Works, the firm having started in Shiplake.

A photo of about 1910 (Fig 15) shows the *Broad Gates* on probably a busy market day, with posters outside advertising what seem to be ploughing matches, of great interest to its farming clientelle some of whom seem to be standing outside. The front of the building in this picture is covered by stucco, unlike its appearance today (Fig 18).

Fig 15 The Broad Gates c.1910 (see also Fig 18)

By 1917 Messrs Stuart Turner had already expanded into the yard behind the *Broad Gates* and had purchased the pub. In July 1917[125] Stuart Turners applied for permission to insert a door leading from their premises into the commercial room of the *Broad Gates.* The object was to provide additional canteen accommodation for their work force, as during the 1914-18 war, they had become Government Contractors, and they proposed that the *Broad Gates* should be closed for the duration of the war. Questions were then asked about buildings in the yard, and whether if the *Broad Gates* were to be re-opened, they would provide extended rooms for the pub. The Magistrates were assured that this would not be the case, and that the buildings were simply

125 Henley Standard 13 & 20 Jul 1917

workshops. Plans were then supplied and the following week the proposals were allowed, and the license was transferred to Sidney Marmaduke Stuart Turner who held the license also in 1918. The *Broad Gates* had closed as a pub in 1917, and at the end of the war in 1918 it did not re-open, and the license was discontinued at the end of the licensing year.

The earliest reference to the *Broad Gates* is in a deed belonging to W H Brakspear & Sons plc, which is dated to the 13th year of the reign of Charles II or 1673. This deed refers to the sale of an inn known as the *Broad Gates* for £320 by John Banister of Finchampstead and John Holt of Swallowfield to Richard Reede of Henley on Thames gentleman. Other deeds of Brakspears show that in 1716 Thomas Springall leased the *Broad Gates*, late in occupation of Anne Havergill, to Edward Evans innholder, who was now in occupation. The release of the same year shows that Springall received £90 from Evans, and then a further £130, which was towards payment of a £500 mortgage owed to John Davis and George Hunt both of Magdalen College. The mortgage was taken out in 1698, which was probably when Springall purchased the property.

In November 1716 Edward Evans mortgaged the *Broad Gates* with its stables, granaries, hop garden, orchard, backsides etc to Thomas Corderoy gentleman. By 1723 the debt was transferred to Mr Havergill and to Mr Andrew Binfield. It was now described as the *Broad Gates* lately occupied by Anne Havergill and now by Edward Evans and included stables, granaries, bowling ground, garden etc. Also in 1723 an agreement was reached by which Edward Evans and his wife Elizabeth would sell the *Broad Gates* to Andrew Binfield.

In 1791 the *Broad Gates,* together with the *King's Arms,* was sold to Robert Appleton and John Shaw brewers, of Benwell's Brewery in New Street, now Brakspear's. In 1791 the *Broad Gates* was described as having been in the occupation of Anna Brooks, and then Richard Willatt or their assigns. Afterwards of John Brown senior and now of John Ilton. It also says that a bowling ground exists where once had been a hop garden. It would seem that the bowling ground had existed since 1723 or just before that[126].

Henley Rentals in 1745 were paid by 'Thomas Evans and now Wall and Willett'. In 1775 and 1785 Binfield was paying for the *Broad Gates*, by 1790 it was Hussey late Binfield for the *Broad Gates* occupied by Allen.

Apart from the bowling ground it seems that there were other entertainments at the *Broad Gates*. According to J S Burn in his 'History of Henley' published in 1861, Sampson Penley and John Jonas in 1798 held a short season of drama at the *Broad Gates,* probably performing in the yard. Penley and Jonas were later in 1805 to build and open the theatre in New Street, now called the Kenton.

In 1784 Mrs Sarah Binfield took out insurance with the Royal Exchange Insurance Co on her two inns, the *Broad Gates* and the *King's Arms.* Mrs Binfield was the proprietor but at that time Robert Appleton and John Shaw were named as mortagees. The insurance description is of a 'house and offices adjoining situate on the south side of the hill. Tenant Joanna Brown an innholder and known by the name of the *Broad Gates* £300. The said buildings' (*Broad Gates* and the *King's Arms*) 'being brick and plaister built and situate in Henley aforesaid.'

By 1826 the Brewery Inventory shows that the *Broad Gates* was then held freehold by Joseph Benwell and W H Brakspear. There was 'stabling for 36 horses, cart lodge, yard and large garden. Land Tax £1 16s 6d. Bridge Rent 10s.'

The *Broad Gates* features in several items in the Reading Mercury & Oxford Gazette[127] and, after 1870, in the Henley Advertiser. In 1787 all the household furniture was to be sold at

---

126 The deeds of 1673,1723,& 1791 are quoted here by courtesy of W H Brakspear plc

127 Reading Mercury & oxford Gazette 7 May 1787, 13 May 1847, 27 Apr 1861, 17 Jan 1863, 14 Feb 1863, 6 Jun 1863

auction, which was probably that of Joanna Brown at the end of her tenure. Later in 1847 the then landlord Robert Irvine, was swindled by two men who claimed that two horses were being sold by a dealer at an exorbitant amount, and that Irvine being unknown to the dealer would get a better price. Irvine duly bought the horses for £34 thinking to please possible future customers, however when he returned with the horses, the men had gone, and the horses were found not to be worth £34. It was remarked in the paper that this type of swindle was common at the time.

After the death of Hannah Irvine or Irving in 1861 her household effects were advertised for sale. It would appear that the tenancy was then taken over by William Rowe, who was also landlord of the *Bull* in Bell Street. In January 1863 both the *Broad Gates* and the *Bull* were advertised to let, since the tenant William Rowe was moving to the *Falcon* in High Wycombe. At that time the *Broad Gates* was described as having a bar, bar parlour and tap room on the west side of the gateway leading into the premises, and on the east a large market room, private sitting room, kitchen and necessary out-offices, seven bedrooms, large club room, excellent cellarage etc, with sheds, stables and loose boxes, coach house, covered skittle alley etc. Extensive yard, piggery and large garden in high cultivation.

Mr Rowe held a sale of his furniture and effects from the *Bull* at the *Broad Gates* in February 1863, and in June a sale of his furniture and effects from the *Broad Gates*. Oddly Mr Rowe was still listed as landlord of both the *Bull* and the *Broad Gates* in a street directory of 1867. Whether this was an error of the directory or that he was still the licensee of both pubs is unknown.

No public coaches are listed in street directories as stopping at the *Broad Gates*, but in 1850 there was a carrier Franklin who went from there to Wargrave, every Tuesday, Thursday and Saturday. By 1883 Mrs Franklin ran the carrier service to Hare Hatch on Thursdays. Although public coaches were not at the *Broad Gates,* it was probably frequently used by both travellers and people from the surrounding district, with their private coaches, chaises, traps, carts and horses.

Towards the end of the 19th century yet another use was found for the yard and sheds behind the pub. An advertisement appeared in the Henley Advertiser in June 1891 announcing that J Barrett, Coach and Waggon builder had premises at the *Broad Gates*.

Mrs Climenson in her 'Guide to Henley' of 1896 says 'A farmer's ordinary is held here on Thursdays, market day. The old tap room, with quaint bar window, and the racks over the fireplace for the horns of old coaching days, is notable, as well as the yard which has much ancient timber work.' It is probable that the 'ordinary' was held in the room described in 1863 as the Market Room, and also was probably the room described in 1917 as the Commercial Room, which Stuart Turner's wished to convert into a worker's canteen. The picturesque 'ancient timber work' is shown in a painting by Miss Lucy Cooper in 1910, entitled 'The Yard of the *Broad Gates*.' The painting like others by Miss Cooper may be seen in the Mayor's Parlour in the Town Hall.

In December 1871[128] the landlord John A Gough was one of six landlords summoned for serving incorrect measures of beer, this was soon after a tightening up of regulations about correct measures. A year later Gough was again before the magistrates for serving beer after 11.0 at night. Police Sergeant James Jannaway deposed that on the night of Good Friday about 12.0 he heard people talking in the tap room, that he heard the name Langley (see the *Jolly Farmer*) and some one said 'Fill this cup' that a person went in the direction of the cellar and returned. Jannaway then tried the door but it was locked. Mrs Gough opened it and when he entered the cups were empty. Hezekiah Langley and Valentine Fletcher were there, both claiming to be lodgers and saying that therefore the drinks were lawful. This was not believed, and Gough was fined 10s and 12s costs.

---

128 Henley Advertiser 18 Dec 1871, 6 Apr 1872, 7 Jun 1873

After this Gough evidently lost his license, as in June 1873 there was an application by W H Brakspear & Sons for a warrant to eject John Gough from possession of the *Broad Gates*. Valentine Fletcher had already been in trouble with the law - in February 1860[129] he was charged with being drunk and disorderly at a Temperance Meeting. He was then described as a beerhouse keeper (see the *Bird In Hand)*, and was charged together with John Wheeler publican (see the *Three Horseshoes)*, and Peter Soundy porter.

The *Broad Gates* in the last thirty years of the 19th century seems to have been a fairly rowdy pub, to judge by the number of court cases[130]. In June 1881 it was again in the news, first a Richard Piercy was accused of assaulting Daniel Lewis in the pub, and then Joseph Ball the landlord, was charged with allowing gaming, that is to say of allowing people to toss for pints of beer. There were so many contradictory witnesses that that charge was dismissed. Joseph Ball was in court again in 1884 over a dispute with John Perrin of Bix about turnip seed, which Ball had sold to Perrin, and which Perrin declared was useless. The claim was for 4s 6d. In 1886 Ball was back in court, though this time as the injured party. Fred Webb, a butcher of Friday Street, was accused of assaulting him.

By 1890 William Bunce was landlord, and he evidently kept pigs in the garden, as he made an application to slaughter them on the premises, an application which was refused. In December of the next year Bunce was in trouble, he was summoned for assaulting Henry Piercy on November 26th. A cross summons was made by Bunce against Piercy for refusing to quit the *Broad Gates* when asked to do so. The events leading to these cases were as follows. Piercy said that his sister had requested him to buy some dishes from some men who were selling them in the market. He had left home at about 9.10, and found that the men had left the market and gone to the *Broad Gates*, where he found them having supper. Piercy bought them two pints of beer, and as the men said they wanted to go to bed early, they agreed to discuss the dishes the next morning. Mr Bunce then came in and seeing the two pints standing, said 'What was the use of having pints ? Why did they not have quarts?' The men then ordered two more pints and they all drank together, and then the men went off to bed. Bunce seeing the two pints not drunk, offered them to a man called May. Piercy objected and said the beer was his, Bunce then took the beer and threw it in Piercy's face, saying that he could have it, and telling him to leave the pub. The case against Bunce, who was also said to have been drunk at the time, was proved. Bunce was fined £2 and 18s 6d costs or a month's imprisonment. The case against Piercy was dismissed. Soon after Bunce lost his license.

Landlords/ Tenants of the *Broad Gates*

pre 1716	Anne Havergill (WHB/D)
1716-23*	Thomas Evans (R)
pre 1745	Thomas Evans (R)
1745	late Thomas Evans now Wall & Willett/Willatt (R,WHB/D)
- ? -	John Brown senior (WHB/D)
*1784-7	Joanna Brown (RE,RM)
1790	Allen (R)
1791*	John Ilton (WHB/D)
1793	William Cox (SD)
*1809-16	Thomas Tanner (RM,CL)
1817-30*	Richard Carter (AKL,CL,SD)
1841-54	Robert Irvine/Irving (RM,C,SD)

129 Reading Mercury & Oxford Gazette 25 Feb 1860

130 Henley Advertiser 4 Jun 1881, 13 Jun 1881, 6 Sep 1884, 8 May 1886, 18 Dec 1890, 5 Dec 1891

*1861	Hannah Irvine/Irving (C,RM)
1861-63 ?7	William Rowe (RM,SD)
1868?	? Richard Blackall (SD)
1869?-73	John Andrew Gough (SSM,C,SD,HA) he may have been landlord since the end of 1865, he is mentioned as landlord of the *Broad Gates* on 13 Jan 1866, when some tame pigeons were stolen from him. RM)
1873-68*	Richard John Bradby/Bradley (HA/SD)
*1877-88	Joseph Ball (RL,C,HA,SD)
1888-92	William Bunce (RL,HA,SD)
Apr 1892-1907	Charles Letchford Shepherd (RL,HA,SD)
1907-14	William Hodges (RL,SD)
1914 -17	Robert Venezi (RL)
(1917-18	Sidney Marmaduke Stuart Turner (RL,HS) for Stuart Turners Ltd)

— Closed —

23

The Bull or the Black Bull

57-9 Bell Street

The *Bull* in Bell Street (Fig 16) although one of the more ancient houses in the town, is not mentioned as a pub until the 16th century, and even then not conclusively.

A document dated 1564/5[131] is an assignment of lease of the *Bull Inne* in North Street (Bell Street) from Elys Webb to Francis Frewyn. The odd thing about this document is that it appears to be one of a series of deeds which clearly relate to the *Bull* in the High Street (Hart Street), which was leased by Thomas Cooper to Ellis Webbe in 1562, and subsequently was leased from Frances Frewen to Hen Lytle or Brooks. Maybe the deed of 1564/5 actually read as 'on the north side of the street'. The north side of Hart Street rather than in 'North Street'.

The premises of the *Bull* may be 15th century or even earlier. Two posts, part of the construction of the front of

Fig 16 The Bull, Bell Street c.1978
Photo by Peter Anderson

131 Hughes 808 AD332 & 244 AD401

the building, have moulded decoration on them, which would be consistent with an early 15th century date. This however does not mean that it was an inn at that time. It is another property which was owned by the Stonor family, and so the early deeds are not available. The building has been much altered, a major alteration probably occurring in the mid 17th century when the upper windows may have been inserted. The walls are said to be 3ft thick, and this has been cited as an indication of great age, but this is not necessarily the case.

Mrs Climenson in 1896[132]said of the *Bull* 'A very ancient structure in Bell Street.one large room upstairs divided into partitions; in one a fine old projecting fireplace. The old tap room, with quaint cupboards by the fire had once with the adjoining room, doors set in a singular way to the street now turned into cupboards.' Traces of one of these doors can be seen on the outside wall, the north door, which inside would be alongside the main fireplace. There are also signs outside of a central door to the main front bar room. This may have been in use in 1896, since the old doors were already cupboards. A central door is shown in two paintings by Miss Lucy Cooper of the *Bull* in 1901, its position can still be seen outside. Traces of a dividing wall can be seen in the central beam of the front bar, but if a wall was there at the same time as the central door, some sort of lobby would have been needed, since the door would have opened directly onto the dividing wall. The central door when it was inserted cut through the supporting post of the central beam. Perhaps originally there was a single downstairs room with a main door at some other point, this on being divided into the two rooms, then had small doors placed at each end, which as suggested may have been awkwardly contrived, so later they were closed up and the central door built. Unfortunately it is not possible to see more of the wall construction.

It is one of the pubs which abound in legends. One claims it as a monk's hospice, and another that it is reputed to be haunted by a presence and the smell of a snuffed candle. Another claims that there is a passage going either in the direction of the church or towards the old malthouse (M12) on the east side of Bell Street. There is the blocked up remains of the beginning of what is claimed to be this passage in the cellar, however as it is about 2ft square it would not have been an easy route.

Oddly enough the ghost with the candle seems the most likely of these tales, and was told me with conviction by one of the landladies, the late Mrs Joy Aston. No records have come to light of a monk's hospice, nor of any monastery or church precincts in or near the town, who might have supplied hostelers or lodgings in the town. As already mentioned (Introduction p 21) priests did stay at the *Bull* icognito, sometimes holding services there, when the Roman Catholic religion was proscribed in the 16th and 17th centuries. The *Bull* and the *Bear* became stopping places for the priests sent out from Mapledurham, but they used packhorses and not tunnels, and did not advertise their presence. These priestly visitations may have given rise to the legend of a monk's hospice.

Although underground passages have been claimed by many residents of Henley as having existed, it seems unlikely, since the water table in the past was much higher than it is today, and many cellars would have been frequently flooded. Perhaps these passages if they did exist, should be seen as flood drains or even sewage drains. There seems to be no reason to build passages as a means of going about the town, they would have been extremely costly to build and maintain, would as already said have flooded, and the town has never been under siege or foreign rule, which would have necessitated secret comings and goings. Even in the Civil War, Henley was an open town merely occupied for short spells by one side or the other, while the townspeople throughout were divided in their loyalties. As for the suggestion that the passages were used for smuggling, this also seems unlikely, it would surely have been simpler to off load any contraband at some quiet stretch of the river and convey any goods by cart. For that matter there was only one Excise Officer

132 Climenson, Mrs Emily J 'Guide to Henley on Thames' 1896

in the town, who could hardly have kept a constant vigil on Henley waterfront.

Henley Rentals in 1745 and 49 say 'Thos Skinner for the *Bull* now Wall.' Soon after 1750 the *Bull* was bought by James Brooks[133], and after 1812 became the property of Joseph Benwell. In 1774 it was said to have been one of the properties which was part of the stock in trade when the partnership was dissolved between J Brooks and R Hayward. Henley Rentals were paid by Brooks up to at least 1800, but by Brakspear in 1807, and by Appleton in 1814 and 1823. It is probable that from 1774 onwards, the *Bull* was leased by Brakspear, certainly by 1790 it appears in the Brakspear Rent Ledgers.

Just before that in 1787 the *Bull* was without a landlord, an advertisement[134] said that it was 'To Lett' at easy rent with immediate possession. In August 1789 another announcement appeared saying that William House, a coachmaker late of London, was taking over the *Bull* and continuing his coach making business there. However by 1790 the *Bull* was again to let, described as old established and well accustomed, comprising a good dwelling house, excellent stabling for 30 horses, a coach house, spacious yard and every other requisite convenience. A most desirable situation for a horse dealer 'as there is no person in the town of that profession'. William House was later discovered advertising his coach business in the Fairmile.

In Brakspear's Rent Ledgers the *Bull* was let to John Rockley 1790-2, to James Taylor on the 5 May 1792-Michaelmas 1793, and in 1793 to Richard Church who remained there until at least 1830. He features in the Alehouse Keepers List of 1817, a church pew faculty of 1820, the Inventory of the Brewery in 1826, and a street directory of 1830. Between 1830 and 1838 a Mr Sturdy must have been landlord. In the Reading Mercury & Oxford Gazette of 24 March 1838 it says 'Died. On Wednesday Mr Sturdy late of the *Bull Inn.*'

In the Inventory of the Brewery of 1826 the *Bull* is listed as being one of the properties held freehold by Joseph Benwell and W H Brakspear. 'The *Bull Inn* in occupation of Richard Church with stabling and other buildings also a capital capacious storehouse occupied by the firm. Land Tax £1 17s 6d. Quit Rent 3s 4d. Bridge Rent 6s 8d. '

Joseph Benwell died in 1830, and his executors sold the *Bull* to Henry Gosse. It was only in 1881 that Brakspears finally bought the *Bull*[135], although they had held it leasehold for many years.

During the 18th and 19th centuries the *Bull* or the *Black Bull* as it was sometimes called, was a busy coaching and carter's inn. On the 24 September 1744 an advertisement in the Reading Mercury & Oxford Gazette announced that the Henley Stage Coach and Horses were to be sold and that the *Bull Inn* at Henley was to let 'where the said coach puts up. Enquire at the *Bull Inn.*' In April 1826[136] the New Regulator Coach to London was advertised by Thomas Stevens. It would call at the *Black Bull* from Wallingford every Monday, Tuesday, Thursday and Saturday mornings at nine. All coaches would go through Maidenhead etc. The same coach the Regulator travelled back to Wallingford calling at the *Black Bull* every Monday, Tuesday, Thursday and Saturday evenings at half past eight.

In May of 1831 Thomas Stevens entered into partnership with Charles Hewett, and they advertised that the coach would now go every morning to London at nine thirty, going through Hurley Bottom and Maidenhead to the *Black Lion*, Water Lane, Fleet Street. The coach would also return from there daily. The fares would be 'Inside 12s. Outside 7s.'

By 1850[137] the coach service from the *Bull* had ceased and carriers had taken over. John

133 Sheppard, Francis 'Brakspear's Brewery 1779-1979' 1979

134 Reading Mercury & Oxford Gazette 21 May 1787, 31 Aug 1789, 25 Jul 1790

135 Same as note 131

136 Reading Mercury & Oxford Gazette 4 Apr 1826, 16 May 1830

137 Street Directories Slater's 1850, Kelly's 1883, 1895 & 1903

Bond Archer went from the *Bull* on Thursdays to Bensington, while Henry Palmer did the same journey on Saturdays. John Bond Archer also on Thursdays had a carrier service to Oxford, this may have been a continuation of the journey to Bensington. James Gibbons had a carrier service to Wallingford on both Mondays and Thursdays, while John Bracey went to Watlington on Thursdays. Thursday has always been a busy day in Henley as it is market day, so these carriers were probably carrying goods purchased at the market to the surrounding districts. Both the *Bull* and the *Bear* were probably much used by farmers and others coming into town from the same areas as served by the carriers.

Indeed in January 1863[138] when the *Bull* together with the *Broad Gates* was advertised to let, since the tenant of both Mr William Rowe, was going to the *Falcon* at High Wycombe, the *Bull* was described as being 'by far the best house of business of its class in Henley, and is supported by nearly the whole of the farmers from a purely agricultural district of great extent. There is also a weekly 'ordinary' held every Thursday very numerously attended, has an excellent Job and Post Horse business requiring 8 to 9 horses and carriages of various descriptions.'

The advertisement also described the *Bull* as having a 'convenient bar, tap room, large parlour, kitchen, scullery etc. and all necessary out offices on the ground floor. A large Market Room with two approaches,' (no doubt the location of the Thursday 'ordinary', and also perhaps the room described later by Mrs Climenson as 'a large upstairs room divided into partitions.') 'Twelve bedrooms, excellent cellarage etc. Stables for about 60 horses with loose boxes and lock-up coach houses, large garden, piggery, barn, etc.'

Although Mr Rowe sold his furniture and effects from the *Bull* at the *Broad Gates* in February 1863, and his effects from the *Broad Gates* in June 1863, he was still listed in a street directory of 1867 as landlord of both the *Bull* and the *Broad Gates*. However this may be an error of the directory since at the *Broad Gates* John Gough was mentioned in 1866 as landlord of that pub. So Mr Rowe before 1866 may have departed for High Wycombe.

By 1883 in all the pubs the coach and carrier services had diminished, but at the *Bull* there was still a carrier service by Amos Prince to 'Binges'. This was probably a printing error for Fingest, as in 1895 and 1903 Prince was going there from the *Bull* every Thursday. In 1883 Charles Gray was also running a service on Thursdays to Lane End, while Hayes was going to Nettlebed.

An advertisement of 1908 says 'horses and carriages of every description let on hire; carriages meet all trains; motor garage for 200 cars, stabling for 250 horses.....' The numbers in this advertisement seem to be excessive, one hopes that the cars and horses were not all there at the same time.

At the Henley Borough Sessions in 1924[139] many licensed houses were said to be badly in need of cleaning and decorating. The *Bull* was one of three singled out for also having unsatisfactory sanitary accommodation, the others were the *Bear* and the *Red Cow.* The following year the accommodation was approved.

In spite of this later criticism, the *Bull* and its yard at the turn of the century proved a picturesque site for Miss Lucy Cooper. Three of her paintings in the Town Hall show the *Bull.* Two of them are of Bell Street in 1901, one looking south with the *Bull* taking its place among the varied shop fronts, and the other looking north with the *Bull* in the foreground on the left. This painting makes much of the fine window box display of flowers in the upper windows. The third painting of 1905 is of the yard, showing the inner side of the main gateway, and is a peaceful scene with birds on the pathway - evidently not a Thursday.

---

138 Reading Mercury & Oxford Gazette 17 Jan 1863, 14 Feb 1863, 6 Jun 1863

139 Henley Standard 8 Feb 1924, 13 Feb 1925

Landlords/ Tenants of the *Bull*

? -* 1564/5	? Elys/Ellis Webb/Webbe (ORO)
? 1564/5-1586	? Francis Frewen/Frewyn (ORO)
? 1586*	? Brooks/Lytle (ORO)
1749	Thomas Skinner now Wall (R)
1789-90	William House (RM) coachmaker
1790-2	John Rockley (WHB/R)
1792-3	James Taylor (WHB/R,SD)
1793-1830*	Richard Church (WHB/R,AKL,CL,PF,WHB/I,SD)
pre 1838	Mr Sturdy (RM)
*1841	B Gallop (C)
1842-7	Thomas/James Collins (SD)
*1850-1	Ann Collins (SD)
1851-63?	William Rowe (C,RM,SD) posting house
1866-72	Horatio John Calcutt (SSM,C,RM,SD)
*1876-95	James Harper (RL,C,SD)
1895-1911	Lewis Edward Froud (RL)
1911-12	Ernest Barton (RL,WHB/C)
Jan 1912-13	Arthur Cook (RL,WHB/C)
Jul 1913-31	Joseph Henry Sherwood Robinson (RL,WHB/C,SD)
Jul 1931-8	William Christopher Grellier (RL,WHB/C,HS,SD)
Sep 1938-48	Mrs Lillian Grellier (RL,WHB/C,SD)
Feb 1948-54	Maurice Mervyn Hussey (RL,WHB/C)
Apr 1954-64	Sidney Arthur Aston (RL,WHB/C)
Oct 1964-7	Owen James Goodchild (RL,WHB/C)
Nov 1967-80	Eric Donald Preston (RL,WHB/C)
Nov 1980-4	David Ernest Gibson-Barton (RL,WHB/C)
May 1984-91	John Hugh King (RL,WHB/C)
Oct 1991-95	Adrienne Camille Menzies & Andrew William Daniel Menzies (RL,WHB/C)
Feb 1995-98	Denis Ball & John Bodsworth (RL)
Feb 1998-99-	Peter Stevens (RL)
1996-99-	Leno & Paula Borg (HS)

(There seems to be a discrepancy between reports in the Henley Standard 1996-99 and the entries in the Licensing Register)

24

The Bull

High Street/ now 27 Hart Street

In about 1478[140] there was a dispute over possession of *Le Boull* in the High Street between Sir William Stonor, Richard Page and John Matthew who were bringing a suit against Margaret Fyssher widow and Thomas Pratte yeoman.

140 Kingsford 'The Stonor Letters' 1919 Vol II

Pratte seems to have claimed the *Bull* as his own property, which was what was contested, though a list of properties contained the words 'Also the londes pat Thomas Pratt holdith, first in his howne place cald the Bole valewr by yere xls.' This may of course mean that he was holding it on lease, the outcome of the dispute is also not clear, though it appears that 'Phelip Fischer was in possession and his dowther after hym in Henley.' This could be the son and grand daughter of Margaret Fyssher widow.

If Thomas Pratte did in fact own the *Bull* in 1478 or was a leaseholder then it is possible that he had inherited it from his father, who might possibly be a John Pratt mentioned in a document of 1437-8 as having at that time a hospice in the town[141].

In about 1491-1500 Henry Grenelefe who by then seems to have owned the *Bull* made a will in which he left a tenement in the High Street called the *Bull* to his son, and if his son had no issue then it was to go as a bequest to the Church and Bridge. This would appear to be what happened as soon after the property belonged to the Church and Bridge. In 1532/3 John Cater was paying rent for a tenement sometime John Gyldon's[142].

On 10 January 1535/6 The Warden Bridgemen etc of the town leased to John Cator son of Thomas Cator and Anne his wife a tenement and garden in 'le Hye Strete'[143]. The Borough Records of 1541 and 43 show first the *Bull* and *Gervys* paying 2s 8d and then the *Bull* and the *Hert* paying 13s 4d[144]. In 1553 the position of the *Bull* is clearly indicated by the Corporation Rental for what is now 25 Hart Street; this says that the property which was leased to J Frost on the north side of the street, was between the heirs of W Cator at the *Bull* on the east and J Pates at the property called the *Hert* on the west.

After this date the property began to change hands with the transfer of leases from one individual to another. A Bridge Rent was still charged, but ownership seems to have changed with the leases. The charge for 27 Hart Street once the *Bull* was 2d in 1886[145], and was one of the rents still being paid in 1967 when the last of the Bridge Rents was commuted into a down payment to provide a similar income.

> 14 August 1558 Will Cater to Thomas Coupper lease of the *Bull Inn* [146] .
>
> 28 June 1562 Thom Cooper to Ellis Webbe lease for 21 years of the *Bull* with Inventory of goods therein.

The next entry is the one which may relate to the *Bull* in Bell Street, although given the sequence of names before and after, that is open to question, might the wording mean on the 'north side of the street' ?

> 1 January 1564/5 Elys Webbe to Francis Frewyn. Assignment of lease of the *Bull Inne* in North Street.
>
> 25 March 1565/6 Francis Frewen to Hen Lytle or Brooks, assignment of lease of the *Bull* in the High Street.
>
> 17 June 1566 Hen Lytle alias Brooke to Thom Browne assignment of lease of the *Bull Inn*.
>
> 27 June 1566 Ric Davye and two others to Thom Browne mortgage of goods in the *Bull Inn* with Inventory.

---

141 Peberdy, Robert B 'The Economy, Society & Government of a small town in late Medieval England: a Study of Henley on Thames from c1300-c1540' Thesis for a Doctorate, Leicester University 1994 O.R.O. B/ IV/ 6

142 & 144 Briers, P M 'Henley Borough Records 1395-1543' 1960 Ox. Record Soc.

143 Hughes 760 AD305

145 Henley Charity Trustees 'Small Bridge Rents' book in Town Hall

146 Hughes 1558-1624 373 AD322, 390 AD326, 808 AD332, 837 AD337, 391 AD339, 821 AD240, 392 AD348, 865 AD419, 274B AD441A, 274A AD448A, 274D AD456A, 274E AD460A

1 October 1569 Dennys Browne to Will Smyth assignment of lease of the *Bull Inn.*

A Corporation Rental of 1590 has Phil Smyth lessee of a tenement and garden on the north side of the High Street called the *Bull* occupied by W Cooper between Nick Wilson on the west and John Stalley on the east. This is the first entry for the *Bull* which suggests a leaseholder not necessarily being the occupier or landlord. It is possible that Philip Smyth was a brewer or maltster living elsewhere in the High Street. Indeed in 1590 on the 23 July the Warden etc granted to Philip Smithe a messuage and garden in the High Street for a rent of 10s, which is probably the house where Philip Smithe lived.

15 December 1596 Phil Smyth to John Bird grant of a messuage known as the *Bull.* Eight years later John Bird evidently discontinued his lease as on 1 January 1604/5 John Birde granted to Phil Smyth a messuage known as the *Bull.*

19 February 1617/8 Phil Smyth to John Woodward grant of the *Bull* and the *Katherin Wheele.*

Finally on 16 June 1624 Dan Harvey to Thom Thomilthorpe lease for seven years of the the *Bull* with Inventory. This last deed could be for the *Bull* in Bell Street, as there is no sequence of names suggesting one in the High Street.

The *Bull* in the High Street possibly ceased trading in the first half of the 17th century, however it was one of the many properties that had a malthouse behind it, which continued in use. Insurance was taken out for this malthouse (M22) by Mr Hugh Keene on 25 October 1787[147]. The property was described as 'A dwelling house situate on the north side of Hart Street in occupation of Mrs Stable. Brick and lath and plaister built and tiled £200. On a malthouse and storehouse adjoining together and to the said house but having no communication with the same. Brick and lath and plaister built and tiled £200.' The malthouse was still shown as a malthouse on the O.S. map of 1879.

The Bridge Rent Book of 1886 entry No 6 says 'The Trustees of Mrs Mortimer late Hugh Barford, formerly Hugh Keene for a house malthouse and garden adjoining No 5 formerly in the occupation of Joseph Brown since of Chas Towsey and now of Miss Hone.' Bridge Rent No 4 was the White Hart while No 5 was the Henley Savings Bank later to become the Trustees Saving Bank, the property which in 1553 was leased to J Frost.

Street directories show Hugh Keene as a maltster in 1784 and in about 1793. Hugh Barford as a maltster 1823-54, at which last date he was also a magistrate. Charles Augustus Towsey in 1854 was a wine merchant in Bell Street, but in 1863-9 was in Hart Street. Mrs Lydia Hone had a ladies boarding school in New Street in 1869, but from 1876-91 had a school at 27 Hart Street.

It is uncertain at what time the malthouse went out of use, if as in 1787 it was entirely separate from the house, there is no reason why it should not have been in use till the end of the 19th century.

Landlords/ Tenants of the *Bull*

1437-8	John Pratt
-*1478	? Phelip Fischer (SL) or Thomas Pratte
1478	Margaret Fyssher (SL) & or Thomas Pratte (SL)
1491-c1500	Henry Grenelefe (ORO)
*1532	John Gyldon (BR)
1553-8	Will Cator (HL)

147 Royal Exchange Insurance Register No 103977 O.R.O. Brakspear X/ 1

1558-62	Thomas Coupper/Cooper (HL)
1562-5	Ellis/Elys Webb/Webbe (HL)
1565-6	Francis Frewen/Frewyn (HL)
1566*	Thom Browne (HL)
*1569	Dennys Browne (HL)
1569*	Will Smyth (HL)
1590	W Cooper (HL)
1596-1604	John Bird (HL)
1617	John Woodward (HL)
? 1624	Dan Harvey (HL)
? 1624*	Thom Thomilthorpe (HL)

These last two may have been at the *Bull* in Bell Street.

— Closed —

25

The Butchers Arms

33 Market Place

The *Butchers Arms* was in existence in the first half of the 18th century and possibly much earlier. It was situated in one of the three buildings, later part of Burgis' Grocery Stores, which were demolished to make way for the entrance from the Market to what is now known as Greys Road Car Park. The *Butchers Arms* was next to the building now on the west side of the entrance, what was once an antique shop then Hackford's Bathrooms and is now a pizza restaurant; which in the 18th and 19th centuries was the *Swan* (Fig 47).

Documents in the Town Hall belonging to the Town Council concerning the *Swan* reveal that on 20 April in the 42nd year of the reign of Elizabeth (1599) John Farmer who was selling the *Swan,* or rather the premises not at that time called the *Swan,* was also the owner of the tenement to the east of that building. Two years later on the 23 January in the 44th year of Elizabeth another document also concerning the *Swan* building, says that at that time to the east was a tenement of Walter Savyn alias Turner. Whether in 1599 and 1601 John Farmer or Walter Savyn were landlords of a pub is not known, there is no mention of the *Butcher Arms,* though that does not rule out the possibility. The south side of the Market Place was known as Butchers Row, since it was where the butchers shops were established.

The earliest known document connected to the premises of the *Butchers Arms* is a lease of 1734/5[148] which quotes a mortgage of 1722, which was between 1) John Havergill the elder deceased 2) Robert Collings of Henley servant and Edward Evans innholder and 3) Andrew Binfield. In 1722 the properties concerned were two houses on the east side of Bell Street and a house on the south side of the Market Place known as the *Butchers Arms* in the occupation of John Eeles. This house had on the east a house in occupation of Widow Rackstraw (No 31) and a house in the tenure of James Kitson on the west (No 35 - James Kitson known to be at the *Swan*). The *Butchers Arms* had stables granaries hop garden, yards, garden etc.

A lease and release of 1735[149] was between 1) William Forster surgeon 2) Elizabeth Havergill the elder widow of John Havergill the elder innholder and 3) John Eeles peruke maker and Ann

148, 149 & 150 O.R.O. Cooper & Caldecott C57 (1), (2), & (3)

Eeles spinster. John Havergill was innholder of the *Bear* see lease of the *Bear* of 1714, he also owned two houses in Bell Street which seem to have been what are now 82 and 84 Bell Street. In the deed of 1735 Elizabeth Havergill was selling the *Butchers Arms* to John Eeles and his sister Ann, William Forster was probably an executor for the late John Havergill. This deed says the messuage on the south side of the Market Place now and for many years in occupation of John Eeles.

Further documents reveal various mortgages until 1754 when Anne and Elizabeth Eeles spinsters of Henley disposed of the property to Joseph Armstrong draper[150]. In the Victuallers Recognizances of 1753 and 54 which give a list of Henley victuallers in those two years, Anne Eeles appears in the list for 1753 but not in that for 1754.

The later documents for the property describe it as at one time the *Butchers Arms*. It would seem that with the transfer to Joseph Armstrong the pub ceased trading. After Armstrong it is possible to trace the ownership right up to the time when it became part of Burgis' Grocery Stores. In the various documents it was still described as having a garden and hop gardens.

Landlords/ Tenants of the *Butchers Arms*

1599 ?	John Farmer (THD)
1601 ?	Walter Savyn /Turner (THD)
1722	John Eeles/Eels (ORO) peruke maker
1735	John and Anne Eeles (ORO)
*1753	Anne Eeles (VR)
1754 pub may have closed	Anne and Elizabeth Eeles (ORO)

— Closed —

26

The Cannon Inn & Brewery

15 Market Place

The *Cannon Inn* and brewery were at what is now the *Argyll* at 15 Market Place. In 1872 the *Cannon Inn* became the *Hop Leaf* (Figs 6, 23 & 26) when bought by H & G Simmonds Ltd of Reading, whose Trade Mark was a hop leaf. Previously in the Census of 1851 Richard Cox brewer was at the same site then called the *North Star*, then employing three men and living there with his wife and one servant. Earlier still in the Census of 1841 Richard Cox brewer was at the *Cannon* beerhouse at 47 Market Place.

Richard Cox started his brewery at the *Cannon* beerhouse, probably in 1838, and in a street directory of 1842 it was already known as the Cannon Brewery. In 1845 the premises at what is now the *Argyll* at 15 Market Place were for sale, Richard Cox bought it and moved his brewery into the back quarters. He then rebuilt the house as a pub, as described in the account of the *North Star.*

In 1851 it was still the *North Star*, but by 1854 a street directory has Richard Cox at the *Cannon Inn* and Brewery. So between 1851 and 54 the pub had changed its name from the *North Star* to the *Cannon Inn.*

In the Reading Mercury & Oxford Gazette of 29 September 1860 Richard Cox thanked his customers for their support and asked them to continue their dealings with his successor Edmund Tanner who was taking over the *Cannon Inn* and Brewery. Edmund Tanner then announced that he would be carrying on the business as Richard Cox had done for the last twenty two years. That he would be supplying Genuine Home Brewed Ales, Pale Ale, Stout and Porter, both wholesale and retail. Also that he would be selling Cognac Brandy, Fine Old Jamaican Rum, Scotch and Irish Whiskey, Gin, Cordials etc., all at lowest possible prices.

In the Census of 1861 Edmund Tanner is listed as a brewer master at the *Cannon* employing five men, and living there with his wife, three daughters, one son, and two servants. This entry is clearly for the *Cannon Inn* at 15 Market Place, not only by its position in the entries, but also because the *Cannon* beerhouse is listed with Daniel Brown in occupation, who in 1841 had been a servant there, when Richard Cox was at the beerhouse. Street directories of 1863 and 1867 have Edmund Tanner at the *Cannon Inn* and Brewery.

In the Magistrates Special Session Minute Book of 1870, Edmund Tanner was listed at the *Cannon Inn* in August of that year. This entry was in the section dealing with those pubs or inns that had full Alehouse & Victuallers Licenses, while at the same date the *Cannon* beerhouse was listed with Henry Jones as licensee. Later in the licensing year of 1870 the name Edmund Tanner was crossed out and replaced by that of James Sharp, who was a maltster and may also have been a brewer. However although James Sharp was listed again in the Minute Book of August 1871, during that licensing year the words '*Hop Leaf* / late' were inserted above the name of the *Cannon Inn*, and the name Richard Hussey Kimber inserted above that of James Sharp which was crossed out.

In the Henley Advertiser in February 1872, there was a notice that Richard Hissey Kimber had taken over the *Hop Leaf*. So it would seem that the second change of name and ownership had occurred before February 1872. It is probable that the Cannon Brewery ceased trading at the same time as the changes, since Simonds Brewery of Reading were the new owners who would not have required the brewery, but an outlet for their own beers. A further proof of the position of the *Cannon Inn* is in the existence in 1870 of a full license, which was handed on to the *Hop Leaf* and then to the *Argyll*. Also the order in which the pubs were listed in later License Registers remained the same as in the 1870 and 71 lists in the Minute Book. The *Hop Leaf* took over the position vacated by the *Cannon Inn,* and later the *Argyll* took over the position of the *Hop Leaf*.

Landlords/Tenants of the *Cannon Inn*

*1854-60	Richard Cox (Cannon Brewery 1838-60) (RM,SD)
Sep 1860-70	Edmund Tanner (Cannon Brewery 1860-70) (SSM,C,RM,SD)
1870-1	James Sharp (SSM)
(1871	Robert William Church (C) Manager of Ale Store)

— Continued as the *Hop Leaf* —

27

The Cannon

Market Place

The *Cannon* beerhouse was situated next door to the *Broad Gates* on the west side. It is now a restaurant (Fig 18).

One of the earliest photos taken of Henley shows the side of the old Town Hall before the ground floor was enclosed in 1870 (Fig 17) In the photograph a cannon may be seen in the right

Fig 17 Photo pre-1870, the Cannon beerhouse, on extreme left the corner of the Greyhound

foreground above a notice board which says 'D Brown - Good Stabling.' Whether it was an actual cannon or a replica is unknown. A similar view of the cannon is shown in a painting by Miss Lucy Cooper of the old Town Hall just before its replacement, her painting is dated 1898.

Street directories show that Daniel Brown was a beer retailer in the Market Place from 1852-67, and the Census of 1851 shows that he was then at the *Cannon*. This is the earliest mention of the *Cannon* beerhouse by name. The Census of 1841 had Richard Cox brewer aged 40 at the position of the *Cannon* though it was not named, and Daniel Brown as a servant there. Between 1845 and 1851 Richard Cox moved to the *North Star* leaving Daniel Brown in charge of the *Cannon*. (see entries for the *North Star* and the *Cannon Inn*) Though the beerhouse is not mentioned by name in 1841, in a street directory of 1842 Richard Cox is given as at the Cannon Brewery. The Cannon Brewery was started at the site of the *Cannon* beerhouse but transferred to the yard behind the *North Star* by Richard Cox when he moved there. Later, soon after 1851 he re-named the *North Star* the *Cannon Inn*. Later still when Cox in 1860 gave up the *Cannon Inn* and the Brewery, it was said that he had had the brewery business for twenty two years. This means that the brewery had started in 1838, at what was probably already the *Cannon* beerhouse.

The last known date for Daniel Brown at the *Cannon* is 1867. In the Magistrates Special Session Minute Book of 1870 Henry Jones was given as landlord, and before the year was out was replaced by Thomas Wyett Wellman who stayed until February 1872. Henry Jones is listed in a street directory of 1869 as a beer retailer on Gravel Hill. It is almost certain that the entry was for the *Cannon*. This means that the photo of the Town Hall showing the cannon above the name of D Brown must have been taken before 1869. The earliest reference to a professional photographer in the town is a Marriage Register entry in 1859 of Jules Nicholaus Guggenheim photographer, who later in a street directory was listed as living in the Market Place. Possibly the photo was one of Guggenheim's early works.

As well as being a beerhouse the *Cannon* was also a lodging house. In May 1892[151] the *Cannon* was noted as being one of the four common lodging houses in the Borough, the others were the *Red Lion* West Street, the *Jolly Farmer* and the *Duke's Head.*

When the license was renewed in 1906[152] it was remarked that 'Charles Edward Ayres, tenant, had been there for 19 years.....a working class trade and he did 4 barrels a week. He did about 120 dozen bottled beer and 200 mineral waters. The Jug trade was largely for the Kings Road. Herbert Henry Long one of the owners of the house, said his mother had a life interest in it under his grandfather's will. The house had been owned by his family for 80 years. His grandfather a Mr Cox, was formerly a brewer in Henley, Hart Street.'

This account makes the date of the *Cannon* possibly as early as 1826. Perhaps the cannon used as a sign was a relict of the Napoleonic wars, part of the equipment of the various troops of soldiers stationed in and around Henley at that time.

In the Register of Licenses in 1877 the *Cannon* was leased by H & G Simonds Ltd of Reading, by 1892 it was leased by Ive Brothers. The ownership in 1905 was divided between Mrs Charlotte Elizabeth Esther Long widow of 110 Southampton Street, Reading; William Simpson of 25 Fielding Road, Bedford Park, gentleman; and Herbert Henry Long of 48 Dorset Street, Portman Square, chemist. The lessees were still Ive Brothers. By 1921 it appears that the property was owned by Mrs Anne Gundry [153], at least when the then landlord Frederick Lewendon had been in trouble over a false claim that a burglary had been committed, it was Mrs Gundry who gave him notice to quit.

In both 1905 and 1914 questions were raised about renewing the license, and in 1929 there was an even more serious problem, largely due to the difficulties of finding a suitable tenant. In 1929[154] the license was not renewed with the other licenses, and the license was temporarily transferred to Mrs Gundry of the Goring Brewery, pending the arrival of a tenant. By February a holdover of the license was made to Albert James Tappern, and in March it was fully transferred. In May, rather oddly an extension of license was granted to Mr F Butler of the *Cannon*, oddly because the license was not transferred to Frederick Butler till July of that year. The following year in 1930 the license was transferred from Butler back to Tappern.

By January 1931 the *Cannon* was closed, and the license suspended. At the Licensing Session in February the *Cannon,* together with the *Olde Bell* and the *Three Tuns* were all recommended for closure. At the *Cannon* it was pointed out that since 1920 there had been eight transfers of license and that it was an unsatisfactory house. It was realised that it was the only house of Mrs Gundry's remaining in Henley, but that it did not do a large trade. It was said that it only did about 1½ barrels a week, though it was conceded that it did better at Regatta times and in the summer. The *Cannon* was referred to the Compensation Authority and was closed finally in May 1931.

Today the building once the *Cannon* is a restaurant, with a narrow passage entrance on the left hand or east side. In March 1871[155] a plan for a new front to the *Cannon* was passed. This

---

151, 152 & 153 Henley Standard 14 May 1892, 2 Mar 1906, 11 Feb 1921

154 Henley Standard 22 Feb 1929, 8 Mar 1929, 17 May 1929, 10 Oct 1929, 13 Feb 1931, 29 May 1931

155 Henley Advertiser 11 Mar 1871

may in fact have been quite an extensive alteration. When a few years ago the restaurant changed hands, and building work was done there, it was possible to see that the building had been much altered in the past. Originally it seems to have been a two floored building with a gable pitched roof with its ridge parallel to the street. It was also probably only one room deep. In order to achieve its present three floors behind a Georgian type facade, the attic had been extended forward so that its front was level with the front wall, which was then built up higher. This increase in living space may have coincided with the *Cannon's* status as an approved lodging house.

The way through to the back yard was probably always a narrow passage, suitable only for those on foot or for a led horse, certainly not wide enough for a cart. This was most likely why Richard Cox having started his brewery at the *Cannon* decided to move, and so acquired the house at 15 Market Place and moved there with his brewery.

In the yard behind the *Cannon* there were several cottages which by 1930 were condemned under the Housing Act of 1925. They were stated to be in appalling condition. There is a possibility that the site of the *Cannon* may have been where the inn of Thomas Garroway was in 1665-8 (Introduction p19). If so there is no suggestion that its use as a pub was continuous, that inn was almost certainly closed by the early 18th century if not before.

Fig 18 On left the Broad Gates on right the Cannon beerhouse Photo 1988

Landlords/ Tenants of the *Cannon*

c1826-c1845	Richard Cox (C,SD,RM,HS)brewer 1838-45 Cannon Brewery
1851-67	Daniel Brown (C,SD) (1841 Daniel Brown servant)
*1869-70	Henry Jones (SSM,SD)
Oct 1870-2	Thomas Wyett Wellman (SSM,C,HA)
Feb 1872-5	Henry Butler (HA)
Nov 1875-8	James Lloyd (RL,HA)
1878-9	William Chapman (RL)

1880-1	Michael Lewis (RL)
1881-7	Daniel Lewis (RL,SD)
1887-95	Joseph Ayres (RL,SD)
Apr 1995-1900	Eliza Ayres (RL)
Aug 1900-12	Charles Edward Ayres (RL,SD,HS)
Nov 1912-20	Frederick Lewendon (RL,SD,HS)
Dec 1920-1	William Edward Cotterill (RL)
May 1921-Sep	Arthur Jesse Norris (RL,HS)
Sep 1921-5	John Goodchild (RL,SD,HS)
Jul 1925-7	George William Curtis (RL,HS)
Feb 1927-9	Thomas Henry Bache (RL,SD,HS)
Mar 1929-Jul	Albert James Tappern (RL,HS)
Jul 1929-30	Frederick Butler (RL,HS)
Oct 1930-Jan 31	Albert James Tappern (RL,HS)

— Closed —

28

The Cannon or Little Cannon

Northfield End

In Billing's Street Directory of 1854 Mrs Spratley is given as a beer retailer at the *Cannon* Northfield End. Other street directories have in 1844 John Spratley, and from 1847-52 Mrs Spratley both as beer retailers in Northfield End.

The Census Returns of 1851 for Northfield End show at entry no.81 Mary Spratley (aged 57) beerhouse keeper, son Edward Spratley (38 yrs) and six lodgers. In these returns the entries go along one side of the road and then down the other side, thereby giving a fairly positive positioning in the road, especially when other entries are positively known. Entry no.60 was for the *White Horse*, at no.69 there was a beerhouse identifiable as the *Windsor Castle/Vine,* at what is now 70 Northfield End. At no.93 was the *Sun* again known and only closed in 1992. As Mary Spratley in the Census was at no.81 it follows that the *Cannon* must have been between the *Sun* and the *Windsor Castle.* The *Cannon* was probably demolished when the two large houses, one of them Easby House, were built, which was in the late 1860s or early 1870s.

Edward Spratley the son, was later landlord of the *Sun,* the *Swan,* and the *Duke of Cumberland.*

Landlords/ Tenants of the *Cannon* or *Little Cannon*

1841-4	John Spratley (C,SD)
1841-54	Mrs Mary Spratley (C,SD)

— Closed —

29

The Carpenters Arms

Greys Road/Lane

In the Census Returns for Greys Road in 1861 the number 131 was given to the *Gas Tap,* while 126 was the *Carpenters Arms,* and 104 was the *Saracen's Head.* Since the *Gas Tap* was at what is now 69 Greys Road and the *Saracen's Head* at 121 Greys Road, it is obvious that the returns were taken going down the road or eastward. The number of households in the Census between the *Gas Tap* and the *Carpenters Arms* was four. It is likely that the *Carpenters Arms* was an early name for the *Rifle,* which depending on the date of the street numbering was either 81 or 83 Greys Road (Fig 40). The street numbering suggests either five or six houses between the *Gas Tap* and the *Rifle,* instead of the four in the 1861 Census. This however can easily be accounted for due to infill building or splitting of houses.

Landlord/ Tenant of the *Carpenters Arms*
1861 Henry Stallwood (C) shoemaker

— Continued perhaps as the *Rifle* —

30

The Carpenters Arms

Remenham

The *Carpenters Arms,* Remenham, was on the south east corner of the bridge where the Royal Regatta building of 1986 now stands (Figs 19 & 50). Like the *Angel on the Bridge* it was built right up to and alongside the old bridge, and it was when the *Carpenters Arms* was demolished in 1984 that a complete arch of the old bridge was found (Fig 4). The front wall of the *Carpenters Arms* had been across the opening of the arch, which was found to be constructed of shuttered flint and edged with Barnack stone from Northamptonshire, and was dated to about 1170. The arch has been preserved and may be seen in the basement of the Regatta building.

The *Carpenters Arms* may well have been built in about 1717, which was the date written on the gable end wall of the pub facing the river. There is no building shown at that end of the old bridge in the painting of about 1690 by Jan Siberechts[156]. In fact at that end of the bridge, whose centre spans at that time were of wood, there can be seen two arches, possibly of stone, one of which could have been the arch later blocked by the *Carpenters Arms.*

Although the *Carpenters Arms* was not in Henley or Oxfordshire, being in Remenham, Berkshire, for the purposes of this book, like its close neighbours the *Little Angel* and the *Two Brewers* at the beginning of the Wargrave Road, it comes into the social orbit of Henley.

The earliest record of the pub is in the Brakspear Rent Ledgers, when from 1791-8 it seems it was owned by Mr James Chaplin, rented to Brakspears who sub-let. In 1798 it was bought by Brakspears for £300[157]. In 1826 the Inventory of the Brewery says freehold of W H Brakspear

156 Siberecht, Jan Painting of Henley from the south east, copy in Mayor's Parlour, Town Hall
157 Sheppard, Francis 'Brakspear's Brewery 1779-1979' 1979

Esq. 'The *Carpenters Arms* at foot of Henley Bridge in occupation of James Butler with stabling for 3 horses and neat garden.' Alongside is a note written in pencil - 'the cottage not included in the calculation.

Where the 'cottage' was is uncertain, over the years the pub was much extended, it could be that the pub was once only partly occupying the original building, which was the part nearest to the road, with the gable end with the date on it. This building had fairly heavy timbering inside, consistent with a date at the beginning of the 18th century.

Fig 19 The Carpenters Arms, Remenham, in the early 1900s (see also Fig 50)

Perhaps a clue to the 'cottage' lies in the second Brakspear Rent Ledger. First a loose list of properties which includes 'a house *Carpenters Arms* and a tenement', and then later an entry in the ledger which reads 'William Brown cottage at Bridge west to *Carpenters Arms'*. Another later entry says 'Cottage on Bridge next *Carpenters Arms* Watkins Yard paid by Overseers of Henley 1811-19.'

This sounds as though originally the *Carpenters Arms* was at the eastern end of two semi-detached cottages, which were eventually both used by the pub. Watkins Yard could have been the area between the house and the river, certainly the part above what had been the old bridge would have belonged to Henley and been the concern of the Henley Overseers. Over the years the pub was definitely enlarged, perhaps first taking over the 'cottage', and then by additions behind and forward towards the river. A photo of about 1870, when the Toll Gate at the north east end of the bridge, dismantled in 1873, was still operating, shows the gable end of the *Carpenters Arms* with an extension behind and what looks like a wooden pole fence. A later photo of about 1895 shows the large boathouse extending to the river from where the fence had been. This boathouse which besides having room at the sides as a dry dock, had a large central wet dock. It was built at the peak of the Regatta small boat and punt era, but in later years was hired by the Regatta Stewards to house the booms and other equipment used at regatta times. The large room above, which had windows with balconies overlooking the river, was connected by passageways to the interior of the pub. This room was used after the closure of the pub and before the pub was demolished in 1984 as a meeting place for Jehovah's Witnesses.

The *Carpenters Arms* closed at the beginning of September 1973, the Henley Standard of the 31 August says that it was 'closing this weekend'.

Landlords/ Tenants of the *Carpenters Arms*

*1792-3	Robert Jackson (WHB/R)
1793-5	Edward Gibbs (WHB/R)
1795-7	Robert Wells (WHB/R)
1797-1804	George Harman (WHB/R) (Rent 9 guineas)
1804	Thomas Bates (WHB/R) (Rent £12)
1804-11*	Mr Carter (WHB/R) (Rent £12)
1815-23	Joseph Wyatt (VR,SD)
1826	James Butler (WHB/I)
1830-47	John Farley (TM,SD)
1850-63	William Pigden (SD)
1864-7	Mrs Sarah Pigden (SD)
*1869-99	Miss Sarah Ann Pigden (RL,SD)
Jan 1900	Mary Ann Pigden (RL)
Mar 1900-8	Alfred Parrott (RL,WHB/C)
Oct 1908-9	Mary Ann Parrott (RL,WHB/C)
Jul 1909-10	George Cartland (RL,WHB/C)
Dec 1910-28	Thomas Henry Vernon Coad (RL,WHB/C)
Oct 1928-Dec	Edith Madeleine Coad (RL)
Dec 1928-50	Edward Thomas Tuckwell (RL,WHB/C)
Dec 1950-66	Edward James Scouse (RL,WHB/C,HS) (known as Jack)
Oct 1966-7	R E Brinsden (WHB/C)
Aug 1967-70	T M Hughes (WHB/C)
May 1970-3	T C W Mansfield (WHB/C)
11 Sep 1973	Vacant (WHB/C)

— Closed —

31

The Catharine Wheel

7-17 Hart Street

The earliest mention of the *Catharine Wheel* is in the will of John Lyde otherwise called John Baker in 1499. In the will he left, amongst other bequests, money for the 'mayntenance of that light kepte by the wevers withyn the chapell of Seint Kateryn in the churche of Henley'. He then goes on to leave his wife Isabel the choice of taking the sum of £10 or receiving the yearly sum of 20s, being the rent from 'my tenemente called the *Katheryne Whyll* in the high strete of Henley.' If Isabel were to take the £10 then the tenement was to go to 'Johan Lyde my daughter for ever'. To his son Robert he left tenements in New Street and also his new barge[158].

There were several chapels within the parish church of St Mary, apart from an altar dedicated

158 Weaver, J R H & Beardwood, A 'Some Oxfordshire Wills 1393-1510' 1958 Ox Record Soc

to the Virgin Mary, there were chapels to St Katharine, St Clement, and St Leonard, as well as one to St Ann which was on the bridge. Of all the chapels the only one still remaining is that of St Leonard on the north side of the church[159].

The connection to weavers mentioned in the will of John Lyde when he left money for the light kept by the weavers in the chapel of St Katharyne, is interesting in that one of his executors was 'John Huntelowe wever' and the other was 'John Andrew dyar'. John Huntelowe in his own will of 1504[160] said that he wished to be buried in the churchyard 'by the tomb of John Lyde lately deceased.' Evidently they were close friends and one wonders whether John Lyde was not only a publican and also a baker, but perhaps was a weaver as well.

The *Catharine Wheel* may have begun as at 'the sign of St Katherine', and she would have been depicted with her wheel, and the name may have contracted to the *Catharine Wheel.* The origin of the local devotion to St Katherine may be connected to the ownership of the Manor of Bensington which included parts of Henley, and was part of the dower of Queen Katharine, wife of Henry V. Katharine married Henry soon after 1415.

In 1541 John Gough alias Powes in his will left 'his tenement in Hart Street called the Cathern's Wheel', giving 6s 8d annually out of its rents to his grand daughter Jane Loveles[161].

In 1564 Thomas Wolley paid £6 to Francis Frewyn of Henley and in consideration of this, received the annual rent of 6s 8d for a messuage with its appurtenances called '*Le Kathren Whele*'. In 1612 William Barnabe owned the premises, and agreed to pay the 6s 8d to Thomas Pearson of Wokingham, to form a charity to be known as the Wolleys Charity, which by 1845 had become known as the Nosegay Charity[162].

In 1609 on 11 April Phyl Smith granted a lease to Martha Smith for 21 years of the *Katherin Wheele* in the High Street. On the 19 February 1617/8 Phil Smith leased to John Woodward the *Bull* and the *Katheren Wheele* [163].

During the mid 17th century trade tokens were often used as there was a shortage of small change, establishments such as inns and the landlords of them started issuing their own tokens. One to do so was William Atkins or Adkines, who was at the *Catharine Wheel* from about 1648-72, he later became Mayor in 1679[164]. The Hearth Tax of both 1662 and 1665 show a William Atkins occupying a house with only two hearths, certainly a modest establishment, but in keeping with a house on a single plot which was what the pub was at that time. Probably the part of the present house nearest to the crossroads. Although the present pub now extends over what were six houses, 7-17 Hart Street, this is a recent development, until 1935 it was only 7-9 Hart Street or two plots (Fig 20). It was while still only two houses that the addition of the porch was made in front of the building. The Court Leet of 26 October 1868 charged W H Brakspear a Quit Rent of 6d p.a. owed to the Lord of the Manor for an encroachment, made since the last Court of 1836, of a portico with two pillars in front of the *Catharine Wheel.*

Bridge Rents have always been paid for the *Catharine Wheel*, in later years at the rate of 13s 4d per annum, which included the 6s 8d for the Wolleys Charity. Since the original rent was clearly only that 6s 8d for the one house, the doubling up to 13s 4d indicates that at some time perhaps during the 17th century the *Catharine Wheel* expanded into two houses or plots, in fact became what was later to be 7 and 9 Hart Street. 13s 4d was still being paid in 1967 when the last rents were commuted into a down payment.

---

159 Radford, Rev E M 'Guide to the Church of St Mary the Virgin'
160 Same as note 158
161 Climenson, Mrs Emily J 'Guide to Henley on Thames' 1896
162 Readwin, T A 'Account of the Charities of the Town of Wokingham' 1845
163 Hughes 274C AD450A & 274D AD456A
164 Peters, George H 'This Glorious Henley' 1950

Fig 20 The Catharine Wheel in the early 1900s

Henley Rentals in 1704 were paid by James Marrick, in 1713/4 by James Harrison, in 1721/2 by G Harrison, in 1727/8 by Underwood, in 1733/4 and 1737 with more for the sign by Eaglesfield, and from 1745-58 by the Rev George Hooper with 'more for the sign'. In 1765 it says the late Rev George Hooper, this is repeated in 1769 but there is added the name J Sanders. In 1775, 1779 and 1785 the Rev Clarke paid for the *Catharine Wheel*. The Court Baron Book of 1785 says that the Rev Clarke paid for the *Catharine Wheel* occupied by Sanders. So it would seem that Sanders was landlord from at least 1769-85. From 1790 Hayward paid the rentals while Mr Marklow was the tenant from 1792. In 1807 Brakspear paid, while from 1814-28, like other similarly owned properties the rentals were paid by Appleton.

Mr Marklow, variously spelt Marklew or Marclue, was the same man mentioned in the account of Gaming at the White Hart in 1800 (Introduction pp15-16) Brakspear's Rent Ledger shows that Henry Sanders was still at the *Catharine Wheel* from 1789-92, and also at that time it was owned by the Rev Arthur Clarke. There is a note in the rent book which says that in 1792 it was bought by Brakspear. From Lady Day 1792 up to 1810 John Marklew was the tenant, after that the ledger does not continue, but the Inventory of 1826 shows him to be still there. 'Freehold of William Henry Brakspear Esq. The *Catherine Wheel Inn* in occupation of John Marklew. Stalled stabling for 9 horses and open stabling for 10 horses. Woodhouse, cowhouse, and other buildings with paved yard. House and shop adjoining in occupation of Mr Nix. Quit Rent 3s.' A note alongside in pencil says £105, this may have been the value of the property at the time.

The accommodation for horses seems slight compared with some of the other inns, the *Bear*, the *Bell* and the *White Hart* for instance, but for a short time the *Catharine Wheel* did cater for public coaches. In 1830 services to London were as follows. A coach from Wantage called at the *Catharine Wheel Inn* every Monday Wednesday and Friday mornings at half past eleven, The Defiance from Oxford every day at twelve, and the Berkeley Hunt every afternoon at half past one. In the other direction to Cheltenham, the Berkeley Hunt called every day at twelve, to Oxford the Defiance called every afternoon at two, while to Reading Thom's Sociable went every afternoon at half past four (Sundays excepted). By 1850 neither public coaches or carriers called or were at the *Catharine Wheel*[165].

The 1841 Census and street directories of 1842 and 44 give Henry Marklew at the *Catharine Wheel*. He was the son of John, the Parish Baptism Register of 1737-1812 has the entry on 26 July

165 Street Directories Pigot's 1830, Slater's 185

1793 of Henry Marklew son of John and Elizabeth (maiden name Kainnard) born 21 June.

By 1877 the inn boasted a billiard table and probably a billiard room, at least of sufficient note to employ John Dunn as a billiard marker[166]. That is how he was described when unfortunately he slipped and broke his leg, when playing with a dog in the yard. He was despatched to a hospital in Reading by Mr D'Oyley Brooks surgeon, and the Henley Advertiser noted that Mr Morgan the proprietor of the *Catharine Wheel* accompanied him there.

In 1937 on Monday 31 May[167] a notable event occurred in Henley, the Emperor of Abyssinia, Hail Selassie, stayed at the *Catharine Wheel* for the night, with two secretaries in attendance. Next morning the car ordered to take them to the station failed to arrive, so the Emperor walked to the station.

During 1961 the Henley Standard reported many discussions in the town about the proposals by developers to demolish the *Catharine Wheel.* However planning permission was finally refused and the *Catharine Wheel* is still open today. It has been much altered and very little if any of the original building remains. The old gateway to the yard has been closed, and even the yard itself is now covered over and used as a tea room and cafe. Many of the changes occurred after 1928. Brakspears had leased the buildings to Ernest Barton for twenty one years, and in 1928 sold the freehold to him[168]. At the same time Ernest Barton bought the two adjacent houses and garage to enlarge the hotel. These were 15 and 17 Hart Street. It was agreed that he could substitute the existing porch and doorway for another further along, and that he would be allowed to make another bay window[169]. A condition of the consent to alterations was that the pavement petrol pump which was outside the garage entrance to no.17, which had been Mr Ratty's shop, was removed. James Alfred Ratty was a motor engineer and motor agent who had been trading at 17 Hart Street since at least 1911.

Landlords/ Tenants of the *Catharine Wheel*

*1499	John Lyde/Baker weaver ?
*1541	John Gough/Powes
1564	Francis Frewyn
Apr 1609*	Martha Smith (ORO)
1617/8*	John Woodward (ORO)
1648-72	William Atkins/Adkines(ORO,HT)
1704	James Marrick (R)
1713/4	James Harrison (R)
1721/2	G Harrison (R)
1733/4	Eaglesfield (R)
*1769-1792	Henry Sanders (R,WHB/R)
1792-1826*	John Marklew/Marklow/Marclue (ORO,WHB/R,WHB/I)
1841-4	Henry Marklew (C,SD)
May 1845-59	Mrs Elizabeth Williams (C,RM,SD)
Jul 1859-76	Miss Mary Eyers/Eyres (SSM,C,RM,SD)
1877-9	Samuel Morgan (RL,HA,SD)
1880-8	Mrs Susanna Morgan (RL,C,SD)
Aug 1888-91	Thomas Shepherd (RL,HA)
Jul 1891-9	Charles Michael Roberts (RL,HA)

166 Henley Advertiser 13 Oct 1877

167, 168, & 169 Henley Standard 4 Jun 1937, 10 Feb 1928, 15 Jun 1928

Jul 1899-1905	Evelyn Stanley Dax (RL)
1905-6	Ellen Dax (RL) widow
Jul 1906-12	Ernest Barton (RL,HS)
1912-35	Rose Harriet Clisby (RL,HS)
Oct 1935-7	Andrew Lorne Hamilton & William Edwin Brooks (RL)
May 1937-9	Andrew Lorne Hamilton & Robert Charles Pearson (RL)
1939-42	Andrew Lorne Hamilton & Winifred Wild (RL)
Sep 1942-3	Arthur Reginald Tucker & Winifred Wild (RL)
Dec 1943-4	Arthur Reginald Tucker & Robert Campbell (RL)
Jul 1944-6	Arthur Reginald Tucker & Sidney Shackleton (RL)
Dec 1946-8	Peter Francis Gordon & Roger Milwell (RL)
Sep 1948-9	Peter Charles Barrett & Roy Henry Billiter (RL)
Dec 1949-52	Peter Charles Barrett & Percy Edgar Martin (RL)
May 1952-Dec	Peter Charles Barrett & Frederick Richard Rhodes (RL)
Dec 1952-6	Peter Charles Barrett & Percy Edgar Martin (RL)
Jan 1956-Jul	Peter Charles Barrett (RL)
Jul 1956-7	Peter Charles Barrett & Arthur David White (RL)
Jul 1957-8	Peter Charles Barrett & Eileen Casswell (RL)
Jul 1958-9	Peter Charles Barrett & Richard Hill Kenyon (RL)
Sep 1959-Dec	Peter Charles Barrett & Harold Joseph Styche (RL)
Dec 1959-60	Peter Charles Barrett & James Richard Robinson (RL)
Mar 1960-Dec	Peter Charles Barrett & Ralph Norris (RL)
Dec 1960-1	Peter Charles Barrett & Colin MacLennan (RL)
Aug 1961-2	Peter Charles Barrett & Idwal Parcel (RL)
Jul 1962-3	Cedric MacGeorge Cockerill & Idwal Parcel (RL)
Dec 1963-4	Cedric MacGeorge Cockerill & Roger Pipe (RL)
Apr 1964-5	Cedric MacGeorge Cockerill & Dennis Keener (RL)
Feb 1965-Nov	Cedric MacGeorge Cockerill & Peter Maurice Powell (RL)
Nov 1965-8	Cedric MacGeorge Cockerill & David John Wood (RL)
Jul 1968-70	Cedric Mac George Cockerill & Leslie Charles Freeman (RL)
Jul 1970-5	Leslie Charles Freeman & Valentine Charles Thynne (RL)
Jul 1975-Nov	Valentine Charles Thynne & Peter Daniel Mousley (RL)
Nov 1975-9	Leo Charles Baker & Peter Daniel Mousley (RL)
Nov 1979-83	Beresford Anthony Brooke & Peter Daniel Mousley (RL)
Feb 1983-4	Beresford Anthony Brooke & Giovanni Giorgione (RL)
Mar 1984-Oct	Graham Thomas Matinson (sic)& Giovanni Giorgione (RL)
Oct 1984-7	Graham Thomas Mattinson (sic) & John William Emery (RL)
May 1987-Dec	Peter Robin Crisp & Patrick Francis McGuire (RL)
Dec 1987-9	Patrick Francis McGuire & Jean Jaques Bickel (RL)
Mar 1989-90	Timothy John Winsey & Paul Reid (RL)
Apr 1990-1	Alan Gary Pountney & Paul Reid (RL)
Jan 1991-95	Paul Reid & Keith Roostan (RL)
Oct 1995-96	Keith Roostan & Simon Peter Stonehouse
Dec 1996-97	Simon Peter Stonehouse
Oct 1997-99-	Simon Peter Stonehouse & Richard John Bodek

32

The Cauliflower

North side of West Street

The only mention of the *Cauliflower* beerhouse by name is in the Reading Mercury & Oxford Gazette, when the premises were for sale. Advertised first in the edition of 22 April 1833, then again more fully described on 6 May 1833.

The sale was in three lots, Lot 1 being for two freehold brick and tiled cottages with small gardens situate on the north side of West Street. Lot 2 was for four newly erected freehold cottages, brick built and slated, situated at the back of Lot 1, and entered from the street by a passage. Lot 3 was for a Retail Beer shop, known by the name of the *Cauliflower* situate on the north side of the street, near the Town Hall, and adjoining Lot 1. Also a brick and tiled tenement adjoining the back of the above. Lot 3 was in the occupation of Thomas Neale and Charles Trotman, at rentals of £13 and £5 15s p.a. Thomas Neale was probably the tenant of the *Cauliflower* at the rent of £13.

The Town Hall mentioned in 1833 was the one before the present one (Fig 17), and until the present one was built there was no road behind the Town Hall and no Kings Road. West Street or West Hill started lower down than it does today, immediately after or at the *Kings Arms*. The *Cauliflower* must have been somewhere between Albion Place terrace and what is now the gateway to the doctors' surgeries, and was in 1833 an entrance to the Workhouse. The occupants of the houses from the *King's Arms* up to Albion Place are known at that time, and Albion Place was already built. To have been described as near the Town Hall, the *Cauliflower* must have been in this lower end of West Street.

It is very probable that the *Cauliflower* was the same beerhouse mentioned in the same paper in a sale of 22 May 1858, when thirteen cottages were for sale in Reform Court. Lot 1 was for nine tenements in Reform Court, Lot 2 was for four tenements on the north side of Lot 1, and Lot 3 was a freehold beerhouse facing West Street and let to Mr Cox brewer of Henley. It was described in an advertisement the previous week as having an excellent cellar, tap room, parlour, wash house and four bedrooms. Also for sale in one lot were thirteen cottages in Reform Court at the rear of the beerhouse.

In the Census Returns of 1841 entries for Reform Court start immediately after those for Albion Place. On the large scale O.S. map of 1879 an entrance is shown as leading to the back of what by then were houses on the east side of Adwell Square; between Albion Place and what is now called Market Cottage. It would appear from another sales notice, this time in the Henley Advertiser of 2 January 1875, that Adwell Square then offered for sale had not long been built. The cottages were described as 'nearly new'. However in the census Returns of 1851 the entrance to Reform Court appears to be on the west side of Market Cottage, which was at one time two houses. In 1851 there are two house entries between Albion Place and Reform Court, and again the map of 1879 shows that there was a passage way also on that side of Market Cottage.

Beyond this second entrance to Reform Court in 1851 the third house to the west was a lodging house. It housed Peter Moore a hatter and lodging house keeper, his wife and their three children, aged 9-11. There were thirteen adult lodgers who had six children between them, aged 2-14. The entries concerning employment in many of the census returns do not always seem to be exact, often being a victualler or beer retailer is omitted in favour of another trade or profession, this is sometimes the case when other records show that the person was actually running a beerhouse.

By the time of the Census of 1861, there were still two houses between Albion Place and the entrance to what had been Reform Court, but by 1861 had become Adwell Square with seventeen houses. There is no mention at that date of either a beerhouse or a lodging house, it perhaps discontinued after the sale of 1858.

Since Reform Court seems to have been where Adwell Square was later built, it is likely that the *Cauliflower*, the unnamed beerhouse of 1858 let to Mr Cox, and the lodging house of 1851, were the same establishment, situated just west of Market Cottage.

Landlords/ Tenants of the *Cauliflower*

1833	Thomas Neale (RM)
1851	? Peter Moore (C)

— Closed —

34

The Chequer

Rotherfield Greys (12 Friday Street ?)

The whereabouts of this pub is uncertain, it appears briefly in the Victuallers Recognizances of the 18th century. Mentioned by name in 1775, when Thomas East was landlord sponsored by himself and Robert Brakspear. There had been entries for Thomas East in 1770 and 74, but in those lists the pub names are not listed. In 1776 and 77 Joseph Jemmett was at the *Chequer* sponsored by himself and William Harris, while East in the same years had moved to the *Plough* in Friday Street. The last mention of the *Chequer* by name was in 1778 when Joseph Jemmett was still there sponsored by himself and Edward Wise.

There are two possibilities for the position of the *Chequer*, first that it later became the *Clubhouse* in Greys Lane/Road. The *Clubhouse* is mentioned in 1780 when the then landlord was sponsored by himself and Edward Wise. Edward Wise later in 1787 was landlord of the *Fox* at Bix, and from 1778-85 sponsored Richard Beckett at the *Ball (Golden Ball)*. Wise also sponsored John Bishop at the *Five Horseshoes* Bix, all three of these pubs fall just outside the scope of this book. The connection through Edward Wise to the *Clubhouse* is a tenuous one, since evidently Wise sponsored several landlords, so the fact that he sponsored Jemmett does not mean that Jemmett was at the house two years later to be called the *Clubhouse*.

The second possibility and perhaps the most likely was that the *Chequer* was in Friday Street, continuing into the 19th century as an anonymous beerhouse. There was one such without a name somewhere near to what is now 12 Friday Street, on the south side of the road and therefore in Rotherfield Greys.

Street directories 1844-67 show a beer retailer in Friday Street called Charles Giles. In the 1851 Census there was a Charles Giles (aged 38) publican and his son, A Giles, also a publican both at the Census number 30. In 1871 the Census had Thomas Haynes beerhouse keeper and bricklayer at the census number 9. This apparent contradiction can be explained by the fact that in 1851 the enumerator started at the river and went along the south side of Friday Street, while in 1871 the returns were taken in the opposite direction starting at the Reading Road. The *Black Horse* in 1851 was numbered 20, while in 1871 it was number 19, so the relative position of the beerhouse was in both cases westward of the *Black Horse* by ten households. Exactly how many dwellings were removed when Queens Road was inserted is uncertain, there may also have been dwellings behind some of the properties. The *Black Horse*, previously the *Plough*, was at the house now known as 16 Friday Street, and since the corner to Reading Road remained unbuilt on until the 1890s, the beerhouse may have been at what is now 12 Friday Street.

In the Rotherfield Greys Tithe map of 1844 (Fig 64), the area occupied by 12 Friday Street was owned by George Rawling and consisted of three small cottages on the street front and a row of cottages extending behind the more easterly house. Susan Harris and others occupied the cottages, while Thomas Woodbridge occupied the house yard and garden on the west side. Sheds on the west side of his yard may have housed a malthouse (M16). The house next door to Woodbridge's house, may have been occupied by Charles Giles and his son, while Susan Harris occupied the third cottage along the street.

In 1875 before the cottages were demolished, a beerhouse license was transferred from Alfred Neale to Joseph Morgan[170]. The rebuilding of the property on the corner of Queen Street seems to have been in about 1881, and Joseph Morgan remained the licensee of an unnamed beerhouse, in the new premises. The beerhouse in 1884 was referred to as *Ye Lion* in the Henley Advertiser when the license was transferred from Joseph Morgan to Adrian Hendrik Hammerslag, however in the License records it was not called *Ye Lion* until 1892.

If the beerhouse was once the *Chequer*, it was a name that seems to have long fallen out of use.

Landlords/Tenants of the *Chequer*

*1770-5	Thomas East (VR)
1776-8	Joseph Jemmett (VR)

of the *Clubhouse*

1780	Thomas Stone (VR)

Landlords/ Tenants of unnamed beerhouse Friday Street, later *Ye Lion*

1844-68	Charles Giles (C,SD)
*1870	Joseph Dyer (HA)
1870-1*	Thomas Haynes/Haines (C,HA)
*1875	Alfred Neale (HA)
1875-84	Joseph Morgan (HA,SD)

— Closed —

34

The Chequers

South side of the Market Place (61-3 Market Place)

The Court Baron Book of 1785 for the south side of the Market Place has an entry which reads 'Jos Benwell messuage called the *Chequers* near the Market Place late Peter Sarney 1s.'

The Henley Rentals of 1785, the same date as the Court Baron Book, has an entry 'Benwell late in occupation Mrs Morse 4s 4d.' In 1779 and 75 'Mr Benwell in own occupation 4s 4d', and in 1769, 65, and 58 it says 'Peter Sarney late Shaw now Andrews 1s', and in 1737 'Mr Sarney late Lee 1s'.

170 Henley Advertiser 24 Jul 1875

Going forward from 1785 the Rentals were, in 1790 and 93 'Benwell occupied Allnutt 4s 4d', in 1795, 1807 and 14 'Sam Allnutt late Benwell 4s 4d', in 1823 'Sam Allnutt own occupation 4s 4d', in 1828 'Cook own occupation 4s 4d', in 1836 'Cook occupied Kirkpatrick 4s 4d', and in 1842 'Cook late occupied Parker 4s 4d'.

Finally the entry in the Bridge Rent Book of 1886 No 46, says 'Misses Geere late Henry Geere late J Cook formerly Samuel Allnutt for a house etc next but one to No 45 on the west side late in the occupation of Samuel Allnutt afterwards Mrs Judson since of Mr Simons and now of Mrs Lind 4s 4d.' Added below in probably about 1920 'Present owner Mr A Walden.'

This places the *Chequers* at Empstead House, 61-3 Market Place, the last house on the south side of the market before it becomes Gravel Hill, and where the firm of Waldens still have their yard and offices. A street directory of 1903 shows them to have been there since at least then.

It is likely that the *Chequers* closed soon after 1785, both Sarney and Benwell were brewers, but after them the brewery connection seems to have ceased.

Landlords/ Tenants of the *Chequers*

c1740	Shaw (R)
1758-69	Andrews (R)
1785	Mrs Morse (R)

— Closed —

35

The Clubhouse

172 Greys Road/Lane

The position of the *Clubhouse* is clearly indicated in a Survey and Fieldbook of the Parish of Rotherfield Greys made for the Rev B C Heming in 1815 (Fig 21). This book gives the various fields owned or farmed by the different farmers of Rotherfield Greys, it consists of plans of the fields of each individual farmer with on the back of each map a list of the field names. The plan of the land of William Chipp of Paradise Farm has on it the position of the *Clubhouse.* It is shown just past the bend of the road, before the junction of Greys Road with the lane to Harpsden, known as Gillott's Lane. Opposite this junction the entire corner plot was called Great Clubhouse field, and was just over 16 acres. Comparing the map of 1815 with a modern O.S. map (1:10,560 or 6ins to 1mile) it can be seen that the *Clubhouse*, to the north of Great Clubhouse field was in the position of what is now 172 Greys Road, and that Elizabeth Road has been built between it and what was the field, Elizabeth Road runs along the northern edge of the old field. 172 may be the actual building which was once the *Clubhouse.*

The first mention of the *Clubhouse* beerhouse and lodging house was in the Victuallers Recognizances in 1780, Thomas Stone was then the landlord sponsored by himself and Edward Wise. There is a slight possibility that it may previously have been the *Chequer*, since that pub was mentioned in the Recognizances up to 1778, and the *Clubhouse* not before 1780 (see the *Chequer).*

In 1781 and 83 the sponsors had changed to Hayward and Brakspear, and later to Appleton and Shaw, so it is probable that Hayward and Brakspear held the lease, especially as the *Clubhouse* in 1790 appears in Brakspear's Rent Ledgers. From 1790-4 Thomas Stone was given as the tenant, with a note that the remainder of the term of his lease (or sub lease) was assigned to William Turpin.

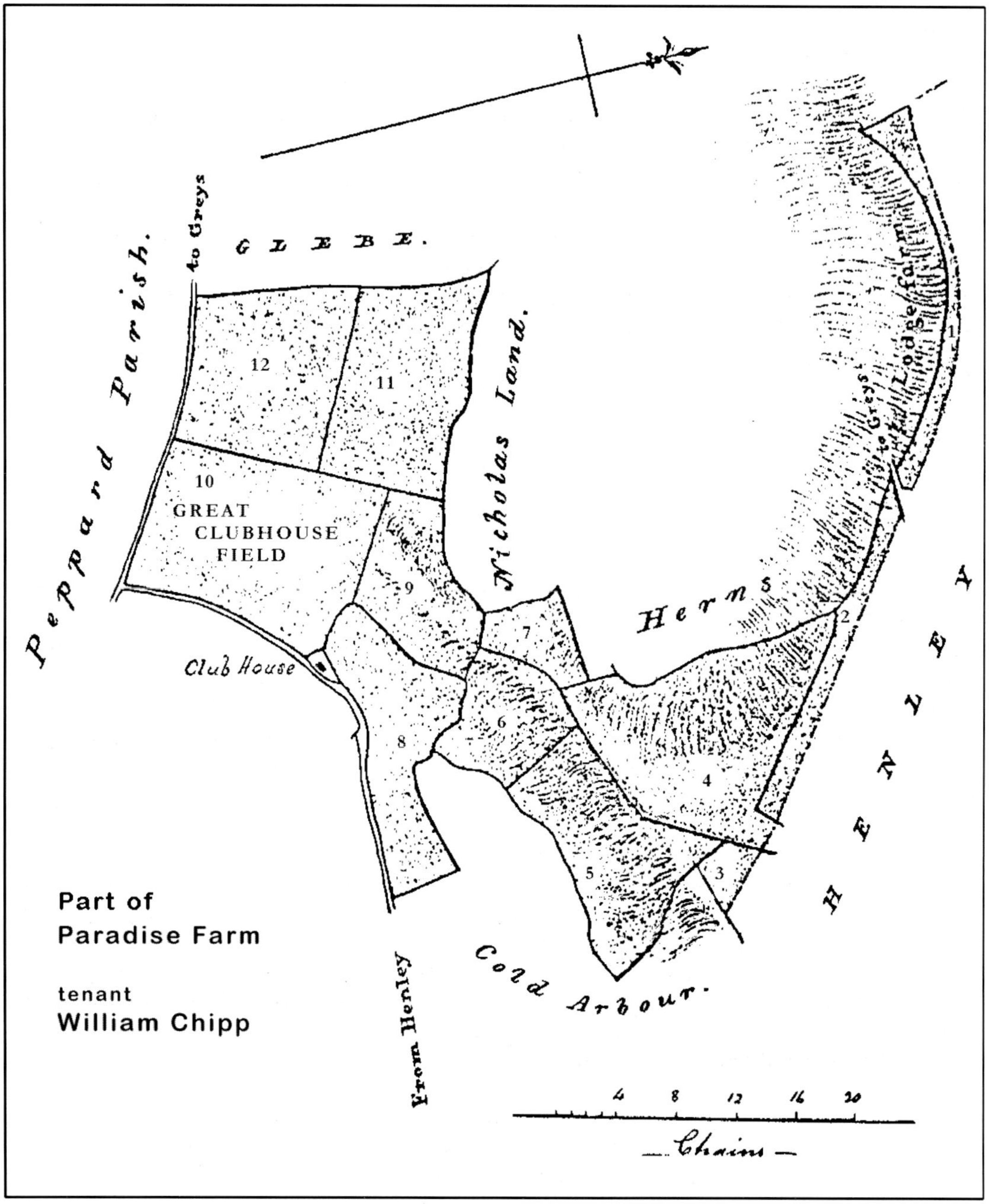

Fig 21 Plan from the Survey & Fieldbook of Rotherfield Greys taken in 1815 for the Rev B C Heming DD. O.R.O.

However by 1797 there was another change of tenant, maybe Stone's lease expired then. The *Clubhouse* does not feature in the Inventory of the Brewery in 1826, so by then it was neither owned or leased by Brakspears.

In April 1797[171]the *Clubhouse* was for sale, together with a house in Bell Street and two tenements at Northfield End, it was described as a freehold dwelling house called the *Clubhouse* at Cold Harbour, in the parish of Greys; divided into three tenements with a garden to each, now in the occupation of John Willis and others. Let on a lease which expires on Lady Day next. So by then there was already multiple tenancy, which may explain the numerous entries to be found in the Rotherfield Greys Parish Registers.

The Parish Registers have an assortment of names for the *Clubhouse*, though some of those mentioned may be related to the beerhouse keepers, others may have been lodgers or living in the adjoining tenements. In the Burials there were in 1818 Mary Webb aged 45, in 1820 Ann Sadgrove aged 70, and in 1839 Tracy Shepherd aged 27. In the Baptisms there were in 1830 Sarah Lovejoy daughter of John and Sarah, also George Akers son of George and Dinah; in 1831 Mary Turner daughter of Mathew and Ann; in 1833 Sarah Lovejoy daughter of John and Sarah, also Ann Turner daughter of Mathew and Ann; in 1834 Samuel Akers son of George and Dinah, also Charles Akers illegitimate son of Rebecca; in 1839 Eliza King daughter of James and Martha; in 1840 Marianne Townsend daughter of Isaac and Jane; in 1841 Rose Ann King daughter of James and Martha; and finally in 1842 Thomas Lanchbury son of Alfred and Jane. All the fathers of the above baptised children were listed as labourers or agricultural labourers, and all gave their address as the *Clubhouse.*

The Census Returns of 1841 indicate that there were three households then living at the *Clubhouse*. The first entry probably being the landlord of the beerhouse. He was Isaac Townsend, aged 30 an agricultural labourer, who had a wife Jane, five children and a 60 year old lodger. The other occupants were William Egleton, aged 34 acgricultural labourer, wife and three children; and James King, aged 30 agricultural labourer, his wife and four children.

The Census of 1851 shows that the *Clubhouse* was then occupied by James Evans aged 35, his wife and three sons. It is possible that the next entries are also for the *Clubhouse* they are a family called Armour, a widow and pauper named Lunnon, and a farm labourer and wife named Marks.

In 1861 Benjamin Kinch aged 39, his wife Sarah aged 34 and three children were at the *Clubhouse*. Kinch was a brewer's labourer. There was also George Willis aged 59 an agricultural labourer, his wife aged 57, a son of 20 and a daughter of 17 both listed as agricultural labourers, and two younger daughters of 13 and 4.

In 1871 and 81 Frederick Tipping was at the *Old Clubhouse,* in 1871 he was termed an agricultural labourer and gamekeeper. He had held the license since October 1870[172], and continued to hold it until the *Clubhouse* was closed in August 1890[173].

Landlords/ Tenants of the *Clubhouse*

*1780-94	Thomas Stone (VR,WHB/R)
1794*	William Turpin (WHB/R)
1797	John Willis (RM)
1840-1	Isaac Townsend (C,BaReg) agric labourer
1851	James Evans (C) labourer
1861	Benjamin Kinch (C) brewer's labourer
Oct 1870-90	Frederick Tipping (RL,C,HA) agric labourer-gamekeeper

— Closed —

171 Reading Mercury & Oxford Gazette 3 Apr 1797
172 Henley Advertiser 15 Oct 1870
173 Rural Register of Licenses

36

The Cock

Waterside/Riverside

The *Cock* seems to have been where the old Rectory and its coach house now exist. Jan Siberechts painting of about 1690, a copy of which is in the Town Hall, shows a terrace of gable ended houses on the site of the old Rectory. A plan of 1793 shows the *Cock* as the third house north of the town ditch. The town ditch until recently diverted, passed under what is now 11 Riverside. Deeds in the Town Hall of the early 18th century refer to a Thameside property having a 'parcel of land on the north side measuring 16ft x 27ft.' This might be a house on the site of what is now the north end of the old Rectory, and it may have been there that the *Cock* was once situated.

In 1793 it was referred to as 'late the *Cock*', in 1629 as the *Cock*, and in 1612 the names of John Stapers and William Jennings are mentioned as connected to the *Cock*. John Stapers would seem to have been the owner, he was a man of means, as he appears as an appraiser of a will and inventory in 1633, he may have been a brewer. The owner in 1793 was a Henry Stevens Esq but by then it was no longer trading, it is the ownership by Henry Stevens that connects it to the deeds in the Town Hall.

Landlords/Tenants of the *Cock*

1612	William Jennings

— Closed —

37

Ye Cocke & another

New Street

Ye Cocke was an inn on the north side of New Street during the 15th century, possibly in the neighbourhood of what is now 37 New Street. There are several property deeds which indicate its position.

> The first deed was dated 10 October 1448, when the will of Margery Sprouk left her messuage in New Street to the Warden, Church and Bridge[174].
> 19 December 1461 Grant of a tenement in New Street to Jon Breche between Will Newnton on the east and Wil Wagge on the west[175] .
> 18 November 1467 Will of John Norris bequeathed to the Warden, Church and Bridge, two tenements in New Street between the doors of his inn (hospitium) and a house belonging to the said Church and Bridge in the tenure of Wm Wagge[176].
> 5 September 1468 Warden to Wil Wagge grant of a tenement called Sprouke's in New Street. (These grants or leases of properties were renewed regularly and this is probably a later version of a grant possibly made soon after 1448, the other renewals may well have been lost.)

174 Hughes 849 AD218

175 Briers, P M 'Henley Borough Records 1395-1543' 1960 Ox Record Soc

176 Hughes 739 AD236 (1467) & 740 AD237 (1468)

9 Sep 1468 Granted to Tho Sugre a tenement with garden in New Street between tenement of the Church and Bridge to the west, and Joh Norys to the east and extending to that garden called Cownteys garden to the north[177].
7 January 1484 Grant to Rob Braye of a tenement with adjacent garden in New Street lately held by Ric Carles taylour, between the tenement of Alisaundri Marten lately called *Ye Cocke* to the east and John Croke to the west.
1 August 1491 Tho Coke carpenter has building lately held by Joh Croke and has laid it to waste and destroyed it. (Presumably he rebuilt it - see 1505)
13 August 1494 Mention of Tho Coke of Henley vyteler.
26 December 1505 Grant to Ludowico Rede of a tenement in New Street lately held by John Croke and before that by Tho Sygar.

It is very likely that Tho Sugre and Tho Sygar are the same person, spelling of names was most erratic. If so the only uncertainty is which of the two tenements he was in. A table of the households makes this a bit clearer

North side of New Street

	west—————	—————	—————	————east
1448	Marg Sprouke	—	—	—
1461	Wil Wagge	Joh Breche	Will Newnton	—
1467	Wm Wagge	2 tenements to Church & Bridge		John Norris(inn)
1468	Wm Wagge	?<—Tho Sugre —>?		Joh Norys
—	—	Tho Sygar	Ric Carles	—
1484	—	Joh Croke	Rob Braye	Alisaundri Marten lately called *Ye Cocke*
1491	—	Tho Coke	—	—
1505	—	Ludowico Rede	—	—

These deeds suggest that the inn of John Norris/Norys was called *Ye Cocke*. That it was on the north side of New Street is certain because of the mention of Countess Garden, which ran behind the properties north of New Street. Originally it had been land belonging to the Manor of Henley, the house of which became derelict in the 14th century[178]. It is a possibility that the four properties may have been in the area of 31-7 New Street, 31, 33, and 37 were still paying Bridge Rents in 1886. Other properties further to the west, such as the land on which the theatre was built were given to the town at a later date, while the small houses 3 and 5 New Street, which were also once town property, are too near the end of the road and therefore not backing on to Countess Gardens.

33 New Street was one of the properties that had a malthouse (M39) behind it, as can be seen on the O.S. map of 1879. It belonged to Roomes in 1828, was then bought by Brakspear, and then in 1897 exchanged for two cottages owned by the Charity Commissioners of the town, so that the Mineral Water Factory could be built on the site of the two cottages[179]. The malthouse was demolished when the large malthouse (M40) was built in 1903.

If the four houses were on the sites of 31-37 New Street, it is interesting to speculate as to whether there was also a pub at 33 New Street. It would seem that *Ye Cocke* no longer existed when Alisaundri Marten was there in 1484, but in 1494 Tho Coke was mentioned as a victualler,

177 Briers as note 175, 1468-1505 pp69, 85, 100, 112, 153 (p85 also Hughes 741 AD259)
178 Burn, J S 'History of Henley on Thames' 1861 pp228-235 see also Gibson, Ruth 'Journal of the H.A.&H.G.' No9
179 O.R.O. Cooper & Caldecott C66 (15) 1897

and in 1491 he had laid waste the building lately held by Tho Croke, next door but one to *Ye Cocke*. In 1505 Ludowico Rede took over the same house from Tho Coke. Ludowico Rede was maybe a brewer or maltster, at the same time in December 1505, he was also granted a tenement opposite the Market Place in the High Street lately that of Tho Hameldon. Before that on 1 August 1491 a tenement at the end of Broke (Duke) Street and a tenement in the middle of the High Street were lately held by Tho Hamulden[180].

From the number of properties with which Rede and Hamulden were connected they both could have been brewers or maltsters, it is just a possibility that malting could have been carried on at the site of 33 New Street from about 1491 up to 1903.

Landlords/ Tenants of *Ye Cocke*

1467-8	John Norris/Norys (BR,HL)
? *1480* ?	Alisaundri Marten (BR)

Landlords/ Tenants of the other possible pub

1491-4	Tho Coke (BR)
? *1553/4*	Matilda Coke ? (see p7)

— Closed —

38

The Cocks

Market Place

It is uncertain where the *Cocks* was situated, it would seem to have been in Middle Row, possibly near to the *Eight Bells* or where the *Victoria* now is. Middle Row until the end of the 18th century extended from the houses above the town hall and where the town hall now stands, down the middle of the market, across the crossroads, and to about the neighbourhood of the *Catharine Wheel*. From the Henley rentals it seems that the *Cocks* was in Middle Row but in the upper part.

The Rentals of 1713/4 say 'John Cook for the tenement called the *Cocks* late in occupation of Edward Stockdale 3s 6d.' Later rentals for the same place are in the name of a man whose surname seems to have several variants - in 1721/2 John Brinkhostes, in 1727/8 John Brinkster, 1733/4 John Brinkies, 1737 John Brinklow, 1745 J Brinkhouse tenement in possession of Vicars, and 1758 and 69 Mrs Whiting late Brinkus.

Since the *Cocks* is not mentioned again by name after John Cook was there in 1713/4, one can only presume that it went out of business soon after that. It could be that Brinkhostes or Brinkus was a publican but there is no proof of this, nor do the other names suggest a brewery or pub connection.

Landlords/ Tenants of the *Cocks*

*1713	Edward Stockdale (R)
1713/4	John Cook (R)

— Closed —

180 Briers see note 175, 1505 p153, 1491 p101

39

The Crown

29-31 Duke Street

The *Crown* was a 19th century beerhouse, it was described in the Register of Licenses as having been a beerhouse 'ante 1869', and therefore old established.

The earliest known beer retailer for the *Crown* was in the Census of 1841, when Robert Coppin aged 30 publican and his wife Ann aged 30 were in occupation. A street directory of 1844 mentioned Robert Coppin as a beer retailer in Duke Street. The earliest mention of the *Crown* by name is a directory of 1854 when John Shaw was listed as a beer retailer and broker.

In 1871 William Jones was one of six landlords in the town summoned for having incorrect cups or measures for the sale of beer. A later court case in 1889 was when the then landlady Mrs Challis sought the help of the court to evict a lodger who had not paid his rent[181].

In 1887 the *Crown* was owned by H & G Simonds of Reading, but before 1891 it was owned by E Wells Esq of Wallingford, who was still the owner when the *Crown* was closed on 31 December 1909. By 1909 half the building had already been rented out for some time to Stanley Mead, a hairdresser, who for many years had his business at 29 Duke Street.

As a pub its situation limited its viability, it had no back entrance or yard, and could therefore only survive as a small beerhouse with no possibility of enlargement.

Landlords/ Tenants of the *Crown*

1841-4	Robert Coppin (C,SD)
*1850-1	Ann Adams (C,SD)
1852-4*	John Shaw (SD) broker
*1869-80	William Jones (SSM,RL,C,SD) domestic gardener
1880-9	James Challis (RL,SD)
Jan 1890-1	Mrs Mary Ann Challis (RL,HA,SD)
Sep 1891-1909	William Whiting (RL,HA)

— Closed —

40

The Crown

9 Market Place

The *Crown* at 9 Market Place, closed at the end of 1952, was first mentioned in the Magistrates Special Sessions Minute Book of 1870 and 1871 when it was described as an inn with an Alehouse and Victuallers License, held by Mrs Emma Kinch (Fig 6). How long it had been an inn is unknown, though it is unlikely that it had existed before the 1860s. It may be that Mrs Kinch was able to acquire the license of the old *Crown and Thistle* which had been next door at 7 Market Place.

A street directory of 1876 and others back to 1863 show Mrs Kinch as a chemist, printer,

181 Henley Advertiser 18 Dec 1871 & 10 Nov 1889

bookseller, stationer, circulating librarian, spirit merchant and tea dealer. Was she also a publican ? In 1854 there was Charles Kinch whose activities added stamp distributor and Agent to the United Kingdom Insurance Co to the above trades. In 1850 Hickman and Kinch were booksellers and stationers, with Charles Kinch as printer and stamp distributor. In 1847 and 1844 Hickman and Kinch were postmasters, printers, chemists and druggists. In 1830 there were Hickman and Stapledon booksellers, stationers and printers.

Deeds in the Oxfordshire Record Office show that the properties now 7 and 9 Market Place were for many years linked together and that 7 Market Place had been first the *Black Horse and Farrier* and then the *Crown and Thistle*[182]. The last of the deeds in the Oxford Record Office concerned with 7 and 9 Market Place, is the will of Susannah Elizabeth Johnson in 1833, and this refers to what was later to be 9 Market Place as being in the occupation of William Hickman and William Stapledon[183], who were chemists and printers. In January 1824 W Hickman announced in the Reading Mercury & Oxford Gazette that he had taken over the business of Mr G Norton and had entered a partnership with William Stapledon. G Norton appears to have had the earliest of the Post Offices in the town, which Hickman took over.

The two houses 7 and 9 included several buildings behind, yards and gardens, fully described in the account of the *Crown and Thistle.* In Brakspear's Inventory of 1826 the *Crown and Thistle* was listed as being held freehold by William Henry Brakspear. The will of Susannah Johnson in 1833 quotes a lease granted in 1825 to William Hickman and William Stapledon which refers to a barn behind the *Crown and Thistle*, a malthouse, a messuage and workshops. This lease indicates that Hickman and Stapledon were occupying 9 Market Place, with the buildings behind it, as well as a barn behind the pub, which at that time was separately owned and occupied.

In 1877 Mrs Kinch had left Henley and was living at 6 The Elms, Princes Park, Liverpool, and A R Awberry was landlord of the *Crown*, and also was a chemist, bookseller and printer[184], though he may have been living at 11 Market Place. In a street directory of 1876 he was in Hart Street, but by 1877 was also in the Market Place, and although for many years he was licensee of the *Crown,* his dwelling place was always at 11 Market Place. By 1897 Mrs Kinch had become Mrs Emma Kinch Seaton Carew, and the premises of the *Crown* were offered for sale[185]. They consisted of a 'Freehold shop, dwelling house, and premises known as the *Crown* situate at 9 Market Place.' The property was bought by Albert R Awberry, who up to that time had rented the premises belonging to the *Crown.*

In 1883 Awberry the licensee, finding that all his activities were becoming too much for him, requested the Licensing Justices to allow him to reduce the hours that he was licensed to open, closing at ten instead of eleven at night, and only opening six days a week instead of seven. This was granted and caused endless problems for his successors who tried for many years to get the order rescinded.

In 1904 the premises were again for sale 'The *Crown Hotel* in the Market Place, the chemists and stationers shop and dwelling house adjoining, with printer's offices at the rear, together with excellent coach building premises and stores, possible frontage to Greys Lane and the Tun's Yard.' Henry Judge bought the property and became landlord of the *Crown* in 1905, in 1908 he sold the *Crown* to Wallingford Brewery but continued as landlord till 1911.

As early in his ownership as 1906 Henry Judge applied for the restoration of the full license and for the opening hours to be extended, this was refused.

In 1920 the then landlord Arthur Staniforth applied again for the seven days opening. He pleaded that the *Crown* had always had a seven day license until Awberry to ease his own work load

182 O.R.O. Cooper & Caldecott C9 see entries for *Black Horse & Farrier,* and *Crown & Thistle*

183 O.R.O. Cooper & Caldecott C9 (7) Will of S E Johnson 1833

184 Register of Licenses & Street Directories

had requested a six day license, which had been granted only as a favour to Awberry. Although it was also claimed that it was an old established house, the request was again refused.

In February 1925 Wallingford Brewery submitted plans to increase the hotel's facilities by using the rooms of the neighbouring house, 11 Market Place, which they had now purchased, in 1908 they had only bought the *Crown*. Albert Awberry had continued to own and live at 11 Market Place until his death, he was buried aged 76 in May 1923[186]. Wallingford Brewery then made a further plea for the seven days opening, citing the extreme inconvenience to guests at the hotel, and pointing out that the *Crown* was the only pub which they owned in Henley. The request was again refused.

In 1930 Wallingford Brewery and its pubs were purchased by Brakspears, the *Crown* being bought for £2,850 as stated in the Henley Standard in July. The following week there was another article about the *Crown* in which it described how the building had been altered during the ownership by Wallingford Brewery. It says how the premises occupied by the late Mr Awberry were included in the hotel, at the rear of which a large new dance hall was erected. The approach to the hall was found inconvenient, and the arrangement of the hotel unsatisfactory. The entrance was in the centre of the premises with a long passage to the saloon bar etc. So a new passage had been constructed on the eastern side of the hotel. The article concluded with the words 'Mr West is the landlord, and Brakspears take over in September.'

Brakspears having taken over the *Crown* in September 1930, at the next licensing session in February 1931, after forty eight years, the seven day license was restored to the *Crown* and the licensee Mr West, a tenant of Brakspears.

Landlords/ Tenants of the *Crown*

1870-1	Emma Kinch (SSM)
*1877-98	Albert Richard Awberry (RL,HS,SD)
Dec 1898-9	Walter Grammer (RL)
Apr 1899-Jul	Edwin James Bussell (RL)
Jul 1899-Oct	Sidney Lyle (RL)
Oct 1899-1905	Albert Richard Awberry (RL)
1905-11	Henry Judge (RL,HS)
1911-18	Henry George Leon Dinham (RL)
Mar 1918-21	Arthur Staniforth (RL,SD)
May 1921-Sep	Edward Henry Museem (RL)
Sep 1921-2	Howard Vivian Ricks (RL,HS)
Mar 1922-4	Charles Edward Green (RL,HS,SD)
1924-8	Frederick William Leftly (RL,HS,SD)
Feb 1928-30	John Rengger/Rennger (RL,HS)
Mar 1930-4	Bertram Jabez West (RL,HS)
Oct 1934-7	Charles Patrick Whistler (RL,HS,SD) RAC appointed hotel
Sep 1937-Dec	Henry Able Noble (RL,HS)
Dec 1937-8	Horace Leopold Rogers (RL,HS)
Dec 1938-40	Harry William Jarman Stevens (RL,HS,SD)
Feb 1940-6	Gladys Eva Stevens (RL) (Sep 46 now G E Drayton)
Sep 1946-9	Gladys Eva Drayton (RL)
Mar 1949-50	Donald Brimmer Budge (RL)
Jul 1950-2	Joseph Gerald Addison (RL)

— Closed —

186 Henley Parish Burial Register 1844-1944

41

The Crown and Anchor

Above the Market Place/Gravel Hill

The *Crown and Anchor* beerhouse above the Market Place, appears in an advertisement placed in the Reading Mercury & Oxford Gazette of 22 September 1838, just before the annual Henley Fair, when the landlord was hoping for more custom.

The house was advertised as a beerhouse, coffee house, chop house, and lodging house, the landlord H Norris had had hopes of obtaining a Spirit License before the Fair took place, as can be seen in the wording of his advertisement.

> 'H Norris begs to return his thanks to those liberal minded friends who favoured him with their signatures to his certificate to assist him in obtaining a Spirit License, and although unsuccessful he assures them that the time is fast approaching when a Legislative Enactment will preclude the necessity of such prejudicial modes of application, so injurious to the Revenue and the Public, and that the Beer and Spirit Monopoly and its combined interests will soon terminate ..... His friends ..... will always find at his house the best articles at the cheapest rate. Pleasant sitting apartments, fine airy bedrooms, and the most comfortable homely accommodation. A part of the spacious house to be let for the Winter Season. A large plot of ground to be let for the Fair.'

Mr Norris was obviously displeased at the refusal of his application, but was pinning his hopes on a change in the Law making it easier to gain a Spirit License. If so he must have been disappointed.

By the 29 June 1839 in the same paper, the property was offered to Let. Described as a highly respectable Free House, opened about three years ago by the present tenant, as a Beer, Coffee and Chop House ..... The house commands a beautiful prospect and is well adapted for Letting Lodgings. Excellent cellars, a good walled-in garden and two acres of meadow land. Would suit a couple with a trade or a small capital. Coming in will be moderate and early possession may be had. Apply at the *Crown and Anchor.*

Whether there was a new tenant in 1839 is uncertain, at any rate in the same paper another advertisement appeared in March 1841again saying that the premises were to let. This time there was a new dimension, it was for a 'newly erected Brewing Plant with 5 barrel copper and appendages, household furniture, utensils and implements of the Beer Trade. *Crown and Anchor* Brewery and Public House, Gravel Hill, Henley. The house and premises to let. Enquire of Mr Webb, Webb's Wharf, Henley.' It would seem that Mr Norris, or possibly some tenant who may have taken over in 1839, having despaired of obtaining a Spirit License, decided to branch out into the brewery business. Perhaps this was not a great success, certainly the advertisement with its instruction to enquire of Mr Webb, implies that Norris, or a later tenant, had departed and left the letting to Webb, who may have been the owner of the property.

In the Census Returns of 1841 for Gravel Hill there is an unidentified beerhouse and lodging house occupied by a Thomas Mumford aged 30, beer retailer, his wife Mary aged 40, two daughters and one female servant. Following the names of the Mumfords there is a long list of what appear to be lodgers, they are in the same entry as Thomas Mumford. There were nine single men, and one single woman, five married men their wives and a total of five children, and another single woman and her daughter.

From the position of the entries in the Census of 1841, the beershop and lodging house was between the house known as Button Juggs or 19 Gravel Hill, and what was the *Basketmakers Arms*. The *Crown and Anchor* was probably in the area where Havelock Terrace once known as Sargeants Row, and the entrance to the College are now situated (Fig 66). The two acre plot of land may have been where part of Henley College is now, and what in 1879 was the entrance to the school.

The entry immediately next to the Mumfords in the Census is for an Ann Norris aged 40 a straw bonnet maker, and her children four daughters and a son named Robert aged 12. From the Baptism Register of St Mary's Church, it seems that Ann Norris was married to, or had been married to a Robert Norris. Robert Norris may have been related to H Norris, and they may have shared the house, perhaps Robert and Ann lived in the part available for letting in the Winter Season. Maybe they stayed on after H Norris left the *Crown and Anchor*. Another possibility is that H Norris and Robert Norris were one and the same person, and that Robert was an alternative name, or even that the use of H was perhaps a printing error.

Landlords/ Tenants of the *Crown and Anchor*

1836-9*	H Norris (RM)
1841	Thomas Mumford (C)
1844	Mary Mumford (SD)

— Closed —

42

The Crown and Thistle

7 Market Place

The *Crown and Thistle* was previously the *Black Horse and Farrier*. Deeds in the Oxford record Office[187] show the descent of the two houses, now 7and 9 Market Place from Robert Cluett in 1744 to his widow Susanna Cluett, who in 1764 left the property to her niece Sarah Blackman, daughter of John Blackman brewer. In 1772 Herald Painter and Sarah Painter (nee Blackman) his wife sold to Josiah Sarney. Both properties were sold, the first mentioned is what is now 9 Market Place as that appears to have been the main dwelling house. It is described as a messuage malthouse garden and stables situated between 'then or late William Rackstraw hatter on the west and the messuage in tenure of Susanna Cluett afterwards Elizth Prince widow and then or late Thomas Gregge on the east' (this would have been the *Crown and Thistle*.) To give an idea of the extent and complexity of the properties concerned it is worth quoting from the document of 1772, after the first mentioned messuage it continues - 'and <u>also</u> malthouse granaries storehouses behind the messuage and adjoining thereto also in tenure of Susanna Cluett then John Blackman then Josiah Sarney and Richard Geere and their under tenants.'

'and <u>also</u> the messuage on the east side of the before mentioned called by the name of the *Black Horse and Farrier* and then or late of the *Crown and Thistle* with the yard and garden thereto heretofore in the occupation of Thomas Davis afterwards James Robinson then or late Lessiter Nichols his undertenants and assigns.'

'and <u>also</u> the messuage lying behind the last mentioned in the yard or garden in the tenure

187 O.R.O. Cooper & Caldecott C9 (1-7)

of Mary Weller widow her undertenants etc formerly in the tenure of Thomas Messenger and then or late of the said Richard Geere.'

'and also all that messuage in Brooke'(Duke)'Street then in tenure of Elizth Jemmett widow her tenants etc adjoining on the north to the last mentioned messuage and on the south to the brewhouses and storehouses of the late John Blackman and then in tenure of Josiah Sarney and Richard Geere.'

This last property is difficult to place, obviously near the north end of Duke Street on the west side. The land of 7 Market Place extended down most of the length of Duke Street, so the cottage behind may have been way down the garden, so if the Brooke Street property was to the south of it, then it would possibly be in the neighbourhood of 20-26 Duke street, though this would place the brewhouse and storehouse even further south. In Henley Rentals there was a brewhouse rented by John Blackman attached to the corner property at the north west corner of Duke Street, possibly once the *George/Crowne*. (see B2 Brewhouses & Malthouses.) This corner was demolished in 1870 when Duke Street was widened. If it were the brewhouse and storehouse of the late John Blackman then the Brooke Street property might have been in the vicinity of 4 Duke Street, however that makes nonsense of the property being south of the cottage behind the *Crown and Thistle*, it should have said east. There is also the problem that in any case the lands belonging to the *Three Tuns* or 5 Market Place were between the land behind 7 Market Place and the backs of the Duke Street houses. Much of this land of the *Three Tuns* has now become Tuns Lane, but when exactly this happened is not known.

The deed continues 'and also all that barn and stable behind the said messuage called the *Crown and Thistle* heretofore in occupation of John Hare and afterwards of John Blackman and then Josiah Sarney and Richard Geere also all that garden enclosed situate on the south side of the garden belonging to the first mentioned messuage' (9 Market Place)'extending to a certain gutter or watercourse called the Town Ditch formerly in occupation of John Gale and then John Saunders also all that void and waste ground adjoining all the houses and outhouses in occupation of Francis Simmonds.'

From the 1772 document it seems that the change of name from the *Black Horse and Farrier* to the *Crown and Thistle* may have occurred in about 1770 or just before, both names were given in 1772 as though the change was recent. However there is a Rental entry of 1762 which says the *Crown and Thistle* on the south side of the Market Place with stabling and extending to the Town Ditch. The will of Susanna Cluett in 1764 calls it the *Black Horse*, so perhaps the change was a slow one. The reason for the change is not known though I have suggested in the entry for the *Black Horse and Farrier* that maybe it was in some way a result of the Jacobite risings of 1745 and was perhaps an indication of support for the continued Hanoverian connection with Scotland.

The last of the tenants mentioned at the *Crown and Thistle* Lessiter Nichols was almost certainly the same person as the Leicester Nicholls mentioned in both the 1770 and 71 lists of licensees, lists with no pub name attached.

It seems that in 1782 Josiah Sarney and Sarah his wife sold to John Wheeler most of the property except for the *Crown and Thistle*. The sale included the messuage (now 9 Market Place) the barn lying at the back of the *Crown and Thistle* and also the malthouse behind 9. Mr John Wheeler maltster took out insurance in October 1782[188] on a house situate in Butchers Row, tenant John Cox cooper (9 Market Place) and also on a malthouse lofts granaries adjoining situate behind the said house in his own occupation. This part of the property was left by will in 1782 to first John Wheeler's mother Elizth Coombes and afterwards to his nephew John Johnson. John Johnson by a marriage settlement of 1786 gave the property to his wife Susannah Elizth Johnson for the use of

188 Royal Exchange Insurance Register No 84746 26 Oct 1782 O.R.O. Brakspear X/ 1

her and her children. In 1825 it was leased to William Hickman druggist, and by will in 1833 all the property in occupation of William Hickman and William Stapledon was left to the Johnson children. It appears that in 1833 the *Crown and Thistle* was still in business, as the will stipulated 'the barn behind the *Crown and Thistle.*'

Meanwhile back in 1782 Josiah Sarney still owned the *Crown and Thistle*, and the Court Baron Book of 1785 says 'Ann Gayer the hill south now occupied by J Ivory.' (Gayer was another spelling of Geere) In Brakspears Rent Ledgers from about 1790 Brakspear rented the *Crown and Thistle* from Josiah Sarney. The sub tenants were 1790-6 John Ivory, Michaelmas 1796-1800 John Godfry, 1800-11 Thos Glover. There was also mention of a tenement in the yard let by Brakspears from 1897-1823 to the Parish of Greys. Brakspear continued leasing the *Thistle Alehouse* from Josiah Sarney up to 1817, when a note says that the premises were bought by Brakspear for £250.

The Victuallers Recognizances and Alehouse Keepers list of 1817 show that Thomas Glover was still at the *Crown and Thistle* in 1817. However in the Court Leet book of the Manor of Henley in 1814 and 1816 under a list of those convicted of selling deficient measures it says Sharp at the *Crown and Thistle.* Maybe after 1816 he was evicted and Glover returned as a replacement. A street directory of 1823 gives the name John Walters, while the Inventory of the Brewery in 1826 has the following :- 'Freehold of Wm Henry Brakspear Esq the *Crown and Thistle* in occupation of James Walter. Stabling for 6 horses yard and skittle ground. A cottage adjoining with two rooms.'

After 1826 and the mention in 1833, there is no further mention of the *Crown and Thistle* it may have closed in about 1833-40. In the Court Leet book of the Manor of Henley on 26 October 1868 W H Brakspear owed the Lord of the Manor an annual Quit Rent of 1½d for the public house called the *Crown and Thistle* now converted into a butcher's shop and in the tenure of Alfred Lester. Later on 9 November 1881 the Court Leet again said that W H Brakspear owed a Quit Rent of 1½d for the public house called the *Crown and Thistle* afterwards converted into a butcher's shop and now in the tenure of Gabriel Machin poulterer. The Census Returns of 1841,51 and 61 suggest that it was already a butcher's shop and continued as such till the present day. Alfred P Lester was there in the 1871 Census, and the shop which is still trading under the name Gabriel Machin first appears in a street directory of 1877.

Landlords/ Tenants of the *Crown and Thistle*

1770-2	Lessiter/Leicester Nichols/Nicholls (ORO,VR)
*1785-96	John Ivory (CB,WHB/R)
1796-1800	John Godfry (WHB/R)
1800-13	Thomas Glover (WHB/R,AKL)
1814-16	Sharp (CL)
1817*	Thomas Glover (AKL)
1823-6 (-33 ?)	John/James Walter/Walters (WHB/I, SD)

— Closed —

43

The Crowne

Corner of Duke Street with Market Place

The *Crowne* appears to have been on the north west corner of Duke Street. It seems that the name of the *Crowne* may have been a short lasting name for a pub previously, and also later called the *George*. There are thre documents which seem to show this [189] :-

> On 1 October 1625 Rich Powle granted to Edm Symeon a lease for 21 years of a corner house in Henley on the south side of the High Street called the *George*.
> On 5 October 1632 Edmund Symeon of Purton in the County of Oxford Esq and John Hampden of Hampden in the County of Buckinghamshire Esq and Elizabeth his wife granted to John Morgan of Henley on Thames a messuage of a corner house on the south side of the High Street called the *Crowne*. In 1634 Henley rentals have an entry for the *Crowne* Market Place.
> On 1 October 1638 John Morgan and others granted to Ric Allen and another the assignment of the remainder of a 99 years lease in a messuage called the *George* in the High Street.

The corner on the other side of Duke Street, which would also have been termed a corner on the south side of the High Street, was in possession of Humphrey Newberry in about 1633-4, see the entry for the *Blue Bell*.

Charles I came to the throne in 1625, and perhaps the name change to the *Crowne* was in a burst of enthusiasm for Charles. However perhaps the gathering dissatisfaction throughout the 1630s may have led to the abandonment of the name of the *Crowne,* and a return to the less contentious name of the *George*, which at that time would have been the saint rather than royalty. It is interesting to note that that stout Parliamentarian John Hampden should have been one of those connected with the pub while it was the *Crowne*, though his probable connection was as a mortagee.

Landlords/ Tenants of the *George/Crowne/George*

*1625	Rich Powle (HL)
1625-32	Edmund Symeon (HL)
1632-8	John Morgan (HL)
1638*	Ric Allen

— Continued as the *George* —

44

The Duke of Cumberland

Now the Bell or Ye Olde Bell, Bell Street

The *Duke of Cumberland* was renamed the *Bell* or *Ye Olde Bell* in February 1920. Though later English history has dwelt upon the Duke of Cumberland, son of George II, as 'Butcher' Cumberland, due to his harsh measures after the defeat of the Jacobites at Culloden in 1746, obviously in Henley at least he was not viewed with repugnance. At the time he was probably the hero of the hour having saved England from both the Scots and the Stuarts, a return of whom was probably looked on with great misgivings.

It is significant that the earliest records of this pub go back to about 1760, so it is fairly safe to assume that the name appeared very soon after the Jacobite rising, when perhaps the people of Henley felt warmly towards the duke. The change of name in 1920 was probably due to the then more romantic image of the Stuarts and the Jacobites, when all actual threat from them was long

189 Hughes 323 AD461, 2 AD474, 1003 AD477

over, and the behaviour of the Duke of Cumberland had been reconsidered.

The site of the *Duke of Cumberland* seems to have been part of a larger plot originally, which included the site of the building next door, known in the mid 19th century as the Assembly Rooms (Fig 32). In the Henley Rentals of 1727/8 Mr Taylor paid 7d for his house in his own possession. Thos Taylor again paid 7d in 1733/4 and 1737. Thomas Taylor continued to pay for his house up to 1758. After that in 1765 the Rentals say 'Taylors now Hayward in occupation Moorhouse and Andrews 7d.' From then on there is a double occupancy, first Moorhouse and Andrews, then in 1793 and 1800 Owthwaite and Andrews. Throughout this period from 1765-1800 Hayward was the owner and the others were tenants, and for most of those years the payment had become 4½d, as it had been in 1745 and 49. In 1807 the owner was Brakspear and the tenants Owthwaite and Andrews, in 1814 Paulin and Andrews, 1823-36 Cooper and Andrews and in 1842 Wright.

In the Bridge Rent Book of 1886, entry no. 93, Messrs W H Brakspear were still paying 4½d for the *Duke of Cumberland* public house. The payment was finally redeemed in 1967.

If one studies the Rentals it becomes clear that the plot became two properties some time between 1758 and 65. It is a possibility that the building still surviving as *Ye Olde Bell* was the original house belonging to Mr Taylor, and that the building later the Assembly rooms was built on its yard or garden. It may have been a public house before 1758, Thomas Taylor may have been a publican, this may be why it was bought by Hayward. Benjamin Moorhouse was described in a deed of 1796 as a wine merchant[190]. Andrews was a publican, in the Victuallers Recognizances lists of 1770 and 71 there was a Joseph Andrews. Owthwaite and Cooper were both furniture dealers, upholsterers and auctioneers[191], it may be that the building later the Assembly Rooms was built as a furniture warehouse and auctioneering rooms. Possibly it was on the site of a malthouse (M 8).

Brakspears Rent Ledgers show that a Joseph Andrews was the tenant of the *Duke of Cumberland* from 1790-1811, the whole period covered by the ledgers. The Alehouse Keepers List of 1817 also has Joseph Andrews. By 1826 the Brewery Inventory says 'Freehold of Wm Henry Brakspear Esq. The *Duke of Cumberland* in occupation of Sarah Andrews with piggery and small yard.' A note beneath in pencil says £8 8s, which was probably the annual rent.

Joseph Andrews died in April 1817 at the age of 79, so he was born in 1738 and in 1765 would have been 27, so it is feasible that he was landlord from about 1760-1817. His wife was Elizabeth, but his daughter-in-law was Sarah, married to his son John who was born in 1761[192]. So it must have been Joseph Andrews' daughter in law who was at the *Duke of Cumberland* in 1826.

Like many other landlords of the time in 1814 Andrews, probably still Joseph, was charged by the Court Leet for selling deficient measures, an easy thing to do before standardised glasses. The Court Leet of 1868 again had an interest in the *Duke of Cumberland* when they charged W H Brakspear for making a cellar flap in front of the pub, which had been made since the last Court of 1836.

Landlords/ Tenants of the *Duke of Cumberland*

*1765-1817	Joseph Andrews (VR,R,WHB/R,AKL,CL)
1817-23*	John Andrews (SD)
*1826-42	Sarah Andrews (WHB/I,SD)
1842-50*	William Wright (R,SD)
1852	George Thompson (SD) carrier to London
1854	Thomas Painter (SD)
1863-7	Thomas Hamilton (SD)

190 Hughes 162 AD703

191 Street Directories

192 Henley Parish Registers

*1870-1	Walter Worrell (SSM)
1871*	Henry Seymour (HA)
1875-6	Henry Punter (HA)
Nov 1876-7	Edward Spratley (HA)
Jan 1877	John Punter (HA)
1877-9	John Hunt (RL,SD)
Apr 1879-Jun	James Belcher (HA)
Jun 1879-80	George Marlin Balchin (RL)
Apr 1880-91	Charles Bailey (RL,HA)
1892-1909	William Bailey (RL)
Sep 1909-11	Annie Dutfield Russell (RL)
Jul 1911-15	William Edward George (RL)
May 1915-20(-24)	Walter Bowers (RL,SD)

(Register of Licenses 1919-24 says that the name was changed from the *Duke of Cumberland* to *Ye Olde Bell* on 12 February 1920)

— Continued as the *Bell* or *Ye Olde Bell* —

45

The Duke's Head

41-3 Duke Street

The duke featured on the sign of the *Duke's Head* in Duke Street, was George Moncke (also spelt Monke/Monk) 1st Duke of Albemarle. He was born in 1608 and became a professional soldier. In 1639 he was a Lt Colonel fighting for Charles I. In 1643 he was arrested on a charge of favouring Parliament, was later released, and, fighting for the king, was defeated by General Fairfax. After three years captivity he entered the Parliamentary service and fought for Parliament in Ireland and Scotland. Cromwell's death and the succession of Richard Cromwell gave Moncke the opportunity of gaining support for a 'Free Parliament.' He went to London with recruits for that cause, and even while arranging a Convention Parliament, he began negotiations with Charles II. At the Restoration Moncke was acclaimed as one of the negotiators, and became a popular figure. Later he served Charles II at the Admiralty, as Governor of London during the plague, and with Prince Rupert helped to defeat the Dutch fleet in 1666. Moncke died in 1670[193].

Moncke seems to have no known ties with Henley, he may have been in the town during the Civil War but that is only speculation. Possibly his popularity at the time of the Restoration made him a suitable candidate for the naming of a beerhouse or pub. It may also have been a tactful move to show support for the restored monarchy. It is ironic that of the two pubs named after dukes in Henley, one the *Duke's Head* should celebrate the return of the Stuarts to the monarchy, while the other the *Duke of Cumberland* should apparently celebrate the final defeat of the Stuarts.

It is not known when the *Duke's Head* first appeared as a beerhouse, though it is a possibility that the houses on the east side of Duke Street were being built or rebuilt at the end of the 17th century. At what is now 33 Duke Street, now the Woolwich Building Society, a coin of Charles II was found within a wattle and daub panel in one of the upper rooms. The *Duke's Head* may well have started during Charles II's reign.

The *Duke's Head* building which remains in Duke Street, is a fine example of an

193 Illustrated Globe Encyclopaedia 1878

Fig 22 The Duke's Head, soon after closure 1988

Edwardian building, dated 1901(Fig 22), and is now shops and offices since its closure as a pub at the end of 1987. It was built back from the previous building line on purpose, with the idea that the street might be further widened in the future. The old *Duke's Head* which it replaced was in line with the other buildings on that side of the street.

The Greys Brewery Rent Ledger for 1885-96 shows that Greys Brewery leased the property from 'the late E Jeggins Esq, executors Thos J Bullen 69 Cheapside.' '*Duke's Head* and cottage adjoining' at a rent of £25 p.a. from 1885-94. The beerhouse and cottage were bought by Wheeler & Co in September 1894.

The Register of Licenses shows that the leaseholders had been Byles & Co otherwise Greys Brewery in 1877. The licenses show that Wheeler & Co of High Wycombe had probably taken over the lease in 1892, and then purchased the property in 1894. In 1892 the *Duke's Head* was noted as being one of the four licensed common lodging houses in the town[194].

Later the *Duke's Head* became the property of H & G Simonds of Reading, and then of Courage Barclay & Simonds. In 1970 it was owned by Courage Brewery Co Ltd. It remained only a beerhouse until 1957 when it was granted a full license.

In 1900 the old building of the *Duke's Head* was extremely dilapidated and unfit for use as a public house. When plans were submitted for rebuilding, there was a suggestion that the pub was not really needed and that it should be closed. This was at a time when many people, led by various teetotal groups, were campaigning for closure of pubs in general. It was pointed out that there were no legal grounds for closure as there had been no misconduct, and that the pub was 'old established.' In order to prove that it had been a beerhouse prior to 1869, Miss Tranter, of 14 Hop Gardens, then

194 Henley Advertiser 14 May 1892

aged 58, was brought before the magistrates, where she declared that her father had occupied the beerhouse 41 years ago[195]. The Register of Licenses says that 'Plans for additions and improvements to these premises' were produced to the Licensing Justices in Special Session on 3 December 1900 and were approved.

The Bridge Rent Book of 1886, no.126, says 'Messrs Holmes and Harper late P B Byles' (all of Greys Brewery) 'late J Jeggins for several tenements formerly occupied by Ambrose Dee Stokes lately occupied by Mrs Harriet Tranter as a beerhouse and now by D Hayes.' In about 1920 Messrs Wheeler & Co of High Wycombe were still the owners.

Henley Rentals 1795-1842 say 'Stokes late Ambrose Dee 4s.' 1779-93 Chas Stokes and in 1775 Mr Ambrose Dee in his own occupation. All the entries were for 4s, the same as in 1886, and the same as finally redeemed in 1967.

Both the names of Dee and Stokes are the names of publicans, an Ambrose Dee was at the *Windmill* 1774-5, and a Charles Stokes was at the *Blue Bell* 1779-85. It is difficult to know whether they were the same Dee and Stokes, one or other could have been father, son, uncle or cousin.

Landlords/ Tenants of the *Duke's Head*

1775	Ambrose Dee (R)
1779-93	Charles Stokes (R)
*1795-1842	Stokes (R)
1841-7	Jesse Prior (C,SD)
1851-4	Dorothy Prior (C,SD)
*1859-77	Thomas Tranter (SSM,SD,HS)
1877-81*	Harriet Tranter (RL,C)
*1884	William Fabry (HA)
Sep 1884-Dec	Benjamin Kinch (HA)
Dec 1884-8	Daniel Hayes (RL,BRB,HA,SD)
Jun 1888-9	Charles L Mays (RL,HA)
Nov 1889-92	William Snell (RL)
Aug 1892-8	Edward Charles Butler (RL)
Oct 1898-9	James Mardall (RL)
Aug 1899-Oct	John Smerdon (RL)
Oct 1899-1900	Joseph Lovejoy (RL)
Mar 1900-2	John Henry May (RL)
May 1902-Aug	William George Wassell (RL)
Aug 1902-3	John Roe (RL) during his tenancy in Feb 1903 the license was refused and only restored in April 1903 on appeal. Roe was convicted under the Licensing Act of 1874 and fined £2 10s with 10s costs.
Oct 1903-4	Daniel Robertson/Robinson (RL)
Jul 1904-Oct	Frederick Charles Fox (RL)
Oct 1904-5	George Trown (RL)
Oct 1905-6	Richard Thomas Whiting (RL)
Sep 1906-7	William James Salter (RL)
May 1907-8	Charles George Lilley Payne (RL)
Nov 1908-11	Alfred Seaman Clough (RL)
1911-12	Arthur Tucker (RL)

195 Henley Standard 21 Sep 1900

Feb 1912-Sep	John Hand (RL)
Sep 1912-28	Thomas William Pine (RL,HS,SD)
1928-9	Harry George Lewis (RL,HS)
Jul 1929-30	Mrs Caroline Bourner (RL,HS)
Jul 1930-3	Harry Jessop (RL,HS)
May 1933-6	Thomas Lake (RL,SD)
Oct 1936-7	Arthur Harry Gladwin (RL,HS)
Oct 1937-9	William Hunt (RL,HS,SD)
1939-49	William Francis Archer (RL)
May 1949-52	Walter Hansell Nelson (RL)
Oct 1952-6	William Charles Williams & Harold Edwin Binfield (RL)
Dec 1956-7	John Patrick McAnulty (RL)
Dec 1957-65	Alexander Donald Sutherland Brisbane (RL)
Mar 1965-6	Reginald Philip Robbins (RL)
Jan 1966-8	Victor Sydney Newman (RL)
Nov 1968-72	Henry Newman (RL)
May 1972-3	Malcolm Sidney John Cooper (RL)
Oct 1973-Dec	Barry Vincent Hughes (RL)
Dec 1973-5	Philip George Hargreaves (RL)
Dec 1975-8	Lawrence George McNally (RL)
Jun 1978-Dec	Judith Mary Clarke (RL)
Dec 1978-84	Alfred George Hedges (RL)
Jul 1984-Aug	Earl George Lyon Mackie (RL)
Aug 1984-7	Sheila Bridget Christiana Richardson & Geoffrey Hopkins (RL)
May 1987-8	Earl George Lyon Mackie (RL)

Last License 1987 closed beginning of 1988.

— Closed —

46

The Edwardian

Station Road

The *Edwardian* was a name given for a brief twelve years to the imposing Edwardian building in Station Road, known before 1981 as the *Imperial* (Fig 28). When new owners took over in the Spring of 1993, they changed the name back to the *Imperial*, as well as refurbishing the building.

Landlords/ Tenants of the *Edwardian*

Nov 1980-2	John Russell Oldman & Elizabeth Mary Clayton (RL)
Oct 1982-5	James Patrick O'Dwyer & Geraldine Ann O'Dwyer (RL)
Mar 1985-6	Andrew Richard Lock & Stephen Paul Cowdrill (RL)
May 1986-7	Timothy Rosamond & Stephen Paul Cowdrill (RL)
Oct 1987-90	Davinder Singh Brar (RL)
Dec 1990-3	Davinder Singh Brar & Philip John Harris (RL)

— Continued as the *Imperial* —

47

The Eight Bells

Middle Row, Market Place

The *Eight Bells* was situated in the Middle Row of the Market Place on the site of the present art gallery, which was the Fire Station from the 1890s.

The *Eight Bells*, or as a street directory of about 1793 says of it, 'Francis Farrow for the *Six Bells*', was previously the *Waggon and Horses*. It was one of the pubs which may have changed its name from the pictorial image of its sign. Possibly the sign showed a team of horses, which may have been six or eight, with a bell on the hames of their collars. What does slightly confuse things is that there appear to have been two pubs called the *Waggon and Horses,* probably next door to each other (see entry for the *Waggon and Horses*).

It seems that the two names, the *Eight Bells* and the *Waggon and Horses* were in use at the same time. Francis Farrow is given as at the *Waggon and Horses* in Brakspear's Rent Ledgers from 1791-1811. At the same time in 1793 in the Henley Rentals Mrs Farrow was at the *Eight Bells,* and Farrow was occupying the same property in 1800 and 1807. There is also the street directory mentioned already.

By 1817 in the Alehouse Keepers List Charles Harding was at the *Eight Bells* and there is no mention of any *Waggon and Horses.*

The Henley Rentals show that the *Eight Bells* was one of the pubs held or leased by Richard Hayward, which later became the property of W H Brakspear, by 1826 he held the freehold. In the Inventory of the Brewery in 1826 the *Eight Bells* was in occupation of Chas Harding. Stable and small paved yard. Land Tax 15s. Quit Rent 3s 4d. Bridge Rent 1s 8d. It was still owned by Brakspears though no longer a pub, when the Bridge Rent was commuted in 1967.

The *Eight Bells* was at the end of Short Hill, which was the name of the footway which led from the Market Place to West Hill in front of the present Fire Station. In a local Government Survey of Roads in 1864, there is the comment that 'the footway from *Eight Bells* to top of Short Hill needs attention'[196].

In 1892 Mrs Middleton, the widow of Thomas Middleton, had the license transferred to her name. Although the license was transferred there was at the same time discussion about closing the pub. As reported in the Henley Advertiser of 28 August 1892 a spokesman for the magistrates declared that 'Mr Brakspear had three other houses in the immediate vicinity of the house and there would be no loss as far as the brewer was concerned, and he hoped that they would deal liberally with the tenant. Mr Piniger on behalf of Mrs Middleton said that he could show that a great number of visitors stayed at the house.' In spite of this appeal the license was then refused and the pub was closed.

Landlords/ Tenants of the *Eight Bells*

1791-1811	Francis Farrow (WHB/R,R,SD)
1817-30	Charles Harding (AKL,CL,WHB/I,SD)
1841-4	Edward Blackall (C,SD)
1847	John Clinch (SD)
1850-4	Robert Wichelow (SD)
*1863-80	Daniel Lewis (SSM,RL,C,SD) furniture dealer
Dec 1880-2	Frederick Webb (RL)

196 Information from Mr John Crocker

Apr 1882*	George Drewett (RL)
*1887-92	Thomas Middleton (RL,HA)
1892	Mrs Kate Middleton (RL,HA)

— Closed —

48

The Elephant

Hart Street ?

The position of the *Elephant* is unknown. A reference to it is made in Burn's History of Henley where he quotes 'Taylor the water poet' who wrote in 1636 'Hendley or Henley is an excellent market town, with these tavernes - The *White Hart*, and the *Elephant,* also there is a taverne with a bush only, at the Bowling Green without the town in Oxford way. Robert Heyborne, Richard Pinder and John Stevens.'

The *White Hart* no longer open is still in existence in Hart Street, and the tavern with a bush only, was almost certainly the *White Horse* or *Old White Horse* in Northfield End, the last house before the Fairmile begins, which is still in business though in a rebuilt form.

It has recently been suggested after excavations there that 20 Market Place might have been a pub. It is possible that it might have been the *Elephant.* However a list of pubs no longer trading in the Henley Standard of 5 June 1931 gives the *Elephant* as being in Hart Street. If in Hart Street a strong possibility is the corner of Hart Street with Bell Street.

The ownership of the corner property in the 18th century, according to Henley Rentals was by Jeffs, then Toovey, then Barrett March from 1785-1814 at which time it was occupied by Hussey. Jeffs, Toovey and Barrett March were all brewers and pub owners, Barrett March being also a publican at the *Catharine Wheel,* while Hussey was also a publican.

In 1808 an Act of Parliament was passed in order to make improvements to Bell Street, Duke Street, and Hart Street. Geoffrey Tyack in an article on 'The Rebuilding of Henley on Thames, 1780-1914' [197] says 'the corners of the streets at the centre of the town were rounded to widen the roadway; the results of this improvement can be seen in the blocks at the corner of Hart Street, Bell Street, Duke Street and the Market Place with their low pitched roofs covered with Welsh slates, characteristic of the period.' In fact the only corner remaining of this improvement is the Hart Street/Bell Street corner. The others were all rebuilt again, though a picture of the *Blue Bell,* shortly before its demolition (Fig 14) shows the Hart Street/Duke Street corner in its post 1808 style.

If this rebuilding of the corners took place soon after 1808 it is probable that if the *Elephant* was the pub on the Hart Street/Duke Street corner, it closed at about that time. Certainly it is not listed in the Alehouse Keepers List of 1817. For later details of the corner see *Long's Stout House.*

Although the Rental entries suggest that the corner was a pub, no name is given to it. In 1636 when three pubs were mentioned it is certain that there were many more than three in Henley, maybe the three mentioned were those that caught the eye of Taylor, who perhaps was travelling towards Oxford. He might well have stopped at the *White Hart* or changed horses there, the *Elephant* if it was the corner house may well have stayed in his mind as there could have been some trouble

197 Tyack, Geoffrey 'The Rebuilding of Henley on Thames 1780-1914' Ox Local History Assoc. Vol 3 No2 Spring1989

rounding the corner. As Geoffrey Tyack quotes from the 1808 Act[198] the streets were 'extremely narrow and out of repair, and at Times so much so that as to render it difficult for Carriages to pass with Safety, and particularly in dark nights, as those Streets are not lighted.' That comment was in 1808, but it was probably even more awkward a corner in 1636, as in those days the centre of the crossing and part of Hart Street were filled with buildings, which were part of Middle Row (see position of the *Feathers* and Middle Row in account of the *Feathers* & Fig 23). The *White Horse* or the 'taverne with a bush only' would also have been noticeable, as apart from being one of the last pubs that side of Henley, the old building of the *White Horse* projected into the roadway.

Landlords/ Tenants of the *Elephant*

1636	Richard Pinder (JSB)
1721/2-49	John Toovey (R)
1769	Sanders (R)
1779-95	Mason (R)
1807	Mrs Swallow (R)
1814	Hussey (R)

— Closed —

49

The Exchequer and Star

North side of the Market Place

The *Exchequer and Star* seems to have been a brief name for a pub better known as the *Sun*. A Rental of 1742 says the *Exchequer and Star* late the *Sun,* now called the *Barley Mow.* Other Rentals, for instance that of 1745 says 'Mr Giles house late called the *Sun.*'

It appears to have been the *Sun* longer than any other name so what details there are listed under the *Sun*, Market Place.

— Continued as the*Barley Mow* —

50

The Feathers or the Plume of Feathers

Middle Row, Market Place

The original pub called the *Feathers* was in the centre of the road, in approximately the position of the main crossroads, it was alongside the old Guildhall, possibly the one built in 1487. The *Feathers* was on a line with an extension of Duke/Duck Street, in 18th century rentals it was sometimes included as part of Duck Street.

A sketch plan belonging to the Town Council shows the position of the *Plume of Feathers.* The plan was probably drawn up in the 1780s when the proposals for the demolition of Middle Row were made, not only does it include the *Feathers* but also the old Guildhall, and other buildings

198 Tyack, Geoffrey as note 197

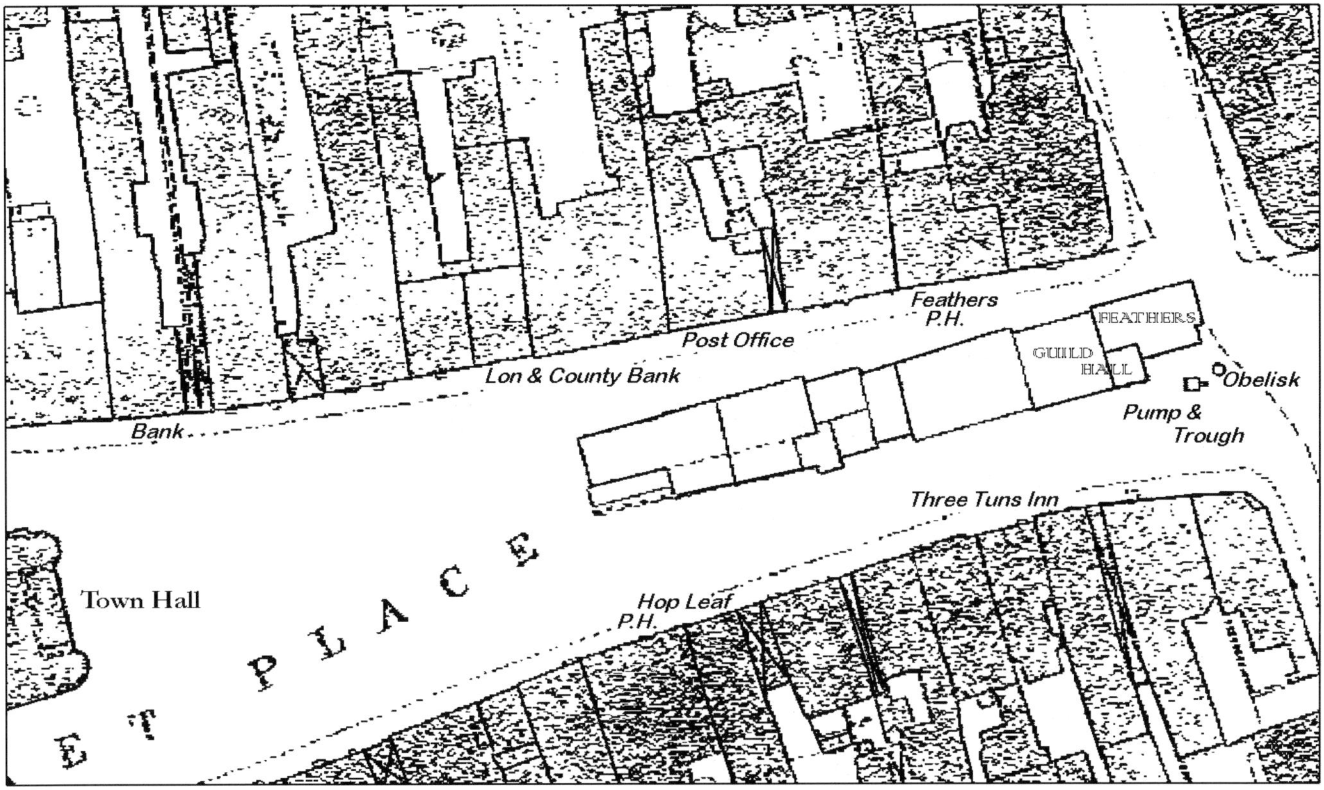

Fig 23 A plan of Middle Row of about the 1780s, superimposed on the O.S. map of 1879 (reduced) showing the position of the original Feathers, the broken lines at the corners of Bell Street and the line down Duke Street, may indicate the original line of those streets.
The O.S. map of 1879 shows the later Feathers, the Hop Leaf & the Three Tuns

which were soon after demolished (Fig 23). The position of the *Feathers* as shown in Fig 23 is not certain, but the result of various considerations. The plan of Middle Row had no measurements on it, except for a note saying '180ft X 24ft roughly'. It did however have the building line of the north side of the Market Place. By reducing the plan so that it was on the same scale as the O.S.map of 1879, it was possible to place it on that plan. The north side of Fisher Row as on the plan, is on the same line as the present day Market Place, excavations in 1984 on the site of where Carpenters shop now called Cargo is built, showed that the line of the shop frontages had remained the same since at least the 16th century. How far down it was placed was a further uncertainty, it is known that Duke Street was considerably widened in 1871, when the whole west side of the street was demolished. A photograph of the street before that date, shows a horse and cart taking up about half the street, from this it is possible to suggest that the width of the street may only have been about 15-17ft. If so the west side may have been on the line of the dashed line shown on Fig 23. All four corners of the crossroads had also been cut back in 1808[199], to allow more road space for turning, again it is not known by how much. However it may be seen that on the O.S.Map of 1879, there is a distinct change of direction on the east side of Bell Street, at a point just to the north of the third house. Again a dashed line shows where the street might originally have been, a line which would have allowed a space of about 15ft between the corner and the *Plume of Feathers,* if the pub was where I have placed it on the map.

It is possible that the *Feathers* was the tavern mentioned in the will of Thom Huberd in

199 Tyack, Geoffrey as in note 197

1359[200], when he left a tavern with solar and shop in the middle of the High Street to Ric Jory mayor. If it were, then the name the *Plume of Feathers* might have derived from the feathers in the badge of the Black Prince, known as the Prince of Wales' feathers. The Black Prince or Edward Prince of Wales held the Manor of Bensington from 1337, which included property in Henley. His fame and success at the battle of Poitiers in 1356 might well have led to the naming of a tavern after his badge.

However the use of the name the *Feathers* is only recorded in 1745 and 49 in the Henley Rentals, which say 'J Dee late Moor for the *Feathers* 4s.' In 1713/4 William Dee junr paid 2d for a tenement in his own occupation, in 1721/2 John Williams paid 2d for Rich Butler and others, in 1733/4 Mr Moor paid 2d for Rich Butler's house, and in 1737 John Dee paid 2d for late Butler's house. After the entries for 1745 and 49, which show a different amount paid, in 1758, 65 and 69 Rich Gibbons late Blagrave paid 2d again for Butler's house. The difference in payments for the years 45 and 49 is to be found in other properties at that time. These Rentals were all listed as for Duck Street, while after 1769 the *Feathers* was included as being 'under and adjoining the Guildhall.' The fact that the *Feathers* was only mentioned by name in 1745 may mean, that although it may have been a pub earlier than that date, it was only named the *Feathers* in 1745. The *Plume of Feathers* could then have also derived from a Prince of Wales, as Frederick, Prince of Wales, the son of George II, lived at Park Place for much of the time from about 1738 till his death in 1752.

Henley Rentals for the *Feathers* continue, in 1775 Mr Binfield paid, in occupation Jas Wilde late Paulin now Rob Arnold. In 1779 Mr Binfield in occupation late of Jas Wilde late Ron Arundell now Wm Finch. In 1785 Binfield occupied Wm Finch and in 1790 Binfield occupied Rob Pairman late Wm Finch.

The Assembly Book of 1790 says 'Committee appointed to find out expense of buying the *Feathers* public house, of taking down the Middle Row and Town Hall and of building new Town Hall on the site of the premises occupied by Cooper cabinet maker.' The Middle Row at that time was as shown in Fig 23, a little earlier it had extended below the crossroads to approximately outside the *Catharine Wheel*. Cooper's cabinet making premises were probably where the present Town Hall stands, in the area west of what is shown on the plan.

In 1790 the *Feathers* appears in Brakspear's Rent Ledgers and was let to Robt Pairman 1790-4, and from 1793-6 to Mrs Sarah Hussey. The slight overlap in the rentings may be explained by the Henley Rentals of 1793 and 95 where they say 'Hussey occupied by R Pairman.' This suggests that although it was let by Brakspears to Mrs Hussey, she sub-let to R Pairman who occupied the premises. After 1796 the Rent Ledgers say 'sold to the Corporation of Henley' and also that further rents from Mrs Hussey had been transferred to a private ledger, perhaps she moved to a private house owned by Brakspear.

On 30 June 1796[201] Rich Hayward and Rob Brakspear brewers and partners, Benjamin Moorhouse wine merchant, Rich Ovey trustee and Will Bradshaw granted to the Mayor etc a 'conveyance of a messuage known as the *Plume of Feathers* near the Market Cross fronting towards Hart Street and adjoining the site whereon the Butchers' shops and the Guildhall lately stood.'

This description makes it clear that the *Feathers* did face down the road towards the river, and could have been on a line with Duke Street. As late as 1886 the Bridge Rent Book entry no. 67 says 'For a house late the *Feathers* adjoining the old Town Hall now pulled down and the site thrown into the Market Place.'

Landlords/ Tenants of the *Feathers* or the *Plume of Feathers*

1713/4	William Dee (R)
1721/2	John Williams (R)

200 & 201 Hughes 635 AD89 & 162 AD703

1733/4	Mr Moor (R)
1737-49	John Dee (R)
pre 1758	Blagrave (R)
1758-69	Rich Gibbons (R)
pre 1775	Paulin and then Jas Wilde (R)
1775	Rob Arundell/ Arnold (R)
1779-85	William Finch (R)
*1790-6	Robt Pairman (WHB/R,R)

— Closed —

51
The Feathers or Plume of Feathers
4 Market Place

The new *Feathers* also sometimes called the *Plume of Feathers* was at 4 Market Place, (O.S. map 1879 Fig 23) now Spiers Travel Agency, but it was not the building that is there today, in spite of the feathers displayed on its fascia. The present building was built on the site as a dairy after the *Feathers* had closed by the instructions of the Licensing Magistrates on 30 December 1908. On 23 December compensation had been paid to Brakspears who owned it, of £1,307 16s[202].

Brakspears owned the *Feathers* from its commencement as a pub on the new site, their Rent Ledgers show the first entry for the *New Feathers* in 1795 when William Finch became the tenant and remained till 1803. At Michaelmas 1803 William Williams took over and was still there in 1823, in spite of being charged by the Court Leet in 1814 for selling deficient measures.

By 1826 the Brakspear Inventory says 'Freehold held by William Henry Brakspear Esq. The *Feathers* in occupation of William Harper. Quit Rent 3d.' A note in pencil beneath says '£16 16s 0d' which may have been the annual rent at a date after 1826. A further Quit Rent was charged in 1868 by the Court Leet for the encroachment and opening of a cellar flap in front of the *Feathers,* which had been made since the previous Court of 1836.

From the Census Returns of 1871 and 81 it is apparent that a grocery business was also established on the premises. In 1871 Charles Bye was innkeeper, victualler and grocer's assistant In 1881 Charles Bye was grocer and innkeeper.

Landlords/ Tenants of the *Feathers* or the*Plume of Feathers*

1795-1803	William Finch (WHB/R)
1803-1823*	William Williams (WHB/R,AKL,CL,PF,SD)
1826-30	William Harper (WHB/I,SD)
1842-4	Richard Burgess (SD)
1847	John/Thos Fitzpatrick (SD)
1850-4	John Thomas Marlow (C,SD) paperhanger
*1861-9	Robert Bye (wife Jane) (C,BReg,SD)
1869-70	Jane Bye (SSM)
1870-84	Charles Bye (SSM,RL,C,HA,SD)grocer's assistant/grocer

202 O.R.O. Registers of Licenses

Dec 1884*	Robert Williams (HA)
*1887-9	Mrs Agnes Williams (RL,SD)
Apr 1889-91	Charles Elliott (RL,HA)
Jun 1891-2	Jeremiah Coleman (RL,HA)
Apr 1892-Nov	Brayfield Williams (RL)
Nov 1892-3	Henry Russell (RL)
1893-4	Sidney Druce Jackson (RL)
Sep 1894-1904	Alfred Holbrow (RL)
May 1904-7	Ernest William Levitt (RL)
Mar 1907—Nov	Thomas Joseph Smith (RL)
Nov 1907-Dec 1908	George William Harper (RL)

— Closed —

52

The Fishermans Cottage

14-16 Market Place

In the Reading Mercury & Oxford Gazette of October 1855 two freehold beerhouses in the Market Place were advertised for sale, known by the names of the *Fishermans Cottage* and the *Waggon and Horses*. The *Fishermans Cottage* contained 8 rooms, a cellar, 2 granaries, stabling for 5 horses, and yard. The *Waggon and Horses* also contained 8 rooms, 2 cellars, stabling for 12 horses with granaries over, cottage and yard. The whole frontage was 33ft with a depth of 131ft, and the situation would be good for either business or as a private residence. Land Tax £1 6s 6d. Bridge Rent 10s.

According to the Bridge Rent Book of 1886 only two properties in the Market Place paid a rental of 10s, one of which later became the Westminster Bank, the other no.61 in the Bridge Book having an entry as follows :- 'Mr William Plumbe formerly George Bennett and Mr Langton of Maidenhead brewer for premises late two beerhouses now pulled down and a shop and warehouse built thereon. 10s.' This rental covers the properties once 14 and 16 Market Place, now part of Carpenters shop or Cargo as it is now called, which also includes what was once 12 Market Place.

On the O.S. map of 1879 the measurements of the frontage of the two houses nos.14 and 16 combined is 33ft while the depth of land is 131ft. This seems to help prove that the two beerhouses were side by side, though which was which is hard to say. A description of the excavation of the site in 1984 is to be found in the account of the *Sheers,* which was a pub occupying the site of both beerhouses in the 18th century. This excavation revealed a brick built cellar with a barrel vault, probably of the 19th century at the front of 16. Under 14 there was a more or less continuous cellar stretching well back under what would once have been yard or garden. This large cellar had been in use up until 1984, and had been much altered and rebuilt, but could possibly have been two cellars in 1855. So it may be that the *Fishermans Cottage* was at 16, since there was no sign of a second cellar behind the brick cellar at the front of that site.

Billings Street Directory of 1854 under Beer Retailers says William Herbert, *Fishermans Cottage,* Market Place. The Post Office Directory of the same date just has William Herbert, Beer Retailer.

Landlords/ Tenants of the *Fishermans Cottage*

*1854 William Herbert (SD)

— Closed —

53

The Fox

Northfield End

The Bensington Manorial Records of 1815 say 'The *Sun* once called the *Fox*.' From this one may assume that the *Sun* at 44 Northfield End, recently closed in 1992, was once called the *Fox*, this may mean that it was called that in the 18th century.

See entry for the *Sun,* Northfield End.

— Continued as the *Sun* —

54

The Gas Tap

69 Greys Road

The house in Greys Road which was once the *Gas Tap*, was used for many years by Jonathan Jerome and his brother as the business premises for their firm of painters and glaziers. Mr John Crocker can remember the business being run by the brothers Jerome, it is still possible to make out traces of their lettered signs on panels on either side of the doorway (Fig 24).

The Gas Works on the opposite side of Greys Road, below the junction with Deanfield Avenue, was started in 1834, so it is perhaps safe to assume that a beerhouse named the *Gas Tap* came into being soon after, while a gas tap was still a novelty. There is also a slight play on words, as a 'Tap' in brewery circles was the term used for a pub near to and serving a brewery, a 'Brewery Tap.'

The earliest date of a publican known to be at the *Gas Tap* is in a street directory of 1842, when John Ayris is listed as at the *Gas Tap*, Greys Lane. In 1847 Abraham Richards is listed as a beer retailer in Greys Lane, and in the Census of 1851 as at the *Gas Tap*, aged 41, a coachsmith with his wife Sarah also aged 41.

In 1871 Jonathan Jerome was summoned by the Inspector of Weights and Measures[203] for having incorrect measure cups for the sale of beer. He was fined 5s and 10s costs. In spite of this he continued as landlord till the *Gas Tap* closed in 1897. It is probable that the Jonathan Jerome who continued the painting and glazing business well into this century, may have been the son of the Jerome who was a publican at the *Gas Tap* from at least 1863.

It was at the end of 1863 that a sales notice in the Reading Mercury & Oxford Gazette on December 26 announced that four freehold tenements were for sale on the south side of Greys Hill including the *Gas Tap* beerhouse and one cottage which was let on lease to T F Byles Esq at an

203 Henley Advertiser 5 Aug 1871

Fig 24 The House on the left was once the Gas Tap Photo 1989

annual rent of £12 and that the two adjoining cottages were let at rents of 2s 6d per week.

Greys Brewery Rent Ledger of 1885-96 shows that the *Gas Tap* was leased by the brewery from T Hamilton of Gravel Hill, from 1885-95 at a rent of £12. It was purchased by Greys Brewery in June 1895. Greys Brewery and all its pubs were bought by Brakspears in 1896, which was the last year that the *Gas Tap* was licensed. In the Register of Licenses it says 'discontinued in 1897.' It is likely that the lease of the property was sold by Brakspears to the Jeromes in 1897.

Landlords/ Tenants of the *Gas Tap*

1842	John Ayris (SD)
1847-51	Abraham Richards (C,SD)
*1863-97	Jonathan Jerome (RL,GB/R,C,SD)

— Closed —

55

The George

North west corner of Duke Street

The corner of Duke Street and the Market Place before 1870 projected further towards Hart Street, in fact the whole of Duke Street was much narrower, and in 1870 the whole west side of the street was demolished and rebuilt further back. So at any time before 1870 when mention is made of the north west corner of Duke Street, it means a building partly on the site of the present corner and partly on what is now roadway (Fig 23).

The *George* on this corner seems to have briefly become the *Crowne,* there are three documents which seem to show this.

On 1 October 1625 Rich Powle to Edm Symeon lease for 21 years of a corner house in Henley on the south side of the High Street called the *George*[204].

On 5 October 1632 Edmond Symeon of Purton in the County of Oxford, and John Hampden in the County of Buckingham and Eliz his wife, to John Morgan of Henley on Thames, grant of a messuage of a corner house on the south side of the High Street called the *Crowne.*

On 1 October 1638 John Morgan and others to Ric Allen and another, assignment of the remainder of a 99 years lease of a messuage called the *George* in the High Street.

The temporary change to the *Crowne* may have been due to fresh hopes of the monarchy with the accession of Charles I in 1625. If so disillusion must have set in during the 1630s, with the growing disagreements between the king and parliament, it was probably safer to return to the name of the *George*, which at that time would have been the saint rather than a king. John Hampden in the deed of 1632 was probably holding a mortgage on the property.

Two deeds seem to show that the *George* continued later in the 17th century. On 21 December 1663 Humphrey Newberry of Henley maultster granted to John Monke of Okingham (Wokingham) in the County of Berkshire, draper, a lease for seven years of a messuage known as the *George* 'nere unto the Crosse of the Town.'

On 23 January 1673/4 the Warden of the town etc granted to Will Thomas a lease for seven years of a messuage called the *George* 'near the Crosse.'

Humphrey Newberry died in August 1665 a victim of the plague[205], and left his property to charities in the town. Some property was left to found almshouses, see the entry for the *Blue Bell*, while the corner site of the *George* was left to a schools charity, and became the property eventually of the United Schools Charity. Hence the Warden , Bridgemen and Aldermen granting the lease in 1673/4.

A deed of 6 September 1726 says the Mayor etc granted to John Blackman of Henley brewer a lease for eleven years of a messuage at the corner of Duck Street west of the *Blue Bell.* The *Blue Bell* was on the north east corner of Duck/Duke Street.

There is an entry in 1732 in the Henley rentals of payment for the sign of the *George*, but that seems to be the last reference to it by name as a pub, but a brewhouse behind or on part of the property continued in use till the end of the 18th century (B2).

Henley Rentals in the 18th century give in 1713 Mr Blackman and Mr Wellbanks for a house in their occupation, from 1721-1727 J Lamborne, in 1737 Rich Miles for Blackman's late Lamborne, and in 1745 Mr Blackman for the tenement Miles lives in. The 1749 entry is the same as in 1745 except it says Mr Blackman's house he and Miles live in. In 1758 there is Ed May for part of Blackman's house, 1765 late Lamden now Lilly, 1769 Mr Blackman late Lamden now Lilly, in 1775 Mrs Blackman late Francis Lilly now M Lilly, 1779 late Blackman in occupation Peckover since Goff now Allen, 1785 Mrs Blackman in occupation Ann Hunt now Richards, 1790 Blackman occupied Richards, 1793 Blackman occupied Hussey, the same in 1795 and finally in 1800 Blackman former occupied Lilly since Hussey now empty.

By 1800 the brewhouse had ceased to exist, in 1798 the materials with which it had been constructed were being offered for sale, it had probably stopped trading in about 1793, or soon after, when an attempt was made to sell it. Blackman, Lilly and Hussey were all probably brewers, Blackman certainly, while Lilly/Lilley appears as surety for licenses in 1770-1, and was therefore

204 Hughes - various deeds- 1625/ 323 AD461, 1632/ 2 AD474, 1638/ 1003 AD477, 1663/ 159 AD302, 1673/ 963 AD525, 1726/ 141 AD566, 1748/ 37 AD603 & 6 AD604, 1776/ 8 AD658

205 Henley Parish Church Registers, Burials 1653-1703

probably a brewer, and Hussey was connected with several pubs, though it is not clear whether he was mainly a brewer or a publican. It seems likely however that although the brewhouse lasted till just before1798, the part used as a pub had already changed to a shop as early as 1748. A deed of 10 January 1748 says the Mayor etc granted to John Hare cheesemonger a lease for eleven years of a messuage at Duck Street corner.

On 9 August 1776 the Mayor etc granted to Leicester Nichols of Henley tinman a lease for eleven years of a messuage at the corner of the High Street and the road to Reading. Both these last two deeds would seem to be for this corner as the other was occupied by the *Blue Bell.*

The Bridge Rent Book of 1886 nos. 119 & 119a say 'The Executors of John E Brown late W F Portello for part of the site of the premises formerly a Brewhouse since occupied by Thos Maynard as a slaughter house and yard, then by Robt Gill, since by Henry Stubbs, afterwards pulled down for street improvements and lotted out for building - new house erected. 119a Mr F Bartlett late W F Portello for the remaining of the above premises - new house now erected.'

The Thomas Maynard mentioned in the Bridge Book was a butcher, the Henley rentals of 1807 say 'Mrs Blackman's house and premises formerly occupied by Mr Lilly now Mr Maynard.' Robert Gill was also a butcher but Henry Stubbs was a grocer according to street directories of 1842-77.

The *George* seems to have closed in the late 1730s, there is no evidence for its continuing later. The brewhouse probably continued till 1793/5.

Landlords/ Tenants of the *George*

*1625	Rich Powle (HL)
1625-32	Edmond Symeon (the *Crowne*) (HL)
1632-38	John Morgan (HL)
1638*	Ric Allen (HL)
*1663	John Monke (HL)
*1673/4	Will Thomas
1713	Mr Wellbanks (R)
1721-7	J Lamborne/Lamden (R)
1737	Rich Miles (R)

— Closed —

56

The George

22 Hart Street

This is a second pub called the *George* which must have been trading at the same time, or possibly a little earlier than the *George* on the corner of Duke Street. The first known reference to this *George* is in a deed of 1629 where the *George* is referred to in the past tense.

The deed of 20 June 1629 is recorded in an Indenture of 1696 and quoted as a past transaction[206]. It was a conveyance from William Walsh of Abborley in the county of Worcester gentleman to John Wells of Grimsby gentleman and his wife Elizabeth of a 'Messuage heretofore

206 O.R.O. Misc Berks (1896) VI/ iii/ 1, (1730) VI/ iii/ 2, (1798) VI/ iii/ 6, (1800) VI/ iii/ 11.

known by the name of the *George*' over and against a messuage called the *Hart* then in tenure of Mistress Wells widow.

Another deed also quoted in 1696 is an Indenture of 1676 between Anne Burlton of the county of Worcester widow, only daughter of John Wells, and Thomas Burlton son of Anne Burlton.

In 1688 (28th year of Charles II) Anne Burlton widow of Lamborne, Worcester, and Thomas Burlton son of Anne, sold to Samuel Turner all that 'messuage called or known by the sign of the *George,* but now divided into several tenements now or late in the tenure of Symon Messenger, Andrew Lovejoye, and John Russell in the High Street over and against a messuage or tenement called or known by the name of the *Hart Inn,*' also land in Southfields.

Samuel Turner left the property by will to William Westbrook who sold to Adam Springall, who sold to William Cock the younger, bargemaster, who died intestate in 1698. Mrs Cock her sons and daughters sold to John Vickers in 1730. In this last document it says 'Heretofore the *George*' but now made into several tenements.

The will of John Vickers baker in 1753, proved in 1762, left the property to his wife Jane, and after her death to his youngest daughter Elizabeth Vickers and to her heirs etc., with the charge that 9d a week should go to his other daughter Martha Fruin, to be paid into her hands weekly on Saturday nights separate and apart from her husband. Evidently he had no love or trust of her husband.

The next transaction was a lease by Peter Pickman maltster of Henley in 1787 to Thomas Smith baker of Henley, who was already in occupation. The leasehold was sold for £180 to Thomas Smith baker by Peter Pickman in 1798, when it says that Peter Pickman survived Elizabeth his late wife, who had been the daughter of John Vicars heretofore of Henley baker. This document also says 'messuage or tenement heretofore known by the sign of the *George* afterwards divided into three tenements and occupied by Simon Messenger, Andrew Lovejoy and John Russell but since converted into one messuage.'

In 1800 a Pew Faculty for the Parish Church awarded to Thomas Smith describes him as the owner and occupier of a house on the south side of Hart Street in Henley, having a house called the *Union* on the west and a house belonging to the Corporation of Henley now in the occupation of Mrs Mary Bennett on the east.

This last document places the position of the *George* most definitely as at 22 Hart Street now the Rope Walk café (Fig 52). The *Union* was at 20 Hart Street, and 24 Hart Street was until fairly recently John Lovering the butcher, the premises having been a butcher's shop since at least the 18th century.

Though it is possible to place the *George* with certainty, it is not possible to know who were the landlords, or for how long it had traded. It may be that at one time the plot of land on which it stood was larger, perhaps including 20 Hart Street. If one studies a large scale map such as that of 1879, it will be seen that most likely the original burgage plot was the width of both 22 and 20 Hart street. Maybe 20 Hart Street was one of the three houses when the property was split in three, and 22 was then divided in two. When it was the *George* before 1629 it probably occupied the whole burgage plot.

— Closed —

57

The Globe

Market Place

The only reference to this beerhouse, so far found, is in the Reading Mercury & Oxford Gazette of 24 March 1838, when there was a report of the Petty Sessions then recently held. William Knight the keeper of the *Globe* beershop in the Market Place, Henley, was fined £5 and 15s costs for keeping a disorderly house.

> 'It was clearly proved that the house was the rendezvous for thieves, prostitutes and other abandoned characters, and that scenes of drunkenness, tumult and vice of the very lowest description were of constant occurrence. The Magistrates performed their duty to the public and the laws, by punishing to the utmost of their powers, the keeper of this den of infamy, and we trust they will cause the police to keep a strict eye on the house in the future.'

It is surprising that the Magistrates were unable or did not choose to close the house, since the licensing laws of 1830-36 gave strict instructions for the regulating of beerhouses (pp12-13), and for a beerhouse license to be forfeited after a conviction. Perhaps however the *Globe* was not a licensed beerhouse, but was operating independently, as seems to have been possible after about 1830, which would mean that there was no license to withdraw.

Where the *Globe* was in the Market Place is unknown, though probably in one of the smaller houses in the upper part of the market. It is unlikely that the *Globe* was in the lower market, since in 1838 the occupants and occupations of those living there are fairly well established. This rules out the north side of the market from Bell Street to the *Kings Arms,* and the south side from Duke Street to where Stuart Turners, once the *Broad Gates,* and its neighbour now a restaurant once the *Cannon* beerhouse are situated. The *Globe* must have been in the upper Market Place.

Landlords/ Tenants of the *Globe*

1838	William Knight (RM)

— Closed —

58

The Greyhound

Middle Row, Market Place

The *Greyhound* was behind the old Town Hall of 1796-1898. There is a painting by Miss Lucy Cooper in the Mayor's Parlour in the present town hall, which is of 'The Old Town Hall from Gravel Hill 1898', which shows the *Greyhound* as being the second house in the row at the back of the town hall. The first house with a portico, was used as extra offices for the Town Hall and was at one time the police station (Fig 17).

Both these houses, and about two others including the old *Victoria,* were demolished in 1898 to make space for the present Town Hall, much larger than the old one, and also for a road to go behind the hall to link up with Kings Road, built at much the same time.

In the Inventory of the Brewery in 1826 the *Greyhound* was owned freehold by Joseph Benwell and W H Brakspear 'Public house the *Greyhound* in occupation of Thomas Jeffries. Land Tax 14s. Quit Rent 1s 8d. and an acre of land in Greys Meadow.'

The house next to the Town Hall with the portico seems in Henley Rentals to be linked with entries for the *Greyhound*; but in the Bridge Rent Book of 1886 no.66 the entry seems only concerned with the house behind the Town Hall. The entry is as follows :-

'Messrs Brakspear and Sons late Alfred Ive formerly C Norton for house and premises formerly occupied by the Corporation of Henley as the Police Station lately occupied by William Harding Relieving Officer and now converted into two houses.' There is no mention of the *Greyhound.*

Going back in time, at first the Henley Rentals also mention only one property, but further back there were obviously two. In 1842 they name Norton occupied by Ive, and in 1836 Norton occupied by Ellison/Ellson, and both Ive and Ellison are named in street directories as landlords of the *Greyhound.* Rentals of 1807 say Thom Neville late Newell house and premises occupied by Francis Hobbs and J Dowling, and also in 1795 and 93 occupied by Hobbs and Dowling. The street directory of about 1793 says Richard Dowling at the *Greyhound.*

So perhaps the Rentals were for two properties, the *Greyhound* and the house next to the Town Hall. In 1790 the rentals say Thomas Hobbs late Rackstraw, and back in 1785 and 79 the entry is for William Rackstraw and there is mention of a cornchandlers establishment, which was probably the house behind the Town Hall.

In 1769 Widow Rackstraw paid 1s 8d for the *Greyhound*, and in 1765 and 58, 1s 8d for garden and encroachment late Norcutt. At this time and earlier when Rich Norcutt was paying there seems to have been no house but just a garden on the site later to be the *Greyhound.*

The explanation may be that the *Greyhound* was built between 1765 and 69 in the garden of the house immediately behind the Town Hall, which may be why the Rentals cover both properties, the house remaining the more important of the two.

In February 1809 the *Greyhound* became untenanted, at least it was in that month that an advertisement appeared in the Reading Mercury & Oxford Gazette saying that the remainder of a lease for some 20-30 years of the *Greyhound* in the Market Place was to be sold. That it was now in full trade and which from its excellent situation cannot fail to command a capital business, both in the beer and spirit line. This or soon after was probably when J or Richard Dowling left the pub.

In August 1898 no renewal of license was applied for, and the house was sold by Brakspears for the erection of the present Town Hall.

Landlords/ Tenants of the *Greyhound*

1769	Widow Rackstraw (R)
1775-85	William Rackstraw (R)
1793-1809	J / Richard Dowling (R,CL,SD)
1814-6	Lewington (CL)
1817	Thomas Livingstone (AKL)
1822	James Alleway (CL)
1823	Jas Spicer (SD)
1826	Thomas Jeffries (WHB/I)
1830-6	Thomas Ellison/Ellson (R,SD)
1841	William Sims (C)

1842-63 Alfred Ive (SD) (Although Alfred Ive was the main tenant and in street directories is given at the *Greyhound*, the Census Returns suggest that he sub-let)

1851	Edmund John Giles (C) assistant victualler
1861	Ada Maria Giles (C) housekeeper
1870-1	Ann Ive for A Ive & Co (SSM)
	(Census 1871 'No person slept in the house on the night of 2 April 1871')
1881	Hannah Brockland (C) barmaid in charge
*1877-82	Ann & Alfred Ive (RL)
1882-3*	Robert Anthony Crouch (RL,SD)
*1887-92	Alfred Vokins (RL,SD)
Jul 1892-8	Mary Ann Vokins (RL,SD)

— Closed —

59

The Half Way House

5 or 9 Bell Street

The *Half Way House* was on the west side of Bell Street, immediately to the north of the entrance to Goff's Yard, the remains of which is the passageway running between Boots and Woolworths. The alternative numbering is due to the change in numbers effected in about 1900.

Fig 25 The Half Way House, Bell Street. On the site of what is now Woolworths

The *Half Way House* features in a photo of about 1880 (Fig 25), in which it can be seen that there were three small shops in the area of Woolworths, with another small shop before what is now Clintons the card shop. At the time of the photo, it can be seen that the *Half Way House* had a shop front, and besides being a pub was also a greengrocery and had rabbits hanging outside for sale.

The premises from 1885-95 were leased by Greys Brewery from George Paulin[207] of 40 New Street[208] at a rent of £25 p.a. On George Paulin's death in 1895 the *Half Way House* was sold by auction together with other property. The catalogue [209]

207 Greys Brewery Rent Ledger 1885-96 O.R.O. Brakspear IV/ ii/ 1

208 This 40 would have been the original New St numbering, possibly Anne Boleyn or Tudor Cottages

209 Auction Catalogue of Sale by Trustees of George Paulin deceased 6 Feb 1896 O.R.O.

describes it thus —

> 'All that valuable freehold Brick built and tiled Beerhouse known as the *Half Way House*, situate in a central position in Bell Street to which it has a frontage of 12ft 6ins. Good bar, tap room, kitchen, three bedrooms, and W.C., with separate entrance from Goff's Yard. Property held by Messrs Holmes and Steward together with the adjoining shop premises on a yearly tenancy under the covenants of an expired lease at rent of £15 p.a. The Tenancy determining by notice (which has been given) at Christmas 1896. Property bounded by property of the vendors, the Misses Monk, and Mr Wm Simpkin, and is sold subject to an easement appertaining to the adjoining property in the occupation of Mr Hawkins consisting of a flue from his kitchen which passes into the chimney of these premises. Land tax 9s 7d.'

The Magistrates Special Sessions Minute Book has John Smith beerhouse keeper of the *Half Way House* in 1870 and 71. The Census Return of 1871 mentions John Smith aged 30 as a brewer's labourer and beerseller, living with his wife and niece. In 1872[210] John Smith was still there, a Caroline Bailey was summoned for being unlawfully drunk and quarrelsome in a beerhouse run by John Smith in Bell Street.

The *Half Way House* was bought by William Simpkin in the sale of February 1896, who for part of the year of 1896 leased it to Greys Brewery, but with the closure of Greys Brewery after it was bought by Brakspears, the *Half Way House* closed in September 1896.

Landlords/ Tenants of the *Half Way House*

1869-76	John Smith (SSM,C,HA,SD)
*1877-88	William Bunce (RL,C,SD)
Apr 1888-95	Arthur George Carter (RL)
1896	Thomas Carter

— Closed —

60

The Hand in Hand

20 Hart Street

In 1774 the *Hand in Hand* is mentioned as part of the stock in trade of the partnership of James Brooks and Richard Hayward[211]. A street directory of about 1793 gives William Finch as the victualler, however in Brakspear's Rent Ledgers in the 1790s it is referred to as the *Union*, which is the name by which it continued to be known. Whether the pub started as the *Hand in Hand* or as the *Union* is uncertain. It is most likely that it started as the *Union* perhaps soon after 1707 when England and Scotland were united. The name of the *Hand in Hand* may have been a colloquial name derived from perhaps a sign of clasped hands.

Landlord/ Tenant of the *Hand in Hand*

1793	William Finch (WHB/R)

— Continued as the *Union* —

210 Henley Advertiser 14 Sep 1872

211 Sheppard, Francis 'Brakspear's Brewery 1779-1979

61

The Holie Bush

near the crossroads

J S Burn in his book 'The History of Henley on Thames' published in 1861 says that the *Holie Bush* was 'situated near the Guildhall,' which was near the crossroads in Middle Row (Fig 23). He continues, in 1589 it was occupied by Richard Dunt, who by his will gave to Edmund Simeon all the wainscot about the hall of the messuage called the *Holie Bush*, two tables with their frames, six joined stools, two joined chairs, one joined cupboard, and all the glass in the windows, one silver goblet, one silver bowl etc.

Richard Dunt in his will of 20 December 1589 also left his property, later known as Floyd's Tenements in New Street, to provide money for the charity known as Dunt's Charity. The only remaining house of these tenements, was later to be known as the *Red Cross,* now closed (see entry for the *Red Cross*). It may be that the *Red Cross* was already trading as a pub in 1589 and that Dunt was a brewer or maltster, owning as it would seem at least two pubs.

— Closed —

62

The Hop Leaf

15 Market Place

The *Hop Leaf* was on the same site as, and later became the *Argyll.* A photo of about 1880 (Fig 26) shows it clearly in that position, and also shows that at that time it was owned by Simonds Brewery, whose trade mark of a hop leaf is on the sign. The house in this photo with its carriage entrance on the east side, with three floors, the top two having a pair of windows, is the house rebuilt by Richard Cox in 1845-6, a 'newly erected house fitted up expressly for the trade.' That was the beer trade, and the house was then the *North Star.*

The *Hop Leaf* was trading before 1872 as the *Cannon Inn* and Brewery. The Magistrates Special Sessions Minute Book for 1870 and 71 lists the *Cannon Inn*. In 1870 Edmund Tanner was at the *Cannon Inn*, and James Sharp took over in July 1871, but in February 1872 it says *'Hop Leaf/* late the *Cannon,* Richard Hussey Kimber'. The Henley Advertiser noted in February 1872 that Richard Hissey Kimber had taken over the *Hop Leaf.* So the pub had become the *Hop Leaf* at the beginning of 1872, probably at the same time as it was purchased by Simonds Brewery. It is also likely that the Cannon Brewery was closed by Simonds, who had their own brewery in Reading.

The lists in 1870 and 71 in the Special Sessions Minutes and the later entries in the Registers of Licenses give the pub names in the same order each year, first there is the list of inns with full Alehouse and Victuallers Licenses, and then the list of beerhouses. The *Cannon Inn*, followed by the *Hop Leaf*, and then the *Argyll*, are all in the same position in the lists, displacing each other, and all have full licenses.

On the 10 January 1885 in the Henley Advertiser a holdover of licenses was mentioned as being granted to Thomas Cleaver and a note was made 'we understand that the name of this house

Fig 26 The Hop Leaf is the third building from the right, with Simmonds sign of a hop leaf on the front. The Crown is the sixth house and next door to it was the Crown & Thistle
Photo c.1880 (see also Figs 6 & 23)

is to be changed to Bodega.' Unfortunately the Register of Licenses for the Borough from 1882-6 is missing. No further mention of the *Bodega* was made in the Henley Advertiser, but in the licenses for 1887 and also in a street directory of 1887, a William Cleaver was given as licensee of the *Argyll.*

Whether Thomas Cleaver and William Cleaver were the same person, is not certain, it could have been an error of the paper. Or they may have been father and son, uncle and nephew or two brothers. The change of name to the *Argyll* probably took place in 1885, and that may indicate the time at which Simonds sold the property to the Ive Brothers, who were listed as owners in the 1887 Register of Licenses. Quite why the name of the *Argyll* was chosen is not known, as the hop leaf was the emblem of Simonds it is obvious that a change of name was needed, but why the *Argyll* ?

Landlords/ Tenants of the *Hop Leaf*

1872-3	Richard Hussey/Hissey Kimber (SSM,HA)
Apr 1873-Jun	George Briginshaw (HA)
Jun 1873-4	Frank Joshua Hudson (HA)
Feb 1874-6	William Barnes (HA)
Nov 1876-Dec	George Thomas Sore (HA)
Dec 1876-8	Mary Ann North (RL,HA,SD) widow
1878-9	Alfred Palmer (RL)
1879-81	Harry Wicks (RL)
1881-5	Daniel Hayes (RL,HA,SD)
1885-	Thomas/William Cleaver (HA)

— Continued as the *Argyll* —

63

The Hope

Hope Cottage, Northfield End

Although the *Hope* is mentioned in Bensington Manorial records in 1815, the Victuallers Recognizances before 1821 only give five pubs for Northfield End, all of which can be identified by the publicans who held them. The five do not include the *Hope*. In 1821 for the first time six pubs are listed in Northfield End, and Frederick Barlow is named as a licensee. The next year all doubt is removed as Frederic Barlow is named as at the *Hope*, while the other five pubs are also named with their respective landlords. It seems that perhaps the *Hope* began trading without a license in about 1815, but was only formerly recognised in 1821.

The Victuallers Recognizances say that Barlow was sponsored by Henry Byles, who was at Greys Brewery. Greys Brewery seems to have owned the *Hope*, as it does not appear in the Greys Brewery Rent Ledger of 1885-96 which dealt with rented property. In the Register of 1892 the owners are given as Holmes and Steward, who were managers of Greys Brewery. After Greys Brewery and its pubs were sold to Brakspears in 1896, the *Hope* was closed and the license discontinued in 1897.

Landlords/ Tenants of the *Hope*

c1815-23*	Frederick/Frederic Barlow (VR,SD)
1830-44	William Matthews (C,SD)
1847	William/John Ibbs (SD)
1850	John Lawrence (SD)
1851-4	John Lovejoy (C,SD)
1861-77	John Dutfield (C,SD) bricklayer
1881	George Arlett (C)
*1882	Edward Spratley (RL)
Nov 1882-5	William Jacobs (RL)
Nov 1885-6	Henry Russell (RL,HA)
Mar 1886-Aug	Amos Richard Peachey (RL,HA) (May 86 accused of assaulting his wife)
Aug 1886-Nov	Charles Martin Holcombe (RL,HA)
Nov 1886-7	Edwin Sherratt (RL)
Jun 1887-Oct	Charles Beckett (RL)
Oct 1887-Nov	W Jelley (RL)
Nov 1887-Dec	George Cresswell (RL)
Dec 1887-9	Thomas Lay (RL,HA)
Jan 1889-Nov	William James Ashworth (RL,HA)
Nov 1889-90	William Stiles Lindforth (RL,HA)
Nov 1890-3	Jesse Fridlington (RL)
Jun 1893-6	Thomas Lay (RL)

— Closed —

64

The Horse and Groom

40 New Street

It is difficult to know when the *Horse and Groom* (Fig 27) began trading, perhaps in the early half of the 19th century, if before that it would have more likely have had an Alehouse and Victuallers License and not have been a beerhouse. The building is certainly older than the 19th century. In the Reading Mercury & Oxford Gazette of June 1855 an old established beerhouse was to let, applications to be made to Harris & Hewett brewers of Reading. Since the *Horse and Groom* seems to be the only pub in Henley owned or connected to Harris & Hewett, it is probable that it was the old established beerhouse to let in 1855.

The first mention of the *Horse and Groom* by name is in the Court Leet Book on 26 October 1868 when Messrs Harris & Co were charged that they owed the Lord of the Manor a Quit Rent of 6d p.a. for making an encroachment, since the last Court of 1836, in front of the *Horse and Groom* beerhouse in New Street opposite St Marys Hall by the opening of a cellar flap in the street there.

Fig 27 Inn sign of the Horse & Groom, the flat front of the building may be the building work of 1870 Photo 1998

In the Magistrates Special Sessions Minute Book of 1870 and 71, George Ayres was given as the licensee of the *Horse and Groom* beerhouse. In the Census Returns of 1871 George Ayres carpenter and beerhouse keeper was there with wife and four lodgers, one of whom had a wife and son. In the Census of 1861 George Ayres was already there at the beerhouse, he most likely took over in 1855.

The Census of 1851, which seems to have been taken in a consistent manner, seems to place James Dobson butcher aged 46 at the house later known as the *Horse and Groom*, with wife, son James aged 11, uncle aged 71, cousin aged 43, both of whom were agricultural labourers, and a lodger of independent means aged 66. These entries may indicate that it was already a lodging house though beer retailing is not mentioned.

However in two street directories of 1854, James Dobson is listed as butcher and beer retailer, and in directories of 1852 and 1850 as a beer retailer in New Street. He was probably the outgoing tenant when the beerhouse was to let in 1855.

The earlier census of 1841 is not so well ordered, but there is a possibility that the premises were then occupied by Harriet Perrin who was 35 and a labourer, and her three children aged 11, 7 and 2. A street directory of 1847 mentions a beer retailer in New Street called Harriet Wetherell, who cannot be placed at any of the other New Street beerhouses. It is tempting to speculate whether Harriet Perrin had married a Wetherell between 1841 and 47, if she did it was not in Henley Parish Church.

In the Henley Advertiser of 10 September 1870 there is an account of a dinner held at the *Horse and Groom*, host Mr Ayres, to celebrate the completion of building works in New Street for Messrs Harris and Hewett, when about 56 contractors and workmen sat down to dinner. According to the Register of Licenses in 1877 Harris and Hewett definitely owned the *Horse and Groom* at that date, and as already said, they most likely owned it in 1855. Where the building work took place is not mentioned except that it was in New Street. Since no other building in New Street seems to have had connections with Harris and Hewett, and given the venue of the dinner, the work must have taken place at the *Horse and Groom.* That the work employed 56 contractors and workmen would imply that it was a fairly extensive building project. Perhaps like many other buildings in Henley an old gabled and perhaps jettied building was given a Georgian type straight front, and extra rooms added, where there were once attics (Fig 27).

In September 1887 a seven day license was granted[212]. In 1892 the *Horse and Groom* was owned by Hewett & Sons of Reading, and by 1898 H & G Simonds of Reading[213]. In the Register of Licenses on 4 May 1955 H & G Simonds agreed to the closure of their beerhouse the *George and Dragon* at Eye and Dunsden, in exchange for the granting of a full license to the *Horse and Groom* in Henley. After 1962 H & G Simonds became Courage Barclay & Simonds, and by 1973 Courage Brewery. In 1991 Morlands of Abingdon bought the *Horse and Groom* from Courage Brewery[214].

The landlord after George Ayres, George Baggs, was not there long. He was charged with selling beer at 11.0 on a Sunday morning, having been previously cautioned for the same offence, and was fined £2 with costs of 12s. This was in July of 1878, and the license was transferred to Robert Bedwell in August[215].

Landlords/ Tenants of the *Horse and Groom*

1841-7 ? Harriet Perrin /Wetherell ? (C,SD)

*1850-5 James Dobson (C,SD) butcher

212 Magistrates Special Sessions Minute Book 1 Sep 1887

213 Register of Licenses 1892-6, 1897-1901

214 Henley Standard 28 Jun 1991

215 Henley Advertiser 3 Aug 1878

1855-77	George Ayres (SSM,C,HA,SD) carpenter
*1878-Aug	Charles Baggs (RL,HA)
Aug 1878-9	Robert Bedwell (RL)
1879-83	John Pain/Paine (RL,CL,C,SD)
*1886-1912	William Robins (RL,BReg, SD) (died Dec 1912 aged 74)
1912-R18	Mrs Laura Robins (RL,BReg, SD) (died Nov 1921 aged 85)
1919-30	Miss Laura Robins (RL,HS,SD)
Jul 1930-5	George Hooper (RL,HS,SD)
Dec 1935-55	George Francis Heath (RL)
Dec 1955-7	Reginald Hughes Plummer (RL)
May 1957-8	Robert Charles Royston Fisk (RL)
May 1958-60	George Anthony Russell & Doreen Patricia Russell (RL)
Dec 1960-2	John Michael Vowles Carpenter (RL)
May 1962-8	George Ernest David Knight (RL)
Aug 1968-70	Angus John Ferguson (RL)
Nov 1970-5	Theophilus Oliver Cammon (RL)
Nov 1975-8	George Howchin (RL)
Jul 1978-9	Valerie Anne Howchin (RL)
Feb 1979-85	John Richard Seymour (RL)
Jun 1985-89	Martin Higdon (RL)
Aug 1989-95	David Christopher Munt (RL)
Mar 1995-96	Lawrence Clive Jordan (RL)
Mar 1996-98	Robert Saunders (RL)
Mar 1998-May	Paul David Hobbs (RL)
May 1998-99-	Martyn Ian Constable (RL)

The Horse Shoes

Reading Road

This appears to have been a brief and alternative name for the *Red White and Blue*. See entry for the *Red White and Blue.*

65

The Imperial

Station Road

The *Imperial* from 1981 to the Spring of 1993 was known as the *Edwardian,* but with a change of ownership in 1993 the name of the *Imperial* was restored.

The *Imperial* and parade of shops on either side of it, were built and completed in 1897 (Fig 28). They were built as one unit, but the *Imperial* in the centre dwarfs the other shops, and was obviously designed as the most prestigious of the group, and also as an eye catching building aimed at Regatta crowds arriving by train. Indeed there is a Post Card of about 1905 which shows the crowds arriving on the station platform, with the front of the *Imperial* facing them.

Like the *Little White Hart* which was rebuilt at the turn of the century, the *Imperial* has a splendid dragon as a ridge finial. These were a common feature of houses in the Thames valley at that period, when chinoiserie was popular, and the dragons were supposed to ward off evil spirits. A firm in Reading, S & E Collier advertised such finials in their catalogues[216]. The dragon on the *Imperial* is larger than that on the *Little White Hart*, in proportion to the size of the building on which it sits.

When the *Imperial* was built it was not licensed. It was owned in 1903 by Joseph Kendall of Penwortham, Birdhurst Road, South Croydon, who on 5 March 1903[217] sent the following letter to the Licensing Justices :-

> 'An application made by me this day for a full license to certain premises known and being the *Imperial Hotel,* Henley on Thames, having been granted by the Licensing Justices subject to confirmation. I undertake promise and affer that there shall be no Bar or Saloon upon the premises in respect to which the licenses is granted.'

Joseph Kendall held the license till 1908, and although he continued to own the *Imperial*, for three years he was not the licensee. However from 1911-16 he again held the license, but in 1917 in the Register of Licenses it says 'Lapsed - License dead and renewal not applied for in February 1917.' The reason for this was that Joseph Kendall had died at the end of 1916, and his widow did not wish to continue the business. The hotel was closed, and until the end of the war the hotel was taken over by the military.

In the summer of 1919 Albert Halliday took over the *Imperial* to re-open it as a hotel. He had previously been at the *Angel on the Bridge*. However when he applied for a seven day license at the Licensing Session of 1920 he was refused. The next year an application was made again, this time by Mr Desire Croce of Milan, who had taken over from Halliday. He assured the Bench that he had no connection with Mr Halliday and applied for a license as it had been before, for the sale to 'bona fide' guests and diners, and on condition that there was no bar or saloon. He also pointed out that the license had been in abeyance and not discontinued. Croce was granted the license, but only stayed till the end of the year. In December Peter Testa became the licensee[218].

Fig 28 The Imperial in the early 1900s

In 1922 Peter Testa applied for a Music and Dancing License to accommodate a Dance Club being

216 Catalogue at Blake's Lock Museum, Reading

217 Register of Licenses 1877-81 O.R.O.

218 Henley Standard 13 Feb 1920, 11 Feb 1921

formed by Capt Fisher Browne and his friends. A dance was to be held every Saturday 8-12 and a dinner dance once a month. The license was granted, and the next week in the Henley Standard of 29 September 1922, a notice appeared saying that the Imperial Dance Club will open next Saturday October 7 at 7p.m for a dinner dance. Tickets (including dinner) 7s 6d. Dancing only at 8.30 p.m. 2s 6d. Applications for membership and tickets for the opening dance from the Honorary Secretary of the Imperial Dance Club.

The Dance Club apparently flourished, and at the next Licensing Session the Music and Dance License was renewed, and was still being renewed in 1931, when at last a full license allowing outsiders and not only guests to buy drinks was granted to the then licensees, Mr Giles and Mr Montgomery .

From 1981-93 as already said, the *Imperial* was known as the *Edwardian*, but in March 1993 the building was bought by Stephen Binns and his wife Nucharee, who comes from Thailand. After extensive re-decorating , including putting in new bathrooms, they re-opened the house as the *Imperial* just in time for the Henley Royal Regatta of 1993. Mr and Mrs Binns brought a Thai influence to the hotel, not only introducing a replica of a Thai temple into the restaurant, but also providing a menu of both Thai and European food[219].

Landlords/ Tenants of the *Imperial*

1903-8	Joseph Kendal (RL)
1909-10	Ernest Baker (RL)
1910	Carl Lewis Ludovic (RL)
1911-6	Joseph Kendal (RL)
1919	Albert Halliday (HS)
1919-21	Desire Croce (RL,HS)
Dec 1921-6	Peter Testa (RL,HS)
May 1926-8	Amelia McCann (RL,HS,SD)
Dec 1928-30	Richard Stanley Redhead (RL,HS)
Dec 1930-1	Clarence Reuben Giles & Samuel Mervyn Montgomery (RL,HS)
Oct 1931-3	Capt Cecil Ernest Curtis & Edwin Percy Augustus Todd(RL,HS)
Jul 1933-7	Mrs Alice Mary Woodbridge & E P A Todd (RL,HS)
Oct 1937-9	Frank Adams (RL)
1939	Dymington West-Symes & John Clifford Hobbs (RL)
1940-1	John Clifford Hobbs (RL)
May 1941-6	Gladys Frances Hobbs (RL)
1946-52	John Clifford Hobbs (RL)
Feb 1952-Sep	Albert Edward Blissitt (RL)
Sep 1952-3	Arthur Leslie Palmer (RL)
Jul 1953-6	Horace William Blows (RL)
Jul 1956-7	Michael Gordon (RL)
May 1957-60	Thasos Georgiou Loizou & Nicholas Georgiou (RL)
May 1960-1	Harry Macgregor Pearson & Edna Vera Pearson (RL)
Feb 1961-9	Richard Geoffrey Patten & May Patten (RL) (May Patten deceased 15 Apr 1964)
Jun 1969-77	John Rowland Herring (RL)
Dec 1977-80	James Manus McGuire (RL)
Nov 1980-2	John Russell Oldman & Elizabeth Mary Clayton (RL)

219 Henley Standard 29 Oct 1993

———The licensees between 1981 & 1993 are listed under the *Edwardian*———

Mar 1993-95	Stephen Lawrence Binns & Nucharee Chalengsakdi (Binns)(RL,HS)
Mar 1995-99-	Raymond Eaken Crockett & Rosemarie Balliol (RL)

66

The Jolly Farmer

39 West Hill/Street

The Census Returns of 1861 and 71 have Hezekiah Langley at the *Jolly Farmer*, as a beerhouse keeper in 1861, and a publican victualler and paper maker in 71. A street directory of 1869 adds marine store. Both Census entries are in lists which come down the street on the south side, in 1861 the entry is next to that for the *Row Barge*, and in 1871 has a household between.

Hezekiah Langley seems to have been a notorious character, not only did he feature in a court case at the *Broad Gates* in 1872, but it was reported in the Henley Advertiser of 31 August 1871, that all licenses in Henley were to be renewed except to Hezekiah Langley of the *Jolly Farmer* beerhouse, 'which by reason of the very indifferent and unsatisfactory way in which the house for some time past has been conducted was refused to him.' The entry in the Magistrates Special Sessions Book is even more specific: 'various complaints having been made by the police against Hezekiah Langley keeper of the *Jolly Farmer* beerhouse for harbouring convicted thieves and persons of bad character in his house the Magistrates refused to grant him a certificate.'

In October 1871 the license was renewed to Samuel Clinch, but he also was soon in trouble. In December he was one of six landlords in the town summoned for having incorrect cups for the sale of beer, and then in February 1872 he was summoned for opening before 12.30 on Sunday February 18th[220]. However he seems to have retained his license as he was still there in 1881, according to the Census and the Register of Licenses. The Census in 1881 shows two households between the *JollyFarmer* and the *Row Barge*.

In 1877 the *Jolly Farmer* was owned by I H W Peel of Watlington[221], and in 1894 sold to Watlington Brewery. In 1903 on 5 March the license was surrendered by the brewers on condition that a full license should be given to the *Victoria* beerhouse Market Place, which they also owned: and which had been recently rebuilt as part of the Town Hall alterations and building.

It seems that the *Jolly Farmer,* though unlicensed, continued for a while as a lodging house, which it had been for some time. It was one of the four common lodging houses in the Borough in 1892, together with the *Cannon,* the *Duke's Head* , and the *Red Lion* West Hill. In the Henley Standard of 1906 mention is made of William Strange as the proprietor of the *Jolly Farmer* Lodging House, West Hill.

Landlords Tenants of the *Jolly Farmer*

*1861-71	Hezekiah Langley (SSM,C,HA,SD)
1871-82	Samuel Clinch (RL,C,HA)
1882-94	Caroline Clinch (RL,SD) widow
1894-5	Jonah Reeves (RL)
Mar 1895-Dec	Thomas Bucket (RL)
Dec 1895-9	Charles Bishop (RL)

220 Henley Advertiser 18 Dec 1871, 2 Mar 1872

221 Register of Licenses 1892-81

May 1899-1901	Henry Thomas Randall (RL)
1901-2	Stephen Aldred (RL)
1902-Mar1903	Jason Harris (RL)
(*1906*	William Strange (HS) lodging house keeper)

— Closed —

67 & 68
The Jolly Waterman, The Old Waterman, The Waterman
175 Reading Road & Reading Road

There were two pubs called variously the *Jolly Waterman,* the *Old Jolly Waterman* and the *Waterman*, near to each other on the Reading Road and both in business at the same time.

Fig 29 The Jolly Waterman after closure. The cottages on the right are those shown on the Tithe Map of 1844 Photo 1998

In the 1844 Rotherfield Greys Tithe Returns and Map, a public house owned by James Partridge occupied by William Strange is shown on a plot of land, now 175 Reading Road, with a row of cottages next to it on the south side, stated to be 8 houses and gardens (Fig 29). To the north of the pub there were three garden plots. Further towards Henley there are shown another row of cottages, which also are still there, five houses with clap boarded exteriors. These houses and gardens were owned in 1844 by William M Soundy (a brewer of Henley) and occupied by Daniel Cartwright and others.

It would seem that one of these five, probably the southern most one, and possibly that occupied by Daniel Cartwright was the *Jolly Waterman.* In other cases where one occupant of several houses is mentioned, it often is the name of the publican, if a public house is one of the group. The position at the south end is because in the Census Returns of 1871 and 81, that appears to be the site by the sequence of entries and the number of households between the pubs. The other *Jolly Waterman*, which for convenience I will call the *Old Jolly Waterman* was the one shown as a pub on the map of 1844 and in the same position as the pub recently closed.

In 'Brakspears Brewery 1779-1979' Francis Sheppard says that the *Jolly Waterman* was bought by Brakspears in the 1860s for £350 and that it was 'since rebuilt on a different site'. The architect of the new pub, the building that stands today, was W G Rambling.

Since the site on the 1844 map and that of the present building are the same, it follows that Brakspears in the 1860s must have purchased the *Jolly Waterman,* once owned by William M Soundy.

The *Old Jolly Waterman* was owned before 1896 by John Noble of Park Place, from whom it was leased by Greys Brewery, Messrs Holmes and Steward, at a rent of £20 p.a.[222]. In 1896 Brakspears bought Greys Brewery and all its pubs, so at that date Brakspears owned or leased both pubs called the *Jolly Waterman*. The license of the *Old Jolly Waterman* was discontinued in 1897[223] and it must have been then that the new pub was built and the two pubs combined in one. In 1897 Brakspears were granted a full license for the *Jolly Waterman*.

Neither pub seems to have existed before 1822, as neither appears in the Victuallers Recognizances for Rotherfield Greys which go up to 1822, with at that time the names of pubs clearly stated. Also the maps accompanying the 'Survey of the Parish of Rotherfield Greys' taken in 1815 for the Rev B C Heming[224], which show the farms of the parish, demonstrate that no houses existed in the whole of the New Town area at that date. The only house on the east side of the Reading Road, after the houses between Friday Street and what is now Station Road, was the farmhouse now at about 165 Reading Road. The house is behind the lane, now flanked by sheds which is between Canadian Terrace and what until recently were police houses and are now (1998) six newly built houses called 'The Copse'.

In July 1996 the landlord James Scott, decided that he wished to retire and gave up his license, Brakspears then decided not to seek a new landlord but to close the pub.

Landlords/ Tenants of the *Old Jolly Waterman*

*1844-71	William Strange (TM,C,SD)
Dec 1871-81*	James Clements junior (C,HA,SD)
*1882-7	Edward Carter (RL,SD)
1887-96	William Titcombe (RL,GB/R,SD)
	discontinued 1897

Landlords/ Tenants of the *Jolly Waterman*

1844	Daniel Cartwright (TM)
1847-54	Thomas Tranter (C,SD) brewer's man
1869	Joseph Tilby (SD)
1871	James Clements (C)
*1873-96	Thomas Rixon (RL,HA,SD)

222 Greys Brewery Rent Ledger O.R.O. Brakspear IV/ ii/ 1

223 Register of Licenses 1892-6

224 Survey of the Parish of Rotherfield Greys 1815 O.R.O. Copy by courtesy of Mr John Crocker

Landlords/ Tenants of the new *Jolly Waterman*

1896-1923	Walter Cordery (RL,WHB/C,HS,SD)
Feb 1923-52	Ernest Victor Cordery (RL,WHB/C,HS,SD)
Dec 1952-68	Stephen Stewart Henry Lewis (RL,WHB/C)
Dec 1968-70	Edward Deans (RL,WHB/C)
Mar 1970-3	Patrick Thomas Wright (RL,WHB/C)
Nov 1973-84	David Albert Kirby (RL,WHB/C)
Dec 1984-96	James Bruce Scott (RL,WHB/C)

— Closed —

69

The King's Arms

32-4 Market Place

The earliest mention of the *King's Arms* is in a deed held by W H Brakspear & Sons plc. This document is the will of a John Bourhez (Butcher?) of New Sarum in the County of Wilts dated 17 July 1684. By this will the inn commonly known as the *King's Arms* in Henley on Thames was left to his kinsman Henry Ringwood also of New Sarum.

However excavations undertaken by Roger Kendal of the Henley Archaeological & Historical Group for Brakspears in the Autumn of 1993 have shown that a pit, which preceded the present barn-like stable, contained a very large number of dismembered animal bones and oyster shells. The quantity of what must have been kitchen refuse was greater than would be expected in a private house, which may indicate that the *King's Arms* was a pub earlier than the documentary evidence shows. On the surface of the pit a very much worn penny of Elizabeth I was found, dating to 1587-8. So it is perhaps possible that the *King's Arms* goes back at least to Tudor times, and possibly before the reign of Elizabeth, since it would more likely to have been the *Queen's Arms* if begun in her reign.

By 1688[225] Henry Ringwood sold the *King's Arms* to John Prosser. At that time it was described as two messuages known by the name of the *King's Arms*, and included outhouses edifices, barns, stables, buildings, orchard, backside garden, yard etc. There is no mention of the then occupant but it may have been someone called Carter, since later his widow was in occupation.

The Henley Rentals in 1704 say that someone named Carter was paying for the *King's Arms*, but this was probably the Widow Carter. By 1713/4 it was W Whitacre for the *Queen's Arms*, evidently a tribute to Queen Anne. By 1721 Whitacre was paying for the *King's Arms* again. Chipp paid in 1727, probably Matthew Chipp who was a maltster living next door at what is now 28-30 Market Place. A Thomas Homens paid in 1733 and Thomas Simmonds in 1737. (These two names may be for the same person as Simmonds is often spelt as Simons, and Homans may be a misreading.) In 1758 Sam Thompson paid, in 1765 it says 'late Thompson since Dobson now Brown' and in 1785 the Court Baron Book says 'Sarah Binfield tenement called the *King's Arms*, late occupied Brown now Randall'. At some point in the 18th century Andrew Binfield bought the

225 Deeds held by W H Brakspear & Sons plc

Fig 30 The Kings Arms, yard entrance through the double doors, the gable beyond them for many years let as a separate cottage

King's Arms from Prosser, and it was then left to Thomas Binfield, Sarah Binfield was probably the widow of Thomas[226].

Sarah Binfield also owned the *Broad Gates* as is shown by the Insurance she took out on 20 September 1784[227]. 'Mrs. Sarah Binfield proprietor. Robert Appleton and John Shaw brewers, mortagees. House and offices adjoining on the north side of the Market Place, tenant Mary Brown, house known as the *King's Arms*. £300.' Also the *Broad Gates* - the 'said buildings being brick lath and plaister built and situate in Henley aforesaid.' The insurance continued till 1805.

The deeds of 1791 held by Brakspears show that the two houses known as the *King's Arms* were occupied in the 18th century by first of all Susannah Carter widow and Susannah Carter spinster. Then by William Whitacre then Daniel Sarney or his assigns, then John Brown, since Mary Randall and then Charles Browne, and finally in 1791 by John Strange and Benjamin Corrigan. By 1791 the two messuages had become one house and were spoken of as formerly two messuages.

The Henley Rentals and the Brakspear's deeds show that the Carter of 1704 was almost certainly Susanna Carter widow with probably her spinster daughter Susanna. The Burial Register of St Mary's Church 1703-32 shows that Susanna Carter widow was buried on the 18 September 1706, while another Susanna Carter 'from London' was buried on 19 March 1708. It is likely that the widow was innholder of the *King's Arms* until her death, and that the daughter may have then moved to London, from whence she was returned to Henley for burial in 1708.

226 Same as note 225

227 Royal Exchange Insurance Register, no. 90423 O.R.O. Brakspear X/ 1

When Sarah Binfield took out her insurance in 1784, it is evident that the *King's Arms* was already mortgaged to Robert Appleton and John Shaw, who were brewers at the brewery of Benwell in New Street, now Brakspears. A mortgage entered upon in 1775 was between Edward Goodenough innholder and the brewers Appleton and Shaw[228]. Although the document is labelled as a Bill of Sale, it is clearly a mortgage of the entire contents of the *King's Arms*, since the goods as listed in a very comprehensive inventory were being placed as security against a loan of £270. The fact that it was the contents and not the buildings which were used as security, and that it was by someone called Goodenough and not Binfield, makes it seem that it was a transaction with a tenant and not the owner. However in 1791 Appleton and Shaw bought a half interest in the property and later bought the whole[229].

The inventory of 1775 is very detailed even down to the colour of the curtains, not only does it list all the furnishings but also the number of rooms. There were five bedchambers, a Maid's Room, a Great Room, two parlours, wash house, granaries, barn, lower granary, ostlery, stable, long stable, pantry, kitchen , bar and cellar.

It was the landlord John Strange who in 1797 wrote a letter about the money owed to him by a soldier (Introduction p14). From the letter one gathers that he had been landlord there for some years, and that the military stores were kept at the *King's Arms*, possibly in the large barn or stable. In 1793 John Strange advertised a flower show to be held at the *King's Arm* 'An Annual Subscription Pink Meeting of 5s each will be held at Mr Strange's the *King's Arms* on Friday 28 June instant when the attendance of Florists and others will be esteemed a favour. To show 7 blooms of 7 different sorts and the subscription money to be divided into six handsome pieces of plate'[230]. Evidently in the 1790s there was a lot of activity around the pub, the comings and goings of soldiers, and events such as the flower show.

The book of the transactions of the Court Leet of the Manor of Henley says that on the 9 October 1801 leave was given to Mr John Strange to build under the projection of his house, a matter of 13ft by 1ft 9ins. This implies that previous to this the building had a jettied front.

John Strange remained at the *King's Arms* until his death in November 1809[231]. A later Court Leet held in 1868 charged W H Brakspear for an encroachment, made since the last session in 1836, of a bow window (Fig 30), for which he was to make an annual payment of 1s.

In the Inventory of the Brewery in 1826 the *King's Arms* is entered among the properties held freehold by Joseph Benwell and W H Brakspear. 'The *King's Arms Inn* in occupation of John Wise with adjoining cottage, good cellarage, two yards one of which is paved, with very large garden, two stables for 18 horses, standing for 12 horses, chaise and wood houses. Land Tax £1 12s 6d. Quit Rent ls 7d. Willis' Charity l0s.'

By 1826 the property was clearly again two houses, though one was now termed a cottage, and refers most likely to the small house now 36 Market Place, between the *King's Arms* and the Police Station (Fig 30). This was possibly a different division of the property to that of the early 18th century, when the 'two houses' appear to have had equal status.

In 1843 the then landlord John Giles had extensive garden land behind the *King's Arms*. The Henley Tithe Map of that date, only shows the garden areas of Henley, and not the houses in the town. However the large garden can be identified, owned by Peter Sarney Benwell with the tenant John Giles. The garden then extended the whole length of what is now Kings Road up to the northern entrance to Kings Road car park. Most of it is now covered by the houses and gardens on the east side of that road.

228 Same as note 225

229 Sheppard, Francis 'Brakspear's Brewery 1779-1979' 1979

230 Reading Mercury & Oxford Gazette 17 Jun 1793

231 Henley parish Burial Register n 1737-1812

From 1847-77 Richard Potter was the tenant, he and several of his family were rope, sail cloth and sacking makers. In 1843 and earlier Richard Potter had lived and had his business at the neighbouring house, now the Police Station, rebuilt in about 1913. The Police moved there in about 1867, so it may be that after moving to be landlord of the *King's Arms* he may have continued his business next door, or he may have moved some of the manufacturing to the *King's Arms*. Towards the end of his tenure in 1873 Richard Potter was summoned for selling a quart of ale after 11.0 p.m. A Mrs Norman was apprehended carrying the quart away under her shawl at 11.15 p.m. Potter was fined 1s and l0s costs[232].

During the early part of the 20th century and probably before that, the stabling at the *King's Arms* was being used by some of Brakspear's dray horses. The horses were still using the stable up to the end of the 1940s.

The *Kings Arms* closed in 1997, and was bought by the Town Council for around £300,000[233] in 1998 to be used as offices. They also are refurbishing the barn or stable across the yard, which dendrochronology has shown the rafters to have a date of c.1603, which may be when it was built.

Landlords/ Tenants of the *King's Arms*

?	Carter ?
*1704-6	Susanna/Susannah Carter (R,BReg, WHB/D)
1713-22	William Whitacre (R,WHB/D)
?	Daniel Sarney (WHB/D)
1727	(Matthew ?) Chipp (R)
1733	Thomas Homans (Simons/Simmonds ?) (R)
1737	Thomas Simmonds (R)
1753-8	Samuel Thompson/Thomson/Tomson (VR,R)
1765	Dobson (R)
1765-71*	John Brown (VR,R)
1775	Edward Goodenough (WHB/D)
1784	Mary Brown (RE)
1785*	Mary Randall (CB,WHB/D)
?	Charles Browne (WHB/D)
*1791-1809	John Strange (WHB/D,CL,BReg,RM,SD) bricklayer
1814-26	John Wise (AKL,CL,WHB/I,SD)
1842-4	John Giles (TM,SD)
*1847-77	Richard Potter (SSM,C,HA,SD) rope, sail cloth & sacking maker
1877-Oct	Michael Lewis (RL)
Oct 1877-1904	John Charles Wheeler (RL,C,SD)
1904-11	Ernest Ivor Hewlett (RL,WHB/C)
Jan 1911-41	Mrs Elizabeth Ann Hewlett (RL,WHB/C)
May 1941-51	Frank Purton (RL,WHB/C)
Jul 1951-72	Alfred Charles Henry Harris (RL,WHB/C)
Mar 1972-8	George William Alfred Clisby (RL,WHB/C)
Jul 1978-80	Nigel Newton (RL,WHB/C)
Jun 1980-8	Clifford John Eyles & Mrs Beryl Christine Eyles (RL,WHB/C)
May 1988-91	Christopher Cherry (RL,WHB/C)
Mar 1991-97	Mrs Robina Pauline Cherry (RL,HS)
Jul 1997-98	Anne Marie Andrews & Nicholas Paul Tilt (RL)

— Closed —

232 Henley Advertiser 12 Apr 1873

233 Henley Standard 15 Jan 1999

70

The King's Head

probably 40 Hart Street

In 1513 by his will of 24 December Thos Devyn left the *King's Head* in the High Street to his son Nicholas[234] 'also his best gown furred with black shanks and his doublet cloke of black camlet'.

Previously in 1467 the Warden, who also happened to be John Devyn, and the Corporation etc had granted a lease to his son Thom Devyn and Sibil his wife of a tenement and garden in the High Street[235]. This may have been the *King's Head.* The will of John Devyn in 1470 left his properties and lands to his wife Joan, all except the tenement 'wherein my son Thomas dwells'. Again this may have been the *King's Head*[236].

In 1501 the will of John Blakkoke left to his wife Alys 'the tenement called the *Kinges Hede'*.... 'that I dwell in after the forme and maner of the Indentures made thereupon'. It then goes on to say that if his wife dies before the expiry of the 'endentures' or lease, that his son John should inherit the property for the remainder of the term[237]. This sounds as though it was on lease to Blakkoke, which had probably expired by 1513 when Thomas Devyn left it to his son.

However in 1503 on the 17 March Joh Bryce seems to have been at the '*Kingeshed',* the Warden received a payment of 13s 4d from him for the Church[238]. This was a payment of what were termed Bridge Rents, and funded both the bridge and the church. The sum of 13s 4d was the same in the Bridge Rent Book of 1886, and had been the same throughout the 19th century.

In 1563 the then Warden, John Froste granted to Thom Haywarde a messuage or hospice called the *King's Head* in the High Street, with Ric Holte on the east, Lane on the west, the street on the north, and the brook on the south[239]. This places it definitely on the south side of the High Street and most likely at what is now 40 Hart Street.

The position of the *King's Head* is further demonstrated by the grant in 1571/2 of a messuage in the High Street to Sibil Stavaton wife of Thomas, between J Cooper on the west, Hayward in the *King's Head* on the east, and the town ditch on the south[240].

The preceding information establishes the following pattern:-

East					**West**
	Holte	Haywarde	Lane		1563
		Hayward	Stavaton	Cooper	1571/2

A Henley Rental of 1775 for what is now 38 Hart Street or was until recently Brakspear's Off License, says 'late Deodatus Staverton in occupation R Brooks now Allen'. The occupancy of Allen continues both before and after this date, and although records for the house are clear back to 1713/4, no Staverton appears, so it is more than likely that he was a 17th century Staverton. He could have been son or grandson of Thomas and Sibil Stavaton, or at least a descendant living in the same house as mentioned in 1571/2. If so then the *King's Head* must have been at 40 Hart

234 Burn, J S 'History of Henley on Thames' 1861
235 Hughes 617 AD235
236 & 237 Weaver, J R H & Beardwood, A 'Some Oxfordshire Willss 1393-1510' 1958 Ox Record Soc
238 Briers, P M 'Henley Borough Records 1395-1543' 1960 Ox Record Soc p143
239 Hughes 872 AD330 & Corporation Rental 1563
240 Hughes 869 AD35

Street, which is now (1999) Café Uno.

Interestingly it is yet another property which formerly had a malthouse behind it (M29). The Bridge Rent Book of 1886 No 22 for 48 Hart Street says 'Mrs Dobson late Wm Powell formerly Thomas Toovey for a house etc formerly a Malthouse adjoining No 21 on the west side late in the occupation of Wm Jackson since of Mrs Crew afterwards of George Pearman and now of Thomas Seymour.' Thomas Toovey held the property from about 1790-1828.

There seems to be no further mention of the *King's Head* after 1572, though since the sixteenth and seventeenth centuries are a time of few references, the pub could well have flourished throughout the 17th century. The fact that a malthouse was still in existence as late as the end of the 18th century may indicate that it did survive that long.

Landlords/ Tenants of the *King's Head*

*1470	Thomas Devyn
*1501	John Blakkoke
1501*	Alys Blakkoke
1503	Joh Bryce
*1513	Thom Devyn
1513*	Nicholas Devyn
1563-72	Thomas Haywarde/Hayward

— Closed —

71

The Lamb and Flag

Market Place

This beerhouse and probably lodging house was in the Market Place in 1840, its exact location is unknown, though probably in the upper end of the market. The only mention of the *Lamb and Flag* seems to be in the Reading Mercury & Oxford Gazette of 23 May 1840.

The entry says 'On Thursday an inquest was held at the *Lamb and Flag* in the Market Place on the body of Pyman, an eccentric character of the town, who in descending the staircase in the dark, unfortunately missed his hold, and in falling dislocated his neck. Verdict - Accidental Death.'

— Closed —

72

Ye Lion

12 Friday Street

Ye Lion was on the north west corner of Queens Street, on the south side of Friday Street therefore in Rotherfield Greys until 1892. The house, now a shop, was built as a pub, probably in about 1881 (Fig 13), Queen Street was being developed in 1881-2. It was in 1884[241] that permission

241 Henley Advertiser 14 Jun 1884, 13 Sep 1884

was given to take up the pavement of Friday Street so that the roadway could go through. A gap had possibly been there for a while before this move.

Although the present building was built in about 1881, it is almost certain that a beerhouse existed on the same site before that date. In the Henley Advertiser of 24 July 1875 a license for a beerhouse 'lately occupied by Alfred Neale' was transferred to Joseph Morgan. It may have been the beerhouse once known as the *Chequer* (see also M16). In a street directory of 1883 Joseph Morgan is given as a beer retailer in Friday Street, and in the Henley Advertiser of October 1884 it says that the license of the *Lion* was held over from Joseph Morgan to Abraham Hamerslag. Both Joseph Morgan and Adrian Hendrik Hammerslag appear as licensees of an unnamed pub in the Henley Rural Register of Licenses 1882-7, Joseph Morgan from 1882-4, and Hammerslag from November 1884. They are followed by Joseph Eaton who was at a pub with 'no sign' until 1891. By 1892 it is called *Ye Lio*n in the Register.

In 1882 *Ye Lion* was owned or leased by H & G Simonds of Reading, but in 1895 the owners or leaseholders were Holmes and Steward of Greys Brewery, so in 1896 it must have become part of Brakspear's holdings, with their purchase in 1896 of the Greys Brewery.

Emily Climenson in her 'Guide to Henley on Thames' of 1896, speaks of *Ye Lion* as a restaurant with a license for beer, wines and spirits, however according to the Register of Licenses it was a beerhouse until a full license was granted in August 1897.

Ye Lion closed in 1977, the Henley Standard of 9 December 1977 says '*Ye Lion* will close next Tuesday.'

Landlords/ Tenants of *Ye Lion*

before 1875	Alfred Neale (HA)
1875-84	Joseph Morgan (RL,HA)
Oct 1884-5	Abraham Henry Hamerslag/Adrian Hendrik Hammerslag (RL,HA)
Mar 1885-94	James Eaton (RL)
1894-6	Walter William Wilmot (RL)
1896-1901	Arthur George Carter (RL)
1901-11	William Thomas Youngs (RL)
1911-22	John Hodsdon (RL,HS,SD)
Jul 1922-3	William John Cheesly/Cheasley/Cheaseley (RL,HS)
Apr 1923-33	Charles Lampard Bundy (RL,HS,SD)
Sep 1933-7	James Edward Hazell (RL,SD)
Dec 1937-9	George King (RL,SD)
1939-48	Edith Ethel/Ellen King (RL)
Oct 1948-53	Claude Albert Lucas (RL)
Sep 1953-7	Frederick Charles Stone (RL)
Jan 1957-Sep	Alfred Henry Jenkins (RL)
Sep 1957-66	John Haydyn Llewellyn Davies (RL)
Jul 1966	Gwynneth Davies & Alan T Farmer (RL)
Aug 1966-9	David William Price Cule Lewis (RL)
Feb 1969-74	Donald James Froud (RL)
Jul 1974-5	Frederick John Rice (RL)
Jan 1976-7	John O'Shea (RL)

— Closed —

73

The Little White Hart or White Hart

20 Riverside/Thameside/Waterside

The *Little White Hart* is occasionally and confusingly called the *White Hart*, but usually has the prefix 'Little'. It seems very probable that the pub on the site may have originally been the *Brewer's Arms,* and could be the house shown with barrels outside it, in the picture painted in about 1699 by Jan Siberechts entitled 'Henley with a Rainbow'[242].

The early 18th century Henley Rentals are quoted in the entry for the *Brewer's Arms*, the first positive naming of the pub as the *White Hart* is in the Court Baron Book of 1785. In that, under Thameside, there is an entry for Hayward & Co for an encroachment of a bow window at the *White Hart Inn*, the position of the bow window may be seen on the plan of about 1793 (Fig 31). From the rental entries during the 18th century it seems that it was the same property previously mentioned as the *Brewer's Arms*, but when the name change occurred is uncertain.

Robert Brakspear, who inherited his uncle Richard Hayward's property, appears to have held the lease of the *Little White Hart* in about 1790, it was then owned by Brooks[243]. Brakspear's Rent Ledgers show that it was leased to Mr B Moorhouse from Lady Day 1789-1811and also to Mr Barrett March from Michaelmas 1793 to 1805. These dates overlap, and the reason may be that the properties leased were not the same, a recently found plan in the Town Hall is a plan of the Waterside which although undated is probably of about 1793 (Fig 31). On the plan it will be seen that on the corner of New Street the cottages are in the name of Mr Clements. According to the Henley Rentals in 1793 the Bridge Rent was paid by Bealey late Clements. In 1790 and 1785 they were paid by Sam Clements. Mr Hollier in 1787 was insuring his property of two granaries on the Waterside, shown on the plan as being where Brakspears now have their small exhibition of artifacts, which was fairly recently vacated by the Henley Rowing Club. Mr March's lease with Brakspears only started at Michaelmas 1793, so that would date the plan to the last months of 1793.

The property leased by Mr March in 1793 was a granary, the site of which is now the Cottage Bar, he also held the lease of the new granary now the Century Galleries. On the O.S. map of 1879 the then *Little White Hart* was situated on the site of the granary, while next to it where the old pub had been, there were then three houses. In 1793 the pub leased to Mr Moorhouse and Mr Hayward who at that time were partners, was next door to the granary, and on the site of what is now the hotel part of the *Little White Hart*, and in 1879 was the site of the three houses. In 1879 one of the houses is shown with a bay window, similar to that shown on the plan of 1793, the bow window which was an encroachment in 1785. It is almost certain that although the two parts of the *Little White Hart* were leased separately, they were both owned as one property.

The tenants during the period covered by Brakspears Rent Book were as follows:- 1791-6 Samuel Clements, 1796-7 John Shephard, 1797-1801 Richard Eldridge, and 1802-5 Richard Harbard.

In July 1813[244] Joseph Benwell through his tenant Appleton bought the *Little White Hart* for the sum of £1,400 from Brooks.

In the Inventory of the Brewery of 1826, the *Little White Hart* was listed as held freehold by Joseph Benwell and W H Brakspear. It was then described as a public house together with cottage adjoining, in occupation of Richard Major, three stables granary and yard. Granaries partly

---

242 Painting by Jan Siberechts in the Tate Gallery, London

243 & 244 Sheppard, Francis 'Brakspear's Brewery 1779-1979' 1979

in hand adjoining to the *Little WhiteHart* with two floors part let to Mr Appleton. Quit Rent 6s p.a. Underneath the entry was written 'Sold by Hodges to W H Brakspear'.

Although listed in 1826 as the freehold of Benwell and Brakspear, who were then in partnership, the *Little White Hart* was still owned by Benwell, who died in 1830.

On 2 April 1832 in the Reading Mercury & Oxford Gazette the *White Hart* was for sale. It was described as a valuable Public House, granary, cottage and coal yard, well situated for business on the banks of the River, the description continues 'divided into numerous rooms, a small cottage, three stables, corn granary with two floors, yard and outbuildings. In the occupation of R Major and Messrs Cox and Swallow, tenants at will.' At this sale it is likely that the *Little White Hart*, was bought by Hodges, who may have been the Hodges of Bolney Court. According to Francis Sheppard in his book on Brakspear's Brewery, it was in the 1840s that W H Brakspear was to buy the *Little White Hart,* which was probably when the note was made under the entry in the Inventory.

By the descriptions of 1826 and 1832 it sounds as though the *Little White Hart* property at that time included both the early pub and what had been Mr March's granary, now described as a granary on two floors. It must have been after it was acquired by Brakspears that the granary became the pub, and the old pub was divided into the three houses shown on the O.S. map of 1879.

It may also have been the time when Brakspears altered the front of the old granary, since it was at a meeting of the Court Leet of the

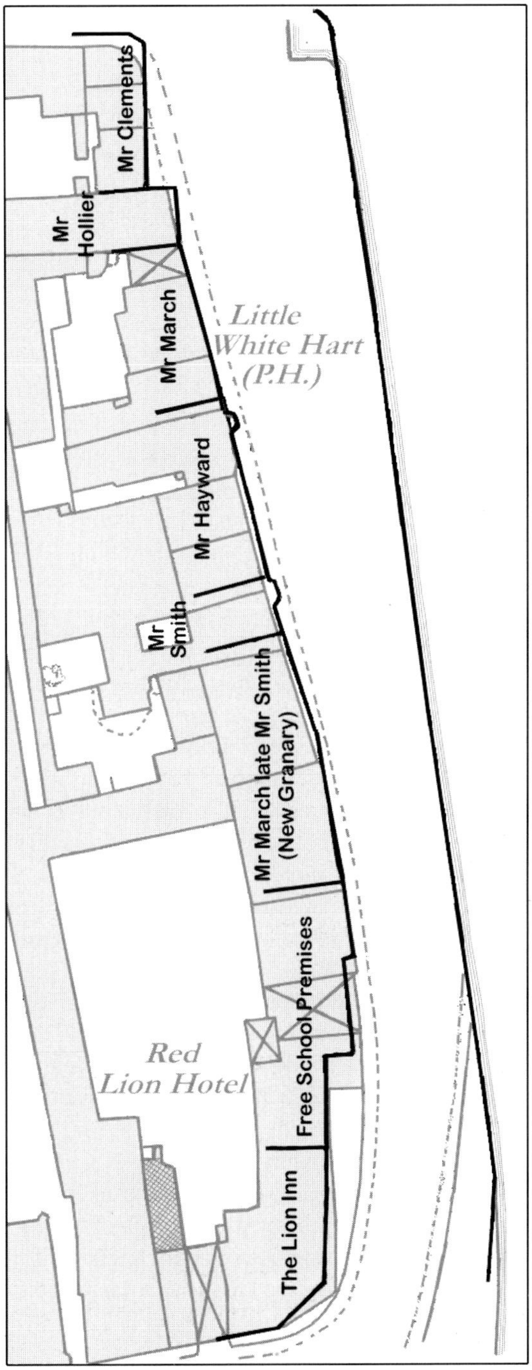

Fig 31 The plan of c.1793 of the waterfromt in black is superimposed on the O.S. map in grey, both have been reduced. It can be seen that the Little White Hart in 1879 is in the position of what in 1793 was the granary of **Mr March**, and that **Mr Hayward** then owner of the Little White Hart is shown at the next property, which in 1879 had become three houses

Manor of Henley on 26 October 1868 that W H Brakspear was charged that he owed the Lord of the Manor a Quit Rent of 5s, for an encroachment onto the Waste of the Manor by setting forward the Granaries on the north side of the *Little White Hart* by 22ins for the length of 54ft. There was no mention of this encroachment in the previous Court Leet meeting which had been on 20 May 1836, though it is again mentioned in the meeting of 9 Nov 1881. An encroachment of the amount described was most likely caused by building below a jettied upper floor, giving more room to the lower floor and a better support to the upper.

The yard of the *Little White Hart* features in a court caseof 1873[245] when Thomas Burns of Henley waterman was accused of assaulting the then landlord Robert Bedwell. Burns had been lodging at the *Little White Hart* for two months. Bedwell claimed that he went into the yard to feed his pigs and saw Burns talking to a female, a few words were exchanged and then Burns pushed him into the pig trough, and he fell and hurt his arm. A witness however said that Bedwell went into the yard and shook his fist in Burns' face, that Bedwell turned away and Burns then pushed him into the pig trough. The case was dismissed.

Apart from the pigs the yard was for a long time also a coal yard. Not only is it mentioned in the sale of 1832 but the Census Returns of 1851 list William Hickman as both publican and coal merchant - at that date there were thirteen people living in the house. Again in 1881 Henry Russell the tenant was both an oarsman and coal merchant, while his daughter Florence was the barmaid.

The rowing connection at the *Little White Hart* has always been a strong one, for many years it was used as the headquarters of the Henley United Rowing Club for river workers, as opposed to the Henley Rowing Club for amateurs and gentlemen. More recently since the two clubs combined, it has been the venue favoured by the Henley Rowing Club who stored their boats in the building next door to the pub, once the granary of Mr Hollier, which became a stable belonging to Brakspears, from which the Rowing Club have removed fairly recently.

The position of the *Little White Hart* on Riverside north, besides leading to it being a favoured pub of oarsmen, must also prior to 1886, have meant that it was very involved with the regatta. The early regatta races, before 1886, had their finish just outside the *Little White Hart*, and, it was on the road outside that a regatta stand was built each year to house the Regatta Stewards watching the finish. The earliest race of all was said to have actually finished at the bridge itself, but that was at once found to be too dangerous.

In 1885 there was an application by Mr Clisby of the Little White Hart to open on regatta days at four o'clock in the morning, which was duly granted[246]. At the same time a similar request was made by the licensee of the *Ship* which was also granted. Both pubs were obviously catering to the work force needed to prepare the stands and organise the regatta. There were also probably bargemen pulling houseboats into position along the Buckinghamshire bank, and perhaps normal barge traffic which on those days had to clear the Henley reach before the day's events began.

The 19th century *Little White Hart* was much smaller than it is today, it was rebuilt in about 1900. There are several photos as it was before rebuilding, the present building is on the site of the old house and the 'granary adjoining'. A feature of the gables of the main house are the dragons which sit on their tops. Unlike the dragon on the *Imperial* briefly the *Edwardian*, they are whole dragons, complete with curling tails. The fashion for these roof dragons was strong in the Thames valley in a lot of properties of about 1880-1905. The idea is thought to have originated in China, the dragons were supposed to protect the property and ward off evil. S & E Collier Ltd of Grovelands, Reading , whose catalogue may be seen at Blake's Lock Museum, was a supplier of such dragons.

245 & 246 Henley Advertiser 6 Sep 1873, 4 Jul 1885

Landlords/ Tenants of the *Little White Hart*

*1791-6	Samuel Clements (WHB/R)
1796-7	John Shephard (WHB/R)
1797-1801	Richard Eldridge (WHB/R)
1802-5*	Richard Harbard (WHB/R)
1809-18	Thomas Neville (AKL,CL,RM)
1820-32	Richard Major (WHB/I,CL,RM,SD)
1842-4	C/Henry Mansey/Mancy (SD)
*1847	Mrs Elizabeth Mancy (SD)
1847-54	William Hickman (C,SD) coal merchant
1854*	George Gray (SD)
1861-7	Henry Williams (C,SD)
*1869-70	James William Pike (SSM,SD,)
1870-6	Robert Bedwell (SSM,C,HA,SD)
1877-84	Henry Russell (C,HA,SD) oarsman & coal merchant
Sep 1884-1901	William Clisby (RL,HA,SD)
Jan 1901-5	Luiz Noraes Gomez Ferreira (RL)
Jan 1905-32	Ernest Barton (RL,WHB/C,HS, SD)
Sep 1932-6	George Frederick Chandler (RL,WHB/C,HS,SD)
Oct 1936-46	A E Booth (WHB/C) manager & Harold Robert Emmett (RL,WHB/C)
1946-56	Stanley Walker (WHB/C,BaReg) manager & Harold R Emmett (RL,WHB/C)
Mar 1956-8	A Hucker (WHB/C) manager & Harold R Emmett (RL,WHB/C)
Dec 1958-66	Thomas Caden Prescott & Mrs Prescott (WHB/C,HS) & Harold Robert Emmett (RL,WHB/C)
Jul 1966-74	Mr & Mrs T C Prescott (WHB/C) managers & Thomas Alexander Warren Wynne & Alan Thomas Farmer (RL)
Apr 1974-7	Tabard Inns (WHB/C) Christopher Joseph Patrick Deegan & Alan Thomas Farmer (RL)
Jun 1977-8	Mrs Pearce (WHB/C) manageress & C J P Deegan & A T Farmer (RL)
Jun 1978-80	Mrs Pearce (WHB/C) manageress - Robert Andrew Simpson & Stephen Rudd-Ludlow (RL)
Oct 1980-96	Eugene Brian Fitzpatrick (RL,WHB/C)
Feb 1996-98	Gillian Tanis Fitzpatrick (RL)
Nov 1998-99-	Philip Arnold Wilkins (RL)

74

Long's Stout House

? 1 Hart Street

Long's Stout House is a name given in a list of pubs no longer trading, published in 1931[247]. George William Long was a grocer and provision merchant at 1 Hart Street, from possibly 1823 and certainly 1830 to about 1840. After that date it was in the name of Mrs Caroline Long. These

247 Henley Standard 5 Jun 1931

dates are from street directories, and although the 1823 directory says Bell Street, the corner houses sometimes were credited to the wrong street.

The placing of the Longs at 1 Hart Street is from the Bridge Rent Book of 1886 entry no.l. 'Mr Charles John Plumbe Coombs late John Simmons Plumbe formerly Joseph May for a house and premises south east corner of Bell Street and west end of Hart Street formerly in the occupation of Thomas Ellson since of George Long then of George Paulin and now of Thomas Clement.'

Henley Rentals of 1823 say 'Jos May late March east corner of Bell Street adjoining Hart Street late Elson now Waddingtons.' Waddington is given in the directory of 1823 under Linen and Woollen Drapers, as J Waddington clothier Hart Street, Elson/Ellson may have been a publican, a Thomas Ellson was at the *Greyhound* 1830-6, if so he must have been at this site before 1817, as he does not feature in the Alehouse Keepers' List, see the entry for the Elephant. The presence of Waddington in 1823 or just before that indicates a change of use from possibly a pub (*Elephant* ?) in the 18th century to that of a shop. Possibly the change occurred after the rebuilding of 1808 (Mentioned in the account of the *Elephant.*)

After the Linen and Woollen Drapers business the Longs probably ran *Long's Stout House*, as a subsidiary of their grocery and provision business, possibly from soon after 1823 to about 1847.

Landlords/ Tenants of *Long's Stout House*

*1823-40 George William Long (BR,SD)
1840-7* Mrs Caroline Long (SD)

— Closed —

75

The Marquis of Granby

on the Bridge

The *Marquis of Granby* was a pub at the north western end of the old bridge, probably opposite the *Angel on the Bridge* and was one of four properties destroyed when the present bridge was built and the old bridge and the houses were taken down in about 1782.

Henley Rentals show that in 1775 a lease was held by Hayward but that it was in the occupation of Samuel Clements, in 1779 'occupied by Sam Clements, the *Marquis of Granby* 2d'. The Court Baron Book of 1785 says 'The Commissioners of Henley Bridge for waste ground whereon stood a messuage occupied by Sam Clements'. In 1800 and 1807 the rentals say 'Bridge Commissioners for premises late in occupations of Sam Clements pulled down called the *Marquis of Granby* 2d'.

It is possible that Sam Clements was already at the *Marquis of Granby* in 1770 and 71 as the Victuallers Recognizance lists of those years mention Sam Clements as a publican in Henley though no pub name is given.

Another of the houses taken down seems also to have been a pub, see the *White Horse on the Bridge*. It is difficult to place the houses exactly, but they probably clustered in the area taken by the roadway of the present bridge. A part of the small strip of land on the north side of the bridge known as the *Red Lion* Lawn, may have originally been used by one or other of the four houses.

The paintings of Henley by Jan Siberechts of about 1690[248] one from the south and the

248 One painting in the Tate Gallery the other a copy in the Town Hall

other from the north of the old bridge, show the cluster of houses to the north west of the old bridge. One of them painted white appears to project over the river on stilts alongside or on the bridge. It may have been the *Marquis of Granby* or more probably the *White Horse* since that was termed 'on the bridge' and appears to have had a cellar not under it but alongside. The *Marquis of Granby* was most likely not on the old bridge but where the north side of the present bridge now is.

In the Corporation Records[249] on 7 December 1781 agreement was reached for the purchase of the public house occupied by Mr Samuel Clements. Also for the house buildings and premises adjoining the said public house late in the occupation of Mr John Allen and for the garden on the bank of the river now in occupation of Mr Barrett March. This last was probably the *Red Lion* Lawn.

Landlords/ Tenants of the *Marquis of Granby*

*1770-81 Samuel Clements

— Closed —

76

The Newe Inn

West side of North/ Bell Street

There are only two positive mentions made of an inn called the *Newe Inn* in Henley. The first is a document dated 1 October 1586[250], when Brooke alias Lyttle conveyed to Thomas Fyelde the *Newe Inn* on the west side of North Street.

The second is in Archbishop Laud's Charity Books[251], when in 1784 Mary Jackson daughter of Joseph applied for funds from the 'Maids' Charity'. She had worked for three years as a maid for 'Mr Francis Waters late of the *Newe Inn*'. That this *Newe Inn* was in Henley seems likely since the charity was only available to maids resident in Henley. Whether 'late of the *Newe Inn*' implies that the *Newe Inn* had stopped trading or whether Mr Waters had merely left the pub, is uncertain, there are no further references to the pub.

Interestingly there is a publican named Francis Waters/Walters who was at what was then the *Plough* but is now the *Plowden Arms* at Shiplake from 1818 to his death in 1848. It is just possible that he was the same Francis Waters referred to in 1784, or he may have been a son of that Waters.

The *Newe Inn* in 1586 was on the west side of Bell Street, if it was still in business up to the 1780s, then it must have been on a site other than occupied by the known pubs, the *Oxford Arms*, the *Bear* or the *Bull*, all of which existed in the 18th century. The *Newe Inn* may have been on one of the sites where malthouses were still operating into the beginning of the 19th century, such as 27, 43, 63 or 91 Bell Street.

Landlords/ Tenants of the *Newe Inn*

*1586	Brooke alias Lyttle (HL)
1586*	Thomas Fyelde (HL)
*1784	Francis Waters

— Closed —

249 Holton, S J Ledger containing transcriptions of 'Corporation Records 1687-c1858' Town Hall 4/ 11/ 12

250 Hughes 244 AD401

251 Archbishop Laud's Charity Books O.R.O. Henley Borough AX

77

The North Star

15 Market Place

The only reference to the *North Star* is in the Census of 1851, when Richard Cox brewer was resident, with his wife and one servant, employing three men. It is probable that Richard Cox, who had been at the *Cannon* beerhouse at 45 Market Place in 1841, and had started the Cannon Brewery there, bought the house at 15 Market Place at an auction in 1845.

The Reading Mercury & Oxford Gazette of 22 February 1845 advertised a Sale by Auction of 'A freehold dwelling house with eight rooms and a cellar, front shop, side entrance and a long range of stabling, sheds and lofts over. Large garden, partly walled, occupying depth of 395ft, and width varying from 22ft to 33ft. Placed in a commanding situation in the centre of the Market. Adjoining premises in the occupation of Mr Binfield and Mr Fletcher, now inhabited by Mr Cook poulterer.'

This property is identifiable as 15 Market Place as Binfield is known to have been at 13, and Fletcher at 17 Market Place. Also the measurements of the plot, including the varying width, tally with those of the *Hop Leaf*, later to be on the same site, on the large scale O.S. map of 1879 (Fig 23).

In 1845 the building was obviously a poulterer's shop and premises, but Richard Cox, who was a brewer, moved his brewery known as the Cannon Brewery into the rear of the premises, and then proceeded to rebuild the house as a pub.

On the 4 April 1846 Richard Cox advertised in the Reading Mercury & Oxford Gazette to 'The Beer Trade'. 'To be let. A very stylish commodious and newly erected house fitted up expressly for the trade, attended with peculiar advantages as the beer is held in high repute. The extensive premises are admirably adapted to facilitate business, and the situation is bold and commanding. Any respectable person possessing business habits, with a very moderate capital, may reasonably calculate upon a good speculation. For particulars apply to Mr Richard Cox, brewer, Henley.'

Whether Cox found a tenant in 1846 is not known, but in 1851 there is no mention of one. By 1854 the name the *North Star* had been dropped, and in a street directory the premises were called the *Cannon Inn* and Brewery (B7). Later it was to become the *Hop Leaf* and finally the *Argyll.* (see entries for the *Cannon Inn,* the *Hop Leaf* and the *Argyll*)

Landlords/ Tenants of the *North Star*

1846-1851*	Richard Cox (C,RM) brewer

— Continued as the *Cannon Inn* —

78

The Oddfellows Arms

2 Church Street

The *Oddfellows Arms* situated at the north west corner of Church Street, was until 1892 in the parish of Rotherfield Greys. It seems that it was in existence in the 1860s, as Francis Sheppard in his book 'Brakspear's Brewery' says that it was bought by Brakspears at that time. It may in fact date back to the late 1840s, in the Reading Mercury and Oxford Gazette of May 1846, there is an announcement that the Oddfellows Lodge in Henley was celebrating its third anniversary. So it is likely that a pub called the *Oddfellows Arms* may well have started soon after 1843, though the corner building close to the street is not on the Rotherfield Greys Tithe map of 1844, so perhaps the house was built as a pub in 1845 or soon after.

In 1871 the Census Returns give Thomas Hone iron moulder and beerhouse keeper. A street directory of 1869 gives Thomas Hone as a beer retailer in Greys Lane. Greys Road was often termed Greys Lane, and the pub situated on the corner of Church Street could be classed as in Greys Lane. Thomas Hone in 1872 tried to obtain a spirits license for the *Oddfellows Arms,* he made a claim that the license of the old *Windmill* which was closing, or had just closed should be transferred to him[252]. This was refused, and it was not till 1897 that a full license was granted[253].

Cecil Towner, landlord from 1884, died in May 1897, leaving his widow Annie Dutfield Towner to succeed him. In August 1899 the Marriage Register of Holy Trinity Church has an entry of the marriage of Annie Dutfield Towner widow to Richard Russell bachelor, police constable. Possibly the police constable was a customer, but sadly he died in October 1905, leaving her once again a widow to carry on the business, which she did for another year.

In 1914 a query was raised as to whether the license should be renewed. At that time the *Oddfellows Arms* was saved, to close eventually in 1985. On the 12 April 1985 the Henley Standard announced 'the *Oddfellows Arms* closed last week.'

Landlords/ Tenants of the *Oddfellows Arms*

*1869-77	Thomas Hone (C,HA,SD)
*1882-4	William Marner (RL,SD)
Aug 1884-97	Cecil Towner (RL,SD)
May 1897-9	Annie Dutfield Towner (RL) widow
Sep 1899-1905	Richard Russell (RL)
Oct 1905-6	Annie Dutfield Russell (RL:) widow
Nov 1906-7	William Bryant (RL)
May 1907-9	Bertie Robert Berry (RL)
May 1909-11	Frederick Howland (RL)
1911-12	Harry Waters (RL)
1912-13	Alfred James Taylor Baiden (RL)
Jul 1913-Sep	Horace Harry Yaindili (RL)
Sep 1913-14	John Batty (RL)
1914-22	James Edward Mills (RL,SD)
Feb 1922-4	Mrs Martha Mills (RL,SD)
Feb 1924-35	Mrs Martha Mary Brooks (RL,SD)
Mar 1935-6	Robert Joseph Beauchamp (RL,SD)
May 1936-7	John Joseph Byrne (RL,HS)
Dec 1937-8	John William Bollands (RL,HS)
Mar 1938-55	James Madgwick (RL,HS,SD)
May 1955-8	John Frederick Carpenter (RL)
Dec 1958-62	Francis Ernest Thomas Norris (RL)
Apr 1962-3	Sidney Leonard Skillings (RL)
Oct 1963-85	Lillian May Skillings (RL)

— Closed —

252 Henley Advertiser 28 Sep 1872
253 Register of Licenses O.R.O.

79

Ye Olde Bell or The Old Bell

Bell Street

This pub has only been known as the *Olde Bell* since the 1920s (Fig 32). A street directory of 1920 listed it as *Ye Olde Bell* but another directory in 1922/3 still listed it as the *Duke of Cumberland* its previous name. The License Register of 1919-24 says that the *Duke of Cumberland* became *Ye Olde Bell* on 12 February 1920.

The Registers of Licenses have Walter Bowers as licensee from 1915-24, and the name of the pub was probably changed by his request. In the early years of this century there was a popular and romantically inspired swing to Jacobite sentiments, and the name of the Duke of Cumberland

Fig 32 Ye Olde Bell once the Duke of Cumberland with the imposing frontage of the building used as Assembly Rooms mid 19th century beyond it, but which may have been built as a Furniture Emporium Photo 1998

would have been viewed with distaste. Walter Bowers was buried in January 1924, and his address in the Burial Register was given as Y*e Olde Bell Inn.*

At the Licensing Session of 1931[254] the *Old Bell*, the *Three Tuns* and the *Cannon* were all recommended for closure. *Ye Old Bell* was said to have a good sort of trade but not much of it, and it was said that the premises were out of date. It had a public bar, small room behind and smoke room behind that, four bedrooms and a dining room upstairs. The kitchen adjoined the outside passage at the rear and there was no rear entrance. Together with the *Cannon* it was sent to the Compensation Authorities for closure. However Y*e Old Bell* was reprieved and it license was renewed.

In September 1937 an alarming incident was reported in the Henley Standard, a Mrs Marie Gibbons was in the kitchen one morning when a customer who had stayed the night at the pub, attacked her with a chopper. Fortunately someone came in and was able to disarm him. The licensee at the time was Mr T J Williams.

For the earlier history of the pub see the *Duke of Cumberland.*

Landlords/Tenants of the *Old Bell* or *Ye Olde Bell*

1920-4	Walter Bowers (RL,BReg, SD)
Feb 1924	Mrs Ellen Bowers (RL) re-married during the licensing year
1924-4	Mrs Ellen Wharton (RL,WHB/C) (same as above)
Feb 1926-7	George Arthur Strange (RL,WHB/C,HS)
Sep 1927-9	George Preedy (RL,WHB/C,HS)
Dec 1929-30	Louis Alfred Rose (RL,WHB/C,HS) manager
May 1930-7	Thomas James Williams (RL,WHB/C)
Dec 1937-9	Percy Samuel Mann (RL,WHB/C,HS)
Feb 1939-57	Alfred Charles Davis (RL,WHB/C,HS)
Dec 1957-77	John Gunning (RL,WHB/C)
Nov 1977-96	Keith Harold Wells-West (RL, WHB/C)
Feb 1996-99-	Sarah Catherine Fitzpatrick (RL,HS)

The Old House at Home

The only mention of the *Old House at Home* is in a book entitled 'Quaint Inn Signs' by G J Monson-Fitzjohn published in 1926. It states that this name is to be found at Westerham, Sheerness, Henley on Thames etc.

In my researches into various sources for names of local inns and beerhouses, this name has never been recorded in Henley as far as I know. It would appear to be a typically 19th century name, probably of a beerhouse, and may well have existed near to Henley in one of the nearby parishes.

However for the purposes of this book I am not including the *Old House at Home* among the Henley pubs.

254 Henley Standard 13 Feb 1931, 13 Mar 1931

80

Our Mutual Friend or The Mutual Friend

53 Bell Street

Our Mutual Friend was at the south end of the building whose fascia remains as part of what was once Waitrose's wine and drinks department, and is now two shops sharing a building plot and semi-detached, 53 and 55 Bell Street.

The Census Return of 1871 gives Thomas Waldron sawyer at *Our Mutual Friend.* This appears to be the first mention as a beerhouse, the book by Charles Dickens called 'Our Mutual Friend' was finished by Dickens in 1865, so it is probable that Thomas Waldron opening a beerhouse soon after that date used the title for his house. Waldron was at the *Blue Bell* up to about 1867, so it may have been then or the next year that he opened *Our Mutual Friend*, he was listed as a beer retailer in Bell Street in a directory of 1869.

In May 1872 Thomas Waldron was in trouble and up before the Town Bench on June 3 for that he 'unlawfully and knowingly suffered gaming in his house, by then permitting Albert Read, William Read, John Wise and Charles Jemmett to play for beer at cards'[255]. He was fined £2 and 12s costs, and by October of the same year the license of the *Mutual Friend* had been transferred to William Wheeler, who in the Census of 1881 was also described as a gardener.

In 1888 main drainage was being installed around the town, and in June it was reported that there was a nuisance caused by the drains at *Our Mutual Friend.* The nuisance was abated at a cost of £4 10s 5d, but the report says darkly 'the closets are still unconnected'[256].

The pub was held on lease by Byles & Co, or Greys brewery, until the sale of the brewery to Brakspears in 1896. At that time the *Mutual Friend*, was closed and the property reverted to Henry Crocker, who had bought the freehold from J J Roake in 1891[257]. The rent of £16 p.a. was payable to Henry Crocker from September 1891, Henry Crocker had also bought 55 Bell Street, where he had established his shoe making business. The *Mutual Friend* subsequently became a butcher's shop, that of Edward Machin.

Landlords/ Tenants of *Our Mutual Friend*

*1869-72 Thomas Waldron (SSM,C,HA,SD)
1872-96 William Wheeler (RL,C,HA,SD)

— Closed —

81

The Oxford Arms

89 Bell Street

The *Oxford Arms* is clearly marked on the O.S. map of 1879 (Fig 61), approximately 27yds north of the *Bear,* its site is now taken into the Adam Court development. Although a mid 17th century token has been known, which had the name Seth Smith and the 'Arms of Oxford' on it, it may not be related to this pub. Seth Smith appears to have lived on the south side of Hart

255 & 256 Henley Advertiser 8 Jun 1872, 16 Jun 1888

257 Greys Brewery Rent Ledger O.R.O. Brakspear IV/ ii/ 1

Street. He may however have owned the *Oxford Arms*.

The earliest positive reference to the *Oxford Arms* is in the Brakspear Rent Ledger, when from September 1790-1811 Joseph Beesley was the tenant. The spelling of Beesley has many variations, the Parish Registers of 1737-1812 reveal 12 versions, all being for the same family group. In the Rent Ledger there is also mention of the adjoining tenement, which was let from 1791-1805 to Robert Seymour.

In 1826 the freehold belonged to W H Brakspear Esq. 'The *Old Oxford Arms* in occupation of Thomas Marshall with work-shop and garden, and house adjoining containing a shop, 5 rooms, yard and piggeries.' The fact that it was then termed the *Old Oxford Arms* may mean that it was older than the 18th century and may well have been trading in the 17th century.

In 1871 William Whatman the landlord was summoned for serving beer after 11.0 at night, he was fined ls with 12s costs[258]. In his defence he claimed that he had fallen asleep at about 10.0. the pub being empty, that someone came in asking for beer and that he did not look at the time, which was actually 11.30. William Whatman who in 1851 was at the *Windmill,* appears at the *Oxford Arms* in the Census Returns of 1861, aged 61 a publican and working bricklayer with a wife, niece and one lodger. In 1871 he appears again now aged 71, a bricklayer and publican, with nephew Elias Piddington aged 29 an unemployed carpenter, whose wife was Arabella Piddington also 29, who is described as assistant publican. Poor William Whatman came to a sad end. On 3 January 1880 the Henley Advertiser reported on the inquest held on William Whatman, an inmate of the Almshouses, who had been burned to death. The old man was in the habit of taking his meals before the fire with his feet on the fender, and it was said 'he was given to drinking'. A verdict of accidental death was reached, he was said to be in his 78th year.

Brakspears were still the owners in 1868 as it was on the 26 October 1868 that W H Brakspear was charged by the Court Leet of the Manor of Henley that he owed a Quit Rent of 6d p.a. to the Lord of the Manor for an encroachment by the opening of a cellar flap in the street. This charge was made in a list of encroachments that had been made since the previous Court Leet of 1836.

The *Oxford Arms* closed between License Registers of 1881 and 1887. A street directory of 1883 lists Mrs Banbury at the *Oxford Arms*, but by June 1886 Mr Ovey, the then owner of the property, was seeking permission to build two new houses on the site of the *Oxford Arms* public house and Cranfield's shop[259]. The two houses were duly built, and were numbered 87 and 89 Bell Street, they were large mock timbered buildings which were finally demolished to make way for Adam Court. The *Oxford Arms* closed in August 1885, when the license was not renewed at the Licensing Session.

Landlords/ Tenants of the *Oxford Arms*

? mid 17th C	Seth Smith ?
1790-1811	Joseph Beesley/Biesley/Bisley/Beaseley/Beseley etc (WHB/R,ORO,SD) tailor
1814-6	William Beesley (CL)
1817	Mary Bisley (AKL)
*1823-50	Thomas Marshall (WHB/I,C,SD)
1851-4*	Charles Lovejoy (C,SD)
1863-71	William Whatman (SSM,C,HA,SD)
*1873-4	Thomas Seymour (HA)
Aug 1874-85	Elizabeth Banbury (RL,C,HA,SD)

— Closed —

258 & 259 Henley Advertiser 10 Jun 1871, 12 Jun 1886

The Oxford Hotel

6 & 8 later 13 Market Place

The *Oxford Hotel* or the *Oxford Temperance Commercial Hotel & Restaurant* is not numbered in this book, however since the name features in some photographs it is mentioned here. It appears first at 6 & 8 Market Place in a street directory of 1907 run by a Mrs Jane Elizabeth Williams, she continued there until the directory of 1915, but after that in the directories of 1920 to 1928 she had moved across the street to 13 Market Place, where she continued running the *Oxford Hotel.*

82

The Packhorse

19 Northfield End

The *Packhorse* (Fig 33) is another pub clearly shown on the O.S. map of 1879. It does not feature in the Brakspear Rent Ledgers, but the Brewery Inventory of 1826 shows it as the freehold property owned jointly by Joseph Benwell and W H Brakspear. 'The *Packhorse* public house in occupation of Mrs Gearing, yard, stable now used as a wood and coal house and a cottage adjoining, containing 5 rooms let to Widow Wood. Land Tax 9s 4d, Cottage Land Tax 6s, Powney's Dower £5 19s 0d.'

The Victuallers Recognizances for Northfield End show Richard Powny as at the *Packhorse* from 1774-80. The Powney's Dower mentioned in 1826 may be a bequest set up by Powney, who probably owned the *Packhorse.* The Victuallers Recognizances continue with Thos Robins 1783-92, Thomas Gearing 1793-1818, and Sarah Gearing 1821-2.

Two events at the *Packhorse* in the 1870s were noted in the Henley Advertiser, the first in December 1873, when the landlord John Boxall was charged with assaulting Police Constable Stephen Whitehead. At about 11.20 at night the constable heard sounds of quarrelling, and on entering the pub he found Boxall who was very drunk, quarrelling with a lodger. Boxall tried to push Police Constable Whitehead down the passage. Boxall was fined £2 with 11s 6d costs, and if he defaulted in the payment, one month's hard labour. Boxall survived this affray, and was still landlord in November 1875 when William Harding labourer was charged with stealing two tame rabbits, value 2s, the property of William Cobb, from a stable at the *Packhorse.* Frances Cobb, wife of William Cobb, said that they lodged at the *Packhorse*, and that she looked after the rabbits. When going to feed them, she found two rabbits missing, and recognised the skins produced in court. Edward Boxall, son of the landlord, saw Harding leaving, presumably with the rabbits; at least they later appeared with Harding at the *Red Lion*, West Hill, where he lodged. Emma Rawlings, wife of Charles Rawlings of Henley, said she lived with her father, who was landlord of the *Red Lion,* and that Harding lodged there. Harding asked her to make a pie with two small rabbits, which he had skinned, she did, and he ate them. William Harding was sentenced to six weeks hard labour.

In 1850 the *Packhorse* was one of the pubs that had a carrier service. Slater's directory of 1850 says that James Farley went to High Wycombe every Tuesday and Friday, and to Reading and Twyford every Monday, Wednesday, Thursday and Saturday.

At the Annual Licensing Meeting in February 1964 it was reported in the Henley Standard that the license for the *Packhorse* had not been applied for, it therefore ceased trading in February 1964.

Fig 33 The Packhorse closed in 1964, on far right the modern flats which replaced the White Horse & Star (see Fig 58) Photo 1989

Landlords/ Tenants of the *Packhorse*

1774-80	Richard Powny/Powney (VR)
*1783-92	Thomas Robins (VR)
1793-1818*	Thomas Gearing (VR,SD)
*1821-28	Sarah Gearing (VR,WHB/I,RM,SD)
1830	Charles Webb (SD)
1842-4	John/Richard Hawkins (SD)
1847-54	Edward Freebody (C,SD)
1861-9	Edward Cable (C,SD)
Apr 1871-5*	John Boxall (C,HA)
1876-7	Edgar Butler (SD)
1881	William Dearlove (C)
1882-3	Andrew Harley (RL)
Nov 1883-91	Walter Richard Bailey (RL,SD)
Jan 1892-1905	Charles Bailey (RL,HA) (License from Mrs Bailey to Charles Bailey late of the *Duke of Cumberland*.) 30 Jan 1892
Jul 1905-6	Caroline Bailey (RL)
Sep 1906-10	Lewis Hart (RL)
1910-21	Robert Brant (RL,HS,SD)
1021-45	William G Neate (RL,HS,SD)
Jan 1946-64	Kate Neate (RL)

— Closed —

83

The Pele

West side of North Street

In 1549 a Corporation Rental shows that R Bolte paid for a tenement and garden on the west side of North Street called the *Pele*, between Arderne to the north, Burton to the south, highway to the east and Arderne garden to the west.

It has been suggested by John Crocker, a local historian, that it could have been the *Bear*, it might have been the *Bull*, or it may have been some other site along the west side of Bell Street.

84

The Plough

16 Friday Street

The *Plough* later became the *Black Horse* (Figs 13 & 64), the changeover officially seems to have come in 1804, when the Victuallers Recognizances which had up to that date listed the then landlord Edward Deane as at the *Plough,* then altered the name to the *Black Horse*. The changeover may well have been due to a pictorial sign, which might have been of a plough drawn by a black horse, which then became the more prominent feature of the sign.

In 1745 the Henley Rentals have 'Ed Taylor for tenement late Dee late Carter now Maskells'. Rental for 1749 is much the same, but in 1775 it had become 'late Mr now Mrs Maskall, in occupation Flight and Benwell now a public house opposite Bird'. Mr Bird occupied the property once the Tan Yard, later the Foundry, and now called Foundry House and Queen Anne Cottage.

This would suggest that the property became a public house in about 1770, in 1779 and 1785 Rentals say 'late Mr and Mrs Maskell in occupation John Flight and Henry Benwell now Thom East'. A Thomas East appears in Victuallers Recognizances for Rotherfield Greys in 1770, with no pub specified and then later in 1776-87 as at the *Plough.* In 1790 Rentals say 'Maskells late Flight and Benwell since Thos East now Ebenezer Humphries'. In 1793 'Darby in occupation Humphries' and in 1795 'Mr Benwell for premises called the *Plough* occupied Deane rented by Hayward'. It is not till 1823 that the Rentals mention the *Black Horse*.

There are certain gaps in the Victuallers Recognizance lists, one of these being between 1789 and 1794, in 1789 George Knapp was at the *Plough,* and in 1794 Richard Deane, and somewhere between the two 1790-93 there must have been Ebenezer Humphries.

Brakspears Rent Ledgers show that from 1791-96 Mr Henry Benwell owned the lease which expired in 1796, the lease contained a clause to abate the £2 a year rent if the premises should lose its license. Brakspear bought the *Plough* in 1796. From 1796-98 Edward Deane rented the *Plough* alehouse, while Ralph Harris leased the house and malthouse (M18) next to the *Plough* from 1796-1812. That house now 14 Friday Street, was sold to Mr Barford in 1813 for £490.

For the later history of the premises see the *Black Horse* Friday Street.

Landlords/ Tenants of the *Plough*, Friday St

1775-87	Thomas East (VR)
1789	George Knapp (VR)
1790-3	Ebenezer Humphries (R)

1794	Richard Deane (VR)
1795-1804*	Edward Deane (VR,WHB/R)
1804-11	Edward Deane (VR) The *Black Horse*

— Continued as the *Black Horse* —

85

The Plough

26 Market Place

The beerhouse called the *Plough* was probably at what is now 26 Market Place, which was previously a hairdressers and until recently was a cut price clothing shop and is now in 1999 used by Oxfam. It is referred to in Henley Rentals first of all in 1704 when Burnham paid 4½d for the *Plough*. In 1713/4 to 1727/8 William Deavon paid 4½d for the *Plough*, in 1733/4 Widow Deavon paid for the *Plough* a painthouse and bulk, and in 1737 she paid 4½d for the *Plough* and a further 5d for the penthouse and bulk. A penthouse or painthouse seems to have been an overhanging jettied building, which by its nature tended to encroach over the street. It is interesting that when work was done on the building recently, that it was clear that the building is indeed an old jettied building, much older than its false Tudor front of the early twentieth century suggests.

In 1758 the Rentals continue Symons for late Devons *Plough* 4½d, and in 1769 late Moorhouse for *Ye Plough* now Mr Cook 4½d. In 1775 and 79 the amount of money on all rentals was increased and Cook in occupation Sam Giles was charged 3s. The Court Baron Book of 1785 says John Cook tenement called the *Plough* late Benjamin Moorhouse 4½d. Although the rentals seem to have been increased, the amount owed to the Lord of the Manor as a Quit Rent seems to have remained the same. In the same year the rentals say Mr Cook occupied Ed May the younger 3s.

This reference in 1785 seems to be the last mention of the *Plough* by name, after this the rentals in 1790 say Robson late occupied May now Ilton., in 1795-1814 Bartlett late Robson 3s and from 1823-28 Mr Bird late Bartlett 3s.

An advertisement in the Reading Mercury and Oxford Gazette of the 12 November 1787 says 'To be sold by auction freehold estate opposite the Market Place in Henley a substantial brick house with a good shop garden and many convenient offices in a most eligible situation for business now in the occupation of Mr Robson apothecary and druggist.' A Pew Faculty in St Marys Church of 1834/5 says 'A faculty granted on 27 January 1787 to the freehold premises on the north side of the Market Place belonging to Mr John Robson druggist and sold by him to Mr Thomas Bartlett. In the year 1817 occupied by Mr Bird tanner'. Later occupants of the premises were in 1842 a hatter called Thomas Allen and then Thomas Rose a currier and leather cutter from about 1847-77, and afterwards a bootmaker and leather seller till about 1900.

The Court Leet of the Manor on 26 October 1868 charged the Carpenters Company of London that they owed 4½d p.a. as a Quit Rent to the Lord of the Manor for a messuage or tenement formerly called the *Plough* afterwards a hatter's shop in the tenure of Thomas Allen and since Mr Rose leather cutter. The Carpenter's Co. were left the property in 1618 by Richard Wyatt of London on condition that some of the money from its rent should pay for meat bread and drink for thirteen poor widows in the town. In 1879 the property was leased to William Perrin when it was described as 'All that messuage and shop with the schoolroom and other buildings at the rear thereof.' It is possible that one of these buildings at the rear may have been a malthouse in the 18th century.

It is probable that Ed May the younger mentioned in the Rentals of 1785 did not actually live at the *Plough* but held the lease and sub-let to a beerhouse keeper. Ed May the younger is named in the Royal Exchange Insurance Register which starts in 1782. On 14 March 1787 Edward May the Younger of Henley maltster took out insurance on his household furniture in his dwelling house in New Street, brick built and tiled for £100 (probably 27 New St). His wearing apparel was put at £30, while his plate was insured for £20. Altogether a man of substance, rather than an alehouse keeper. Later in 1789 he moved to his 'new dwelling house brick built on the Hill above the Market Place', and his trade goods removed to his office and malthouse adjoining nearby.

It is very probable that the *Plough*, which may have ceased trading soon after 1785, had a malthouse behind it, the reason for Ed May's interest. After Ed May the younger maltster, a following tenant was Ilton a corn chandler. Very often maltsters and corn chandlers used the same type of premises.

Landlords/ Tenants of the *Plough*, Market Place

The names in the Rentals seem to be lessees rather than publicans but maybe:-

1775-9 Sam Giles (R)

1785 Ed May

— Closed —

86

The Portobello

Reading Road

The *Portobello* alehouse was the old pub which became the *Wheatsheaf*, the present building only dates from about 1882. In the 18th century the *Portobello* as it then was called, was in Rotherfield Greys. It changed its name in about 1787-9.

The Victuallers Recognizances for Rotherfield Greys show that a John Jemmett was landlord of a pub from 1753-74, and then from 1775-82 was landlord of the *Portobello*, it was only in 1775 that names of pubs were given. It is extremely likely that he was at the *Portobello* throughout. After John Jemmett, from 1784-87 John Heath was given as landlord of the *Portobello*, and then from 1789-1822 as landlord of the *Wheatsheaf*. There is no further mention of the *Portobello*, and 1789 is the first mention of the *Wheatsheaf*.

John Heath died in 1824 and was buried at Rotherfield Greys, in the Burial Register alongside his name, it says '40 years publican at the *Wheatsheaf*.' This means he was at the *Wheatsheaf* then called the *Portobello* in 1784.

The land behind the *Wheatsheaf*, in the area of St Marks Road was once known as Portobello Hill and Portobello fields

Landlords/ Tenants of the *Portobello*

1753-82 John Jemmett (VR)

1784-87 John Heath (VR) the *Portobello*

(1784-1824 John Heath (VR,BReg) the *Wheatsheaf*)

— Continued as the *Wheatsheaf* —

87

The Portobello

further along Reading Road

There seems to have been a faint revival of the name, the *Portobello* in 1851. The Census Returns of that year give a Charles Webb sawyer and beerhouse keeper of the *Portobello*. From its position in the Returns, it would seem to have been much further along the Reading Road, beyond the Toll House which was approximately at the southern corner of Hamilton Avenue, possibly as far as where Harpsden Road branches off. There were very few properties in that area in 1851. This *Portobello* does not appear again in any records, it may have only been there a few years.

Landlord of the *Portobello*
1851   Charles Webb

— Closed —

The Queen's Arms

Market Place

The *Queen's Arms* was a very short lived name for the *King's Arms* in the Market Place. It was only referred to in a Henley Rental of 1713/4, and quickly reverted to the *King's Arms*. There is no evidence that it traded under that name, so it is not numbered here.

88

The Queen's Head

30 Duke Street

The *Queen's Head* is on the corner of Duke Street and Greys Road. The queen on the sign is Queen Victoria in whose reign this pub started its life. The present house, like all the other buildings on the west side of Duke Street was rebuilt in the early 1870s, when the previous buildings were demolished in 1870 for road widening. It seems however that a pub existed here before 1870.

An Indenture of John and Charles Plumbe in 1840[260] made between Mary Barrett of Remenham, George Dyer Morgan of Henley waggonmaster, Charles Plumbe and Samuel Cooper concerns 'all that yard with stables sheds etc on the west side of Duke Street formerly Duck Street at lower end of said street and near a place called Dirty Bottom otherwise Greys Lane which lies on the south part thereof, the said Duke Street lying on the east part and a road leading to the *Three Tons* on the west, in occupation of George Dyer Morgan'.

This clearly describes the area now taken by the *Queen's Head*, the Queen's Hall, and also buildings to the north, in fact a large corner plot. There is however no mention of the *Queen's Head* or any pub, the site was a waggoner's business and yard. It also seems to have been a coach building and harness business.

260 Chambers & Co, Estate Agents. Papers of John & Charles Plumbe 1840

The Bridge Rent Book of 1886 and previous Henley Rentals show that the whole corner area, including what was once the site of the Wesleyan Chapel (1874-1980), now 26 & 28 Duke Street was part of the same rental. The Bridge Book entry is in two parts:- 'No.122. The Trustees of the Wesleyan Chapel for part of the site of premises lately belonging to Mark Woodbridge formerly used by John Cottrell as a coachmakers shop since pulled down for street improvements and chapel erected. No.122a. Mr Chamberlain for the remaining part of the site above described premises - new house now erected.' John Cottrell appears in street directories 1842-7 as coach builder and harness maker, while Mark Woodbridge in 1844-63 appears as saddler and harness maker. According; to the Reading Mercury & Oxford Gazette, John Cottrell took over the business from his late employer N W Philip in March 1835. Philip who was from Reading had succeeded to the coach building and wheelwrights business in June 1830. Previously it had been owned by Paul Richardson and later by his widow Charlotte Richardson. So the coach building business was of long standing.

Edmund Chamberlain who in the Bridge Rent Book of 1886 was paying for the remainder of the site, was listed in the Post Office directory of 1854 as a brewer, beer retailer and grocer. In Billings directory of the same year he was listed as both a shopkeeper in Duke Street and a brewer at the Union Brewery, Duke Street. The brewery was behind the *Queen's Head*, where the Queen's Hall now stands. In the beating of the bounds in 1868[261]the route of the Town boundary crossed from Tuns Lane diagonally through the site of the Queens Hall, and is described as going 'in an oblique direction through the corner of Mr Paulin's Brewery' (Fig 64). Evidently by 1868 the Brewery belonged to or was leased to Mr Paulin. In the Greys Brewery Rent Ledger in 1885, Greys Brewery were leasing from Chamberlain the *Queen's Head*, the *Rifle* and Greys Hall (1885-96). In the ledger before the words 'Greys Hall' there was written 'Union Brewery' which was then crossed out. The rent of the three properties 1885-96 was £60 p.a.

Although Edmund Chamberlain still owned the corner property in 1885, it seems that he had for some time leased out the *Queen's Head* and the brewery. It is probable that Chamberlain began selling beer and opened the *Queen's Head* in about 1854 or just before that. Whether the Union Brewery had started at the *Union* pub in Hart Street and was transferred to Duke Street in about 1850 is unknown, though there do not seem to be any records of it as at the Union, though there was a malthouse at the *Union* (M28). The *Queen's Head* is first mentioned by name in Dutton Allen's street directory of 1863 when the landlord was given as Thomas Hart Grimsdale brewer.

At some time after 1867 it seems that the lease of the brewery was taken by Frederick Paulin who by coincidence was landlord of the *Union* Hart Street in 1868-9. At any rate in the Henley Advertiser of 10 January 1874 it was said that Frederick Paulin had sold the Union Brewery to Messrs Byles & Co of Greys Brewery on 20 December 1873. Since the property was owned by Chamberlain, it may have been the lease which was sold by Paulin. The Union Brewery was probably closed by Greys Brewery before 1885 since in their records they are listed as renting Greys Hall (now Queens Hall), and not the premises of the Union Brewery.

Meanwhile the *Queen's Head* continued in business after the rebuilding of 1870 when the whole of the west side of Duke Street was demolished for road widening. In 1872[262] the landlord of the *Queen's Head* Thomas Gregory took out an action against H W Thomson, butcher's apprentice to Walter Hudson of Duke Street, for recovery of £10, which Gregory claimed was the value of a large black retriever dog alleged to have been killed by Thomson. The dog was known as a stealer of meat from the shop, and Thomson took a whip to it, but claimed that the blow missed and the

261 The Court Leet Book of the Manor of Henley 1786-1881 in Town Hall
262 Henley Advertiser 21 Dec 1872

dog ran off. Gregory claimed that the dog had been struck with a broom and had died of his injuries. The case was dismissed due to lack of evidence or witnesses. One can imagine that feelings ran high in Duke Street.

In the 1880s the *Queen's Head* seems to have had a rough clientele. In 1883 in both January and August there were cases brought by the landlord taking action against customers who were drunk and disorderly[263]. In 1886 Mr Rowden was one of the landlords applying for a special license for refreshments at the Show Ground. In 1896 when Brakspears acquired Greys Brewery and its pubs, they at once made additions to the *Queen's Head*. The License Record which mentions this unfortunately does not say what the alterations were.

In 1937 there appears to have been a shortage of public lavatories in the town[264] a problem still arising in 1994. In 1937 Brakspears magnanimously agreed that the lavatories at the back of the *Queen's Head* should be open to the public. How long this lasted is not known.

Landlords/ Tenants of the *Queen's Head*

1854	Edmund Chamberlain (SD) brewer Union Brewery
1863-7	Thomas Hart Grimsdale (SD) brewer
1865	Henry Jones (RM)
1870-7	Thomas Gregory (SSM,C,HA,SD)
1881	Samuel Smith (C)
*1886-8	James Robert Rowden (RL,HA,SD)
Mar 1888-94	William Cleaver (RL,SD)
1894-5	William Vinnicombe (RL)
Aug 1895-6	Charles Stuart (RL)
1896-1905	Walter William Willmott (RL,SD)
Jul 1905-11	Alfred John Batzer (RL,SD)
May 1911-Sep	John Crabbe (RL)
Sep 1911-13	William Larner (RL)
Nov 1913-15	Thomas Albert Scott)RL)
Sep 1915-33	Charles Alfred Kennett (RL,WHB/C,SD)
Oct 1933-5	Peter Testa (RL,WHB/C,HS)
Sep 1935-7	Mrs Ivy Irene Elizabeth Testa (RL,WHB/C)
Jun 1937-8	Henry George Styles (RL,WHB/C)
Sep 1938-41	Leonard Darnell (RL,WHB/C)
Oct 1941-6	Dorothy Darnell (RL)
Feb 1946-50	Leonard Darnell (RL,WHB/C)
Sep 1950-9	Frederic George Turgis (RL,WHB/C)
Dec 1959-73	Henry Edward Ellott (RL,WHB/C)
Nov 1973-4	Barry Vincent Hughes (RL,WHB/C)
Oct 1974-7	William Beresford Bays (RL,WHB/C)
May 1977-82	Keith Jackson (RL,WHB/C)
Aug 1982-99-	William Dobson (RL,WHB/C)

263 Henley Advertiser 6 Jan 1883, 18 Aug 1883
264 Henley Standard 3 Dec 1937

89

The Red Cow or The Cow

80 West Hill/Street

The *Red Cow* or a beerhouse on the same site probably began trading in 1830-1(Fig 34). In the Reading Mercury & Oxford Gazette of 18 October 1830 there were advertised for sale 13 freehold messuages or tenements and a spacious building in front, occupying a frontage of 38ft and a depth of 150ft, well supplied with water, in West Street. The advertisement continued 'calculated for a Retail Brewery, Manufactory or for investment....the first building having excellent cellar room and at a trifling expense might be converted into a Public House.'

Fig 34 The tile fronted house was the Red Cow, entrance to the Workhouse was beyond it Photo1989

By 1 August 1831 what seems to be the same property was again advertised for sale, but this time as a 'Public House and a row of 13 tenements.'

The house then the *Red Cow* can be seen on the O.S. map of 1879 as having a row of tenements behind it, and its frontage was still 38ft. The tenements in 1879 were known as Smith's Row, by then there were only 12 of them, and they were in use by the Workhouse. They lined the west side of the walkway to the Workhouse grounds, now the grounds of the Hospital and Doctors' Surgeries.

A street directory of 1844 lists a Joseph Smith as a beer retailer in West Hill. The Henley Rentals for the premises show that in 1842 Barnett owned the building but it was occupied by J Smith; prior to that it was 'Miss Barnett late Stannford now Plumridge,' The name Stannford is variously spelt Stainford, Staniforth and Stanniford. It seems that Henry Stanniford was there from 1745-79, but there is no suggestion that it was then a beerhouse or public house. It is likely that Joseph Smith may have been the first landlord, starting perhaps in 1830-1, when the house was converted into a beerhouse.

In the Register of Licenses in 1877 an unnamed beerhouse on the 'north side of West Hill' was licensed to Thomas Smith, as also in the Magistrates Special Sessions Book of 1870 and 71. In the list of 1870 the words the *Red Cow* were pencilled in. The owner in 1877 was given as James Smith of Remenham Hill. By 1878 the license was held by Eleanor Smith, and the house was owned by John Pittman of Goring. By 1880 it was listed as the *Cow.*

In 1883 J Pitman of Goring Brewery advertised a beerhouse to let[265] 'Beerhouse with bakehouse and grocer's shop. West Hill, Henley.'

After the death of John Pitman/Pittman in 1887, Pitman's Brewery, together with 37 licensed houses were put up for sale. The Sales Catalogue[266] described the *Red Cow* as follows :-

265 Henley Standard 27 Jan 1883

266 O.R.O. Misc Lee III/ vi

'Lot No.37. The *Red Cow*. A freehold beerhouse the *Red Cow*, situate in populous district in West Hill contains - shop, bar parlour, tap room, bakehouse with, oven, wash house, cellar, 4 bedrooms, boxroom and attic. Passage at side leads to garden and outhouse. Back portion newly and substantially built. Let till recently for £15 p.a. but now in hand. Mr Parkman is caretaker.'

After the sale of the Goring Brewery and its pubs to Mrs Ann Gundry, and after several short term tenants, Walter Norris became landlord in April 1890[267]. The *Red Cow* is remarkable in that it was held by a Walter Norris from 1890 till its closure seventy years later, at the end of January 1960, when no application was made for renewal of the license[268]. Although throughout this time the landlord was Walter, it has to be said that the first Walter had a son Walter James, who in turn had a son Walter John[269]. The first Walter had the license for 42 years, in May 1932 the license was transferred to Walter James, the first Walter died in 1940 aged 75.

Apart from the beerhouse the main occupation of the first Walter, and later of his son, was as a baker. In 1886 when his son was baptised, the father's profession was given as baker and his address as the Fairmile. Probably one of the attractions of becoming licensee of the *Red Cow* was the 'bakehouse with oven'. Indeed in later years the bakery and shop became the most important part of the business, and the Norris' were known as bakers rather than as publicans. They had a well known delivery cart which carried their bakery goods around the town.

In 1924 at the Borough Brewster Sessions many licensed houses were said to be in need of cleaning and decorating. The *Red Cow* was one of three singled out for having unsatisfactory sanitary accommodation. The other two were the *Bear* and the *Bull.* In February 1925 it was said that the accommodation was now satisfactory[270].

In 1940 after the decease of Mrs Ann Gundry, her brewery and most of its pubs were bought by W H Brakspear & Sons, and after that till its closure in 1960 the *Red Cow* was owned by Brakspears[271].

Landlords/ Tenants of the *Red Cow*

1830?-44*	Joseph Smith (R,SD)
*1863-77	Thomas Smith (SSM,RL,SD) baker, grocer, beer retailer
1878	Eleanor Smith (RL)
1878-9	Henry Prince (RL)
1879-80	George Arlett (RL)
1880-7	John Lewis Coates (RL,HA,SD)
1887	(Mr Parkman (AucC) caretaker)
1887	Joseph Henry Harris (RL)
Nov 1887-8	James Parkway (RL)
Mar 1888-Aug	Alfred Beckett (RL)
Aug 1888-Dec	George Cresswell (RL,HA)
Dec 1888-90	Samuel Englefield (RL,HA)
Apr 1890-1932	Walter Norris (RL,HS,SD) baker
May 1932-60	Walter James Norris (RL,HS,SD) baker

— Closed —

267 Register of Licenses & Henley Advertise 12 Apr 1890
268 Register of Licenses & Henley Standard 5 Feb 1960
269 Henley Parish Registers
270 Henley Standard Feb 1924 & Feb 1925
271 Register of Licenses & Henley Standard 22 Nov 1940

90

The Red Cross or Assendon Cross

Assendon Road

The *Red Cross* was sometimes referred to as the *Assendon Cross* or simply the *Cross*. In the Bensington Manorial Records of 1815 it says the *Red Cross* once the *Assendon Cross*. It was at the Junction of the Fairmile with the road through Assendon, on the north east side, opposite the *Travellers Rest* which was on the V between the two roads. The *Red Cross* and the *Travellers Rest*, were both in Henley parish, but the *Golden Ball*, a few doors from the *Travellers Rest*, on the west side of the Assendon Road was in Bix parish. The *Golden Ball* is therefore not included in this survey of the pubs of Henley (one has to stop somewhere)

Fig 35 The Red Cross at Assendon in about 1890

The house that was until about 1900 the *Red Cross* (Figs 35 & 36) is still standing as a private house, and I have been told an eerie story about it by Mrs Bruce, who lived there for a time. While there she several times saw the ghost of a woman, dressed in a mob cap, with a crossed over bodice or draped shawl, above a full skirt. Mrs Bruce woke up to find the woman by her bed, she was not frightened but was impressed by an air of desperation coming from the woman; who said her name was Mary, that she was buried in the cellar and wanted Christian burial. Mrs Bruce a Quaker, not wanting to alarm her family, decided herself to say some prayers as a form of exorcism, and to give the spirit a Christian blessing. Mrs Bruce does not know how well it worked. However she was not alone in having seen the poor unquiet spirit, several others who have lived there have seen her, including Mrs Bruce's daughter, who later said that the woman had frequently come to her room, when she was younger, but that she had not spoken of it as she thought she would not be believed. Apparently at no time was the spirit frightening, all who have seen her speak of her as a sad and gentle spirit.

The description of dress though evocative, unfortunately would fit any servant girl from about 1700 to 1840 or even later. The name Mary is not much help either, being far too popular in all centuries. Altogether a sad story, and one wonders who she was and when she lived.

The house was probably a pub for most of the 18th century, if not before, it is possible that William Webb was landlord in 1753, and Annie Webb 1754-64, followed in 1774-88 by John Webb and in 1789-93 by Grace Webb[272].

There is some uncertainty after that, as Brakspears Rent Ledgers for the *Bix Cross* give 1791-5 James Ivermy, April 1795-1800 Edward Baylis and 1800-11 John Cox, while the Victuallers Recognizances mention none of these names. It is possible that Brakspears who were leasing the property, let the premises to Ivermy, Baylis and Cox, who in turn sub-let to others. The others seem to have been, according to Victuallers Recognizances, 1794-1812 Joseph Dyer/Dyor, 1816 John Gomm, 1817-18 Thomas Reeves and 1821-22 Sarah Reeves.

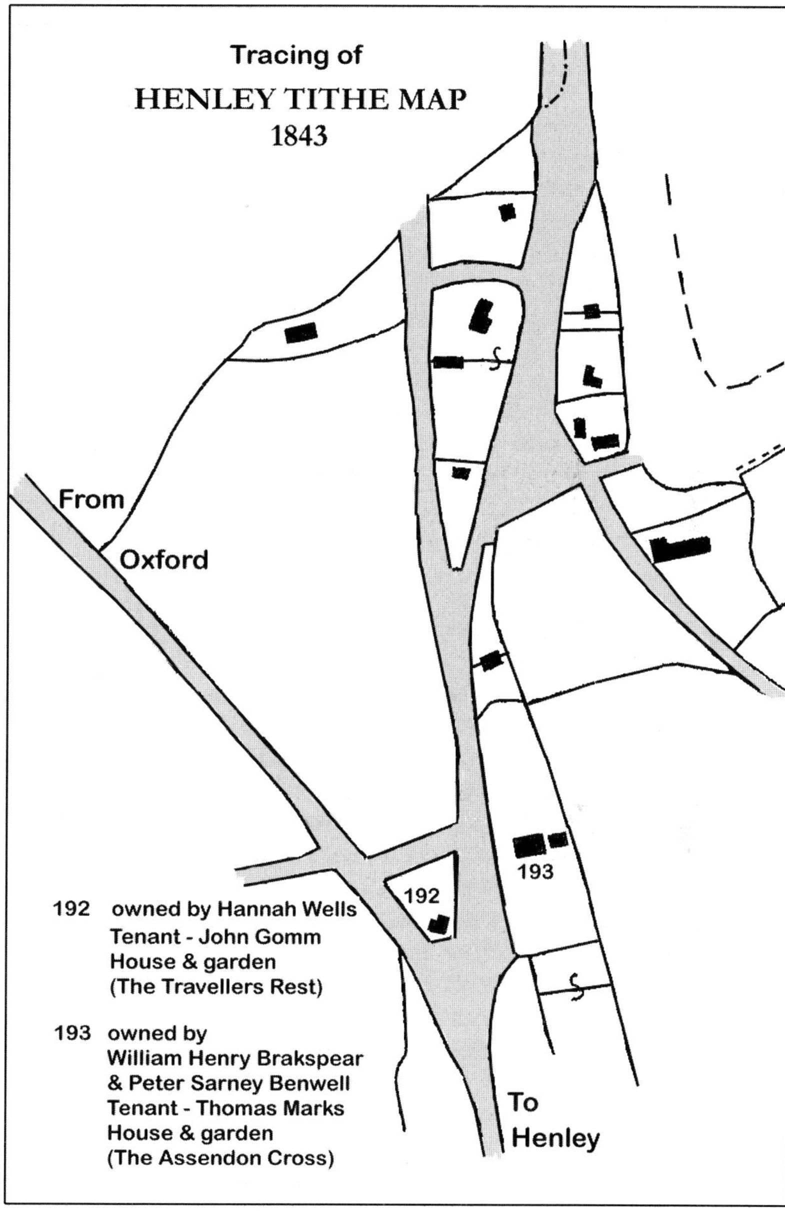

Fig 36 Part of the Henley Tithe Map 1843, showing positions of the Red Cross & the Travellers Rest at the end of the Fairmile

The problem is further confused by the Street Directory published in about 1793, in that James Ivermee is given at the *Red Cross* while Grace Webb is given as victualler at the *Cross*. If the *Cross* is the Assendon pub, which agrees with the Victuallers Recognizances, then Ivermee/ Ivermy must have been at the other *Red Cross* which was at 51 New Street. This not only was in Henley Town, which means that it does not feature in the Victuallers Recognizances at all, but also by no stretch of the imagination could be the *Bix Cross*. There is another possibility, that is that there was yet another *Red Cross* or *Cross* in Bix, which could have been the *Bix Cross* but if so it should have featured in the Victuallers Recognizances.

A reference in the book detailing the actions of the Court Leet of the manor of Henley

272 O.R.O. Victuallers Recognizances

says that an encroachment was made in 1801 by Joseph Dyer at the Cross in the Fairmile. This would support the evidence of the Victuallers Recognizances, and Ivermee etc must have been at the other *Red Cross*, Brakspears Rent Ledger must have had an error, substituting the word Bix for Red. A second entry in the Court Leet book of 1804 confirms that Joseph Dyer was at the Assendon *Cross,* when he was taken to court for an encroachment of inclosing a piece of ground of about 30 poles being the ditch belonging to the Lord of the Manor, and on which he had built a privy.

The Alehouse Keeper's List for Henley in 1817 gives a Daniel Reeves at the *Red Cross* (New Street), and he is known to have continued there until 1854, and appears in the Census of 1851 as aged 66. He would therefore have been 32 in 1817. On the other hand Sarah Reeves in 1822 is clearly at the *Cross* in Assendon, and she evidently took over from Thomas Reeves. The problem is aggravated by the coincidence of the name Reeves.

More definite is the Inventory of the Brewery of 1826, and this is clearly the *Red Cross* at Assendon. 'Public house held leasehold on 2 lives AC 66468. by Benwell and Brakspear. In occupation Richard Goddard with large garden. Rent £10 l0s 0d p.a. Land Tax 8s'. A note beneath says 'lease renewed WHB'. By the time of the Tithe Returns of 1844, it says Thomas Marks tenant of Benwell and Brakspear.

In September 1897 an occasional license was granted to Robert Carpenter Bratchell of the *Red Cross*, Assendon[273], to sell liquor in a field at Lambridge Wood on the occasion of the Volunteer Annual Prize Shooting on 2 October 1897. In February of 1903 the death of Robert Bratchell of the *Travellers Rest* was announced in the Henley Standard, it said that he was formerly landlord of the *Red Cross* on the opposite side of the road to the *Travellers Rest*, and that upon the *Cross* being done away with, Mr Bratchell went to the new *Travellers Rest* which was erected some two or three years ago. The new *Travellers Rest* was built in 1900, so if Mr Bratchell went there then, it would seem that the *Red Cross* must have closed in either 1900 or perhaps 1899.

Landlords/ Tenants of the *Red Cross* at Assendon

*1753	William Webb (VR)	
1754-64*	Annie Webb (VR)	
*1774-88	John Webb (VR)	
1789-93	Grace Webb (VR,SD	(1791-5 James Ivermy (WHB/R))
1794-1812*	Joseph Dyer/Dyor (VR,CL)	(1795-1800 Edward Baylis (WHB/R))
1817-18*	Thomas Reeves (VR)	
1821-22	Sarah Reeves (VR)	
1826	Richard Goddard (WHB/I)	
*1842-61	Thomas Marks (C,TM,RM,SD)	
Nov 1861-7	James Nurse (RM,SD)	
1868	John Adey (SD)	
1869-77*	Stephen Parson (SD)	
*1881	William Budd (C)	
1882-97*	Robert Carpenter Bratchell (SSM,RL,HS,SD)	

— Closed —

273 Special Sessions Minutes Book 30 Sep 1897

91

The Red Cross

51 New Street

The *Red Cross* in New Street was also sometimes known as the *Cross*, which leads to the confusion over landlords already mentioned under the *Red Cross* at Assendon, in the period 1790-1815. The landlords for the *Red Cross* named in the Victuallers Recognizances are for a pub outside Henley Town and therefore cannot be for the *Red Cross* New Street

The names Ivermee/Ivermy, Baylis and Cox mentioned in the Brakspear, Rent Ledgers could be for the New Street *Cross*, the only problem is that they are listed as at the Bix *Cross,* but as suggested in the previous entry for the *Red Cross* at Assendon this must have been an error.

Fig 37 The Red Cross, New Street after closure as a pub. On left the yard of Brakspear's large malthouse, M40 Photo 1989

The *Red Cross* in New Street was a small building now a private house (Fig 37), alongside what, from about 1900 was the yard of Brakspears main malthouse (M40) and stables (Fig 66). The house is the only remaining house of what were originally ten dwellings, known for many years as Floyd's Tenements. The Bridge Rent Book of 1886 says 'Messrs W H Brakspear & Sons for Floyd's tenements', added afterwards it says 'the *Red Cross* public house 8s.' In 1879[274] there were still five cottages stretching back behind the *Red Cross*, along the eastern side of the yard. There remain today traces of a fireplace of the one which was immediately behind the *Red Cross*.

The tenements or perhaps a single house on the site, were given to the town by the will of Richard Dunte in December 1589[275] to provide income for Dunte's Charity, which gave 8s p.a. to

274 O.S.map of 1879 Scale 10,560 or 6 ins to 1 mile (41.66 ft to 1 in)

275 Cooper, John 'An Account of the Charities under the Management of the Corporation of Henley on THames' 1858

eight aged and impotent men' (the word 'impotent' then meant infirm or frail). Dunte had acquired the property from Francis Stonor Esq. and in 1589 one of the occupants was William Ellis. Like other properties 'given to the town', they were often sold later but with the obligation of continuing to pay the Rental, in this case 8s from 1589, the same was still being paid in 1886, and was finally redeemed on 31 March 1967.

Henley Rentals 1733-69 say Floyd's tenements late Normans, 1775-79 Mr Shaw late Floyd's, and in 1785 Hayward. Floyd, Shaw and Hayward were all brewers, so it was likely that there was already a public house there by 1733. One wonders if William Ellis in 1589 was a publican. Often in a case of multiple tenancy of tenements, where one building is a public house, the name of the landlord is the only occupant mentioned. There is also the possibility that Richard Dunte was connected to the brewing or public house trade, his other property left in his will was of a tenement called the *Holie Bush.* (See the entry for the *Holie Bush.*)

By the 1790s Robert Brakspear had inherited from his uncle Richard Hayward, and Floyd's tenements feature in Brakspears Rent Ledgers. As already stated in the account of the *Red Cross* at Assendon there is some confusion about the tenants of the two *Red Cross* pubs in the 1790s. The Victuallers Recognizances place Grace Webb in 1793 at the Assendon pub, which means that of the two entries in the Street Directory of about 1793, 'Grace Webb victualler (Cross)' means Assendon, while 'James Ivermee victualler (Red Cross)' means New Street.

Brakspears Rent Ledgers having listed various other properties says 'The Bix *Cross* James Ivermy 1791-95, Edward Baylis Apr 1795-1800, Jno Cox Lady Day 1800-11.' This is followed immediately by the New Street tenements (Floyds) in the following order - Nos 4,3,2,1, then 10,9,7,8,6. It will be noted that there is no number 5, and it is as though the numbering went back from the street at one side, and that, whoever was collecting rents then went back to the road in the reverse order of numbers on the other side. Was number 5 the *Red Cross* ?

In 1826 in the Inventory of the Brewery the freehold was held by W H Brakspear Esq. 'In occupation of Daniel Reeve with 3 stalled stable, loft and garden and 8 brick erected cottages with gardens to each one, the yard contiguous to the Red Cross, and occupied by tenants - Wayman, Austin, Anderson, Hunt, Hussey, Trimming, Alloway and Gosby. A range of newly erected Pig Styes on brick piers with slated roofs.' In pencil a note says 'Rent one cottage £25'.

This meant that by 1826 one of the cottages had gone, in fact 6 was marked in the ledger as 'Condemned' on 3 October 1801, although tenants are given for it up to 1811.

Of the tenants in 1826 Austin (James) had been there since 1800, Hussey (Bristow) since 1791, and Gosby (John) since Lady Day 1808. Interestingly a John Cox was a tenant of one of the cottages from 1808-11.

The position of the *Red Cross* near the bottom of New Street meant that it must often have had extra trade at Regatta times. In August 1923[276] Mr Woodley of the *Red Cross* was given permission to open for the afternoon of the Henley United Rowing,Club Regatta.

The *Red Cross* remained open until October 1977 when on the 21st the Henley Standard announced that the *Red Cross* 'closed last week'.

Landlords/ Tenants of the *Red Cross,* New Street

*1791-5	James Ivermee/Ivermy (WHB/R,SD)
1795-1800	Edward Baylis/Bayliss (WHB/R,CL)
1800-11*	John Cox (WHB/R,CL)
1814-54	Daniel Reeves/Reeve (AKL,CL,PF,C,SD)
1863-71	Thomas Seymour (SSM,C,SD)
*1876-94	Thomas Pusey (RL,C,SD)

276 Henley Standard 24 Aug 1923

1894-6	William Jarvis (RL,SD)
1896-9	Charles Prior (RL)
Apr 1899-Dec	Stephen Eggleton (RL)
Dec 1899-1902	Henry Jemmett (RL)
Oct 1902-4	Alfred Thomas Kent (RL)
May 1904-7	Charles Edmund Collins (RL)
Jan 1907-Sep	Walter Robert Carter (RL)
Sep 1907-10	Alfred Robert Pothecary (RL)
Sep 1910-39	Charles Thomas Woodley (RL,HS,SD)
Jul 1939-53	Violet Mary Prior Woodley (RL)
Sep 1953-4	Edward George Chapman (RL)
Jul 1954-7	Cecily Edith Davis (RL)
Mar 1957-63	Harold Jefford Davis (RL)
May 1963-4	Sheila Grace Davis (RL)
Nov 1964-5	Philip Edward Putnam & Sheila Grace Davis (RL)
Jul 1965-77	Mrs Winifred Sim (RL)

— Closed —

92

The Red Lion

Hart Street or Thames side

The *Red Lion Hotel* is situated on the corner of Hart Street and Thames side north. It has a large yard behind, and buildings which circle the yard. It was very much altered in 1889, when the main yard entrance, which went under the house into the yard from the Hart Street side, where the present porch now stands (Cover photo), was converted into a reception room and hallway, while a billiard room and other rooms were built out into the yard at the back (Fig 39). The only entrance for carriages or carts after this to the yard was the one still there on Thames side.

The oldest part of the *Red Lion* is on the west side, running back from the road and alongside the path leading to the Chantry House, behind the east end of the church. This part of the *Red Lion* like the Chantry House, which abuts the north wall, is built in three storeys. A ground floor level with the yard of the *Red Lion*, a middle floor on a level with the churchyard, and a top floor. The wing of the *Red Lion* shares its north wall with the south end of the Chantry House, and it is not at all clear which came first[277]. The Chantry House has been dated to about 1400. The present top floor of this wing of the *Red Lion* is divided into three bedrooms, and it used to be evident from the timber mullion remains of windows on their east side, that the passage now connecting them on that side, did not once exist, that the windows were on an outside wall. Recent changes, 1987-91, to install 'en suite' bathrooms have destroyed all but one of the mullions. At the south end, of the building, there was an enormous chimney breast, now also destroyed to make a bathroom. The chimney came up through the upper floors from what must have been a large fireplace on the ground floor, its base may be seen in the kitchen area of the plan Fig 39. The whole of this three storied wing was probably the original *Red Lion*.

277 Steane, John; Gibson, Ruth; & Cottingham, Ann 'The Chantry House & the Oldest Part of the Red Lion' 1997 pub. Henley Archaeological & Historical Group

This old part of the *Red Lion* is a building reputed to house a ghost, apparently sighted by several different people. He is said to have long hair and to be a cavalier, but who he was is unknown. Others merely say that they have felt a presence in the room, but no one seems to have been unduly frightened, even the person who said that they felt themselves being pushed.

The Chantry House is alleged to have been the residence of the Chantry priests, though viewing the fact that those priests were of the lowest ranks of the clergy, and the so called Chantry House is a grand three storeyed residence, this seems somewhat unlikely. At any rate from the 15th century to the 18th century it was used by two of the schools of Henley, at other times it was let out to the *Red Lion*, was sold to the *Red Lion* in 1846, and in 1922 bought back by the Church. The ground floor or basement is still leased by the *Red Lion*, as it has been for several centuries. Indeed a lease of 1732, mentioned in more detail later, includes in the lease 'all the stables under the Blewschool Roomes with the Brewhouse standing in the said yard or backside.' Although the Chantry House is connected on its middle floor to the churchyard and thence to the church, its main aspect is to the yard of the *Red Lion*. It is on this side that one sees the imposing three storeys and the two projecting jetties. However Ruth Gibson[278] suggests that the timbers on the churchyard side may indicate that its front face was perhaps to a road or path leading from New Street to between the Red Lion and the church, and that its yard side was only the working side of the building.

Recent work sorting and cataloguing documents in the Town Hall by the Henley Archaeological & Historical Group, has revealed early deeds concerning the Chantry House and its land. The earliest of these is dated to the 23rd year of Henry VI (1444) when Sir John Say who had become the Rector of Henley in 1443, sold the property to the two merchants John Elmes and John Devene. There is at that time no mention of priests, chantry or otherwise. The property consisted of the house backing on to the churchyard, a yard or vacant place of land and two granaries on the east side or river side (See plan of Schoolhouse & Storehouse of 1726 Fig 38). On the south side of these there was a vacant place of land sometime of Henry Bradley. To the north there was a granary of John Lytching and a vacant place of land and a messuage of Henry Martin called the Wollhouse.

From the deed of 1444 it is clear that the *Red Lion* if it then existed, may have been occupied by a Henry Bradley, that there was no building on the land to the south east and that possibly the only building which could have been the *Red Lion* was the one adjoining the Chantry House (on Fig 39 labelled the kitchen, scullery & service area with cellars beneath). This old building was a contemporary of the Chantry House and probably also built in about 1400. The earliest mention of the building as the *Lyon* is in the will of Robert Kenton dated 1532[279], he left tenements in Henley, lands and the *Lyon*. This seems to be the earliest available mention of the *Red Lion* as a hostelry, the earlier mention of Henry Bradley and later Michael Wolley in 1553, do not name a pub.

The deed concerning the Chantry House in the 6th year of Edward VI (1553) was for the sale of the property described as a messuage or tenement in the churchyard in Henley called the Schoolhouse four chambers or tenements in the churchyard called the priests chambers one woodhouse or portage with the granaries and cellars thereto belonging and barn thereto adjoining two granaries. All that messuage between the churchyard of Henley on the west and the highway which is between the said messuage and the River Thames on the east and the tenement in which dwelleth Michael Wolley on the south and the tenement of John Bradley and John Assendon on the north. This may mean that by 1553 there was no longer a vacant plot at the corner but that possibly

278 Same as note 277

279 Peberdy, Robert B 'The Economy and government of a small town in Medieval England: A study of Henley on Thames from c1300-c1540' 1994 Thesis for a Doctorate at Leicester University

the *Red Lion* had extended from the old building on the church side, and was then occupied by Michael Wolley.

It was not till 1578 that the Chantry House was sold to the Warden Burgesses etc of the town, by then in the 20th year of Elizabeth the building was termed the Schoolhouse, and the granaries at the front facing the river were known as the Storehouse. In 1604 the 2nd year of James the Warden etc sold the Schoolhouse and Storehouse to the Governors of the Free Grammar School of Henley. They remained in the ownership of the Grammar School and later the United Free Schools until 1846, but long before that the *Red Lion* had enlarged its premises by leasing the Storehouse building and the yard.

John S Burn in his 'History of Henley' has an entry for the *Red Lion*, and a footnote says that in 1621 the proprietor was Rice Freeman. Rice Freeman was baptised on 28 Jan 1570/1, the fourth son of his father Henry. Rice married three times, to Jane, Agneta and Jana, and had seven children, one son and two daughters by his first wife, and one son and three daughters by his third wife, the last being born in 1636. There seems to be no local record of Rice Freeman's death or burial, nor does he appear in the Protestation Returns of 1641-2. His third wife Jana/Jane was buried in 1640, when she was described as wife not widow[280].

Fig 38 Plan of Schoolhouse (Chantry House) & Storehouse of 1726 superimposed on part of the O.S. map of 1879 showing the Red Lion's original plot size

In 1723 in a document belonging to the United Schools Charities, the lease holder of the Storehouse for the next eleven years was John Eaglesfield of Henley innholder. At that time the property was described as the stables, granaries, and other buildings commonly called the Storehouse late in the occupation of Sarah Stevenson widow, and now in the occupation of John Eaglesfield. Also all that Wharf on the west side of the river partly adjoining the said storehouse, shown on the plan of 1793 as the old Campshot.(Fig 31).

In 1726 the Schools' Charities had a plan drawn up showing the properties which they owned, a plan also discovered in the Town Hall. In

280 Parish Registers. Baptisms, Marriages & Burials 1558-1653

this there was a plan of the Schoolhouse and the Storehouse, in which the yard is called the Red Lion Yard. When the plan of 1726 was reduced to the same scale as the O.S.map of 1879, and then superimposed upon the map of 1879 (Fig 38) it can be seen that the Storehouse occupied the riverside frontage of the *Red Lion* from the end of what is now the Century Galleries to the middle of what is now the dining room.

A lease[281] of the Storehouse in 1732 by the Governors of the Schools to Robert Underwood of the *Red Lion* says that the previous tenants were Sarah Stevenson, John Eaglesfield and then George Harison. It then goes on to describe all that stable with hay loft over, lying near the Thames between that part of the messuage or tenement or Inn of Sarah Stevenson 'called the *Red Lyon Inn* now in the occupation of the said Robert Underwood which was lately new built on the south part thereof and another part of the said Storehouse and building (being a cross building) lying on the north part thereof.' The cross building would seem to be the building shown in the plan in Fig 38, as going from east to west, and it sounds as though it was fairly recently that the *Red Lion* to the south had been new built. It is difficult in deeds to ascertain what is meant by the term 'new built' it could refer to the previous twenty years or so, or it might mean a slightly longer time. The building to the south, that of Michael Wolley in 1553, was perhaps demolished, and the corner building and frontage as it is today, built either at the end of the 17th century or beginning of the 18th century.

In the part of the *Red Lion* probably built perhaps in the late 17th century in an upstairs room[282] facing the river and the bridge, a painting of the Royal Arms with the monogram of Charles I dated 1632, was discovered in the restorations of 1889. It is said that Charles I stayed here in 1632 on his way to Oxford and again in 1642, on that occasion accompanied by Prince Rupert. This suggests that the 'new built' part was much earlier, indeed it would seem to imply that it was built at least a hundred years before the lease of 1732, which is unlikely. The coat of arms was most probably a later painting than the date given, maybe painted during the reign of Charles II to commemorate the visit of Charles I, when royalty was again in fashion towards the end of the 17th century when the building was perhaps 'new built'.

An Indenture made on 26 January 1712 between (1) Hanway (2) G Jemmett of Shiplake (3) Gregory Stevenson innholder & Sarah his wife & (4) John Blackman brewer & others concerns the messuage called the *Red Lyon*[283] on the west side of the bridge formerly in occupation of Nathaniel Worley deceased, afterwards of Widow Frances Worley and now in occupation and tenure of Gregory Stevenson. The churchyard in Henley lying on the west side of the messuage, the school house storehouse and yard on the north side the highway to the south and the Thames to the east. It also concerns various plots of land around Henley, and land in Watlington.

In 1716 Gregory Stevenson innholder made a settlement of the *Red Lion* and some of the land on his wife Sarah, the trustee was William Worley of London tobacconist. In 1720 Gregory Stevenson made his will, he was buried on 4 March 1720/1, he left all his property to his wife Sarah, and it would seem that by 1723 she had handed over the running of the *Red Lion* to John Eaglesfield, when he was the named innholder taking out the lease, previously held by Sarah Stevenson.

The will of Sarah Stevenson widow in 1734 left £20 p.a. from rent of the *Red Lion* to her sister Elizabeth Floyd. To various nieces and nephews £100 each and various other bequests, the residue and presumably the *Red Lion* itself she left to her nephew Nathaniel Worley. The overseers of the will each received £10, one of them was Francis Blandy the ill fated father of Mary (see the *Angel* Remenham).

281 Document among papers of the Schools Charities now removed to O.R.O.

282 Climenson, Mrs Emily J 'Guide to Henley on Thames' 1896

283 O.R.O. Misc Cooper IV/ 1-7 Documents of 1712, 1716, 1734, 1751, 1756

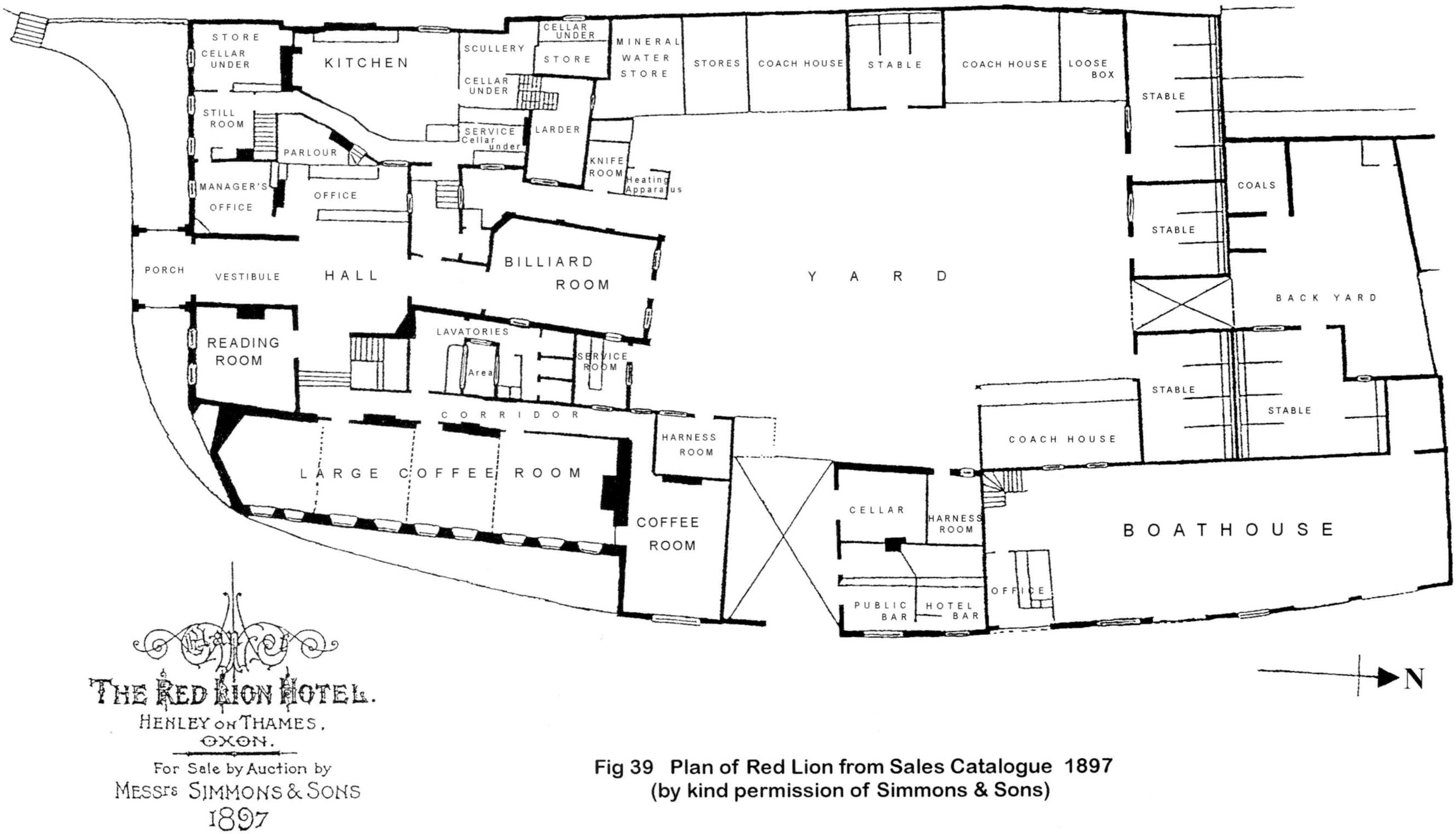

Fig 39 Plan of Red Lion from Sales Catalogue 1897
(by kind permission of Simmons & Sons)

In 1751 Nathaniel Worley of Staples Inn, London, gentleman sold the *Red Lion* to Solomon Toll, all that messuage called the *Red Lyon* formerly in tenure and occupation of Gregory Stevenson deceased, now in occupation of Edward Prascey, together with some land.

In 1756 Solomon Toll had an abstract of title to the *Red Lion* drawn up, and in 1757 a mortgage that says now in occupation Edward Prascey. This is the last in a series of documents concerning the *Red Lion* at the Oxford Record Office.

Henley Parish Burial Register 1653-1703 shows that the first Mr Nathaniell Worley mentioned as deceased in the deed of 1712, was buried on the 3 January 1678/9 and his widow Frances innholder on 23 February 1705/6. Nathaniell had nine children baptised in Henley, two of whom were called Sara, one born in 1665 and the other in 1666. However one daughter called Sara died and was buried on 29 June 1665. Her death was the last entry in the Register before the plague, which raged in Henley from the beginning of July 1665 to September 1666. Sarah Stevenson was almost certainly the daughter born in 1666 of Nathaniel and Frances, which would have made her 68 when she died in 1734. It could be that it was her father Nathaniel Worley, who had part of the *Red Lion* 'new built'.

In 1665 the Hearth Tax was listed in Henley, and the residents had the number of their hearths counted. Unfortunately no other information is forthcoming from the lists, but there is the name (on Membrane 3) of Nathaniell Worley and alongside the number xiij. This number of hearths is consistent with him occupying a large inn such as the *Red Lion*, and maybe proves that he was in occupation at that time, indeed he may have been there in 1656, as that is the date of the baptism of Christopher, his first child to be christened in Henley. There is no record of Nathaniell's baptism or marriage, so it is likely that he was not a Henley man, he probably came from London, as the later connections suggest.

A plan of the waterfront belonging to the Town Council and kept in the Town Hall vault has recently come to light. The plan (Fig 31) is undated but would appear to be of about 1793, property further along the Waterside was listed as belonging to Mr Hayward who died in 1797,and Mr Clements on the corner no longer rented that property after 1793 (see entry for the *Little White Hart*). On the plan the measurements are given from the front of the buildings to the river wall, and after the one at the north of the School premises, the next says Middle of the new granary, and the one after that, the North corner of the New Granary.

These two granaries, now the Century Galleries, had for a long time been the property of or leased by the innholders of the *Red Lion*. They continued however as granaries and only were incorporated into the Red Lion in 1888 when Mr T Shepherd bought the *Red Lion.* He converted the granaries into a large boathouse (Fig 39), which has now become the Century Galleries. The boathouse contained upstairs boat building facilities, while the ground floor was used for boat storage and a boat hiring business. This boathouse was included in the sale description of the *Red Lion* in 1897[284]. Although the Sale Catalogue was drawn up in 1897, Mr Shepherd was listed as licensee in 1898, and it was not till November 1898 that his death was reported in the Henley Standard, when he was described as proprietor of the *Red Lion.* He apparently had an accident falling down some six stairs and died soon after.

There are two entries in the Bridge Rent Book of 1886 which apply to the *Red Lion* No.19 'Messrs W H Brakspear & Sons late Philip Barrett Cooper formerly Barrett March for a house etc known as the *Red Lion Hotel* formerly in the occupation of James Dixon, and now of Mrs Elizabeth Williams' added after 'now Mr T Shepherd and now the *Red Lion Hotel Co.*' No.20 same ownership, a house 'now used as a Granary being part of the premises of the *Red Lion*

284 Simmons & Lawrence Auction Catalogue, the Red Lion 1897

Hotel'. No.19 was for the main part of the *Red Lion,* while No.20 was for what are now the Century Galleries.

Following these entries back in the **Henley Rentals** one finds the entries as follows:-

The Red Lion	**The Granaries, now the Century Galleries**
1842-36 Dixon for the Red Lion	1842-36 Dixon late Jeffs
1828 P B Cooper for Red Lion occ. Dixon	1828 late Jeffs
1823 Barrett March	1823 late Jeffs, late Gleed now Dixon
1814 B March	1814 late Jeffs now Dixon
1807 Mrs Barrett March occ. Dixon	1807 Mrs Barrett March own occ. late Jeffs
1800,1795,93 Barrett March	1800,1795, 93, 90 Barrett March own occ. late Jeffs
1790 B March late Babbage now Andrews	

Court Baron Book 1785 :- Mr Andrews tenement called the *Red Lion* and B March lately converted two tenements to a stable and encroached on Waste of the Manor and hath built a stable thereon and for granaries late Benj Sarney and late Darby near the Waterside.

Rentals again :-

1785,79,75 Mr Andrews for the *Red Lyon*	1785 late Jeffs now Barrett March 1779, 75 late Jeffs now Barrett March own occ late Gleeds
1769 late Mr Pracey for the *Red Lyon* now March & Andrews	1769 Mrs Jeffs late Falleys & Widow Robinson, now Widow Smith
1765 Pracey for the *Red Lion* & more for sign & garden	1765 Jeffs late Falleys & Benj Sarney late John Darby
1758 Same as above	1758 Robt Jeffs Esq late Falleys more in possession Widow Smith & Benj Sarney late Darby
1737 Mr Underwood for the *Red Lion* more for sign garden & encroachment	1737 Mr Jeffs tenement late in his possession, more for Widow Smith, Mrs Darby tenement Thameside
1733/4 Underwood for the *Lyon*, more for sign, encroachment of a wall, & garden	1733/4 Mr Jeffs ten. occ. Jas Farsley (Falley?)more for house occ. Rich Smithe & Mr Darby tenement
1727/8 Mr Harrison for *Red Lyon*, encroachment of a pale & a garden	1727/8 Mr Jeffes occ by John Eponsley(?) & House occ Richard Smith, & Mr Darby for ten. Thameside
1721/2 Mr Stevenson for the *Red Lyon*, wall & garden	1721/2 Mr Jeffes occ James Hallay (Falley?) & house occ. Richard Smith, & William Darby ten.
1713/4 Mr Stevenson for *Redd Lyon,* & for wall	1713/4 John Darby house in occ & for tenement occ Rich Smith & others

These entries show that the two houses or tenements taken in to the *Red Lion* and demolished to make way for stables in about 1780-5, were previously not part of the *Red Lion.* They stood on the land behind the granaries, and one of them may have been the messuage of Henry Martin in 1444, called the Wollhouse. In the plan of 1897 (Fig 39), stables can be seen behind the boathouse, and there is a dividing wall which may indicate the division between the two houses.

The area to the south, consisting in the plan of the *Red Lion* in 1897 as being the space occupied by the Public & Hotel Bars, the Yard Entrance, the Coffee Room, and about half of the north section of the Large Coffee Room, was shown in 1793 as being the property of the Free Schools, in fact the Storehouse of earlier deeds.

In the 19th century the part that had been the Storehouse to the north of the yard entrance, had become known as the *Red Lion Tap,* it is referred to as such in the Court Leet Book in 1809 when someone called Tidy was in charge, then in 1813 it was B Neighbour, evidently separate from the main Inn. By the Court Leet session of 26 October 1868 Mr Welch was charged for making an encroachment since the last meeting of the Court in 1836, by projecting a bow window in front of that part of the Red Lion premises by the Thames side which lies to the north of the Gateway there and which is now used as a Tap.

Many well known people since Charles I have had connections with the *Red Lion.* The first Duke of Marlborough is said to have furnished a room in the hotel, so that he could stop there on his frequent journeys from London to Blenheim and back. The poet William Shenstone, who died in 1763 and is sometimes referred to as the 'water poet', wrote on the glass of one of the windows part of the poem which is in the frontispiece to this book. Dr Johnson and Boswell stopped at the *Red Lion* in 1776, and Boswell commented on the poem on the window. It was also on the same trip while staying at Chapel House near Blenheim that Dr Johnson made his comment on Inns in general and their delights, also quoted in the frontispiece.

George III, whose parents had lived at Park Place, also knew the *Red Lion*, and on 12 July 1788 the king, the queen, the Princess Royal, and the princesses Augusta and Elizabeth all had breakfast there. The Prince Regent was another habitué, his friend the Earl of Barrymore lived at Wargrave, and the prince was often in Henley. It is said that at one sitting he ate fourteen mutton chops.

The visits of royalty continued, culminating in the visit to Henley in June 1814, of the Allied Princes on their way to Oxford to receive academic honours. Among them were Alexander of Russia, the King of Prussia with his nephews, one of whom became William I of Germany, and lastly General Blucher. The procession passed in front of the *Red Lion*, and did not stop, except for General Blucher who was brought back to drink wine with Lady Malmesbury, who had been watching from a window of the *Red Lion.*

Robert Dixon and Mrs Deborah Dixon had presided over many of these glamorous events, it appears that Robert Dixon was the landlord in 1799, since it was he who was accused by the Court Leet of making an encroachment by taking in a piece of land of 38 square yards in a triangular line on the east front of the *Red Lion.* Barrett March was still the owner and it was he who was taken before the Court Leet in 1808 for another encroachment. This time it was for placing railings at the south front of the *Red Lion* on each side of the gateway before the windows. Railings which were removed in the Second World War, and which have now (1999) been replaced. Robert Dixon was buried on 12 February 1810 aged 58, and his widow Deborah died aged 66 in 1832, and their son James took over, helped by his brother George. James aged 64 and George aged 62 were both buried on 11 September 1849. Their death at the same time suggests some disease, perhaps cholera, though rumour insisted that they were poisoned. After their death the *Red Lion* was closed, and in the Reading Mercury & Oxford Gazette of 1855 and 1856 was advertised for sale, and it was added that since Mr Dixon's death the business had been suspended. Mrs Elizabeth Williams who had been at the *Catharine Wheel* took over the *Red Lion* and re-opened it in May 1859, and ran it till her death in 1887. It was soon after her opening in 1859 that there occurred the visit of the 11th Hussars (Introduction p15).

Although coaches and travellers must always have been a feature of the *Red Lion*, and indeed the enlarging of the premises by building new stables in about 1780 is an indication of this, it was probably busier with private coaches and chaises belonging to the gentry rather than with public coach services. It also may have been busy in 1794 with another sort of customer. The Reading Mercury & Oxford Gazette of May 1794 offers a Five Guineas Bounty to those joining the Oxfordshire Light Dragoons, 'not to go out of England but to serve their King and Country at home. Commandant the Hon. Major Parker.' It continues:-

> 'All lads of spirit willing to enlist in the above corps, may have a horse, pay and quarters immediately by applying to Capt. Auriol in Caversham, at the *Red Lion* in Henley, or to Sergeant Hyde at his house in Broad Street Reading. None but young men of good character and appearance from 5ft 4ins to 5ft 8ins high will be accepted. GOD SAVE THE KING.'

In the heyday of public coaching in 1830 there were coaches to London from the *Bell* calling at the *Red Lion* every morning (Sundays excepted) at seven, every morning at five and every Saturday morning at nine. By 1850 when coaching was beginning to give way to the railway, Dixon's coach from the *Bell Tap* to London called at the *Red Lion* every morning at nine. There was also the Train Coach to Twyford from the *Bell Tap* calling at the *Red Lion* every morning at eight and a quarter before one noon. This of course was before the branch line of the Great Western Railway came to Henley from Twyford in 1856.

Brakspears seem to have purchased the *Red Lion* in 1872, it was sold to Shepherd in 1888, and sold again after 1897, possibly not till 1899, when it was bought by Walter Henry Harris of the *Red Lion Hotel Co*. In 1918 it was bought by Messrs Hobbs & Sons Ltd. Shortly after the *Red Lion* became the property of Messrs Hobbs, the licensee, A J Hobbs was in trouble before the Magistrates[285] for serving beer at excessive prices above the maximum price. He was fined fairly heavily, but retained his license for some years. Of recent years the *Red Lion* seems to have frequently changed ownership, and has been owned by various individuals or hotel companies. Since 1946 two individuals seem to hold the license, one of whom has probably been the Manager.

Landlords/ Tenants of the *Red Lion*

1444 ?	Henry Bradley(THD)
1532	Robert Kenton (THD)
1578 ?	Michael Wolley (THD)
1621-36?	Rice Freeman ?
*1656-78/9	Nathaniel/Nathaniell Worley (ORO,BaReg,BReg,HT)
1678-1705	Frances Worley (ORO,BReg)
1705-1720/1	Gregory Stevenson (ORO,BReg,R)
1720-34	Mrs Sarah Stevenson owner but as landlords:-
1723	John Eaglesfield (TH), 1727/8 Mr Harrison/Harison (TH,R)
1732-47	Mr Robert Underwood (TH,R,RM)
1751-65	Edward Prascey/Pracey (ORO,VR 1753-4)
*1766?-9?	March & or Babbage ? (R)

285 Henley Standard 26 Sep 1919

1769-90	Andrews (R,CB)
1793-1800	Barrett March (R, VR lists as innkeeper 1770-1,CL)
*1799-1810	Robert Dixon (R,CL,BReg)
1809	*Red Lion Tap* —Tidy(CL)
1813	*Lion Tap* B Neighbour (CL)
?1836-68*	*Red Lion Tap* Mr Welch
1810-32	Mrs Deborah Dixon (R,AKL,CL,SD,BReg)
1832-49	James & George Dixon (R,C,SD,BReg)
1849-59	————closed————
1859-87	Mrs Elizabeth Williams (SSM,RL,C,RM,SD)
1887	Mrs Morgan of the *Catharine Wheel* (HA)
Sep 1887-8	Frederick Francis Williams (SSM,RL)
Mar 1888-98	Thomas Shepherd (RL,HA,HS,AucC,SD)
Mar 1899-1905	Henry William Boston (RL)
Jul 1905-8	Charles Hans Burkard (RL,SD)
Jul 1908-9	Grace Augusta Waghorn (RL)
Nov 1909-10	Francis Spencer Colson Phillips (RL)
May 1910-15	Herbert Medland Manley (RL)
1915-17	Gerald Blewett Manley (RL)
1917-37	Arthur John Hobbs (RL,HS,SD)
Feb 1937-46	Maj Arthur Wilfred Farwell (RL,HS,SD)
May 1946-7	Jessica Amelia Beecham & Ivy Florence Gertrude Fleming (RL)
May 1947-8	Leslie Harold Smith & — Browill (RL)
May 1948-50	Leslie Harold Smith & Desmond William Lionel Alexander (RL)
Feb 1950-Jul	Clifford Firth Middleton & Michael Henry Hengell Elphinstone(RL)
Jul 1950-1	Clifford Firth Middleton & Rene David Duquenoy (RL)
Jan 1951-May	Clifford Firth Middleton & Rosemary Duquenoy (RL)
May 1951-2	Clifford Firth Middleton & Cyrus Retablock (?) (RL)
May 1952-3	Maxwell Joseph & Leonard David De Pinna (RL)
May 1953-4	Maxwell Joseph & Cynthia Grace Baker (RL)
Dec 1954-5	Maxwell Joseph & Alfred Brigden (RL)
May 1955-66	David James Summerby (RL)
Aug 1966-72	Richard John Elsden (RL)
Feb 1972-3	Peter Alan Kirby Ottewill (RL)
Sep 1973-88	Charles Anthony Ractliffe (RL)
Apr 1988-95	Jean Paul Leveque & Charles James Benjamin Miller (RL)
Feb 1995-97	Charles James Benjamin Miller &Richard Sharland Burwell(RL)
Aug 1997-99-	Charles James Benjamin Miller & JamesWilliam Ellis Shawcross (RL)

93

The Red Lion

86 West Hill/Street

The *Red Lion* in West Street probably goes back to the 18th century or beyond, but records of properties in West Hill are confusing, and some of the Rental entries which maybe for the *Red Lion* could also be for the *Row Barge*, as the ownership seems at times to be similar.

Again there is confusion in the entry of the Bridge Rent Book of 1886, when the entries nos.53 and 54 for the *Red Cow* at 80 West Hill/Street and the *Red Lion* at 86 West Street have been run together. The entry reads—'Messrs Holmes & Harper late P B Byles late Joseph Barnett formerly James Reeves for houses late in the occupation of Josh Eades and others now the *Red Lion* beerhouse late in the occupation of Thomas Clements afterwards of Charles Rawlings and now of W Poffley now owned by Mr W Norris.' Most of this is for the *Red Lion* and not for the *Red Cow*, it is the last sentence which seems to be misleading, W Norris was landlord of the *Red Cow* and as far as is known was not at the *Red Lion*. However he may have owned the *Red Lion* though he lived and worked at the *Red Cow*.

Henley Rentals for the *Red Lion* can be traced back as follows—1842-36 Jas Reeves late Jos Eades, 1828 Jas Reeves occupied by Eades, 1823,1814,1807,1800 Augustus Reeves late Rance now Reeves, 1795-75 Augustus Reeves occupied by Thos Rance. Both Rance and Reeves are names that appear at the *Row Barge*, so earlier entries become too confusing to have any certainty about them.

West Hill in the l9th century was a very rough area, connected as it was to the Workhouse, now the hospital, which was built in 1790 when the Workhouse was removed from New Street. The Tramps' wards were along the pathway to the hospital near to both the *Red Cow* and the *Red Lion*. It was an area of slum housing which grew worse and worse. Towards the end of the 19th century many of the houses were in appalling condition and badly overcrowded. The squares and yards were full of rubbish and debris, there was poor ventilation and the sewage and refuse disposal was almost non-existent. It comes as no surprise to find that Mrs Emma Rawlins, landlady of the *Red Lion* in 1884 was summoned for having stolen lead at her house in June of that year. She lost her license, and there was much discussion as to whether the license should be retained[286].

At the Licensing Session a Mr Knight suggested that the *Red Lion* was not needed and he continued that there are 'so many public houses in the town, and so much misery and crime caused by them, he thought the Bench should adopt some plan which would reduce the number by half....' There was then a long discussion but the Clerk advised 'that this being an old beerhouse, they could not legally refuse the transfer on the grounds it was not required. It could only be done by the holder of the license conducting the house improperly....'

It appears that the *Red Lion* was also a lodging house of some size or that the lodgers were packed in. The Census of 1861 had Thomas Clements a shoemaker, in 1871 Clements had 12 lodgers plus his wife and daughter, and in 1881 Charles Rawlins bricklayer's labourer, had 19 lodgers plus 3 family. (Introduction pp19-20)

The accommodation available was described in sales notices in the Reading Mercury & Oxford Gazettes of May, 5 June and October of 1866. At that time T Clements was the occupant, and it was leased to Messrs Byles & Co until Michaelmas 1877. The house contained five bedrooms, a parlour, tap room, kitchen, good cellar, and back yard with side entrance, and a well of good water. There is no mention of the size of the rooms, and it is probable that they were not very large. It is likely that the house was bought in 1866 by Messrs Byles & Co., since it appears to have been their property in 1896.

In 1899 the *Red Lion* was referred to as one of the four licensed common lodging houses in the Borough , the others were the *Jolly Farmer*, the *Cannon* and the *Duke's Head*. Also in 1892 there was a directive from the Bench that the *Red Lion* beerhouse needed to be cleansed and whitewashed

In 1896 the *Red Lion* was acquired by Brakspears when they bought Greys Brewery, and it was Brakspears that agreed to close it when the license expired on 9 June 1906, they were paid

286 Henley Advertiser 30 Aug 1884 also following events 16 Jan & 14 May 1892

compensation of £382. In August 1907 the sale was announced of the freehold house originally the *Red Lion*, now known as 86 West Street[287] .

Landlords/ Tenants of the *Red Lion*, West Street

1775-95	Thomas Rance (R)
1800-23	Augustus Reeves (R)
1828	Joshua Eades (R)
1836-42	James Reeves (R)
*1844-77	Thomas Clements (SSM,C,RM,SD)
1877-81	Charles Rawlins/Rawlings (RL,C,SD)
1881-4	Emma Rawlins (RL,HA,SD)
1884-92	William Poffley (RL,HA)
Feb 1892-1906	Joseph Ayres (RL,HS,SD)

— Closed —

94
The Red White and Blue or The Horse Shoes
Reading Road

The Red White and Blue is mentioned by Henry Tomalin in his 'Book of Henley on Thames', but there is no mention of it in either License Records or street directories. It is however mentioned in a list of pubs no longer trading which was published in the Henley Standard on 5 June 1931. Both these mentions of the *Red White and Blue* were probably derived from the same source, the only positive record of the pub, the Census Returns of 1861 for Reading Road.

In the Census for 1861 the original *Three Horseshoes* was numbered 209, the Manse 210, the *Red White and Blue* 211 with the occupant George Simmons blacksmith, then there was another house, and then the *Wheatsheaf* was 213. This order of the returns show that there were two households, one of which was the *Red White and Blue*, between the Manse and the *Wheatsheaf.* Since the area immediately north of the *Wheatsheaf* now flats, but previously a garage, was before that an open field, then the site of the two cottages may have been in the neighbourhood of where the British School was built, and is now the carpet shop and carpet cleaners. That is somewhere on the Norman Avenue/Reading Road corner.

George Simmons blacksmith was probably the father of Joseph Simmons blacksmith who later became licensee of the *Bird in Hand*. Joseph is mentioned in a street directory of 1867 as a blacksmith in Reading Road. Indeed in the Reading Mercury & Oxford Gazette of 11 June 1864 J Simmons was advertising to sell his stock in trade as a blacksmith, and what may have been a coach and waggon repairing business. His stock consisted of about 500 coach spokes, 100 elm stocks, 200 waggon vellies, 100 coach vellies, a quantity of well seasoned beech and ash planks and half round ash, 3 beech axles, smith's tools, sundry useful iron and iron works, a pair of blacksmith's bellows, anvils, new and secondhand wheels, wheelbarrow, ladders, coach makers' trussels and stands etc.

In the following weeks in the same paper, a notice was placed to say that a beerhouse and blacksmith's shop and yard were to let.

287 Henley Standard 2 Aug 1907

The stock in trade for sale was described as being the property of Mr J Simmons who is leaving the *Horse Shoes,* Reading Road. This indicates that either the name of the beerhouse had been changed since 1861, or that the *Horse Shoes* was an alternative name for the *Red White and Blue*, perhaps derived from horse shoes on display in the blacksmith's shop.

There is no possibility that the sale referred to the *Three Horseshoes* sometimes also called the *Horse Shoes*, which was on the town side of the Manse and Chapel. Firstly the *Three Horseshoes* was an old established public house with a full license and not a beerhouse. Secondly - and perhaps more importantly the old *Three Horseshoes* was built close to the road (Figs 48 & 64), and in 1826 was said only to have a small shed and yard. There was no room for a blacksmith's shop and yard, certainly of the size and type suggested by the stock in trade of 1864. Whether J Simmons failed to sell in 1864 and stayed on till 1867, when a street directory lists him as a blacksmith in Reading Road, is unknown. Nor is it known whether by that time the beerhouse by whichever name had closed.

Landlords/ Tenants of the *Red White and Blue*

1861	George Simmons (C) blacksmith
1864-7	Joseph Simmons (RM,SD) blacksmith

— Closed —

95

The Rifle

83 Greys Road/Lane

The *Rifle* was a beerhouse at what is now 83 Greys Road, which was once 81 (Fig 40). In 1885 and probably for some years before that it was owned by Edmund Chamberlain, together with

Fig 40 The white house on the left was once the Rifle, and may have been once the Carpenters Arms Photo 1989

the *Queen's Head* and the Queen's or Greys Hall, all three of which were leased to Greys Brewery at a rent of £60 p.a.[288]. As with other property of Greys Brewery, the lease of the *Rifle* was taken over by Brakspears, and by agreement Brakspears closed it after the license expired on 28 December 1907, they were then paid £712 in compensation.

Already in 1873 the *Rifle* had been under consideration for closure after the Licensing Act of 1871, in which it stated that for a beerhouse to remain open, it had to be, of at least the value of £12 p.a. Frederick Paulin, the landlord, contested the matter then and maintained that as a private house it would let for at least £12 p.a., so in 1873 the license continued[289].

The name the *Rifle* may indicate that the beerhouse was named soon after 1853. It was in that year that the Enfield Rifle was adopted by the British Government for the army[290]. A type of rifle was first used by the British Army in America in 1776, known as the Ferguson Rifle[291]but 1853 was when the rifle was generally adopted. However in 1861 the beerhouse may have been known as the *Carpenters Arms*, so the change of name to the *Rifle* would have been after the 1861 Census Returns were made.

Landlords/ Tenants of the *Rifle*

*1870	Henry Jones (HA)
1873	Frederick Paulin (HA)
May 1875-7*	James Arlett (HA,SD)
*1881	William George Wells (C) gardener
1882-6	Henry Fordham (RL)
Apr 1886-9	Frederick James Wise (RL)
Jan 1889-1907	William Carter (RL,HA,SD)
Jan 1907-Dec	John Henry Hearn (RL)

— Closed —

96

The Rose and Crown

27 Market Place

The *Rose and Crown* in the Market Place was the original pub of that name in the town, it was closed in about 1785 or soon after. The name of the pub suggests that it may have dated from Tudor times, the Tudor Rose being a popular image.

William Barnaby by a deed of feoffment dated 6 September 1582[292] granted 13s 4d for upkeep of the bridge, 20s for bread for the poorest on Good Friday, 20s for 10 smocks for the oldest and poorest women and the remainder to the poor in the Almshouses. Any residue to go to the Bridge. All this was to be taken yearly from the rents of a house in High Street, Henley. In 1858 when an account of the charities in the town was written this house was termed 'formerly the Rose and Crown', let on lease to the late Wm Bennett (and by him assigned to Mr Thomas Reeves) for 33 years from 24 June 1835 at the rent of £22 p.a.

288 Greys Brewery Rent Ledger 1885-1896 O.R.O. Brakspear IV/ ii/ 1

289 Henley Advertiser 29 Aug 1873

290 Illustrated Globe Encyclopaedia 1879 Ed. Ross, John pub. Fullarton & Co Edinburgh

291 'American War of Independence 1775-83' Catalogue pub. by British Library & British Museum

292 Cooper, John 'An Account of the Charities under the Management of the Corporation Of Henley on THames' 1858

TO BE LET,

On a BUILDING or REPAIRING LEASE,

For a Term of 33 Years,

FROM MIDSUMMER NEXT,

ALL THAT

MESSUAGE

OR

Dwelling House,

With the Gateway, Yard, Stables, and other Buildings, Situate on the South-Side of the Market-Place, in Henley, lately Occupied by Mr. BURNETT, and now by Mr. HYSLOP, and used as a Waggon-Office; containing a Frontage in the Street, of 27 Feet, and a Depth of 429 Feet.

All Persons desirous of taking the same, are requested to send in Tenders, stating the Rent they are willing to give, and the Extent of Improvement they propose to make to the Premises, together with a Plan of the same, to the Office of the Town-Clerk, on or before the 1st Day of JUNE next.

Town-Clerk's Office, Henley,

May the 1st, 1835.

HICKMAN AND STAPLEDON, PRINTERS, HENLEY.

Fig 41 Sales notice of Rose & Crown building after closure

There was also a piece of land adjoining the above, being Mr Owthwaite's Gateway, let on lease to Mr Owthwaite for 99 years from Michaelmas 1831 at the rent of £5 p.a. Four cottages in Friday Street, Henley let to James Paulin, William Hunt, Charles Goodey and James Allen as yearly tenants, at rents amounting in aggregate to £22 5s 0d. Lastly a messuage on Gravel Hill called 'Button Juggs' let on lease to Mr Nathan Curtis for 77 years from Michaelmas 1835 at a rent of £8 p.a. The whole deed of 1582 concerning these four groups of property was known as William Barnaby's Bridge Book Charity.

After the house in the High Street ceased trading as the *Rose and Crown*, it first became a Waggoner's Office under William Atkins, waggoner. Henley Rentals in 1842 say 'Bennett late the Waggon Office'. William Bennett was a cooper, and in 1835 he took on the lease advertised in the poster published here (Fig 41). The 33 years lease was on condition that he spent £250 in altering and improving the messuage[293] formerly an inn called the *Rose and Crown* and now a private dwelling house on the south side of the Market Place formerly in occupation of Wm Atkyns afterwards of Abraham Brangwin since of Alfred Hyslop and now unoccupied. Length fronting the street of about 27ft and in depth north to south about 429ft having a messuage the property of George Bennett to the east and a gateway and premises in occupation of Robert Owthwaite to the west, also barns outhouses stable etc.

The improvements to be made were extensive, and probably explains why the frontage has now no indication of an inn, or of a passageway for coaches,carts or waggons. The improvements were as follows :-

> 'to dig a cellar underneath the front room or shop. To put in a shop front and take in part of the present gateway into the shop. To pull down and remove the stack of chimneys in the front room and rebuild them in a more convenient place. To make a parlour from part of the present kitchen and pull down the stack of chimneys therein and rebuild the same. To erect a new staircase to the first floor. To lower the flooring over the gateway and to build two attics in front over the said premises and a staircase to the same. To pull down a portion of the present building at the

293 O.R.O. Cooper & Caldecott C18 (17)

> bottom of the yard and rebuild the same on the space adjoining the dwelling house for workshops so as the same buildings shall be as much in extent as that which is now erected upon the said demised premises.'

After such rebuilding it is not surprising that there are now no traces of the *Rose and Crown*. However its position at what is now Facys, becomes very clear when the deeds of the houses to the west, taken down for the entrance to Greys Road Car Park, are studied[294], they are the houses which were 29,31 & 33 Market Place (33 was at one time the *Butchers Arms*, while 29 was once the *Seven Stars*). Robert Owthwaite owned both 29 and 31, and later Burgis' Stores were to own all three houses. The deeds for 29 show that the *Rose and Crown* was next door on the east side.

The earliest mention of the *Rose and Crown* is in the Quakers' Minute Book of 1705.

> 'About the year 1658 our honourable friend Ambrose Rigge came to Henley with two more in his company on the 5th day of the week being Market Day: they setting their horses at the *Rose and Crown Inn*......... After market was a little over they got a stool or form and set it in the gateway of the said inn, which was against the Corn Market: and there the said Ambrose Rigge declared Truth: there being many people gathered about them. Some were very attentive and sober, and I believe that two or three of them were so reached that afterwards they came to owne Truth: yet some were very rude and abusive and throwing things at him, as guts they got from the butchers.'

The corn market in the 17th century was probably in the area now known as Falaise Square. At that time the Town Hall or Guildhall was near the crossroads, just on the market side of the crossing (Fig 23). As far as one can tell it had shops beneath it and not the corn market. The later Town Hall built in 1796 and demolished in 1898, was situated in much the same position as the present Town Hall. The hall of 1796 originally had open pillars on the ground floor (Fig17), and the space was used as a corn market, but that was long after the time of Ambrose Rigge. The Butcher's Row was on the south side of the row of buildings known as Middle Row, with butcher's shops in Middle row and also on the south side of the Market Place. Middle Row stretched from about the level of the *Catharine Wheel* in Hart Street right up the centre of the market, and included the old Guildhall. The lower part was demolished in about the 1780s the upper part in the 1790s, this was the part shown on the plan which I have shown superimposed on the O.S.map of 1879 (Fig 23). So the 'rude and abusive' inhabitants of Henley did not have far to go for their 'guts'.

In 1727 and 1738 leases were granted of the *Rose and Crown* to Chas Brigstocke brewer, and then in 1756 to John Brigstocke brewer[295].

A deed of sale in 1751 of 29,31 & 33 Market Place says on the east messuage in possession of James White, a second deed of sale of the same houses in 1776 says on 'the east formerly in occupation of James White now or late James Whitley'[296]. In 1771 James Whiteley appears in a list of Alehouse licenses for Henley. There are two lists, one of 1770 and the other 1771, since Whiteley is on the list of 71 but not on that for 70, it would seem that he took over from someone who had been on the first list but not on that of 71. There are three posssible names, William Fluister, Thomas Guy or Mary Purbrick, all of them had Richard Hayward as one of their sureties.

In 1776 the *Rose and Crown* was leased to Richard Hayward and William Newell of Henley brewers and partners[297]. In 1780 Rich Hayward obtained the lease again, though this time for only 8 years[298], all other leases had been for 11 years, so may be it closed in 1788. Hayward and

294 & 296 O.R.O. Cooper & Caldecott C58 (1-13)

295, 297 & 298 Hughes 33 AD 569, 36 AD583, 53 & 186 AD612 & 613, 181 & 91 AD657 &661, 35 AD662

later Brakspear continued holding the lease until about 1823, though by 1790 the Rentals say 'Hayward occupied Cooper late the *Rose and Crown.*'

In the year 1766 on 16 December a fire evidently swept the stables and outhouses of the *Rose and Crown.* There is a document dated 16 December 1771[299] apparently written five years later, which outlines 'Proposalls for repairing the Stables at the *Rose and Crown Inn* Henley lately damaged by Fire and for building a new Stable adjoining the lower end of the above mentioned stable, one hundred and thirteen feet long and fifteen feet wide from out to out where the old stable was lately burned down.'

> 'The foundation to the east side of lower end of the new intended part to be carryd up 1½ft high above ground with brick and flint work 1 brick and a ½ thick. To erect a timber frame on this 5½ft high from the underside of the sill to the upper side of the Raising plate and board the same with fetheridge of elm boards. To make good the roof of the old stables, part out of the old timber that is sound and what is wanting with new timber. To make good the boarding of the upper end of the old stable to frame and put on a roof over the new part. The lower end of the new roof to be hipped back. The roofs to be covered with plain tiles on good heart oak lathes.'
>
> 'To put up a rack and manger the whole length of the new part and make good the Rack and Manger the whole length of the old. The manger parts to be oak, the Rale and boarding to the manger to be Deal. The Rack to be Deal Rales with cleft oak staves.'
>
> 'To make and hang 5 ledged doors out of inch yellow Deal to the east side, with iron hinges and wood latches.'
>
> 'To make good the pitching to the additional length of the new stable. All the materials that are good and sound to be reserved in the building.'
>
> 'Dimensions of timber as follows :-

Oak	- Sills to side & end	8" x 4"
	- Door posts	7" x 6"

Fir -

Corner posts	8" x 8"	Middle principal posts	6" x 6"
Braces to side and end	5" x 3"	Quarter to side and end	4"x 3"
Plates	7" x 4½"	Beams	10" x 8"
Principal rafters	5" x 4" (in the middle)	Purlins	6" x 6"
Hipps	8" x 1½"	Struts	9" x 2½"
Running rafters	4" x 2"		

> 'To erect a Boghouse 5'x 4' on some part of the premises as shall be thought most convenient and cover the same with plain tiles. All above be done in workmanlike manner with good and sound materials for the sum of £139 and all the old materials.'
>
> '16th December 1771 Wm Bradshaw'

299 O.R.O. AD 4/ 37 F119

William Bradshaw was one of the leading builders in the town and was at one time Mayor. It is interesting to see the sizes of timbers considered necessary, much heavier than would be used today. It is difficult to ascertain whether any of this stable remains in existence .

Landlords/ Tenants of the *Rose and Crown*

1751	James White (ORO)
*1770	William Fluister ?, Thomas Guy ?, Mary Purbrick ?
1771-6*	William Whiteley/Whitley (ORO)

— Closed —

97

The Rose and Crown

56 New Street

There seems to be no indication that these premises were a beerhouse before the 1840s or even the 1850s, although John Strange who occupied the house from about 1812-42 may have been the son of a publican. In all street directories in which he is listed, it is as a bricklayer and plasterer and not as a beer retailer. His father may have been John Strange of the *King's Arms*, who wrote the letter quoted in the Introduction (p14) and who probably remained at the *King's Arms* till his death in 1809. The father was a builder, bricklayer and victualler, but the John Strange of New Street was not a beer retailer, his business was as a stone mason and kiln owner, manufacturing bricks and pottery, he had a kiln in Henley and in March 1824 took over Comp Kiln in Sonning Common.

The Bridge Rent Book of 1886 says 'Mrs Champion late Sarah Strange formerly John Strange for a house and premises late in the occupation of Mrs House and now of George Green'. Henry House in 1850, and later Harriet House were listed as beer retailers, but it is not till a directory of 1854 that the *Rose and Crown* is mentioned by name.

Henley Rentals show J Strange in occupation from 1814-42, before that, in 1807 there was 'Sam Hucks in occupation Mr Richards now Mr Brown.' In 1800 and 1795 'late in occupation Richards now Brown.' In 1793 and 85 'occupied Riche' (Richards/Riche/Riches/Richies all are variants of the same name). In 1779 it was 'occupied T Davies now T Woods', and in 1775 'Fowler occupied Thos Davies.' Any of these names might have been beer retailers but they are not mentioned as such.

The *Rose and Crown* (Fig 7) in 1877 was owned by J Pitman of Goring, and like the other pubs owned by him was put up for sale in 1887 on his death. The Sales Catalogue says 'Lot 36. The *Rose and Crown*. A capital beerhouse, in good position known as the *Rose and Crown* New Street. Accommodation - Parlour, Tap Room, small Sitting room, scullery, cellar, 9 bedrooms. In rear approached by carriage way (sub-let to tenant Mr W H Feesey) is stabling for 6 horses, loft over, and large timber cartshed, harness room and W.C. Let to Mr George Green on monthly tenancy at low rent of £16 p.a . Held upon a yearly tenancy from Lady Day Quarter at £20 p.a.'[300].

Like the *Red Cow* the *Rose and Crown* was bought by Mrs Ann Gundry of the Goring Brewery. In 1940 twenty five of the houses owned by the Goring Brewery together with the brewery itself were bought by Brakspears[301]. The *Rose and Crown* was one of the pubs acquired at that time, it was then still a beerhouse, it only gained a full license in 1960[302].

300 Sales Catalogue 1887 O.R.O. Misc Lee III/ vi

The whole plot is fairly narrow, and it was probably the neighbours who complained in 1906 about the Manure Heap in the yard[303]. It was probably the long accumulated manure belonging to Mr Feesey, and then Mr Keene and possibly by some later tenant of the yard and stables. After Mr Feesey, Mr William Keene rented the yard and stables etc. and ran his business from there. He advertised Horses and Carriages for Hire, Riding and Driving lessons, and Hunters and Hacks for Hire. He moved out to the slightly larger premises of the *Bear* yard in May 1890.

When building work was being carried out in 1988, a well was uncovered more or less in the entry to the yard. The well was about 12ft deep and 26-29ins in diameter, not a true circle. The body of the well was lined with clunch, with brick only near the top. From the materials it could have been any date from the 16th to 19th century. The depth of the well is such as would be expected in that part of Henley, not very deep, and would have been fed by underground streams. The Town Waterworks were opened in 1882, and after that there was a movement to connect up as many houses as possible. At that time many of the wells in Henley were regarded as supplying sub-standard water. It is probable that New Street was connected to the mains by the mid 80s, and it is likely that that would be when the well was closed.

The whole frontage of the *Rose and Crown* is just less than 20ft, and almost half of it was taken up by the carriage way. The house itself is narrow, and runs back from the road. In front there is one room with two sash windows, with a fireplace on the east wall. Behind is a small stair to the cellar, and behind that the bar, with the kitchen and other room beyond. The alterations of 1988 have extended the bar room across the carriageway to occupy the whole width of the plot. Beneath the front room is the cellar, the walls of which are mostly brick with a few flints, the floor also used to be brick. At the front of the cellar, projecting under the pavement is a small projection with a narrow arched entry to it. Although it was spoken of as a passage there is no sign on any of the walls of any exit, and no sign that any exit had ever been there. Most likely it was designed as a coal cellar with a chute from the pavement separated from the main cellar by the arch, which may well have had a door.

There has probably been a house on the site for a very long time, the well may be the remnant of an earlier house, but the present building has every appearance of being built at the beginning of the 19th century. Even the cellar shows no sign of being of an earlier date. Indeed it seems that the premises were rebuilt during the tenancy of John Strange builder. In the transactions of the Court Leet of the manor of Henley in 1816, John Strange was summoned for allegedly building the front of his house in New Street so that it projected onto the Waste of the Manor. John Strange replied that this was not the case as he had rebuilt his house on the foundations of the old house. When the premises were examined it was found that this was true, but that a step forming the approach to the front door projected 10inches upon the Waste and that two spur posts to the gateway adjoining the house projected 9 inches. Strange was therefore ordered to pay 6d annually for the encroachments, and this was to be back dated to Michaelmas 1812. This probably means that that was the date of the building of the house in its present form, and that John Strange was there from at least 1812 and most likely slightly before that. It also seems that in 1816 there was a front entry to the building, a door where there is now a window. Perhaps it was after 1816 that to avoid the encroachment payment, the door was moved under the archway to the yard, and the offending step removed.

In the Reading Mercury & Oxford Gazette of 13 April 1835 a substantial and recently built freehold dwelling house with extensive stabling and outbuildings situated in New Street was advertised for sale. It was in the occupation of Mr John Strange who held a lease with 54 years unexpired, at a yearly rent of £10 5s payable quarterly.

301, 302 & 303 Henley Standard 22 Nov 1940, 5 Feb 1960, 27 Jul 1906

Later in the same paper on 29 December 1838 the property was again offered for sale, still occupied by John Strange. This time the description was more detailed. 'Two sitting rooms, kitchen, counting house, wash house, good cellarage and eight bedrooms. Side gate entrance to commodious stables, sheds and other buildings. Well situated, substantial brick built and slated in the last 25 years, upon a most convenient plan. Well adapted for a Brewery or any Tradesman requiring a long range of buildings.' It would seem that at that time it was most definitely not yet a beerhouse.

Landlords/ Tenants of the *Rose and Crown* , New Street

(*1812-42*	John Strange (R,CL,RM,SD) not a beer retailer)
*1850-1	Henry House (C,SD)
1852-83*	Mrs Harriet House (SSM,RL,C,SD)
*1886-1917	George Green (RL,BRB,SD)
1917-8	Helen Thernal (RL) wife of Frank Thernal
Oct 1918-9	Amelia Taylor (RL,HS)
Jul 1919-39	Alfred William Irving (RL,HS,SD)
May 1939-53	Edwin George Hooper (RL,WHB/C,SD)
Sep 1953-80	David Reginald Beck (RL,WHB/C,SD)
Apr 1980-4	David James Bethel (RL,WHB/C)
Jun 1984-6	Chadwick Douglas Frank Buckler (RL,WHB/C)
Jun 1986-92	Christine Diane Buckler (RL,WHB/C)
Oct 1992-94	P Morris (RL)
Nov 1994-99-	Michael Charles Matthews (RL)

98

The Row Barge

37 West Hill/Street

In the Oxford Record Office[304] there are some papers relating to the *Row Barge* (Fig 42). They concern a case of trespass in 1759, when Thomas Smith the plaintiff, brought a case against Thomas Clements, James Clements, Thomas Freeman, Jenkins Sharp, William Hughes, John Gibson, William House, Philip Drew, George Heath, Henry Horne and Nathan Heath defendants. Unfortunately the rights and wrongs of the case are not recorded in this document, nor what position Thomas Smith held. It is possible that he was landlord of the *Row Barge* at the time. Were all these people using a passage as a way through from perhaps West Hill to the Market? The document is an instruction that Mr Keeley the owner or leaseholder of the *Row Barge* should bring certain documents with him to court.

The documents that he had to bring were three. A lease from the Mayor and Gislingham Cooper dated 25 March 1705, to Mr Wm Brooks of a cottage or tenement in Henley. A license, dated 5 April 1712 from the Warden and Wm Whitelocke to Moses Rance to let or assign premises in Henley. Lastly a lease, dated 12 September 1758 from the Mayor and Gislingham Cooper Esq. to Anna Brooks of a tenement or cottage in Henley.

Oddly no mention is made of the lease dated 25 September 1758[305], when the Mayor and Gislingham Cooper Esq. granted to Mr Robert Rance victualler, a cottage or tenement in Henley called the *Row Barge*.

304 O.R.O. Cooper & Caldecott C1(16)

305 Hughes 92 & 138 AD618 & 619

Whitelocke, and after him Gislingham Cooper were owners of Fawley Court and because also owners of Phyllis Court, became Lords of the Manor of Henley, and were also owners of property in the town. Gislingham Cooper was Lord of the Manor from 1723-68. The estates then went to Sambrook Freeman, in 1782 they passed to Strickland Freeman and from him in 1821 to Admiral William Peere Williams Freeman until 1831, and then to the Admiral's grandson William Peere Williams Freeman until 1853[306].

Fig 42 The Row Barge Photo 1989

The earlier Henley Rentals confirm the names mentioned in the three documents of 1705, 1712, and 1758. The Rentals say 1713/4 Will Brooks for cottage occupied by Moses Rance. 1721/2 and 1733/4 Moses Rance for one cottage. 1737-69 Rob Rance for a cottage and more for a woodpile. It would seem that the Brooks, first William and then Anna held the lease and sublet to the Rances. The only difficulty in this is where was Thomas Smith?

The lease of September 1758 places Robert Rance at the *Row Barge*, while the Court Baron Book of 1785 says 'J Keeley tenement called the Row Barge late occupied by Rob Rance'.

During the mid 18th century it is difficult to be certain as to the various Rentals in West Hill. As already said in the account of the *Red Lion* West Hill, there is confusion in some of the 18th century entries for West Hill. It seems that Thomas Rance may have been at the *Red Lion*, while Robert Rance was at the *Row Barge*. There are entries for 1779, and 75 which say Robt Rance late Facer, and then in 1745 Mr Facer tenement in possession of Widow Fowler. These entries could refer to the *Row Barge*, equally they could be for the *Red Lion*, or for some other property.

The later Rentals after 1785 are clearer, 1785-1807 they say 'J Keeley in own occupation'.

306 Burn, J S 'History of Henley on Thames' 1861 p254

Whether this was the same Keeley who as leaseholder was asked to bring the documents to court in 1759 is not certain, it could be his son. In 1814 the Rentals say 'J Keeley occupied by J Reeves' and 1823-36 'J Keeley occupied J Reeves the *Row Barge*'. In 1842 the entry says 'Brakspear the *Row Barge* occupied by J Reeves'.

In the Brewery Inventory of 1826 the *Row Barge* was held leasehold by Joseph Benwell and W H Brakspear. It was in occupation of James Reeves. The lease due to expire 29 September 1827. Rent £30 p.a. Bridge Rent 1s 8d. A note beneath says 'Purchased of W P W Freeman by W H B.' No date is given to the purchase, though it would seem likely to have been when the lease expired in 1827. Francis Sheppard in his book 'Brakspear's Brewery 1779-1979' says however that the *Row Barge* was purchased in 1830. Whichever date it was the W P W Freeman was almost certainly the Admiral.

Landlords/ Tenants of the *Row Barge*

1712-34	Moses Rance (ORO,R)
1737-71	Robert Rance ? (ORO,VR,R) (He is listed as a Victualler in the VR lists of 1753-4 and 1770-71)
?1745	Widow Fowler ?
?1759	Thomas Smith ?
1785-1807	J Keeley (R,CB,CL)
1814-42	James Reeves (AKL,CL,R,WHB/I,SD)
*1847-8	Mrs Reeves (RM,SD)
*1854-67	Mrs Rebecca Chase (SD) grocer
1868-71	Thomas Hamilton (SSM,C,SD)
Dec 1871-87	Thomas Hamilton junior (RL,HA,SD)
Nov 1887-91	Joseph Henry Harris (RL,HA,SD)
Mar 1891-1928	Joseph Harding (RL,WHB/C,HA,HS,SD)
Dec 1928-32	Samuel Hunter (RL,WHB/C,HS,SD)
May 1932-6	Bertie Wilfred Nunn (RL,WHB/C,HS,BReg)
Sep 1936-8	Mrs Ethel Annie Nunn (RL,WHB/C,HS) (in Sep 1938 Mrs Nunn married Thomas Hancock labourer of 74 West Hill)
1938-51	Mrs Ethel Annie Hancock (RL,WHB/C)
Mar 1951-6	Alfred Leonard Swell (RL,WHB/C)
Dec 1956-9	Arthur Jesse Bowers (RL,WHB/C)
May 1959-68	Wilfred Kyte (RL,WHB/C)
Mar 1968-Oct	Richard Albert Roach (RL,WHB/C)
Nov 1968-70	Anthony Robert Coombs (RL,WHB/C)
Apr 1970-8	Norman Mitchell (RL,WHB/C)
Feb 1978-99-	William David Cheney (RL,WHB/C)

99

The Royal Exchange

7 New Street

The *Royal Exchange* beerhouse, keeper Charles Howarth, features in the lists of 1870 and 1871 in the Magistrates Special Sessions Book. The Census Returns of 1871 which started on the north side of New Street at the west end, have as the third entry Charles Howarth aged 54 beerhouse keeper his wife also a beerhouse keeper, an adopted daughter and two lodgers. The two preceding entries are of people known to have been at 3 and 5 New Street, 1 New Street being included in the Bell Street corner property.

The Register of Licenses in 1877 confirms that the *Royal Exchange* was on the north side of the street, and by then the licensee was Charles Webb, while the owners were H & G Simonds Ltd.

There is little information before 1870, and no mention of Charles Howarth as a beer retailer in street directories. There is however in a directory of 1869 mention of George William Spencer as a beer retailer in New Street, who might have been at the *Royal Exchange*, since the other beerhouses in the street all seem to have had other occupants at that time.

The Census of 1851 places Job Gunnell shoemaker aged 44 at what is now 7 New Street, plus wife, three sons and three daughters, ranging in age from 1-18. There is no mention of him being a beer retailer, though that is not conclusive, but there is also no mention of him as a beer retailer in any street directory.

The Census of 1841 is not as reliable as to order as that of 51, but there is a possibility that a James Paulin baker aged 55, wife, son and daughter were at 7 New Street. If so he may have been the same James Paulin who appears as a baker in an 1842 directory, and as a beer retailer in New Street in 1844. He does not seem to be at any of the other beerhouses in the street.

If James Paulin was at the *Royal Exchange* and was a baker, it is not unlikely that later the business was taken over by Mrs Harriet Wetherell a beer retailer in New Street in 1847, who may have been at the *Royal Exchange* rather than the *Horse and Groom* (see suggestion in account of the *Horse and Groom*.) The connection could well be the bakery business, in I847 and 1850 David Wetherell is listed as a baker in Bell Street. A business apparently run in 1852 by Julia Wetherell and in 1854 by Judith Wetherell.

Whether Paulin and later Wetherell and Gunnell were involved in running a beerhouse and whether that beerhouse was the *Royal Exchange* does not seem provable. It is likely that the beerhouse was one of the many started in the 1830s or soon after. What is known is when it stopped trading, which was at the end of the licensing year of 1878, no license was taken out in August 1879.

Landlords/ Tenants of the *Royal Exchange*

? *1841-4*	James Paulin ? (C,SD) baker
? *1847*	Mrs Harriet Wetherell ? (SD)
1851	Job Gunnell (C) shoemaker
? *1869*	George William Spencer ? (SD)
*1870-1	Charles Howarth (SSM,C,HA)
Dec 1871-2	Stephen Wise (HA)
Nov 1872-7	Henry Belcher (HA,SD)
1877-79	Charles Webb (RL)

— Closed —

100

The Royal Hotel

Station Road

The *Royal Hotel* was originally built as a grandiose private house in about 1864 by Robert Owthwaite one time Mayor, and a successful business man and entrepreneur. Both Robert Owthwaite and his father, also a Robert Owthwaite, were auctioneers, furniture dealers and property owners (see the *Duke of Cumberland*, the *Rose and Crown* and its neighbouring gateway, also the *Seven Stars*). The *Royal Hotel* when a private house was known as Baltic House, and only when Owthwaite changed its use to a hotel did it become the *Royal Hotel* in 1872 (Fig 43).

Fig 43 The old Royal Hotel, on extreme left the part of the hotel which later became a convent

The building in 1872 was extensive, far larger than the present building, as can be seen on the O.S. Map of 1879. There were two distinct wings, a later O.S.map of 1925, shows a remnant of the old building, now demolished which in 1925 was a convent (Fig 44).

The other wing of the old building, the River Wing, faced south towards Marsh Meadows and lock (Fig 43). In the Harrod's Directory of 1876 it says that the *Royal Hotel* 'is quite detached, and is specially adapted for the accommodation of visitors to this favourite place of summer resort.... the hotel stands in its own grounds of 14 acres which comprise croquet lawn, and beautifully laid out garden with meadow attached. Mr R Owthwaite proprietor.'

Mr Robert Owthwaite had tried to sell Baltic House in 1872, but was unsuccessful. It was offered for sale as part of the Portobello and other freehold estates. The sales catalogue describes it as a spacious modern mansion admirably adapted for a First Class Hotel or Club House, 'substantially built in the Italian Villa Style'. It is divided into what is called the River Wing and the Garden Wing.

Robert Owthwaite died in October 1887, but earlier in the year, a report in the Henley Advertiser in April says that 'extensive alterations are going on at this hotel which has been purchased by Messrs Holmes, Harper and Neame of the Greys Brewery. The ugly high wall near the station has been cut down, so that the hotel is now visible, and four windows have been inserted in the dead wall of the hotel close to River Terrace....' In July another report in the same paper says 'We are glad to hear that this hotel under the able management of Mr Hardwicke is steadily gaining favour.......'

In spite of this it was never much of a financial success, in 1892 [307] it was owned by Frederick Trotman who was also the licensee, and in 1894-99 was owned by the Official Receiver in Bankruptcy.

In 1899 it was bought personally by Archibald Brakspear, and it was he who had the old River Wing demolished and rebuilt to designs of G W Webb of Reading [308]. These designs included the row of gabled buildings facing the river, which was the hotel accommodation. Meanwhile the Garden Wing became a detached building and was taken over by the Ursuline Nuns as their convent.

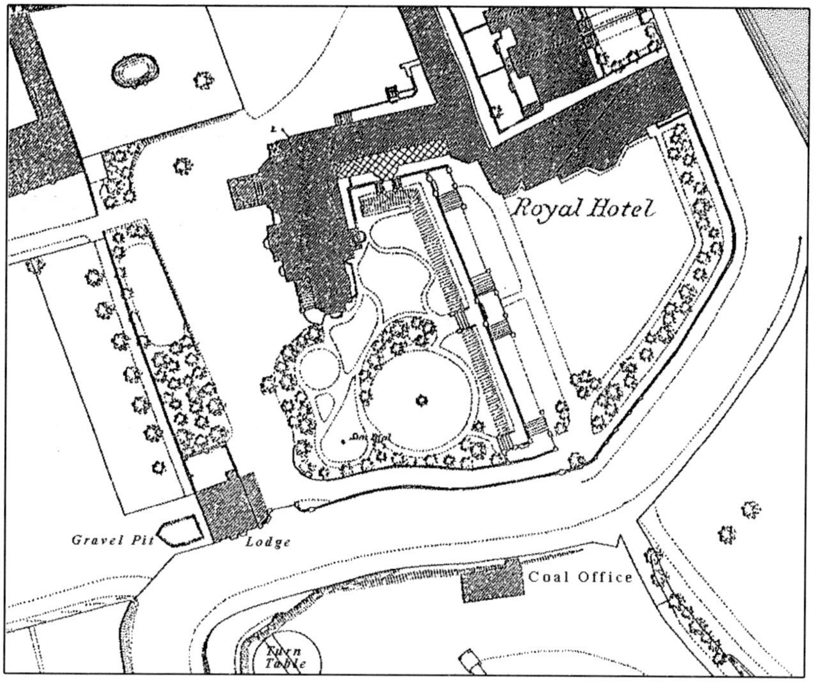

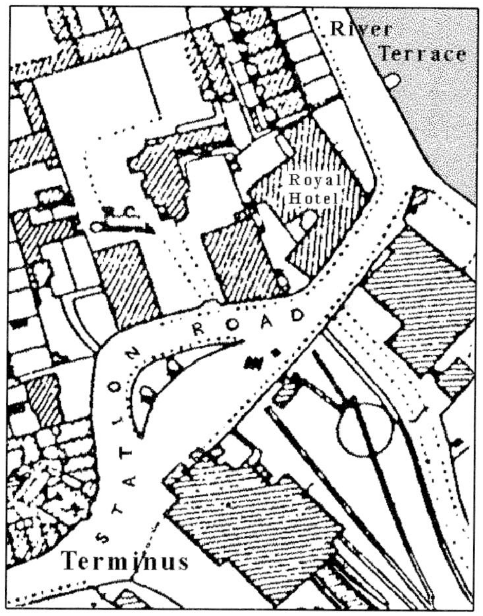

Fig 44 Part of O.S. maps of 1879 & 1925 showing the original Royal Hotel and the later hotel. The map at top of 1879 greatly reduced that of 1925 only slightly reduced

In 1925 the *Royal Hotel* was bought by Brakspear & Co., the hotel accommodation was sold off as flats, and the main entrance, public rooms and bar continued to be run by Brakspears as a pub, until early in 1993, when the *Royal Hotel* closed.

Landlords/ Tenants of the *Royal Hotel*

1872-87 Robert Owthwaite (AucC,HA,SD)
(1887 George Peacey boat builder &steam Launch Proprietor The Bridge & *Royal Hotel* , one minute walk from the station (SD))
1887-90 William Hardwicke (RL,HA)
Jul 1890-1 John Gates (RL,HA)
Jun 1891-5 Frederick Trotman (RL,HA)
(1894-9 Official Receiver in Bankruptcy) (RL)
May 1895-9 Charles James Singleton (RL)
Oct 1899-1908 Alexander Groves (RL)
1908-9 Robert Arthur Buddicon (RL)

307 O.R.O. Register of Licenses

308 Sheppard, Francis 'Brakspear's Brewery 1779-1979' 1979

1909-11	Robert Marshall (RL)
1911-23	Frederick William Dee (RL,SD)
Sep 1923-9	Leonard James lFord (RL,HS)
Jul 1929-30	James Martin Hill (RL,WHB/C,HS)
Jul 1930-3	Edwin Talbot Ball (RL,WHB/C,HS)
Jan 1933-Nov	Charles Edward Vaughan Burr (RL,WHB/C,HS)
Dec 1933-6	Henry Algernon Panting (RL,WHB/C,HS,BaReg)
Feb 1936-40	George Atkinson (RL,WHB/C,HS,SD)
Jul 1940-54	Joseph Davis (RL,WHB/C)
Jul 1954-5	Arthur John Parker (RL,WHB/C)
Nov 1955-7	Charles Edwin James (RL,WHB/C)
Dec 1957-9	Norman Owen Colbeck (RL,WHB/C)
Dec 1959-62	Edward William Robert Turtle (RL,WHB/C)
Mar 1962-5	Vincent Melville Wingate (RL,WHB/C)
Mar 1965-79	Francis Roland Holland (RL,WHB/C)
Feb 1979-88	Norman Mitchell (RL,WHB/C)
Sep 1988-91	Clive Beverley Foley (RL,WHB/C)
Oct 1991-3	James Lawrence Brown (RL,WHB/C)

— Closed —

101

The Royal Oak

6 Greys Road

The *Royal Oak* just up Greys Road (Fig 45), was until 1892 in Rotherfield Greys. The Henley/Rotherfield Greys boundary came up the centre of Friday Street from the river, crossed over the crossroads, started up the centre of Greys Road, but turned north up the entry to Tuns Lane, and then ran west behind the houses on the north side of Greys Road (Fig 64).

It is very probable that until 1811 the *Royal Oak* was called the *Blue Blacksmith*, by 1818 it had changed its name. The Victuallers Recognizances for Rotherfield Greys give the pub named the *Blue Blacksmith* up to 1811, then there is a gap in the records, but in 1818 that name disappears from the lists, and in its place, in the same order of pubs, is the name the *Royal Oak*, which was not mentioned before. The landlord was then Joel Perrin/Perryn.

In 1826 the freehold was owned by Joseph Benwell and W H Brakspear and the Inventory says '*Royal Oak* public house in occupation of Joel Perrin stabling for 2 horses and woodhouse, also cottage adjoining with 4 rooms.'

However on the Tithe Return for Rotherfield Greys in 1844, the owner is then given as Henry Gosse, while the premises were occupied by William Pierce and another. Later, before 1882, Brakspear & Sons were to buy back the *Royal Oak*, they appear as owners in the Register of that date.

The Henley Standard of 11 November 1977 said that the *Royal Oak* closed over six years ago, the actual date of closure was 11 January 1971. The building stood for many years after the closure, empty and desolate, gradually becoming more dilapidated. Eventually in 1981 it was demolished and a new building put on the site.

(see the *Blue Blacksmith* for earlier information)

Fig 45 The two cottages once the Royal Oak closed in 1971 and became derelict Photo c.1978 by Peter Anderson

Landlords/ Tenants of the *Royal Oak*

*1818-40	Joel Perrin/Perryn (VR,WHB/I,SD) (RGreys BReg May 1840)
*1842-7	William Pierce/Pearce (TM,SD) (RGreys BReg Feb 1847)
1847*	Mrs Jane Pearce (SD)
1851-4	William Tucker (C,SD)
1863-77	William Wenman (C,SD)
*1881-5	Joseph Tranter (RL,C,SD)
Apr 1885-97	Joseph Foster (RL,HA,SD) well appointed open and closed carriages, brakes, pony traps, waggonettes etc to Let & Hire
Jan 1898-1900	Francis Smith (RL)
Apr 1900-1	Richard White (RL)
Jul 1901-4	Walter Bowley (RL)
May 1904-5	Lavinia Bowley (RL) widow
May 1905-6	John Cook Read (RL)
Mar 1906-28	Tom Leslie Mason (RL,HS,SD)
May 1928-40	Alfred Pearce (RL,HS,SD)
Feb 1940-53	Albert Ralph KIrby (RL,HS,SD)
Dec 1953-62	John Wheeler (RL)
Oct 1962-7	Donald Albert Stark (RL)
Dec 1967-70	Percy William Roberts (RL)
Aug 1970-71	Norah Frances Roberts (RL)

— Closed —

102

The Saracen's Head

112 Greys Road/Lane

The *Saracen's Head* is another pub that was in Rotherfield Greys, it did not exist however in 1844, when the Tithe Returns of that date were made. The Tithe Map shows an empty plot of land (Fig 60).

Brakspears bought the land in 1844 [309] and soon after erected the *Saracen's Head*. It was a time when that part of Rotherfield Greys was expanding. Holy Trinity Church was opened in 1848 on Greys Hill, which runs parallel to Greys Road just behind the *Saracen's Head*, the school opened in 1850 was also on Greys Hill.

Edmund Butler the first landlord, in the Census of 1851, is described as a brewer's man aged 45, and he was still there in the Census of 1871. In a street directory of 1854 he is given as the landlord of the *Black Prince*, there is no other mention of this pub, and it is possible that it was a colloquial name given to the *Saracen's Head*, referring to the picture on the sign. The name obviously did not take, and it has always remained the *Saracen's Head.*

Edmund Butler's career came to an end in November 1873[310] when he was charged with receiving two loads of coal knowing them to be stolen (66 lbs of coal), which were delivered to the *Saracen's Head.* (In the newspaper account he is mistakenly named Edward) He was charged jointly with James Willis of Rotherfield Greys labourer, who was charged with stealing 93 lbs of coal. Both were committed for trial, and in January 1874 the license of the pub was transferred to Henry Russell.

Butler was not the only landlord of the *Saracen's Head* to be in trouble with the law, in October 1903 [311] William Norcott was charged with selling one pint of beer in a bottle, not corked and sealed, to a child of under 14 years, that is to say of the age of 10 years, at his licensed premises. Contrary to the Intoxicating Liquor (sale to children) Act of 1901. He was fined £1 and costs.

Landlords/ Tenants of the *Saracen's Head*

*1847-74	Edmund Butler (C,HA,SD)
1874*	Henry Russell (HA)
1877	Cornelius Turner (SD) coal dealer
*1882-5	William Holloway (RL,SD)
Sep 1885-6	Rhoda Holloway (RL)
Mar 1886-7	Thomas Maddox (RL,WHB/C,HA,SD)
Jun 1887-1904	William Norcott (RL,WHB/C,HA,SD)
Nov 1904-5	Walter Martin (RL,WHB/C)
Mar 1905-11	James Edward Vaughan (RL,WHB/C)
Dec 1911-13	George James (RL,WHB/C)
May 1913-Sep	Arthur Bunkle (RL,WHB/C)
Sep 1913-33	George James Hull (RL,WHB/C,SD)
Oct 1933-6	Joseph Michael Fenn (RL,WHB/C,HS,SD)
Feb 1936-7	William George Wheeler (RL,WHB/C,HS)
Jul 1937-54	Ernest Frederick Cook (RL,WHB/C,HS,SD)
Dec 1954-67	Leonard Darnell (RL,WHB/C)

309 Sheppard, Francis 'Brakspear's Brewery 1779-1979' 1979

310 Henley Advertiser 8 Nov 1873

311 O.R.O. Register of Licenses

Mar 1967-8	Mrs Dorothy Darnell (RL,WHB/C)
Jun 1968-88	Louis Stargatt (RL,WHB/C)
Apr 1988-94	Michael Trevor Mills (RL,WHB/C)
Nov 1994-99	Colin Richard Roberson & Melanie Jane Roberson (RL,HS)

103

The Seven Pigeons

Station Road

The *Seven Pigeons* was listed as one of the pubs no longer trading in the Henley Standard of 5 June 1931.

If it was in Station Road as stated, it would have had to have been after 1856, as the road did not exist before then. Even in 1879, the date of the O.S. large scale map, there were no buildings in the road except the Station, coal depot and the *Royal Hotel* and its Lodge House (Fig 44). By the time other buildings were being built in Station Road, any pub would have appeared either in the Register of Licenses, street directories or after 1870 in the Henley Advertiser accounts of licensing sessions.

One possibility is that it could have been on the Waterside before the *Royal Hotel* or its predecessor Baltic House was built, which would mean a date of about 1856-64. Robert Owthwaite built Baltic House in about 1864, and later converted it into the *Royal Hotel.*

— Closed —

104

The Seven Stars

29 Market Place

The *Seven Stars* was next door to what is now part of Facy's, and was in one of the three buildings demolished to make the northern entrance to Greys Road Car Park.

The Bridge Rent Book of 1886 No.39 says 'John Weyman late Robert Owthwaite formerly William Cooper adjoining next but one to No.37 on the west side late in occupation of William Cooper since of Robt Owthwaite and now of George Fuller 7s.' (added after) 'now Mr D Burgis'.

In the Bridge Rent Book No.38 should be for 27 Market Place, now Facy's, which was once the *Rose and Crown*, but for some reason unknown that entry is omitted. The entry referred to as No.37 is at 25 Market Place.

Burgis' Stores, a grocery business, can be traced back in the street directories to 1903, it also occupied 31 and 33 Market Place. All three premises were demolished in the 1960s. Before 1903, 29 Market Place was briefly John Hatton & Co drapers, before that Weyman & Co furnishers and decorators, before that George Fuller cabinet maker, preceded by Robert Owthwaite furniture dealer in about 1854-63, and William Cooper corn dealer in 1823.

Henley Rentals for 29 Market Place, have in 1842 & 1836 Robert Owthwaite in own occupation 7s. 1828,1823, & 1814 Hill now Cooper 7s. 1800 Hill late Arnold late Farmer since Marshall now Dobson 7s. 1795 Hill late Arnold late occupied Farmer 7s. 1793 Hill occupied

Marshall 7s. 1790 & 1785 Hill occupied R Farmer 7s. 1779 J Hill occupied J Cooper now White 7s. 1775 late Arnold now John Hill in occupation J Cooper now White 7s. Finally back in 1749 it says Mr Willis for Tidd's *Seven Stars* and in 1745 Humphrey Newberry for Tidd's *Seven Stars* 7s.

Documents in the Oxford Record Office[312] show the sale of the building from 1751, which seems to be the date when it ceased functioning as a pub.

In 1751 Thomas Tidd of Leicester Fields in Middlesex gentleman, son of Mary Tidd late of the parish of St James Westminster, widow deceased, and Elizabeth his wife, sold to Joseph Arnold fishmonger two messuages with backsides, gardens, granaries and malthouse on the south side of the High Street near unto the cornmarket (cornmarket- see *Rose & Crown*)between the messuage late in possession of James White on the east (see *Rose and Crown*) and the messuage in possession of Zachary Sarney on the west (see *Butcher's Arms* 33 Market Place), extending to the High Street on the north and towards Dirty Bottom (see *Queen's Head* & Greys Lane) on the south.

Joseph Arnold sold the two houses to John Hill on 2 October 1776, between a messuage formerly in occupation of James White now or late James Whitley on the east (*R.ose and Crown*) and a messuage formerly in possession of Zachary Sarney now or late James Armstrong (*Butcher's Arms*) on the west.

John Hill son of John Hill sold in 1803 to Ann Pauling, and in 1814 John Paulin sold to William Cooper. By now the sale was of the one house 29 Market Place. The description of it is as follows :-

> 'all that messuage backside, garden, malthouse and workshops etc. adjoining south side of the High Street near the corn-market between a messuage belonging to the Corporation of Henley' (*Rose and Crown*) 'heretofore in occupation of James White since James Whitley late William Cook and now Atkyns on the east and a property late of Ann Paulin deceased late in occupation of Hayes and now of Richard Paulin on the west' (the second house 31 Market Place). It continues 'all of which messuage, malthouse etc. are in occupation of William Cooper and are in width along the front 24ft and at the back of the garden 23ft 3ins and north to south 260ft, all excepting a room at the west end of the premises extending over and belonging to the messuage adjoining' (31 Market Place) 'lately occupied by William Cooper which is now parted off and laid to the messuage now occupied by Richard Paulin'.

From these documents and the Henley Rentals the position of the *Seven Stars* is clearly defined, and the two houses linked together, not only by ownership but also actually by an overlapping room, were probably originally one property. The *Seven Stars* in the 17th century was probably a large and prosperous inn, which by the mid 18th century had become only a small beerhouse, occupying only half its original site. The buildings behind, including as they did a malthouse, sound like the appurtenances of an important inn, and together with the length of the plot of 260ft give the impression of a large burgage plot, which might well have been 47ft 4ins wide, that being the width of 29 and 31 Market Place as given in their deeds.

Landlords/ Tenants of the *Seven Stars*

1745	Humphrey Newberry (R)
1749	Mr Willis (R)

— Closed —

312 O.R.O. Cooper & Caldecott C58(1-5)

105

The Sheers/ Shears

14-16 Market Place

The *Sheers* or *Shears* beerhouse was most likely already trading in the 17th century and continued to the last years of the 18th century when it briefly became the *Turk's Head*. It was at 14-16 Market Place, later, perhaps in the 1830s, to become two beerhouses (see the *Fisherman's Cottage* and the *Waggon and Horses*). After 1855 it was re-built as a shop and warehouse for William Plumbe draper, who also had No 12. At the turn of the century the properties became three separate shops, and then later were combined in a building for the Co-Op, which in turn was demolished and re-built as Carpenters in 1984, now called Cargo.

The Bridge Rent Book of 1886 No 61, which is for 14 and 16 Market Place, says 'Mr William Plumbe formerly George Bennett and Mr Langton of Maidenhead brewers for premises late two beerhouses now pulled down and a shop and warehouses built thereon'.

Henley Rentals in 1704-06 say 'Whitacre for the *Sheers*'. 1713/4-1721/2 'Stephen Shadwell for the *Shears*'. 1727/8 'Mr Lovegrove'. 1733/4 'Mr Lovegrove and Mr Wyatt'. 1737-69 'Daniel Wyatt for the *Sheers*'. 1775 'Dan Wyatt now Mrs Wyatt for the sign of the *Sheers*'. 1779 'late Dan Wyatt for late the sign of the *Sheers* now the *Turk's Head*'. 1785 'Mr Wyatt for the *Turk's Head* late the *Sheers*'. In 1795 it says 'late the *Turk's Head*'.

Evidently it had ceased being the *Sheers* by 1779. Two burials are recorded of a Daniel Wyett/Wyatt in the 1770s, one in 1772, and another in 1776. It seems likely that the second of the two may have been at the *Sheers*, and it may have been his widow and son who changed the name. The *Turk's Head* appears to have closed shortly before 1795. The Henley Rentals up to at least 1836 say 'late the *Turk's Head*'. From 1814 there were two occupants named as Loftin/Loften/ Lofting and Bennett.

In 1984 before the present building of Carpenters was built, the Henley Archaeological & Historical Group had the chance of doing a small excavation on the site, under the direction of Brian Durham of the Oxford Archaeological Unit.

A brick barrel vaulted cellar made of what appeared to be 19th century bricks, was found at the west end of the site, occupying what would have been the front of 16 MarketPlace. It may have been the cellar of *Fisherman's Cottage*. Behind it there was a fireplace which might have been in the back room or parlour of the shop at the beginning of the 20th century. Beneath lay another fireplace, which could have been in the parlour of the shop or beerhouse at the beginning of the 19th century. Even further down, and slightly to one side, there was the remains of a much older fireplace, with tiles set on their edges, which may have been 17th, 16th or even 15th century. This may have been a fireplace belonging to the *Sheers*, it extended beyond the division between 16 and 14 Market Place, and obviously belonged to a larger house. There was no sign of any old wall dividing the property, not like the wall between 16 and 18 which was an old wall built of clunch. One interesting point was that as far as could be ascertained the front wall abutting the Market Place had always been in the same position. The cellars beneath 14 had been entirely rebuilt.

Landlords/ Tenants of the Sheers/*Shears*

1704-6	Whitacre (R)
1713-22	Stephen Shadwell (R)
1727-34	Mr Lovegrove (R)
1737-69	Daniel Wyatt

1775	Mrs Wyatt
1779-94	Mr Wyatt (R) the *Turk's Head*

— Closed —

106

The Ship

Waterside or Wharf Lane

A house down Wharf Lane on the left hand side, was the *Ship* at the end of the 19th century and when it closed in 1897. It was also there when the large scale O.S. map of 1879 was drawn. However a map accompanying a sales catalogue of 1853, when Fawley Court and its properties were sold[313], seems to show the *Ship* nearer to the river and a house on the lane as Wharfe House. However another Fawley Estate map probably of about 1821 (Fig 46) shows the *Ship* as on the left of Wharf Lane, with Wharf House further along on the same side, it also shows the stables of the Ship as across the lane, end on to the river, with a yard and shed behind it. The sales map of 1853 was probably indicating the whole property and not just the house. The stables

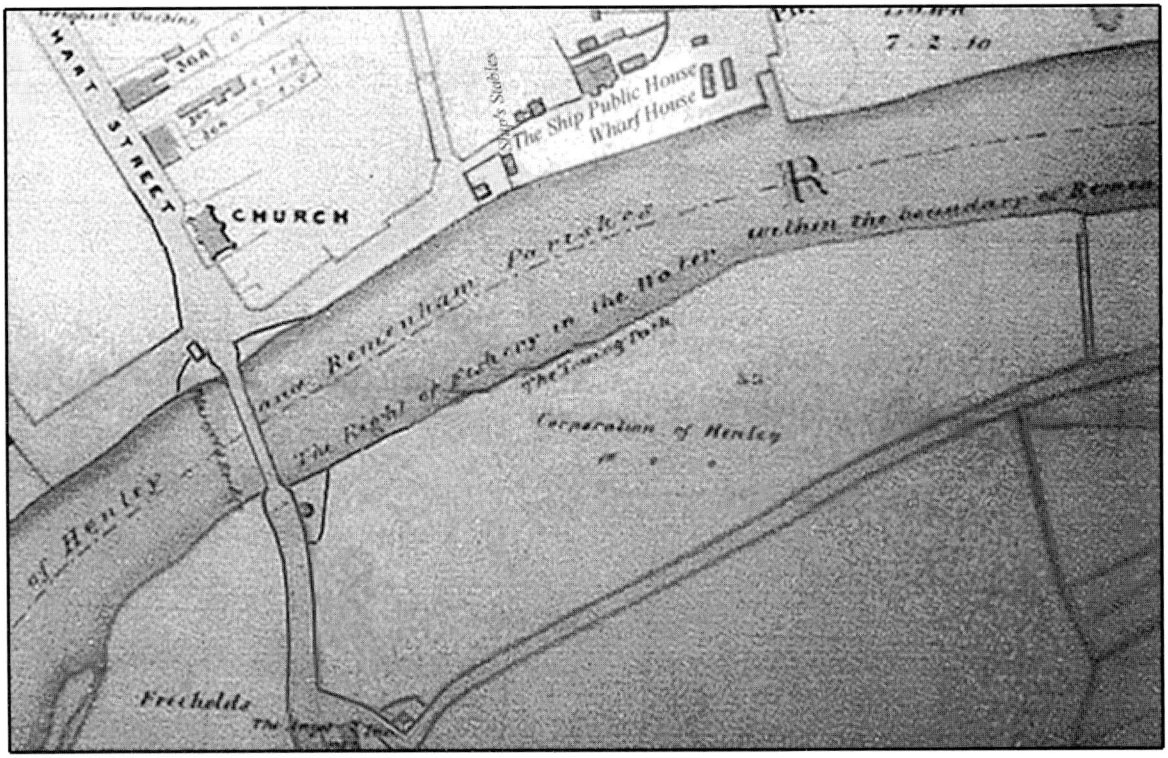

Fig 46 Part of the Fawley Court Estate plan c.1821, showing the ship & Wharf House. Building nearer the river with yard & shed behind it along the river side, inscribed 'The Ship's Stables'

313 See entry for the *Bell*, the Freemans of Fawley Court

and the yard were on the site of what became part of a wood yard, and a working boathouse at the end of New Street built in about 1880. Later in about 1886 this was converted into the desirable residence still there today, and two other residential boathouses were built alongside, probably by Hobbs, landlord 1871-1897.

The sales catalogue of 1853 says 'Freehold beershop on Henley Wharf with stabling and a small yard in front. Let to Messrs Brakspear as yearly tenants at £14 p.a. Land Tax 11s 5½d .'

An earlier sale in 1724 of Fawley Court and properties[314] does not mention the *Ship*, but only the Wharfe and Wharfe House. 'The messuage or tenement heretofore called Wharfe House and now Fortune's Wharfe situate near Phyllis Court heretofore in the occupation of William Fortune and now or late George Hawkins. And also all that Wharfe called Phyllis Court Wharf in tenure heretofore also of the said William Fortune and now or late George Hawkins. adjoining on the north end to Phyllis Court on the south to the street called New Street in Henley on the east side to the river Thames and on the westside to the messuage aforementioned (Wharfe House) and abutting on a large garden called Countess Garden'.

Although there is no mention of the *Ship* in this deed, a George Hawkins appears in the Victuallers Recognizances for Northfield End 1759-67, he may have been a son of the George Hawkins of 1724, and possibly at the *Ship*. This deed also clearly places Wharfe House to the west of the wharf, and backing on to Countess Garden, the position of the house shown in the map of 1821, with its land occupying the whole area between New Street and Phyllis Court.

The sale of Phyllis Court and Fawley Court in 1768[315] by Mrs Cooper to Sambrooke Freeman says 'all that part adjoining the said wharf called the *Ship* alehouse late in occupation of Jeremiah Rose now of William Axon'. The Victuallers Recognizance lists of 1770 and 71 both mention a William Axson whose surety was William Bennett.

By 1826 and the Brewery Inventory, Joseph Benwell held the leasehold of the *Ship* 'in occupation of Thomas Lintell with stabling for 6 Horses lofts over, workshop, small yard and wharf. The lease expires 29 September 1833. Rent £20 p.a.' There is a note written later beneath which says 'purchased of Freeman by T Scott'. This may have been at the sale of 1853, as later than that it could not have been purchased from Freeman. T Scott may have been an agent or representative of Brakspears, since by 1877 and the Register of Licenses the '*Ship* Waterside Wharf' was owned by Brakspears.

The *Ship*, adjoining the wharf, which by the 19th century had become Webb's Timber Wharf, was obviously a pub frequented by bargemen and river workers. Like the *Little White Hart* it became used by Regatta workers, and in 1885 also made an application to open at 4.0 in the morning on Regatta days[316].

In 1888 it was the scene of 'an affray'[317] when James Wilkins was charged with assaulting Henry Hobbs the landlord. 'Police Constable Russell found the defendant and four other men quarrelling.... James Wilkins went to the *Ship* to have a drink with his brother in law, who had just come down river in a tug.' Wilkins apologised and instead of a penalty of £5 was charged 23s 6d including costs.

Landlords/ Tenants of the *Ship*

1724 ?	George Hawkins (ORO,VR) ?
pre 1768	Jeremiah Rose (ORO)
1768-71	William Axon/Axson (ORO,VR)
1793-1817	Edward Ward (AKL,CL,SD)

314 O.R.O. MS DD Henley DIV 2

315 O.R.O. Cooper & Caldecott C1(12)

316 & 317 Henley Advertiser 4 Jul 1885, 24 Mar 1888

1820	Benjamin Garraway (CL)
1823	A Manuel (SD)
1826	Thomas Lintell (WHB/I)
1830	Thomas Martin (SD)
1844	Thomas Goodey (SD)
1847	Robert Pratt (SD)
*1850-4	Benjamin Allum (C,SD)
*1860-71	James/George Hooper (SSM,RM,SD) boat builder
Apr 1871-97	Henry Edward Hobbs (RL,C,HA,SD)

— Closed —

107

The Sun

North side of Market Place possibly the site of 2 West Hill

This pub called the *Sun* is only mentioned in Henley Rentals. In 1704 Widow Luen paid for the *Sun*, in 1713/4 'Chris Fennell for the *Sun* late Widow Luen'. In 1742 the rental was for 'The *Exchequer and Star* late the *Sun* and now called the *Barley Mow*'. In 1745 the rentals say 'Mr Brigstocke for Mr Gyles house late called the *Sun*'.

It is not certain where this pub was, except that it was most likely on the lower north side of West Hill or where the Kings Road is now situated.

One possibility is that it existed on the site of the house now 2 West Hill. Mr Gyles mentioned in 1745 owned the house that in 1769 and 1775 was let to Humphrey Gainsborough. Maybe that house was built on the site of the *Sun* in the 1760s or just before.

Landlords/ Tenants of the *Sun*

1704	Widow Luen (R)
1713/4	Chris Fennell

— Continued as the *Exchequer and Star* —

108

The Sun

44 Northfield End

An entry of 1815 in the Bensington Manorial Records is for 'The *Sun* once called the *Fox*. W Towsey and Rev J Joyce.' The Rev Joyce appears in other property records, he was brother in law to W H Brakspear, being married to Sarah the eldest daughter of Robert[318]. She had inherited two houses in Henley from her father, and so these became the property of her husband.

318 Sheppard, Francis 'Brakspear's Brewery 1779-1979' 1979

The Victuallers Recognizances for Northfield End show that Thomas Buckett was at the *Sun* 1774-85, John Ayres 1786-91, Mary Ayres 1792-3, Isaac Hunt 1794, John Hobbs 1801-4, Elizabeth Hobbs 1808-18 and Thomas Poor 1821-2. There is confirmation of some of these names in Brakspear's Rent Ledgers from 1790, John Aries(sic) 1791-4, Isaac Hunt 1794-7, and then John Hobbs 1797-1812.

In Archbishop Laud's Charity books Mary Hobbs in 1805 applied for the 'Maid's Charity', she was described as the daughter of John and Elizabeth Hobbs of the *Sun* [319].

In the Inventory of the Brewery in 1826 the *Sun* was held as a 'lifehold' by Wm Henry Brakspear Esq. 'The *Sun* in occupation of Thomas Poore with stabling piggeries and yard on lease dated - for three lives of the following ages:- R H Brakspear 35 years, W H Brakspear 22 years, Sarah Joyce 34 years.' A note beneath in red ink says 'Lease for 75yrs. Michaelmas 1848'. (The 7 is indistinct it could be a 2 or a 1.) A lifehold was a form of lease to last for the lifetime of any of the persons designated, something of a gamble.

The present building though probably on the site of the *Fox*, has almost certainly been much altered and possibly rebuilt in the 19th century, it also seems to have been extended on the east side.

The *Sun* closed at the end of September 1992, after the last landlord Kenneth Crocker and his wife Sheila transferred to the *White Horse*[320].

Landlords/ Tenants of the *Sun*

*1774-85	Thomas Buckett (VR)
1786-91 ?94	John Ayres/Aries (VR,WHB/R)
1792-3	Mary Ayres (VR)
1794-7	Isaac Hunt (VR,WHB/R)
1797-1808	John Hobbs (VR,WHB/R) (John Hobbs buried 1 Feb 1809)
1808-18*	Elizabeth Hobbs (VR)
1821-6	Thomas Pooor/Poore (VR,WHB/I,SD)
1830	Jeremiah Heath(SD)
1847-54	John Hitchcock (C,SD)
1861-8	Edward Spratley/Spratly (C,SD)
May 1871-2	James William Pike (HA)
Jun 1872-90	Daniel Buckett (RL,C,HA,SD)
Jan 1890-4	Hannah Buckett (RL,HA)
Nov 1894-7	Samuel White (RL)
Apr 1897-1905	Ernest Edward Phillips (RL)
1905-7	John West (RL)
May 1907-10	Joseph Patrick Casey (RL)
Jul 1910-12	William Oliver Sherry (RL)
Jul 1912-27	Henry John Coxford (RL,WHB/C,SD)
Oct 1927-8	Walter Edgar Welch (RL,WHB/C,HS,SD)
Sep 1928-31	George Turner (RL,WHB/C,HS)
May 1931-5	Thomas Greygoose (RL,WHB/C,HS,MReg)
Feb 1935-Apr	Ernest Andrew Jeston Page (RL,WHB/C)
May 1935-8	Alfred William Sweetzer (RL,WHB/C,HS,SD)
Feb 1938-48	Somerset Reginald Tapsfield (RL,WHB/C,HS,SD)
May 1948-50	Ora Kate Tapsfield (RL)

319 Archbishop Laud's Charity books O.R.O. Hen Bor AX35

320 Henley Standard 2 Oct 1992

Oct 1950-77	George William Laye (RL,WHB/C)
Sep 1977-Nov	Victoria Maude Laye (RL)
Nov 1977-92	Kenneth George Crocker (RL,WHB/C,HS)

— Closed —

109

The Swan

72 Greys Hill

Greys Hill and the build up of houses along Greys Road or Lane appears to have begun in about 1800. By the time of the 1844 Rotherfield Greys Tithe Map there were quite a few houses in Greys Hill, and the one now 72 Greys Hill was noted as a beershop and garden owned by Henry Byles (Greys Brewery) and occupied by Elizabeth Lewis and another (Fig 60). There is no mention of the *Swan* beerhouse in the Victuallers Recognizances for Rotherfield Greys which go up to 1822, and which from 1775 mention the pubs of Greys by name. So it is reasonable to assume that the *Swan* opened between 1822 and 1844 to cater for the growing population of the district. It is interesting to note that in this case the pub arrived before the church and school. Holy Trinity church opened in 1848, and the old Trinity Infants School also in Greys Hill opened in 1850.

After Elizabeth Lewis the tenants of the *Swan* are hard to trace, as beershops in the early street directories are seldom mentioned by name, and beer retailers only listed as being in certain streets. However in 1850 and 1854 Henry Lambourn is given for Greys Hill, and in 1869 David Waller was in Greys Hill, both were most likely at the *Swan.* Charles Hamilton in 1877 was a beer retailer in South Hill. This street name crops up now and again, and was probably another name for Greys Hill, though it could have been Gravel Hill or a part of Greys Lane. However since the Census of 1881 places Charles Hamilton at the *Swan*, Greys Hill, and a Register of Licenses shows him there in 1882, he was probably already there in 1877.

By 1882 the Register shows that the *Swan* was then owned by Ive Brothers, later in 1914 it was the property of Dymore Brown & Son Ltd of Reading, and in 1940 of Morland & Co of Abingdon.

By the 1950s it seems to have become the custom to hold Harvest Festivals at the *Swan*. The Henley Standard reports festivals in 1957 and 1959, when Mrs Porter and Miss Joyce thanked the donors for their contributions. Mrs Porter was the last publican of the *Swan*, which closed in February 1962, when at the Annual Licensing Session no license was applied for.

Landlords/ Tenants of the *Swan*

1844	Elizabeth Lewis (TM)
1851-4	Henry Lambourn (C,SD)
1869	David Waller (SD)
Jul 1875*	Hanry Walkling (HA)
*1877-83	Charles Hamilton (RL,C,SD)
Jul 1883-7	William Norcott (RL)
Jun 1887-1902	Edward Alleway (RL)
May 1902-3	Annie Alleway (RL)
Oct 1903-13	Alfred Clinch (RL)

Dec 1913-4 Alfred George Bushell (RL)
Nov 1914-6 Sidney Liney (RL)
Mar 1916-24 Ernest Victor Evans (RL,HS,SD)
Oct 1924-30 Harry Percy Bint (RL,HS,SD)
Feb 1930-7 Charles Henry Burley (RL,HS,SD)
Jul 1937-8 Mrs Rose Burley (RL,HS,SD)
Jul 1938-49 Herbert Edward Porter (RL)
May 1949-62 Mrs Florence Mary Porter (RL,HS)

— Closed —

110

The Swan or The White Swan

35 Market Place

The *Swan* was in the house on what is now the west corner of the north entrance to Greys Road Car Park (Fig 47), and was occupied in 1991 by Hackford Bathrooms, having previously been an antique shop, it is now (1999) a pizza restaurant. Before the demolition of numbers 29-33 Market Place (see the *Seven Stars* and the *Butcher's Arms*) 35 was in a continuous row of houses on the south side of the Market Place, and not on a corner.

Fig 47 Shop once the Swan, on right brick house once the site of the Woolpack. Far left tower on top of malthouse once part of Ive's Brewert B8 & M33 Photo 1989

There is an entry in the Borough Records[321] on Friday September 8 1486 'Item for a tenement called *le Swanne* 10d.' This might be an early record of the *Swan* at 35 Market Place or it might not, there is no following reference nor indication where '*le Swanne*' might have been.

321 Briers, P M 'Henlery Borough Records 1395-1543' 1960 Ox Record Soc

The earliest positive reference to the property later known as the *Swan* in the Market is a document[322] of the 39th year the reign of Elizabeth (1596) when on the 1 March the then owner, Henry Lord Norris of Rycot conveyed the property to his son Sir Henry Norris. Later in the same year on 21 March Henry Lord Norris and his son conveyed all the messuage, garden orchard etc to John Farmer of Henley gentleman. John Farmer on the 20 April in the 42nd year of Elizabeth then assigned the property to Humphrey Douglas of Henley blacksmith. The house is then described as being on the south side of the High Street between a tenement of the said John Farmer on the east and a tenement of Agnes Maynard widow on the west. At that time, 1599, it was said that the building had been late in the occupation of William Cole weaver.

So far in these deeds there seems no indication that the property was an inn or public house, but since landlords often later had other occupations there is no reason that it could not have already been the *Swan*. However it is interesting that John Farmer who sold the property to Douglas, should also have owned the neighbouring house on the east side, since that too at the beginning of the eighteenth century was a pub, the *Butchers Arms*.

Two years later on 23 January in the 44th year of Elizabeth, Humphrey Douglas took out a mortgage with Zachary Alnutt of Skirmott, Hambleden. By then his neighbours had changed, on the east there was a tenement of Walter Savyn alias Turner, and on the west Richard ffrowen (Frewen). On 10 February in the 45th year of Elizabeth (1602) Humphrey Douglas assigned the premises to William Gravett. In 1604 on 2 June Gravett leased the property on a 99 years lease to John Kenton, who signed a covenant in October agreeing to pay a rent of 5s p.a., to keep the premises in good repair, and to allow Gravett or his representatives to visit and inspect the premises twice yearly. In this agreement Gravett was said to be of the parish of St Clements Danes in Middlesex. Almost immediately after this lease to John Kenton, William Gravett sold the property for £70 to the Governors of the Grammar School of Henley on Thames, this was on 26 December in the 2nd year of James. It was agreed that the lease to John Kenton should remain unchanged.

On 21 February 1697 the Governors of the Grammar School agreed that William Haster of Henley blacksmith should take over the remainder of the 99 year lease at the same rent of 5s p.a. It was also agreed that a further lease of 99 years would be available in 1704 which would terminate in 1803. Was there a blacksmiths business on the premises ? This is the second occupant to have been a blacksmith.

In 1803 the then holder of the lease, probably James Brooks was buried on the 18 June[323], the heir of the estate designated in a document merely as A.B. (Anne Brooks ?) was unaware of the terms of the lease, by which renewal should have been applied for before 1803. Her tenants remained on the premises until 1805, when the Governors suddenly woke up to the fact that the lease had expired, and ordered their eviction. A renewal of the lease was refused, but the occupants claimed that they should have had six months notice to leave and that they would stay.

In another document[324] held by the Schools Charities the lease expiring in 1803 was described. The lease of 99 years granted in 1704, when for £5 p.a. 'a house and premises in the Market Place now the *Swan Inn*' was leased to William Haster. This 99 year lease was held from 1775 to 1803 by James Brooks. The wording of this document possibly suggests that it had not been an inn long, so maybe the *Swan* only started trading in 1704 or just before. In which case *le Swanne* of 1486 was probably elsewhere.

The house and the *Swan* when it existed was, and is still, owned by the Governors of the Henley United Schools, it is one of the properties from which funds are provided to the United Schools' Charities.

---

322 & 324 Documents 1596-1803 belonging to Henley Educational Charities removed from Town Hall, now in O.R.O
323 Henley Parish Burial Register 1737-1812

When in 1803 the 99 year lease expired, and after the problems that arose from its expiry were sorted out, it was leased to Robert Brakspear. Described as 'the *Swan* public house, stables, outhouses, garden orchard etc. now in the occupation of John Wiswould as under tenant, on the south side of the High Street in the Market Place between messuage formerly in the occupation of Richard Martin late of J A Rackstraw and now of George Deane and Joseph Soundy on the west side and the messuage formerly in occupation of Nicholas Eeles since of Joseph Armstrong draper and now of R P Culham on the east side, and extending from the street on the north to the town ditch on the south.' Nicholas Eeles was the father of John, Elizabeth and Ann Eeles of the *Butcher's Arms*, while Richard Martin was probably at the *Woolpack.*

In Henley Rentals for 1733/4 under Friday Street, there are entries for those in the town renting sheep and hog pens in Friday Street. There are eight entries, the second and third being for the *Woolpack* and the *Swan*. Previously in 1727/8 in the same order of the list there are Widow Webb and Edward Marten, in 1721/2 Widow Webb and James Kitson, and in 1713/4 Mr Stevens and James Kitson.

As further proof of James Kitson's presence at the *Swa*n, there is an indenture of 1734[325] concerned with 33 Market Place, then the *Butcher's Arms,* which quotes an indenture of 1722 and says 'a house in tenure of James Kitson on the west.'

Although the main 99 years lease appears to have been held by James Brooks until 1803, it is evident that it must have been sub-let to Brakspear by 1786, as at that date entries appear in Brakspears Rent Ledgers. From 1786-95 the Swan was let to Mr Joseph Avery, and then 1795-1811 to John Wiswould.

At the beginning of October 1814[326] Richard Paulin became landlord and advertised that there were 'good beds and stabling'. He was still there in 1826 when the inventory of the brewery was taken. 'Leasehold of the *Swan Inn* in occupation of Robert Paulin stabling for 35 horses small yard and garden. Lease expires Michaelmas 1828. Rent £35 p.a.' A note scribbled below appears to say 'renew lease' The lease was in 1826 held by Joseph Benwell. It is probable that the name Richard in the paper of 1814 was an error, and that he was Robert. A Robert Paulin was baptised 2 March 1777.

Part of the stabling was probably being used in 1830[327] by Stephen Banks, who ran a carrier service from the *Swan* to London every Friday and to Cirencester every Sunday.

Brakspears did renew the lease, and held it till the closure of the *Swan* at the end of the licensing vear of 1877.

There was no application for a license in 1878. The pub had probably been in difficulties for some years. In July of 1870[328] the landlord Henry Alfred Collcutt was summoned for the non payment of £2 11s 7½d, the amount of the poor rate assessed. Later in October a distress warrant was made against Collcutt, this would seem to imply either poor custom or mismanagement of the pub. In the next seven years there were several changes of landlord, and a few attempts to improve the premises, but by 1877 a decision to close had been taken.

After the closure of the *Swan* the premises were sometimes referred to as the White House, this may have been because the front of the premises (which then was the only part visible from the street) was plastered and whitewashed, which again may be the reason for the pub occasionally being called the *White Swan.*

---

325 O.R.O. Cooper & Caldecott C57 (1)

326 Reading Mercury & Oxford Gazette 3 Oct 1814

327 Pigot & Co Street Directory 1830

328 Henley Advertiser 16 Jul 1870 & 8 Oct 1870

Landlords/ Tenants of the *Swan*

pre 1599	William Cole (THD) weaver
1599-1602	Humphrey Douglas (THD) blacksmith
1604-	John Kenton (THD)
1697-1703*	William Haster (THD)
1713-22	James Kitson (ORO,THD,R)
1727/8	Edward Marten/Martin (THD,R)
*1786-95	Joseph Avery (WHB/R,SD)
1795-1814	John Wiswould/Wiswold (WHB/R,CL,USC,THD)
Oct 1814-26*	Robert/Richard Paulin (AKL,CL,WHB/I,PF,RM,SD)
1830	Thomas Greenwood (SD)
Jan 1841*	John Shrimpton (RM)
*1841	Charles Little (C)
1842-57	Arthur Eaton (C,SD,BReg)
Feb 1857-67*	Mrs Susannah Eaton (C,SD,BReg)
1869	Henry Deller (SD)
*1870	Henry Alfred Collcutt (SSM,HA)
Oct 1870-1	Edward Spratley (SSM,C,HA)
1871-2	John Weyman (HA)
Apr 1872*	George Henry Mathews (HA)
*1876	Joseph Ball (SD)
1877	Thomas Rogers (HA)
Jan 1877-8	Jeremiah Windebank (RL,HA)

— Closed —

111

The Three Horseshoes , The Horseshoes or The Five Horseshoes

(12) Reading Road

This *Three Horseshoes* is not the pub open today of the same name at the junction of Harpsden Road with the Reading Road, but the original pub (Fig 48). This was situated on the west side of the Reading Road, where there is now a wide pavement in front of the monumental mason's yard of E T Sheppard. It was once numbered as 12 Reading Road.

The *Three Horseshoes* was a small pub with adjacent cottages, between the garden wall of Southfield House, now the row of shops on the west side of the street, and the land of what is now the United Reformed Church (Figs 63 & 64). It is shown in several photos and postcards of the street, and it can also be seen why there was such a wish to remove it in the early years of this century. Its trouble was that it stuck out into the road, it was built when the Reading Road was a lane, and by the 1920s it was a hazard to traffic. Its porch in particular extended into the road.

The *Three Horseshoes* was owned by Brakspears, who also owned the house built as a pub in 1898 at the junction of Harpsden Road. However they were refused a license for that house, and still did not have one in the late 1920s. As pressure mounted to close the *Three Horseshoes*, Brakspears came to an arrangement with the Licensing Magistrates. In return for allowing the sale and closure of the old *Three Horseshoes*, they were to be granted a license for the house at Harpsden Road corner. Accordingly the license, the name and the licensee were all transferred in July 1930, to the house built in 1898 but not used as a pub for thirty two years.

The old *Three Horseshoes*, which was till 1892 in Rotherfield Greys, was an old established pub which had been trading since the 18th century, and probably for a long time before that. The Victuallers Recognizances for Rotherfield Greys give the landlords from 1774, and Brakspear's Rent Ledgers from 1791-1811. It is Brakspear's Rent Ledgers which sometimes name the pub the *Five Horseshoes.*

Fig 48 The original Three Horseshoes just before demolition. Earlier photos show the buildings without timbering, brickwork painted white Photo 1930 by the late W G Reeves (see also Figs 63 & 64)

It is also from the Rent Ledger concerning the new tenancy by Robert Irving in 1811 that the following letter comes:-

> 'Sir, Robt Irving having applied to me to sanction his taking the adjoining public house, I have conversed with him, and have reason to hope, he is steady himself, he promises to keep order, not to suffer riots and to observe good hours, as such I should be sorry to throw the least difficulty in his ways. Indeed I shall recommend him any time while his conduct comports with the above intimation.
>
> Yours respectfully - James Churchill.'

It is not surprising that after this commendation Robert Irving got the job and became landlord. James Churchill was the Minister of the Congregational Chapel, now the United Reformed Church, from 1807-15, and lived in the Manse which is still alongside the mason's yard.

The Rent Ledgers also supply information on the tenants in the adjoining three cottages. The pub was listed as no.l, in no.2 in 1791-7 there was Samuel Heath, in 1798-1800 Chris Holmes, 1801-4 Robt Irving, 1805-10 Mrs Irving and 1811-2 James Cordery. In no.3 in 1791-7 there was Thomas Fukes and in 1798-1811 Thomas Hickman. In no.4 in 1791-7 there was Thos Hodges and in 1798-1811 Henry Bliss. From these rentals it seems that the Irvings lived from 1801 next door to the *Three Horseshoes*, though it is possible that the Robert of that date was the father of the Robert who became landlord, and the Mrs Irving may have been his widowed mother. The Irvings do not appear in the Henley Parish Registers, they were probably Congregationalists.

Another tenant who seems briefly to have been licensee of the *Three Horseshoes* is Chris Holmes who was at no.2 before the Irvings. In the Victuallers Recognizances Chas Holmes had the license 1798 and 1801. The discrepancy between Chris and Chas can easily be seen as a writing or reading error, what is strange is that he is not named as licensee in the Rent Ledger. Perhaps he held the license while still living at cottage no.2.

The Inventory of the Brewery shows that Robert Irving was still at the *Three Horseshoes* in 1826, indeed a street directory of 1830 lists him as being there then. The Inventory says freehold belonging to Wm Henry Brakspear Esq. 'The *Three Horseshoes* in Grays in occupation of Robert Irving, small shed and yard.'

The question of closure seems to have hovered over the pub for 30 years, as early as the Annual Licensing of 1900, questions were raised and the license was actually refused, only being re-instated on appeal. Again in 1907 while closure was discussed and referred to the Compensation Authority, only a Provisional License was granted. At that time it escaped closure, until as already related it was finally closed in 1930, and soon after demolished.

Landlords/ Tenants of the *Three Horseshoes*

*1774-97	Henry Godliman/Godley (VR)
1789-94	Grace Godliman (VR) /1791-4 Widow Godley (WHB/R)
1794-7	Thos Wargent/Wargeant (WHB/R)
1797-8	Thos Eggleton/Egleton (VR,WHB/R)
1798-1801	Chris/Chas Holmes (VR)
Oct 1801-11	Edward Clark/Clarke (VR,WHB/R)
Feb 1811-30*	Robert Irving/Irwin (VR,WHB/R,WHB/I,SD)
1841-4	James Wix/Wicks (C,TM,SD) carrier
1847-54	John Wheeler (C,SD) carpenter
1868	Frank Austen (SD)
*1869-81	John Coker (C,SD)
1882-96	Samuel Piggott (RL,SD)
Mar 1896-1900	James Pickerbnell (RL)
Mar 1900-3	Robert George Wilson (RL)
Dec 1903-7	William Walters (RL,WHB/C)
1907-16	William John Hayns/Haynes (RL,WHB/C)
Dec 1916-8	Herbert Ayers/Ayres (RL,WHB/C,SD)
1919-30	Mrs Brigid Ayres (RL,WHB/C,HS,SD) removed to the *Three Horseshoes,* Picked Piece, Reading Road 1930

— Continued as the *Three Horseshoes* at 38 Reading Road —

112

The Three Horseshoes

38 Reading Road

The *Three Horseshoes* open today, as explained in the account of the old *Three Horseshoes*, was built as a pub in 1898 by Brakspears to serve the fast expanding population of New Town and the houses along the Reading Road. It was built on land known as Picked Piece, which had been a small triangular plot at the junction of Reading Road with Harpsden Lane.

However when a license for the new pub was applied for, it was refused. In 1903 it was suggested that the license of the old *Three Horseshoes* should be transferred to Picked Piece, but it was again refused. As early as 1923 Brakspears offered to demolish the old *Three Horseshoes* in exchange for transference of the license, but it was not till February 1930 that the suggestion was approved [329].

329 Henley Standard 14 Feb 1930

The approval though was subject to conditions. When the license was refused, the house at Picked Piece became a shop, selling groceries, confectionaries and non alcoholic drinks. By 1924 Mrs Emma Giles was installed running it as a grocery and sub-post office[330] so when in February 1930, at long last the long awaited transfer of the license was granted, Mrs Giles had to be accommodated. Mrs Giles described as being Post Mistress and having a newspaper and general store, was to have new premises built by Brakspears, behind the house already there. In March[331] agreement was reached that the transfer of license should be on 30 July 1930, so as to allow time for the building of the new premises. However after all these arrangements, the Standard of 2 May 1930 reported the death of Mrs Giles, Post Mistress of Picked Piece Post Office for the last ten years, and newspaper and general store shopkeeper. Whether the building of the new premises continued is not mentioned.

In July 1930 the name of the *Three Horseshoes*, its license and its licensee, Mrs Brigid Ayres, were transferred to Picked Piece, Reading Road.

Landlords/ Tenants of the *Three Horseshoes*

1930-48	Brigid Catherine Ayres (RL,WHB/C,HS,SD)
Sep 1948-50	William Barson (RL,WHB/C)
Dec 1950-5	Donald John Herbert (RL,WHB/C)
Jan 1956-71	Mrs Edith May Herbert (RL,WHB/C)
Fen 1971-81	Trevor Ernest Herbert (RL,WHB/C)
Nov 1981-96	Evelyn Joan Herbert (RL,WHB/C)
Oct 1996-99-	Dawn Lesley Kirby (RL,HS)

113

The Three Tuns

5 Market Place

The *Three Tuns* is well documented back to the 18th century, but although probably in existence long before that, no earlier references have been found. The building is almost certainly much older.

The name of the *Three Tuns* as illustrated on its sign, of three barrels, one above and two below, is very similar to the coat of arms of the Vintners Co., who may have at one time owned the property. 3 Market Place is still owned by the Vintners, and two of its coats of arms of three barrels, two above and one below, may be seen on either side of the house just above the fascia board of 3 Market Place.

During the 18th century the, *Three Tuns* was owned, or at least the Henley Rentals were charged to James Maynard 1713/4, then to Abraham Darby 1721-8, Mrs Darby 1737, and then Thomas Higgs late Darby in 1765 and 69. The Victuallers Recognizance lists of 1753 and 54 show an Elizabeth Darby as a victualler, and in the lists of 1770 and 71 there is a Thomas Higgs, whose sureties were William Rackstraw and John Deavon.

The Court Baron Book of 1785 says 'Mrs Benwell tenement called the *Three Tuns* occupied by Higgs'. It was probably after Higgs left that the pub became empty, and was then advertised in the Reading Mercury & Oxford Gazette of September 1787 as that 'old and good accustomed house the *Three Tuns*'........'situated in the centre of the Town of Henley'........'now in very good

330 Post Office Directory 1924

331 Henley Standard 14 Mar 1930

trade with stabling for forty horses and may be entered upon immediately' applications to be made to Messrs Appleton and Shaw.

A street directory of about 1793 gives John Griffiths at the *Three Tuns*, but soon after it may have been taken by Harry Williams, as in the Reading Mercury & Oxford Gazette of 22 October 1798 there is an announcement of the sale at the *Three Tuns* of the furniture and effects of Mr Harry Williams deceased.

There seem to have been problems about finding a suitable landlord, as in both January and June of 1800 Appleton and Shaw advertised in the Reading Mercury & Oxford Gazette that the *Three Tuns* was to let, that it was in full trade and had stabling for upwards of sixty horses. A temporary manager must have been employed to keep the trade going.

In 1822 there was another sale at the *Three Tuns*, Mrs Stacey was being forced to sell her possessions under a Distress Warrant. The Reading Mercury & Oxford Gazette of 14 January announced that the sale was for paying her rent and for the benefit of her creditors. The sale included all her household furniture, a two pull beer engine, a horse, young sow, neat gig and harness, and other effects. In spite of the sale Mrs Stacey was still at the *Three Tuns* in 1823 according to a street directory.

By 1826 in the Inventory the freehold was held jointly by Joseph Benwell and W H Brakspear. 'The *Three Tuns* public house in occupation of John Barker with yard and stabling for 26 horses. Land Tax £1 2s 0d. Quit Rent 92d.' Evidently the stabling had diminished since 1787 and 1800.

According to Francis Sheppard in his 'Brakspear's Brewery 1779-1979' the *Three Tuns* was bought in 1865 from Joseph Benwell's estate by Brakspear, at the same time that he bought out Benwell's interest in the brewery and other properties.

There is quite a large amount of ground behind the *Three Tuns* today, and originally it had a strip of land running down as far as the Town Ditch or Town Boundary. The boundary ran up the centre of Friday Street, across the crossroads, then down the entrance to Tuns Lane, then along behind the houses on the north side of Greys Road, all of which had small gardens. Today the boundary might be said to have gone along the south side of the car parks. The strip of land behind the Three Tuns would have been comparable to the burgage plots in Hart Street, as would all the house plots on the south side of the Market Place westward of the *Three Tuns*. In fact they are shown as being so on the O.S.map of 1879.

Tuns Lane which runs behind the houses on the west side of Duke Street, can only be entered from Greys Road, the northern end being part of the pub, and closed as a throughway. The lane may once have been part of the burgage plot of the *Three Tuns*. The lane is now used as a back way to the shops in Duke Street and a back entrance to the *Three Tuns*. For many years there was also a public right of way to the Market Place through the passage at the side of the pub, now discontinued.

How much of the land of the roadway belonged to the *Three Tuns* in 1826 is uncertain. However some of the stabling mentioned then would have been used by the carriers who worked from the *Three Tuns*, and presumably used the lane as a means of reaching the stabling. In 1830 Thomas Appleby had a carrier service to London every Monday, and to Watlington every Thursday. Thursday was Market Day hence the more local service. In 1850 Edie Elys had a van for passengers and goods to Reading every afternoon at four - Sundays excepted. In 1883 Joseph Jones had a carrier service to Hambleden every Thursday [332].

The Census of 1861 reveals that Charles Lovell general dealer was at the *Three Tuns* together with his wife, son and daughter. He also had five boarders, five lodgers and six males aged

332 Street Directories 1830,1850 & 1883

about 20, names unknown, who were horse copers and keepers. Perhaps in 1861 the stables were also being used by the horse copers. One wonders too whether it was the horse copers or their friends who were involved, when in January 1863, John Day who was by then landlord, was charged with permitting 'notoriously bad characters to assemble at his house'[333]. On that occasion John Day was fined £3 with 16s costs it being his second offence of a similar kind.

In 1872[334] plans were allowed for building a shed and loft behind the *Three Tuns.* In 1873 the landlord had trouble with a customer who was drunk and quarrelsome and refused to leave; in the report the landlord's name was given as Nathaniel Richardson. This seems to have been incorrect as the landlord was a Nathaniel Robinson. Three street directories of 1868, 69 and 76 all list him as Robinson, that of 68 adding that he was a cattle-dealer. The Census of 1871, and also the Magistrates Special Sessions Minute Book of 1870 and 71, all give the name Nathaniel Robinson.

In 1931 at the Licensing Sessions[335] it was recommended that the *Three Tuns*, together with *Ye Olde Bell* and the *Cannon* should be closed. William Edward George was said to have been licensee for '11 years come May', before that he had been four years at the pub known by 1931 as *Ye Olde Bell*, after which he had been recruiting for the National Reserve, with whom he had served till 1919. There was nothing against him, but there was very little trade. The house contained an ordinary bar, smoking room and garage. There were eight bedrooms, three unfit for use. A kitchen and a pantry, and the Saloon Bar was used as a private sitting room. The licensed rooms were the bar and the Saloon Bar. After considerable debate the license was renewed.

Robin Gladman became landlord in 1991, and in January 1993 the bar area was extended with a new bar in what the Henley Standard described as a four hundred year old stable. This bar was to be aimed at younger people and have a juke box and regular performances by live bands. The character of the stable was to be retained with the stalls remaining, which were said to have been still in use after the Second World War, but a new terra cotta floor and wood burning stove had been added. The 'Stable' bar had an entrance from the car park behind, which combined with the bar being somewhat secluded proved to be disastrous for Robin Gladman. Inspector Dizaei of the Thames Valley Police in August 1996 made an application to the Magistrates for Gladman's license to be revoked, after a drugs raid by the police had arrested nine people in the bar. The police claimed that the bar and its situation, and the general running of the pub, created an atmosphere where drug dealers felt comfortable, they also claimed that customers from the pub had caused a disturbance in the Market Place the previous summer. Gladman was also accused of serving drinks to under age customers, and keeping a disorderly house. In August Robin Gladman lost his license, but he determinedly denied all the accusations and his license was restored on appeal.

In September 1997[336] Robin Gladman and his wife Jenny left the *Three Tuns* to take over the *Grouse and Claret* at Kingwood Common. Brakspears who own the *Three Tuns* have decided to transfer the pub to become part of the brewery's managed house division, and in future it will be run by Brakspear employees, the first to do so will be Simon Charman and Lynne Whitehouse.

Landlords/ Tenants of the *Three Tuns*

1713/4	James Maynard (R)
1721-8	Abraham Darby (R)
1737-54	Mrs Elizabeth Darby (R,VR)
1765-85	Thomas Higgs (R,VR,CB)
1793	John Griffiths (SD)

333 Reading Mercury & Oxford Gazette 31 Jan 1863

334 Henley Advertiser 9 Mar 1872, 4 Jan 1873

335 & 336 Henley Standard 13 Feb & 13 Mar 1931, 12 Sep 1997

*1798	Harry Williams (RM)
Nov 1799	Thomas Glover (CL)
*1814-May 19	Richard Stacey (AKL,CL,BReg)
1819-3*	Mrs Mary Stacey (PF,RM,SD)
1826-30	John Barker/Barckus (WHB/I,SD)
*1841-61	Charles Lovell (C,SD) in 47 fishmonger & in 61 general dealer
1862-3*	John Day (RM,SD)
*1868-76	Nathaniel Robinson (SSM,C,HA,SD) cattle dealer
1877	Mrs Ann Robinson (SD)
1877-87	Henry Worskett (RL,C,SD)
Sep 1787-8	Edmund Henry Lawrence (SSM,RL)
Dec 1888-1904	William Jose (RL,SD)
Mar 1904-5	Walter Messenger (RL)
1905-9	Frederick George Dickson (RL,WHB/C)
Sep 1909-12	Jesse Miles (RL,WHB/C)
Mar 1912-May	Leonard James Ford (RL)
May 1912-13	William Wood (RL,WHB/C)
Sep 1913-14	Henry James Brown (RL,WHB/C)
Oct 1914-20	William Edwards (RL,WHB/C,SD)
Jul 1920-37	William Edwin George (RL,WHB/C,HS,SD)
Jul 1937-64	Thomas Albert Cain (RL,WHB/C,SD)
Jun 1964-8	Mrs Marjory Ettie Cain (RL,WHB/C) widow
Jul 1968-71	Brian Edward Courtier/Courtice (RL,WHB/C)
Jan 1971-5	Kenneth Leonard Thomas Johnson (RL,WHB/C)
Jan 1975-6	Gerrard Ormond Gyngell (RL)
Dec 1976-91	Robert Jack Gortley Knowles (RL,WHB/C,HS)
Sep 1991-97	Robin Gladman (RL) (From Mar 1996-Mar 97 the license alternately revoked & adjourned)
Sep 1997-Oct	Simon Darren Charman & Lynne Joyce Whitehouse (RL,HS)
Oct 1997-Nov	Kenneth George Edwards (RL)
Nov 1997-99-	David Forbes Denham (RL)

114

The Travellers Rest

The end of the Fairmile

The *Travellers Rest* was at the junction of the Toll road to Nettlebed and the road to Assendon (Fig 36). It was demolished in 1939 to make way for the dual carriageway up the hill on the Nettlebed road. Both the name and the licensee were transferred to the newly built large roadside pub at Caversham, opposite where the road runs down to Reading and Reading bridge.

The *Travellers Rest* demolished in 1939, was built in 1900, it replaced an older pub and was built immediately behind the old *Travellers Rest*. There is a photo taken by the late Miss Sybil Reeves' father in 1900, showing the old pub with the new pub under construction behind it (Fig 49). Henley Standard of 8 June 1900 recorded that a holdover of the licenses of the *Travellers Rest* was granted to Robert Carpenter Bratchell late of the *Red Cross* (Assendon). The new premises

Fig 49 The Travellers Rest during rebuilding in 1900. Photo by the late W G Reeves (see also Fig 36)

having been completed and built in accordance with the plans approved by the Magistrates at the last licensing day. As usual the license was confirmed a week or two later.

The *Travellers Rest* seems to have been a haven for publicans who had suffered the closure of their pubs, Bratchell in 1900 after the closure of the *Red Cross*, and in 1892 George Lay had come from the *Plough* at Bix, when that pub closed.

The Fairmile and the way into Henley appears to be flat, but there must be a slight gradient, as it was noted in 1906 that the window sill on the ground floor of the old *Travellers Rest* was said to have been on a level with Henley Church clock[337] .

Although new in 1900, like most buildings of that time, there was no electricity installed, and only in 1935 was it put in. It seems an odd expense to have gone to in 1935, considering discussions were already going on about altering the road down Bix Hill. The Henley Standard reported on 8 February 1935 that electric light was installed at the *Travellers Rest*, and by 3 November 1936 it reported that work had begun on the dual carriageway.

The license, name and landlord were all transferred to the new pub at Caversham on the Henley road on 1 June 1939[338].

Landlords/ Tenants of the *Travellers Rest*

*1844-50	John Gomm (TM,SD)
1851*	Ellen Gomm (C)
1854-68	Stephen Parsons (SD)
*1871	George Taylor (C)

337 Henley Standard 21 Sep 1906
338 Rural Register of Licenses 1935-40

Aug 1871-92	Isaac Brown (RL,C,HA,SD)
Mar 1892-3	George/Thomas Lay (RL,HA)
Jun 1893-6*	James Yeatman (RL)
1900-3	Robert Carpenter Bratchell (HA)
1903-5	Mary Ann Bratchell (RL)
Mar 1905-27	William Grove (RL,HS,SD)
Oct 1927-39	Walter Willcocks (RL,HS)

— Continued as the *Travellers Rest* at Caversham —

115

The Turk's Head

16 Market Place

The *Turk's Head* was previously the *Sheers* or *Shears*, it became the *Turk's Head* in about 1779, and closed in about 1794. See the entry for the *Sheers.*

Landlords/ Tenants of the *Turk's Head*

1779-93	Mrs Wyatt

— Closed —

116

Le Turnours & another

High Street

Le Turnours is mentioned in a document listed by Hughes dating to 21 October 1337[339] Thom Schireburne (Schyrborne) and Elizth his wife to John de Harewelle (Herwell) Warden etc. Grant of 13sol 4den (13s 4d) rent of a tenement called Le Turnours in the High Street.

Early rents such as this 14th century rent for 13s 4d tended to continue as Bridge Rents. This was a rent charged for the upkeep of the Bridge and Church at a time that by feudal custom property in the town was owned by the Town Corporation, as represented by the Warden, Bridgemen, Aldermen etc. Even later when properties were bought, sold or leased by individuals for other amounts of money, a Bridge Rent continued to be charged for the same early specified rent. Rents charged in the 14th century remained the same until the final Bridge Rents were commuted to a down payment in 1967.

According to the Bridge Rent Book of 1886, four properties in Hart Street and one in Middle Row were then paying 13s 4d. They were, on the south side - 40 Hart Street, recently the Tandoori restaurant and now (1999) Café Uno: on the north side - the corner of Bell street with Hart Street, - the *Catharine Wheel,* and - 31/33 Hart Street.

40 Hart Street may have been a pub, but in the 15th century it was most likely the *King's Head.* The corner property was also probably a pub, certainly it was in the hands of brewers in the 18th century (see the *Elephant*), and may have been *Long's Stout House* in the 19th century. The

339 Hughes 556 & 624 AD40 & 41

Catharine Wheel has been known as such since 1499, and its early rental was for 6s 8d, thereby putting it out of consideration as a possibility for *Le Turnours.* The only rental of 13s 4d being paid in 1886 in the Market Place was for the then beerhouse the *Victoria.*

The presence of a malthouse behind 31/33 Hart Street in the 17th century[340] may indicate an earlier use of the site as a pub, it is possible that it may have been the site of *Le Turnours.* However it must be considered that other properties which in the past paid Bridge Rents may have ceased to pay before 1886. It is just possible that *Le Turnours* might have been in Middle Row, that is if the build up of Middle Row had taken place by 1337. Certainly it seems that it may well have done since the deeds mentioned below concern Middle Row only twenty years later.

Also referring to a pub in the 14th century but probably not the same pub as *Le Turnours,* there were two deeds concerning a nameless pub in the Middle Row of the Market (see entry for the *Feathers* Middle Row & also the *Two Brewers*).

6 November 1359[341] the will of Thom Huberd. Bequest of a tavern with solar and shop in the middle of the High Street (in reversion) to Ric Jory, Warden etc. and messuages in New Street and South Street.

12 November 1363[342] Thomas Jory to Regin Warbeltone. Grant of a shop and solar in the middle of the High Street.

25 March 1382/3[343] Regin Warbeltone to John Morcote and Juliana his wife. Grant of a shop and solar in the middle of the High Street.

Landlords/ Tenants of nameless pub

pre 1359	Thom Huberd
*1363-82	Regin Warbeltone
1382/3*	John Morcote

— Closed —

117

The Two Brewers

2 Hart Street

The *Two Brewers* appears to have been in business at 2 Hart Street from about 1785 to 1840. The relationship of the *Two Brewers* to the pub known as the *Blue Bell* is confused, as explained in the account of the *Blue Bell.* The Bridge Rent Book of 1886 entry no. 31 says 'Trustees of Thomas Cobb Binfield late Mrs Stokes for a house formerly '*The Old Blue Bell*' afterwards '*The Two Brewers*' since a private house and now a shop. Formerly in occupation of Mrs Hiatt since of Josh Jeffreys afterwards of A W Awberry then of Miss Peacock now of Miss Gear now Miss Morshead.'

The site was incorporated into the rebuilding of the corner site when the *Blue Bell* was demolished , and was then part of W H Smith and then Fosters, and now (1999) has become a Hairdressers.

The Thomas Cobb Binfield Charity, set up in 1724, originally held a property in the lower Middle Row of the Market Place which was demolished in about 1785. The Trustees then bought

340 O.R.O. Cooper & Caldecott C14 (2-4)

341, 342 & 343 Hughes 635 AD89, 623 Ad107, 560 AD124

the house next to the corner house on the Hart Street/Duke Street corner. This house was once part of the *Blue Bell* which from that time was only at the corner house. It is possible that the *Two Brewers* opened when the Charity first purchased the house, or it may be that the house demolished in Middle Row was already a pub which might have been the original *Two Brewers*, if so there are no available records of it. Whether Thomas Cobb Binfield was a brewer is uncertain, however other members of the Binfield family in the 18th century were owners or suppliers of mortgages for pubs, so the property in Middle Row left for charity may well have been a pub.

Mrs Hiatt was a stationer, bookseller, glass and china dealer in Hart Street according to the street directories. From the same source, Josh Jeffreys was a grocer in 1863, and A W Awberry a chemist and stationer in Hart Street in 1876 (later he moved to 9 &11 Market Place, see the *Crown* Market Place.) Miss Peacock and Miss Gear both sold ladies underclothing in 1883 and 1887 respectively.

The Henley Rentals show that up to 1842 it was a pub, entries for 1823-42 are for 'Binfield former *Old Blue Bell* since *TwoBrewers*.' Before Binfield (the charity) it was held by Mrs Geere. In 1795 the entry says 'Geere for *Old Blue Bell* since *Two Brewers* late occupied Hewitt since Peperlow now Allan.' There is no clear indication when exactly the change from the *Blue Bell* to the *Two Brewers* took place, as the rentals make no earlier mention of the two names before 1795. In 1785 the entry says 'late Blackman now Jos Sarney occupied Fullock.' Since in the same year the entry for the *Blue Bell* says 'Humfrey Newberry's Trustees occupied Chas Stokes,' one can only assume that the *Two Brewers* had already taken over 2 Market Place and it had ceased to be the *Blue Bell*.

Landlords/ Tenants of the *Two Brewers*

1785	Fullock (R)
1790-93	Hewett/Hewitt (R)
pre 1795	Peperlow/Peploe (R)
1795-1800*	Allen (R)
1807-42	Binfield (R)

— Closed —

118

The Two Brewers

Wargrave Road, Remenham

The *Two Brewers* like the *Little Angel* and the *Carpenters Arms*, is outside both Henley and Oxfordshire, but situated as it is only just across the bridge at the junction of the road up White Hill with the Wargrave Road (Fig 50), it comes naturally into the orbit of Henley.

The Victuallers Recognizances for Berkshire seem to be very slight, in fact there is only one entry, on 11 September 1815, when for the *Two Brewers* it says William Gibbs of Remenham victualler and John Cox of Henley on Thames cooper, paid a surety of £10 each, and that William Gibbs was licensed to keep a Common Alehouse or Victualling House.

It was owned freehold by Joseph Benwell and Wm Brakspear in 1826, at the time of the Inventory of their brewery, when it was still in the occupation of William Gibbs. There was stabling for 7 horses, piggery and garden.

In the Reading Mercury and Oxford Gazette of 20 December 1845, there is an advertisement of a coach service from the *Two Brewers* to Twyford, presumably as a connection to the new Great

Western Railway already operating through Twyford. At the same time as advertising the coach, there is a comment about the iniquitous charges made to pass through the Toll Gate on Henley Bridge, which prevented the service from continuing into the town. It is worded as follows:-

'REBECCA AND HER DAUGHTERS ARE MUCH WANTED

Henley Bridge & Bar Toll Gates

The Twyford and Henley Omnibus leaves the Two Brewers over Henley Bridge every morning at a quarter before seven, and half past four (in the) afternoon; from Twyford to Henley at quarter past one and quarter past 6 afternoon. On Sunday quarter before eight morning from Henley; from Twyford half past eight evening.

Fare one shilling

The enormous charge of 28s per week for this Omnibus at these Gates, prevents their going into the town

AND CALLS LOUD FOR REBECCA AND HER DAUGHTERS'

In 1843 there had been a series of attacks on Turnpikes and Toll Gates by a group of Welsh rioters, who were led by a man calling himself Rebecca, dressed in woman's clothing. The connection to the biblical Rebecca and the reason for the choice of name, is to be found in Genesis 20, v 60, where Rebecca on leaving her father's house was told 'let thy seed possess the gate of those which hate them'[344].

The *Two Brewers* had already, in 1838, had trouble with Tolls and the Henley-Maidenhead Turnpike Trust. The Reading Mercury & Oxford Gazette of 26 January 1839 carries an article expressing the uproar and outrage of the people of Henley and district about the action of the Turnpike Trust in placing a Toll Bar on the Wargrave Road at Wargrave Marsh. The gate was at the south end of the cottages beyond the *Two Brewers,* known as Marsh cottages. The Trust apparently had acted to prevent people using the Wargrave Road to avoid paying tolls at the Hurley Gate on the road to Maidenhead. However the locals were protesting that not only were travellers to Maidenhead being stopped and having to pay, but also locals on their daily business. Even those who were going through the Toll Bar to visit the *Two Brewers*, though in doing so they were not setting foot on the Turnpike Road, and were about 60 yards from it, had to pay. There was also the outrage that if someone from the Wargrave Road were going to Henley two Tolls had to be paid within a few hundred yards of each other.

Arguments over the Marsh Toll Bar continued for some years, until finally the Henley-Maidenhead Turnpike Trust decided to discontinue the Marsh Bar as from 16 January 1852. Even then the Bondholders objected and decided to file a Bill in Chancery to prevent the closure[345]. However nothing further seems to have been done and the Trust itself ceased in 1878.

It is probable that the *Two Brewers* was rebuilt in the 1860s, possibly after the severe gales at the end of February 1860. It was reported in the Reading Mercury & Oxford Gazette of 3 March, that a large elm at the junction of the Wargrave and Hurley roads, had fallen on the *Two Brewers* carrying with it the corner of the roof, cutting through the roof, the chamber, and the tap

344 Brewer's Dictionary of Phrase & Fable

345 Crocker, John 'Transactions of the Turnpike Road Trusts' 1993 Henley Archaeological & Historical Group

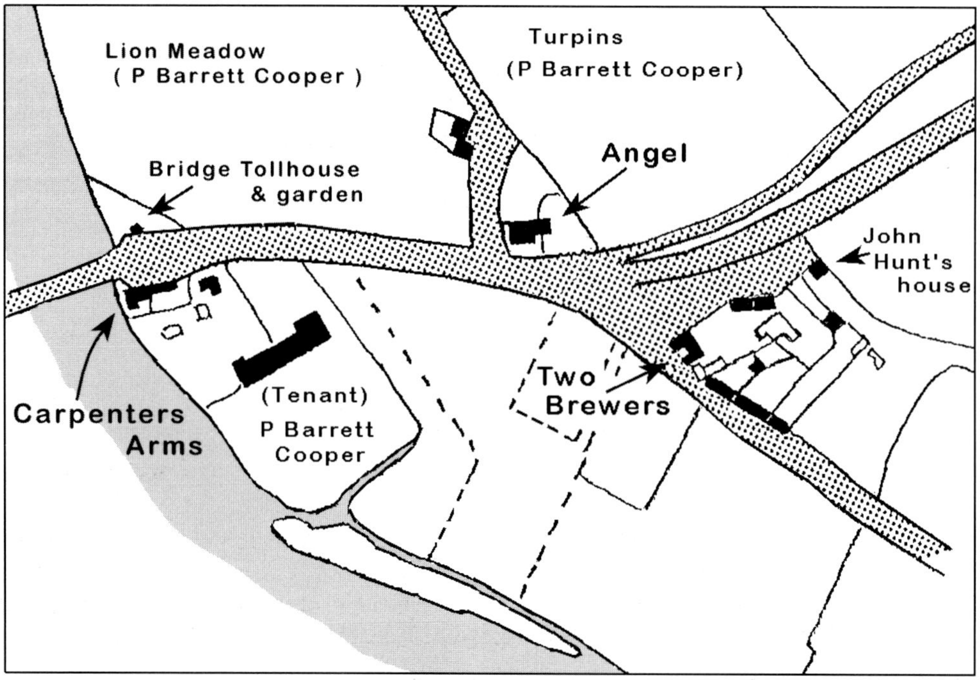

Fig 50 Part of Remenham Tithe map 1841 (O.R.O.)
The Two Brewers, the Angel & the Carpenters Arms

room and ending in the basement. The damage was said to be considerable, so maybe W H Brakspear who owned the pub decided to rebuild entirely. Certainly the house shown on the Remenham Tithe Map of 1841 was an E shaped house, without the centre bar, with two projecting wings facing, and right up against the Wargrave Road. While the present house faces towards the Henley - Hurley Road, and may be slightly south of the old house.

Like the *Little Angel* across the road, it was a pub that suffered from periodic flooding. In 1894 the Henley Standard reported that 'the *Two Brewers* was inundated, the water being nearly up to the counter, and the cottagers in the Wargrave Road were in a terrible plight, being confined to upper rooms, provisions carried to them in boats....'

The *Two Brewers* closed temporarily at the beginning of September 1996, when the then landlord Derek Tomlin was declared bankrupt. However it was re-opened shortly after.

Landlords/ Tenants of the *Two Brewers*

1815-30	William Gibbs (VR,WHB/I,SD)
1841-51	Ann Quiney (TM,C,SD)
1863-76	Daniel Hayes (SD)
*1883-92	Henry Stevens (RL,SD)
Mar 1892-1923	Joseph Henry Williams (RL)
Jan 1923-5	John Arthur Arlett (RL)
Sep 1925-8	Arthur Shopland Johnson (RL)
Dec 1928-9	Christopher Button (RL,WHB/C)
Aug 1929-31	Thomas Frank Gillett (RL,WHB/C)
Apr 1931-6	Herbert Edward Carmichael (RL,WHB/C)
Feb 1936-Dec	Frank G Prewett (RL,WHB/C)
Dec 1936-40	Alwyn Dales Wright (RL,WHB/C)
Sep 1940-1	Arthur Wilfred Farwell (RL,WHB/C)

Jan 1941-4	Beatrice May Farwell (RL,WHB/C)
Apr 1944-6	John Edward Chalcroft (RL,WHB/C)
Jan 1946-66	Katie Elizabeth Gift Waugh (RL,WHB/C)
Nov 1966-77	F E Howard & Mrs Howard (WHB/C)
Feb 1977-89	M A Blumire & Mrs A Blumire (WHB/C)
Sep 1989-	Graham Godman & Deanna Godman (WHB/C,HS)
-96	Derek Tomlin (HS)

119

The Two Magpies

Northfield End

In Billing's Directory of 1854 the *Two Magpies* is mentioned by name, and the landlord is given as George Dunn, and as being at Northfield End. Other street directories give George Dunn as a beer retailer Northfield End 1844-54. Other than this there are no further mentions of this pub.

It is the Census Returns which give a clue as to its position. George Dunn appears both in

Fig 50 The Two Magpies in the 1850s, the men were probably the work force of John Moss agricultural machinist whose premises were in the same yard

1841 and 1851. In 41 as a beer retailer with a wife and two children, and in 51 as a beerhouse and lodging house keeper, wife Ann, three children and twelve lodgers.

The Census of 1851 is one of the more orderly lists, households, as far as one can check, being taken in correct order, and going up one side of a street and down the other. The entry for George Dunn and therefore for the *Two Magpies* is no.46, between the *Packhorse* at no.8 and the *Hope* at no.52. This places it, using the large scale O.S.map of 1879 between Leicester House and the *Hope,* near a smithy, shown as part of a large yard, and about halfway between the Friends Meeting House and the *Hope.* The smithy seems to have been used by the firm of Moss agricultural machinists, the family of Moss living at a house to the west of Leicester House. This information comes from a letter published in the Henley Standard on 15 September 1950 from T H Moss, who wrote to the paper after seeing the publication the previous week of a picture, taken probably around 1860 of Leicester House. In the photo a boy stands in the road, whom T H Moss recognised as being one of his uncles, the one who lost a leg when he fell from a tree, when bird's nesting in the Fairmile.

Another picture of about the same time (Fig 51) shows the workforce of Moss and Sons with some of their machinery on the pavement outside a pub. The pub was selling Clarkson's Beer and was most likely the *Two Magpies*. The whereabouts of Clarkson's Brewery is not known

Landlord/ Tenant of the *Two Magpies*
1841-54 George Dunn (C,SD)

— Closed —

120

The Union

20 Hart Street

The *Union* beerhouse was sometimes known as the *Hand in Hand* in the 18th century, but by 1800 a Pew Faculty license granted to Thomas Smith of 22 Hart Street (previously the *George*) says on the west the *Union* public house (Fig 52). Also in Brakspears Rent Ledgers of 1790 it is called the *Union.* It is possible that officially it was always the *Union,* and may have dated from soon after 1707, the time of the union of England and Scotland. One can imagine that perhaps a sign of two hands clasped might have given rise to the colloquial name of the *Hand in Hand..*

It is said to have been the property of James Brooks[346] and passed to Robert Brakspear from Richard Hayward who bought James Brooks' property in 1774. Unlike the other properties acquired by Robert Brakspear and then passed on to W H Brakspear, in the Inventory of 1826 it is not listed as a freehold owned by W H Brakspear but as one jointly held by Joseph Benwell and W H Brakspear. In 1826 it was described as a 'public house in occupation John Hunt with small yard, woodhouse and skittle ground'.

By the 1860s there was a brewery called the Union Brewery, which may have started production behind the *Union.* There was a malthouse on the *Union* premises which was demolished in 1829 (M28) and there was also a large malthouse next door at 18 Hart Street (M27), but there is no mention of a brewhouse. Frederick Paulin landlord of the *Union* 1868-9, was also a brewer at the Union Brewery. However a notice in the Henley Advertiser of 10 January 1874, says that in December 1873 Frederick Paulin sold the Union Brewery in Duke Street to Messrs Byles & Co of

346 Sheppard, Francis 'Brakspear's Brewery 1779-1979' 1979

Fig 52 The Henley Money Shop was once the Union, which together with the Rope Walk was once the George. Behind the house on the right was malthouse M27 Photo 1988

Greys Brewery. So by then it would appear that the Union Brewery was no longer at the *Union*, if indeed it ever was there. The brewery's position in Duke Street seems to have been behind the *Queen's Head* (see entries for the *Queen's Head* and B3).

Henry Clinch who followed Paulin as landlord, does not seem to have had an additional trade such as brewer. His claim to notice was that he was one of six publicans in the town charged with selling beer in incorrect measures, this was in 1871[347] soon after the Act of 1870 which regulated measures to be used.

A painting of 1892 by Miss Lucy Cooper in the Town Hall, shows the *Union* as it was then. In 1911 it was decided not to renew the license, and on 23 December 1911 compensation of £581 15s 10d was paid to Brakspears, and the house closed on 30 December 1911.

Landlords/ Tenants of the *Union*

1793	William Finch (SD) (The *Hand in Hand*)
*1790-95	William Finch (WHB/R)
1795-1808	Robert Pearman (WHB/R)
1808-18*	Isaac Hunt (AKL,CL,WHB/R)
1822-6	John Hunt (WHB/I,SD) John Kent (CL)
*1830-51	Frederick Leaver (C,SD)
1852-4*	Thomas Penn (SD)
1861	William Webb (C)
*1868-9	Frederick Paulin (SD) brewer Union Brewery
1869-76*	Henry Clinch (SSM,SD)
1883	Ann Clinch (SD)
Apr 1885-1906	John Blackett (RL,HA)
1906-9	Thomas William Tranter Wheeler (RL)
1909-10	Frederick William Dee (RL)
1910-11	Samuel Henry Riley Mountain (RL)
1911	Alfred George Brown

— Closed —

347 Henley Advertiser 18 Dec 1871

121

The Victoria

48 Market Place (Middle Row)

The present building of the *Victoria* on the corner of West Street and the Market Place was rebuilt in about 1900 when the road between the Town Hall and the *Victoria* was built connecting with the Kings Road. Before the present Town Hall was built, there was no road behind the previous Town Hall (Fig 17), merely a row of houses joining the hall to the site of the *Victoria*. It was in this row that the *Greyhound* and the original *Victoria* were situated.

The *Victoria* probably started trading in about 1850, the first publican to be definitely connected with it was Josiah Wheeler, who in a street directory of 1869 was both a barge owner and beer retailer. Later in 1871 he was one of the six publicans charged with selling incorrect measures of ale[348]. In 1874[349] Josiah Wheeler of the *Victoria* begged to be excused paying a rate of 13s 4d on account of poverty, he having been bed-ridden for several months. The application was not allowed, and a few months later he lost his license.

The *Victoria* features in the Bridge Rent Book of 1886, no.64 which says 'Messrs Wethered formerly Richard Tayler for a house and premises late in the occupation of Wilmot afterwards of Ward and now occupied by Joseph Bond as a beerhouse. 13s 4d.' Added afterwards it says 'now Watlington Brewery Co. since Wethereds, Marlow Brewery'.

It was obviously the Bridge Rent of 13s 4d that Wheeler was trying to evade paying. The entry also seems to imply that the house had not always been a beerhouse or pub, and that Richard Tayler owned it as a house. According to the Henley Rentals he owned it from about 1814 to at least 1842, and William Willmott appears to have been in occupation from about 1807-36. Earlier in 1779-85 a Thomas Wilmot seems to have been there.

There seems to be no connection between either of the Willmotts/Wilmots and beer selling. However in 1842 against an entry which says 'Taylor late Gale' there is a note in pencil which says 'Miss Wethered'. When this addition was made is unknown, but it may indicate a purchase which later became the property of Messrs Wethered

The only Ward traceable in the street directories is a William Ward who is listed as a beer retailer in the High Street in the Post Office Directory of 1854. It is possible that William Ward was the first landlord of the *Victoria,* but he does not appear in other directories before or after. If a beerhouse was opened in the early 1850s, it is a reasonable date for the naming of it as the *Victoria.*

The Court Leet session of 26 October 1868 charged that Messrs Wethered owed the Lord of the Manor a Quit Rent of 1s 6d p.a. for the messuage or tenement late Taylors in occupation of Nicholson but now a beerhouse in the tenure of Joseph Wheeler.

In the 1890s although the Register of Licenses give Henry Russell as landlord from 1891-1901, there were in fact two Henry Russells. The Henley Advertiser on 26 November 1892 reports the Holdover of the license to H Russell son of the present proprietor. Subsequently the license was transferred.

After the rebuilding of the pub in about 1900, a full license was granted in 1903, when it was owned by the Watlington Brewery, on condition that the Watlington Brewery surrendered the license of the *Jolly Farmer,* which they also owned[350]. By 1909 the *Victoria* was again owned by Thomas Wethered & Sons Ltd of Marlow, who still own it today.

---

348 & 349 Henley Advertiser 18 Dec 1871 & 18 Jul 1874

350 Register of Licenses 1903-18

Landlords/ Tenants of the *Victoria*

1854	William Ward (SD)
*1868-74	Josiah/Joseph Wheeler (SSM,CL,HA,SD) barge owner
Nov 1874-86	Joseph Bond (RL,BRB,CL,HA,SD)
Sep 1887-8	Edwin Clarke (SSM,RL)
Jun 1888-91	George Clacy (RL,HA)
Aug 1891-2	Henry Russell (RL,HA)
Nov 1892-1901	Henry Russell junr (RL,HA,SD)
Aug 1901-2	Frederick Silver Heydon (RL)
Mar 1902-4	William Henry Jeffery (RL)
1904-5	George Foster (RL)
Jan 1905-May	Francis George Wheeler (RL)
May 1905-6	John Waitman (RL)
Mar 1906-Nov	Robert John Wheeler (RL)
Nov 1906-7	Symons James Simpson (RL)
Jul 1907-9	Alfred Patmore (RL)
Jul 1909-11	Sidney George Smith (RL)
Nov 1911-35	Charles Hobbs (RL)
Sep 1935-48	Percy James Bartlett (RL,SD)
Dec 1948-59	Ernest Swadling (RL)
Dec 1959-64	William George Benson (RL)
Nov 1964-6	Arthur John Neams (RL)
Sep 1966-83	Reginald Stanley Greve (RL)
Aug 1983-5	Robert John Worsdell (RL)
Mar 1985-6	Philip Edwin Chadwick (RL)
Dec 1986-9	Martin Busby (RL)
Nov 1989-90	Adrienne Camille How (RL)
Mar 1990-91	Adrienne Camille How & Andrew William Menzies (RL)
Oct 1991-?	Scott David Barker (RL)
? - 95	A C How & A W Menzies (RL)
Feb 1995-99-	Nicholas Davies (RL)

122

The Vine

10 Hart Street

This small pub called the *Vine* was on the site of where Barclays Bank now stands. The bank was built soon after 1895 on the site of two houses 10 and 12 Hart Street. The bank was built by J & C Simmonds & Co Bank, who had previously been at 24 Market Place, and was a branch of the Reading Bank, and had connections with William Deacon Bank Ltd. It was not until some time between 1911 and 1915 that it became Barclays Bank.

At 12 Hart Street before it was demolished, Thomas Bosley a saddler and harness maker had been there since about 1869, previous to him there was from 1854-63 William Powell saddler, and before him Mrs Collier and John Collier saddlers harness makers and collar makers since about 1807[351].

351 Rentals & bridge Rent Book 1886

At 10 Hart Street there was the *Vine* public house owned in 1868 by Messrs Lucas (late Glover) who were charged at the Court Leet on 26 October that they owed the Lord of the Manor a Quit Rent of 8d p.a. for a messuage or tenement formerly in the tenure of William Biddle and now of William White and used as a beerhouse. By 1877[352] Blandy and Hawkins of Reading owned it and in 1879 Fuller & Co of Maidenhead.

The *Vine* was closed in 1895 and pulled down in September and October of the same year. The earliest positive landlord of the *Vine* was William White who seems to have been there from about 1847-78, in a 77 directory he was also a fish-monger. It is possible that a John White mentioned in a directory of 1844 as a beer retailer in Hart Street was also at the *Vine,* and William Biddle may have been there before him.

Landlords/ Tenants of the *Vine*

? ?	William Biddle
? *1844*	John White (SD)
*1847-78	William White (SSM,RL,CL,SD)
1878	Thomas Jemmett (RL)
1878-9	Thomas Gregory (RL)
1879-81	Charles Smoker Bance (RL)
1881-2	James/William Bowsher (RL,HA)
Apr 1882-7	William Thomas Holley (RL,HA)
Sep 1887-8	Campbell Prout (RL)
Sep 1888-9	Thomas Parsons (RL,HA)
Jan 1890-1	Joseph Drake (RL,HA)
Nov 1891-4	Frederick Hill (RL)
Dec 1894-5	Wallace Henry Fitt (RL)

— Closed —

123

The Vine

70 Northfield End

This second pub called the *Vine* was at at Northfield End, and came to light in the Greys Brewery Rent Ledger of 1885-96, a ledger which became the property of Brakspear when they bought Greys Brewery in 1896.

The entry says 'Leased from George Paulin, New Street, house late the *Vine,* Northfield End, Henley. Rent £12.'

George Paulin died in 1895, and his estate was sold by auction on 6 February 1896. Other property of Paulin's sold at the same time were the *Half Way House* and Everly House, until recently Brakspears' off-license premises in Hart Street.

> The *Vine* was Lot 3. 'Freehold premises brick built and slated situate at Northfield End within the Borough of Henley on Thames, and containing 2 sitting rooms, 5 bedrooms, kitchen, scullery laundry and W.C. A frontage of 29ft to the main Oxford Road with a depth therefrom of 100ft and is occupied as a laundry by Mrs Wright at a rent of £15 p.a. This lot is held by Messrs Holmes and Steward

352 Register of Licenses

on the terms of covenants of an expired lease at a rent of £12. The tenancy determining by notice (which has been given) at Christmas 1896. Lot 3 is bounded by the properties of Mr John Child and Mr R Blackall.'
In 1896 Mr John Child was at Easby House.

The *Vine* was at 70 Northfield End, and was once called the *Windsor Castle* (Fig 53). The Census Returns of 1871 show a William Wright carpenter and beerhouse keeper. The Census of 1871 is one of the more reliable returns as to order of households, the *White Horse* was at no.39 while Wright was at 48, which using the O.S.map of 1879 as a guide, allows for the right number of houses between. On the same 1879 large scale map it is possible also to measure the size of various properties. 70 Northfield End is one of the only plots in the main Oxford Road which has a frontage of 29ft and a depth therefrom of 100ft.

Fig 53 The house once the Windsor Castle then the Vine Photo 1989

That William Wright was the landlord of the *Vine* is clear from the following accounts:- The Henley Advertiser reported on 10 May 1873 that William Wright beerhouse keeper of the *Vine* was found unlawfully drunk on his own premises on Sunday 27 April. He also according to the constable resisted arrest and was abusive. This was about 3.15 p.m., but another witness claimed that Wright was sober at 2.30 p.m The case was dismissed for lack of evidence. However two years later on 26 June 1875 it was reported that William Wright of the *Vine* beerhouse, Northfield End was charged with being drunk on his own premises on 13 April last. He was fined 10s and 15s 6d costs or in default to serve 14 days hard labour. After this Wright probably lost his license, and the *Vine* would have been closed in 1875.

However it seems that the Wrights continued to live at the house, in 1877 and 1883

William Wright was listed in street directories as a carpenter at Northfield End. In 1883 and 1891 Mrs Wright was listed as a laundress in North-field End, and was obviously still working there in 1896. William Wright died and was buried on 5 December 1893 aged 73, the address being Northfield End, according to the St Mary's Burial Register. So by 1896 Mrs Wright was a widow.

For earlier details see the *Windsor Castle*, which it was probably called until William Wright took over.

Landlords/ Tenants of the *Vine*

*1871-5	William Wright (HA,AucC) carpenter

— Closed —

124 & 125

The Waggon and Horses

Market Place, (Middle Row)

Though listed here as one pub, it seems there were two, both called the *Waggon and Horses* and both in the Market Place at the same time. They may in fact have been next door to one another, as one became the *Eight Bells*, which was where the old Fire Station in the market once was, and is now the Art Gallery. The other which seems to have been closed in about 1810, was then let as a private house, and may have been the small cottage between the Art Gallery and the *Victoria,* only in the last few years sold by Brakspears.

Brakspears Rent Ledgers give tenants for the *Waggon and Horses* and for the *Old Waggon and Horses.*

At the *Waggon and Horses* from Michaelmas 1790 William Cook, and from 10 October 1791-1811 Francis Farrow.

At the *Old Waggon and Horses* in 1799 William Cook and from 1806-10 Thos Atkins. Tucked into this ledger is a letter of 23 March 1807 which says:-

> 'Mr Thos Atkins (alias) Adkins, I do hereby give you notice to quit and deliver up to me at Michaelmas next ensuing peaceable and quiet possession of the messuage or tenement with the yard garden buildings and appurtenances thereto belonging situate in the Market Place Henley on Thames Oxon and now in your possession let by me to Mrs Mary Cook.' signed 'R Brakspear'.

What happened after this letter, which I presume to be a copy of that sent to Atkins, is not recorded, though it does seem that Atkins was there till 1810. Perhaps Mrs Cook entered into 'peaceable and quiet possession' after that. Mrs Cook was possibly the widow of William Cook who had been first at the *Waggon and Horses* and had then transferred to the *Old Waggon and Horses* in 1799, and was probably there till 1805, a William Cook is recorded in the Parish Burial Register as being buried in August 1805, aged 52. One possibility is that after the death of William Cook, Thos Atkins was brought in to continue the business with Mrs Cook remaining resident, that subsequently in 1807 the date of the letter, Brakspears decided to close the *Old Waggon and Horses* as a pub, and therefore no longer had need of Atkins. Mrs Cook meanwhile had the tenancy of the building as a private house.

The *Waggon and Horses* on the site of the Art Gallery, seems to have become the *Eight Bells* during the tenancy of Francis Farrow. As suggested in the Introduction the name change might be connected to the visual impact of the pub sign, which may have depicted a team of horses with bells on their harness hames. The street directory of about 1793 gives Francis Farrow as landlord at the *Six Bells*. A list loosely placed in one of the Brakspear Rent Ledgers of properties owned or leased by Brakspears, says 'House in the Market Place known as the *Eight Bells* - Farrow'. For the later history see the *Eight Bells.*

The earlier Henley Rentals seem to have applied to one pub called the *Waggon and Horses* and they feature William Cook before Farrow. It may be that the Rentals applied to both buildings, which may have been one pub, with William Cook in 1790 as landlord of the whole. That the split into two pubs came in 1791 when Farrow took over the one half called the *Waggon and Horses* later to become the *Eight Bells,* leaving Cook at the *Old Waggon and Horses* later to become a private house.

The Rentals are as follows 1790 'Hayward and Newell occupied Cook'. 1785 'Hayward and Newell late Mrs Mary Parker now Cook', while the Court Baron Book also of 1785 says 'Hayward now Wm Cook'. The Rentals for 1779,75,69,65 and 58 all say 'now Parker' or 'in occupation Parker' (which probably all meant Mrs Parker) though that of 1779 also says 'Nicholas late Wyatt'.

Henley License lists of 1770 and 71 give a Mary Parker, while the lists of 1753 and 54 a Robert Parker. They were both probably at the *Waggon and Horses.*

In 1745 in the Rentals there is an entry which says 'Mr Toovey late Simmons', in 1737 'Mr Toovey for a house late F Wyatt'. In 1733-22 Francis Simons/Symonds, and in 1713/4 'Wyatt in occupation Francis Simons premises and yard'.

Landlords/ Tenants of the *Waggon and Horses*

1713-34	Francis Simons/Simmons/Symonds etc (R)
1737-45	Mr & Mrs Toovey (R)
*1753-56 or 68?	Robert Parker (VR,BReg,R) (one Robert Parker buried 11 Mar1756 & another Robert Parker buried 15 Dec 1768 - no ages given)
1756?68-79*	Mrs Mary Parker (VR,R,CB)
*1785-90	William Cook (R,WHB/R)
1791- ?	Francis Farrow (WHB/R,SD)

Landlords/ Tenants of the *Old Waggon and Horses*

*1799-1805	William Cook (WHB/R)
1806-10	Thos Atkins/Adkins (WHB/R)

— Continued as the *Eight Bells* —

126

The Waggon and Horses

14 Market Place

The *Waggon and Horses* beerhouse was one of two freehold beerhouses in the Market Place offered for sale in an advertisement in the Reading Mercury & Oxford Gazette of October 1855. The other beerhouse, the *Fisherman's Cottage* contained 8 rooms, cellar, 2 granaries, stabling for 5 horses and yard. The *Waggon and Horses* contained 8 rooms. 2 cellars, stabling for 12 horses with granaries over, cottage and yard. The combined frontage was 33ft and the depth of the plot was 131ft. Land Tax £1 6s 6d. Bridge Rent l0s.

The Bridge Rent Book of 1886 has the entry for 14-16 Market Place as follows:- 'Mr William Plumbe formerly George Bennett and Mr Langton of Maidenhead brewer for premises late two beerhouses now pulled down and a shop and warehouses built thereon. l0s.'

Only two properties in the Market Place had a Bridge Rent of l0s, the Westminster Bank property and 14-16 Market Place, or what is now two thirds of the shop known as Cargo.

On the O.S. map of 1879 the measurements of 33ft and 131ft are correct for Nos 14 and 16. As explained in the entries for the *Fisherman's Cottage* and the *Sheers,* a pub that preceded both beerhouses, the excavations of 1984 revealed apparently only one cellar in the position of No 16, while under 14 there was an extensive cellar which could well have been two cellars in 1855. This would seem to place the *Waggon and Horses* at 14 Market Place, or in the middle of the present plot.

When the two beerhouses began trading is unknown, maybe in the 1830s when beerhouses became more numerous, it is almost certain that they closed in 1855.

Landlords/ Tenants of the *Waggon and Horses*
Unknown

— Closed —

The Welcome Tavern

58 West Hill

The *Welcome Tavern* should probably not be here at all, it may have been a coffee house. In 1898 and 1904 a Welcome Coffee House is listed in Duke Street. There is also a mention of the Welcome in 1904 in the Henley Standard, and another street directory mention in 1909, these last two not specifying an address. In the Burial Register 1884-1944 there is an entry in August 1909 for an Arthur Lewington who was only 6 months old, and his address was given as the *Welcome Tavern* 58 West Hill. However this was at a period when licenses were exactly recorded in the Register of Licenses, and there is no license for the Welcome, before or after this date. So it was probably a Temperance Hotel or a Coffee House, and therefore is not numbered in this book.

127

The Wheatsheaf

Reading Road

The *Wheatsheaf* before 1892 was in Rotherfield Greys, and was called the *Portobello* in the 18th century. In the Victuallers Recognizances John Heath was at the *Portobello* from 1784-87, and then at the *Wheatsheaf* from 1789-1822. John Heath was buried at Rotherfield Greys aged 74 on 11 April 1824. The entry in the Rotherfield Greys Parish Register adds '40 years landlord of the Wheatsheaf.' This takes his tenancy back to 1784, for earlier details see the entry for the *Portobello*. Another landlord also buried at Rotherfield Greys was John Wingrove aged 60 who was buried on 11 October 1840.

An estate map of property belonging to Jeremiah Hodges Esq drawn up in 1802[353] , shows

353 Plan of Estate of Jeremiah Hodges 1802, now removed from Town Hall to O.R.O.

the Wheatsheaf Public House as being part of Portobello Farm owned by Hodges and let to Henry Chipp, who was not a publican but a farmer. The Wheatsheaf on the turnpike road, was just north of the position of the Turnpike Gate, which appears to have been approximately where the south corner of Hamilton Avenue now is situated. The footpath, running diagonally across the fields from Harpsden which now terminates in Vicarage Road opposite the top end of Singers Close, in 1802 ran on and joined the main road between the Wheatsheaf and the Turnpike Gate. Henry Chipp in 1802 obviously had no interest in running the pub and appears to have sub-let to John Heath.

After John Heath in 1824, Thomas Heath became landlord. In the Brakspears Inventory of 1826, the *Wheatsheaf* was held by leasehold in occupation of Thomas Heath, with stabling for 3 horses, woodhouse, loft, piggery and small garden. Lease expires 29 September 1828. Rent £15 p.a. A note beneath says 'purchased of Hodges by WHB'.

J F Hodges in about 1850 was a landowner and owner of Bolney Court possibly the son of Jeremiah Hodges of 1802, and Brakspears are said to have bought the *Wheatsheaf* from him in the 1850s for £650[354]. Possibly in about 1853, which would have been the expiry date of a renewed 25 year lease. However there seems to be a contradiction, as evidenced below.

In 1844 at the time of the Tithe Awards for Rotherfield Greys the *Wheatsheaf* was then owned by the Trustees of Mary Atkins Wright who owned Crowsley Park, and numerous other properties in Shiplake, Harpsden, and Rotherfield Greys. If the pencilled note was correct and it was bought by Brakspears from Hodges it must have been before 1844 and then sold again to the Trustees of Mary Atkins Wright, which seems unlikely. More probably the pencil note was incorrect and should have said bought from the Trustees of Mary Atkins Wright, unless of course after 1844 and before the 1850s it was sold back to the Hodges.

In 1844 the *Wheatsheaf* was occupied by Matthew Ball, who died in January 1862, when an inquest on his death was held at the pub[355]. He had been knocked down by an omnibus when returning from the station, he was aged 68.

Plans for alterations to the buildings were submitted in 1882[356] and were passed with the provision that a later plan should detail the drainage. This was the era when Henley was being connected to piped water and main drainage.

The building work, which was more like a complete rebuild rather than an alteration, was done under the direction of the architect, W G A Hambling[357] .

The position of the *Wheatsheaf* near to the station, and comparatively near the coal wharves at the end of Friday Street and Station Road, probably led to some of the extra activities of the landlords. William Ayre/Eyre was also a coal merchant, H W Green in 1896[358] was a 'job and post master' and had horses and carriages for hire, and flys to meet each train. The next landlord Walter Frewin Mott continued the business and was a 'Fly Operator'.

Landlords/ Tenants of the *Wheatsheaf*

1784-1824	John Heath (VR,BReg)
1826*	Thomas Heath (WHB/I)
1830	Mary Heath (SD)
*1840	John Wingrove (BReg)
1840-2*	Fanny Wingrove (C,SD)
*1844-62	Matthew/Mathew Ball (TM,C,RM,SD)
*1865-8	Thomas Parker (RM,SD)

354 , 356 & 357 Sheppard, Francis 'Brakspear's Brewery 1779-1979' 1979
(357 see also Fig 49 architect of Travellers Rest)

355 Reading Mercury & Oxford Gazette 11 Jan 1862

358 Climenson, Mrs Emily J 'Guide to Henley on Thames 1896'

1869-77*	William Ayre/Eyre (C,SD) coal merchant
*1882	William Wenman (RL)
Oct 1882-6	Richard Peach (RL)
Mar 1886-7	George Harris Wood (RL,HA)
Jun 1887-9	John Thomas Youngs (RL)
Nov 1889-91	Ralph Harper (RL)
1892-1901	Herbert William Green (RL,WHB/C,SD) job & post master
Apr 1901-11	Walter Frewin Mott (RL,WHB/C,SD) fly operator
Jul 1911-4	William John Musto (RL,WHB/C)
1914-29	Sidney Sheppard (RL,WHB/C,HS,SD)
Sep 1929-31	Christopher Button (RL,WHB/C,SD)
Jul 1931-5	John James Smith (RL,WHB/C,HS)
May 1935-7	Mrs Ada Lizzie Smith (RL,WHB/C,HS)
Sep 1937-48	Frederick Thomas Ball (RL,WHB/C,HS)
Oct 1948-55	Norman Howard Tickner (RL,WHB/C)
Feb 1955-63	Stanley William Overall (RL)
Mar 1963-Apr	Olwin Elizabeth Overall (RL)
Apr 1963-75	Ernest Ronald Abraham (RL,WHB/C)
Jun 1975-8	Michael James Tanner & Mrs V M Tanner (RL,WHB/C)
Aug 1978-99-	Mrs Valerie Margaret Tanner later Mrs Valerie Margaret Thomas (RL,WHB/C)

128

The White Hart, The Old White Hart, The Hart or The Hert

23 Hart Street

In spite of the fact that the *White Hart* was the oldest pub trading in Henley, and therefore of great potential attraction for tourists to the town, it was closed in the beginning of December 1996. It had then been trading for over five and a half centuries and possibly for even longer.

It is known from the 15th century for certain. A Court Roll of 1428-9[359] mentions a tenement in the High Street called '*Le Herte'*. A will of William Barneville made in August 1466 and proved in March 1467[360] left the *Hert* hospice in the High street, the cottage to the west of the *Hert* and several other properties. In 1490 the will of another William Barnevyle[361] left a cottage to Isabel his daughter. The cottage was described as 'near to his Inn called the Hert', it may have been the same cottage as in the will of 1466, when the first Barneville left the *Hert* to his sons, and in default of heirs to them, to the Church and Bridge. His sons may have left no heirs as the property was subject to a Bridge Rent of 3s 4d. This Bridge Rent continued to be paid until it was redeemed at the closure of the Small Bridge Rents on 31 March 1967.

There is said to be a mention of the *Hert* in 1483, when there was an affray in the street, when William Barnevyle saved Giaccome Pisani, a Florentine merchant, from attack by watermen,

359 & 360 Peberdy, Robert B 'The Economy, Society & Government of a small town in late Medieval England: A Study of Henley on Thames from c.1300-c.1540' Thesis for a Doctorate at Leicester University 1994

361 Burn, J S 'History of Henley on Thames' 1861

by sheltering him in the *Hert.*

A white hart was one of the badges of Richard II, whose reign was 1377-99, and it is tempting to imagine that the pub dated from that time, but this at the moment seems unproveable. According to the Rev M T Pearman in his book 'The History of Bensington' (1896), the land of Bensington in about 990 included the land later to become Henley. Later still Bensington only included Northfield End and stopped at the town boundary. In 1337 the Manor of Bensington was conferred on Edward the Black Prince the father of Richard II. Richard II is known to have held property in Henley town, in the second year of his reign he assigned the rents from 115 messuages in the town to provide an income to support the upkeep of the Church and Bridge, the start of Bridge Rents in the town. A gift which could well have led to the naming of the pub after his well known badge.

In 1537/8 Clem Burne held a tenement called the *Hert* for a rent of 3s 4d[362]. In 1553 a Corporation Rental concerning the neighbouring property 25 Hart Street, until recently the T.S.B., says 'J Frost on the north side of the High Street between the heirs of W Cator at the Bull on the east, and J Pates called the *Hert* on the west'. There is a similar mention in 1541.

On 20 June 1629[363] a document referring to the *George* (22 Hart Street) describes it as being 'over and against a messuage called the *Hart* then in tenure of Mistress Wells widow'. Other than this there are only tentative suggestions in the 17th century of names of landlords. In 1636 it was one of only three taverns mentioned by 'Taylor the water poet'[364] as being in Henley. From the order in which first the pubs and then the landlords are named, it seems likely that Robert Heyborne was at the *White Hart.* The other pubs were the *Elephant,* which may have been on the Hart/Bell Street corner, and a pub in the Fairmile, which almost certainly was the *White Horse*. However there is no Heyborne in the Protestation Returns of 1641/2, which could mean that he had left soon after 1636.

Tokens, which were a form of local cash of low denominations, were issued by inns and other traders, mostly between about 1648 and 1672. Some have been found in Henley, one token had the name Robert Sury on it, and is said to be from the *White Hart* [365]. Another token of 1668 for 2d, has the name John Hathaway on it together with a picture of 'a man driving a carriage and pair'. In a footnote to the account of this in his 'History of Henley' John S Burn says that Hathaway was at the *White Hart*. However in the Hearth Tax of 1665 there is no Sury or Hathaway, though this could mean that Sury was there before 1665 and Hathaway after. The only John Hathaway traceable, is one who was buried on 26 November 1700, when he was described as a coachman not an innkeeper. According to George Peters in his book 'This Glorious Henley' John Hathaway or Gibbs was of Bell Street and had three hearths in 1662. Perhaps he was at the *White Hart* not as a landlord but running a coaching service, the picture on the token could represent his business.

An Abstract of Title[366] from 1694, drawn up in 1739 when Daniel Sarney bought the *White Hart* from Mary Sayer, is a confusing list of deeds which seem to relate to various leases, mortgages and trusts made first by Thomas Springall who owned the *White Hart* in 1694, and then by Jonathan Sayer, husband of Mary Sayer and others. Jonathan Sayer appears to have acquired an interest in the property in 1701, finally buying outright in 1711, though even then it seems to have been heavily mortgaged. One of the mortgages was transferred in 1704 to Henry Benwell. Joseph Benwell eventually was to own the *White Hart* at the end of the 18th century.

---

362 Briers, P M 'Henley Borough Recvords 1395-1543' 1960 Ox Record Soc

363 Conveyance 20 Jun 1629 O.R.O. Misc Berks VI/ iii/ 1

364 Burn, J S 'History of Henley on Thames' 1861

365 Peters, George N 'This Glorious Henley' 1950

366 O.R.O. Cooper & Caldecott C15 (19)

Whether Springall or the Sayers were actual landlords or innkeepers is uncertain, they may have been some of the time, Mary Sayer in 1739 was perhaps living at the *White Hart* or near to it, as she retained the back yard area as her garden, when she sold the property. She may have had a small house or cottage at the back.

Fig 54 The yard of the White Hart, showing the back range and the second yard or garden beyond. On right above, the end of the closed in gallery, and to right of arch, the kitchen door which may be a genuine Tudor doorway Photo 1985

What further confuses ownership and occupancy is that though the *White Hart* today has the single frontage with the yard entrance on its left or west side, at various times in the past it has also included, either owned or leased, part of, or the whole of the buildings on both sides.

In the yard, which has a second yard or garden beyond, it can be seen that the *White Hart,* unique in Henley, has the remains of a gallery along its west or yard side (Figs 54 & 55). This was covered over probably in the 18th or early 19th century, and upstairs one can see in the timber work lining the house side of the gallery, that there were a series of doorways to individual rooms, leading off the gallery. What is most probable is that the gallery continued across the bottom end of the yard, and along buildings on the west of the yard. Part of this west side still belongs to the *White Hart*, was reconstructed as stabling and until recently housed a yard bar. Between this bar cum stable and the road there lies a small house, the ground floor of which was used by the *White Hart*, while the upper floor belonged to someone else.

This small house is of great interest, the timbers that can be seen at the northern end, are very heavy and are possibly 16th century. The roof line shows that originally the roof did not cover the part of the building nearest to the yard, that the gallery on the yard side was an open gallery. It is very likely that it was a continuing gallery with that on the east side of the yard.

The small house may be that mentioned in a deed of 1727[367] when it seems that Jonathan

367, 368,369 & 370 O.R.O. Cooper & Caldecott C15 (7), (9), (9), & (20)

Sayer who then owned the *White Hart* sold to Henry Shepherd 'all that little chamber or room being part of and lying on the west side of a certain messuage situate in Hart Street being in the tenure of John Eaglesfield called the *White Hart*'. It continues 'and all that little room or passage with the said little room or chamber, which little chamber or room and little room or passage are situated on the east part or side of the front kitchen of and belonging to the messuage called the *White Hart*, and which contains in length from south to north 18ft 2ins or thereabouts and in breadth from east to west 6ft 4ins approximately. Together with roof buildings timbers etc. above or under the said chamber or room and little room and passage'.

This seems to indicate that there was a passage or gallery connected to the upper room, and also that the *White Hart* kitchens at that time lay on the west side of the courtyard, partly beneath and alongside the little room. The kitchens were probably in the back area of what is now 21 Hart Street. Perhaps the reason for sale was that the proximity to the kitchens meant that it was not a popular room for guests.

Also in 1727 Jonathan Sayer bought 25 Hart Street, the house next to the *White Hart* on the east side. Three deeds show that John Shepherd who owned 25 had in 1723 mortgaged the property, which was leased to John Eaglesfield. It is described as lately in occupation of John Sheppard, leased to John Eaglesfield and being between Mrs Stevens on the east and the *White Hart* on the west[368].

Fig 55 The yard of the White Hart in the early 1900s, the gallery is on the left and the small house which may have had a continuation of the gallery on the right

In 1736 Jonathan Sayer in his Will, left all his property to Mary Sayer his widow. Almost immediately there is a deed which recites how the property which he had owned in 1718 was mortgaged then, and what that property consisted of [369] 'All that messuage tenement or inn with barns stables granaries etc on the north side of Hart Street called the *White Hart* then in tenure of Sarah Brasier widow, George Harrison, Joel Chapman and Joseph Woodware or some or other of them <u>also</u> all that messuage on the west side of the messuage tenement or inn then in tenure of Elizabeth Freeman widow <u>also</u> all those three messuages or tenements on the west side of Bell

Street then in tenure of William Smith, Francis Brat, and Sarah Dashwood'. This deed ends with the statement that the mortgage can be redeemed for £256.

When in 1739 Mary Sayer sold the *White Hart* to Daniel Sarney brewer of Henley, the description is as follows:-

> 'Two messuages on the north side of Hart Street formerly one messuage then called or known as the *White Hart* now in several tenures or occupations of Henry Stevens innholder, and Katharine Gunnis widow also barns stables granarys yard etc and little garden (on the east side of the barn) and wall at north end of little passage between the stables (leading into the yard belonging to Mary Sayer widow the whole width of the stables) and all outhouses edifices buildings ways passages lights casements sinks gutters sign, sign post and appurtenances purchased by Daniel Sarney and also from Thomas Springall and Henry Shepherd and others etc and given in the last will and testament (of Jonathan Sayer) to Mary Sayer widow lying between the garden formerly belonging to the *White Hart Inn* and now in possession of Mary Sayer (and not intended to be conveyed by this deed) on the north end thereof and the messuage or tenement back-side and garden of Benjamin Sarney and Anne his wife on the east side thereof and the little garden and yard belonging to Mary Sayer widow, and the yard or backside belonging to Mr Staverton and the messuage or tenement of William Chesssall on the west side and the street called Hart Street and the messuage of William Chessall on the south.'

This deed appears to indicate that the back part of the present *White Hart*, with the passage through to the back yard, and the present kitchens to the right or east side of the passage, was in 1739 the stable block (Fig 54). The yard beyond was that retained by Mary Sayer as a garden, 'the whole width of the stables'. The two houses were possibly 21 and 23 Hart Street, Katharine Gunnis being at what is now 21, while Henry Stevens innholder was at 23 the present *White Hart*. That William Chessal was at 19, which property overlaps the west side of the *White Hart* yard and western range of buildings, which would place him south of the *White Hart* although his garden would have run alongside on the west. Mr Staverton would have been at 17 whose garden or backside extended further than the land of Mr Chessall, thus making him also a neighbour.

Benjamin Sarney and his wife Anne in 1739 owned what is now 25 Hart Street, they had probably bought it from Mary Sayer in the previous couple of years, certainly they are there listed in the Henley Rentals of 1737, with Eaglesfield still there as occupant or tenant. It was being used as part of the *White Hart* until at least 1842 according to the Rentals.

The Henley Rentals during the time that the Sayers owned or were concerned with the *White Hart* seem to suggest that most of the time, the landlords were tenants of theirs. Starting in 1704 and 1706 George Marrick is given for the *White Hart*. In 1713/4 there was George Brazier, presumably the late husband of Sarah Brasier widow who was there in 1718. In 1721/2 Sayer paid the rental but it was occupied by Fletcher. After that it just says Sayer, until 1745 when Sarney paid. This must be Daniel Sarney who bought from Mary Sayer in 1739. In 1747 Daniel Sarney died a bachelor[370], and left his property to his brother Peter Sarney, who paid the rentals up to 1779. In 1785 it says 'late Mr P Sarney', and the Court Baron Book of the same year says 'Ann Benwell of Mortimer for a messuage called the *White Hart* now occupied by Taylor'. Ann Benwell was maybe a descendant of John Benwell who married Elizabeth Sarney in 1740.

It is probable that the neighbouring house (25 Hart St), which had also been owned by Daniel Sarney and leased to Eaglesfield, was left in 1747 to Benjamin Sarney, as his name appears

370 see note p246

in the rentals for that property from 1758-79. In 1785 the Court Baron Book says 'Eaglesfield of Oxford, land now part of the *White Hart* and where a bow window is B Sarney 9d' (This bow window had been removed by the time of the Court Leet session of 1868 when the Quit Rent for it was ordered to cease.) The Rentals of 1785 say 'Rob Eaglesfield occupied by Ed Nicholas 9d', and in 1790 'R Eaglesfield late Nicholas now Taylor'. It would seem that 25 Hart Street was owned by Sarney but leased to Eaglesfield who then leased it to Nicholas and then Taylor. Whether Nicholas was also landlord of the *White Hart* is uncertain.

Taylor probably took over the *White Hart* in 1785,as it was in November of that year that he placed an advertisement in the Reading Mercury & Oxford Gazette. Before that and before Nicholas, in 1770 the landlord was John Cooper, who was named as landlord in an account of the arrival at the *White Hart* of a post chaise whose occupant a Mr Bodington travelling from Benson to London had died on the journey[371]. His brother travelling with him said that he was alive on the hill about one and a half miles from Henley, but that his countenance appeared to change on the hill, but where exactly he died he did not know, only discovering him dead when trying to assist him from the chaise at the *White Hart.* The account in the Corporation Record seems more concerned with the affront to the Mayor, who by the Constitution of 1720 was accredited to act as Coroner, and who had been superseded by a Coroner sent from Oxford. John Cooper is also listed in the Alehouse Licenses[372] of 1770 and 1771 sponsored by Thomas Bennett and Jonathan Dobson for £5 each. These two lists only give the name of the licensee and not the name of the pub.

In the Reading Mercury & Oxford Gazette of 30 January 1786 it says that Daniel Tindall 'late of the *White Hart*' had taken over the *White Horse and Star.* Tindall was probably at the *White Hart* before 1785. In 1781 he advertised in Jackson's Oxford Journal that he was running a post coach service to London, an activity typical of the *White Hart.* By 1785[373] Richard Taylor was advertising his coach service from the *White Hart*. In 1789 Bett Taylor widow of the late Richard Taylor begged leave to inform her friends and the general public that she was continuing the business of the *White Hart* and the coaching business[374] . By 1793 which is the approximate date of the street directory of the period, Thomas Burrett was landlord, the same Burrett who was one of the participants in the gambling incident at the *White Hart* in 1800 (Introduction pp15-16).

By 1807 the rentals say 'Joseph Benwell for *White Hart* occupied Mr Burrett' and 'Robert Eaglesfield for house used as part of the *White Hart*', and while J Benwell continues for the *White Hart* in 1814 and 23, 'Burrett late Eaglesfield' pays for 25 Hart Street in 1823. By 1826 Brakspear was paying for the *White Hart* and 'E Barford late Burrett' for the house used as part of the *White Hart.*

In 1826 in the Inventory of the Brewery, the freehold of the *White Hart Inn* was held by Joseph Benwell and W H Brakspear in occupation of William Venables (a portion is leasehold at £45 p.a.) with double coach house stalled stabling for 33 horses and open stabling for 40 horses. 2 granaries, hay and straw house, numerous lofts and spacious yards. House adjoining in occupation of James Chissall with detached spacious bakehouse. Quit rent 3s 9d. Leasehold - part of *White Hart* with detached offices yard and garden Rent £45 p.a.

The White Hart was finally bought by W H Brakspear in 1865 after Joseph Benwell's death, when he managed to buy out Benwell's share of the firm, and also all the pubs then owned by Benwell[375].

The leasehold property at a rent of £45 was what is now 25 Hart Street, the property lived

371 Holton, S J Ledger containing 'Transcriptions of the Corporation Records 1687-c.1858' Town Hall 4/11/12

372 O.R.O. Alehouse Licenses A XVI 30/1 F114 & F115 1770& 1771

373 & 374 Reading Mercury & Oxford Gazette 7 Nov 1785, 22 Jun 1789

375 Sheppard, Francis 'Brakspear's Brewery 1779-1979' 1979

Fig 56 Advertisement for a Coach Service at the White Hart 1717

in by Chissall may have been 21 Hart Street, perhaps the bakehouse occupied what had previously been the main kitchens of the *White Hart*. James Chissall may well have been a relative of the William Chessall[376] who in 1739 was to the west and south of the *White Hart.*

The *White Hart* apart from being the oldest pub in Henley, of which there are available records, until recently still in business, was also the main public coaching inn. An advertisement of 1717[377] announced that 'Henley Stage Coach begins on Monday December 9th 1717 and sets out from the *White Hart Inn* in Henley every Monday and Friday at 6.0. and comes to the *White Horse Inn* in Fleet Street the same nights, with a good coach and 6 horses. Performed (if God permits) by John Alleway. Note the Stage will begin to go three times a week from the 25th March next ensuing during the Summer Season. Likewise they will call at the *Black Bear* in Piccadilly every Journey.' (Fig 56)

An advertisement by Richard Taylor in November 1785[378] is for 'The Henley Machine', and he 'respectfully informs his friends and the public in general that his coaches will set out from the *White Hart Inn* on Monday, Tuesday, Wednesday, Thursday and Friday mornings at eight o'clock and Sunday mornings at ten o'clock to the *Angel Inn* behind St Clement's church in the Strand, London, and will return from thence every morning (Sunday excepted) at ten o'clock. Calls at the *Old White Horse Cellar* Piccadilly going in and coming out of town for the convenience of passengers and parcels. Performed by the public's most obedient and humble servant - Richard Taylor. Mourning coaches and a hearse to any part of England. Neat Post Chaise with able horses and careful drivers.'

The following April, Richard Taylor advertised again in the same paper, with much the

376 The alternative spelling Chessall or Chissall was common until the end of the 19th century

377 Henley Standard 13 Jan 1961

378 Reading Mercury & oxford Gazette 7 Nov 1785

same itinerary, the only differences were that his coach was now termed 'The Henley Fly', and it set out at six o'clock and returned the same day at one o'clock. He also had a Post Coach which goes to town every Sunday at one and returns on Monday at eight. In this advertisement there is a note at the end 'N.B. No parcel above the value of five pounds will be accounted for unless entered and paid for as such.' Again he announced his mourning coach and hearse, and a post chaise to any part of England.

Richard Taylor died in 1789, the *White Hart* was then taken over for a year or two by his widow Bett, but by 1793 Thomas Burrett was landlord and advertising his coaching service. A street directory of about 1793 says 'a stage coach goes from the *White Hart Inn* every morning at six o'clock (Sunday excepted) to the *Angel Inn* behind St Clement's Church, the Strand, and returns again in the evening stopping at the old and new *White Horse Cellar*, Piccadilly, alternately going in and coming out - the following Stage Coaches pass through to and from London every day viz: Holyhead and Shrewsbury, Worcester, Birmingham and Liverpool, Cheltenham and Gloucester, and Tedbury, Wantage and Wallingford, Abingdon, Cirencester, and several from Oxford.' Also there were '2 stage waggons every week, one by William Cook the other by John Wakling, both set out on Monday mornings and return Wednesday evenings - the former to the *White Horse* and the latter to the *Saracen's Head*, Cheapside....'

In January 1813 a Henley Coach from the *White Hart* was advertised[379] by Richard Taylor & Co (late Thomas Burrett & Co). This may have been a son or grandson of the earlier Richard Taylor, and in this case is not the landlord but the proprietor of the coaching business at the *White Hart*, which seems to have been a separate concern. Perhaps a similar situation to John Hathaway over a hundred and forty years before, or even to John Alleway in 1717.

Pigot's Street directories of 1823 and 30 both give coach information. In 1823 to London from the coach office in Hart Street (the *White Hart*), every morning at seven o'clock (Sunday excepted) and to Oxford and the west every four hours. By 1830, probably the heyday of the coaching era, the directory is more detailed.

> **To LONDON**: The Royal Mail (from Gloucester & Stroud) calls at the *White Hart Inn* every morning at half past two. The Rocket (from Shrewsbury) every morning (Sunday excepted) at five. The Alert (from Oxford) every morning at half past eleven. A coach (from Faringdon) every Tuesday Thursday and Saturday afternoon at half past one. The Magnet (from Cheltenham) every afternoon (Sunday excepted) at two. A coach (from Stroud) every afternoon during Summer and every Monday Wednesday and Friday afternoon during Winter at half past two. The Sovereign (from Worcester) every afternoon at four, and the Triumph (from Holyhead) every afternoon at half past four.

The coaches going west from the White Hart in 1830 were as prolific.

> **To CHELTENHAM**: The Magnet calls at the *White Hart Inn* every morning (Sunday excepted) at ten, goes thro' Dorchester, Oxford, Witney, North Leach. **To FARINGDON**: A Post Coach calls at the *White Hart Inn* every Monday Wednesday and Friday at twelve. **To GLOUCESTER**: The Royal Mail calls at the *White Hart Inn* every night at half past twelve goes thro' Nettlebed, Bensington, Dorchester, Oxford, Ensham, Witney etc. **To HOLYHEAD**: The Triumph calls at the *White Hart Inn* every morning at half past ten goes thro' Nettlebed, Bensington, Dorchester, Oxford, Woodstock, Stratford on Avon, Birmingham, Shrewsbury, Llangollen and Bangor. **To HIGH WYCOMBE & MARLOW**: Thomas Hall's Sociable from his house & the *White Hart Inn* every

379 Reading Mercury & Oxford Gazette 11 Jan 1813

Tuesday and Friday morning at nine. **To OXFORD**: The Alert calls at the *White Hart* every afternoon at half past one. **To READING**: Thomas Hall's Sociable from his house & the *White Hart* every morning (Sunday excepted) at nine. **To SHREWSBURY**: The Rocket calls at the *White Hart* every morning (Sunday excepted) at half past eight goes thro' Oxford, Woodstock, Stratford on Avon, Birmingham etc. **To STROUD**: The Royal Mail calls at the *White Hart* every night at half past twelve and a Post Coach every day at twelve during Summer, and every Tuesday Thursday and Saturday during Winter, goes thro' Nettlebed, Bensington, Dorchester and Abingdon. **To WORCESTER**: The Sovereign calls at the *White Hart* every morning at eleven goes thro' Oxford etc.

This list conjures up a picture of the *White Hart* bursting with activity day and night. At least 18 coaches stopped there on some days, and most were a daily service - Sunday excepted. The clatter and the noise must have been prodigious. When one realises that each coach probably had four horses, with possibly extras on trace for the climb up White Hill, and that all would probably have required a change of horses, except the Sociables to Reading, one is talking of a resident number of horses, between 60 and 70, so the stabling mentioned for 73 horses is not excessive.

The coming of the railway as said in the Introduction, abruptly terminated all this busy traffic, which must have supplied employment for innumerable people, ostlers, stable lads, cooks, kitchen workers, maids and menservants and others. When the coaches pulled in to the *White Hart* to change horses, the passengers would have rushed to get what food and drink they could, while porters would have been removing luggage and stowing more on board, and the stable staff would have been working as quickly as they could to change the horses, and make any repairs to the harness. Some passengers may have decided to stop over to complete their journey another day, and they would have been seeking rooms and beds.

By 1850 the decline had set in, the street directory of that year lists as going from the *White Hart* one coach to Marlow and High Wycombe at nine o'clock on Mondays, Wednesdays Thursdays and Saturdays. There was also a carrier service from the *White Hart* to London every Monday and Thursday. In the Reading Mercury & Oxford Gazette of the 19 June 1858, almost exactly a year after the opening of the railway branch line to Henley, the proprietor of the Henley Reading Omnibus trading at the *White Hart*, was to discontinue his service to Reading, and to sell 7 capital horses, a roomy omnibus, a fly, a gig, a spring cart, 2 sets of pair horse harness and sundry other useful harness. By 1883 there was only a carrier going from the *White Hart* to London on Mondays and Thursdays.

It was sometime between 1836 and 1868 that a cellar flap was opened in the street by W H Brakspear who was charged a Quit Rent by the Court Leet in 1868 for making that encroachment since the last Court session.

The landlord in 1854 James Farley was licensed to let horses, and in the Census of 1861 he is listed as a baker as well as innkeeper. By the time of the Census of 1871 Rosina Pickernell was at the *White Hart* as hotel keeper, and her living in work force consisted of two men and a boy.

From being an important stop on so many routes with connections westwards, the *White Hart* and the town must have become a complete backwater with problems of employment. The *White Hart* instead of catering to the long distance traveller had to exist on local custom. Locals like Mr W Wickens of Knowl Hill who had an accident in 1877 when entering the gateway[380]. His horse shied at a basket in the entrance, collided with the wall 'precipitating Mr Wickens from the vehicle'. Fortunately though shaken he was unhurt, but 'the vehicle was broken in several places'.

380 Henley Advertiser 22 Dec 1877

The White Hart is owned by Brakspears, but in 1971 was leased to Tabard Inns, and then from 1985 to Beefeater Steak Houses' whose non-renewal of the lease led to the closure of the pub.

Landlords/ Tenants of the *White Hart*

*1466-7	William Barneville
*1483-90	William Barnevyle (JSB)
1537/8	Clem Burne (BR)
1541-53	John Pates (BR,R)
1629	Mistress Wells (ORO) widow
1636	Robert Heyborne (JSB)
?	Robert Sury ? (HTom)
? 1668	John Hathaway (JSB) coachman?
1704-06	George Marrick (R
1713/4	George Brazier (R
(1717*	John Alleway - coachman) (HS)
1718	Sarah Brasier (ORO) also George Harrison, Joel Chapman & Joseph Woodware
1721/2	Fletcher (R)
1739	Henry Stevens (ORO) also Katharine Gunnis widow
1770-1	John Cooper (TH,VR)
*1781-5	Daniel Tindall (RM,OJ)
(1785	Ed Nicholas) ? (R)
1785-89	Richard Taylor (RM,CB,BReg)
Nov 1789*	Bett Taylor (RM)
*1793-1814	Thomas Burrett/Barrett (RM,ORO,R,CL,SD)
1814-8*	Bet Burrett (AKL,CL)
Sep 1821-3*	Edward Burford (RM,SD)
1826	William Venables (WHB/I)
1829-45	John Williams (RM,C,PF,SD)
1847	Samuel Kent (SD)
*1850-62	James Farley (C,SD,BReg)
Jan 1862-7	Lydia Farley (SD)
1867-71	Jonathan Pickernell (SSM,RM,SD,BReg)
Jan 1871-7	Rosina Pickernell (SSM,C,SD)
1877	Elizabeth Williams (RL) widow
1877	Henry Wilcox Adams (RL)
1877-8	Ann Robinson (RL) widow
1878-9	Thomas Smith (RL)
1879-82	John Davis (RL,HA)
1882-8	Henry Thomas Whitby (RL,BRB,SD)
1888-90	Thomas William Goddard (RL)
Aug 1890—1	Francis James Pinniger (RL)
Nov 1891-1903	Charles Butler (RL,SD)
1903-5	James Sullivan (RL,WHB/C)
Jul 1905-11	Walter Fox (RL,WHB/C)
1911	Frank Reginald Clark (RL,WHB/C)

1911-12	Ernest Barton (RL)
1912	John Batty (RL)
1912-23	Leonard James Ford (RL,WHB/C,SD)
Jul 1923-5	Herbert Austin (RL,WHB/C,HS)
Feb 1925-Oct	William Edward Grinter (RL,WHB/C,HS)
Oct 1925-7	John Spooner (RL,WHB/C,HS)
Dec 1927-30	Cuthbert Bede King (RL,WHB/C,HS,SD)
Oct 1930-2	Bernard Henry Ramsden Sant (RL,WHB/C,HS)
Jul 1932-8	Leslie Harris Cuthbert (RL,WHB/C,HS)
Mar 1938-51	Cecil Lennox Foreman (RL,WHB/C,HS,SD)
Feb 1951-62	Mrs Florence Maud Foreman (RL,WHB/C,HS,SD)
Oct 1962-71	Henry David Stewart (RL,WHB/C)
Nov 1971-81	Tabard Inns (WHB/C)
	Christopher Joseph Patrick Deegan & Anthony Fincham (RL)
Jul 1981-Dec	Anthony Fincham & Colin Arthur Bycroft (RL)
Dec 1981-5	George Anthony Cromack (RL,WHB/C)
Dec 1985-	Beefeater Steak Houses (WHB/C)
Dec 1985-8	Jonathan Salmon & Glen Farrar (RL)
Jul 1988-Oct	Richard Cook (RL)
Oct 1988-9	Robert Raymond Cook (RL)
Mar 1989-90	Robert Cook & Brian Keighley-Sauden (RL)
Feb 1990-1	Robert Cook & Mary Bridget White (RL)
Jun 1991-96	Robert Cook & Michael Peter Huysinga (RL)

— Closed —

129

The White Horse

on the Bridge

The *White Horse* was one of four properties destroyed when the present bridge was built and the old one taken down. The old bridge ran alongside the new bridge, and occupied the space between the present bridge and the *Angel on the Bridge* (Fig 4). In the Court Baron Book of 1785 there are two entries 'Commissioners of the Bridge for House pulled down on the part thereof the present bridge is built, which house was formerly in the possession of Rob Usher.' The second entry says 'the Commissioners owe for some cellars and rooms that they have destroyed for Bridge building formerly Mr Merratt.'

In the painting by Jan Siberechts of Henley from the south east of about 1690[381], it can be seen that the old bridge at its west end had a single stone arch, now part of the cellar of the *Angel* (see the *Angel on the Bridge*), and on the northern side of the arch a cluster of buildings. In the second painting by Jan Siberechts of Henley[382], taken from the north east side, these buildings are shown as projecting slightly into the river on piers as though part of the bridge. The position of these houses would have been where today the roadway across the bridge runs.

381 Copy of painting by Jan Siberechts in Mayor's Parlour, Town Hall
382 Painting by Jan Siberechts in Tate Gallery, London

There are various deeds which relate to the *White Horse* on the Bridge, the earliest being on 22 December 1587, when the Warden granted to John Lewis at a rent a tenement newly built upon the bridge[383] (There is just a possibility that this deed could relate to one of the other three houses.)

On 10 April 1629 the Warden etc. leased to Roger Shard of Henley Osteler (Osteler means at that time Hosteler and not ostler, though the two words are probably related) for 21 years of a messuage adjoining the Hermitage at the west end of the bridge[384].

In 1631 Roger Sharde Innholder died, and left not only a Will which deals mostly with financial bequests to his family, and not to disposal of property, but also an Inventory[385]. The fact that he apparently did not leave land or houses ties in with his having been a leaseholder. His property consisted of items and goods within his house, tables, chairs, stools, beds etc.

The house contained the following rooms, a Hall, a 'Newe Parlour', a buttery, a 'Newe Chamber', a chamber at the 'Stayres Head', a Hall Chamber, a chamber over the Buttery and a Garrett. After listing the main furnishings in all the rooms, there follows a list of Linen, of Pewter, of Brasse and of Iron.

Under Lynnen there were :-'thirteene pairs of sheetes and one odd sheet- 2 flexen table clothes, fower table clothes of Hemp, one drinking towel, fower hand towells, twoe Holland pillowebeeres, one dozen & a half of flexen napkins and one dozen of hempe napkins'. The value of the sheets was £3 7s 6d, while the rest amounted to 30s.

Of Pewter there were:-'Nine great platters, ten smaller platters, ffower fruite dishes, nine sausers, three basons, seaven Chamber pottes, six eared porrenger & one wyne cupp, one beaker, one pynte, one halfe pynte & a quarterne of wine measure, three ale quartes & a pynte pott, one pair of Bell candlestickes & a broken Candlestick, one double salt two single saltes, one paire of tyn Candlestickes and one tonnell of tyn.' The pewter was valued at 46s 8d.

Of Brasse there were :-'one brass spice mortar with a pestle of Iron, one Chafering dish, two brasse pottes, 2 posnettes of pott mettle, two skyllettes of other mettle, one brewing kettle, three smaller kettles, one warmeing pan, one basteing ladle and one skymer.' This lot was valued at £2 13s 4d.

Of Iron there were :-'one dryppinge pann - frying pan - spittes one Iron to set before the dripping pan, one sredding knyfe, two paire of Iron dogges, one paire of racke Andirons, two fyer shovells, two paire of tonges, two potthangers, and a pair of potthookes.' The Iron was valued at 15s 4d.

It will be seen from the above items that Roger Sharde was fully equipped for catering and for lodgers, as well as for brewing his own beer. His premises may not have been very large, probably the Hall, newe parlour and Buttery were on the ground fioor with the other rooms above, and the garrett in the roof. One thought comes to mind were the 'newe Parlour' with perhaps the 'Newe Chamber' above it, an extension ?

Besides the rooms already mentioned there was also a cellar which is separate from the other rooms and after the itemised lists. It comes at the end together with the 'Backside' which contained 'one hovel'. This could be because the cellar was not under the house, but alongside on the river bank, as the house projected over the river. It is significant that later in Henley Rentals a cellar appears as a separate property.

At the end of the Inventory there is lastly the item of 'the lease of the howse wherein the Testator late dwelt'. This sounds very like the 21 year lease of 1629.

On 14 April 1649 the Warden etc. leased to Rob Shard yeoman, for 21 years a messuage

383 & 384 Hughes 681 AD406, 765 AD471

385 Will & Inventory transcribed by evening class taken by Miss Joan Dils 1984

adjoining the Hermitage at the west end of the bridge[386]. The Hearth Tax of 1665 shows that Robert Shard had 3 hearths, if as is likely he was at the same house as his father, these hearths were probably in the Hall, the 'Newe Parlour' and either the Hall Chamber or 'Newe Chamber'. No kitchen is mentioned in the Inventory, so it is very likely that cooking was done at the Hall fire, and the room was used both as a kitchen and general room.

In 1679 repairs were needed to the house on the bridge, called the *White Horse*, this seems to be the first mention by name[387].

On 2 September 1681 the Warden etc. granted a lease to William Usher of Henley bargeman for 11 years of a messuage on the bridge called the *White Horse*[388]. On 3 February 1723/4 the Mayor granted to Robert Usher of Henley bargemaster, a lease for 11 years, of a piece of land in the Thames on the north side of the bridge with buildings thereon[389].

Meanwhile in 1713 the Henley Rentals have 'Widow Usher for an encroachment belonging to the Hermitage'. In 1721,27 and 33 there is John Usher's house on the bridge and in 1733 Rob Usher had adjoining cellar and two rooms.

The Victuallers Recognizance lists of 1753 and 54 have the names of Robert Usher in 1753 and Elizabeth Usher in 1754.

In 1775 the Rentals say 'Mrs Usher in occupation Widow Jackson', who could be the Sarah Jackson who appears in the Henley License lists of 1770 and 71.

The last Rental before the buildings were demolished to make way for the new bridge was in 1779, when it says 'Rich Hayward late Rob Blackman sometime Usher since Jackson now Marrott, Binfield and Geere are tenants.' Although Binfield and Geere are listed in the Rentals as tenants, they were probably leaseholders. In the Bridge Book recording transactions at the time of the building of the bridge[390] on the 7 December 1781 agreement was reached for the purchase, authorised by Mrs Elizabeth Blackman and Mrs Anne Gear[391], of the public house situate on the north side of the bridge now in the occupation of Daniel Curtis.

(The Hermitage mentioned in the various deeds was probably a name by which the Almshouses of Bishop Longland, established in 1547, were then known. The almshouses were on the site of Bridge House, and the Rector's garage, and owned the land down to the river. The Trustees of Longland's Charity own the *Angel on the Bridge* built on the riverside land in the 18th century, probably in about 1730)

Landlords/ Tenants of the *White Horse* on the Bridge

1587	John Lewis (HL)
*1629-31	Roger Sharde/Shard (HL,ORO)
1649-65	Robert Sharde/Shard (HL,HT)
1681	William Usher (HL)
1713	Widow Usher (R)
1721-33	John Usher (R)
1723-65	Robert Usher (R,VR)
1754	Elizabeth Usher (VR)
pre 1770	Jackson ?
1770-5	Sarah Jackson (R,VR) widow
1776?	Merratt/Marrott ? (R)

386, 388 & 389 Hughes 85 AD486, 105 AD536, 240 AD564

387 Burn, J S 'History of Henley on Thames' 1861 p297

390 Holton, S J Ledger containing Transcriptions of Corporation Records 1687-c.1858 Town Hall 4/11/12

391 Spelling of names at that pweriod was arbitrary, Gear might be spelt as Geare, Geer, Geere, or Gayer

1779	Binfield or Geere ? (R)
*1781	Daniel Curtis (TH)

— Closed —

130
The White Horse or The Old White Horse
100 Northfield End

The *Old White Horse* as it is today, is a pub which was entirely rebuilt and re-opened in October 1938. The original building was much further forward on the roadside, slightly projecting into the road (Fig 57). When the plans for rebuilding were passed in February 1937[392] it was stated that the new pub was 'to be set back 40ft from the roadway'.

Fig 57 The old White Horse c.1905, the present White Horse was built 1937-38, and was placed back from the road

John S Burn in his 'History of Henley on Thames' thought that the *White Horse* was meant when Taylor in 1636 mentioned an inn having only a bush for a sign 'at the Bowling Green without the Town in Oxford way'. In this list of three pubs this one is mentioned last, so it is reasonable to assume that the innkeeper was the last named of the trio, a John Stevens. Burn continues by saying 'This house at the Bowling Green was most probably the *White Horse*, for in some legal proceedings in 1810 respecting the wall on the east side of the Fairmile, it is stated that there was a skittle alley at the White Horse, and the farm adjoining was called Bowling Green Farm in the Fairmile'.

A Will and Inventory[393] of Thomas Lea/Leay of Henley yeoman, dated 1664 was maybe connected to the *White Horse,* listing as it does a Bowling Alley. Although one has to say that it may have been at another pub more centrally situated, or about which comparatively little is known, such as perhaps the *Broad Gates* or the *Kings Head.*

In the Inventory the rooms listed were 'His Lodging Chamber' in which there were 'one highbedsted one trundlebedsted' and other furniture. There were also 'one fether bed & bolster, one flockbed' and various blankets & covers, also 'Eight payre of Sheetes, ffower dozen of napkins, ffower Tablecloaths & six Handtowells'.

392 Henley Standard 12 Feb 1937

393 Will & Inventory transcribed by evening class taken by Miss Joan Dils 1984

'In the Chamber over the Kitchin & the Garret' there was only a table, a chest, a set of cock pens, a tub & some lumber. 'In the Chamber over ye Parlor' there was beside tables, cupboards and stools, a 'trundle bedsted', there were also 'Iron dogges & a payre of tongs', evidently the room had a hearth.

The Kings Head chamber was the grandest, it had tables, joyned stools, a joyned form, and eight 'Lether Chaires'. It also had 'one fetherbed & bolster, a fether pillow, one greene Rugge, one blankett, one carpett, a payre of Curtaines & Valience & ffower Cushions'. Oddly there is no mention of a bedsted. It did however have a fire, 'a payre of Andirons a payre of doggs a fire shovell & a payre of tongs'.

The 'parloure' had a chair, eight stools, a cupboard and a 'payre of doggs a fire shovell & tongs'. The other rooms were the 'Shovellboord Roome', the 'Hall or Brewing Roome' the 'Kitchin', and the 'Seller'. This is followed by the 'Stable & Backside' and the 'Bowling Alley & belonging to it', in which there were 'one Rowle & ffower payre of Bowles 11s'. The total for all Thomas Lea's possessions came to £50 9s 4d.

After Thomas Lea/Leay in 1664 who may after all have been elsewhere, there is a large gap before any positive references to the innkeepers of the *White Horse* appear. Being in Northfield End there are Victuallers Recognizances from 1753 but the early records do not name the particular pubs. From 1774-7 the *White Horse* was occupied by Henry Sawny, John Neal took over in 1778 and remained till 1793. Brakspears Rent Ledgers which start in 1790 show in fact that he was there 1790-4. The Ledgers continue with Edward Thorn March 1794-1800, George Penny Lady Day 1800-2, and John Kentfield 1802-11. Back in 1753 the Victuallers Recognizances had listed a Mary Neal but she could have been at any Henley pub, there is no reason to suppose that she was at the *White Horse* in spite of a John Neal being there in 1778. Later entries show that John Kentfield continued at the *White Horse* till 1818, and after that Mary Kentfield was there in 1821 and 22.

In 1790 and after the *White Horse* was held by Brakspears on a normal lease, until 1815 when William Henry Brakspear or probably his trustees took out a Lifehold on the property. It is listed in the Brewery Inventory of 1826. 'Lifehold belonging to William Henry Brakspear Esq. The *Old White Horse* in occupation of Widow Kentfield with stabling for 5 horses and large garden. Held on lease dated 21 June 1815 for 3 lives of the following ages. Richard Hayward Brakspear 25 years, William Henry Brakspear 12 years, Mary Brakspear 15 years. Land Tax 10s'.

The Henley Parish Registers do not have entries for the burials of Richard and Mary Brakspear, but William Henry was buried in February 1882. So at least until that date the lifehold would have continued. So probably the *White Horse* was purchased by the Brakspear company after then.

In 1874 a tramp was summoned for breaking a pane of glass at the *White Horse*[394], he was fined Is 6d. William Barney the son of the landlord said that the tramp William Lennox, sat in the Tap Room and played tunes on some glasses. Thomas Barney the landlord, was having his supper and Lennox asked if he might have some, he was then given some supper. However later he became quarrelsome, was thrown out, at which Lennox picked up a stone which he threw through the window.

Landlords/ Tenants of the *White Horse* or the *Old White Horse*

1636	John Stevens (JSB)
? *1664	? Thomas Lea/Leay (ORO)
*1774-7	Henry Sawny (VR)
1778-94	John Neal (VR,WHB/R)
1794-1800	Edward Thorn (VR,WHB/R)

394 Henley Advertiser 4 Jul 1874

1801-2	George Penny (VR,WHB/R)
1802-18*	John Kentfield (VR,WHB/R)
1821-30	Mary Kentfield (VR,WHB/I,SD)
1841-54	Jeremiah Heath (C,SD)
1858-77	Thomas Barney/Barnes (C,RM,HA,SD)
*1881-4	William Barney (RL,HA,SD) carpenter & joiner
Sep 1884-98	Emily Ann Barney/Barnes (RL,HA,SD)
Jan 1898-1900	Isaac Fletcher (RL)
Dec 1900-9	Thomas Holloway (RL)
Jul 1909-14	William Froud (RL)
Nov 1914-21	Frederick MacQueen (RL,WHB/C,SD)
Sep 1921-3	Harry George Batchelor (RL,WHB/C,HS,SD)
Oct 1923-4	Frederick Simmons (RL,WHB/C,HS)
Oct 1924-5	George Tom Charlton (RL,WHB/C,HS)
Oct 1925-30	Cecil H Gramshaw/Grimshaw/Gramstraw (RL,WHB/C,HS,SD)
May 1930-Dec	William George Hatch (RL,WHB/C,HS)
Dec 1930-9	James Aaron Rawle (RL,WHB/C,HS, BReg)
Jul 1939-40	Jack Edward Rawle (RL,WHB/C)
1940-5	John Speakes (RL)
Feb 1945-8	Jack Edward Rawle (RL)
May 1948-59	Jack Edward Rawle & James William Rawle (RL)
Sep 1959-64	James William Rawle (RL,WHB/C)
Feb 1964-8	Philip Featherstone Holland (RL,WHB/C)
Nov 1968-87	Martin Graham Perryer (RL,WHB/C)
Aug 1987-91	Kenneth George Ryder (RL,WHB/C)
Oct 1991-2	Francis Lindsay Reynolds (RL)
Oct 1992-6	Kenneth George Crocker (HS)
Oct 1996-99-	Robert & Marie-Anne Slater (HS)
	(Robert Edward David Slator & Marian Elizabeth Slator (RL)

131

The White Horse and Star

29 Northfield End

The *White Horse and Star* closed in 1887, it had been run by the Drewett family since about 1844. John Drewett established a Wheelwrights and Carriage Building business in 1849, which gradually became more important as a business than the pub. A photo of 1887 (Fig 58), at the time of Victoria's Golden Jubilee, shows both the carriage business and the old pub. About two thirds of the frontage is taken up by the workshop, above which the fascia says 'T M DREWETT Coachbuilder', and it is above this that the Jubilee display is shown. Together with variously placed VRs, there is a sign saying 'Royal Patronage of Her Highness Princess Louise'. To the left of the works the *White Horse and Star* is a small house with a single door, to the left of which there was probably just one room, to judge by the one window. Above the doorway there was a rather grand projecting clock.

John Drewett who founded the coach building business appears as landlord of the *White Horse and Star* in 1847. He had married a daughter of the previous landlord Thomas Marlow, who had been there since 1822. The Drewett's son was Thomas Marlow Drewett the T M Drewett of the 1887 photo. Mrs Mary Ann Drewett, nee Marlow, stayed at the *White Horse and Star* as landlady until its closure in September 1887. Later she moved to Queen Street where she died in 1890. The coach building business continued after the pub closure, Thomas Marlow Drewett was taking on Apprentices for a five year period starting in 1887[395].

Fig 58 The White Horse & Star, 1887 Jubilee photo

At the time of the Brewery Inventory of 1826, the freehold of the *White Horse and Star* public house was owned by Joseph Benwell and W H Brakspear. 'In occupation of Thomas Marlow three stables in yard for 26 horses with lofts over, detached wash house and garden. Land Tax 20s.'

It is probable that before John Drewett took over, the pub may have been larger, with another room to the right of the main door, and part of the later workshop space being used as part of the pub. There would also probably have been a carriage entrance to the yard behind.

The *White Horse and Star* was bought in 1750 by James Brooks, and was part of his stock in trade when he dissolved his partnership with Richard Hayward in 1772[396].

The earliest mention of the pub is in a deed of 1693[397] when a mortgage was taken by Richard Brinklow Gibbs on a messuage known as the *White Horse* now in possession or occupation of John Davis. Richard Brinklow Gibbs had inherited the property by the will of his grandfather William Brinklow, proved in 1679. In this will there is also mention of another messuage on the south side of the main property occupied in 1679 by William Pratt carpenter.

By the will of Richard Brinklow Gibbs in March 1713 the property was left to his son, another Richard Brinklow Gibbs. Included in this will were two stables and a piece of ground at Northfield End now in tenure of John Davis, formerly belonging to and used together with a messuage in occupation of John Pusey.

A mortgage of 1719 on the *White Horse and Star* says late in the occupation of John

395 Apprentice Indentures, Municipal Charities' documents 6, in Town Hall

396 & 397 O.R.O. Brooks C1 (5) & C5 (1-21) from 1683-1750

Davis now in tenure of Priscilla Pearman. This mortgage also included the house previously occupied by William Pratt and now by John Patey.

By August 1720 Richard Brinklow Gibbs and others (the mortgagees) sold the *White Horse and Star* to James Brandon or Brandin, who was already in occupation. Also sold were the two stables and piece of ground together with a garrett of four rooms occupied by John Pusey. It is possible that James Brandon became the tenant by marrying Priscilla Pearman, in his will in 1728 he left his property to his wife Priscilla. Before that however in November 1720 Brandon had mortgaged the *White Horse and Star* occupied by himself to James Prosser.

In 1749 a William Tiller bought the house to the north of the *White Horse and Star* from Thomas Gibbs. Then in 1750 the *White Horse and Star* together with the stables and other houses etc was sold to James Brooks by William Tiller and his wife Priscilla late Brandon, in exchange for payment of mortgages, the sum of £200 and an annuity of £17 p.a. for life to Priscilla.

In the Clerk's Book of Burials, a supplement to the Register of 1724-39, on the 8 June 1739 there was buried 'William Davis at ye Wit Hors and Star'. He may have been a relative of John Davis and perhaps took over as landlord from Priscilla Brandon after the death of James Brandon in 1728. The Davis/Daves family may have been connected to two English Brown Stoneware mugs or tankards, one inscribed with the name 'John Davis Bargman of Henley 1740' and the other John Daves senr born March 2 1688/9 followed by a list of his children born between 1714 and 1726, ending with the words 'The Lord bless us all Henly 1740'. The first tankard is in a museum in Kansas City, while the other was exhibited in 1985 by a firm in Kensington[398] .

In the Victuallers Recognizances it is probable that in 1774 Henry Pepple was landlord, followed in 1775-80 by Ann Pepple. From 1783-6 Mathew Taylor was there, then from 1786-90 Daniel Tindall, and then John Bringlow or Bringloe from 1791-4, the Victuallers Recognizances and Brakspear's Rent Ledger disagree as to spelling.

The *White Horse and Star* was not a coaching inn, but catered to carriers and waggons. Daniel Tindall decided in 1789 to branch out, and advertised [399] to 'Bargemasters and Cost Bearers' that he intended to keep a good team of horses 'for the purpose of towing barges from Marlow to Henley, and if required from thence to the Kennett's mouth, and that he likewise purposes providing Waggons for the Conveyance of Goods to and from the Boats viz. loading and unloading '.

By 1797 the landlord had evidently changed, as the following notice in the Reading Mercury & Oxford Gazette of the 1 May shows.

> 'Whereas, I Noah Ford of Henley on Thames in the County of Oxford, labourer, did on Sunday the 14th instant very much abuse the character of my then Master Mr Thomas Hunt of the *White Horse and Star Inn* without any foundations whatever, for which he did threaten to proceed at law against me; but upon my publicly acknowledging my fault and asking his pardon, which I hereby do, he hath consented to withdraw all proceedings against me, for which I consider myself under many obligations to him.
>
> The Mark X of Noah Ford. Witnessed - Wm House'.

Announced in the same paper on 7 April 1800 there was to be a forced sale by order of the Sheriff, of part of the 'Household furniture, near 100 gallons of British compounds, 40 of Foreign spirits and other effects of Mr Thomas Hunt of the *White Horse and Star*'. This sale was most likely due to the insolvency of Thomas Hunt, and by June the same paper had the announcement that a Waggon Inn was to let, and might be entered upon immediately. With stabling for horses whose consumption was 11-12 quarters of horse corn and 3 tons of hay per week.

---

398 Reeves, Ivy article in 'Journal of the Henley Archaeological & Historical Group' No7 Dec1989

399 Reading Mercury & Oxford Gazette 5 Oct 1789

When Job Middleton took over the *White Horse and Star* in October 1817[400] he advertised the pub as a 'Waggon Inn'. He also stated that he had 'good beds and every accommodation for man and horse at reasonable terms. N.B. an ordinary every Market Day'.

In the 1830 Pigot's Directory under Carriers it says 'To London Waggons from Sodbury call at the *White Horse and Star* twice a day'. A waggon probably had a team of from six to eight horses, which if they were changed would mean having 24 to 32 horses constantly available every day.

The buildings were demolished in the 1960s and a block of flats erected on the site (Fig 33).

Landlords/ Tenants of the *White Horse and Star*

1693-1713	John Davis (ORO)
1719	Priscilla Pearman (ORO)
*1720-8	James Brandon/Brandin (ORO)
*1739	William Davis (BReg)
*1762-74	Henry Pepple/Papel (VR)
1775-80*	Ann Pepple (VR)
*1783-6	Matthew Taylor (VR,RM)
1786-91	Daniel Tindall (VR,RM)
1791-4*	John Bringlow/Bringloe (VR,WHB/R)
*1797-1800	Thomas Hunt (RM)
1801-2*	William Davis (VR)
1804-12	Isaac Bolton (VR)
1816	James Poore (VR)
Oct 1817-18*	Job Middleton (VR,RM)
*1821	Thomas Lentall (VR)
1822-Oct 43	Thomas Marlow (VR,WHB/I,C,SD,BReg)
1843-Jun 79	John Drewett (C,SD,BReg) wheelwright
1879-87	Mrs Mary Ann Drewett (RL,C,SD) née Marlow
	License discontinued 1 September 1887

— Closed —

Thomas Marlow Drewett continued with the Wheelwright & Carriage Business

132

The White Lion or The Lion

23/5 Friday Street

The *White Lion* is not to be confused with *Ye Lion*, which was a comparatively modern pub on the south side of Friday Street, on the corner of Queen Street. The *White Lion* was situated opposite Queen Street on the north side of Friday Street and therefore was always in Henley town, and not in Rotherfield Greys. It was one of the row of cottages known as Gravett's Gift (Fig 59).

By the Will of William Gravett, of the 10 April 1624, three messuages in Friday Street were left for the benefit of the Corporation of Henley, for the curbing of the turbulent of the town, and 40s for the use of the Bridge. In 1858 John Cooper[401] wrote that the Corporation are now in

400 Reading Mercury & Oxford Gazette 20 Oct 1817

401 Cooper, John 'An Account of the Charities under the Management of the Corporation of Henley on Thames' 1858

possession of three messuages in Friday Street now converted into six tenements, and comprise the *White Lion* public house and five cottages adjacent - and they pay 40s to the Bridgemen.

William Gravett who died in 1624 was christened on 30 January 1568/9, he was the second son and fourth child of John Gravett and Joan Bannyster, who were married on 10 October 1562[402]. William had four sisters, Joan Gravett was buried in 1574 and John Gravett in 1600.

Fig 59 Gravett's Gift cottages, the White Lion was the one with dormer windows. On extreme right one of two cottages also re-built by Bradshaw, behind which was the Simmonds' malthouse M14

After 1624 there is a lapse of over a hundred years before anything further is recorded. On 4 July 1746[403] the Mayor etc. leased to Benjamin Bradshaw of Henley carpenter for 9 years, six new erected messuages on the north side of Friday Street.

It is interesting that on examining the buildings, there is evidence that the three original houses were converted into six, without taking them down to the ground. The roof spaces and the original timbering show that walls were inserted, and it was more of a conversion than a re-building. On a brick to the right of the door into 23 Friday Street there can be made out the date of 1744 and what could be a K. (The numbering of 23/25 dates to a time after the closure of the *White Lion,* when the house was divided yet again, thus making seven cottages in all.)

The K scratched into the brick by the doorway, may be an indication that Kislingbury/Killingsbury/Kislinbury might have been landlord as early as 1744. Jonathan Kislingbury is in the Henley License lists of 1770 and 71, and was buried in October 1772[404]. The Insurance Register of the Royal Exchange Insurance Co.[405] Policy no.103975, taken out by the Mayor, Aldermen, Bridgemen & Burgesses of Henley on the 25 October 1787 says 'on a house and woodhouse adjoining, brick, timber, lath and plaister built and tiled and thatched. Tenant Mary Kislingbury victualler and known by the sign of the *White Lion*. Value £100'.

Henley Rentals for 1775-1807 say Bradshaw occupied by Kislingbury/Killingsbury or Kislinbury, these entries are probably for Mary Kislingbury, who may have been widow, sister or

402 Baptism Marriage & Burial Register 1558-1653

403 Hughes 143 AD601

404 Burial Register 1737-1812

405 Royal Exchange Insurance Register O.R.O. Brakspear X/1

daughter of Jonathan.

The date of 1744 on a brick is not conclusive evidence of the date of the rebuilding of the houses, but it could be that they were rebuilt at about that time. In the Assembly Books for 1745 there is an entry that says that Benjamin Bradshaw had a lease of tenements in Friday Street adjoining the east end of tenements 'he has lately built' for periods of four terms of 11 years. He is to repair and rebuild the same. These tenements are the two to the east of 23, now numbered 27 and 29 Friday Street (see M14). The significant part is that the tenements are east of those 'lately built'.

The Assembly Books continue in 1746, the six tenements in Friday Street that are new built are leased to Bradshaw. The two adjoining eastward were built in place of two old houses and malthouse that were in the possession of Widow Simmons. In the Henley Rentals for 1745 and 1749 it says 'Widow Simmons for Gravett's Gift'. Widow Simmons seems to have been a maltster of the day, and she may well have leased the *White Lion* and the other cottages to install her own tenants.

Specific leases of the properties are as follows:- on 11 March 1791[406] the Mayor etc. to Wm Bradshaw of Henley builder Lease for 11 years of six messuages on north side of Friday Street. On 5 October 1804[407] Mayor etc to Wm Parker of Henley builder, executor of Wm Bradshaw lease for 8 years of six messuages on the north side of Friday Street.

On 9 January 1824[408] the Corporation leased the six messuages to Joseph Appleton, lessee of the Brewery of Joseph Benwell and W H Brakspear. The Brewery Inventory of 1826 says 'Leasehold public house in occupation of Edward Richardson with five cottages adjoining of 4 rooms each, in the occupation of Bloxam, Lambert, Riggs and Cooper. Lease expires 29 September 1834. Rent £45 p.a.'

On 17 June 1835[409] lease for £45 p.a. to W H Brakspear and Peter Sarney Benwell. Public house and 5 messuages in occupation of Elizabeth Usher, Widow Lamport, William Johnson, Richard Cooper, Widow Eustice. *White Lion* licensed as a common alehouse or public house.

In 1846[410] there was a repeat lease the same as above except for the occupants who were now - Charles Goodry, David Stevens, Martha Wise, Daniel Philip, James Player, and Widow Eustace.

The Bridge Rent Book of 1886 no.132 says 'The Treasurer of the Corporation for six tenements in the occupation of Mrs Collins and others'. At this time the *White Lion* was leased to Greys Brewery, the Greys Brewery Rent Ledger of 1885-96 says 'leased from Henley Corporation the *White Lion* and five cottages. Lease expires 29 September 1889. Rent £60 p.a.'

The Henley Advertiser records during July and August 1889 various discussions about whether the *White Lion* and the five cottages should be re-let, and whether they needed extensive renovations. After viewing the dilapidations it was recommended that the Corporation should retain the *White Lion*, repair it and then let it out as tenements.

It was during 1889, that water and drainage were being introduced into the town, and in December 1889[411] the Corporation had a discussion as to whether they were liable for the Water Rate of £2 16s 3d for the premises. Messrs Holmes and Steward for Greys brewery said they would not pay, as the water and drainage had been laid on without consulting them, just before their lease expired in September. The Council tried to maintain that by not renewing their lease Messrs Holmes and Steward were being saved the cost of £30 for dilapidations.

In the Henley Advertiser there seems to be a problem about the licensees of the *White Lion* just before its closure. A street directory of 1887 gave the landlord as John Titcomb but the Advertiser of 8 December 1888 says that the license of the *White Lion* had been transferred from

406, 407 & 408 Hughes 171 AD691, 69 AD712, 351 AD740A

409 & 410 O.R.O. Cooper & Caldecott C18 (14) & (15)

411 Henley Advertiser 14 Dec 1889

Thomas Wood to George Brown, but in the issue of 19 January 1889, just over a month after the December transfer, it says that the license was transferred from Thomas Meads to George Breuse. However the Register of Licenses of 1887-92 makes it clear that the final sequence of landlords was Titcombe, Wood and then Brown.

The license for the *White Lion* was discontinued in August 1890, but it appears to have been closed after the lease, held by Greys Brewery, expired in September 1889. After the closure there were many discussions about what was to be done about the *White Lion* and the other cottages belonging to Gravett's Gift Charity. Finally in August 1892[412]six cottages and the *Lion* were sold by the Council.

Landlords/ Tenants of the *White Lion*

*1744?-1772	Jonathan Kislingbury/Killinsbury/Kislinbury etc (VR,BReg)
1772-1807*	Mary Kislingbury (R,RE)
*1809-12	Thomas Jones
1812-17*	Elizabeth Jones (AKL,CL)
1820	John Lewington (CL)
1822-6	Edward Richardson (CL,WHB/I,SD)
1830-47	Charles Goodey/Goodry (ORO,C,SD)
*1850-1	Dan/Charles Phebe/Phebey (C,SD)
1852-68?	James Middleton (C,SD) (it is likely that he may have ceased being landlord in 1866, he was charged and committed to the assizes for stealing rags from his neighbour who caught him in the act - Reading Mercury & Oxford Gazette 13 Jan 1866)
*1869-71	James Wilder (SSM,C,SD) bricklayer
Jun 1872*	William Wyatt (HA)
*1876-83	John Dearlove (RL,C,SD)
1886	Mrs Collins (BRB)
1887-8	John Titcomb/Titcombe (RL,SD)
Mar 1888-9	Thomas Wood (RL,HA)
Jan 1889-Sep	George Brown (RL,HA)
Sep 1889-Aug1890 ?	George Brown ?

— Closed —

133

The Windmill

alongside the Mill, Parkside

The *Windmill* public house was outside the town boundary, but within the Parish of Henley. like the *Bell* it was mentioned in the Victuallers Recognizances of the 18th century as being of Henley, but not in it.

In the Recognizances there was a Thomas Dee at the *Windmill* in 1770, Ambrose Dee in 1774-94, then Henry Hester/Hesther from 1797-1818, and Martha Hester 1818-21. Brakspears Rent Ledgers confirm these names from 1790-1812, and also state that the lease had been owned by Mr Henry Chipp but was later transferred to Appleton. Henry Chipp was not a publican but a

412 Henley Advertiser 20 Aug 1892

farmer, and the Windmill Public House and garden in 1802 was part of Paradise Farm, it is listed as such in the plan of the estate belonging to Jeremiah Hodges Esq[413] and was let to H Hewett and H Chipp. They must have sub-let to tenants, who were, up to 1794 Ambrose Dee, and 1795-1818 Henry Hester. The rent in 1807 was raised on 25 September to £5 5s 0d p.a.

The Inventory of 1826 states 'Leasehold. Windmill public house in occupation of John East with skittle ground and small garden. Lease expires 29 September 1828. Rent £10 p.a.'

The estate map of the property of Jeremiah Hodges drawn up in 1802 shows a house in an enclosure in the middle of Windmill Close, which is west of what is now called Pack and Prime Lane and south of the road to Greys. In the list of properties at the side of the map, the house is referred to as the Windmill Public House.

In the Henley Tithe Award of 1844, which deals with the outlying parts of Henley Parish, and excludes the town, Windmill Close can be found in a similar position as in 1802, as an isolated house within an enclosure shown in the middle of the field. The house in 1844 was occupied by William Whatman, but no other description is given. William Whatman was a publican, later he was at the *Oxford Arms*, but in the Census of 1851 he was at the *Windmill* public house aged 51, bricklayer and publican, with his wife Sara aged 50. Street directories of 1852 and 1854 also place Whatman at the *Windmill*.

The Census Returns of 1851,61, and 71 all confirm that the position of the *Windmill* was in the area of the plot of land shown isolated in Windmill Close in 1802 and 1844. In 1864 a Local Government Survey of Roads says 'Lane leading to Windmill public house and to Greys Road needs to be put in order both as a road and a footway'.

O.S. Maps of 1879, 83, 99,and 1925 show the same house and garden incorporated into the grounds of Parkside, after the Windmill pub had closed in 1872. It was in September of 1872[414] that Thomas Hone of the *Oddfellows Arms* suggested to the County Bench that the full spirit license or Alehouse Victuallers License, of the *Old Windmill* should be transferred to him. His request was refused, but it does suggest that the *Windmill* closed that year.

In 1986-7 the Henley Archaeological & Historical Group conducted an investigation at Parkside then derelict, into a mound which was within the enclosed area of the small house and garden as shown on the map of 1802 and the 1844 Tithe Map. The investigations of the mound revealed the remains of a round tower made of flint, of about 7 metres wide, with an interior of about 3 to 3.5 metres. It was concluded that the tower was the remains of a small tower windmill, probably of the late 16th or early 17th century, and that it had ceased use in the first quarter of the 19th century. A map of Thomas Pride in 1790 marks the position of the windmill in this area. (For more details of the windmill and its excavation see the Journal of the Henley Archaeological & Historical Group, No.6 Winter 1988)

The presence of a skittle ground in 1826, suggests that the mill was still doing business, as it would have provided an occupation for those waiting for their corn to be ground. It is logical that a windmill on a hillside outside a town should provide both refreshment and entertainment for those having business there, and that a pub called the *Windmill* should be nearby. The demise of the windmill was probably due to its small size, and to the development of large water mills on the Thames which could deal with larger quantities of grain.

During the excavation a fair quantity of 18th and early 19th century pottery were found, kitchenware, drinking vessels and remains of glass bottles. There were also a number of clay pipes ranging in date from one of about 1610-40, up to the mid 19th century. All these finds were in keeping with the refuse from a public house, and also suggest that it might have been in existence for about the same time as the windmill itself.

413 Estate map of Jeremiah Hodges 1802 now transferred from the Town Hall to O.R.O.

414 Henley Advertiser 28 Sep 1872

Landlords/ Tenants of the *Windmill*

1770	Thomas Dee (VR)
*1774-95	Ambrose Dee (VR,WHB/R)
1795-1818	Henry Hester/Hesther (VR,WHB/R)
1818-21*	Martha Hester (VR)
1826	John East (WHB/I)
1841	Thomas Brooker (C) lodging house
1844-54	William Whatman (TM,C,SD)
*1861-8	Arabella Brooker (C,SD) & 2 lodgers
1869-71	George Gale (C,SD) painter

— Closed —

134

The Windsor Castle

70 Northfield End

In Billing's street directory of 1854 it says 'Thomas Briant Beer Retailer, baker & shopkeeper Windsor Castle, Northfield End.'

In the Census Returns of 1851, Sarah Hemmings beerhouse keeper and three lodgers are at entry no.69, while the *White Horse* is at 60, and the *Little Cannon* at 81. The 1851 returns seem to have been taken in an orderly manner, and this places the beerhouse at what is now 70 Northfield End. In 1861 Thomas Briant baker and Gas Co. was in the same locality, as was William Wright carpenter and beershop keeper in 1871.

Under Thomas Briant from about 1854-61 the beerhouse was clearly known as the *Windsor Castle*, but later in 1873 it had become the *Vine* (Fig 53), with William Wright the landlord. (see the *Vine* Northfield End)

Landlords/ Tenants of the *Windsor Castle*

1851	Sarah Hemmings (C)
1854-61	Thomas Briant (C,SD)

— Continued as the *Vine* —

135

The Woolpack

Market Place

The *Woolpack* in the Market Place is briefly mentioned in Henley Rentals. In 1733/4 for sheep and hog pens in Friday Street the *Woolpack* paid 5s, and in 1745 Mrs Stiles now Rackstraw paid 2s rental for the *Woolpack.*

The list of sheep and hog pens comes under Duck Street and Friday Street but were obviously used by the whole town. The *Swan* Market Place also paid 5s in 1733/4. The lists of 1727/8 and 1721/2 give the names of the licensees of the *Swan* and the *Woolpack,* Widow Webb at those times seems to have been at the *Woolpack*, and earlier in 1713/4 Mr Stevens.

There seem to be no other references to the *Woolpack*, but moving forward in the Henley Rentals, using the guide line of its position in the various lists of successive names, and also the rent charged of 2s, it is possible to find 1790-1800 Rackstraw 2s, 1807 Rackstraw occupied Soundy 2s, 1814-36 G Deane occupied Soundy and self 2s, 1842 Deane own occupation. Finally in the Bridge Rent Book of 1886 no.43 there is 'Messrs Ives Brothers late Anna Deane for a house and premises adjoining No.42 (the *Swan)* on the west side part thereof lately in the occupation of Anna Deane, the other part formerly occupied by Joseph Soundy since by H W Godfrey and now converted into a brewery 2s.'

There is also a deed of 1803 belonging to the United Schools Charities, concerning the *Swan* which states that to the west was late Richard Martin now J A Rackstraw, and now Deane and Soundy. Two earlier deeds concerned with the *Swan* at 35 Market Place belonging to the Town Council also give the occupiers of the property to the west of the *Swan.* The first dated 20th April in the 42nd year of Elizabeth (1599) says that to the west is the tenement of Agnes Maynard widow. The second document of 23rd January in the 44th year of Elizabeth was a mortgage again describing the *Swan* and saying that to the west was a tenement of Richard ffrowen (Frewen). In neither of these two Elizabethan documents is there a mention of an inn either at the *Swan* or at the *Woolpack,* but this does not mean that neither of them were then trading.

The conclusion is that the *Woolpack* was at what is now 37-9 Market Place, almost certainly in an earlier building on the site where there are now two semi-detached houses, which appear to be mid or late 18th century. The brewery was the Ives Brewery (B8 & M33) which was behind 39, the malthouse of which is now known as St Mary's Hall (Fig 47).

Landlords/ Tenants of the *Woolpack*

1599	Agnes Maynard widow
1601	Richard ffrowen
1713/4	Mr Stevens (R)
1721-8	Widow Webb (R)
1745	Mrs Stiles (R)
? ?	Richard Martin (USC)

— Closed —

136

Beerhouse - name unknown

Grays Hill

On 10 June 1854 a For Sale notice appeared in the Reading Mercury & Oxford Gazette by order of the Trustees of the late Mr W Sargeant. Offered as of interest to brewers and rope and sacking manufacturers, the property consisted of a freehold house, established for some years for the sale of beer, with a double frontage, together with a long range of workshops with loft over, a cottage, stabling and yard, situated on Grays Hill. For many years occupied by the present tenant Mr Norris, rope maker etc. Both frontages were 36ft wide, and the depth of the site was 108ft, the workshops and loft occupying the whole depth. The dwelling house contained 4 bedrooms, 2 parlours, 2 kitchens, wash house, yard, well of water, and side entrance. The cottage of 4 rooms was at the back frontage. Annual rent £29.

The main house was on Grays Hill, while the cottage on the back frontage was on Grays Lane. The enlarged section of the Rotherfield Grays Tithe Map (Fig 60) and the Tithe Returns show that in 1844 Elizabeth Sargeant owned a property, described as a house and manufactory, whose tenant was Francis Norris. This property was situated on the west side of what in 1844 was an empty plot, where the *Saracen's Head* was to be built in the late 1840s. The map clearly shows the houses fronting Grays Hill, the shed or manufactory immediately behind the more easterly of the houses and stretching the length of the plot to Grays Lane, the cottage is shown in the north west corner of the plot fronting Grays Lane.

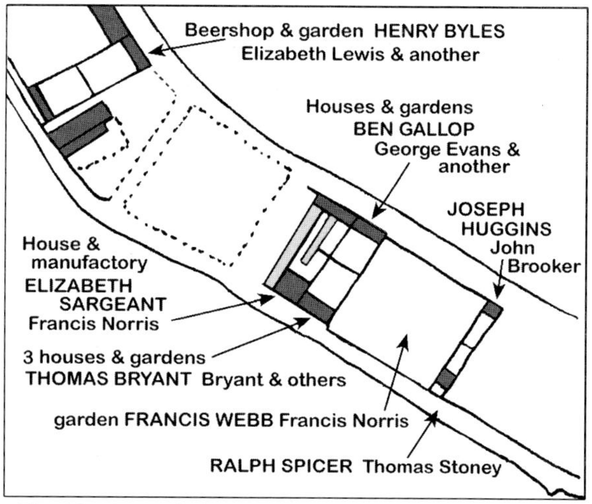

Fig 60 Part of the Rotherfield Greys Tithe map of 1844, the Henley section drawn to a larger scale showing individual houses. Houses in dark grey, sheds outhouses etc. in light grey. Owners in capitals - Tenants in lower case

The property was again offered for sale in the same paper in May 1860, when Mr Norris was still the occupant. It was then described as two freehold houses now used as a retail beerhouse, with an extensive rope and sacking manufactory. It also said there was a skittle alley to the rear.

Both Mr Norris and his wife Hannah seem to have died in 1860, Hannah Norris on the 6 December. On 16 February 1861 her Trustees were disposing of her furniture and the stock in trade of the Rope and Sacking manufactory. It is probable that the beerhouse closed in 1860.

Landlords/ Tenants of the beerhouse with no name

*1844-60	Francis Norris (TM,RM)
*1860	Hannah Norris (RM)

— Closed —

137

Unknown

? behind Longland's House, Hart Street ?

The only evidence for what might have been a pub or beerhouse is in the building and a tentative suggestion from Henley Rentals.

Behind Longland's House there is a building on the east side of the garden, which extends beyond the kitchen extension, and has apparently been used as a garden shed or perhaps wash house. In this building there is the curious remains of what may be an earlier building, or even the front bay of a house beyond the wall dividing Longland's garden from the churchyard. This part of the churchyard is where Longland's Almshouses were built in 1830, on the site of two houses, which were between Longlands and the church, and their back gardens yards etc would have been alongside the wall of Longland's garden. These houses were previously the site of a Brewhouse, in 1704 -1714 the property of Springall, who was also at Longlands, and then of Sayer until about 1735. The Henley Rentals which supply this information cease after that to mention a Brewhouse but in 1737 say 'Rich Bullock late Sayer for two houses next the churchyard'. In 1845 they say two houses formerly a Brewhouse.

Whether the building within the shed behind Longland's House, belonged to Longlands or the neighbouring property, it now consists of a room which is enclosed within the later shed. It is entered through a door, half glass paned, with alongside it a wood wall, with the top half glass paned. This joins a small section which cuts the corner, giving a section of about 2-3ft which is at an angle of 45 degrees with the front and side wall. The side wall on the outside can be seen to be of a brick and timber construction, such as can be found in many late 17th and early 18th century houses, when brick was thought not to have sufficient strength on its own.

Inside on the same wall there is a fine piece of panelling about 4-5ft tall, consisting of top and bottom panels, each panel being well defined with sturdy mouldings round them. The panels may well be early 18th century. Across the top row of panels there is a worn rub mark such as might have been made by the back of a settle.

The panes of glass in the window panels on the front and corner wall are much cracked, but on them writing is scratched on the glass. Little of the four lines of what seems to be poetry is decipherable, but the name above the lines seems to be Snowden. Separately written on another pane of glass is 'S J Snowden' and underneath the date '1766'. It seems unlikely that any one should bother to write so lengthily on glass which was part of a garden shed, moreover the presence of the panelling indicates a room with some social pretensions. The type of window in which the panes are situated, has something of the appearance of the windows which often used to be seen in older pubs, where a window was the place through which drinks were served. (An example is in the bar of the *George* in the Borough, London, and another at the *Bottle and Glass* Binfield Heath.)

The room today unfortunately has been adapted for use as a boiler room, and to accommodate the boiler the floor has been lowered by about 4ft and replaced by concrete, thus effectively removing any information which might have been gained from a study of the floor.

The street directories, the Bridge Rent Book of 1886 and the Henley Rentals show that at Longland's House prior to a succession of doctors who were there from about 1886-1935, it was occupied by George Edward Brakspear from about 1876-86, while even earlier W H Brakspear was there in 1847. The property has been owned by Brakspears up to the present day.

Through most of the 18th century and later, Longlands was owned by a family called Prince, first in 1721 by W Prince, later by Ann Prince and then up to at least 1836 by J Prince. Even earlier in 1713 it was owned by Mr T Springall and in tenure of Widow Cocke. Rentals of 1721 and 1728 have the occupant as Widow Clocke, it was probably the same person. An Adam Springall prior to 1698 was concerned in the buying and selling to William Cock the property, previously the *George* in Hart Street. However that transfer of property seems to have had no connection to the brewery or pub trade since the *George* had already been closed for some time, but a Thomas Springall owned the *White Hart* in 1694, and held the lease of the *Broad Gates* in 1716. So perhaps there was a pub connection at Longlands.

There certainly seems to have been a brewing connection as it appears that the house on the site of what is now Longlands was held by the Lewes/Lewys family from at least 1555 to 1624, and Thomas Lewes appears five times as a guarantor in the list of 'Typplers' of 1532 (p7).

The present house called Longland's House was built possibly in the mid 18th century. Under a window near to the front door there is graffitti scratched on the bricks which give the dates 1768 and 1769. This is no proof that the house was built then, but one may suppose that it was built before those dates. So it is possible that a previous house on the site may have been a pub, and just possibly the curious room may have been part of it. If the date of 1768 was for the newly built house, perhaps the writing on the glass by S J Snowden was a farewell to an old and much loved pub.

BREWERIES & MALTHOUSES

Breweries and Malthouses
Bell street West side

M 1 27 Bell Street, now W H Smith

It seems that there were two houses on this site at the beginning of the 19th century. In the Reading Mercury & Oxford Gazette of 20 November 1815, two houses were to let, both the property of the late Mrs Bacon deceased, who had lately lived in one of the houses, the other being occupied by Mr Joseph Cowx. Behind the house late occupied by Mrs Bacon there was a malthouse to let. It is described as being capable of 'wetting 15 quarters, with good barley lofts, plenty of stowage rooms and every convenience, with a two stall stable, likewise a small meadow with stable.'

In the same paper on 24 September and 5 November 1832 the same property was again advertised for sale. Described as two excellent and substantial freehold houses with a gateway between. Together with a Malthouse capable of wetting 15 quarters, a two floored granary, stabling, piggery and numerous domestic offices, also a plot of meadow adjoining. In occupation of Mr Hugh Waite at the very low rent of £60 p.a. Land Tax redeemed.

Henley Rentals show that for much of the 18th century the property was owned by Thomas Bartlett, but that in 1793 the rental was paid by 'Bacon in occupation Miss Wytchelow.' The street directory of about 1793 lists a John and Stephen Bacon both of whom were maltsters. Rentals of 1800 have 'Bacon late Bartlett occupied Mrs Wichelo,' and in 1807 and 1814 'Bacon late Bartlett occupied Cowx.' In 1823-36 the rentals say 'Butler occupied Waite' and in 1842 'Carter late Butler occupied Cobb.'

Street directories 1823 and 1830 give a John or Hugh Waite as a corndealer and mealman, while William Cobb in 1842-54 was a brewer, corndealer, beer retailer and maltster. After that, the directories show that the property from 1863-1915 was used as an ironmongers, first by William Stevens, then George Roberton, and then Frank Ward, who in 1903-15 was also at 63 Bell Street (M3).

It would seem that the malthouse went out of use between 1854 and 1863, the two houses probably became one at about the same time, since the rentals up to 1842 give two names as occupants. Modern building has removed all trace of either the houses or of the malthouse.

M 2 43 Bell Street

In the Reading Mercury & Oxford Gazette of 26 March 1821 there was announced a sale by auction of a freehold property lately occupied by Mr William Harper at a rent of £55 p.a. It was in Bell Street and consisted of 'a dwelling house with malthouse attached, substantially built and replete with every requisite for business, and sufficiently capacious to work 25 quarters at a wetting. Together with a large walled garden and excellent vinery therein. The premises are 29ft in width in front and 252ft in length.'

The measurements given exclude any property on the east side of the street, since only 32/4, now Simmons & Lawrence, of the properties on that side have ever been able to extend to a length of 252ft, the rest are curtailed by the properties of Hart Street and New Street. On the west side of Bell Street only properties between about what are now 27-71 had the necessary length. South of that the properties on the north side of the Market prevent the length, and to the north the curving of the road makes the plots smaller at that end.

Of the malthouses in the area, the one behind 63/63a, although having the frontage of 29ft was on the O.S. map of 1879 actually longer than 252ft. Moreover it is probable that that malthouse had become an ironmongers by 1804.

The most likely position for the malthouse was behind what used to be 43 Bell Street, where until recently there was the entrance to Waitrose's public car park, and is now blocked by a new shop property. The old 43 Bell Street was a house with a side yard entrance and a way through to back premises. Recent excavations by the Oxford Archaeological Unit showed several buildings had been in the back area. The present 43 Bell Street is the next house on the south side and is a comparatively modern house.

There is also the consideration that in the Census Returns of 1841 the property was occupied by Thos Riggs maltster, his wife, three sons and two daughters. In 1851 it was occupied by Thomas B Riggs maltster and corndealer employing six men, and living with him two sons and two daughters all unmarried. By 1861 Thomas B Riggs maltster was still there but now with a son, daughter in law and one servant.

It may have also been the property, or part of the property advertised in a Sales notice of 1810, when Mr Sumner corn dealer may have been there. The sale in 1810 by Mr J Cloase was for several buildings including three houses with well accustomed shops, gardens, granaries, workshops, and other extensive buildings. The other houses were then or lately occupied by Mrs Shaw grocer and Mr Munday shoe maker, and they may have been in the houses to the south of Mr Sumner, since in 1820 a Pew Faculty awarding a pew in the church to Mrs Sumner says to the north Elizabeth Rhodes, who owned and lived at 45 Bell Street for many years. John Barney Sumner was buried in March 1810, and his widow may have continued living there, while the corn dealing and malting was in the hands of William Harper, who probably also lived there. At the sale in 1821 it was only the single house malthouse and garden etc. being sold.

It is probable that the malthouse went out of use after a disastrous fire, reported in the Reading Mercury & Oxford Gazette of 10 November 1866. The fire raged for some time and the roof and upper floor of the malthouse were totally destroyed, together with a large amount of malt and corn. The premises were insured by the Phoenix Insurance Co, but perhaps the owner, by then George Riggs, a son of Thomas Riggs, decided not to rebuild. At any rate by the Census of 1871 the occupant was B Reeves who was a corn merchant, and in 1881 Thomas Hayes who was a corndealer and shopman. There seem to be no further mentions of malting, maltsters or a malthouse at this site.

M 3 63-63a Bell Street

Behind 63 Bell Street, to the north of the *Bull* and adjacent house, there was a building marked on the 1879 O.S. map, not then called a malthouse, but a building of the same shape and size. It is said to be the original malthouse belonging to Richard Hayward.

In the 1920s the premises were occupied by William Lawrence, cycle maker, but from 1842-1915 had been an ironmongers. Street directories show that from 1842-50 there was John Pescud, 1863-69 Mrs Sarah Pescud, 1877-87 Alfred Pescud, 1891-98 Robert Sizeland and from 1903-15 Frank Ward.

The Bridge Rent Book of 1886 no. 73 says 'Messrs Brakspear & Sons for house & premises formerly occupied by Mrs Ducron since of John Pescud afterwards A W Pescud and now by Robert Sizeland.'

The Inventory of the Brewery in 1826 says 'Freehold of Joseph Benwell & W H Brakspear'. The *Bull Inn* is next described; then the dwelling house adjoining the *Bull* (now 61); then the house adjoining occupied by Mr Pescud, shop & parlour, workshop, 4 chambers & other domestic conveniences (63); and also house adjoining (63a) occupied by Mrs Whiteway 8 rooms, yard and shed.

Henley Rentals show that Richard Hayward was there from 1779, when the entry says 'Mr Hayward late Rich Lowe.' In 1775 it was 'Mr R Lowe in his own occupation.'

Brakspear's Rent ledgers give John Prescud/Pescud as a tenant from 1804-14, rent £10 p.a. Also that the premises were sold to Appleton in 1815 for £150 but given up to Mr Benwell, Michaelmas 1816, the title not being satisfactory. It therefore seems as though the malthouse of Richard Hayward was not used as such after 1804 and probably had fallen into disuse before that.

Earlier the four properties now 61,63,65 and 67/9 Bell Street were all owned by James Brooks who had acquired them from John Green in about 1744. In deeds lodged in the O.R.O. under the name Brooks[415], various previous transactions and occupants of the four houses are recorded. The earliest is a deed of 1657 which is the sale by Richard Barnes shoemaker to Richard Leaver of the house (now 63) built on the land of Margery Sharpe widow, then in the occupation of Elias Skinner, between the house of Margery Sharpe to the south (61) and that of Thomas Perlinge to the north (65). The house (63) was said to be late in the occupation of Phillip Nash and Thomas Evannes, and Richard Barnes had lately purchased it from Humphry Foster. Perhaps Humphry Foster was a descendant of John Foster an innkeeper in 1533 (Introduction p7)

B 1 Brewhouse 67-9 Bell Street

This is where Richard Hayward's brewery, and before that Brook's brewery was situated. The Henley Rentals for the property say '1749 Mrs Brooks for house in her possession 6s 8d. 1775 late Mr James Brooks for Brewhouse 6s 8d. 1785,90,93, & 95 James Brooks for Brewhouse 6s 8d. 1800,07, Brakspear for Brewhouse 6s 8d. 1814 Appleton for Brewhouse. 1823 W Parker former Brewhouse occupied by Wiggleworth.'

From these Rentals it would seem that although Hayward occupied the Brewhouse in 1779, it was still the property of the Brooks family until at least 1795. By 1800 it had been acquired by Brakspear, and after Robert Brakspear's death in 1812, was probably bought by Appleton. It ceased use as a Brewhouse between 1814 and 1820, as Wiggleworth/ Wiglesworth was already in occupation when a Pew Faculty was granted in 1820 to Mr Parker. This says 'to the north Benjamin Wiglesworth'. Mr William Parker lived at Merton House (65 Bell Street) and owned both that property and the Brewhouse property. Both properties had previously belonged to James Brooks, as did the neighbouring properties (now 61 & 63), Parker probably bought what are now 65 and 67/9 at the same time.

James Brooks had purchased the properties from the Green family in about 1744. The earliest deed concerning 65 Bell Street was in 1678 when William Leaver sold it to John Greene. At that time the house to the north was said to be in the occupation of Thomas Painter (67/9 Bell Street). A later deed of 1725 says to the north late Thomas Painter now John Green. The Painter/Peynter family had long associations with the beer trade. John Peynter in 1533 was an innkeeper (p7), and in 1772 it was Herald Painter and his wife, daughter of John Blackman brewer, who sold the *Black Horse and Farrier* to Josiah Sarney.

M 4 77-9 Bell Street, the *Bear*

In 1686 John Stonor son and heir of Thomas Stonor sold the *Beare Inn* to William

415 O.R.O. Brooks 3 (1-14)

Hyne yeoman of Pishill[415]. This included the barns, stables, malting house, yard gardens etc. In 1714 James Phelps/Philps labourer sold the *Beare Inn* together with stables malthouse etc to John Havergill innkeeper.(See entry for the *Bear*)

These two deeds seem to be the only mention of the malthouse, though since the *Bear* was bought by James and Anna Brooks in 1732, it is likely that the malthouse remained in use for most of the 18th century and possibly into the early 19th century.

M 5 85 Bell Street

A sales notice in the Reading Mercury & Oxford Gazette of 12 March 1864, announced the sale of 'two freehold brick and tile messuages or tenements on the west side of Bell Street. A dwelling house with bow windowed shop, parlour, kitchen and six bedrooms, closets, underground cellars, good brewhouse, three store rooms and warehouses (formerly used as a malthouse), courtyard with side entrance, good supply of water, lately occupied by Mr. Hunt upholsterer.' the second house, which was what would now have been 83 Bell Street, was a 'comfortable private residence under the same roof, containing front sitting room, entrance passage, four bedrooms, kitchen, wash house, back garden and offices, now occupied by the Misses Hills. Land Tax redeemed. Bridge Rent l0s.' The whole property having a frontage of 39ft 6ins and a depth of 86ft.

There is no doubt that the two houses were once on what is now the wide entrance to Adam Court. The measurements as given are exactly the same as for 83 and 85 Bell Street on the O.S. map of 1879. The Bridge Rent of l0s also identifies the position of the houses.

In the Census Returns of 1861, the Misses Hill appear at a position on the list, no.40, which is consistent with 83 Bell Street, given that the entries proceeded in a fairly orderly manner from the south end of the west side of Bell Street. Mr Hunt upholsterer in the same Census, appears before the *Bull* at Census no.26. He does not feature at all on the west side of Bell Street in 1851. It is quite possible that he had moved to 85 Bell Street between the taking of the Census in 1861 and March of 1864.

Neither the Census of 1851 or 41 reveal any malting connections in the occupants of the houses, however Henley Rentals in 1842 and 1836 say Rickford two houses occupied by self and Benwell. Rickford was a grocer and not a maltster, the fact that Benwell was part occupying the premises in 1836 and 1842 may mean that the malthouse was then in use. The house (85) was perhaps sub-let to someone else or maybe Rickford was occupying both houses, one part being his business premises.

The fact that the sale of 1864 mentions the 'store rooms and warehouses (formerly in use as a malthouse),' suggests that the usage must then have been fairly recent, certainly not much longer than 25 years. It is probable that it ceased as a malthouse in the early 1840s.

Although a brewhouse is mentioned in the sales notice of 1864 there is no evidence that it was used as a commercial brewery. However it may have been, or perhaps it was merely a brewhouse for domestic use like others mentioned in house sales around Henley.

M 6 91 Bell Street

The malthouse behind 91 Bell Street shown on the O.S. map of 1879 (Fig 61)was demolished when the Adam Court development was built. The original house still stands, though altered, and what was the carriageway to the yard and malthouse is now an entrance to Adam Court.

The property was bought in 1822 by Mrs Jane Ovey, and the Ovey family have various documents concerning the property.

An indenture of 1792 says 'a malthouse and garden on west side of Bell Street otherwise North Street, bounded on the north by property of Thomas Mason, occupied by Edward Toomer, and on the south by property of Hayward & Co now occupied by Joseph Biesley.' This last named property was the *Oxford Arms*

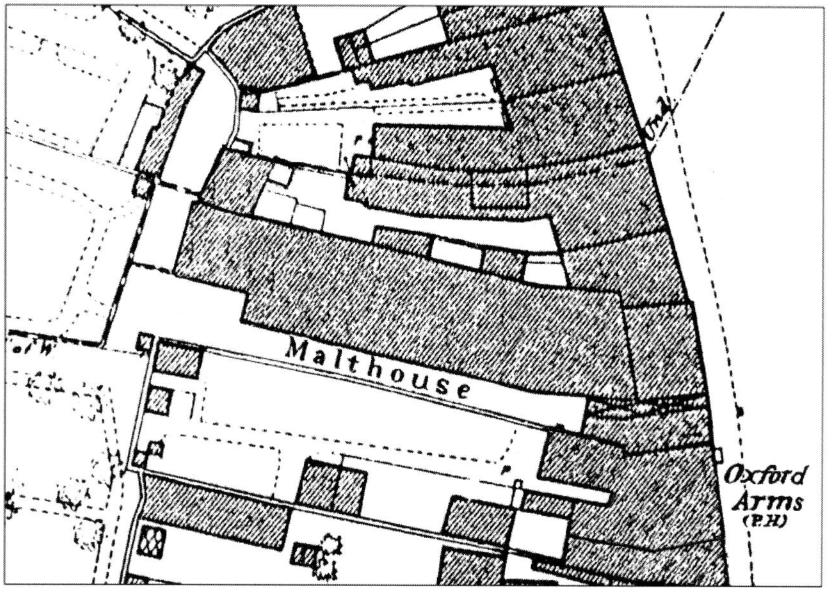

Fig 61 Malthouse M6 at 91 Bell Street O.S.map 1879

In another deed of 1772 the property bought by Mrs Jane Ovey was described as 'a newly erected malthouse in the occupation of Mary Hollyman.' While in 1752 the property was 'one messuage one malthouse and one garden.'

In April 1978 a small excavation took place in what then remained of the malthouse, at that time it appeared to be an open ended barn with no upper flooring, though there were marks on the walls indicating that there might once have been an upper floor. The whole front end had been removed, so that what was left was the part on the map back from about where the 'o' of the word malthouse appears. The excavation was an attempt to find evidence of Ravenscroft's glasshouse, but no trace of it was found. It has later been suggested that the glasshouse was off Bell Lane.

Northfield End

M 7 Somewhere at Northfield End

In 1789 there was a malthouse at Northfield End when on 25 March Mr Edward Ladd of Henley maltster took out a policy with the Royal Exchange Insurance Co (No 111143) on household furniture in his 'dwelling house brick and flint (except a small part lath and plaister) and tiled situate at Northfield End £150. On Utensils and Stock in Trade in a malthouse adjoining brick timber lath and plaister built and tiled £300'.

A note alongside the entry said 'Removed to the house and malthouse late in occupation of Mr May on the hill in Henley' (M34).

Where exactly this Northfield End malthouse stood it is difficult to say, though unless it was in the area just past the old *Bell* at the beginning of the Marlow Road, it was most likely on the other side of the Oxford road perhaps between Badgemore Lane (once Hog Lane) and Hope Cottage (once the *Hope*) and the place where Northfield End becomes the Fairmile.

Bell Street East side

M 8 18-20 Bell Street

The buildings now known as the *Olde Bell* and the Assembly Rooms (Fig 32), were at one time one property, and one Bridge Rent covers them both. The *Olde Bell* was called the *Duke of Cumberland* till 1920, and the Assembly Rooms were only known as that from the late 1840s. Before that they were not Assembly Rooms but the premises of various auctioneers and furniture dealers. In Henley Rentals of 1823-36 the auctioneer was Cooper, before that Paulin, and back in 1793-1807 it was Owthwaite. Before 1793 in the Court Baron Book of 1785 Richard Hayward was paying for two messuages occupied by Moorhouse and Andrews, Andrews being the publican of the *Duke of Cumberland*.

The Rentals go back further, and in the 1770s and 1769 it was 'late Tyrrell now Hayward in occupation Moorhouse & Andrews.' From 1727-58 the payments were by Thos Taylor for his house. (The Tyrrells also owned M34; in the Market Place).

Two indentures in the Record Office show that in 1765 John Taylor and Hamal Taylor sold the property to John Tyrell of Hambledon for £350. A later deed of 1769 sold it on to Benjamin Moorhouse of Henley cabinet maker[416]. The property at that time was described as 'Messuage or tenement now divided into two, with the malthouse, granary and storehouse on the east side of Bell Street, formerly in the tenure of John Taylor and Ralph Pain and now of Joseph Andrews and Benjamin Moorhouse.'

Although in these documents Benjamin Moorhouse is described as a cabinet maker, later he was termed a brewer when in 1791 he entered upon a joint lease for the *Blue Bell* in company with Richard Hayward and Robert Brakspear[417], (see also M11). The building which became the *Duke of Cumberland* was probably the house of Thomas Taylor, and may even have been a pub when owned by Taylor, who was described in 1735 as a maltster (M26). The Auctioneers/Assembly Rooms were built on the site of the malthouse, which had most likely been built on the garden area of the house, which explains the one rental covering both properties.

M 9 36-38-40 Bell Street

These premises were once one property and paid a single Bridge Rent of 6s 8d. In 1886 in the Bridge Rent Book it says 'Mr C Simmons late Mr C Poynder formerly Joseph Sharp for a house since pulled down and rebuilt and now in the occupation of the Misses Geere. Also a house formerly occupied by Knapp stone mason, since Josh Bisley and now Gosby. Also a house formerly occupied by Mrs White since G R Mummery and now of Honey. All included in one Bridge Rent. 6s 8d.'

In a list of property offered for sale by auction in the Reading Mercury & Oxford Gazette of 24 September 1821, it says that Lot 5 was a leasehold house and extensive premises divided into three tenements, and now in the occupation of Mr Jos Sharp, Messrs Smith & Nunn, and Robert Simmonds in Bell Street. Containing eight sleeping rooms, two garretts, six rooms below, a garden, a large malthouse now used as a workshop, two granaries, summer house, piggery, gateway etc. Let at £34 p.a. Held lifehold for life of a lady aged about 67 years at a peppercorn rent. Frontage of 61ft and depth of 198ft. Land Tax £1 l0s. Bridge Rent 6s 8d.

It appears to be the same malthouse advertised as part of an estate for sale in the same paper on 27 June 1803. Lot 3 was described as a spacious malting and premises in Bell Street to be

416 O.R.O. Mercer 111 1(1-3)

417 Hughes 110 AD692

sold for the life of a lady aged 50 years - clear from rent - large malting and chambers, various out buildings, roomy dwelling house and garden. On lease to William Toovey which lease expires at Midsummer 1803.

The malthouse, by 1821 no longer in use as such, must have been behind what are now the three houses 36,38 & 40 Bell Street, whose frontage on the O.S. map of 1879 was 61ft, while the depth of the property was about 198ft. The advertisement of 1821, and Henley Rentals from 1823-42 name Joseph Sharpe/Sharp, who in street directories was mentioned as a pork butcher.

M 10 42 Bell Street

The Bridge Rent Book of 1886 No 89 says 'Messrs Brakspear & Sons for a malthouse in their own occupation adjoining No 88 on the south side.' Added later it says - now owned by H H Peck.

In 1907 Herbert Peck builder and plumber was listed in a street directory at 42 Bell Street. The O.S. map of 1879 labels 42 as a malthouse. The frontage is now two shops, one recently a wineshop, with a yard entrance on the north side of the property. It probably ceased being used as a malthouse soon after 1900, when Brakspears built their new large malthouse in New Street (M40), opposite to the brewery.

M11 62 Bell Street

A malthouse was at 62 Bell Street, 18th century deeds concerning the whole corner block at the Bell St/New St corner mention the malthouse.

In 1779 Meliora Newell widow of Thomas Newell, from whom she had inherited the property by the will of Thomas in 1776, granted a lease for one year[418] to Benjamin Moorhouse cabinet maker and George Robinson of Henley gentleman for the sum of 5s. The properties concerned in this lease were :-

> 1) A messuage or tenement situate on the east (sic) side of New Street formerly in the occupation of Edward Saywell and now of Catherine Gomm spinster, lying between the messuage belonging to and in the occupation of John Deavon cooper on the east and the messuage hereinafter mentioned late in the occupation of Thomas Cooper and now Francis Bennett on the west. (Deavon was at what is now 3 New St so this property is 1 New St.)
>
> 2) Also the messuage or tenement being a corner house late in occupation of Thomas Cooper and now of Francis Bennett situate in North Street adjoining the aforesaid premises in occupation of Catherine Gomm.(now 60 Bell St)
>
> 3) And also all that Malthouse in North Street or Bell Street adjoining to and being part of the premises late in the occupation of Thomas Cooper and now of Francis Bennett a tenement late in the occupation of — Marshall and now of Thomas Bowling being on the north side thereof. (62 Bell St.)
>
> 4) And also all that garden lying behind the premises lately occupied by Thomas Newell deceased and now by Meliora Newell. (64 Bell St.)

All the above mentioned properties were sold to Benjamin Moorhouse and George Robinson by a conveyance of September 1779.

418 O.R.O. Cooper & Caldecott C11(11)

In February 1790 in the Royal Exchange Insurance Register (No 114986), Mr Benjamin Moorhouse brewer took out insurance on a tenement outhouses and storehouses adjoining lath and plaister built and tiled situate at the corner of Bell and New Streets in Henley, tenant - William Hewett grocer and others - £350. Also on a tenement adjoining brick built and tiled lately in the occupation of John Deven but now empty - £150.

This seems as though Moorhouse had by 1790 acquired 3 New Street. There is no mention of the malthouse but since Moorhouse was now termed brewer rather than cabinet maker, perhaps he was retaining the malthouse for his own use, and only insuring the property he had leased to others.

M 12 74-76-78 Bell Street

Two of these properties are now known as Granary Cottage and the Maltsters House. All three, before the large malthouse was built in New Street (Fig 67), were part of the premises of Brakspear's main malthouse. The 1879 O.S. map shows that the malthouse at that time was attached to the back of what are now numbers 74 and 76, occupying the whole garden space (Fig 62). A yard entrance was on the south of 74.

It is possible that before the malthouse was built in the garden, malting may have been carried on in a large room which extended along the back of the three houses. Although this room is now divided between the three houses, the structure of the rooms show a continuity, and the building is of a later date than the main parts of the houses, and may have been added to give floor space for malting in the 18th century.

Before the 18th century there is no record of malting, though it may have gone on, but the houses themselves are much older and were originally one house. The centre house is the remains of an open hall with fine cusped windbraces in its roof, it may have been a medieval manor house, some of its timbers have been dated to 1405[419].

The Bridge Rent Book of 1886 No 86 says 'Messrs Brakspear & Sons for a Malthouse late Woodalls in their own occupation 1s.'

Back to 1800 the Henley Rentals show that it belonged to Brakspear 'late Woodalls.' In 1800 it was owned by James Brooks who had bought it in 1750 from Woodall, who in the rentals of 1737,1745 and 1749 paid ls for his house. In 1750 when sold to Brooks it was described as a Malthouse and two cottages. James Brooks leased the property to Hayward in 1772 and Brakspear probably inherited the lease and later bought the property.

The Inventory of the Brewery in 1826 describes it as a freehold of Joseph Benwell and W H Brakspear. 'No 1 Malthouse Bell Street. 2 working floors and a 28 quarters steep with suitable Malt and Barley chambers and a screen room. A tenement contiguous of 4 rooms in occupation of Daniel Lovegrove. A tenement occupied by William Martin 4 rooms cellar and garden. A plot of land attached to the malting and formerly part of the yard in occupation of Wm Godfrey.'

On the map Fig 62, No78 is the house with the garden behind it, in which the word Malthouse is written. 76 is the house with a small yard between it and the malthouse, and includes the passageway from the street on the left, and the part of the malthouse in line with the back of 78. What is now 74 is the square bottom left, the narrow area to the right of it, and part of what was the malthouse in a line with the back of 78 The rooms along the back of the houses that were once one room, probably used for malting in the 18th century, lie above this back area.

In 1826 the property was still two tenements or cottages, and indeed remained as two up

419 Gibson, Ruth 'A late Medieval Manor House in Bell Street' &
Miles ,D W H, & Haddon-Reece, D 'Tree Ring Dating of 76 Bell Street' H.A.& H.G. Journal No9 Spring 1993

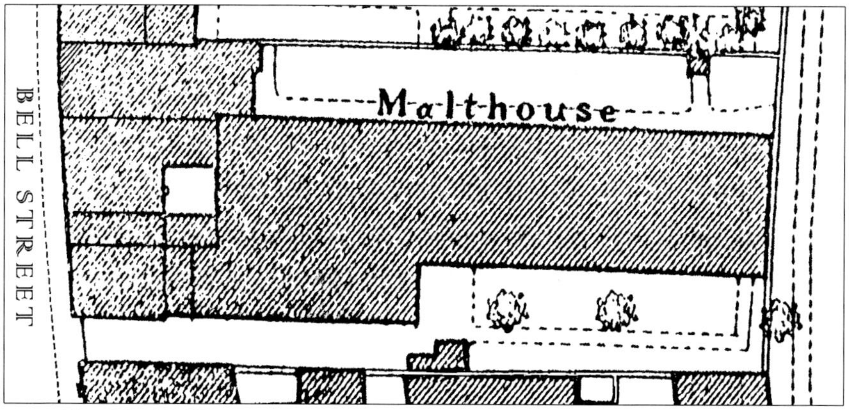

Fig 62 Malthouse M12 at 74,76,78 Bell Street O.S.map 1879

till 1926 when it was divided into three. Daniel Lovegrove was probably the maltster occupying what is now 76 and 78, only part of which would have been his four room living quarters. William Martin was probably at 74 , which is the only part with a cellar, and is the part on the map on the lower left, above the broad carriage or cart entrance.

As part of the insurance of the brewery in February 1786 Messrs Robert Appleton and John Shaw brewers took out a policy (No 96425) with the Royal Exchange Insurance Co. 'On utensils and stock in trade in a malthouse and on the lofts storehouses granaries and offices adjoining, brick and timber pannelled with brick except a small part of the front of one of the lofts which is lath and plaister built and tiled situate in Bell Street. £800.'

The whole property was sold by Brakspears in 1900.

Duke Street West side

B 2 2-4-6 Duke Street and 1-3 Market Place

It is difficult to make out where exactly the brewhouse was situated, whether in Duke Street or Market Place. Although rentals are often for Market Place, the brewhouse was probably behind 4-6 Duke Street. A further complication is that the whole of the west side of Duke Street was demolished in 1870 to widen the street, and it may be that the corner block originally projected more into both Duke Street and the Market Place.

The actual corner house is owned by the Humphrey Newberry's Charity, the Bridge Rent Book of 1886 No 33 says 'James Thackara late the Trustees of Humphrey Newberry's Charity for a house etc late in the occupation of James Baggalley since pulled down for street improvements and a new house built, now being the corner house on the west side of Duke Street late in the occupation of Ruth Thackara and now of her son William Thackara 2d.'

The next entry No 34 says 'Mrs Bate late Henry Stubbs late W F Portello formerly Thomas Maynard for a house etc late in the occupation of Thomas Maynard then of Robert Gill afterwards of the said Henry Stubbs and now of Walter C Williams 5s.' This is 3 Market Place.

Under Duke Street in the Bridge Rent Book Nos 119 and 119a there is the following. 'The Executors of John E Brown late W F Portello for part of the site of the premises formerly a Brewhouse since occupied by Thomas Maynard as a slaughter house and yard, then by Robert Gill since by Henry Stubbs afterwards pulled down for street improvements and lotted out for building - and new house now erected 5s.' For 119a it says 'W F Bartlett late W F Portello for the remaining part of the above premises and new house erected 5s.'

It seems likely that the last two entries covered the area now taken by 2-4-6 Duke Street, and provided back premises to the two properties in Market Place, forming a corner block.

According to street directories Thomas Maynard was a butcher 1823-30, Robert Gill was a butcher in 1842 and Henry Stubbs a grocer 1842-77. Henley Rentals give Thomas Maynard from 1807, while in 1800 and 1795 the premises were empty, owned by Mrs Blackman. Robert Blackman was a brewer (see both the *Black Horse and Farrier* and the *Crown and Thistle*) the rental for 1779 says 'late Rob Blackman now widow late in occupation F Lilly.' Earlier rentals throughout the 18th century show that the occupants were mostly brewers. It is probable that it remained a brewhouse until just before 1795.

The whole corner property seems to have been for sale in 1793, when on 8 July in the Reading Mercury & Oxford Gazette the sale was announced of two houses with shops both of which face Bell Street. One in the occupation of Mr John Dowling shoemaker, the other of Mr Hussey but lately of Mr George Richards grocer, containing together 32ft in front. Likewise the Brewhouse storehouses and stables with large yard, lately in the occupation of Mrs Ann Gear but now of Messrs Hayward & Co. The premises extend from east to west about 63ft and from north to south about 178ft. The corner of Duke Street before the widening of the road in 1870 (Fig 23) was further east, and houses on the north of the corner would have been facing up Bell Street.

By 1798 the Brewhouse had definitely closed. In the Reading Mercury and Oxford Gazette of 8 October, building materials were offered for sale, being the materials of the Brewhouse in Duke Street; consisting of a large quantity of oak beams, rafters and joists, old flooring boards, and a large quantity of firewood, bricks, tiles etc.

B 3 The Union Brewery

The Union Brewery was behind the *Queen's Head* in Duke Street (see the *Union*, M28 and the *Queen's Head.*)

M 13 Somewhere in Duke Street (Reading Road ?)

A rental of 1755 says that 'John Teffle peruke maker has malthouse and tenement' in Duke Street. This is the only reference to any malthouse in Duke Street, but it seems that sometime at the beginning of the 19th century, and perhaps before that, buildings along the Reading Road up to where Station Road was later built, were referred to as in Duke Street. So it may be that the peruke maker's malthouse was actually in what is now called Reading Road.

It might have been the malthouse offered for sale in the Reading Mercury & Oxford Gazette on 24 December 1821. A dwelling house and malthouse to be sold by private contract, situate at entrance to the town of Henley. To view the property and to treat for the same contact Mr George Deane, Market Place,Henley.

Later in the same paper on 21 April 1823, a longer advertisement described a dwelling house malthouse and good garden situate in Southfield End on the road to Reading. The house had three chambers, one garret, a large parlour, kitchen, pantry and wash house. There were two cellars and good garden with shed and well of water. The malthouse had a cistern capable of wetting 16 quarters, with five malt lofts etc. A most eligible site for building upon having delightful views of Park Place and the River Thames. Frontage 70ft depth 90ft. Land Tax 16s p.a.

The most likely position for this property was on the east side of the Reading Road, where the four houses of South Place, nos17,19,21,&23 Reading Road are now built (Figs 63 & 64).

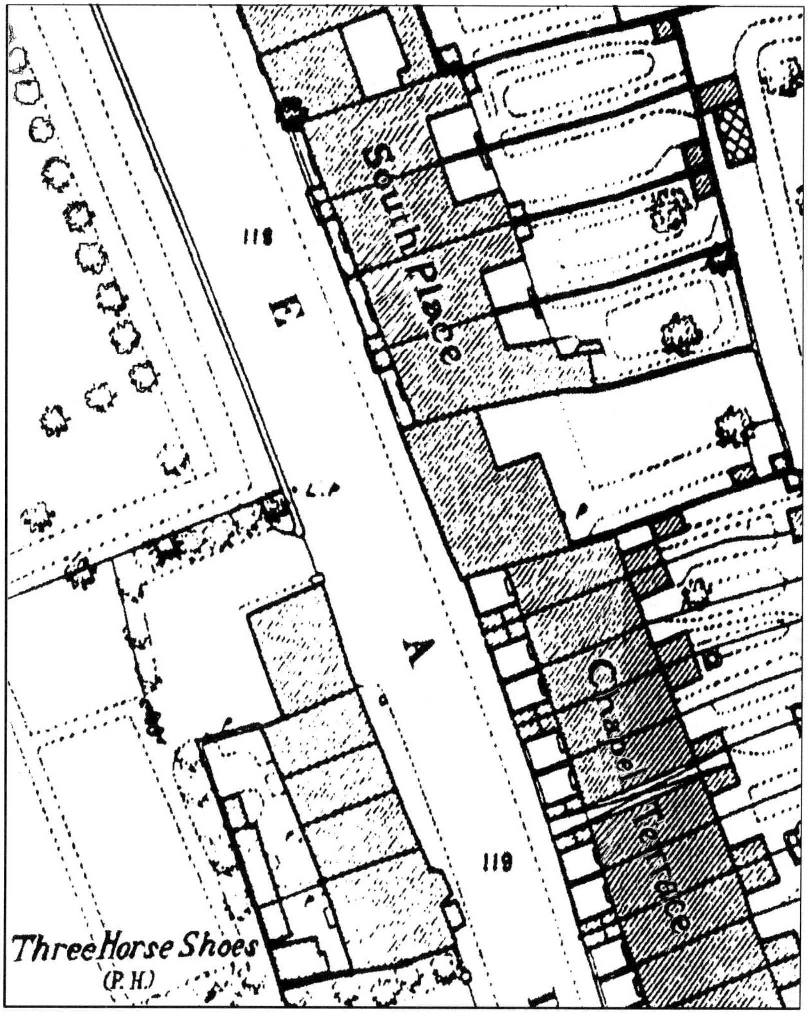

Fig 63 O.S. map 1879 shows position of South Place and the original Three Horseshoes

They were probably built in about 1824 after the sale. Their frontage on the O.S. map of 1879 measures exactly 70ft, while the depth of the property to a boundary wall is about 85ft. It is possible that 5ft may have been lost to the road or the pavement since 1823. No other properties in the vicinity come near to the given measurements.

Friday Street North side

M 14 31-33 Friday Street

In the Assembly Books for 1746 it says 'The six tenements in Friday Street that are now built are leased to Bradshaw. The two adjoining eastwards were built in place of the two old houses and malthouse that was in possession of Widow Simmonds.' The six tenements in modern street numbering are 17-29, the slightly larger one having been divided and now numbered 23 and 25 (see the *White Lion* & Fig 59).) The two adjoining eastwards would have been 31 and 33.

Earlier than 1746 on 24 January 1719 the Warden etc granted to William Symonds of Henley maltster a lease for 11 years of two messuages on the north side of Friday Street.

On 20 September 1731 William Symonds of Henley yeoman was granted another lease of 11 years of two messuages on the north side of Friday Street [420].

The Assembly books in March 1745 say 'Benj Bradshaw has lease of two tenements in Friday Street adjoining at the east end of the tenements he has lately built, for periods of 4 terms of 11 years at a rent of £3. He is to repair and rebuild the same.' The lease mentioned may have been either the one of 6 April 1744 when Bradshaw was granted a lease for 11 years of two messuages on the north side of Friday Street; or the lease of 6 February 1745 [421] when he was granted a lease of another two messuages in Friday Street. For some time Bradshaw had leases of two pairs of houses, the other two being 'next the parsonage gateway,' now 57-59-61 Friday Street, which were probably two properties converted by Bradshaw into three.

B 4 45 Friday Street

Information from deeds, and an account by Air Vice Marshal Baker written in 1963, of the history of 45 and 47 Friday Street, now known as Queen Anne Cottage and the Old Foundry, show that behind Queen Anne Cottage there was a brewhouse. That it may have been a brewery is perhaps evident from its ownership or leasing in the past.

Both houses were considerably renovated in about 1947/8, Queen Anne Cottage being less drastically altered than the Old Foundry, which had previously been the industrial end of the two plots, and had been a foundry since about 1860 or shortly after that. Before 1860 the site had been a tannery since about beginning of the 17th century, if not earlier. The name Queen Anne Cottage is of fairly recent usage, before that it was the house of the foundry owners, and previously that of the master tanner.

In 1734 a policy was taken out with the Sun Insurance Office by Robert Underwood innholder on a brick and tiled house on the north side of Friday Street valued at £250 and also on a brick brewhouse valued at £50. The insurance plaque is on the front wall today. Robert Underwood was the landlord of the *Red Lion* and he probably required more brewing facilities than were at the *Red Lion.* Later in a will of James Bird of 1766 who held the lease of the whole property including the tannery, and was leaving it to his son, it says that it was lately purchased from James Underwood, presumably the son of Robert. In the same will it describes the lease as being an unexpired lease of 99 years begun in 1699 which had been made between the Trustees of the Grammar School and Benjamin Wheeler tanner.

The whole premises had been bought by the Trustees of the Grammar School on the 26th December 1604 to provide income to support the then newly established Grammar School, King James' letters patent founding the school and endowing it were signed on the 17th December 1604. At the time of the purchase the property consisted of four houses, a barn tan house tanyard and other hereditaments. Part of the property was already on lease to Augustine Springall.

Although the brewhouse is not mentioned either in 1604 or 1699, the fact that Augustine Springall is mentioned as having a lease on part of the property, suggests that a brewhouse might have been his interest, the Springalls or Springals were a family much concerned with both pubs brewing and malting. Again the acquiring of the lease by Robert Underwood, who was definitely not a tanner, and who had adequate living accommodation at the *Red Lion* , would seem to suggest that the brewhouse was the attraction. There may well have been a brewery on the site at the end of the 16th century, which may have lasted until the mid 18th century.

420 & 421 Hughes 84 AD562 (1719), 135 AD572 (1731), 158AD597 & 180 AD598 (1744), 20 AD600 (1745)

M 15 67-69-71 Friday Street

These three properties were probably originally one house and had a malthouse behind it, as may be seen on the O.S.map of 1879 (Fig 65), however it appears that originally the whole corner block to the east of the malthouse, may have been one property. This would have included the house now known as the Old Granary, and the house now Barry Keene's art gallery.

In 1823 an agreement was reached for the lease of the property, by the then Lord of the Manor of Henley[422], to William Soundy, Thomas Eisdell and John Curtis Byles. It then consisted of three messuages, three warehouses, three storehouses, three stables, three curtilages & three gardens in Henley on Thames. John Curtis Byles was a coal and corn merchant and wharfinger[423],and his brother was Henry Nathaniel Byles also a coal and corn merchant and brewer, who together with Thomas Soundy started Greys Brewery. In a book about William Byles, it is said that a stone set in the warehouse wall, commemorated a flood in which William Byles, then an infant had to be lowered from a window. William was born in July 1807, so the flood was that of January 1809, the height of which is marked on a stone in the wall of 11 Riverside, which is now part of Barry Keene's art gallery.

Much earlier than the early 19th century occupation of the houses, in Hughes List of Archives dated 23 September 1670[424], the Warden granted to Roger fforster (Forster) a lease for 11 years of a malthouse and garden in Friday Street.

That this malthouse in 1670 and the properties mentioned in 1823, were on the north side of the street is definite as otherwise in both cases they would have said in Rotherfield Greys and not Henley. However in 1670 it may have referred to the malthouse at 31-33 Friday Street (M14).

Henley Rentals for the property at 67/69/71 Friday Street in 1745 say 'Widow Stevens and in 1749 Widow Stevens house now Toovey'. In 1795 they say 'Thomas Toovey malthouse,' in 1800 'Toovey occupied Harman malthouse' and from 1807-42 'Byles malthouse.' By 1886 in the Bridge Rent Book No 136 it says 'W D Mackenzie Esqre late Margaret Byles formerly John B Byles for a malt-house late in the occupation of Thos A Byles 16s 8d.'

From the Rentals one gets the impression that it was a single property, but it may be that the three messuages mentioned in 1823 may have been the houses now known as 67/69/71 Friday Street, that the three malthouses were combined into one large malthouse, and that perhaps the warehouses and storehouses were the houses fronting onto Riverside. In 1886 the property was still owned by the Lord of the Manor, at that time W D Mackenzie.

Friday Street South side

There were at least five malthouses on the south side of Friday Street. The O.S. map of 1879 shows two malthouses, one of them part of Greys Brewery, behind what is now 54 Friday Street, between the yard of the brewery and the *Anchor* pub. The other is marked as behind the house now demolished for the entry to Queens Street, which was next but one on the west side of the *Plough/Black Horse*. Queens Street was built in about 1881, the Henley Advertiser of the 14 May said plans had been submitted by Owthwaite for ten cottages in the proposed new road.

---

422 & 423 Copy of deed & extract from Byles, F G 'William Byles' printed for private circulation 1932, sent to me by Ralph Byles of Inglewood, S.A., Australia, who has researched the Byles family John Curtis Byles the father of William Byles

424 Hughes 322 AD518

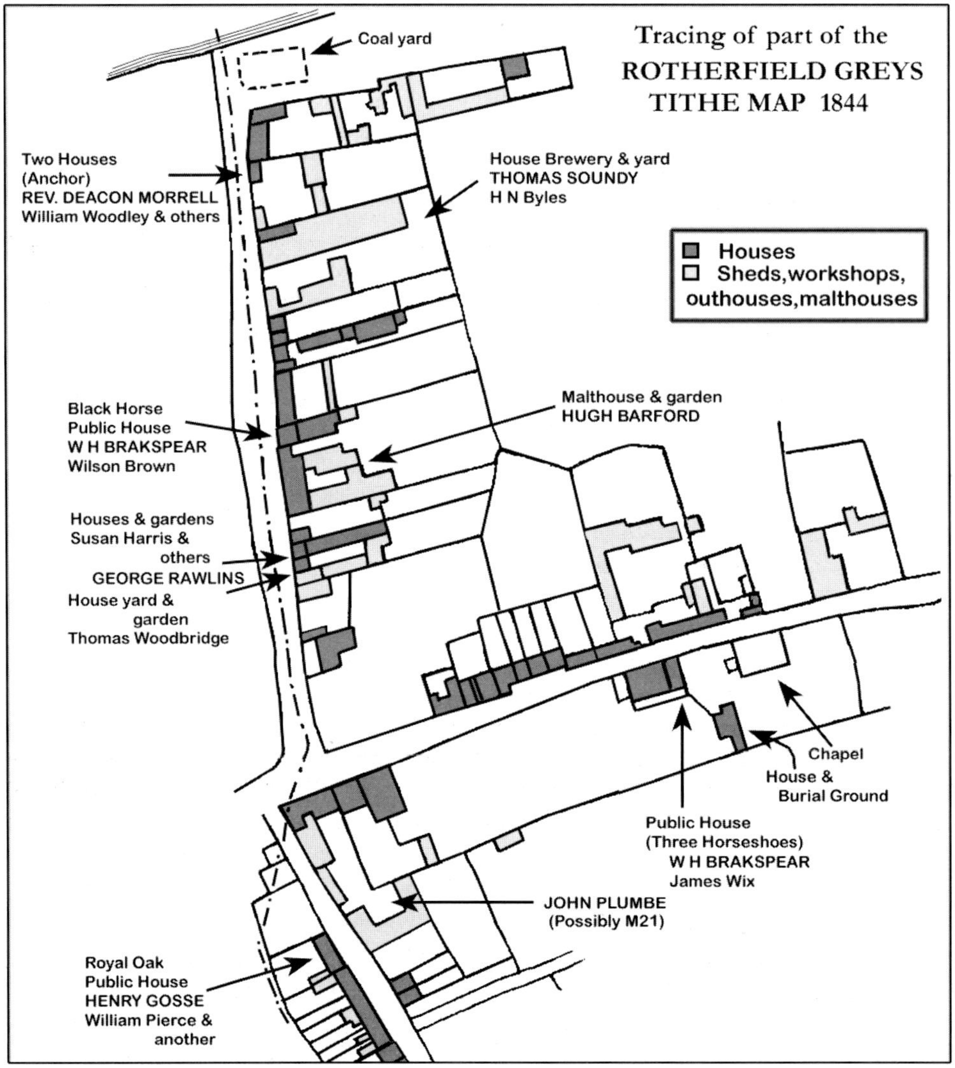

Fig 64 The Rotherfield Greys tithe map has the section dealing with Henley drawn to a larger scale showing individual houses. Information in brackets not from Tithe Map.

M 16 12 Friday Street, once *Ye Lion*.

The entry in the Bridge Rent Book for the south side of Friday Street No 128 says 'GeorgeRawlins late William Toovey for several cottages formerly a house and Malthouse afterwards a silk manufactory now in the occupation of — 2s.' There is a note written probably about 1920 which says 'Present owners the Royal Hotel Co.' and then another note 'purchased in 1926 by Messrs Hobbs & Sons Ltd.'

The Henley Rentals in 1842 & 36 say Rawlins/Rawlings late Toovey late malthouse now cottages 2s. In 1828 'Edwards late Toovey malthouse occupied by Byles 2s.' From 1814-23 J Byles paid and occupied the malthouse himself, and in 1807 he occupied the premises and malthouse though the rent was then paid by Edwards. In 1800 the occupant was Pickman and in 1795 Harris.

In 1793 when Edwards was paying the occupant was Toovey. In 1790 it says Wm Toovey late occupied by J Pickman now Jeggins, in 1785 Wm Toovey occupied by J Pickman and in 1779 & 75 Wm Toovey late in occupation of Mr Byles now Pickman. All the entries being for 2s.

The situation of this malthouse, west of the other malthouses is clear from a study of the Tithe Map of Rotherfield Greys in 1844 (Fig 64). At that time George Rawlins owned three cottages along the street frontage, with other cottages behind, also a range of sheds or buildings enclosing a small yard. All these cottages and buildings were on the site of where *Ye Lion* was built, and also partly in the area which is now Queen Street. The occupants of the cottages in 1844 were 'for houses and gardens Susan Harris and others' and Thomas Woodbridge who had a house yard and garden.

From the rental entries it seems that the malthouse went out of use between 1823 and 1836, possibly in about 1830, when G Rawlins was at the Crown Brewery (see B10).

M 17 Malthouse on site of Queen Street

This malthouse demolished in about 1881, was shown on the O.S. map of 1879. The Bridge Rent Book 1886 entry No 130 says 'George Riggs late James Wheeler for a malthouse and premises late in the occupation of Richard Harris and now of Robert Owthwaite 6d.' A note following the entry says 'These premises were pulled down and the site thrown into and forms part of the road known as Queen Street.' (The cottages whose plans were submitted in 1881 were possibly for the houses on the east side of Queen Street, on land which had been part of this malthouse).

Henley Rentals show that it was owned by R Harris and occupied by James Wheeler 1823-42, that previously it was owned and occupied by Ralph Harris 1807-14, and occupied by Jackson and Usher from 1793-1800. From 1749-90 it was owned by Keene.

M 18 14 Friday Street

In Brakspears Rent Ledgers, Brakspear was paying Land Tax in July 1797 of £1 6s 0d for a house in Friday Street Rotherfield Greys in occupation of Ralph Harris and £1 8s 0d for the *Plough* alehouse adjoining (see the *Plough/Black Horse*). The Rent Ledgers from 1796-98 show Edward Deane at the *Plough* and the 'house and malthouse' (next to the *Plough*) leased to Ralph Harris from 1796-1812. A note says 'sold to Mr Barford in 1813 for £490.'

The Reading Mercury & Oxford Gazette of 12 April 1813 announced this sale as part of an auction in four lots. Lot 2 was for a freehold dwelling house and malthouse in Friday Street in occupation of Ralph Harris. A house malthouse and kiln capable of wetting 13 quarters, with five malt lofts that will hold 600 quarters, and other extensive buildings, the whole of which covering nearly 20 poles of ground, exclusive of a passage leading to stables, which must be fenced off at purchaser's expense, and a right of way maintained through the same for — years to come to the occupants of the house adjoining known by the name of the *Black Horse* also a good well of water and about ¾ of an acre of garden.

The Tithe Award and the accompanying map of 1844- (Fig 64) show that the property was then still owned by Hugh Barford, while an occupant of the house was George Beck. The Tithe map of Rotherfield Greys near to Henley town is supplemented by a more detailed plan drawn to a larger scale so that individual houses can be identified, even when huddled together as in Friday Street. On this map the two properties with the malthouses M17 and M18 are shown as a continuous house along the road, probably semi-detached. The two malthouses seem to project behind the houses, with a yard between them. As both seem to have been operated for some time with the same maltster in charge, they probably shared the yard.

The Henley Rentals for Hugh Barford's property seem to have discontinued after 1823, when Barford paid ls. Previously in 1807 Rob Brakspear paid late Benwell house and premises in occupation of Ralph Harris ls. and in 1795-1800 it was Henry Benwell occupied by Ralph Harris ls.

M19 House now demolished on east side of 16 Friday Street

A marriage settlement between Richard Darby and Dinah Day on 23 April 1735[425] concerned three lots of property owned by Richard Darby who was a maltster, as was his father Samuel. Two of the properties were in Hart Street and both having malthouses they are discussed under Hart Street malthouses.

The property in Friday Street is described as a messuage tenement malthouse situate on the south side of Friday Street now in the tenure of George Soundy between the house of Cornelius Bland butcher on the east and William Dee mason on the west. Inherited from Richard Whiteseed after the death of Richard Darby's brother Samuel who was under 21 years old.

The position of this malthouse is determined by the Henley rentals charged to 16 Friday Street once the *Plough* and then the *Black Horse* (Figs 13 & 64). The *Plough* does not appear to have existed as a pub much before 1775 when the rentals say 'late Mr & Mrs Maskall in occupation Flight and Benwell now a public house opposite Mr Bird.' (Mr Bird was at the Tannery later to be the Foundry) Previous rentals for 1745 say 'Ed Taylor for tenement late Dee late Carter now Maskells.'

This rental of 1745 suggests that Dee in about 1735 may have been at 16 Friday Street and therefore Darby's property, the malthouse previously owned by Richard Whiteseed, would have been to the east of the *Black Horse*.

B 5 & M 20 Greys Brewery & Malthouse

The brewery and malthouse were behind what are are now 52 & 54 Friday Street. The brewery yard was behind 52 while the malthouse was directly behind 54, on the east side of the yard, as can be seen on the O.S. map of 1879 and the tithe map of 1844 (Figs 64 & 65). In 1879 next to 54 there was an entrance into the yard behind and then a small house in the front corner of the *Anchor* yard. The *Anchor* as shown in early postcards, was known as the Brewery Tap (Fig 1).

The brewery was called Greys Brewery because of its position, being on the south side of Friday Street it was in Rotherfield Greys. The Tithe Award for Rotherfield Greys in 1844 shows that the owner of the property at that time was Thomas Soundy while the occupant was H N Byles.

The date for the starting of Greys Brewery is unknown, though it was claimed by Thomas Soundy's great grandson Samuel Soundy, when he was aged 91 in about 1930[426], that it was started in about 1760 by Thomas Soundy. However there seems to be no confirmation of this and it does not seem likely. Thomas may have been a maltster and also may have shipped malt down river, but before 1800 his interests appear to have been mainly in shipping. Thomas Soundy and H N Byles were trading as partners in the Coal and Coke trade for some time before 1800, Soundy owning a wharf near the end of Friday Street. In 1798 they advertised in the Reading Mercury & Oxford Gazette of 7 May that they would be holding their Annual Ash Feast with a dinner at the *Red Lion*

425 Marriage settlement papers were with Chambers & Co. now closed, an abstract of papers among Town Hall deeds

426 Byles, F G 'William Byles' printed 1932 for private circulation see notes 422 & 423

on 17 May. Their advertisement continued; 'Best Sea coals, Coke and Welsh Coals (good measures), Charcoal, Rags, Peat and Ashes on lowered terms.' Almost as an afterthought, but in capital letters this was followed by **'LONDON PORTER'**. This may have indicated that they were brewing London Porter, or more probably that it was an import brought up river by the same barges as the coal.

In the same paper on 27 June 1803 a malthouse was offered for sale, which by its description sounds like the malthouse later part of Greys Brewery. A dwelling house, offices, garden and spacious malting, malt and corn chambers, stabling and out buildings and large yard, on lease to Mr William Toovey which lease expires Midsummer 1803. None of the other malthouses in Friday Street would meet the requirements of this advertisement, and significantly there is no mention of a brewhouse.

By 25 June 1804, when in the paper, a meeting of all Maltsters and Brewers was being called to convene at the Catharine Wheel, Soundy and Byles, and Thomas Soundy were named among those calling the meeting. What it does not say is whether the participants were maltsters or brewers.

Fig 65 Greys Brewery B6, M19 & the Anchor, also M15 on north side of Friday Street O.S. map 1879 (reduced)

Henry N Byles was also a draper, linen and wool merchant, with premises on the corner of Bell Street and Market Place. Premises that his father John Byles had had in 1784. In 1809 H N Byles leased that property to John Butler finally selling to him in 1823[427]. However already on 23 April 1821 Byles announced in the Reading Mercury & Oxford Gazette that he was giving up the drapery business and handing over to J Butler. He also stated that he was continuing at his brewery in Friday Street 'where families may be supplied with Genuine Ales, Table Beers and Porter.' Also that because of the lowered price of barley and hops that he was lowering his price for ale to 10s the barrel.

It is probable that the brewery was started by Thomas Soundy and H N Byles in about 1803 or soon after. Street directories of 1823,30,44 and 47 say Henry Byles brewer Friday Street,

427 O.R.O. Cooper & Caldecott Abstract of Title C11 (29)

some giving his full name Henry Nathaniel Byles. By 1850 a directory says 'Byles & Son (East India Pale Ale & Porter) Friday Street'. In 1852 and 54 it is still Byles & Son, though one 1854 directory says 'Thomas Fox Alexander Byles, brewer Friday Street.' In 1863,67,and 1869 T F A Byles was still there, but by then it had become 'Byles & Co.' In 1877 it was 'Byles & Co brewers, maltsters, & Wine & Spirit Merchants, Greys Brewery Friday Street.' By 1883 it is just 'Greys Brewery Co Ltd. Walter Henry Harrison manager.'

The Registers of Licenses show that Byles & Co were still running the Greys Brewery up to 1880, but after that it was just listed as Greys Brewery, until 1885 when Holmes and Harper are named as managers. In 1892 up till 1896 the managers were Frederick Herbert Holmes and John Henry Steward.

In 1896 Greys Brewery together with its various pubs, many of which were leasehold, was bought by Brakspears. Soon after, the brewery, the malthouse and also some of its pubs were closed.

Greys Road

M 21 Malthouse at Dirty Bottom

Dirty Bottom was the common name for the lower end of Greys Road in the 18th and early 19th centuries.

Where exactly the malthouse was situated is not known, it is mentioned in the Will of James Roomes written in 1828 and proved in 1833. As it was said to be in Rotherfield Greys, it must have been either on the south side of Greys Road, or if on the north side of the road west of Tuns Lane. There is no mention of it in the Tithe Award of 1844 for Rotherfield Greys, but a study of the map (Fig 64) shows that the houses at the corner of Reading Road with Greys Road had behind them a yard with sheds running along the Greys Road side, and an extremely large shed across the end of the yard. This large shed may have been a malthouse, by 1844 no longer in use as such, the whole of the corner premises were then owned by John Plumbe and let out to various tenants.

Before 1793 it was owned by Joseph Rackstraw. The Reading Mercury and Oxford Gazette of 26 August 1793 announced the sale of property belonging to the late Mr Rackstraw, amongst which was a freehold estate consisting of 'a large malthouse which will wet 30 quarters a week, with barley loft over that will contain 300 quarters, and a dry loft for 1,000 quarters. A large screening room and every convenience for Welsh coals, conders and billets. A very good pump, two stables, a cow house, two piggeries and a large yard. All situated at Dirty Bottom, Henley late the property of Joseph Rackstraw.'

Earlier on 6 August 1782 Joseph Allright Rackstraw tallow chandler, soap boiler , grocer and maltster took out insurance with the Royal Exchange Insurance Co (No 84227) on various properties and on his malthouse lofts granaries and sheds adjoining brick stone and timber pannelled with brick (except part of one side of the malthouse which is lath and plaister) in the Parish of Greys. On adjoining house also. Tenant - Thomas Gregge grocer.

Rackstraw probably purchased the malthouse in 1782, shortly before taking out insurance, since on the Fawley Court Estate Map of about 1782, now in the River & Rowing Museum, there is written in the corner between Reading Road and Greys Road the words 'late Peter Sarneys Malthouse.'

It probably ceased being used as a malthouse after 1833 when James Roomes died.

Hart Street North side

M 22 27 Hart Street

The malthouse behind 27 may still have been in use till the mid 19th century, or even slightly later.

The Bridge Rent Book of 1886 No 6 says 'The Trustees of Mrs Mortimer late Hugh Barford formerly Hugh Keene for a house malthouse and garden adjoining No 5' (25 Hart St) 'formerly in the occupation of Joseph Brown since of Chas Towsey and now of Miss Hone. 2d.'

Charles Augustus Towsey was a wine and spirit merchant listed in Hart Street in directories of 1863-9. Hugh Barford was listed as a maltster 1823-54, and Hugh Keene as a maltster in 1785 and about 1793.

On 25 October 1787 Mr Hugh Keene took out insurance with the Royal Exchange Insurance Co. (No.103977). 'On a dwelling house situate on the north side of Hart Street in the occupation of Mrs Stable. Brick lath and plaister built and tiled £200. On a malthouse and storehouse adjoining together and to the said house but having no communication with the same. Brick lath and plaister built and tiled £200.'

Evidently the house and malthouse were separately occupied as early as 1787, and may have been for a hundred years before that. It is the same site as the *Bull* in Hart Street, which seems to have ceased trading during the 17th century, the malthouse may have originated when the *Bull* was in business.

M 23 31-33 Hart Street

The malthouse behind this house which is sometimes referred to as Armistice House, a name by which it was known in the 1920s and 30s when it was a temperance hotel, has a long history.

Deeds in the Oxford Record Office go back to an indenture of 1621[428]. A will of Anne Gooding widow dated 13 February 1698/9 left the property for life to her nephew Thomas Frost maltster, it was then described as a messuage malthouse orchard and garden in Hart Street then in tenure of William Toovey. The property after the death of Frost was to go to his daughter Anne, who however died an infant. There was another daughter Elizabeth, and later after the death of Anne two more daughters Anne and Elianor. In 1717 Frost before his death sold the lease to Thomas Grassingham. However Samuel Smith husband to Elizabeth claimed the property and there followed a series of transactions. In 1723 Smith sold to Sarah Froysell of Henley widow for £175. At that time the property is described as being between the messuage of Francis Blandy on the west and the messuage of William Forster surgeon or his under tenant on the east.

By 1812 a lease granted to Mr John Paulin all that messuage with malthouse buildings lofts and granaries garden yard etc heretofore in the occupation of Thomas Staverton since of Mrs Anne Staverton (both deceased) and late of Mr Pickman.

The Henley Rentals echo the descent of the property starting in 1713/4 with 'Thomas Frost late in tenure of Ford. Grassingham who was in occupation 1721-1734 and then in 1737 Staverton. In 1807 it was Mrs Staverton's executors, in occupation P Pickman and in 1814 occupied by Paulin. In 1836 and 1842 it was Matthews late Staverton occupied by Prowse. Street directories from 1842-69 show Richard Prowse was a corn dealer, so it is possible that the malthouse remained in use up to about 1869.

428 O.R.O. Cooper & Cadecott C14 (1-42)

According to the Bridge Rent Book of 1886 the property at that time was occupied by Harry and Tom Marsh, who were photographers. The rent book continues 'late by Richard Prowse formerly Peter Matthews for a house gateway and garden formerly in occupation of Richard Prowse then of the Misses Prowse and now of Messrs Marsh Bros.'

There is no mention in 1886 of a malthouse but it had been a well built brick construction. In 1789 Mrs Anne Staverton widow had taken out insurance with the Royal Exchange Insurance Co (No 110568) 'on her dwelling house brick except a small part lath and plaister and tiled situate in Hart Street £500. On a granary and malt loft over brick built and tiled belonging £50. On a malthouse lofts and granaries adjoining belonging brick built and tiled £100. On a Granary belonging timber built and tiled £50.' The insurance expired in 1793.

B 6 & M 24 Adjoining the churchyard

A Brewhouse is mentioned in the Henley Rentals of 1704-06 when Adam Springall paid 11d for a Brewhouse next door to the house now Longlands, the Brewhouse was between Longlands and the church. In 1713-14 Mrs Bridget Springall paid, and in 1721-22 Mr Sayer paid the 11d for the Brewhouse in tenure of — and Rudyard. Mr Sayer was paying the 11d in 1733-34 though now it was in the tenure of Hemscombe, and he was also paying for an encroachment of railings. In 1737 Mr Rich Bullock late Sayer paid 11d for two houses next the churchyard, and by 1745 he was paying for two houses formerly a Brewhouse. By 1758 the payments were being made by W Prince and the two houses were described as Bullock's houses.

From theses Rental entries it would seem that the Brewhouse ceased operating between 1734 and 1737, and was replaced by two houses on the site. Adam and Bridget Springall were relatives of Thomas Springall who owned the house now known as Longlands, and the Prince family continued at Longlands until about 1836. The Springalls and Mr Sayer were owners of pubs in the town and probably used the brewhouse to supply them with beer. There is a strong possibility that at the beginning of the 18th century there may have been a pub at Longlands, or rather at the house on the site, before Longlands was built in possibly the mid 18th century.(See Unknown pub No 137).

The malthouse may have been at the back of the Brewhouse and later behind the houses which were between Longlands and the west end of the church. The houses were taken down in about 1830 to enlarge the churchyard and to give space to rebuild Longland's Almshouses. However there is no sign of any malthouse in a sketch made in 1830 showing the houses and the churchyard, at that time there were piggeries in the back gardens. The malthouse may have gone out of use at the same time as the Brewhouse in about 1735, its only mention is earlier than that.

The malthouse is mentioned[429] as 'a parcel of ground where a malthouse and dwellings lately stood in the churchyard.' The deed is dated 19 May 1699, when Will Barrett and Ursula his wife and others granted the property to James Lane.

Earlier even than 1699 there seems to be proof that the site of the house now Longlands and the neighbouring houses may have been a Brewery with probably also a malthouse. Deeds recently found in the Town Hall, owned by the United Schools Charities are concerned with a property in New Street, shown in Fig 67 as houses 2 & 3. These were afterwards exchanged by Brakspears for 33 New Street as explained in M39. On a plan drawn up in 1726 of all the property owned by the Charities, it shows what was then a single house with to the south the garden of Mr Prince, who was then at Longlands. The earliest deed for the same house is one dated to the 7th year of Edward VI (1554 or 1555) when it says extending to the garden of John Lewys to the

429 Hughes 786 AD514

south, and in 1610 another deed says William Lewys to the south. The will of William Gravett in 1624 left the New Street property which he had lately purchased from Nicholas Woolley to the Warden Bridgemen etc of Henley for supplying money to the Free Schools. In this deed of 1624 its says the property to the south was that of William Lewes.

That the Lewys/Lewes' were brewers is very likely as in the list of 'Typplers' of 1532 or 1533[430] the name of Thomas Lewes appears five times standing as surety to five alehouse keepers. It is probable that he was at the site of Longlands and was the father of John Lewys/Lewes.

If the malthouse was behind a Brewhouse it seems very likely that the two buildings formed a brewery, in use during the 16th , 17th and early 18th centuries.

Hart Street South side

M 25 Malt Mill & Malthouse 6-8 Hart Street

The malt mill seems to have been situated at about 6-8 Hart Street which may have been at one time a single plot. Henley Rentals of 1713/4 mention a malt mill. The position of the entry in the Rentals, which says 'Mr Arthur for part of his shoppe where a malt mill stood,' places it on the corner of Barlows Yard. The entry to the yard was between 6 and 8 Hart Street. In 1721/2 the Rental says 'Mr Brinscombe for his shoppe where the mill stood.'

Although Barlow's Yard had by the 19th century become a back yard containing slum housing, and the houses on the front divided into small properties, it was probably originally a working yard behind a substantial house with a central yard entrance.

In 1735 Richard Darby and Dinah Day had a marriage settlement drawn up[431] which concerned property on the south side of Hart Street, there were two houses with malthouse which may be identified as at 14-16 Hart Street (M26) and another messuage malthouse garden etc which was at 6-8 Hart Street. The information about this last malthouse comes from a document found among the Town Hall documents, when on 11 June 1818 the last owner of the property William Day appears to have died intestate, and a limited administration was granted.

This deed of 1818 refers to the original marriage settlement and says a messuage malthouse garden etc on south side of Hart Street in possession of Richard Darby between a messuage late in the possession of Thomas Rickford Taylor and then John Mattingley on the east and of — on the west. Given to Richard Darby by the will of Richard Whiteseed. Since the position of the two messuages at 14-16 Hart Street says that they were between Thomas Taylor maltster on the west and William Turpin butcher on the east it seems to show that the properties were separated by the house of Thomas Taylor. Also in the Henley rentals for 10 & 12 Hart Street in 1769 and 1765 it says Mr Harris late Taylors now Abe Round, and back in 1745 it was Mr Taylor for his house.

10-12 Hart Street ?

It is possible that there was another malthouse behind 10-12 Hart Street, since it was clearly occupied in 1735 by Thomas Taylor maltster. However so far no mention of a malthouse on those premises has been found. Interestingly 10 was the site of the *Vine,* until it was demolished to make way for the bank, now Barclays.

---

430 Briers, P M 'Henley Borough Records 1395-1543' 1960 Ox Record Soc also Introduction p7

431 See note 425 p288

M 26 14-16 Hart Street

These two houses in the 18th century were jointly owned and 16 had a malthouse behind it. A marriage settlement of 23 April 1735 between Richard Darby of Henley maltster, Miss Dinah Day and Samuel Darby of Henley maltster says 'Two messuages or tenements with malthouse, bakehouse, granary, outhouses, yards gardens etc. on the south side of Hart Street in occupation of Thomas Alleway glazier and Thomas Viccars maltster between the messuage in possession of Thomas Taylor maltster on the west and the messuage in possession of William Turpin butcher on the east' (see M25)

Subsequent entries in Rentals, street directories and the Bridge Rent Book of 1886, place the malthouse as behind 16 Hart Street.

M 27 18 Hart Street

The Bridge Rent Book of 1886 No 25 says 'George Riggs late Hugh Barford formerly Hugh Keene for a house and malthouse etc. The malthouse being now in his own occupation and the dwelling house lately occupied by Mr George Pearson now Mr John Roberton 6s.'

This malthouse was probably in use right up to the end of the 19th century, street directories show that George Riggs maltster was in Hart Street in 1877, and Thomas Riggs maltster in 1887 and 95.

On 25 October 1787 Mr Hugh Keene of Henley maltster took out insurance with the Royal Exchange Insurance Co (No 103977) 'On household furniture in his house in Hart Street £100. On utensils and stock in trade in his malthouse, granaries, storehouses and offices adjoining together to his said house but having no communication therewith. Brick and stone and timber panelled with brick (except part of the said granaries and part of the upper part of a woodhouse which is timber built and tiled) £400. On utensils and stock in trade in his malthouse lofts granaries adjoining situate in Hart Street £400.'

The Reading Mercury & Oxford Gazette 26 November 1798 advertised that the three storied house was to let together with a good malthouse which will wet 39 quarters per week, with granaries and store rooms late in the occupation of Mr Hugh Keene deceased.

Henley Rentals and the Reading Mercury & Oxford Gazette show that 'Hugh Barford late Keene' had this malthouse 1823-62, and Mr Keene from 1775. Before that there were from 1765-9 Thomas Lovejoy, 1758 C H Sayer, from 1737-49 Turpin and from 1721-34 Thos King. It is possible that the malthouse was only built in the mid 18th century as Turpin was a butcher and not a maltster (M25). Though given the pattern of later lettings, the house seems often to have been let separately from the maltings, so it is a possibility that William Turpin butcher merely rented the house.

In the Reading Mercury & Oxford Gazette of 20 December 1862 the malthouse was advertised for sale by the executors of the late Mr Hugh Barford. It was described as malting premises with a dwelling house. The house and gardens were let to the Rev William Chapman at the rent of £25 p.a. and consisted of an entrance hall, two sitting rooms, kitchen and scullery with rooms over, wash house and brew house. Six bedrooms and water closet, together with china and linen closets. At the back there was a courtyard and the malthouse. The malthouse was 90ft long and had two working floors, 15 quarter cistern, barley and malt lofts, screening room and every convenience for an extensive trade. At the rear of the malthouse there was stabling, a piggery, sheds and a walled garden. The maltings were let at £26 p.a. to Mr T B Riggs. Land Tax £2 4s 6d. Bridge Rent 6s. The whole property was held for the residue of a 2,000 year lease which commenced on the 5 December 1676 at a peppercorn rent.

Since the date given is 1676 that may have been the date when the present house (Fig 52) was built. Stylistically that would be a possibility. Its position on the main street, as one of the more important burgage plots in the town probably means that it replaced another house on the site. Whether there was a malthouse behind it in 1676 or even earlier is unknown, but that is also a possibility, though a malthouse before that date may have been behind the kitchen, as said by Dr Plot (see Introduction p2) so it could be that the malthouse also dated from 1676.

(B 3) & M 28 20 Hart Street

The Union Brewery may have started at 20 Hart Street, at the *Union* pub, in the mid 19th century. There was a malthouse behind the *Union* (Fig 52). In the Reading Mercury & Oxford Gazette of 1 June 1829 there were building materials advertised for sale, being part of the materials of a large malthouse, pulled down and lying on the premises of Mr Leaver's in Hart Street. A street directory of 1830 shows Frederick Leaver as landlord of the Union, and he was probablv there in 1829. Nothing except the name connects the brewery to the *Union,* and the fact that Frederick Paulin landlord of the pub in 1868-9 was a brewer at the Union Brewery.

However Edmund Chamberlain of the *Queen's Head* was also a brewer connected to the Union Brewery, and it is likely that the brewery was at the *Queen's Head* (see entry for the *Queen'sHead.*)

M 29 40 Hart Street

The Bridge Rent Book of 1886 No.22 says 'Mrs Dobson late Wm Powell formerly Thomas Toovey for a house etc formerly a malthouse adjoining No.21 on the west side, late in the occupation of Wm Jackson, since of Mrs Crew afterwards of George Pearman and now of Thos Seymour.'

Street directories give George Pearman as a boot and shoemaker 1863-77, Mrs Maria Crew's girls' school 1847-50, and William Jackson's school in 1830.

Henley Rentals in 1828 and 23 have Toovey occupied by Jackson 13s 4d. In 1807 it was 'Mrs Toovey house and premises late Flight now Brakspear 13s 4d.' In 1800 it was Toovey late occupied Flight now Hayward, and in 1795 Toovey late Milner now Hayward & Co. Earlier rentals have in 1793 Toovey occupied by Milner and in 1775 Mr Rose in occupation of Floyd, Branscombe and others 13s 4d.

On 16 April 1788 Mr Thomas Toovey of Nettlebed gentleman took out insurance with the Royal Exchange Insurance Co (No. 106301) 'On a house malthouse, granaries and lofts adjoining in Hart Street, brick and timber pannelled with brick and tiled. Tenants Messrs Milner and May.'

It would seem that it was a malthouse throughout the 18th century, the names of the occupants are those of maltsters, and that it ceased functioning between about 1807 and 1820. Again it is a property which may have been a pub (see the *King's Head*).

Market Place South side

M 30 9 Market Place

There was a malthouse behind 9 Market Place, which together with the house during the 18th and early 19th centuries was always linked with 7 Market Place. The malthouse and both

7 and 9 Market Place are described in the accounts of the *Black Horse and Farrier*, the *Crown and Thistle* and the *Crown*, all of which were at 7 and 9 Market Place.

B 7 The Cannon Brewery, 15 Market Place

15 Market Place is now the *Argyll*, but was the *Cannon Inn* at the time of the brewery, which was probably started at the *Cannon* beerhouse in the upper Market Place in about 1838. The brewery was transferred in about 1843 to 15 Market Place, where it remained till its closure in about 1871. Further details are given in the accounts of the *North Star*, the *Cannon Inn*, and the *Hop Leaf*, all three of which preceded the *Argyll* on the same site (Figs 6, 23 & 26).

M 31 21-23 Market Place

The Bridge Rent Book of 1886 No 37 says 'Ann Ive late Joseph Dobson formerly Charles Slater for a house and malthouse etc. adjoining No 36 on the west side, late in the occupation of Charles Slater since of George Bennett and William Dobson and now of A Ive & Co and H Simons. 6d.'

No 36 was the Bridge Rent for 19 Market Place, and was also in the possession of Ann Ive, widow of Alfred Ive. 19 and 21 Market Place were taken over later by John Lovibond & Sons Ltd. and then Victoria Wine. However on examination of the actual houses and roof lines, it is evident that 21 Market Place was joined to 23 Market Place rather than to 19. The Bridge Rent No 37 applies to the two houses 21 and 23, and the malthouse shown on the O.S. map of 1879 was behind 23.

Street directories show the Ives as brewers and maltsters, and from 1823-63 William Dobson was also a maltster. Henley Rentals have in 1842 'Bennett occupied by Dobson 6d.' In 1836 'Bennett occupied by Dobson and Benwell 6d.' and in 1828 'Matt Slater occupied Dobson and Bennett.' From 1814-23 it was 'Slater occupied Dobson and self 6d'. Slater whose trade was 'breeches maker' seems to have been in occupation from 1769, and there were usually at least two occupants of the two houses, though it is probable that the malthouse was separately run.

Two advertisements in the Reading Mercury and Oxford Gazette of 20 May 1811 and 29 June 1812 refer to the houses now 21 and 23 Market Place and the malthouse behind. In May 1811 the premises were for sale by tender and were described as two messuages or tenements, malthouse, garden and premises. The two dwelling houses were brick and tile, and the malt-house will wet 12 quarters at a wetting. Now in the occupation of Mrs Harman, Mrs Sharp and Mrs Rance. The second advertisement of June 1812 has almost identical wording, including that the premises were extensive and well adapted for trade being in the centre of the Market Place or suitable for conversion as a manufactory. The occupants in 1812 are given as Mrs Harman, Mr Sharp and Mr Slater.

On 3 November 1789 Mr Mathew Slater breeches maker and Walter Knight of Ruscomb, Berks, Esquire took out insurance with the Royal Exchange Insurance Co. (No 113799) 'On a building in two tenements and malthouse adjoining, brick timber lath and plaister built and tiled, situate in the Market Place in Henley. Tenants the said Matthew Slater and others £300.' This insurance continued until 1792.

A fortnight earlier, on 21 October 1789, another insurance was taken out by Mr Pickman of Wallingford maltster (No 113597) 'On utensils and stock in trade in a malthouse lofts granaries and outhouses adjoining, brick and timber pannelled with brick and plaister built and slated, situate behind the dwelling house of Matthew Slater breeches maker near the Market Place in Henley.'

M 32 29-31 Market Place

These houses were two of the three demolished to make a northern entrance to Greys Road Car Park. Before demolition in the 1950s the three properties were used as one, being the site of Burgis' Stores since about 1903. Before that the two houses 29 and 31 had often been linked together, and had probably been at one time one house (see the *Seven Stars*).

The sale of the two houses in 1751 was by Thomas Tidd who sold to Joseph Arnold. They were described as 'two messuages with backsides, gardens, granaries, and malthouse, on the south side of the High Street near unto the Cornmarket between the messuage late in the possession of James White on the east' (the *Rose and Crown*) 'and the messuage in possession of Zachary Sarney on the west' (the *Butcher's Arms*) 'extending to the High Street on the north and towards Dirty Bottom on the south.'

The malthouse is mentioned in the sale of both properties in 1776, and again when offered for sale in the Reading Mercury and Oxford Gazette of 31 August 1812. At that time they were advertised as two freehold dwelling houses, a Malthouse, and seven brick and tiled new erected granaries, as well as lofts sheds etc. and a walled garden. The whole property 390ft in depth and 51ft wide. In occupation of Mr Richard Paulin and Mr William Cooper, both tenants at will .

It appears that up to 1812 the malthouse was still in use, since the granaries were 'new erected.' The properties were sold in 1814 but separately, and after that the malthouse does not seem to have been used for malting. From the deeds of 1814 it is clear that the malthouse was behind the more easterly house or what would have been 29 Market Place.

B 8 & M 33 37-39 Market Place, the Ive Brewery

The two houses have one entry in the Bridge Rent Book of 1886 No 43 which says 'Messrs Ive Brothers late Anna Deane for a house and premises adjoining No 42 (the *Swan* Fig 47) on the west side, part thereof lately in the occupation of Anna Deane the other part formerly occupied by Joseph Soundy since by H W Godfrey and now converted into a Brewery. 2s.'

If street directories are a guide, the brewery only came into being in about 1883 or just before. In 1883 Ive & Co are listed as brewers, wine, spirit and beer merchants at 19, 21 and 37 Market Place. Before that in 1877 and 1876 Ive & Co were wine, spirit and beer merchants at 19 and 21 Market Place only, and even earlier from 1842-69 Alfred Ive is given as a wine and spirit merchant in the Market Place. The last entry in street directories for the Ive Bros is that of 1915, by 1920 they are no longer listed.

Henley Rentals show that in 1842 Deane was in his own occupation paying 2s, in 1836, 1828,1823 and 1814 it was George Deane occupied by self and Soundy 2s. In 1807 Rackstraw paid 2s and the premises were occupied by Mr Soundy, and before that in 1800, 1795, 1793, 1790, 1785 and 1775 it just says Jos Rackstraw.

A deed of the School Charities concerned with the *Swan* (35 Market Place) in 1803 says 'to the west late Richard Martin and J A Rackstraw now Deane and Soundy.'

The only earlier Rental that can be linked to the property is that of 1745 which says 'Mrs Stiles for the *Woolpack* now Rackstraw 2s.'

It seems that although the brewery only began in the late 19th century, the property had malting and inn keeping associations long before. Joseph Rackstraw is listed in a street directory of 1784 as a grocer, soap boiler, tallow chandler and maltster. In the directory of about 1793 Joseph Soundy is listed as a maltster and farmer.

There is also the malthouse which still stands behind 37 Market Place, now known as St Mary's Hall. Interestingly on the side of the building, let into the wall now facing Greys Road

Car Park, there is a stone plaque which has the letters **R J H** and the date **1778** carved on it. If this stone genuinely belongs to the malthouse, then there is a possibility that it might have been built by Richard J Hayward. However since the stone is positioned on a side wall, it is unlikely that it is in its original place. In 1778 and up until the 1950s the wall would have been on the boundary of the property, and would have faced into the garden of 35 Market Place. If the stone belongs to the malthouse it would probably have been placed on its front wall, facing the yard of 37 and 39 Market Place.

M 34 55 Market Place

The Baptist Chapel, built in 1878, now stands on the site of where the malthouse and a house once stood. The Bridge Rent Book of 1886 No 45 says 'The Trustees of the Baptist Chapel late James Dobson formerly Tyrrell for a house and malthouse etc. late in the occupation of Wm Dobson and James Wm Talbot afterwards of Joseph Dobson and Elizth Townsend part whereof has since been pulled down and a chapel erected 3s 6d.'

According to the Rentals the Tyrrell family seem to have owned it from 1737-1842, though the occupancy varied. They also owned the malthouse M8 in Bell Street in the 18th century. Street directories give Joseph Dobson as a maltster in 1869, and William Dobson as a maltster 1847-63. They also show that James Wm Talbot was a clothier 1847-54. No Elizth Townsend appears in the directories but in 1863 a Mrs Sarah Townsend was a dressmaker and in 1877 a staymaker.

In the Henley Advertiser of 17 October 1874 Mr Joseph Dobson advertised his property for sale, as he had decided to leave Henley. Lot 1 was a dwelling house on Gravel Hill (the upper market was often referred to as Gravel Hill, and Gravel Hill as part of the Market Place) occupied by Mr Dobson and a shop and premises adjoining let to Miss Townsend at a rent of £20 p.a., and also the malthouse behind with a 15 quarter cistern.

It seems that the Bridge Rent Book of 1886 concerned two houses 55 and 57 Market Place, and while one remained with a malthouse behind it until its demolition to make way for the Chapel, the other was a shop and clothier's business.

However earlier Rentals seem to suggest that there were once three properties, which might have included 59 Market Place now called 'The Malthouse.' In 1842 the rentals say 'Tyrrell occupied Talbot,' in 1828, 1823 and 1814 'Tyrrell occupied Taylor and Maskell,' in 1807 'Tyrrell occupied C Applegarth,' in 1800,1793,1790 and 1785 'Tyrrell in own occupation,' and in 1779 and 1775 'Tyrrell in occupation Jas Armstrong.' The Court Baron Book of 1785 gives the first indication that there might have been three houses, it says 'J Tyrrell three messuages in occupation of Bowen Howard and Tyrrell.' The Rental of 1769 also gives three names 'J Tyrrell, Peter Stokes late Brinkus, Hollier and Armstrong.' Although there were three tenants and in 1785 three houses, it does not follow that the third house was 59 Market Place, there may well have been another house behind either 55 or 57, or one or the other was divided.

In the Royal Exchange Insurance Register (No 112575) John Tyrrell of Henley gentleman took out insurance on 27 July 1789 on his dwelling house brick lath and plaister built and tiled situate on the south hill above the Market Place in Henley £150. On his household furniture £50. On a malthouse and offices adjoining together and to his dwelling house but not communicating therewith brick lath and plaister built and tiled - Tenant Edward May. On a house adjoining his dwelling house - Tenant the said Edward May brick built and tiled £150. On offices adjoining brick and timber built and tiled - Tenant Charles Ballwood Esq £200. On a wash house and offices adjoining brick and timber built and tiled belonging £30.

Earlier on 14 March 1787 Edward May the younger of Henley maltster had taken out insurance on his belongings in a house in New Street, and a later note was added in 1789 that he had removed his belongings to his new dwelling house brick built on the hill above the Market Place and his trade to a malthouse and offices adjoining.

Mr Edward Ladd on 25 March 1789 had insurance on his house and malthouse at Northfield End (M7), and again added later, though the date was not specified, there was a note saying 'Removed to the house and malthouse late in occupation of Mr May on the hill in Henley.' He probably remained as maltster at these premises till 1799, since in the Reading Mercury & Oxford Gazette on the 17 June it was announced that a sale would be held of the furniture and effects of Mr Edward Ladd deceased of Market Place Henley.

Gravel Hill
or a continuation of the south side of Market Place

M 35 Possibly 13 Gravel Hill

This malthouse is mentioned in an advertisement in the Reading Mercury & Oxford Gazette of 5 November 1798. 'To be let a house and shop in Grocery and Bacon trade late in occupation Mr James Parsons deceased, together with a malthouse adjoining that will wet 24 quarters per week. Between 300 and 400 Hogs (besides porkers) are killed and sold at the above house during the season. Enquire of Mrs Parsons on the premises or of Mr Applegarth builder of Henley on Thames.'

That the premises were on Gravel Hill is confirmed by the advertisement in the same paper on 24 December 1798 when Elizabeth Parsons grocer and bacon seller of Gravel Hill widow of the late James Parsons thanked her friends, customers etc and said that her business had been taken by Mr William Taylor who begs the favour of their custom etc.

Mr Applegarth builder was probably nearby and the most likely houses for the Parsons and the Applegarths may have been what are now 13 and 15 Gravel Hill. On the O.S. map of 1879 (Fig 66) there is shown a long building projecting and attached to 13 which could have once been a malthouse, while the neighbouring house, which may once have included both 15 and 17 Gravel Hill had a yard with workshops behind it (In Fig 66 the modern house numbers are entered in brackets). Mr Applegarth is known to have lived in property somewhere on Gravel Hill since in his will of 1803 [432] his property was described as being 'situate in the Liberty of Baggeridge (Badgemore) in the Parish of Henley.' The houses on Gravel Hill until the end of the 19th century were still in Badgemore.

It is likely that the Parsons had been in occupation since at least 5 February 1788, since on that date Mr James Parsons took out a policy (No 105407) with the Royal Exchange Insurance Co on his household furniture in his dwelling house brick lath and plaister built and tiled situate on the hill in Henley. Also on his wearing apparel, and stock in trade.

There seems to be no suggestion that the Parsons or William Taylor were maltsters so perhaps the malthouse had gone out of use before 1788.

B 9 The Crown and Anchor Brewery, Gravel Hill

This brewery is mentioned in an advertisement in the Reading Mercury & Oxford Gazette

432 Information & copy of the Will kindly supplied by Mr E G Applegath of Alton, Hants a descendant of William Applegarth/Applegath

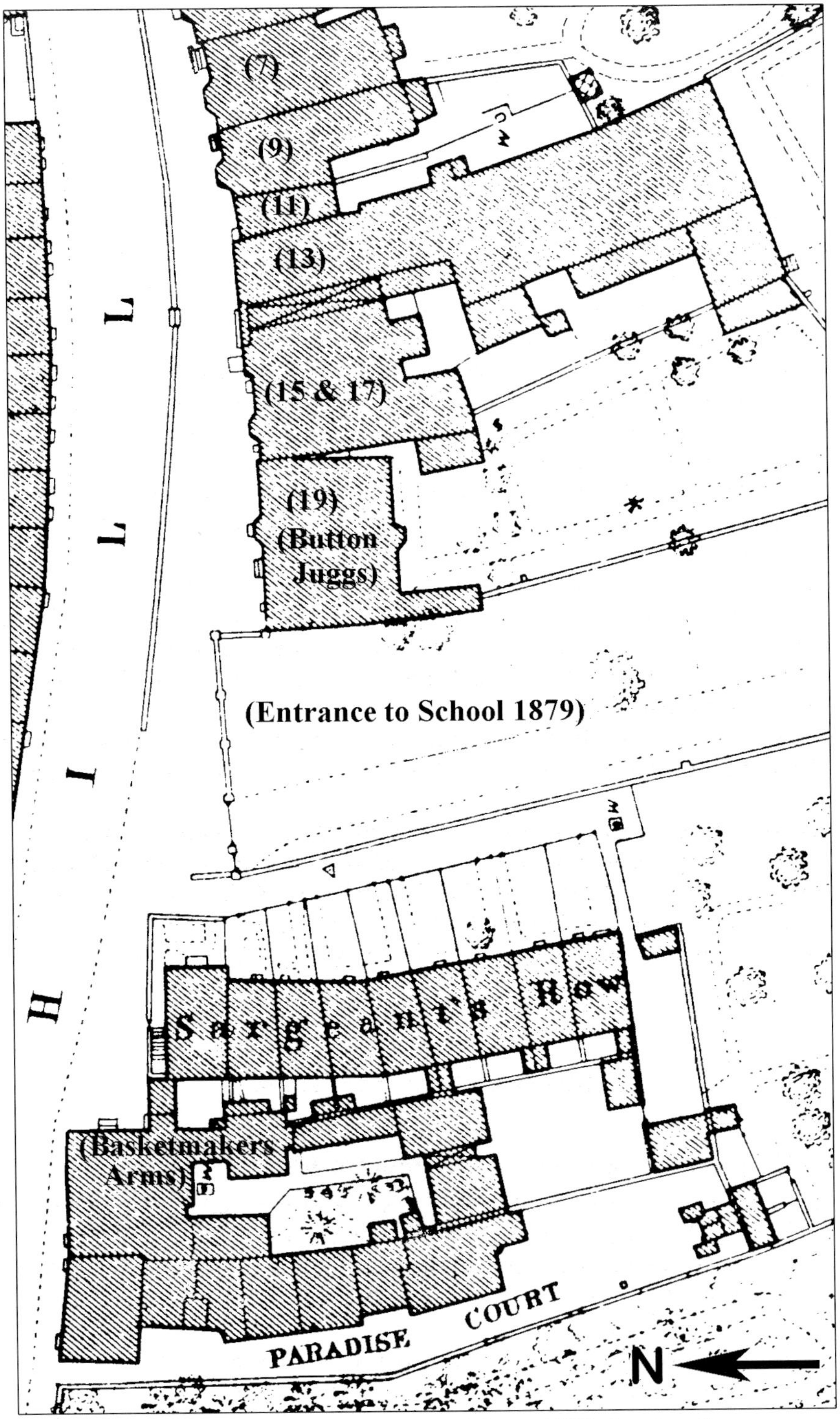

Fig 66 Part of O.S.map 1879 of Gravel Hill showing the Basketmakers Arms (see also Fig 8), and possible sites of B9,M35, & M36. (Modern numbering in brackets)

of March 1841, situated on the premises of the *Crown and Anchor* pub (see entry for the *Crown and Anchor*)

M 36 Above the Market Place on the hill

In the Royal Exchange Insurance Register (No 97350) on 22 April 1786 Mr Henry Newell of Shiplake took out insurance on a house brick (except a small part which is lath and plaister) built and tiled - Tenant - Francis Pease - situate above the Market Place on the hill in Henley £400. On a malthouse storehouses granaries and offices adjoining brick and timber pannelled with brick lath and plaister built and tiled situate near - Tenant - Thomas Drewitt £200.

Following insurance policies appear to be for the same property. (No 112000) 12 June 1789 Mr Joshua Rutland on household furniture in his dwelling house brick built and tiled situate on the south side of the hill above the Market Place in Henley £100. On his wearing apparel £30. On his plate £10. On his stock in trade in a malthouse lofts and granaries adjoining brick lath and plaister built and tiled situate near £450. On utensils and stock in trade in a barn belonging timber built and thatched £50.

(No 115097) 13 February 1790 Mr William James of Henley tallow chandler, soap boiler and grocer took out insurance on his house etc in Bell Street and also on a house brick except a small part which is lath and plaister built and tiled situate above the Market Place on the hill - Tenant - Joshua Rutland. On a malthouse storehouses granaries and offices adjoining brick lath and plaister built and tiled situate near.

(No 115635) 1 April 1790 Mr Joshua Rutland maltster on utensils and stock in trade in a malthouse lofts and granaries adjoining lath and plaister built and tiled situate in the Market Place Henley.

The whereabouts of this malthouse remains in doubt, it may have been above the Market Place on Gravel Hill or perhaps on West Hill. If on Gravel Hill it would not have been at 13 since the Parsons seem to have been there already in 1788, and although there is a suggestion that there could have been a malthouse behind Button Juggs (now 19 Gravel Hill - Fig 66), at that time it was two small cottages and not a single house. It seems more likely to have been on West Hill.

Market Place North side

B 10 The Crown Brewery 22 Market Place

This brewery was started by G Rawlins in 1829. He advertised in the Reading Mercury & Oxford Gazette on 10 August 1829 that he had opened a Retail Brewery in the Market Place next door to the bank. The bank was John Charles & Henry Simmonds' Bank at 24 Market Place, which was already there in 1823 and remained there till the 1890s when it moved to the new building in Hart Street now Barclays Bank.

Rawlin's advertisement for the Crown Brewery continued that he would be selling superior home brewed beer, and that no beer was allowed to be drunk on the premises being contrary to the law.

In the same paper G Rawlins advertised again on the 4 October 1830, when he said that due to the repeal of Beer Duties on the 10 October instant, he would be able to sell his beer at the following prices :-

X	Ale strongly recommended to families 27s per barrel
XX	Ale 36s per barrel
XXX	Ale 48s per barrel
XXXX	Stout at 72s per barrel

The Bridge Rent Book, no.60, for the premises in 1886 said 'R Mackay late William Lovegrove late William Hunt formerly G Rawlins for a house and premises on the north side of the Market Place formerly occupied by J T Mattingley since by Henry Horne afterwards by Frederick Haslam since by Wm Lovegrove and now by J W Walker.'

J W Walker provision merchant was there till at least 1928, after which it became the Worlds Stores. Lovegrove was a boot and shoe maker, while Mattingley was an auctioneer upholsterer and cabinet maker. Horne and Haslam are untraceable. Oddly none of the names appear in the Census Returns of 1841, 1851, 1861 or 1871, except for Mattingley in 1841, when he is entered as for 18 Market Place. However street directories show that in 1877 Lovegrove was at 22, while in 1883 Walker was at 22.

How long the Brewery continued is not known, in 1834/5 Mr Rawlins was given a Pew Faculty in St Mary's Church, which was awarded to the house in Market Place for ever.

26 Market Place ?

It is possible that there was a malthouse behind these premises in the 18th century, see the entry for the *Plough* Market Place. However no definite reference has yet been found.

M 37 28-30 Market Place

These two properties are now separate shops, but at one time were a single establishment. In 1752 the property, then a single house, came into the ownership of the Lord of the Manor, who at that time was Gislingham Cooper of Phyllis Court. This was because it had been owned by a Miss Jeffryes who was convicted of murdering her uncle, a retired butcher who had left her the property. According to J S Burn in his 'History of Henley,' published 1861, she was abetted by her uncle's gardener Swan, who committed the murder. The uncle, who lived at Walthamstow, had disapproved of his niece's loose behaviour with Swan, and had threatened to disinherit her. J S Burn continues 'the houses which came to the Lord of the Manor by this eschaet are those now occupied by Mr Bisley and Mr Neville in the Market Place.'

Gislingham Cooper died in 1768, and his widow Ann, together with their son the Rev Edward Cooper sold the Manor of Henley and Phyllis Court to Sambrook Freeman of Fawley Court. A deed of 1768 [433] says 'Messuage with malthouse and garden adjoining the *Kings Arms* in the Market Place of Henley' sold by Ann Cooper widow of Gislingham Cooper to Sambrook Freeman of Fawley Court.

The malthouse was almost certainly there in the 17th century as a deed of 1688 belonging to Brakspears concerning the *Kings Arms* (Fig 30) says that the messuage to the east was occupied by Thomas Coomey maltster. Another deed of 1791 says that to the east there was a messuage late of Matthew Chip, and then of William Irons maltster and then of John Neville baker. There is no further mention of the malthouse, the Neville's bakery business was at the property from at least 1785, and continued in the single house until 1846.

433 O.R.O. Cooper & Caldecott C1 (12-14)

In the Reading Mercury & Oxford Gazette of 6 June 1846 it says 'On Monday night about twelve o'clock the back part of the house occupied by Mr Neville in the Market Place fell in with a great crash. It had long been in a dilapidated state, and dangerous to the farmers attending the Market. The-premises are now in the course of demolition and two modern erections will be built on the site.'

After the rebuilding, Neville remained at 28 Market Place. In 1854 Benham a grocer was at 30 Market Place, and was already there in 1853 when Fawley Court was for sale, and Neville and Benham were the occupants of two houses in the Main Street. By the time of the Census of 1861, and which was also the date of J S Burn's 'History of Henley', Benjamin Neville baker was at 28, while Joseph Bisley master tailor was at 30.

West Hill/Street
or a continuation of North Side of the Market Place

M 38 Albion Place, West Hill/Street — possibly B11

In the will of James Roomes, written in 1828 and proved in 1833, he left a bed and bedding to his daughter Mary Ann Roomes, and the rest of his property to his wife Ann Roomes, which comprised 'the house or messuage where I now dwell with malthouse yard and appurtenances on the north side of West Street, also malthouse and storehouse at Dirty Bottom in Rotherfield Greys in own occupation (M21) also granaries and storehouses by Waterside at bottom of New Street and also farm land rented or held.'

It seems that the house in which James Roomes dwelt was on the site of Albion Place, and was demolished soon after his death, Albion Place already featured as a row of five dwellings by the time of the Census in 1841. In 1868 in the Court Leet Book of the Manor of Henley it says Joseph Partridge (late Bowling) owes the Lord of the Manor for five tenements and a gateway called Albion Place erected on the site of a house and malthouse late of Samuel Roomes. The Quit Rent owed was 2s 2d p.a.

Thomas Bowling in the Census of 1841 was living at 4 West Street, and it appears that he either bought or inherited Roomes' house and premises and was probably the builder of Albion Place. Thomas Bowling married Elizabeth Roomes, another daughter of James Roomes on 1 April 1820 [434], and their two eldest children had the second name of Roomes. At their marriage Mary Ann Roomes was one of the witnesses.

It is likely that the malthouse together with the neighbouring property on the west side may have constituted a brewery in the 18th century. The Court Leet Book again in 1868 has the entry 'H B Reynardson Esq (late Swallow) for a messuage and premises formerly a Brewhouse and on part of which premises part of Adwell Square hath been built by the late Mr Birch.

Adwell Square was probably built between 1858 and 61 on the site of Reform Court, the census of 1861 has entries for the square. A sale of 1875 describes the houses of Adwell Square as nearly new, while a sale of 1858 was for the sale of the houses in Reform Court, which featured in the Census Returns of 1841 and 51. Reform Court was probably in existence by 1820, since a Pew Faculty for Mr Roomes describing his house says to the west 'The Barracks'.

The Bridge Rent Book of 1886 says 'W J Birch Reynardson Esq late H B Reynardson late J W N Birch formerly Mr Swallow for house and premises formerly in the occupation of Thomas Swallow.' The Henley rentals shows that Swallow was there from 1765-1842, whether it was one

434 Parish Registers, Marriages 1813-43, Baptisms 1737-1812 & 1813-34

person or father and son is not clear, though perhaps the use of the name Thomas as separate from Mr Swallow in the Bridge Rent Book implies at least two people. The entry for 1785 in the Court Baron Book suggests a third generation, as it says 'Rich Swallow a Brewhouse formerly a Gateway next adjoining his dwelling late Wilkins'.

The Brewhouse was evidently there in 1785 and it is a possibility that it was used in conjunction with the malthouse next door to form a brewery. The Brewhouse must have gone out of business soon after 1800, and this may have been when Mr Roomes acquired the Malthouse.

New Street North side

B 12 & M 39 33 New Street

The Bridge Rent Book of 1886 No 103 says 'Messrs W H Brakspear & Sons Ltd late Roomes since John Sharp for a house and malthouse and premises adjoining No 102.'

Henley Rentals for the same property say in 1842 'Brakspear occupied by Alleway,' and in 1836 'Brakspear occupied Sharp.' In 1814-28 it was 'James Roomes occupied Sharpe,' in 1807 'Bush house and premises occupied Mr Pickman now Mountford,' and from 1785-1800 'Bush occupied by Pickman.' A street directory in about 1793 says Peter Pickman maltster of New Street, and another in 1830 says Richard Pickman and John Sharp both as maltsters in New Street.

On 5 January 1785 Peter Pickman took out insurance with the Royal Exchange Insurance Co (No 91595) 'on a tenement - tenant Dorothy Harris £150. On a tenement and malthouse adjoining £150. On utensils and stock in trade in malthouse £300. The above buildings are situate on the north side of New Street in Henley, they are brick and timber pannelled with brick except some small parts which are lath and plaister and weather boarded and tiled.' This insurance was continued till 1808.

In July 1789 an advertisement appeared in the Reading Mercury & Oxford Gazette. 'To Lett and entered upon immediately. A good House, newly improved and neatly fitted up, situate in New Street, consisting of two parlours, kitchen, pantries, cellars, four chambers, two servants rooms, wash and brewhouse, laundry, stable and hay loft, a well enclosed garden and summerhouse - Enquire of Peter Pickman in New Street aforesaid.' It would seem that Pickman did not wish to use the house, and so was letting it out, retaining the use of the malthouse for himself.

The Rentals 1814-28 show that James Roomes owned the premises at that time, but they were occupied by Sharp. It is probable that soon after 1828 John Sharp brewer and maltster bought the property and began a small brewery, possibly using the brewhouse attached to the house. In about 1830 beer duties were altered (see the Crown Brewery B10) and so small breweries became a better financial proposition.

According to Francis Sheppard in his book 'Brakspear's Brewery,' the brewery of John Sharp was bought in 1836 by W H Brakspear for the large sum of £700, thus removing a potential rival brewer from the vicinity of Brakspears.

The whole property seems to be one featured in a transaction on the13 August 1897 [435] when an exchange of property took place between Brakspears and the Charity Commissioners of Henley. The two properties exchanged were '1) a piece of land containing 34 sq yds or thereabouts and having a frontage to the south side of New Street with two cottages thereon. Nos 52 and 54 now or late in the occupation of Enos Clarke and George White.' (The street numbering is

435 O.R.O. Cooper & Caldecott C66 (15)

misleading, the south side of New Street was re-numbered drastically later to include the properties lying back from the street in the back alleys, which are many on that side of the road. The numbers quoted as 52 and 54 would by more recent numbering be in the 80s.) '2) a messuage No 33 or 35 New Street now in the occupation of Arthur Wright and containing 860 sq yds or thereabouts. They shall accept a lease for 21 years at £38 p.a.'

The purpose of this exchange was so that Brakspears might build the Mineral Water Factory, which was erected in 1897 on the site where the Charity Commissioners cottages had been (Fig 68 Houses nos 2 & 3). The two cottages were part of the Schools Charities, and in 1842-7 were in use as the National School, the Master and Mistress of which were John and Matilda Buckingham. The Bridge Rent Book of 1886 No 110 said of the site 'The Governors of the Henley United Schools for the old School House now two houses formerly in the occupation of Mrs Pottinger and Wm Bevan and since of Josh Bisley and Chas Johnson and now of C Bateman and Miss Littlewood.'

M 40 39 New Street

The O.S. map of 1879 shows that at that time there was a malthouse behind 39 New Street, which by then belonged to Brakspears. In 1879 there was a solid row of houses fronting the street, with only gateways beneath parts of the houses into the yards behind. There was no driveway to Phyllis Court at about 37 New Street, nor any wide entrance to the malthouse yard, neither was there a low wall topped by railings as there is today.

Fig 67 Brakspear's large malthouse M40 in New Street, with what was once the stable block at the back of the yard Photo 1998

It is probable that Brakspears bought the property in 1846. In the Reading Mercury and Oxford Gazette of 28 November there is an announcement of a sale of property which belonged to the late Mr R Pickman. Lot 1 was a freehold residence 'erected in a very substantial manner of modern elevation situate on the north side of New Street.' Together with a capital malthouse adjoining. 'Cistern capable of wetting 26 quarters, kiln in good order, well arranged lofts and every convenience for carrying on a first class trade.'

Since Brakspears seem to have bought the Brewery and malthouse of John Sharpe at 33 New Street in 1836 (B12 & M 39) and according to Henley Rentals were in possession in 1836 and 1842, it is likely that the property for sale in 1846 was 39 New Street and was then purchased by them. R Pickman was Richard Pickman; and is listed as a maltster in New Street in a street directory of 1830.

Soon after 1900 Brakspears re-built the malthouse into the massive three storied building which still exists, now turned into offices (Fig 67). The yard was also cleared and opened up, the old cottages known as Floyd's tenements being removed in the process (see entry for the *Red Cross* New St. Fig 37). At the same time a block of stables was built across the north end of the yard, which had all the latest features of stable design installed. They are now converted into apartments.

This malthouse became the main and only malthouse of Brakspear's Brewery, being large enough to deal with sufficient malt for the entire needs of the company. As a result the company closed all their other malthouses in the town, and by the 1920s after the closure of Ive's Brewery, when Brakspears remained the only brewery in Henley, this malthouse was the only one still working. It was closed down in 1972.

New Street South side

M 41 44 New Street

The malthouse behind 44 New Street is shown on the O.S. map of 1879. The Bridge Rent Book of 1886 No 117 says 'George Riggs for a house malthouse and premises in own occupation 2d' a note beneath says 'now owned by Mr J Putnam and the late Mrs J Putnam.' In 1903 Joseph Putnam and Sons tent makers are listed in a street directory in New Street, so it is likely that the malthouse closed between 1886 and 1903, it may have closed at the same time as the building of the large malthouse at 39 New Street by Brakspears.

Henley Rentals show that the Riggs family had been there since at least 1775, owning it probably from about 1790. Street directories show that in 1850 Henry Riggs, in 1830 Thomas Riggs, in 1823 Riggs and Son, and in 1793 John Riggs were all maltsters. The Rental of 1785 says 'Mr Mills occupied J Riggs 2d,' in 1779 and 1775 it says 'late Blackman now Mills in occupation of J Riggs' and in 1749 'Mrs Blackman now Nicholas.'

Presumably it was purchased by Riggs soon after 15 February 1790 when the Reading Mercury and Oxford Gazette advertised 'To be sold by Auction. Freehold estate in New Street consisting of a brick dwelling house containing a front shop and parlour, two front bedrooms and a garrett, a roomy kitchen with store room and convenient closets, good cellaring, with an extensive malthouse, two working floors, steeping cistern, drying kiln and barley loft, with every other requisite, out office, a small convenient garden walled round. The whole let to Mr Riggs tenant at will, at an old rent of £13 p.a.'

M 42 52 New Street

In the Royal Exchange Insurance Register on 20 December 1788 (No 109694) Mr William Deane of Henley maltster took out insurance 'On his dwelling house, wash house, malthouse and offices adjoining, stone built and tiled situate in New Street' value '£550. On household furniture therein £50. On Wearing apparel £20. On Utensils and Stock in Trade in the same £380.'

William Deane also paid insurance 'on two tenements lath and plaister built and tiled situate in New Street. Tenants — £50.' These were next door at what is now 50 New Street. The Bridge Rent Book refers in 1886 to 50 New Street as owned by Mr N Mercer and formerly owned by 'John Smith for two houses and premises then in the occupation of Gillot and Stone since pulled down and one house built.' Later from at least 1920 the house was used as offices by Blaker and Mercer solicitors and is still in use by Mercers.

An earlier insurance was taken out on 52 New Street on 20 March 1782 by Messrs Robert Appleton and John Shaw brewers and maltsters (No 83339). This was insurance 'On Utensils and Stock in Trade in malthouse, granaries and warehouse adjoining built in brick and stone and tiled on the south side of New Street behind a house occupied by Mrs Deane. £700.'

Henley Rentals of 1775 say 'late Mr Hayward in occupation of Mr Bowen now Abe Deane in own occupation.' In 1779 'late R Hayward late in occupation Mr Bowen now Mrs Deane.' In 1785 and 1790 'Dean in own occupation.' In 1795 and 1800 'Matt Haskey late Deane.' From 1807-1828 there is Smith, and in 1836 and 1842 W C Strange.

In 1823 Widow Smith in a street directory is named as a maltster in New Street, but W C Strange was a builder and manufacturer of Kiln wares at Fawley Court Kilns, and after his death in 1845 his sons sold off many of his goods and stock in trade; according to an advertisement in the Reading Mercury & Oxford Gazette. So it is likely that the malthouse, which was in use in the 18th century, ceased being used after W C Strange took over, which was between 1820 and 1834.

Pew Faculties give some indication as to the change over from Smith to Strange. In 1820 for Pew 37 it said 'A faculty to Elizabeth Smith, New Street, on the east John Strange, on the west — Gillett.' It is almost certain that at that date 54 New Street did not exist, it was described in a sales notice in May 1834 as 'newly erected' and that particulars could be had from 'Mr William Strange-builder at the house adjoining.' The neighbour to the east in 1820 was therefore John Strange at what later was to become the *Rose and Crown* (Fig 7). Gillett or Gillott as already mentioned was one of the occupants of the two houses then at 50 New Street.

The later faculty again for Pew 37 was in 1834/5, 'A faculty to the use of Elizabeth Smith now W C Strange and his family so long as they shall continue to occupy their present dwelling house situate in New Street.'

The Census Returns of 1841 has Wm Strange aged 35 bricklayer and his wife aged 40, together with their 13 year old servant at what is now 52 New Street. W C Strange was related to both the late John Strange of the *King's Arms* and the younger John Strange at 56 New Street, both of whom were also bricklayers.

By the 1851 census the house (52 New Street) was occupied by Nicholas Mercer and one servant. Nicholas Mercer continued there in both Census returns and street directories until between 1887 and 91, when William Mercer took over the house. Later Harry Blaker was there and by 1928 it was a private residence of a Mrs Durand

B 13 Brakspears Brewery, 80-88 New Street

This brewery is now the only remaining brewery in Henley and is situated at the end of New Street on the south side (Figs 68 & 69). The brewery was not originally Brakspear's, it was built by the Sarneys and Benwells, and Joseph Benwell continued to own it until about 1830, although he entered into a partnership with Robert Brakspear at the end of the 18th century.

The Mineral Water Factory already mentioned is at 80 New Street, while the company offices are at 82, 84 and 86, this last known as 'The Old Brewery House'. The premises extend across Church Lane to 88, which housed the coopering sheds and yard, and to the cottages on the river front, which were also owned by the company (see the *Anchor* Waterside & Fig 3).

There are four entries in the Bridge Rent Book of 1886 for the whole property, Nos 107-110. The entries for 107 and 110 have already been quoted (see the *Anchor* and B12 & M39 exchange of properties). The other two, are for 'a house and premises late in the occupation

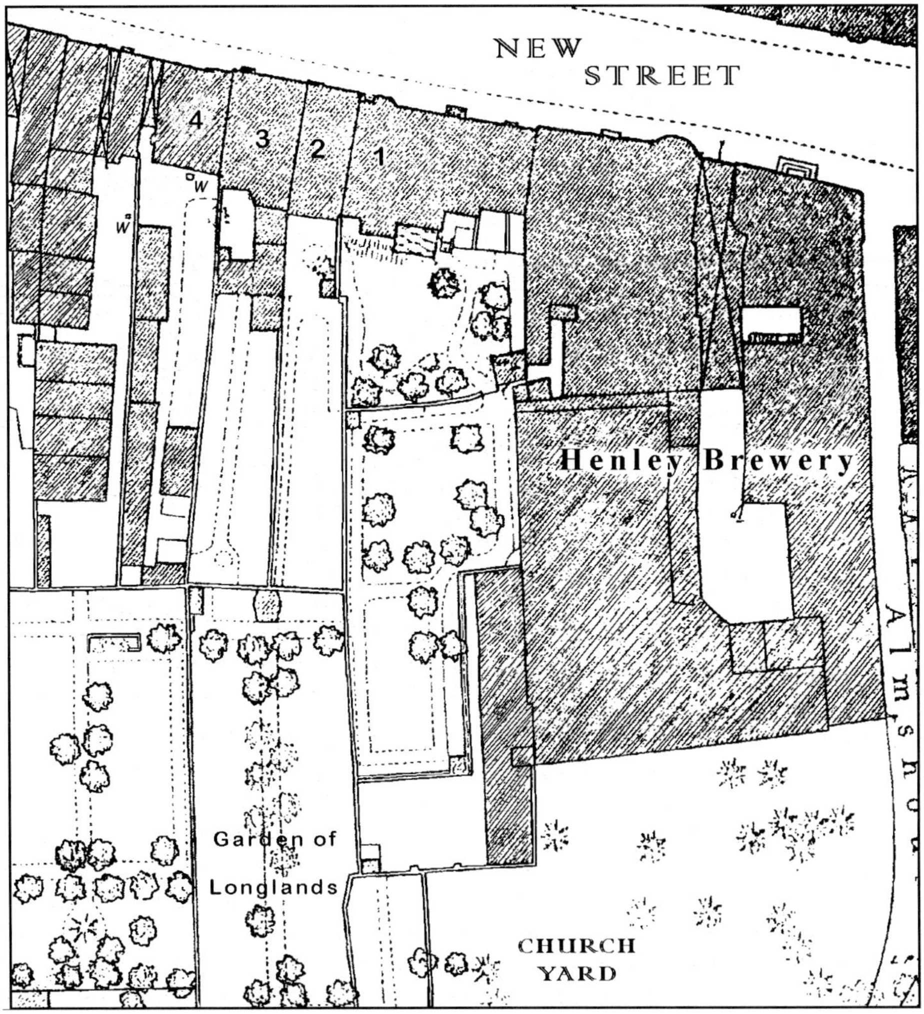

Fig 68 Part of the O.S.map of 1879 showing Brakspear's Brewery to the west of Church Lane and the four houses demolished for the Mineral Water Factory, here labelled 1-4. No1 appears to have been divided, half remains

of George Wright but now used as the Counting House 2s 4d.' and 'for an obit 6s 8d'. George Wright brewer in the Census of 1871 was living at the Old Brewery House, east of the yard entrance, together with a wife, 2 daughters 2 sons and 1 servant.

The Henley Rentals have the entries for 1836 and 1842 as Brakspear and Co. in own occupation, but prior to this from 1793-1828 it was Benwell occupied by Appleton. In 1790 it was J Benwell late Jemmett occupied by Appleton and Shaw and in 1779 and 1775 Mr P Sarney late occupied Sam Jemmett late Read and others now Appleton and Shaw.

On 1 February 1786 Messrs Robert Appleton and John Shaw of Henley brewers took out insurance with the Royal Exchange Insurance Co. (No 96425) 'On utensils and stock in trade in their Brewhouse storehouses and offices adjoining brick lath and plaister built and tiled £1500.' This was a vast sum of money in those days and far exceeds the value put on other property or stock in trade at the same period. The same policy continues 'On utensils and stock in trade in a malthouse and on the lofts storehouses granaries and offices adjoining brick and timber panelled with brick except a small part of the front of one of the lofts which is lath and plaister built and tiled situate in Bell Street £800.' This last was the malthouse at 74-78 Bell Street (M12) and even its value is greater than most house properties, which were around £250-£300.

Fig 69 Brakspear's Brewery B13, entrance to yard. On right curved bay of offices Photo 1995

A Pew Faculty of 1834/5 for the north gallery in the church says 'Granted 27 January 1787 to the freehold premises situate on the south side of New Street in the Parish of Henley in the occupation of Mr Robert Appleton brewer and to the occupiers of the said premises for ever. In 1817 occupied by Mrs Appleton.' This seems to have been the Old Brewery House to which this faculty was granted. At the same time another faculty was granted also dating from 27 January 1787, 'to the freehold premises situated on the south side of New Street in the Parish of Henley in the occupation of Mr John Shaw Brewer and to the occupiers of the said premises for ever, in 1817 occupied by Mr Joseph Appleton'. This faculty would probably have belonged to the house to the west of the Brewhouse (1 Fig 68).

In December 1808 at a meeting of the Court Leet of the Manor of Henley, it was noted that an encroachment had been made at the Brewhouse in New Street belonging to Joseph Benwell Esq of Battersea, in the occupation of Robert Appleton, by the building of a Bow Window in the front of the dwelling house, for which a charge was made of 2d. This refers to the projecting bow in front of the house and would mean that it was added between 1804, the date of the previous Court Leet, and 1808 when the charge was made (Fig 69).

The fullest account of the brewery is given in the Inventory and Valuation of the Brewery made on 1 January 1826, when the freehold was owned jointly by Joseph Benwell and W H Brakspear

> 'Brewhouse, New Street, on east brick erected residence formerly occupied by Mrs Appleton, fitted up and adapted to the accommodation of a respectable family with numerous rooms and cellarage and entrance from gateway of Brewery Yard and now used as a store. Faculty pew in church belongs to premises above. Counting House overlooking brewery entrance and yard.'
>
> 'No 2 a storehouse.
>
> No 3 Mens tap between which and the Tun room is a staircase leading to room over the Counting House and to mens sleeping room. No 2 Table beer. Tun room No 4 spacious store with lumber room over. This completes line of building on East side.'
>
> 'At extreme top of the yard is a spacious store No 5 with corn and hop lofts over, in the front is a lean to cooper's shop. This forms the boundary on the south side.'
>
> 'On thc west side is the brick erected Mill house with three floors and lofts over a lofty brewhouse with cooler room over.'
>
> 'No 1 Strong beer store and Tun room in front of which and towards the yard is a lean to shed. Nos 6, 7,and 8 vat and strong beer stores.'
>
> 'The whole enclosed by folding gates.'
>
> 'Separated from the Brewery premises by Church Lane (Fig 68) is a tenement for two families with paved stable yard, newly erected Dray house and stable and loft over. Chaise house and Riding Horse stable enclosed by gates.'

(This would have been what was later to be the coopering shed and yard). Next come the four cottages on Waterside

> 'A cottage near the Waterside at extremity of New Street, brick and timber built but in bad repair and at present untenanted. 3 rooms.' The other three cottages of the same size are listed with their tenants, Mrs Ivermee, Edward Pearce and J Bucket.

After this comes the house to the west of the Brewhouse, (1 Fig 68).

> 'Spacious and well arranged Family house, New Street, adjoining the Brewhouse now in the occupation of Mr Appleton. Numerous well arranged rooms and domestic offices, cellar (part of which is used in the trade), well planted garden, yard and well of water. Faculty Pew in church.'

This Mr Appleton would be Joseph Appleton mentioned as having the faculty in 1817. Lastly in this section of the Inventory is the next house.

> 'Dwelling house adjoining the above for accommodation of a family, with yard and garden, now in the occupation of Mr T Knight. Right to a pew in church.'

In the Pew Lists of 1834/5 there seems to be no separate faculty awarded to this property but a

Mrs Knight had a seat in a pew (No 32) together with a Mr Hussey and wife. It may be that in 1826 there were two houses, which by the time of the O.S. map of 1879 are shown as one house (1 Fig 68), and the Right to a pew was derived from the faculty awarded to the larger section of the property.

The house lived in by Mr Knight cannot have been the house shown as 2 in Fig 68 as up until 1897(see exchange of properties M39), that was part of the schools property and not owned by Brakspears. As early as 1726 when plans were drawn up of all the properties owned by the Schools Charities[436] , the house which on the plan of 1879 is shown as two cottages (2 & 3) was termed the Free School Master's House, and on the east side of it the occupants of the neighbouring house were listed as the Rev Mr Jas Birch, Tho Colier & Danl Smith. So clearly in 1726 there was already multiple tenancy of the property.

The Inventory after these houses begins its list of pubs and other properties owned jointly by Benwell and Brakspear, then the copyholds and leaseholds, then the freeholds of Brakspear alone, followed by his lifeholds and leaseholds. Following these there is a comprehensive list of the Plant and Utensils of the Brewery. The value of the entire business including Good will was £ 47,772 19s 0d in 1826.

---

436 Plan of properties belonging to United Schools' Charities 1726 now in O.R.O.

INDEX

Index of Personal & Company names

Names of Publicans accompanied by dates, other persons without dates. When Fore-names or Initials not known names shown as **. Position in Text indicated by name of pub, page number or by B or M, which refers to numbered Breweries or Malthouses.

****

Ladd
Edward M7,M34
Lake
LThos 1933-6 *Dukes H*
Lamb
J M G 1957-72 *Angel on B*
Lamberd/Lamport
widow ** *White Lion*
Lamborne/Lamden
J 1721-7 *George* DkSt/MkPl
Lambourn
Henry 1851-4 *Swan* GsH
Lanchbury
Alfred,Jane,Thomas *Clubhouse*
Lane
James B 6, M24
John p14
Mr & Mrs ** *Angel R*
** *Kings H*
Langley
Hezekiah 1861-71 *Jolly Farmer, Broad Gates*
Langton
Mr ** *Shears/Turks H,Fishermans Cot, Waggon & Hs*
Large
Henry 1887-8 *Anchor* FSt
Larner
William 1911-13 *Queens H*
Latter
The Misses ** *A E Hobbs*
Laud
Archbishop Wm *Bell*
Laud's Charity
Sun NEnd
Lawrence
Edmund H 1887-8 *3Tuns*
John 1850 *Hope*
William M3
Lay/Laye
George 1892-3 *Travellers R*
G W 1950-77 *Sun* NEnd
Thomas 1887-9 & 1893-6 *Hope*
Victoria M 1977 *Sun* NEnd
Lea/Leay
Thomas 1664 *White Horse*, p18
Leadbetter & Bird High Wycombe
Bird in Hand , p5
Leaver
Fredk 1830-51 *Union*, B3, M28
Richard M3
William 1789-97 *Blue Black-smith*
William B1
** *Blue Bell*
Lee
Major ** p14
** *Chequers*
Leftly
Fredk W 1924-8 *Crown* MkPl
Lennox
William *White Horse*
Lenthall/Lentall
Thomas 1821 *White H & Star*
Lester
Alfred P *Crown & This*
Leveque
Jean P 1988-95 *Red Lion*
Levitt
Ernest W 1904-7 *Feathers*
Lewendon/Lowendon
Fredk 1912-20 *Cannon* MkPl
Lewington
Arthur *Welcome Tavern*
John 1769-87 *Blue Blacksmith*
John 1820 *White Lion*
** 1814-6 *Greyhound*
Lewis/Lewys/Lewes
Daniel 1863-80 *8Bells*
1881-7 *Cannon* MkPl
Daniel *Broad Gates*
D W P C 1966-9 *Lion*
Eliz 1844 *Swan* GsH
Harry G 1928-9 *Dukes H*
John 1587 *White H on B*
John B6, M24
Michael 1877 *Kings A*
1879-81 *Cannon* MkPl
Thomas pp7,8, B6, M24, *Unknown pub* No139
S S H 1952-68 *Jolly* ***Waterman***
William B6, M24
Lilly./Lilley see also **Lylly**
Francis *George* DkSt/MkPl, B2
Lind
Mrs ** *Chequers*
Liney
Sidney 1914-16 *Swan* GsH
Lindforth
William S 1889-90 *Hope*
Lintell
Thomas 1826 *Ship*
Little
Charles 1841 *Swan* MkPl
Littlewood
Miss ** B12 M39
Livingstone
Thomas 1817 *Greyhound*
Lloyd
James 1875-8 *Cannon* MkPl
William 1882-3 *Black Horse*
Lock
A R 1985-6 *Edwardian*
Lockyer
Arthur 1917-19 *Bear*
Lofting
Samuel 1845-7 *Blue Bell*
Loftus
William 1800-7 *Turks H*
Loizou
T G 1957-60 *Imperial*
London
** *Blue Bell*
Long
Caroline 1840-7 *Longs Stout H*
Charlotte E E *Cannon* MkPl
George W 1823-40*Longs Stout H*
Herbert H *Cannon* MkPl
Longland's Charity
Angel on B
Losewell
Hen p7
Lothian
S P 1992-93 *Argyll*
Louise
'Princess' *White H & Star*
Lovegrove
Daniel M12
William B10
** 1727-34 *Shears*
Lovejoy/Lovejoye/Lovjoy
Andrew *George* HSt
Charles 1851-4 *Oxford A*
John 1851-4 *Hope*
John,Sarah,Sarah,Sarah *Clubhouse*
Joseph 1899-1900 *Dukes H*
Mary 1851 *Hope*
Thomas M27
Loveles
Jane *Cath W*
Lovell
Charles 1841-61 *3Tuns*
Lovering
John *George* HSt
John Lovibond & Sons Ltd
Rose & C MkPl, M31
Lowe
Rich M3
Lowendon see **Lewendon**
Lowthman
Wil p7
Lucas
C A 1948-53 *Lion*
Richard *Bird in Hand*
Messrs ** *Vine* HSt
Ludlow see **Rudd-Ludlow**
Ludovic/Ludwig
C L 1910 *Imperial*
Luen
Hen pp7,8
widow ** 1704 *Sun* MkPl
Lunnon
widow ** *Clubhouse*
Lyde
Johan *Cath W*
John pre1499 *Cath W*, p8
Ric p8
Robert *Cath W*
Lyle
Sidney 1899 *Crown* MkPl
Lylly see also **Lilly**
Olyver pp7,8
Lytching
John *Red Lion*
Lytle see **Brooks**

****

McAnulty
J P 1956-7 *Dukes H*
McCann
Amelia 1926-8 *Imperial*
McDermott
William p20
McGuire
J M 1977-80 *Imperial*
P F 1987-9 *Cath W*
Machin
Edward *Our Mutual F*
Gabriel *Bear, Crown & This*
Mackay
R B9
Mackenzie
W D M15
Mackie
E G L 1984 & 1987-8 *Dukes H*
MacLennan
Colin 1960-1 *Cath W*
McNally
L G 1975-8 *Dukes H*
MacQueen
Fredk 1914-21 *White Horse*
McVicker
Mary 1890-3 *Angel on B*
Maddox
Thomas 1886-7 *Saracens H*
Madgwick
James 1938-55 *Oddfellows A*
Maidment
Chas W 1903-21 *Basketmakers A*
Kate 1921-7 *Basketmakers A*
Major
John 1811-23 *Blue Bell*
Richard 1820-32 *L W Hart*
Malmesbury
'Lady' *Red Lion*
Mancey/Mancy/Mansey
Eliz 1847 *L W Hart*
Henry 1842-4 *L W Hart*
Manley
Edward J 1957-72*BasketmakersA*
(cont...)

Perlinge
Thomas M3
Perrin
Harriet 1841 *Horse & G*
Joel 1818-40 *Royal Oak , Blue Blacksmith*
John *Broad Gates*
Perryer
M G 1968-87 *White Horse*
Pescud/Prescud
Alfred, John, Sarah M3
Peynter see **Painter**
Pfyl
E R 1968-86 *Bear*
Phebe/Phebey/Pheby
Dan 1850-1 *White Lion*
Phelps/Philps
James 1714 *Bear,* M4
Philip
Daniel *White Lion*
N W *Queens H*
Phillips
Ernest E 1897-1905 *Sun* NEnd
Francis S C 1909-10 *Red Lion*
** 1769 *Barge Pole*
Phoenix Insurance Co M2
Pickernell
James 1896-1900 *3Horseshoes*
Jonathan 1867-71 *White Hart*
Rosina 1871-7 *White Hart*
Pickman
Eliz *George* HSt
J M16
Peter*George*HSt,M23,B12M39
Richard p3, B12 M39,M40
** M31
Pierce see **Pearce**
Piercy/Piercey
Henry *Broad Gates*
John *Chequer*
Richard *Broad Gates*
Thomas p16
Pigden
Annie *Basketmakers A*
Sarah 1864-7 *Carpenters A*
Sarah A 1869-99 *Carpenters A*
William 1850-63 *Carpenters A*
Piggott
Samuel 1882-96 *3Horseshoes*
Pike
James W 1869-70 *L W Hart*
1871-2 *Sun* NEnd
James *Jolly Waterman*
Pinder
Richard 1636 *Elephant*
Pine
Thomas W 1912-28 *Dukes H*
Pinna see **De Pinna**

Pinniger
Francis J 1890-1 *White Hart*
Mr ** *8Bells*
Pipe
Roger 1963-4 *Cath W*
Pisani
Giaccome *White Hart*
Pither
J L *British Workman*
Pitman's Brewery Goring
John & Anne Pitman *Red Cow, Rose & C* NSt, *Angel* R
Player
James *White Lion*
Plot
Dr ** pp2,4, M27
Plumbe
John & Charles *Queens H*
John S *Elephant,Longs Stout H*
John M21
William *Shears/Turks H FishermansCot, Waggon & Hs*
Plummer
R H 1955-7 *Horse & G*
Plumridge
** *Red Cow*
Poffley
William1884-92*RedLion*WSt,p24
Poore
James 1816 *White H & Star*
Thos 1821-6 *Sun* NEnd
Portello
W F *George* DkSt/MkPl, B2
Porter
Florence M 1949-62 *Swan* Gsh
Herbert E 1938-49 *Swan* GsH
Joyce *Swan* GsH
Pothecary
Alfred R 1907-10 *Red Cross* NSt
Potter
Richard 1847-77 *Kings A*
Pottinger
Mrs ** B12 M39
Pountney
A G 1990-1 *Cath W*
Powell
Peter M 1965 *Cath W*
William *Kings H ,* M29
William *Vine* HSt
Powes see also **Gough**
John 1541 *Cath W*
Powle
Rich 1625 *George/Crowne* DkSt/MkPl
Powney's Dower
Packhorse
Powny
Richard 1774-80 *Packhorse*
Powys
Mrs Lybbe *Bell*

Poynder
C M9
Pracey/Prascey
Edward 1751-65 *Red Lion*
Pratt/Pratte
John 1437-8 *Bull* HSt
Robert 1847 *Ship*
Thomas 1478 *Bull* HSt
T *Angel on B*
William *White H & Star*
Preedy
C H 1927-9 *Olde Bell*
Prescott
Thomas C & Mrs 1958-74 *L W Hart*
Preston
E D 1967-80 *Bull* BSt
Prewett
Frank G 1936 *2Brewers* R
Pride
Thomas *Windmill*
Prince
Amos(carrier) 1883 *Bull* BSt
Ann, W & J *unknown pubNo139*
Eliz *Black H & F/ Crown & This*
Henry 1878-9 *Red Cow*
W B5, M24
Prior
Charles 1896-9 *Red Cross* NSt
Dorothy 1851-4 *Dukes H*
Jesse 1841-7 *Dukes H*
Prosser
James *White H & Star*
John *Kings A*
Prout
Campbell 1887-8 *Vine* HSt
Prowse
Richard & Misses M23
Prussia
'King of" *Red Lion*
Pullen
O T 1898 *Royal Hotel*
Punter
Henry 1875-6 *Duke of C*
John 1877 *Duke of C*
Purbrick
Mary 1770 *Rose & C* MkPl
Purton
F 1941-51 *Kings A*
Pusey/Puzey
John *White H & Star*
Thomas 1876-94 *Red Cross* NSt
Putnam
Joseph & Mrs J M41
P E 1964-5 *Red Cross* NSt
Putnam & Sons M41
Pyman
** *Lamb & Flag*
Pyrry
Hen p7

****

Quelch
** 1745-9 *Rose & C* MkPl
Quiney
Ann 1841-51 *2Brewers* R

****

Rackstraw
Joseph A 1745 *Woolpack, Swan* MkPl, B8, M21,M33
Timothy *Greyhound*
William 1775-85 *Greyhound*
William *Black H & F*
William *3Tuns*
widow ** 1769 *Greyhound, Butchers A*
Ractliffe
C A 1973-88 *Red Lion*
Rames
Mr** p11
Rance/Rannie
J 1823 *Row Barge*
Moses 1712-34 *Row Barge*
Robert 1737-71 *Row Barge*
Thomas 1775-95 *Red Lion* WSt
Mrs ** M31
Randall
Henry T 1899-1901 *Jolly Farmer*
Mary 1785 *Kings A*
Ratty
J A *Cath W*
Ravenscroft
George *Boar,* M6
Rawle
Jack E 1939 &1945-59 *White Horse*
James A 1930-9 *White Horse*
James W 1948-64 *White Horse*
Rawlings/Rawlins
Charles 1877-81 *Red Lion* WSt
Emma 1881-4 *Red Lion* WSt,p24
Emma & Charles *Packhorse*
George *Chequer,* M16
G B10
Rawlyns
Ralph *Bull* HSt
Rawlynson
Rob p7
Read see also **Reid, Rede, Reede**
Albert & William *Our Mutual F*
John C 1905-6 *Royal Oak*
** B13
Rebecca
2Brewers R

Saywell
Edward M11
Scheibner see also **Brice**
Fredk H R 1913-7 *Angel on B*
Schireburne/Schyrborne
Thom & Eliz 1337 *Turnours*, p5
Schomaker
W p7
Scott
James B 1984-96 *Jolly Waterman*
Thomas A 1913-15 *Queens H*
T *Ship*
Scouse
Edward J 1950-66 *Carpenters A*
Seaton Carew see **Carew** &
Kinch
Selassie
Hail *Cath W*
Seymour
Henry 1871 *Duke of C*
John R 1979-85 *Horse & G*
Robert *Oxford A*
Thomas 1863-71 *Red Cross* NSt
Thomas 1873-4 *Oxford A*
Thomas *Kings A*, M29
Shackleton
Sidney 1944-6 *Cath W*
Shadwell
Stephen 1713-21 *Shears*
Shard
Rob 1649-65 *White H on B*, p18
Roger 1629-31*White H on B*, p18
Sharp/Sharpe
James 1870-1 *Cannon Inn, Hop Leaf*
James (sen) p3,
James (jun) pp3,4
Jenkins *Row Barge*
John p3, B12, M39, M40
Joseph M9
Margery M3
Mr ** & Mrs ** M31
— 1814-16 *Crown & This*
Shaw
James *Bear*
John 1852-4 *Crown* DkSt
John *Anchor* Wside, *Broad Gates*, *Kings A*, *Red Cross* NSt, *3Tuns* pp2,17, B13, M12,M42
** c1740 *Chequers*
Mrs ** M2
Shawcross
James W E 1997-99- *Red Lion*
Shefford
Thomas *Bear/Boar*
Shenstone
William *Red Lion*
Shenton
David J A 1995-98 *Argyll*

Shephard/Shepherd/Sheppard/Shepperd
Charles L 1892-1907*Broad Gates*
E T *3Horseshoes*
Francis *Jolly Waterman, L W Hart,Oddfellows A, Row Barge, 3Tuns* B12, M39
Henry *White Hart*
Sidney 1914-29 *Wheatsheaf*
Thomas 1888-91 *Cath W*
Thomas 1888-98 *Red Lion*
Tracy *Clubhouse*
** 1828 *Blue Bell/2Brewers* HSt
Sherratt/Sharratt
Edwin 1886-7 *Hope*
Sherry
Wm Oliver 1910-2 *Sun* NEnd
Shrimpton
John 1841 *Swan* MkPl
Siberechts
Jan *Angel on B, Brewers A , Carpenters A ,Cock, Marquis of G, White H on B*
Sim
Winifred 1965-77 *Red Cross* NSt
Simeon/Symeon
Edmund *Holie Bush Crown/George* DkSt/MkPl
Simmonds/Simonds/Simmons/Simon/Simons/Symonds/Symons etc.
C *Brit Workman*, M9
Francis 1713-34 *Waggon & Hs*
Francis *Crown & This*
Fredk 1923-4 *White Horse*
George 1861 *Red White & B*
H M31
Henry B10
James 1906-7 *Victoria*
Joseph 1864-7 *Red White & B* 1869-71 *Bird in Hand*
Mary 1728 *Angel on B*
R F 1957-64 *Bear*
Robert M9
Thomas (**Homans** 1728 ?) 1728-37 *Kings A*
William M14
widow ** *Kings A, White Lion*,M14
** *Chequers*
** *Plough* MkPl
C&H SimmondsBank B10
J &C Simmonds&Co*Vine*HSt
Simmons & Lawrence M2
H & G Simonds & Co
Seven Bridges Brewery, Reading
Bird in Hand,BlueBell,Cannon Inn,Cannon MkPl,*Crown*DkSt, *HopLeaf,Horse &G,Lion,Royal Exchange*,p5

Simpkin
William *Half Way H*
Simpson
Symons J 1906-7 *Victoria*
William *Cannon* MkPl
Sims
William 1841 *Greyhound*
Singleton
Charles J 1895-9 *Royal Hotel*
Sizeland
Robert M3
Skillings
Lillian M 1963-85 *Oddfellows A*
Sidney L 1962-3 *Oddfellows A*
Skinner
Elias M3
Thos 1749 *Bull* BSt
Slater
Charles *Rose & C* MkPl, M31
Mattthew M31
Mr ** *Red Cross* Ass
Slator
Marian E 1995-99- *W Horse*
Robert E D 1995-99- *W Horse*
Smerdon
John 1899 *Dukes H*
Smith see also **Smyth**
Ada L 1935-7 *Wheatsheaf*
Arthur B 1893-4 *Angel on B*
Daniel B13
Eleanor 1878 *Red Cow*
Eliz M42
Francis 1898-1900 *Royal Oak*
James *Red Cow*
John 1871-2 *Half Way H*
John J 1931-5 *Wheatsheaf*
John M42
Joseph 1842-4 *Red Cow*
J *Red Lion*
Leslie H 1947-50 *Red Lion*
Riche *Red Lion*
Samuel 1881 *Queens H*
Samuel M23
Seth *Oxford A*
Sidney/Sydney G 1909-11 *Victoria*
Thomas *George* HSt
Thomas *Union*
Thomas 1759 *Row Barge*
Thomas 1863-77 *Red Cow*
Thomas 1878-9 *White Hart*
Thomas J 1907 *Feathers*
Thomas 1909 *Crown* DkSt
William *White Hart*
Corporal ** p14
Mr** M9
widow ** *Red Lion*
widow p3
W H Smith & Sons Ltd
Blue Bell, *2Brewers* HSt, M1

Smyth
Martha 1609 *Cath W*
Phil 1617/8 *Bull* HSt, *Cath W*
Ric p7
Will 1590 *Bull* HSt
Snell
William 1889-92 *Dukes H*
Snowden
S J *unnamed pub* No139
George T 1876 *Hop Leaf*
Soundy
George M19
Joseph *Swan* MkPl, *Woolpack*, B8, M33
Samuel B5, M20
Thomas *Anchor*FSt,B5,M15,M20
William M *Jolly Waterman*
William M15
Southwood
P A 1973- *Angel on B*
Spalding
Ruth *Bell*
Speakes
John 1940-5 *White Horse*
Spencer
George W 1869 *Royal Exchange*
Spicer
James 1823 *Greyhound*
William 1869-77 *Anchor* FSt
Spooner
John 1925-7 *White Hart*
Spratley/Spratly
Edward 1861-8 *Sun* NEnd
Edward 1870-1 *Swan* MkPl
Edward 1876-7 *Duke of C*
Edward 1882 *Hope*
Edward *Cannon* NEnd
John 1841-4 *Cannon* NEnd
Mary 1841-54 *Cannon* NEnd
Spray
L F 1937-8 *Angel on B*
Springall/Springal
Adam & Thomas *unnamed no139*, B6,M24
Adam *George* HSt
Augustine B4
Mrs Bridget B6, M24
Thomas *Broad Gates,White Hart*
Sprouk
Margery *Cocke*
Stable
Mrs ** M22
Stacey
Richard 1817 *3Tuns*
Mary 1820-3 *3Tuns*
Staley
Adrian N 1991-95 *Argyll*
Stalley
John *Bull* HSt

Stallwood
Henry 1861 *Carpenters A* GsR
Mr **(architect) *Blue Bell*
Staniforth
Arthur 1918-21 *Crown* MkPl
Stannford/Stainford/Staniforth/ Stanniford
Henry *Red Cow*
Stapers
John *Cock* Wside
Stapledon
William *Crown & This/ Crown*MkPl
Stargatt
L 1968-88 *Saracens H*
Stark
Donald A 1962-7 *Royal Oak*
Stavaton/Staverton
Deodatus *Kings H*
Sibil & Thos *Kings H*
Thomas & Anne M23
Mr ** *White Hart*
Steer
H F 1936-40 & 45-52 *Anchor* FSt
Stevens
Abraham,Eliz,Margaret *Bell*
David *White Lion*
Gladys E (see also **Drayton**) 1940-6 *Crown* MkPl
Harry W J 1938-40 *Crown* MkPl
Henry 1739 *White Hart*
Henry 1883-92 *2Brewers* R
Henry *Cock* Wside
John 1636 *White Horse, Elephant*
Peter 1998-99- *Bull* BSt
Richard 1699-1701 *Bell*
William 1885 *Blue Bell*
William M1
widow (Mary?) 1701-8 *Bell*
Mr ** 1713/4 *Woolpack*
Mr ** *Swan* MkPl
** 1721/2 Red Lion
Mrs ** *White Hart*
widow ** M15
Stevens & Co
Thomas *Bull* BSt
Stevenson
Gregory 1705-20 *Red Lion*
Sarah 1720-34 *Red Lion*
Stewardsee also**GreysBrewery**
John H B5, M20
D Graham & Celia B 1993-99- *Bird in Hand*
Stewart see also **Stuart**
H D 1962-71 *White Hart*
Stiles see also **Styles**
Mrs ** 1745 *Woolpack,* M33
Stock
Charles 1737 *Brewers A*

Stockdale
Edward pre1713 *Cocks* MkPl
Stoke
Robert Dove 1886-7 *Blue Bell*
Stokes
Charles 1779-85 *Blue Bell*
Charles 1779-93 *Dukes H*
Peter M34
** 1795-1842 *Dukes H*
** pre1779 *Blue Bell*
Mrs** *Blue Bell, 2Brewers* HSt
Stone
F C 1953-7 *Lion*
Thomas 1780-94 *Clubhouse*
Thomas *Chequer*
Thomas p7
Mr ** p14
** M42
Stonehouse
Simon P 1995-99- *Cath W*
Stonor
Francis *Red Cross* NSt
Georgina *Bear/Boar,Bull* BSt,p21
John Bear, M4
Thomas *Bear,* M4
William *Bull* HSt
Strange
George A 1926-7 *Olde Bell,*
John 1791-1809*KingsA*, p15,M42
John *Rose & C* NSt, p13, M42
Sarah *Rose & C* NSt
William 1844-71 *Jolly Waterman*
William 1906 *Jolly Farmer*
William & Sarah M42
W C M42
Street
George 1901-2 *Bear*
Strong
Rob p7
Stuart see also **Stewart**
Charles 1895-6 *Queens H*
Stubbs
Henry *George* DkSt/MkPl, B2
Sturdy
** pre1838 *Bull* BSt
Styche
Harold J 1959 *Cath W*
Styles see also **Stiles**
H G 1937-8 *Queens H*
Sugre/Sygar
Tho *Cocke*
Sullivan
James 1903-5 *White Hart*
Summerby
David J 1955-66 *Red Lion*
Sumner
Mr & Mrs JB M2
Sury
Robert *White Hart*

Swadling
Ernest 1948-59 *Victoria*
Swallow
Rich M38
Thomas M38
Mr ** M38
Mrs ** 1807 *Elephant*
** *L W Hart*
Swan
** M37
Sweetzer
Alfred W 1935-8 *Sun* NEnd
Swell
A L 1951-6 *Row Barge*
Sygar see **Sugre**
Symes see **West-Symes**
Symons/Symonds see **Simmonds**

****

Tabard Inns *L W* ***Hart***
Talbot/Talbott
Eliz 1818-19 *Black Horse*
James W M34
Richard 1798-1811 *Angel* R
Tallant/Tallent
James 1830-54 *Angel* R
Tanner
Edmund 1860-70*Cannon Inn* , B7
Edmund *Blue Bell, Hop Leaf*
M J 1975-8 *Wheatsheaf*
Thomas 1809-16 *Broad Gates*
Valerie M (see also **Thomas**) 1978-99 *Wheatsheaf*
Tappern
Albert J 1929 & 30-1*Cannon* MkPl
Tapsfield
Ora K 1948-50 *Sun* NEnd
S R 1938-48 *Sun* NEnd
Tayler/Taylor/Taylour
Amelia 1918-9 *Rose & C* NSt
Bet 1789 *White Hart*
Ed *Plough* FSt, M19
George 1868 *L W Hart*
George 1871 *Travellers R*
Hamal M8
James 1792-3 *Bull* BSt
John M8
Matthew 1783-6 *White H&Star*
Richard1785-9 *White Hart*,p21
Richard *Victoria*
Richard p15
Thomas *Duke of C* , M8
Thomas M25, M26
William M35
William (poet) *Elephanrt, White Hart, White Horse*
** *Victoria*

Taylor & Co
Richard *White Hart*
Teffle
John M13
Terry
Mrs S *Brit Workman*
Testa
Ivy I E 1935-7 *Queens H*
Peter 1921-6 *Imperial*
1933-5 *Queens H*
Thackara
James,Ruth, William B2
Thackery
William 1815 *Angel* R
Thernal
Frank *Rose & C* NSt
Helen 1917-18 *Rose & C* NSt
Thomas
Valerie M (see also **Tanner**) 1978- 99 *Wheatsheaf*
Will 1673/4 *George* DkSt/MkPl
Mrs ** *Brit Workman*
Thomilthorpe
Thom 1624 *Bull* HSt
Thompson/Tomson/Thomson
George 1852 *Duke of C*
H W *Queens H*
Sam 1753-8 *Kings A*
Thorne/Thorn
Edward 1794-1800 *White Horse*
Thomas 1930 *Angel on B*
Thornett
Charles p20
Thurston
William D 1995-99- *A E Hobbs*
Thynne
V C 1970-75 *Cath W*
Tickner
N H 1948-55 *Wheatsheaf*
Tidd
Eliz,Mary,Thomas *7Stars,* M32
Tidy
** 1809 *Red Lion (Tap)*
Tilbury
Mr ** *Angel on B*
Tilby
Joseph 1869 *Jolly Waterman*
Tiller
Wm & Priscilla *White H & Star*
Tilt
Nicholas P 1997-98 *Kings A*
Tindall
Daniel pre 1785 *White Hart*
1786-91 *White H & Star*
Tipping
Fredk 1870-90 *Clubhouse*
Titcomb/Titcombe
John 1887-8 *White Lion*
William1887-96 *Jolly Waterman*

Todd
E P A 1931-7 *Imperial*
Toll
Solomon *Red Lion*
Tomalin
Henry *Red White & B*
Tomson see **Thompson**
Tonnjon
William P16
Toomer
David 1770-5 *Angel on B*
Edward M6
Hanah 1785-8 *Angel on B*
Toovey
John *Elephant*
Thomas *Kings H*, M15,M29
William B5, M9,M16,M20,M23
Mr * Mrs**1737-45*Waggon &Hs*
Mrs ** M29
Topping
John A & A 1991-92 *Argyll*
Towers
C 1904 *Oddfellows A*
Towner
Annie D (see also **Russell**) 1897-99 & 1905-6*Oddfellows A*
Cecil 1884-97 *Oddfellows A*
Townsend
Eliz M34
Fredk E 1915-17 *Bear*
Isaac 1840-1 *Clubhouse*
Jane, Marianne *Clubhouse*
Sarah M34
Towsey
Charles A *Bull* HSt, M22
W *Blue House, Sun* NEnd
Tranter
Harriet 1877-81 *Dukes H*
Joseph 1881-5 *Royal Oak*
Thomas 1847-54 *Jolly Waterman*
Thomas 1863-77 *Dukes H*
Miss ** *Dukes H*
Trimming
** *Red Cross* NSt
Tripp
Charles 1787-93 *Bell*
Trotman
Charles *Anchor* FSt
Charles *Cauliflower*
Fredk 1891-5 *Royal Hotel*
Trown
George 1904-5 *Dukes H*
Tucker
Arthur 1911-12 *Dukes H*
Arthur R 1942-6 *Cath W*
William 1851-4 *Royal Oak*
Tuckwell
Edward T1928-50 *CarpentersA*
Tunnell
Charles 1713 *Sun* MkPl
Turgis
F G 1950-9 *Queens H*
Turner
Ann,Mathew,Ann,Mary *Clubhouse*
Cornelius 1877 *Saracens H*
George 1928-31 *Sun* NEnd
Richard J 1996-99- *Argyll*
Samuel *George* HSt
Sidney M S 1917-18*Broad Gates*
Walter (see also**Savyn**)*Swan*MkPl
Stuart Turner Ltd *Broad Gates*
Turpin
William 1794 *Clubhouse*
William M25,M26,M27
Turrell
Mr ** *Brit Workman*
Turtle
E W R 1959-62 *Royal Hotel*
Twyford
Henry p10
Tyack
Geoffrey *Elephant*
Tyrrell
John *Duke of C*, M8,M34

****

Underwood
James B4
Robert B4
** 1727/8 *Cath W*
** 1733/4 *Red Lion*
Union Brewery
Queens H, Union, p4, M28
Usher
Eliz 1754 *White H on B*
Eliz *White Lion*
John 1721-33 *White H on B*
Robert 1723-65 *White H on B*
Robert *Angel on B*
Thomas *Angel on B*
Thomas 1841-69 *Basketmakers A*
William 1681 *White H on B*, p14
widow ** 1713 *White H on B*
** M17

****

Vaughan
James E 1905-11 *Saracens H*
Venables
Arthur 1816-21 *Bell*
William 1826 *White Hart*
Venezi
Robert 1914-17 Broad Gates
Vicars/Viccars/Vickers
John,Jane,Eliz *George* HSt
Thomas M26
** *Cocks* MkPl
Victoria
'Queen' *Queens H,*
Victoria'sJubilee *White H & Star*
Victoria Wine Co M31
Villiers
'Lord' *Bell*
Vinnicombe
William 1894-5 *Queens H*
Vokins
Alfred 1887-92 *Greyhound*
Mary A 1892-8 *Greyhound*

****

Waddington
J *Longs Stout H*
Wagge
Wil *Cocke*
Waghorn
Grace A 1908-9 *Red Lion*
Waite
Hugh p3, M1
John p3, M1
Waitman
John 1905-6 *Victoria*
Waitrose & Co M2
Wakling /Walkling
Henry 1875 *Swan* GsH
John(carrier) 1793 *White Hart*
Walden
A *Chequers,* p19
Waldron
Thomas 1861-3 *Blue Bell*
Thomas 1869-72 *Our Mutual F*
Wales
Edward 'Prince of ' *Feathers* p5
Fredk 'Prince of ' *Feathers* p5
Walker
Charles L 1950-1 *Angel* R
Hubert (**Walter**?) 1946-8 *Basketmakers A*
James pp19, 20
Stanley 1946-56 *L W Hart*
Walker's Stores B10
Walkling see **Wakling**
Wall
** 1745 *Broad Gates*
** 1749 *Bull* BSt
Waller
David 1869 *Swan* GsH
Wallingford Brewery
Crown MkPl, p5
Walsh
William *George* HSt
Walstead/Wilstead
William 1826-30 *Bear*
Walter/Walters/Waters
Francis 1784 *Newe Inn*
Harry 1911-12 *Oddfellows A*
Hubert see **Walker** (cont...)
Walter/Walters/Waters (cont...)
John/James1823-6*Crown&This*
William 1903-7 *3Horseshoes*
Warbeltone
Regin *Turnours*
Warcupp
Sir Ed p14
Ward
C C 1940-5 *Anchor* FSt
Edward 1793-1817 *Ship*
Frank M1,M3
Mary *Clubhouse*
Reginald G H 1899-1900*Anchor* FSt
Mrs R G H *Anchor* FSt
William 1854 *Victoria*
William(carrier) 1850 *White Hart*
Wargent/Wargeant
Thomas 1794-7 *3Horseshoes*
Waring
Mary 1755 *Bear*
Warner
J *Barge Pole*
Warrell
Walter 1868-9 *Duke of C*
Warren see also **Conti**
Leslie J 1948-50 *Angel on B*
Vera A 1948 *Angel on B*
Wassell
William G 1902 *Dukes H*
Waters see **Walter**
Watlington Brewery
Jolly Farmer, Victoria, p5
Waugh
Kate E G 1946-66 *2Brewers* R
Wayman see **Weyman**
Webb/Webbe
Anne 1754-64 *Red Cross* Ass
Charles 1830 *Packhorse*
Charles 1851 *Portobello*
Charles 1877-9 *Royal Exchange*
Ellis/Elys 1562-5 *Bull* HSt & BSt
Fredk 1880-2 *8Bells*
Fred *Broad Gates*
Grace 1789-93 *Red Cross* Ass
G W (architect) *Royal Hotel*
John 1774-88 *Red Cross* Ass
Mary *Clubhouse*
T *Blue Bell*
William 1753 *Red Cross* Ass
William 1861 *Union*
William 1887-8 *Bird in Hand*
Mr ** *Crown & Anc*
widow ** 1721-8 *Woolpack*
widow ** *Swan* MkPl
** *Bear/Boar*
Webb's Timber Wharf *Ship*
Webb's Travels p6
Webster
James W 1894-8 *Angel on B*

General Bibliography & References

1 Alehouse Keepers List O.R.O. AXVI 30 1817
2 Brakspear's Rent Ledgers O.R.O. Brakspear IV/i/l & IV/i/2
3 Briers,P M 'Henley Borough Records - Assembly Books i-iv 1395-1543' pub by Oxford Record Soc. Vol XLI 1960
4 Burn,John S 'History of Henley on Thames' 1861
5 Census Returns 1841-81
6 Climenson, Mrs Emily J 'Guide to Henley on Thames' 1896
7 Cooper, John 'An Account of the Charities under the Management of the Corporation of the Town' 1858
8 Court Baron Book 1785 - from copy made by Mr John Crocker- Rentals of 1785 made for the Lord of the Manor, contains similar Rental information to the Henley Rentals but with a few variations
9 Court Leet Book of the Manor of Henley 1787-1888 In Town Hall records
10 Gretton, Mary Sturge 'Oxfordshire Justices of the Peace in the 17th Century' pub Oxford Record Soc 1934
11 Greys Brewery Rent Ledger 1885-96 O.R.O. Brakspear IV/ii/l
12 Heming, Rev B C 'Survey & Fieldbook of the Parish of Rotherfield Greys, Oxfordshire' 1815 O.R.O.
13 Henley Advertiser - Microfilm Henley Library
14 Henley Charity Trustees 'Small Bridge Rents' 1886 -Town Hall
15 Henley Church Pew Faculties 1820, 1834 & 35
16 Henley Church - Registers of Baptisms, Marriages & Burials
17 Henley Rentals 1704-1842 - from copies made by Mr John Crocker
18 Henley Standard —Microfilm Henley Library & recent editions
19 Hughes, M W 'List of the Archives of the Borough of Henley on Thames' compiled Aug 1928-Oct 1930
20 Inventory & Valuation of the Brewery, New Street the property of Joseph Benwell & W H Brakspear. 1 January 1826. O.R.O. Brakspear VI/1
21 Kingsford, Charles L'The Stonor Letters & Papers 1290-1483' Vol II ed for the Royal Historical Soc 1919
22 Magistrates Special Session's Minute Book 1870-97 - Magistrates Court
23 Oxford Record Office various individual documents & deeds
24 Pearman, Rev M T 'History of the Manor of Bensington' 1896
25 Reading Mercury & Oxford Gazette 1785- Microfilm Henley Library
26 Registers of Licenses -
O.R.O. AXVI 30/1 F 114 & 115 1770-71,
O.R.O. AXVI 141-4 1877-81, 1892-1918
27 Registers of Licenses - Magistrates Court -
Borough Licenses 1887-91,1919-1999
Rural Licenses 1882-96, 1903-1999
28 Registers of Licenses for Berkshire - Berkshire Record Office- 1815, 1873, 1887-1955
29 Royal Exchange Insurance Register 1782- O.R.O. Brakspear X/1
30 Sheppard, Francis 'Brakspear's Brewery 1779-1979' 1979
31 Spalding, Ruth 'The Improbable Puritan' 1975
32 Street Directories -
Part of directory 1784, directory of c 1793,
Pigot & Co 1823,1830, 1844
Post Office 1842,1847,1854,1869,1877)
Snare's 1847 Slater's 1850
Robert Gardner's 1852 Billing's 1854,
Dutton Allen 1863 Melville 1867
Cassey 1868 Harrod 1876
Kelly's 1883,1887,1891,1895, 1903,1911, 1915,1920,1924,1928,1931,1935,1939,1942
Bennett's Business 1898,1904
Oxford & District Trade 1908-9
Cope's 1910
Reading Berks & OxfordTrade1922-3,1925-6
33 Tyack, Geoffrey 'The Rebuilding of Henley on Thames 1780-1914' Oxfordshire Local History Assoc.Vol 3 No 2 Spring 1989
34 Victuallers Recognizances 1753-1822 (not Henley Town) O.R.O.
35 Weaver, J R H, & Beardwood, A, 'Some Oxfordshire Wills' pub Oxford Record Soc 1958
36 Wills & Inventories of 17th C. from Henley Evening Class under the direction of Miss Joan Dils

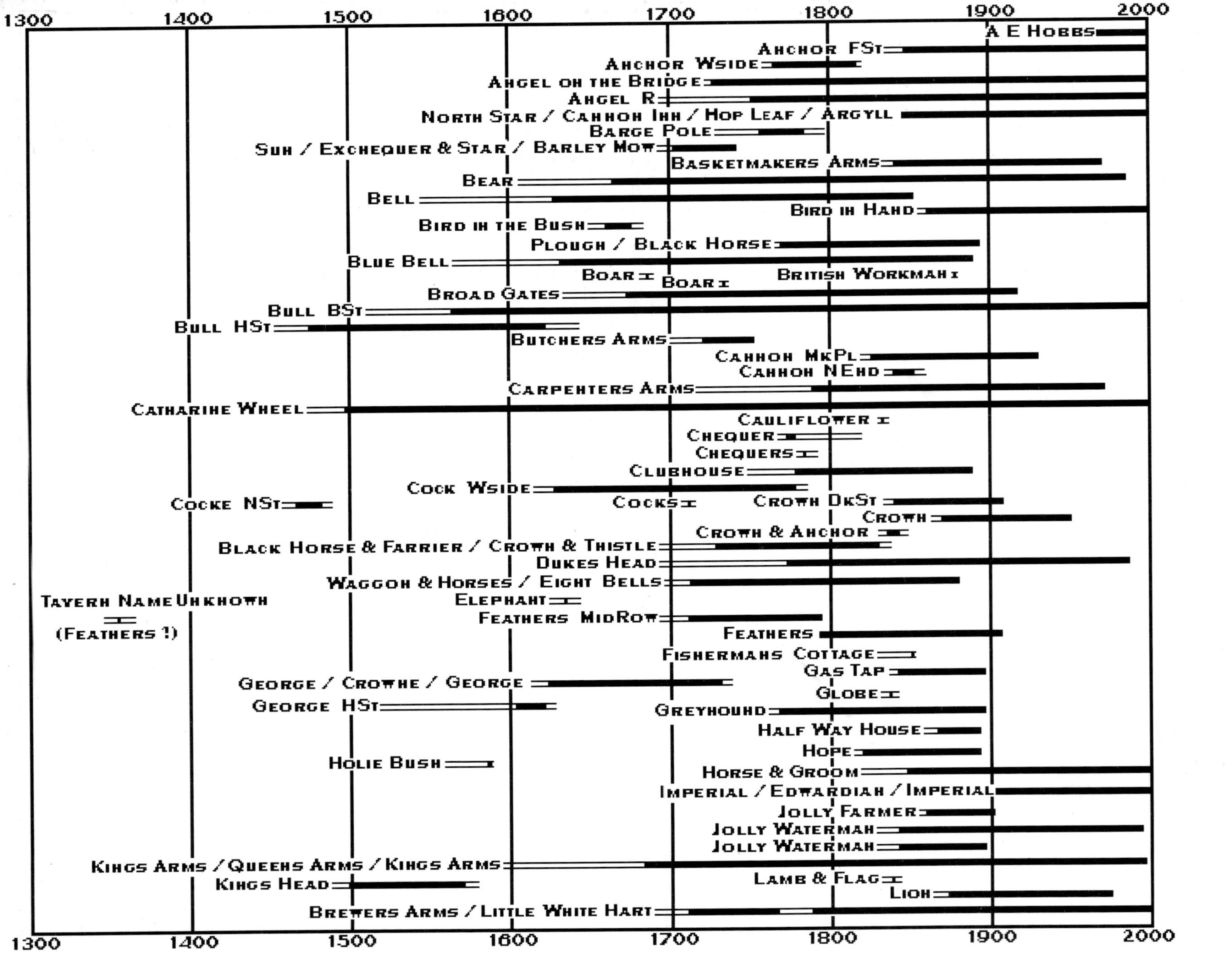
1300
1400
1500
1600
1700
1800
1900
2000
A E Hobbs
Anchor FSt
Anchor Wside
Angel on the Bridge
Angel R
North Star / Cannon Inn / Hop Leaf / Argyll
Barge Pole
Sun / Exchequer & Star / Barley Mow
Basketmakers Arms
Bear
Bell
Bird in Hand
Bird in the Bush
Plough / Black Horse
Blue Bell
Boar
Boar
British Workman
Broad Gates
Bull BSt
Bull HSt
Butchers Arms
Cannon MkPl
Cannon NEnd
Carpenters Arms
Catharine Wheel
Cauliflower
Chequer
Chequers
Clubhouse
Cock Wside
Cocke NSt
Cocks
Crown DkSt
Crown
Crown & Anchor
Black Horse & Farrier / Crown & Thistle
Dukes Head
Waggon & Horses / Eight Bells
Tavern Name Unknown
(Feathers ?)
Elephant
Feathers MidRow
Feathers
Fishermans Cottage
Gas Tap
George / Crowne / George
Globe
George HSt
Greyhound
Half Way House
Hope
Holie Bush
Horse & Groom
Imperial / Edwardian / Imperial
Jolly Farmer
Jolly Waterman
Jolly Waterman
Kings Arms / Queens Arms / Kings Arms
Kings Head
Lamb & Flag
Lion
Brewers Arms / Little White Hart